fodor's

GREAT BRITAIN 1970

Illustrated edition with atlas and city plans

EUGENE FODOR
ROBERT C. FISHER
Editors

BETTY GLAUERT
Associate Editor

ROLAND GRANT
Area Editor

Introduction by
SIR DENIS BROGAN

DAVID McKAY COMPANY, INC.-NEW YORK

PUBLISHED 1970

✱

ALL RIGHTS RESERVED

No part of this book may be reproduced in any form without permission in writing from the publisher

Travel Books Edited by Eugene Fodor
1936 ON THE CONTINENT
1937 IN EUROPE
EUROPE IN 1938
MEN'S GUIDE TO EUROPE
WOMAN'S GUIDE TO EUROPE

1970 Area Guides, Revised Yearly
GUIDE TO EUROPE
GUIDE TO THE U.S.A.
JAPAN AND EAST ASIA
CARIBBEAN, BAHAMAS AND BERMUDA
SOUTH AMERICA
INDIA

1970 Country Guides, Revised Yearly
AUSTRIA
BELGIUM AND LUXEMBOURG
FRANCE
GERMANY
GREAT BRITAIN
GREECE
HAWAII
HOLLAND
IRELAND
ISRAEL
ITALY
MOROCCO
PORTUGAL
SCANDINAVIA
SPAIN
SWITZERLAND
TURKEY
YUGOSLAVIA

FODOR-SHELL TRAVEL GUIDES, U.S.A.
(8 volumes)

Printed in the Republic of Ireland by Cahill & Co. Limited, Dublin 8.

EDITORS' FOREWORD

Because a new product demands a new package, we have replaced the old *Britain & Ireland* title of the Fodor series with a completely new volume on Great Britain alone. (Ireland is also featured in a separate, all-new book.) The new product, of course, is modern Britain, the home of electronic music, mini-skirts, vinyl jackets and equal rights for long-haired boys *and* girls. In this book, however, we will not bore the reader with a monochrome picture of a wild England, a rebellious Wales or a depressed Scotland. We've even cast a sceptical glance at "swinging" London. It's not a simple country to describe.

Britain is a paradox. This most insular of countries has spread its language and its way of life to all corners of the earth. This most taciturn of peoples has given the world its greatest literature. This most industrous of manufacturers insists upon living in a green park of a land. Penetrating this paradox is an absorbing travel experience. Everywhere Britain offers you handsome rewards—in the scenic beauty of her countryside, the dignity and elegance of her capital, the lessons of her ancient and recent history—most of all, her people, whose qualities are so exceptional.

In this guide we have sought to present modern Britain— from museums to family trees, shops to horseraces, palaces to pubs—not overlooking the unique British pageantry or the many opportunities provided for pursuing your professional interests. In particular, we have considerably expanded our practical information on London, the mother of the English-speaking world. But London alone is not England . . . nor is England Britain. To meet the demands of that ever-growing number of travelers who set out to explore all of this island of explorers, new chapters on storied Scotland and more information on Wales and Northern Ireland have been added.

Traditional Britain is very much in evidence today, as you will discover to your delight. So come to see it while the ferment of progress is carefully controlled, and pray, with us, that the approach of the affluent society in the United Kingdom will not mean the end of this love of tradition which means so much to the visitor.

(This volume actually covers the entire United Kingdom of Great Britain and Northern Ireland—as a title, however, this long monicker leaves us cold, so we have dubbed the whole lot *Great Britain*. If fans of Northern Ireland feel put out by this, they can be consoled with the thought that the six counties are described in two volumes of our series, appearing in *Ireland* as well.)

* * *

We wish to acknowledge and express our thanks for the help we have received from the British Travel Association in general, and in particular, from its representatives in London: Mr. Raymond V. Hewett, Chief Overseas Public Relations Officer; Mr. David H. Jones, Chief Press & Public Relations Officer; Mr. Ian Richards, U.K. Public Relations Officer; Mr. Peter ffrench-Hodges, Press Facilities Officer; Mr. A. W. Paveley, Manager of the Tourist Information Department; Mr. Bernard A. Hammond, Assistant Sales & Circulation Manager; Miss Sheila Sweeney of the Photo Library and Miss Jennifer Booth, secretary to Mr. Hewett. Thanks are also due to Mr. W. D. Cormack, Press Officer of Thomas Cook and Sons, London; and to Mr. Noel Ranns and Miss Eileen Rolph for editorial assistance in preparing this book and to BTA's Overseas Press Officer, Mr. W. M. P. Kemmis, for keeping us abreast of new developments.

* * *

Although we make a last-minute check just before going to press, much information contained herein is of a perishable nature, and we cannot be responsible for the sudden closing of a restaurant, bankruptcy of a hotel, or bad mood of an otherwise excellent chef, any (or all) of which can make one of our comments out-of-date overnight. We count on our readers to give us their opinions, too, and look forward to hearing from them.

* * *

As faithful readers of the Fodor series know, merely listing an establishment in one of our books is sufficient recommendation. Needless to say, no establishment pays to be listed, and establishments will not know if they are listed, or dropped, until the book is published.

CONTENTS

	Page
EDITORS' FOREWORD	5
WHY COME TO BRITAIN?—America's "Parent" in the Throes of Change *Sir Denis Brogan*	11

FACTS AT YOUR FINGERTIPS

Planning Your Trip: *When to go, Seasonal Events, Festivals, Where to go, How to go, What will it cost.*	23
How to Reach Britain: *From North America by Plane or Ship, From the Commonwealth, India and the Far East, From the Continent, From Ireland.*	33
Arriving in Britain: *Customs, Money.*	41
Staying in Britain: *Hotels, Restaurants, Shopping, Country Workshops, Tracing Your Ancestors, Guides, Meeting the People, Sports, Hiking and Camping, Closing Days, Mail, Telegrams, Telephone, Photography, Tobacco.*	42
Traveling in Britain: *Train, Bus, Canal Boat, Air, Car.*	48
Leaving Britain: *Customs, Nuisance Taxes.*	51

THE BRITISH SCENE

BRITAIN TODAY—A Fascinating Blend of "Swinging" and Sensible *Karl E. Meyer*	55
THE BRITISH—Portrait of an Island People *John Barr and J. P. Martin*	66
THE ROLE OF TRADITION—Living Links with the Past	77

CONTENTS

	Page
A MINI HISTORY OF BRITAIN—Kings and Queens and All That	82
CREATIVE BRITAIN—The Sceptred Isle's Poetry in Word and Form *John Lehmann*	86
WHAT'S ON IN BRITAIN—Sports and Special Interests for the Connoisseur *John Barr*	103
FOOD AND DRINK—Stamping Out the Bad Food Myth *Kato Frank*	115
COMING OF AGE—A Satirical Glance at Cuisine, Manners and Class *George Mikes*	122

THE FACE OF BRITAIN

LONDON—"Swinging", but Satisfyingly Static *Roger Baker*	133
LONDON'S ARTISTIC ATTRACTIONS—Museums, Theatre, Music and Cinema *Julian Aston*	153
WINING AND DINING IN LONDON—International Choices and Very Varying Standards	166
LONDON BY NIGHT—Dancing, Dining and Afterwards	179
SHOPPING IN LONDON—The Hallmark is Quality and Style	184
EXPLORING LONDON—Yesterday's Charm and Today's Clever Chaos	196

Map of Central London 200-1; Underground Map 202

LONDON'S OUTSKIRTS—Pastoral Beauty in the Capital's Environs	232

CONTENTS

	Page
THE THAMES COUNTRY—From the Cotswolds to London Map of Oxford 265	250
THE SOUTHERN COUNTIES—History's Sweep from Canterbury to Stonehenge *Peter Whelpton*	277
THE SOUTHWEST—A Sunny Corner of England	307
EAST ANGLIA—Rural Beauty and Pleasant Towns *Pat Barr* Map of Cambridge 343	331
THE SHAKESPEARE COUNTRY—The Bard as Dignified Tourist Magnet *Sydney Moorhouse* Map of Stratford-upon-Avon 351	346
THE MIDLANDS—Hunting Shires and Industrial Heart	355
THE NORTH—Backbone of England Map of York 397	379
THE ENGLISH LAKELAND—A Quietly Beautiful National Park	407
THE ISLE OF MAN—"Necromancer's Island"	417
WALES—Land of Poets and Singers *Jean Wakeman* and *James E. Thomas* Map of Cardiff 433	423
SCOTLAND—Britain's Northern Giant *Patricia Barclay*	449
EXPLORING SCOTLAND—The Lochs and the Highlands	481

CONTENTS

	Page
EDINBURGH—"Auld Reekie", Scotland's Capital	496
Map of Edinburgh 504-5	
GLASGOW—Scotland's Industrial Heart	510
THE CHANNEL ISLES—England with a French Accent	518
NORTHERN IRELAND—"The Six Counties" *Martin Wallace*	524
Map of Belfast 539	

SUPPLEMENTS

AN ENGLISH-AMERICAN VOCABULARY—Explaining the Common Language that Divides Us *Ransom Bradford*	546
INDEX	555
16-PAGE FOUR-COLOR TOURIST ATLAS OF GREAT BRITAIN	561

Color illustrations and black-and-white photographs are by courtesy of the British Travel Association.

WHY COME TO BRITAIN?

America's "Parent" in the Throes of Change

by

SIR DENIS BROGAN

(Britain's leading authority on the United States—and France—Sir Denis has spent a great deal of his time explaining Great Britain to his American and French friends. Author of many outstanding books, the latest of which is Worlds in Conflict, *he was until his recent retirement professor of political science at Cambridge University and a fellow of Peterhouse.)*

The British public learned, or at any rate was told, in 1969 that Britain had more than 5 million visitors from overseas in 1968—and most of them were tourists. This news was both gratifying and surprising to the man in the street. For as he has increasingly taken his own holidays outside Britain, he is rather surprised to find that people have come to a wet and chilly island which he, if he can afford it, is usually anxious to leave during the summer and would even more gladly leave during the winter. Yet the fact remains that Britain is one of the great tourist attractions of Europe, above all for Americans, but increasingly even for the French, and there must be something to attract here people who can choose where to spend their holidays—why come to a country without the visible charms of Italy, above all, without the charm of the sun, and which has no great reputation for catering to the whims of any foreigner, tourist or otherwise?

To amend Holy Writ, "what come they forth to see?" There are, of course, a great many traditional "sights" to be seen. London, if not a beautiful city, is a magnificent one. The view from Westminster Bridge is almost as fine as it was when Wordsworth described it in a famous sonnet a hundred and fifty years ago. Any foreign guide book finds a good many places to recommend as "must-see" objectives. Even if Baedeker, in his last complete edition on England (1937), marked Oxford and Cambridge with two stars, and added, "If pressed for time, omit Cambridge", it does not deny the charm of either of the old university cities. Windsor Castle, Edinburgh Castle, some of the great country houses, the British Museum (which the French always erroneously call "le British")—all of these are sights of the greatest magnitude, comparable to the Louvre, the Metropolitan Museum in New York or the Vatican. But it should be said that to go to Britain looking for sights is not quite to waste your time, but to miss a great deal of what is most rewarding in this island kingdom.

Britain, outside southern England, is not so thickly clustered with sights as is France, and of course is far less favoured in this respect than Italy. The National Gallery is not as good a picture gallery as the Louvre (although it is one of the greatest galleries in the world) and the British Museum has its rivals in European and in American cities. London is not any longer the largest city in the world, having been overtaken by Tokyo (and even by New York), and a great deal of the splendour of English life which fascinated Americans like Henry James before the First World War, is rather tatty today. "All the Queen's horses and all the Queen's men" still march as they did in the famous pre-war song, but they are no longer symbols of an empire on which the sun never sets; they are almost as much relics of an empire that is dead as is Williamsburg in Virginia or the Hofburg in Vienna.

The most important thing to look for when coming to Britain is the character of the society and the character of the state which is based on that society. The great French historian

Michelet laid down the law, "England is an island". (Like many foreigners, he equated England with Britain, to the indignation of the Scots and the Welsh.) And certainly, the insular character of Britain is one of the features which mark it off from its nearest neighbour, France, "that sweet enemy", as Sir Philip Sidney called it in the 16th century. Also, the small scale of the island and of many of its visible institutions marks it off from the United States and from Russia. England is a "precious stone set in the silver sea", and must be treated as such, not simply as an extension of Europe or simply as the mother of the United States of America.

A City's Character

This is reflected in the character of London itself. It is not only that London was for two hundred years the largest city in the world—it was the largest city in the Roman Empire north of the Alps—it was the largest city in Europe for three hundred years, and still is. Yet its immense size, which led William Cobbett, the great Radical polemical writer, to call it "the Wen", is not dramatized as is Paris, in the great sweep from the Arc de Triomphe down to the Louvre, or as is New York, by Fifth Avenue or Park Avenue, by the great bridges or by the most topless of its towers. The power of London is widespread. It is because it is so endless that it is in many ways so varied (and so maddening to drive into).

But in the City of Westminster and what used to be called the inner suburbs, one can find a reflection of the aristocratic character of the English state. The most conspicuous public monument in London is the Houses of Parliament, which themselves were built in the middle of the 19th century after fire had destroyed the old and rather ramshackle building in which parliament was addressed by Queen Elizabeth I and disbanded by Oliver Cromwell. Almost all that remains of the old royal city of Westminster is Westminster Hall, which just escaped destruction in the Second World War and is now an appendix to the modern Houses of Parliament. Quite rightly, the English Parliament is known as the "Mother of Parliaments", but she is a mother who has had her face lifted a good many times.

There are, of course, very fine things to be seen in detail in London, but above all, see the whole of London itself and, especially, see its survivals from the past. Look for things like the Inns of Court, where the lawyers hang out, or some of the smaller museums, some of the 17th- and 18th-century houses. Running all through London is the Thames, "liquid history", as John Burns (the politician) once called it, the river which is the explanation of the importance of London since Julius Caesar crossed it near where the Tower of London now stands. London's history is continuous—rebuilding in the City of London over a badly-bombed area, the contractors found a Roman temple to Mithras. All building had to be stopped till it was excavated, studied, and recreated on a nearby site as a museum piece. Until now, there has been no breach with history here such as you had in Paris, with the deliberate destruction of the Bastille and the Tuileries.

Continuity—Physical and Political

This continuity is seen all over the country with good and bad results. It is one of the illusions of the English (though not of the Scots) that they are, above all, a country-loving people. In fact, England is one of the most completely urbanized nations in the world. There can be few countries where fewer people know anything about agriculture than England. Yet what agriculture there is, is of the very highest quality. Few, however, live on the land as farmers. A great many live in the country for the sake of their gardens or commute to the great cities or have their weekend cottage where they can relax and cast themselves as bogus squires. All over southern England you have the relics of the great noble names, their magnificent noble houses. Woburn Abbey, the huge central estate of the Russell clan, has a wall fourteen miles long round its park. This is what the English call an estate, not what goes by that name in Westchester County, New York, or Fairfield County, Connecticut. The great country houses themselves sometimes have architectural interest, but by and large, they are a relic of this continuous and rich aristocratic society which still survives as a ghost—but a ghost which has still some life in it!

So when tourists come to see the sights of England, they ought not to miss the greatest sight of all, which is the continuity of English society. This continuity means a comparative absence of the social conflict which produces dangerously revolutionary areas like Harlem, or Watts, or the Paris "red suburbs". It may be paradoxical to say of England (it would be untrue to say it of Scotland) that snobbery is the remedy for class consciousness. Every foreigner moving into England, for a shorter or a longer period, runs up, sooner or later, against the bewildering entanglements of English snobbery. I have often asserted that American snobbery is an artificial fence having to be continually repainted and restored while English snobbery is like a wild hedge which simply grows. Nothing is more distressing to the class-conscious Englishman than the ignorant way in which American and other tourists mix up titles and miss the fine shades of social differences which make life in England so infuriating and so entertaining.

All of the great country houses, many of the significant institutions of the City of London, the leading colleges of Oxford and Cambridge and the old "public schools" (like Eton and Winchester) are aspects of a hierarchical society threatened, but not, I think, yet seriously shaken. This society exists independently of contemporary life. The tourist who visits Stratford upon Avon to see Shakespeare performed in his native town, for example, is near one of the greatest industrial agglomerations in the world, Birmingham, a city about which there is little more of the aristocratic than there is about Birmingham, Alabama. The hierarchy tries to ignore the British Birmingham, as they do every city which "doesn't count". A brilliant Anglo-Irish journalist, Gerard Fay, once said that the only British provincial city that looked like a big city of the American type was Glasgow, and Glasgow is a very large city in which not a *single* alumnus of Eton resides!

The Two Britains

There is another factor worth noticing about Britain: there are *two* Britains—the south of England, prosperous, rich, complacent and accepting "the aristocratic embrace" with very little resentment; and the Britain of Scotland, Wales, Northern Ireland and the North of England, poor, grimmer, more resentful, more modern in many of its attitudes. Glasgow has an ancient cathedral and an ancient university, but it is a modern city with its eyes turned to the west. Edinburgh is, if not a modern city, at any rate a capital city, resentful of London, although obedient to it. No greater mistake can be made by the tourist than to think that the differences between England on the one hand and Scotland and Wales on the other are trivial, like the differences between North and South Carolina or North and South Dakota. Of course, there are differences between North and South Carolina, but they are not as serious as the differences between Scotland and England. And it is after experience of both countries that American soldiers on leave felt themselves more at home, as did the Australians and Canadians, in the north than in the south. In the north, there were fewer trip wires to fall over, fewer affronts to the egalitarian spirit of the New World.

Here we come to another question as to what the intelligent tourist, who has something more in his mind than seeing the places that Shakespeare and Dickens and Walter Scott wrote about, should look for. He will, for instance, see some of the oldest and most depressing areas in the world. When Henry Adams made his first visit to England just before the Civil War, he realized as he took the t ain from Liverpool to London, passing through the "Black Country", that he was seeing an unique phenomenon, at that time the only great industrial area in the world. It was not an attractive sight then, and it is not an attractive sight now. Even less attractive are the relics of that industrialization in Scotland, Lancashire and South Wales. Nevertheless, these are the places from which the modern world sprang. Professor Adam Smith of Glasgow University protected the young, self-taught mechanic James Watt, who was inventing the first practicable steam engine in the university workshops. In Birmingham, the first modern technological industry was created by James Watt, who moved south from among the barbarous Scots to the company of the more sophisticated working men of the English midlands. There are many things to be seen north of London which are still pioneering achievements—like the great radio-telescopic observatory of Jodrell Bank, run by the University of Manchester.

In the same way, if a great deal of British rebuilding since the war has been banal or worse (this is especially true of the rebuilding of London), there has been much good modern building which should interest the enlightened tourist (by definition, one who is willing to regard Britain as a living society and not as an immense museum piece anchored northwest of Paris). For example, some of the best new school buildings in Europe can be found scattered all over England; and in Scotland is one of the most successful specimens of modern town planning in Europe (perhaps in the world), the new town of Cumbernauld, outside Glasgow.

There are, of course, other things to be seen which may excite pity rather than admiration—for example, the twenty miles of the shipyards that used to line the Clyde, now, alas, dwindling. The Clyde is trying desperately to keep its place behind Japan instead of leading the whole world, as it once did, in shipbuilding. The same is true even of some modern industries like our aviation industry. But for the American interested in the technology of the modern world, there is a great deal to be seen. And embedded in the middle of these unattractive industrial agglomerations, flourishing or stagnant, are often things well worth seeing for their historical or aesthetic importance. There is a magnificent country house north of Leeds, Temple Newsam, which is the property of the city of Leeds. Hadrian's Wall strides across from east to west, between Scotland and England, near the great industrial complex on the Tyne. The city of Glasgow has a splendid art gallery as well as a fine second-class cathedral. Edinburgh is an admirable background for its August festival, as well as a centre of banking, insurance, printing and brewing.

But, again, it is not a question of sights new or old, but of sights, new *and* old, set in a peculiar society (or set of societies). For example, there are very fine Gothic cathedrals in England, of which I think the most charming is Wells, but France has even finer Gothic cathedrals and many more great churches of all kinds. There is more variety of artistic pleasure to be got in an hour's driving in Italy than in three or four hours' driving in Britain.

On Manners and Snobbery

But what can be seen and felt here, with a little attention, is the peculiar character of British society. The main pattern of British society is set by the English, who are by far the most numerous of the populations of the United Kingdom, the people who have created most of the literature, and those whose role in the world has been so magnificent (including the role of being the somewhat ungrateful parent of the United

States). The tourist who comes with preconceived ideas or who comes from America expecting to see an effete, aristocratic, obsolete society full of quaintness (but not of life), or a Frenchman irritated by the incomprehensible attitude of the inhabitants of what is traditionally "perfidious Albion", will learn a great deal if he takes advantage of the intrinsic friendliness of most of the islanders. It seems to me the manners of the Londoners are very much better than the manners of the Parisians or the New Yorkers. (I cannot speak of the manners of the inhabitants of an even larger city, Tokyo.)

The snobbery, the careful avoidance of conscious aggression makes life easy for the tourist, and profitable, if he himself will keep an open mind. He will find the average Englishman a good deal more forthcoming to him than he would be to one of his own countrymen. For the average Englishman does not mind talking freely to an American or a Frenchman because he is not giving himself away, taking the wrong tone to somebody who is above him or below him. (Everybody in England is above or below somebody, except the Queen, who is above *everybody*.)

This friendliness is best tasted if the tourist has time to settle down either in a small town or in a village. True, there will be no such ostentatious friendliness as you get in an American small town. Although the "welcome wagon" has arrived in England, it is not very much welcomed, and the elaborate social filaments of an American small town do not exist in England. Yet a tourist will usually find service which is friendly, if not necessarily very competent. He will find this on the railways, as well as in the often backward hotels. He will suffer from the absurd licensing laws, which make it a matter of speculation when he can get a drink, and he will suffer from the fact that the English go to bed early. (The whole of London is more dead at midnight than many a small western town in America is at 2 o'clock in the morning.)

The tourist will, strangely enough, see the results of snobbery in a slightly more agreeable form than he might have expected when he landed. A great many of the English people are not desperately anxious to climb the ladder of social or economic success. They not only "know their place", they *like* it. This does not mean that they are easily pushed around.

They are much more set on "having their rights" and much more conscious of what their rights are than the average American or Frenchman is. The fact that the police all over Britain go unarmed reflects well not only on the police, but on the employers of the police, the mass of the British people. Even if today the English boast ironically that "we used to have the best cops in the world; now we have the best robbers", the impressive crimes in which they take a sardonic pride are seldom crimes of violence.

The New Democracy

The whole country, perhaps not quite consciously, is becoming more democratic in the American sense of the term. Education, using that loose word loosely, is far more widely spread. The post-war generations are more ambitious than their parents, although their ambitions are often those of the beatnik rather than the ambitions of the simple industrious apprentice. The great country houses like Woburn, Longleat, Beaulieu are aristocratic Disneylands now. Lord Montagu of Beaulieu specializes in a collection of old cars; Lord Bath of Longleat specializes in lions; the Duke of Bedford at Woburn specializes in a zoo he inherited as well as a number of tourist attractions he has invented. This is not the English aristocratic society which so fascinated Henry James! But it is a more democratic society—by paying quite a small sum, you can visit the great aristocratic houses and even have a cheap meal, on which the noblemen make a slight profit.

There is an increasing equality in dress and manners, although the give-away character of speech is still overwhelmingly important in England, if not so important in Wales or Scotland. There is one sense in which Britain is more democratic in many ways than either the United States or France—here, social conflicts are very muted. At the moment, the whole country is going through an agonizing reappraisal of its position in the world. It has just been slowly realizing that the days of Britain as a world power are over, that Britain is either an offshore part of Europe or a transatlantic dependent of the United States. But a great deal of the self-criticism and self-denigration is ironical. A great part of the public, the mass of the working class for example, never took the empire very seriously. What they did take seriously was England or

Scotland or Wales. In the crisis of 1940, they displayed an astonishing versatility and power of self-discipline which would have surprised people who did not know them, or who judged them by the temper of 1938.

It may be that the English people, if not the Scots and the Welsh, have decided to call it a day and are willing to coast along, not so much revelling in past glories as deciding that the great historical effort has come to an end. I do not believe it is as simple as this, and I believe that there are great resources of energy and initiative as yet untapped. And one of these sources of initiative and energy is a comparative absence of detestation of the governing class. (For the average man, "the governing class" is the government, whether the government calls itself Conservative or Labour.)

It is not quite accidental that the motto of the royal arms is *Dieu et mon Droit* ("God and My Right"). It is characteristic that the motto is in French and recalls the Norman Conquest. (What other country has ever celebrated its own conquest as England did in 1966?) It may be that faith in God is not what it once was; certainly, England is no more a Christian country than is France and a great deal less a Christian country than the United States. But the faith in his "rights" is deeply embedded in all Englishmen, whether they are the rights of a duke or the rights of a bus conductor. And if the tourist finds an irritating number of things that are badly done in Britain— and he will—he should remember he will find a great many things extremely well done that are much worse done elsewhere because they are done there in a more violent and aggressive temper.

The greatest asset of England is that its citizens are still a people who are conscious of having had a happy history, unlike the Scots, the Irish, the Welsh and the French, and who are convinced, despite momentary grumbling, that they will continue to have a happy history, if not a happy history of the same expansive and glorious kind as they have had earlier in this century.

FACTS AT YOUR FINGERTIPS

FACTS AT YOUR FINGERTIPS

For information about:	See Page:	For information about:	See page:
ADDRESSES	29-30, 47-8	HOTELS AND RATES	42-3
AGENTS, TRAVEL	27-30	IRELAND, TRAVEL FROM	40
AIR TRAVEL		MAIL	46
From North America	33	METHODS OF TRAVEL	27-9
From the Commonwealth	39-40	MONEY	41-2
From the Continent	40	MOTORING	48-9
From Ireland	40	NORTH AMERICA, TRAVEL FROM	
In Britain	51	By air	33-5
AIRPORT TAX	52	By sea	35-9
BONUS STOPOVERS	34-5	PACKING	31-2
BUDGETS, TRAVEL	30-1	PASSPORTS	32
BUSES	50	PHOTOGRAPHY	47
CALENDAR OF EVENTS	23-5	RESTAURANTS	43
CANAL BOAT TRAVEL	50-1	SEA TRAVEL	
CLOTHING	31-2	From North America	35-9
CLOSING TIMES	45-6	From the Commonwealth	40
COMMONWEALTH, TRAVEL FROM	39-40	From the Continent	40
CONTINENT, TRAVEL FROM	40	From Ireland	40
COUNTRY WORKSHOPS	44	SEASONS, TRAVEL	23
CUSTOMS REGULATIONS	41, 51-2	SHOPPING	44
ELECTRIC CURRENT	46	TELEPHONE & TELEGRAMS	46-7
FARES		TIPPING	36-7, 43-4
Ocean liners	36	TOBACCO	47
Transatlantic planes	33-4	TOURIST OFFICES	29-30
Trains in Britain	50	TRAINS	49-50
Buses in Britain	50	VISAS	32
FESTIVALS	26-7		
GUIDES	45		
HEALTH CERTIFICATES	32		
HISTORIC BUILDINGS	44-5		

Additional practical hints about hotels, restaurants, transportation, etc., of a regional and local character, not contained in this section, will be found throughout the book.

PLANNING YOUR TRIP TO BRITAIN

WHEN TO GO? The regular tourist season in Britain runs from mid-April to mid-October. The spring is the time to see the countryside at its fresh greenest, while in September and October the northern moorlands and Scottish highlands are at their most colorful. June is a good month to visit Wales, the Lake District and Ireland. July and August are the months when most of the British take their vacations and that is when accommodation is at a premium. The winter season in London is brilliant with the Covent Garden opera, Royal Ballet and theater among the main attractions. In the main, the climate is mild, though the weather is changeable and unpredictable. London has summer temperatures in the 80's and 90's at times, and can be humid.

Annual rainfall varies from about 23 inches in London and most of the southeast, to upwards of 60 inches in the Lake District and west Highlands.

Temperatures. Average max. and min. daily temperature in degrees Fahrenheit (average daylight temperature exceeds 60° on only 60 days in the year!)

	Jan.	Feb.	Mar.	Apr.	May	Jun.	Jul.	Aug.	Sep.	Oct.	Nov.	Dec.
South	44	45	51	56	63	69	73	72	67	58	49	45
(Greenwich)	35	35	37	40	45	51	55	54	51	44	39	36
North	43	43	47	50	55	62	65	64	60	53	47	44
(Edinburgh)	35	35	36	39	43	48	52	52	48	44	39	36

Off-Season Travel. This has become increasingly popular in recent years as tourists have come to appreciate the advantages of avoiding the crowded periods. Transatlantic sea and air fares are somewhat cheaper and so are hotel rates. Even where prices remain the same, available accommodations are likely to be better. Many resorts and inland spas enjoy a mild winter climate and offer first-class entertainment in the way of theater, concerts, exhibitions, etc. And, because this country is one in which you might as well ignore the weather, it provides one of the very best places to go if you have the good fortune to be able to travel out of the regular tourist season.

SEASONAL EVENTS. Among the special attractions that might influence you in selecting the date for your vacation in Britain are the following:

January. Specific events include Plough Sunday celebrations (Sunday after Twelfth Night) at Exeter and Chichester; Cake and Ale ceremony the following day at Bury St. Edmunds; Wassailing the Apple Tree in mid-January at Carhampton; Burns Night celebrations on the 25th at Ayr and elsewhere; Up Helly Aa at Lerwick in the Shetland Islands at the end of the month; and the King Charles I Commemoration Ceremonies on the 30th in London. During the *winter* in London you can enjoy the brilliant attractions this great and ancient city offers— opera at Covent Garden, the art shows at Burlington House, the Royal Ballet, symphony concerts, variety shows, and, above all, the one place in Europe where you can have your fill of English-speaking plays.

February is the month of Cruft's Dog Show in London, and the Pancake Race on Shrove Tuesday at Olney, when housewives compete against their transatlantic cousins in Liberal, Kansas, who are doing the same thing.

March has among its famous events the Grand National Steeplechase at Liverpool and the Ideal Home Exhibition, Olympia. The Oxford v. Cambridge boat race on the Thames takes place just before Easter. The All-England Badminton Championships are held during the last week of March at Wembley.

April is the month of the Badminton Horse Trials and of the opening of the flat-racing season at Doncaster. April also sees the Royal Maundy Presentations at Westminster Abbey; Good Friday Orange Rolling at Dunstable; the Easter Parade at London's Battersea Park; Shakespeare's Birthday Celebrations on the 23rd at Stratford-on-Avon; and the Spring Flower Festival at Southend-on-Sea.

May sees the Royal Windsor Horse Show; the International Trophy Race (automobiles) at Silverstone; the Chelsea Flower Show in London; Skye Week in the island of that name, Scotland; the annual cart horse parade in London; London's fashion fortnight; and it's a good month to go out to Kew Gardens for the spring display. Maypole celebrations (of recent origin) during early May at Elstow; the Chelsea Spring Antiques Fair in London; scrambling for hot pennies on the 23rd at Rye; and the Court of Arraye in Lichfield. May also sees the start of a summer-long programme of festivities at Plymouth to celebrate the 350th anniversary of the sailing of the "Mayflower".

In **June**, there's the Derby at Epsom, possibly the world's most famous horse race; the international motorcycle races on the Isle of Man; Trooping the Colour for the Queen's birthday; the Antique Dealers' Fair at Grosvenor House; the Druid pilgrimage to Stonehenge on the 24th; racing at Royal Ascot; the lawn tennis championships at Wimbledon; the Royal Horse Show at Richmond (Surrey); and the yachting fortnight on the estuary of the Clyde. On Whit Monday at Birdlip Hill, there is cheese rolling; and at Bangor, Northern Ireland (date varies), an Irish folk dance festival.

July. In July there are two special events this year; the Commonwealth Games at Edinburgh (16th-25th), and the start of the Tall Ships Sailing Race from Plymouth. Then there's the Royal Regatta at Henley-on-Thames, where American crews and scullers often compete with the British; the British Open, often in the home of golf, Scotland; and a selection of examples of that very British and very thrilling spectacle, the military tattoo. On the Isle of Man in the first week of July, you can see the Tynwald Ceremony and the Peel Viking Festival; at Belfast on the 12th, Battle of the Boyne Celebrations; at Builth Wells, the Royal Welsh Agricultural Show (third week in July); and on the last Thursday of the month, the Battle of Flowers at St. Helier on the Isle of Jersey. In London during July you might wish to take in the Royal International Horse Show at White City or the Royal

Tournament at Earls Court. Also the Riding of the Marches in Annan, Scotland, or the Braw Lads' Gathering at Galashiels. One completely new event this month; a 1,700-mile Round Britain powerboat race, starting Portsmouth July 26.

In early **August**, Cowes Week, the big event for yachtsmen; the 12th sees the opening of the grouse shooting season; in Ulster there is the Grand Prix Classic International Road Race; the International Sheep dog Trials are staged in each country in turn. The International Festival of Music and Drama opens in Edinburgh; regattas take place at Torbay, in Devon. In August, Cricket Week is observed at Canterbury; and in London, you can see the International Sports Festival and Exhibition at Crystal Palace. Around the 1st of the month, watch the Doggett's Coat and Badge Race from London Bridge. Grasmere has its Old English Games, while Scotland is the site for Highland Games at Edinburgh and Crieff, and Highland Gatherings at Dunoon and Strathden (all from the middle of the month). On the 24th, a Frankenstein-like creature named Bartle is burned in effigy at West Witton (Yorkshire).

In **September**, the partridge shooting season starts. The Royal Autumn Show is held in Edinburgh, and the Royal Highland Gathering at Braemar. The St. Leger is run at Doncaster. The Flying Display and Exhibition is held at Farnborough during the first week of this month. More Highland Games and Gatherings at Aboyne, Oban and Pitlochry (first half of month); while down in England, you can watch the Horn Dance (a very old custom) at Abbots Bromley, the St. Giles Fair at Oxford or the Cricket Festival at Scarborough. The lawn tennis professional indoor cups are fought for at Wembley.

In **October**, a third bird joins the list of permissible game, the pheasant. Birdies, not birds, interest the gallery at the Ryder Cup matches. And the International Motor Show comes off in London.

November is the month for fairs, with a Goose Fair at Nottingham, Mop Fairs at Stratford upon Avon and Warwick, and the Chelsea Autumn Antiques Fair in London. Colchester has its Oyster Festival. On the 5th, in Leamington Spa, boys kick a burning football around the streets. You can watch the children burn the guys on Guy Fawkes Day (Nov. 5), and a few days later see the Lord Mayor's Show pass through Fleet Street. You can also observe the state opening of Parliament during the first week or watch the veteran car run to Brighton.

In **December**, in addition to the Closing of the Gates of Derry on the 18th and the Mason's Walk at Melrose, Scotland, there are many events connected with the Christmas season, such as: the Festival of Carols in King's College Chapel, Cambridge; mumming plays at Andover and Marshfield; and carol services everywhere. On New Year's Eve, the Hogmanay Celebrations at Dundee and the mild revelry in Trafalgar Square, London, climax the evening, although the parading with blazing tar barrels on the head in Allendale (Northumberland), is hard to top!

Finally, if you are interested in old British customs, there's something going on almost all year round: best check on the spot for exact dates, as these can vary.

Festivals of Britain. From spring until fall various music and drama festivals are held throughout the country. Actual dates may vary from year to year, so best check in advance. Among the best known are:

Aldeburgh. 10 days in June. Benjamin Britten's leadership.

Bath. 10 days in May or June.

Belfast. The Belfast Festival in November.

Bexhill-on-Sea. Festival of Music in the latter part of July.

Birmingham. April Spring Festival.

Bolton. Music Festival in April.

Brighton. Festival of Music and the Arts in April and May.

Broadstairs. Dickens Festival, 5 days in June and Festival of Music in July.

Buxton. International Music Festival, with Hallé Orchestra, in July.

Cheltenham. First half of July, British Contemporary Music; first half of October, Art and Literature.

Chester's miracle plays are held in the last week of June, every 5 years (1972 is next). Regular Festival of the Arts in July features drama.

Chichester. From late May. Theater Festival under direction of Sir Laurence Olivier in the ultra-modern arena-style theater. Also see *Winchester*, below.

Durham. Twentieth Century Festival, August.

Edinburgh. August-September (for 3 weeks). International Festival of Music and Drama, Film Festival.

Gloucester. See Worcester.

Glyndebourne. May to mid-August. Opera Festival in a country setting.

Harrogate. 1 week in July, Hallé Music Festival.

Haslemere. Festival of Early Music and Instruments, 9 days in July.

Hereford. See Worcester.

Hexham Abbey. October Festival.

Invercauld. August Drama Festival.

Keswick. Theater Festival during July.

King's Lynn. Festival of Music and the Arts, in July.

Leeds. Triennial Musical Festival during April.

Llandaff. Llandaff Festival, June.

Llangefni. National Drama Festival, October.

Llangollen. 1 week in July. International Musical Eisteddfod. In August the 1-week National Eisteddfod is held alternately in north and south Wales (the proceedings are all in Welsh, with instantaneous English interpretation, using transistorized hand-sets).

London. The City of London Festival, July.

Ludlow. Summer Festival, 2 weeks in June and July.

Neath. Craig-y-Nos Opera Festival in July.

Norfolk & Norwick. Triennial Music and Drama Festival late May/early June.

Oxford. Bach Festival, 10 days in June-July.

Pitlochry. Mid-April through October. Drama Festival.

Reading. Summer Festival of the Arts in June.

Richmond (Yorkshire). Richmond Festival, September.
Salisbury. See Winchester.
Selby. Triennial Festival in June. (Next will be 1971.)
St. Pancras (London). Arts Festival. 3 weeks in March.
Stratford-upon-Avon. March or April through November. Shakespeare Season at the Royal Shakespeare Theater.
Stroud. Festival of Music and Arts, October.
Swansea. 1 week in October. Festival of Music and the Arts.
Tilford. Festival of Music in May.
Winchester, Salisbury and Chichester. 3 days in July. Southern Cathedrals Festival, each taking turn as host.
Wolverhampton. Festival of Music in June.
Worcester, Hereford and *Gloucester.* 1 week in early September, the Three Choirs Festival. Choirs of the three cathedral cities, each taking turn as host.
Wye. Stour Festival of Music and Painting, first week in June.
York. 3 weeks in June and early July. Mystery Plays and Festival of the Arts, held every three years, next 1972.

WHERE TO GO? Unless you travel on a packaged tour with a fixed itinerary and schedule you can't modify, it's most unlikely that you will follow unchanged any detailed plans you make in advance. Nevertheless it is advantageous to rough out your trip. This gives you an opportunity to decide how much you can comfortably cover in the time at your disposal. It also allows you to relate the extent of your travels to the limits of your pocketbook.

Highlights of Britain. Undoubtedly, London is the number one tourist mecca, with its history, top entertainment attractions and services: the surrounding countryside is easily explored on day trips, including Oxford, Cambridge, Windsor and the south coast. Yet no main provincial center is further away than 8 hours by train (except Ireland and northern Scotland).

Other highlights: the Shakespeare country, the Cotswolds and the Thames Valley, the Lake District, Oxford and Cambridge, the Peak District, Devon and Cornwall.

In Wales, the national parks and the Eisteddfodau; in Scotland, Edinburgh, the Burns country and the Highlands. In Northern Ireland the Glens of Antrim, the Giant's Causeway and the Mountains of Mourne.

HOW TO GO? When you have decided where you want to go, your next step is to consult a good travel agent. If you haven't one, the American Society of Travel Agents, 360 Lexington Avenue, New York, or the Association of British Travel Agents, 50-54 Charlotte St., London W.1, will advise you. Whether you select *Maupintour, Diner's Club-Fugazy, American Express, Cook's,* or a smaller firm is a matter of preference. They all have branch offices or correspondents in the larger European cities. The *American Automobile Association* also runs escorted tours.

Travel abroad today, although it is steadily becoming easier and more comfortable, is also growing more complex in its details. As the choice of things to do, places to visit, ways of getting there, increases, so does the problem of *knowing* about all these questions. A reputable, experienced travel agent is a specialist in details, and because of his importance to the success of your trip, you should inquire in your community to find out which organization has the finest reputation.

If you wish your agent to book you on a package tour, reserve your transportation and even your first overnight hotel accommodation, his services should cost you nothing. Most carriers and tour operators grant him a fixed commission for saving them the expense of having to open offices in every town and city.

If, on the other hand, you wish him to plan for you an individual itinerary and make all arrangements down to hotel reservations and transfers to and from rail and air terminals, you are drawing upon his skill and knowledge of travel as well as asking him to shoulder a great mass of detail and correspondence. His commissions from carriers won't come close to covering his expenses, and thus he will make a service charge on the total cost of your planned itinerary. This charge may amount to 10 or 15 per cent., but it will most likely *save* you money on balance. A good travel agent can help you avoid costly mistakes due to inexperience. He can help you take advantage of special reductions in rail fares and the like that you would not otherwise know about. Most important, he can save you *time* by making it unnecessary for you to waste precious days abroad trying to get tickets and reservations. Thanks to his work, you are able to see and do more.

> *Credit travel.* Americans and many other countries' citizens can arrange with one of the travel credit organizations for a European charge account that enables them to sign for hotel and restaurant bills, car rentals, purchases, and so forth, and pay the resulting total at one time on a monthly bill. This is particularly advantageous for businessmen traveling on an expense account or on business trips whose cost is deductible for income tax. Offering this service are the *American Express*, with branch offices in all major cities, *The Diners Club*, 10 Columbus Circle, New York, Hilton's *Carte Blanche*, *Eurocard International*, *Barclaycard*, and many others.

There are four principal ways of traveling:

The *group tour*, in which you travel with others, following a prearranged itinerary hitting all the high spots, and paying a single all-inclusive price that covers everything—transportation, meals, lodging, sightseeing tours, guides. And here your travel agent can book you with a *special interest* group, so you needn't spend a high proportion of your tour trotting round museums if you would much rather be wandering round botanical gardens, for example, and you will be among people with similar interests to your own.

The *prearranged individual tour*, following a set itinerary planned for you by the travel agent, with all costs paid in advance.

The *individual tour*, where you work out the itinerary for yourself,

FACTS AT YOUR FINGERTIPS 29

according to your own interests, but have your agent make transportation and hotel reservations, transfers and sightseeing plans.

The *free lance tour*, in which you pay as you go, change your mind if you want to, and do your own planning. You'll still find a travel agent handy to make your initial transport reservation and book you for any special event where advance reservations are essential.

AMERICAN AGENCIES SPECIALIZING IN BRITISH TOURS

American Express, 65 Broadway, New York, N.Y. 10006.

Brownell, Brownell Blds., Birmingham, Alabama 35201.

Caravan, 401 North Michigan Avenue, Chicago, Illinois 60611.

Cartan, 108 North State St., Chicago, Illinois 60602.

C.I.E., Irish Suite, Hotel Lexington, New York, N.Y.10017.

Colpitts, 85 Franklin Street, Boston, Mass. 02110.

Cook's, 587 5th Avenue, New York, N.Y. 10017.

Diners Club-Fugazy, 488 Madison Ave., New York, N.Y. 10022.

Esplanade/Swans, Charles Street, Boston, Massachusetts 02110.

Fourways, 30 E. 42nd St., New York, N.Y. 10017.

Frames, 114 East 32nd St., New York, N.Y. 10016.

Gateway, 10 E. 44th St., New York, N.Y. 10017.

Global, 230 Park Ave., New York, N.Y. 10017.

Globus, 521 Fifth Ave., New York, N.Y. 10017.

Maupin, 711 W. 23rd St., Lawrence, Kansas 66044.

Skyway-Ensign, (Male Travel Bureau), 274 Madison Ave., New York, N.Y. 10016.

SOURCES OF INFORMATION. A large selection of brochures, booklets and general information may be had from *British Travel*, the national tourist organization, which has offices in several countries:

U.S.A.: 680 Fifth Avenue, New York, N.Y. 10019.
39 South La Salle Street, Chicago, Ill. 60603.
612 South Flower Street, Los Angeles, Calif. 90017.
Canada: 151 Bloor Street West, Toronto 5.
602 West Hastings Street, Vancouver 2.
France: 6 Place Vendôme, Paris 1er.
Germany: Neue Mainzerstrasse 22, Frankfurt/Main.
Holland: 6-8 Nieuwe Spiegelstraat, Amsterdam C.

In Britain

British Travel, 64 St. James's St., London W.1.
Northern Ireland Tourist Board, 10 Royal Ave., Belfast 1; 13 Lower Regent St., London S.W.1.
Scottish Tourist Board, 2 Rutland Place, West End, Edinburgh 1.
Wales Tourist Board, 3 Castle Street, Cardiff.

Regional Tourist Offices

The London Tourist Board, 170 Piccadilly, London W.1.
Guernsey States Tourist Committee, States Office, Guernsey, Channel Islands.

States of Jersey Tourism Committee, Weighbridge, St. Helier, Jersey, Channel Islands.
Isle of Man Tourist Board, 13 Victoria St., Douglas, Isle of Man.
Southwest Travel Association, 229 High St., Exeter, Devon.
Yorkshire Travel Association, 1 Harcourt Place, St. Nicholas Cliff, Scarborough, Yorkshire.
Northumberland and Durham Travel Association, 8 Eldon Square, Newcastle-upon-Tyne, Northumberland.

171.5
13.0
201.0

385.5

WHAT WILL IT COST? This is about the hardest travel question to answer in advance. A trip to Britain (or to Europe) can cost as little (above a basic minimum) or as much (with virtually no limit) as you choose. Budgeting is much simplified if you take a prepackaged trip. As an indication: A five-day stay in London, including hotel, meals except lunches, but with lunch included on two full-day sightseeing trips, visits in London and to Windsor and Hampton Court and theater, costs anything between £20 ($48) and £45 ($108), depending upon the hotel category required. A package 6-day coach tour of Britain can be had for £42 ($100).

DEVALUATION OR INFLATION?

Devaluation in some European countries, with consequent rising taxes and costs throughout, and possible inflationary trends to come, make accurate budgeting in advance an impossibility in any country. Prices mentioned throughout this title are indicative only of costs at time of going to press. Check with your travel agent near the time of your trip for latest details.

For the pay-as-you-go, go-where-you-please, traveler, budgeting is more difficult. There can be a wide spread of price levels, as you can spend a lot of money in London if you want to go in for deluxe living; but it will be real luxury, the absolute tops in this line, and you can enjoy yourself very adequately for much less. In provincial centers, costs will be less for hotels and entertainment.

A typical day might cost one person this:

Hotel, with breakfast (moderate)	£2 15s
Lunch at a restaurant (inexpensive)	15s
Transportation, say four buses	2s
and two taxis	10s
Dinner at restaurant, one drink (moderate)	£1 10
Theater (cheap seat)	12s 6d
Coffee	1s 6d
Two half-pints of beer (at a pub)	3s
Cigarettes	5s 5d
In other words, this day will cost you about £6 14s ($17.08)	

Other items: man's haircut 4s 6d; a woman's anywhere from 6s 6d to 15s. A set is 10s 6d to 25s, a manicure 6s 6d. It costs about 3s 6d to have a shirt laundered, 7s 6d to 10s 6d to dry-clean a dress or a man's suit. A local paper will cost you 5d. Your evening out means spending 7s 6d to £2 for theater or opera, 7s 6d up to 15s at the cinema, 15s to 30s in a restaurant, and about all you have at a nightclub—exact figures vary greatly, since you have to pay a membership fee to "join" a nightclub the first time you go, and the fee is highly elastic.

WHAT TO TAKE? The first principle is to travel light, and fortunately for the present-day traveler, this is really possible due to the manufacture of strong, lightweight luggage, and drip-dry, crease-resistant fabrics for clothing. If you plan to fly, you have a real incentive to stay below the first-class transatlantic limit of 66 pounds and economy limit of 44 pounds; each pound overweight costs extra money. Moreover, most bus lines as well as some of the crack international trains place limits on the weight (usually 55 pounds) or bulk of your luggage.

Even if you are traveling by ship, resist the temptation to take more than two suitcases per person in your party, or to select luggage larger than you can carry yourself. Porters are increasingly scarce in these days of European prosperity, and you will face delays every time you change trains (or hotels), go through customs, or otherwise try to move about with the freedom that today's travelers enjoy. Motorists need to be frugal, too. You should limit your luggage to what can be locked into the trunk or boot of your car when you make daytime stops. At night, everything should be removed to your hotel room.

Don't carry coals to Newcastle. Whether you need a new suit or not, this is your opportunity to have some of the best cloth in the world put together by some of the best tailors in the world, at about three-fifths of what you would pay in the United States. Most men's accessories are of excellent quality in England (special tip: this is a fine place to buy a set of golf clubs, so why bring yours?), and women may want to pick up tweeds or sweaters here. Raincoats are a necessity in the British Isles and are consequently of excellent quality.

Travelers cheques are the best way to safeguard travel funds. They are sold by various banks and companies in terms of American and Canadian dollars and pounds sterling. Most universally accepted are those of *American Express*, while those issued by *First National City Bank of New York* and *Bank of America* are also widely used. Best known and easily exchanged British travelers cheques are those issued by *Thos. Cook & Son* and the "Big Four" banks: *Barclays*, *Lloyds*, *Midland*, and *National Westminster*.

If you wear glasses, take along the prescription. There is no difficulty about getting medicines, but if you have to take some particular preparation, better bring a supply.

Clothes. Britain is sometimes cool even in midsummer. You will want sweaters and you will certainly need rainwear. In keeping with the climate, ordinary everyday dress, especially for traveling, runs very much to the casual and to sportswear; tweeds and non-matching jackets for men, mix-and-match separates for women. Dressing in the evening during summer is not practised widely in England these days, but if you want to go to the very best places (top night clubs or elegant theaters with hit shows) better bring a black tuxedo (white is usually worn only by headwaiters and band-leaders).

TRAVEL DOCUMENTS. Getting a passport should have priority in your plans. U.S. residents must apply in person to the U.S. Passport Agency in New York, Chicago, Boston, Miami, New Orleans, San Francisco, Washington, D.C., or the local courthouse. Take with you a proof of citizenship, birth certificate, two recent photographs, 2½ inches square, and $10.

If you are not an **American** citizen, but are leaving from the United States, you must have a Treasury Sailing Permit, Form 1040D, certifying that all Federal taxes have been paid; your travel agent, steamship company, or airline can tell you where to get it. To return to the United States, you need a re-entry permit *only* if you intend to remain abroad more than 364 days. If abroad less, your Alien Registration Card will get you in on return. Apply for the Re-entry Permit at least six weeks before departure in person at the nearest office of the Immigration and Naturalization Service, or by mail to the Immigration and Naturalization Service, Washington, D.C. This permit entitles the non-citizen resident to stay abroad a total of two years. (Naturalized American citizens may now stay abroad an unlimited length of time, even in the country of their origin.)

Canadian citizens entering the United Kingdom must have a valid passport, application forms for which may be obtained at any post office; these are to be sent to the Canadian Passport Office at 40 Bank Street, Ottawa, together with a remittance of $5.

Visas. Not required for entry into Britain by American citizens, nationals of the British Commonwealth and most European and South American countries. Citizens of Ireland coming from Ireland do not even need passports.

Health Certificates. These are not required for entry to Britain, unless you arrive from Asia, Africa or South America. The United States modified its requirements in 1968: citizens and non-citizens without a valid certificate of vaccination against smallpox are only subject to vaccination at the port of entry if, within the previous 14 days, they have visited a country where smallpox is present or have been exposed to a smallpox case somewhere en route.

England, we've known you for 20 years.

Since 1950, TWA has flown more than a million people to England.

This experience has taught us how to anticipate your needs. To find out what problems you might run into. And how to solve them before you even run into them.

We've learned how to keep you entertained with music and movies*.

And how to prepare a meal good enough to tell your friends about.

And most of all, we know what you expect from a tour. And we know how to give it to you for less than you expect.

For reservations, call your travel agent or TWA.

If we didn't know how to make you happy, we never could have convinced a million people to fly with us.

TWA
**Our people make you happy.
We make them happy.**

*Entertainment optional at nominal cost.
Movies by In-Flight Motion Pictures, Inc.

Travel carefree...go Maupintour

MORE FOR YOUR MONEY! Why go it alone and take potluck seeing and spending carelessly? Go Maupintour instead and have fun sharing new adventures and being an <u>expected</u> guest. Travelers wanting the best, without frustrations, have enjoyed Maupintour travel over 18 years.
COMPARE! Ask for Maupintour's new escorted tours of Europe (eight of which include the <u>Oberammergau Passion Play</u>!) plus Grand Italy, Greece/The Aegean, Dalmatia/Balkans, Alpine Countries, Salzburg Festival, British Isles, Scandinavia, USSR/Eastern Europe, Spain/Portugal, and Morocco/Madeira.
ASK YOUR TRAVEL AGENT for folders or write Maupintour, 270 Park Ave., New York, N.Y. 10017.

Maupintour
standard of travel excellence

Ride a Rolls-Royce to Great Britain

Sit back and enjoy deluxe Comfort Class service on our smooth Rolls-Royce Jet Prop 400s. Fly Icelandic direct to London and Glasgow at the lowest fare of any scheduled airline—all year round! (Then use the saving for one of our special Shoestring Tours.) We'll treat you to excellent food and liqueurs, and give you lots of room to stretch out. It's the best buy in the sky. From New York to Iceland · London · Glasgow · Luxembourg Sweden · Norway · Denmark. See your travel agent or write us for the folder FB.

Icelandic Airlines, 630 Fifth Avenue (Rockefeller Center) New York 10020 · 212 PL 7-8585 · Chicago · San Francisco Washington, D.C. · Miami

LOWEST AIR FARES TO EUROPE
ICELANDIC AIRLINES
LOFTLEIDIR

ANYWHERE YOU'RE GOING

Diners Fugazy Travel will help you arrange it all. Business and vacation travel. Incentive and group charters. And with a Diners Club Card extended payments are available.

With over 150 offices worldwide, there's one near you.

DINERS FUGAZY TRAVEL

The WESTBURY Hotel

The highest standards of comfort and cuisine. 285 rooms, finest central location in heart of London's West End.

The Westbury Hotel, *Bond Street, London W.I.Y. O.P.D.*
Tel: 01-629 7755 *Telex:* 24378 *Cables: Westburotl, London W.1.*

PRUNIER

French cooking at its best — wonderful sea-food, exquisite wines, no music.
Open every day including Sundays (except Bank Holidays) for lunch and dinner.
72 ST. JAMES'S STREET LONDON SW1
01-493 1373

Paris: Prunier, 9 rue Duphot; Traktir, 16 ave Victor Hugo

CRIME & BANDITRY DISTRESS OF NATIONS & PERPLEXITY

will increase

until the Bishops open

Joanna Southcott's
BOX OF SEALED WRITINGS

What the Bible says about the Box & the Bishops:

"And the temple of God was opened . . . and there was seen . . . the Ark (Chest or Box) of his Testament (or Will)."

"And round about the Throne were four-and-twenty . . . Elders (Bishops) sitting . . . (and they) fall down . . . and cast their crowns (their wisdom) before the Throne."

Rev. xi 19: iv 4, 10

THE PANACEA SOCIETY
BEDFORD, ENGLAND

HOW TO REACH BRITAIN

From North America

BY AIR. With jet service cutting the flight time from New York to London to 6 hours, Britain is closer than ever to the New World. From New York, there are direct flights to London on the following scheduled airlines: *TWA, Pan American, BOAC, Alitalia, Qantas, Air India, Japan Airlines, El Al, Irish* and *Icelandic Airlines.* Over the pole flights to London operate from San Francisco on *Pan American* and *TWA.* There are also services by various airlines from Baltimore, Boston, Chicago, Cleveland, Dallas, Denver, Detroit, Honolulu, Houston, Los Angeles, Miami, New Orleans, Philadelphia, Portland (Oregon), Seattle, St. Louis and Washington.

From Canada, there are direct flights on *BOAC* and *Air Canada* from Montreal, Toronto, Vancouver, Edmonton and Winnipeg. Direct flights to Prestwick airport, near Glasgow, are available from New York on *BOAC, KLM,* and *Pan American,* from Montreal on *BOAC* and *Air Canada,* and from Toronto on *BOAC.* There are also direct flights from New York to Belfast on *BOAC* and *Irish Airlines,* and nonstop New-York, Manchester flights on *BOAC.*

Of course, there are some disadvantages to air travel even in this new age of vibrationless, over-the-weather flying. One is limited space. Except on first-class flights, seats are arranged three on each side of a narrow aisle, and on Jumbo Jets, 9 abreast with 2 aisles.

Another drawback is the luggage allowance, 66 pounds (30 kilos) for first-class, 44 pounds (20 kilos) for economy classes. If you are the kind that travels light as a matter of principle, this will be no hardship especially since you can carry a camera, a pair of binoculars, an umbrella, a laprobe, an overcoat, and a couple of books in addition to the luggage that is weighed. If you are not, then you'll be paying 1% of the standard first-class fare for every kilo (2.2 pounds) of overweight.

```
171.5
 13.0
201.0
─────
385.5
```

AIR FARES. Transatlantic airlines have first and economy class only, tourist class having been dropped in 1960. From New York or Montreal to London the one-way jet fare is about $375 first-class, $255 economy. Round trip is roughly double the single rate. Fares and accommodations are subject to change and regulation by the International Air Transport Association and the above rates are only indicative of the maximum. A complicated structure of reduced air fares obtains at this writing, based on the dates of flight, Consult your travel agent on this in order to achieve the minimum rate. He will also supply information about group rates, charter flights, credit facilities, and other savings. A round trip excursion fare with minimum stay in Europe of 14 days, maxiumm 21 days can be had for $300 (economy). Moreover, *BOAC* offer 21-day holidays to London from New York for $300, including jet round trip, country hotel accommodation within 100 miles of London, and 1,000 miles of rail travel around Britain.

With one exception, all North Atlantic air carriers charge identical fares, established by the International Air Transport Association. As a non-member of IATA, and because its flights (New York-Glasgow via Iceland) take a few hours longer, *Icelandic Airlines* is able to provide average economy standards of comfort at a lower fare.

Children between the ages of 2 and 12 travel at half the adult tariff, but are entitled to a full luggage allowance. Infants under 2 not occupying a seat and accompanied by an adult are charged only 10% of the full fare. Although they are not entitled to a free luggage allowance, their food, clothing, and other supplies needed in flight are not weighed. Most airlines provide special bassinets if notified in advance.

Airline tickets can be bought on the instalment plan. A down payment of as little as 10% secures the reservations, and the balance can be paid off, after your trip, during the next 12 to 24 months. Interest charges make this arrangement more expensive. If you buy your ticket with a credit card, no downpayment need be made at all.

BONUS STOPOVERS TO BRITAIN

by

DAVID GOLLAN

(*The author is Executive Editor of* The Travel Agent *and* Interline Reporter, *two North American travel trade publications.*)

If you are going to Britain with a ticket to London, why not stopover en route at Reykjavik (Iceland) or Dublin, Glasgow or Belfast? These and several other points may be visited without extra charge when you buy a ticket from New York to the British capital.

You'll be pleasantly surprised at the way an ordinary roundtrip can be broadened in scope into a comprehensive circle trip. When you buy a ticket to London you are entitled to 4,147 miles of transportation in each direction. This allows you to add cities which lie off the direct route and saves you paying for separate side trips.

Stopovers are, of course, entirely optional. You can fly nonstop to London. However, if you wish to add cities en route these stopovers are certainly useful.

Let's examine some of the available routings to London. These are only a sampling of the total number offered and you should discuss the complete range of possibilities with your travel agent.

Leaving New York you may fly first to Glasgow and stopover in Scotland which is gaining in popularity as a tourist destination. Glasgow is a good headquarters for sightseeing trips to the Highlands, the Firth of Clyde resorts and the Hebrides, a group of islands located off the north-west coast.

Continuing from Glasgow to London, you have a choice of stopovers en route or you may fly nonstop. Edinburgh can be visited at no extra charge and the city is particularly worth including in your itinerary during the Aug.-Sept. music festival. It has fine shops, gardens and is a good base for sight-seeing on Scotland's east coast and the Border country.

Another routing from Glasgow to London takes you first to Belfast (Northern Ireland), another area which is gaining increasing attention. Liverpool, Manchester and Birmingham also can be included on this particular itinerary. Liverpool is a convenient gateway for Southport and St. Annes, two of England's leading northern seaside resorts. Manchester and Birmingham are good jumping-off points to the Shakespeare countryside and rental cars can be hired at both airports for the road trip.

The Irish Republic also can be visited at no extra charge on a New York to London ticket. You fly first to Shannon, gateway to western Ireland, and then continue into Dublin, the capital. Between Dublin and London, you can add Glasgow and Manchester if you wish.

What about circle trip possibilities between New York and London? On the outward trip, you can fly to Glasgow, Belfast, Liverpool, Manchester, Birmingham and London. Homeward, you can travel via Dublin and Shannon.

Fares are approximately: $750 first class and $510 economy class, both roundtrip jet. Check with your travel agent for details of special excursion and tour basing rates as low as $270.

Reykjavik (Iceland) also may be included at no extra charge on your trip from New York to London, when you fly on non-IATA Icelandic Airlines, which offers lower rates than members of the International Air Transport Association. IAL operates via Reykjavik and Glasgow to the British capital. Iceland is worthwhile visiting as a stopover and sightseeing trips can be arranged to the hot springs near Reykjavik and Gullfoss, a towering waterfall.

Yet another suggestion for Americans is to buy a ticket only to Glasgow from New York, a saving of about $30. This can be applied toward a rental car, rail or bus ticket for a lesiurely trip through the British countryside to London.

BY SHIP. Although today more transatlantic tourists travel by air than by sea, many prefer the relaxation of life aboard ship before a hectic European tour. For the high season, berths on the most popular ships have to be booked several months in advance, particularly for tourist and cabin class. As new ships enter service, and the older ones are refurbished, the standard of accommodation grows steadily more comfortable. Crossing time takes from 5 to 11 days, depending on the route and the speed of your particular vessel.

Some of the larger ships still carry three classes—first, cabin, and tourist; there is an increasing tendency, however, to change to two-class, or even one-class accommodations. First class may be cosmopolitan or stuffy, depending entirely on the crowd. Cabin class is usually less formal, less pretentious, and more relaxed. Tourist class is often the most fun of all, expecially in summer, when many students and younger people set the pace. It is also the most crowded. Cargoliners, generally carrying about 12 passengers, offer the most informal—and slowest—transportation.

FARES. When you travel by sea, your transportation cost is an elastic if not actually elusive quantity. In addition to tipping, which adds at least 5% to your fare, you will also need to allow for incidental spending over the time you're on the ocean: in the shops, at the barber or hairdresser, the bar, etc. Moreover, the minimum fares quoted by the major lines are just that, minimum, and in tourist and cabin class, you're again almost certain to pay more, either because the cheaper accommodations have been sold out for months before you made your reservation, or because you want an outside cabin, one for only two persons, one in the middle of the ship, or whatever. Round trip fares save you 10% in the off season (eastbound, January 1 to Mid-April and August 23 to December 31; westbound, January 1 to June 21 and November 1 to December 31); at other times they are double the one-way fare.

```
171.5
 13.0
201.0
-----
385.5
```

Some shipping lines have an arrangement with an airline enabling a tourist to travel by sea one way and by air the other for the price of half a round trip by each carrier.

First-class, of course, is the most variable of all. It starts as low as $275 on an old ship off season and runs as high (still minimum) as $455 in season on the most popular ships. $550 is a fair average (a suite can run up to $1,200 per person) plus another $75 for tips, drinks, and other extras.

Cabin-class fares off season start at about $220. Your total for transportation, tips, and shipboard fun, therefore, can't be kept much below $320.

Tourist-class berths can be had as cheaply as $195 to $215 off season on various older vessels that shuttle between Canadian ports and Liverpool or Southampton, to which sum American passengers have to add the expense of overland travel to Quebec or Halifax. Minimum in-season fares on any of the big-name ships are in the $235 and up range to Atlantic ports. Thus, for the New York-Southampton run in season on a better ship in average cabin, count on spending $285, tips and incidentals included.

Cargoliner fares range from about $195-250, depending upon port of embarkation, and incidentals are minimal.

Children under 1 year old not occupying a separate berth are carried for $40 in first class and $20 in cabin or tourist class. Children from 1 to 12 travel at half the adult fare, but get the full adult baggage allowance.

TIPPING. Perhaps the most annoying feature of ocean travel is the ritual of tipping that signals the end of every voyage. Since your cabin steward and dining room steward will normally have done the most for you during your trip, they are tipped most generously. The deck steward should also be remembered if you have occupied a deckchair. The bath steward, barman, wine steward, and lounge steward are tipped according to services rendered. The ship's officers, from the purser on up, are not tipped, of course, The table below is generous for one person on the average crossing. If there are several people in your party, increase the suggested amounts by about 50% for each additional person. *Holland-America Line* says it does not allow tipping—a bright note for travelers!

	First Class	Cabin	Tourist
Cabin steward	$10 to $15	$7 to $8	$5
Dining room steward	10 to 15	7 to 8	5
Deck steward	3	2	2

WHICH SHIP? The answer to this one depends on what type of atmosphere you prefer. British boats are probably unsurpassed for unobtrusive service, experience, and seamanship. Cuisine is anywhere from good to outstanding and a certain formality prevails. Canadian ships are about the same, but a shade less formal. American ships have the strictest safety regulations and devote the greatest attention to air-conditioning, plumbing, and efficiency. Service is anywhere from casual to downright folksy, and the food can be excellent. French boats are probably the gayest, with good service and top-notch cuisine of the continental variety. They are less formal than the British, less aseptic than the American. Dutch boats are generally functional, spotlessly clean, conscientiously served, and unpretentious. Food is good to excellent. Greek ships are noted for their thoroughness, American-continental cuisine, and entertainments. German liners are noted for their exceptional comfort in tourist class.

CUNARD LINE. The Cunard Line is the company with the longest experience on the North Atlantic. On the route New York-Cobh (Ireland)-Le Havre (France)-Southampton (England) is the new, superbly equipped liner:

Queen Elizabeth 2, 58,000 tons. Basically one class, this is a dual purpose ship, built for cruising and for the transatlantic run. The 5 decks of staterooms and cabins have mostly outside locations; all have bath or shower and toilet. There are 3 decks of public rooms, the restaurants being high in the superstructure; 2 outdoor and 2 indoor swimming pools.

Cunard officials, now that their once-mighty fleet has been decimated, plan to operate the *Queen Elizabeth 2* in co-operation with the *SS France,* alternating sailing dates instead of racing in competition across the Atlantic. The new *Elizabeth 2* will spend much of its sailing time (especially in winter) as a cruise ship in the Caribbean, almost exclusively out of New York.

UNITED STATES LINES. Besides the *United States,* the holder of the North Atlantic speed record, this company operates a large fleet of cargo vessels on the North Atlantic that accommodate from 4-12 passengers each. The *United States* shuttles from New York to Le Havre (France) and Southampton, extending her voyage to Bremerhaven (Germany) on alternate trips.

United States, 53,330 tons, built in 1952. Carries 871 passengers in first class, 508 in cabin, and 549 in tourist. Set North Atlantic record of three days, 10 hours, 40 minutes. Completely air-conditioned with individual thermostats in every room. Except for pianos and carving blocks, the entire ship and its furnishings are non-inflammable. Lavish use of colors, modern fabrics, imaginative decor. The most modern ship afloat plus international cuisine. Five-day crossing.

FRENCH LINE. The super-modern *France* made her maiden voyage early in 1962 as flagship of the French Line, and is now the only French Line vessel operating on the New York, Southampton and Le Havre run. A 67,000-ton ship, she carries 2,000 passengers in first and tourist class. She has the same superb cooking, vintage wines and good service that have won such a devoted following for the French Line among seasoned travelers. Five-day crossing.

HOLLAND-AMERICA LINE. Seafaring is an ancient tradition with the Dutch, so it's hardly astonishing that the fleet of the Holland-America Line alone numbers 29 vessels. Five ships are in regular passenger service from New York to Southampton, Le Havre, and Rotterdam, with occasional stops at Cobh (Ireland). "No tipping" is the rule on these ships.

Rotterdam, 38,645 tons, put into service late 1959. New flagship. Completely air-conditioned, largest and fastest. Carries 1,400 passengers first and tourist class. Seven-day crossing, eight to Rotterdam. (May be withdrawn in 1969.)

Nieuw Amsterdam, 36,640 tons, commissioned 1938. Recently converted to a two-class ship, carrying about 1,200 passengers. Often used for winter cruises. Air-conditioned and equipped with stabilizers. Seven-day crossing, eight to Rotterdam.

Statendam, 24,294 tons, commissioned 1957. Only 84 in first class, the rest of the ship is dedicated to the 867 tourist class passengers. Equipped with stabilizers. Seven-day crossing, eight to Rotterdam.

CANADIAN PACIFIC. Two ships comprise the ocean-going division of this versatile company that also runs a transcontinental railroad, an international airline, and a chain of hotels. Sailings are from Montreal and Quebec to Liverpool (England) in summer, from St. John (New Brunswick) to Liverpool in winter. Several calls are made at Greenock (Scotland) during summer.

Empress of England, 25,500 tons, put in service 1957. Carries 158 passengers in first class, 900 in tourist. Completely air-conditioned. One of the most attractive ships on the North Atlantic. Has stabilizers. Six-day crossing.

Empress of Canada, 27,300 tons, came into service in 1961. A two-class ship, with 200 passengers in first and 856 in tourist accommodation. Specially designed to serve also as a cruise ship. Six-day crossing.

NORTH GERMAN LLOYD. Re-entered the North Atlantic run with the 23,000-ton *Bremen* in 1959, which links New York with Bremerhaven via Cherbourg and Southampton, carrying 200 first class and 900 tourist passengers; 6-day crossing. Also on this route is the *Europa* (21,000 tons).

JOHN SON LINE operates cargo liners several times monthly from US and Canadian west coasts through Panama to Europe, some ships calling at London.

LYKES LINES. Operate cargoliners between U.S. Gulf and various United Kingdom ports.

FJELL-ORANJE LINE. A Dutch company, operating cargo vessels with accommodation for 4 to 12 passengers, with frequent sailings from Montreal to Le Harve and Rotterdam (in winter from Halifax), also from Montreal to London. Largest in the fleet is the 8,173-ton *Ornefjell*.

FURNESS PACIFIC LINE. Operates four cargo/passenger vessels between Los Angeles Harbor and Glasgow, taking 22 days. Vessels carry up to 12 passengers.

MANCHESTER LINES inaugurated in 1960 a mixed cargo service between Montreal and Halifax to Manchester as well as southern U.S. ports to Manchester and Glasgow with a fleet of nine vessels.

GDYNIA-AMERICA LINE. The well-known m/s *Batory*, which has a displacement of 14,300 tons, plies regularly between Montreal and Gdynia, calling in both directions at Southampton and Copenhagen. The liner is provided with first and tourist class accommodation.

Several shipping companies and air lines have interchange agreements providing one-way-by-ship, one-way-by-air tours, with the usual round-trip discounts available.

From the Commonwealth, Africa and the Far East

BY AIR. From Australia, direct flights to London are available on *BOAC* and *Qantas* from Sydney and Perth. From New Zealand, direct flights to London from Auckland on *BOAC*.

Direct flights from Johannesburg to London on *BOAC* and *South African Airways*.

Australians and South Africans traveling to London may make numerous stopovers en route without paying a penny more. A passenger originating in Sydney can travel in one direction via the USSR and return via the Middle East, thus completing a very comprehensive circle trip at no extra fare. North America also may be visited in conjunction with trips to Britain.

A typical itinerary takes the traveler from Sydney via Djakarta, Singapore, Bangkok, New Delhi, Moscow, Copenhagen to London. Homeward bound, he can visit Geneva, Rome, Athens, Beirut, Karachi, Bombay, Colombo.

A South African bound for London can fly in one direction via Luanda (Angola), Las Palmas and Lisbon. Returning, he can stop at Athens, Tel Aviv and Teheran. These are just two of many examples.

BY SEA. From New Zealand, Australia, or South Africa a travel agent can be especially helpful because of the many different ways of traveling. New Zealanders and Australians may take the *Shaw Savill Line* via the Panama Canal or the same line via South Africa. The *P. & O.* runs a number of ships between Australia and London via the Suez Canal (when open), as do the *Holland-America, Lauro, Cogedar* and *Sitmar* lines. The *Blue Star Line* covers the Australian-South Africa route with a large fleet of cargo ships with accommodation for 12 passengers.

India, Pakistan, Singapore. The *P. & O. Line*, in addition to Hong Kong and Singapore, en route to Australia, also serves Bombay and Colombo. These ships are usually booked months in advance. There are many cargo ships with good passenger accommodation.

From the Continent

BY AIR. From the continent to London and other English cities, there is a wide variety of services by practically every European airline. In addition, there are direct flights to Scotland from the continent, and even a few to Wales.

BY SEA. In addition to the cross-channel railway ferries, the following services by sea will get you to Britain: *Drive-on/drive-off* car ferries: Cherbourg to Southampton, Le Havre to Southampton, Dieppe to Newhaven, Boulogne to Dover, Calais to Dover, Dunkerque to Dover, Ostend to Dover, Zeebrugge to Dover, Antwerp to Tilbury, Rotterdam to Tilbury, Gothenburg to Tilbury. Bremerhaven, Esbjerg, Ostend and Kristiansand to Harwich; Rotterdam, Antwerp, Bremen, Hamburg and Gothenburg to Hull; Amsterdam and Gothenburg to Immingham; Copenhagen to Leith; also a hovercraft service, Calais to Pegwell Bay, near Ramsgate.

There are passenger-only services from Iceland to Leith, and from Esbjerg, Oslo, Kristiansand, Bergen and Stavanger to Newcastle upon Tyne.

From Ireland

BY AIR AND SEA. From Ireland, in addition to excellent air services between most important cities across the Irish Sea, there are *drive-on/drive-off* car ferries between Rosslare and Fishguard, Dun Laoghaire and Holyhead, Belfast and Liverpool, Larne and Preston, and Larne and Stranraer. *Passenger ferries* (all with car-loading facilities) operate between Cork and Fishguard, Dublin and Liverpool, Dublin and Glasgow, Belfast and Heysham and Belfast and Glasgow. Book ahead as far in advance as possible, especially for summer car-ferry crossings, as space for the vehicles is necessarily limited.

FACTS AT YOUR FINGERTIPS

ARRIVING IN BRITAIN

CUSTOMS REGULATIONS. You may bring in 400 cigarettes or one pound of tobacco in any other form duty free; one bottle of spirits, one of wine and half a pint of toilet water and one quarter pint of perfume, if arriving from outside Europe (if arriving from Europe, only 200 cigarettes allowed). In general all articles you are carrying with you for your personal use may be brought in free of duty.

MONEY. You may take into the United Kingdom any amount of currency of any kind in the form of travelers checks, letters of credit and so forth and any amount of notes in any currency. You are entitled to take out of the country foreign currencies in the amount brought in, or in an amount equivalent to £50 sterling, whichever is the greater. At this writing you may not take out of the United Kingdom more than £15 worth of sterling or British Commonwealth notes (except Canadian and Rhodesian notes).

The monetary unit is the Pound Sterling (£1) which is divided into 20 shillings (20s). Notes are issued to the value of £10, £5, £1 and 10 shillings (10s). Shillings are divided into 12 pennies. Silver coins are issued to the value of sixpence (6d), one shilling (1s) and two shillings—sometimes called a *florin* (2s). The penny (1d) piece is made of copper. In addition, there is one nickel coin worth 3d. The old half-penny was demonetized in 1969, the old half-crown (2s 6d) on January 1, 1970.

The abbreviations are £ for the pound, s or a dash for the shilling, d for the penny.

A guinea is 21 shillings or £1 1s. There is no note or coin for a guinea, but if you see a dress advertised at 5 guineas, you'll know that means £5 5s. All of this seems perfectly logical to Britons.

Below is a quick conversion table.

American	British	American	British
$.01	1d	2.40	£1
.06	6d	5.00	£2 1s 8d
.10	10d	10.00	£4 3s 4d
.12	1s	12.00	£5
.30	2s 6d	20.00	£8 6s 8d
.50	4s 2d	50.00	£20 16s 8d
1.00	8s 4d	100.00	£41 13s 4d

GOING DECIMAL. By 1971 Britain will have changed over completely to the decimal system and there are already 3 new decimal coins in use. These are the 5 new pence (5p.) coin, the 10 new pence (10p.) coin, and the 50 new pence (50p.) coin. The 5p. coin is silver, is exactly the same size as a shilling, and the same value. The 10p. coin is also silver, and is the same size and value as a two-shilling piece. The 50p. coin is silver, and 7-sided, about the size of the 10p. coin.

DEVALUATION. An important change took place in late 1967 when the British Government announced the devaluation of the pound from the old level of $2.80 to the present one, $2.40. This means that your dollar will buy more pounds than before, and your trip will consequently be much cheaper. As a quick currency guide, remember that an English penny is now the same value as an American one.

Note:

When you change dollars or travelers' cheques, unfortunately, you will probably lose a few cents, from 2¢ at banks, to 4¢ at hotels and shops, as the former convert at "bank rates" and the latter at any rate they feel like.

STAYING IN BRITAIN

HOTELS. It is advisable to make reservations in advance, especially in London during the summer tourist season. Post-war rebuilding has accelerated the provision of amenities that American visitors have been more accustomed to taking as a matter of course than do the British, such as central heating, air-conditioning and private bathrooms. Especially outside of London, however, many of the older good hotels are still not so fully equipped.

Unlike most continental hotels, except the most luxurious, British hotels put a cake of soap on the washbowl. As part of the service you may put your shoes outside your door at night, and retrieve them, neatly polished, in the morning. Usually your room charge includes breakfast the next morning as well, and British breakfasts are extremely hearty meals. A few London hotels quote European Rates, but almost everywhere else, bed and breakfast is the rule.

Rates. Hotels in this guide have been grouped in categories according to their price range, service, facilities offered, and similar considerations. *Super deluxe:* speaks for itself, but about £8 ($19) up; *luxurious:* £5 to £7 ($12–$17); *first-class superior:* £4 to £5 ($10–$12); *first-class reasonable:* £3 to £4 ($8–$10); *moderate:* £2 10s to £3 ($6–$8); *inexpensive:* 35s to £2 ($4–$5); *rock bottom:* 25s to 30s ($3–$3.60). These approximate rates are based on single room with breakfast. Rooms with private bath are usually extra. Similar categories in the provinces are usually much lower in price.

Boarding or guest house charges, based upon single room with all meals for one week, are : *superior,* £16 16s; *moderate,* £14 14s; *inexpensive,* £12 12s.

Trust Houses. All over, especially in county and market towns, you'll find Trust Houses. These are comfortable, usually first class reasonable to superior in category, and are often atmospheric old coaching inns. Their motels, called "Post Houses", are excellent. For information: *Trust Houses Ltd.,* 81 Piccadilly, London W.1. (GRO 1846).

Rank Hotels can be found in several major business and tourist centers. All are the last word in modernity, and have a reputation for good service. Most in luxurious or first class category. For details, write to Rank Hotels Ltd., 11 Belgrave Rd., London S.W.1. 834-6633).

Motels. There are now a number of motels strategically situated along main roads in Gt. Britain (see regional chapters under *Practical Information*). Most have private bathroom with the studio room, tea-making equipment and an adjacent restaurant. Charges are from about 30s ($3.60) single.

Country House Hotels and Clubs. If you like accommodation with a difference, try one of the many country house hotels or country clubs that dot the countryside on the outskirts of towns and touring areas. Often of historic interest, these former homes of the landed gentry usually have traditional furnishings and large gardens or parks with sports facilities, as well as a cocktail bar. Service can be variable, but the atmosphere is worth a stay. (See regional hotel listings.)

Farm Houses. At a simpler level, and deeper in the countryside, there are farms which take a few visitors in summer. Accommodation will be homely and you are more likely to eat good regional dishes here than anywhere else, since the farmer's wife is usually the cook. Charges are very modest: under £1 ($2.40) for bed and breakfast, about £7 to £9 per week including evening meal, but not lunch ($20–$25). Advisable to book in advance and, if possible, have a recommendation from a former guest or a local authority—you *can* rough it too much! A list issued by *British Travel* gives brief details, including the type of farming carried on: write for their booklet (3s 6d or 42¢), *Camping & Caravan Sites and Farmhouse Accommodation in Britain*. (Address on p. 29.)

RESTAURANTS. Prices vary widely according to region, but in a top restaurant in London or the provinces you will pay from 18s 6d for lunch and from £2 for dinner ($2.22 and $4.80 respectively)—more if you dine *a la carte*. An average in lesser establishments is 10s 6d for lunch, 17s 6d for dinner ($1.26 and $2.10, respectively). Popular chain cafés provide a reasonable 3-course lunch for about 7s 6d (90¢), and at a snack bar or self-service restaurant you can make out for less.

A bottle of wine will cost from £1 ($2.40) or a half pint of beer around 1s 6d (18¢). A cocktail runs about 4s and up (48¢), whisky or gin 2s 8d to 3s (32¢–36¢) depending on the bar you are in; coffee is 1s to 1s 6d (12¢–18¢) a cup. Water has to be asked for, and it's not likely to be iced.

TIPPING. Some hotels will put a service charge of 10 to 12½% on your bill. (12½% works out to 2s 6d (30¢) per £.) If they fail to do so divide about the same among your chambermaid, waiter (if you eat at the hotel), headwaiter, hall porter, and bellboy, the greater part of it to the first two. If a service charge has been made, note whether it applied to the restaurant bills; often it does not, in which case you give the waiter up to 15% of the price of your meals, and to the same in outside restaurants.

Taxi drivers should get 1s on all short journeys up to a 5s fare, and 2s for fares up to 8s—after that, 15% of total. Give station or air terminal porters at least 1s, then 6d for each piece of luggage over two, and a little more for long distances or waiting. Barbers and hairdressers get 20%. Give a cloakroom attendant 6d when you take your coat back, and 3d to 6d in hotel or restaurant washrooms where there is some service. However, in many women's washrooms, the penny-in-the-slot system still operates, so have a supply of pennies in hand. Hatcheck girls: sixpence to one shilling, doormen a shilling for finding you a cab. If Americans tip as at home, pretending that the shilling is a quarter, there will be smiles all around. You do not tip while drinking at the bar in a pub. Do not tip cinema or theater ushers unless they serve you tea, nor elevator operators. Croupiers at the big gambling clubs *expect* a 10-20% tip, but you don't *have* to give them anything.

SHOPPING. Visitors to Britain (except residents of Europe) will find the Personal Export Scheme an advantage for major purchases (over £5—$12—for any one item), because they are not subject to the purchase tax, which applies to most products. The goods must be delivered direct to the port of departure for exportation as baggage (so allow time for delivery when buying), or the firm can send them to your home address. Take your passport when shopping as you will be asked to show this. Shops and stores operating the scheme generally display a notice in their windows, but it is worthwhile to ask anyway.

COUNTRY WORKSHOPS. For the best of Britain's craftmanship and handmade products in wood, wrought iron, pottery, fabrics, furniture and so on, try one of the workshops that exist in country areas: they are worth a visit on your tour. For a complete listing of the shops write: *Rural Industries Bureau,* 35 Camp Rd., Wimbledon, London, S.W.19.

HISTORIC BUILDINGS AND GARDENS. Opening days and admission charges for houses, etc., are liable to change from season to season, especially as many are still privately-owned and inhabited. We therefore list only approximate days and times throughout this book. British Travel (629-9191) London can confirm the current times and charges if you are in doubt.

In our regional chapters we are able to list only a few of the outstanding stately homes, castles, and other properties that may be visited. An extremely useful publication, giving opening times and admission fees of over 500 houses and gardens open to the public, is *Historic Houses, Castles and Gardens in Great Britain and Ireland,* Index Publishers Ltd., 27/28 Finsbury Square, London E.C.2 (6s including postage, or 5s from booksellers). The entrance fee to most of the houses varies from about 2s to 5s, but is usually 2s 6d or 3s. A few houses have Connoisseurs' Days (a specific day of the week), when the charge may be as much as 6s.

Many houses belong to The National Trust, a private organization, founded to help preserve the national heritage. An annual membership (£2) entitles you to visit free over 120 historic properties; for information write *The National Trust,* 42 Queen Anne's Gate, London S.W.1. Or, for Scotland only, *The National Trust for Scotland,* 5 Charlotte Square, Edinburgh 2. Further information about gardens can be obtained from: *National Gardens Scheme,* 57 Lower Belgrave Street, London S.W.1, and *Scotland's Gardens Scheme,* 26 Castle Terrace, Edinburgh 1.

A 12-month "Open to View Ticket" is offered in the U.S.A. through travel agents. The cost ($10) covers free entry to over 600 historic monuments and buildings whose normal entry fee is 6d to 2s 6d. Total admission would cost $300, so this is quite a saving. All famous places are included.

FOR STUDENTS. Summer courses in economics, history, art, music, literature, etc., are offered by such universities as Oxford, London, Edinburgh, Bristol, Liverpool and others. Information may be obtained from the *Institute of International Education*, 1 East 67th Street, New York; *British Information Services*, 845 Third Avenue, New York; or in Canada from *United Kingdom Information Services* at Quebec, Montreal, Ottawa, Toronto, Edmonton, Vancouver.

The *General Bureau for Educational Visits and Exchanges*, 55a Duke Street, London W.1., issues a booklet and advice on a wide variety of activities available to young overseas visitors (individuals or groups). These activities provide an opportunity to meet local young people, whether through student groups, special interest holidays, working holidays or college courses.

Package student tours are operated by a number of American tour operators, including *American Express* and *University Travel*, 18 Brattle St., Cambridge, Mass., as well as by the U.S. National Student Association's *Educational Travel, Inc.*, at 265 Madison Ave., New York.

GUIDES. *Take-a-Guide Ltd.*, 11 Old Bond Street, London W.1 (HYD 1688) has a 24-hour personal sightseeing service operated by Oxford and Cambridge graduates with a fleet of modern cars. *Undergraduate Tours*, 6 S. Moulton St., London W. 1 (MAY 5267), provides the same kind of service, using Oxbridge students or graduates. Both highly recommended. Nowadays in London you can even carry your own guide around with you—in the form of a small tape-player which is carried by a shoulder strap and gives a commprehensive comentary on the city's sightseeing highspots. Details from *Audioguides Div., Microfacts Corporation*, 18415 W. Eight Mile Rd., Detroit, Michigan 48219.

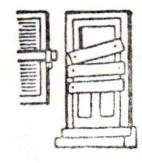

CLOSING DAYS AND HOURS. Legal holidays (bank holidays is the English term) are not uniform throughout Great Britain. In England and Wales, the holidays are Good Friday, Easter Monday, May 25 (late Spring holiday), August 31 (August 3 in Scotland), Christmas Day, and Boxing Day, (Dec. 26). Northern Ireland adds St. Patrick's Day, March 17 to this list, and Orangeman's Day, July 12. Scotland does not universally observe Easter Monday or Boxing Day, but to make up for it, New Year's Day, January 2, and the spring and autumn holidays in Edinburgh and Glasgow are observed. The Channel Isles add New Year's Day and Liberation Day, May 9.

Usual shopping and business hours are 9-5 p.m. Banks open at 10 a.m. and close at 3 p.m. (Monday to Friday) and are open 9:30 a.m. to 11:30 on Saturdays. Shops and most retail houses have a half holiday one day a week, in addition to Sundays. Shops in the West End of London, and some other districts, close at 1 p.m. on Saturdays, though country towns and London suburbs usually close on a Wednesday or Thursday. Big West End of London stores stay open until 7 p.m. one day a week, generally Thursday. The changeover to a five-day week is resulting in many stores throughout the country closing for a whole day (often Monday).

Drinking hours. Approximately 11 a.m. to 10:30 or 11 p.m., with the exception of about 2½ hours in the afternoon, usually 3 to 5:30 p.m, depending on the area. On Sundays, hours are 12 noon to 2 p.m., and 7 to 10:30 p.m. (In Wales, Sunday opening only in several areas—see *Practical Information for Wales* section. In Scotland, young people under 18 are not allowed in licensed bars and rooms for the consumption or purchase of liquor—nor even for a soft drink.

ELECTRIC CURRENT. If you're bringing electric shavers, irons, hair-driers, etc., with you, it's best to check that they can be safely used on British voltages. The most general are 200 to 250 volts, A.C., 50 cycles. Since most American appliances are designed to operate on 120 volts, 60 cycles, visitors from the United States will need transformers.

To be on the safe side before plugging in, ask your hotel or, in London, phone the *Electricity Council*, 30 Millbank (VIC 2333).

MAIL. The postage rates: *Inland:* letters and postcards up to 2 oz , 4d (slow), 5d (fast). *To Europe:* letters up to 1 oz., 9d; postcards 5d. Letters and postcards go by air at these rates if this makes for earlier delivery, so there is no need to use airmail stickers, though lightweight paper will make for minimum postal rates. *To the United States:* letters up to ½ oz., 1s 6d; postcards 9d (airmail stickers should be used). These rates apply also to South and Central America, Canada, Rhodesia and South Africa. *To Australia and New Zealand:* letters up to ½ oz., 1s 9d; postcards 10d. These rates are liable to increase in the near future.

The post office near St. Martin's Church, at the corner of Trafalgar Square, has a 24-hour service.

TELEGRAMS. You may send telegrams from any post office or by telephone (dial 190; 100 for overseas). If sending from a public phone booth, have the correct amount ready for insertion when the operator has counted the words. Telegrams can be sent by telephone any hour of the day or night, but few main post offices are open at all hours if you want to hand one in at the counter. The internal rate is 5s for twelve words. Additional words cost 5d each. Full-rate telegrams for priority delivery usually reach their destination within an hour. Overnight telegrams can be sent for 2s 6d for twelve words (2½d each additional word). They are delivered with the first post next morning.

The rate for telegrams to Europe varies according to distance, from 7d per word, overnight letter telegrams 6s 5d for 22 words. To the United States and Canada, 1s 5d per word; overnight, 15s 7d for 22 words. To Australia, New Zealand, Rhodesia and South Africa, 1s 10d per word, overnight 22s 2d for 22 words.

TELEPHONE. Dial more slowly than you would in North America. Overseas rates can be had on application at a post office or from any operator. Telephone kiosks are plentiful in the streets (they are painted red) and in post offices. The working of coin-operated telephones varies but instructions are affixed to the kiosk. Most have STD (timed) calling and you'll need a supply of sixpenny coins. Sixpence buys you 3 minutes' speaking time.

FACTS AT YOUR FINGERTIPS 47

Dialling codes in the greater London area: for general enquiries 191; for all inland directory enquiries 192; for inland long-distance calls 100; for continental calls 104 (except Austria, Germany, the Netherlands, Scandinavia 105); for overseas calls 108, cables 557.

For *emergency calls* throughout the country dial 999.

All-figure telephone numbers are being introduced in London, Birmingham, Edinburgh, Glasgow, Liverpool and Manchester. For the time being, though, calls to the old numbers are still being connected.

PHOTOGRAPHY. American, continental and British color films are obtainable in Britain. Most types can be processed in the country in about three days during the slack season, and in 10 days during July and August. Kodak International has depots in Kingsway and Regent Street, London; they also have agents in other large towns. Black and white film costs from 5s 10d a roll of 20 exposures, color from 20s 8d (which includes processing). Color slides of the British scene can be bought for a few shillings a set at most stores and photographic shops.

TOBACCO. English cigarettes cost 5s 5d (65¢) for a pack of 20, American cigarettes 5s 11d; a cigar will cost anywhere from 1s 9d up. Pipe tobacco costs about 6s to 7s 6d an ounce. Smoking is permitted on railway trains, except in those compartments where a notice appears on the window pane forbidding it. If you want to smoke on a bus, climb to the top deck or the rear of a single-decker. You can smoke in most cinemas, but the practice in theaters varies; look for the notice concerning smoking in the auditorium. At formal banquets you do not smoke until after the toast to the Queen.

USEFUL LONDON TELEPHONE NUMBERS	
Dial	
TIM (or 123)	for the correct time.
ASK 9211 (or 246 8041)	for information on the principal events of the day. (If from a call box refer to the instruction notice.)
WEA 2211 (or 246 8091)	for the local weather report. Essex coast, WEA 3311, Kent coast, WEA 4411, Sussex coast, WEA 5511. For forecasts in other areas, dial the Meteorological office, TEM 4311.
ASK 6611 (or 246 8021)	for road conditions within 50 miles of London (Oct. through April only).

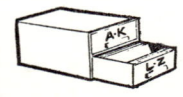

USEFUL ADDRESSES. The *United States Embassy* is at No. 1 Grosvenor Square, W.1 (GRO 9000). A good bet for all questions is the *Tourist Information Centre*, at 64-65 St. James's St., London S.W.1 629 9191). The *London Tourist Board* has information bureaus at West London Air Terminal, Cromwell Road (FRE 4933),

BOAC Terminal, Semley Place (SLO 1596) and at Victoria Station, opposite platform 9 (TAT 5556).

American Express has offices in London (Haymarket) and at 25 Smallbrook Ringway, Birmingham; India Buildings, Water Street, Liverpool; Havelock Chambers, Queen's Terrace, Southampton; 139 Princes Street, in Edinburgh; 115 Hope Street, Glasgow.

Thomas Cook has offices in London and all major cities. *Robert Fisher Ltd.*, 32 Lexington Street, London W.1., will take care of shipping home your overweight luggage.

American Automobile Association, 15 Pall Mall, London S.W.1 (TRA 3077).

TRAVELING IN BRITAIN

BY CAR. The visitor bringing his own car to Britain has the efficient assistance of the two principal motoring clubs, the *Automobile Association*, Fanum House, New Coventry St., London W.1 and the *Royal Automobile Club*, 83 Pall Mall, London S.W.1. Both of them maintain highly organized touring departments which are represented at all the principal ports. It's a good idea to get advice on documents required from your own automobile club before leaving for Britain. On your arrival, the port authority will issue an International Circulation permit which must be displayed on the windshield, and British registration plates, which will cost about 30s. These will not be necessary if you hold an International Certificate for Motor Vehicles, and have a nationality plaque on your car. Your current home driving license is now valid in Britain.

In Britain, you drive on the left-hand side of the road. The speed limit in cities and built-up areas is 30 miles per hour and 40 m.p.h. on many suburban roads. A limit of 50 m.p.h. is sometimes imposed on other roads at weekends in the summer, and there is a limit of 70 m.p.h. on all roads, including motorways. The Automobile Association and the Royal Automobile Club maintain highway patrol services that will help you in any sort of emergency, such as changing a tire or making small repairs, if you are a member (or temporary member).

Motorists wishing to avoid long drives can take advantage of the car-passenger train services ("*Motorail*") operating between London-Newcastle-Edinburgh; London-Plymouth or Penzance; London-Fishguard (summer only, for S. Ireland); London-Perth or Stirling and several others.

The price of gasoline (ask for petrol in Britain) averages about 6s (72¢) per gallon for the ordinary grade, and 6s 6d (78¢) for super. Lubricating oils average around 30¢ (2s 6d) a pint. The British Imperial gallon is substantially larger than the American. Five of the former equal six of the latter.

Car Purchase or Hire. Buying or renting a car is preferable to bringing your own, as American models are unwieldy on narrow English roads and consume more gas than do the small native models. There are

FACTS AT YOUR FINGERTIPS 49

many firms specializing in the hire of self-drive or chauffeur-driven cars, by the hour, day, week, or month. Prices vary according to the size of the car and length of hire. The average summer weekly rate for a small 4-seater is about £15-£25 ($36-60), with unlimited mileage. All firms require a deposit, normally £10 ($24), plus the estimated cost of hire, unless you use a recognized credit card, with which all charges can be paid later. Winter rates are lower. Rates for chauffeur-driven cars range between £10-£15 per day plus a mileage charge, inclusive.

Avis Rent-a-Car 12a Berkeley Street, London W.1 (GRO 4881).
Hertz Rent-a-Car, 243 Knightsbridge, London S.W.7 (KNI 5050).
International Car Hire Ltd., 31 Notting Hill Gate, London W.11 (PAR 1467).
Godfrey Davis, Wilton Road, London S.W.1 (VIC 8484).
J. Davy Ltd., Logan Place, Earls Court Road, London W.8 (FRE 6000).
Martins, 57 Park Road, London N.W.1 (PAD 7950).
Kennings, 84 Holland Park Avenue, London W.11 (PAR 5077).
Autohall, 302 King Street, Hammersmith, London W.6 (RIV 8781).

It is possible to arrange for a self-drive car to be waiting for you at your port of arrival, or any railway station.

If the visitor intends to buy a car in Britain it is best to make arrangements with a distributor at least six weeks in advance. If this is done the car can be waiting at the port or airport on your arrival. Formalities and arrangements to take the car home will be handled by the manufacturers or car purchase agents, some of whose London addresses are listed here:

Auto-Europe, Ltd., 23 Piccadilly, W.1; *British Motor Co. Export Sales*, 41 Piccadilly, W.1; *Ford Motor Co. Ltd.*, 88 Regent St., W.1; *Jaguar Export Sales, Ltd.*, 88 Piccadilly, W.1; *Panocean Ship-A-Car System, Ltd.*, Mount Royal Hotel, W.1; *Rolls Royce & Bentley*, 150 Old Park Lane, W.1; *Rootes, Ltd.*, Devonshire House, Piccadilly, W.1; *Rover Motor Cars*, Devonshire House, Piccadilly, W.1; *Standard-Triumph International, Ltd.*, 15/17 Berkeley Square, W.1; *Vauxhall Motors, Ltd.*, 112 Wardour St., W.1.

BY TRAIN. East-west distances in Britain are so short there is little need for sleepers. North-south is another matter and several sleeper trains are operated, but the British tend to favor their high-speed daylight expresses equipped with restaurant and buffet cars. Where sleeping cars are carried, these are of particularly high standard in 1st class, while the newer 2nd-class cars are probably better than on any other railway system in the world. In any case, sleepers should be reserved well in advance and this applies to famous expresses where accommodation is limited.

You may find the multiplicity of railway stations in London confusing. There are 15 that you might possibly need to use at one time or another —Paddington, Victoria, Waterloo, Charing Cross, Euston, King's Cross, Cannon St., Holborn Viaduct, Blackfriars, London Bridge, Fenchurch St., Broad St., Liverpool St., St. Pancras and Baker Street— and to explain which region is served by each would be so complicated that the best advice that can be given the traveler is to make sure, when

D

he looks up a train, never to think of its point of departure as "London" but as King's Cross or Victoria or whatever.

Here are some of Britain's famous trains to Scotland: *The Flying Scotsman, The Elizabethan, Talisman, Heart of Midlothian, The Royal Scot, Midday Scot, Caledonian, Queen of Scots* (an all-Pullman express), *Royal Highlander,* and *Aberdonian.*

Railway fares start at 3¼d per mile second class, and 50% more first class. Round trip reductions are available for midweek tickets in summer in second class for distances over 100 miles and some same-day journeys. Many inexpensive full-day and half-day excursions are offered. *All-Line Railrover* tickets permit 14 days' unlimited travel by rail in England, Wales and Scotland (also on Clyde and Loch Lomond steamers); price £30 ($72) second class, £45 ($108) first class (plan also available for 7 days); children travel half price and there are reductions for family travel. Also 7-day *Regional Railrover* tickets for shorter journeys; the *Freedom of Scotland* ticket costs £7 15s ($18.60) second class, £11 5s ($22.80) first. Reserving your seat in advance costs 3s (36¢). Sleeper charges between any two stations in Britain are £2 5s ($5.40) for a first class single berth compartment, and £1 10s ($3.60) for a second class two-berth compartment.

If you're in a spending mood, you can charter an 8-coach train for a whole day from about £350 ($840) up.

TRAVEL BUYS

Best rail travel buys for visitors are:

"Thrift" plan, a book of coupons good for up to 1,000 miles of 2nd-class or 675 miles of 1st-class rail travel in Britain at an app. saving of 10% over ordinary fares. The coupons are also good for steamer tickets between Gt. Britain and Ireland and on some services in Scotland. The price per book is $30 2nd class and $45 1st class.

These special tickets can be bought only in the U.S., Canada, South Africa, Australia and New Zealand. (The last 3 countries have a slightly varied plan).

For information: British Railways, 270 Madison Avenue, New York, N.Y.

BY BUS. A network of express bus services links London with the remote country districts and offers a fine way to see the countryside. Prices are not standardized but are approximately 2d a mile There are also both local and long-distance bus lines covering all parts of Britain in an extraordinary close and excellent network. They are too numerous for any attempt to be made to list even the principal lines, but the tourist who wants to use buses to get about is advised to contact Victoria Coach Station, Buckingham Palace Road, London S.W.1, or to invest in a copy of the official *ABC Coach and Bus Guide* (10s.), or $2 post-free from *Iliffe-NTP Inc.,* 300 E. 42nd. St., New York, N.Y. 10017, which lists the principal routes and gives their fares.

FACTS AT YOUR FINGERTIPS 51

BY CANAL BOAT. Information about boat hire companies (for independent travel), and organized all-inclusive cruises, can be obtained from the *Inland Waterways Association* (4 Emerald Street, London W.C.1), the *Association of Pleasure Cruise Operators* (The Wharf, Braunston, Northamptonshire), and the divisional offices of *British Waterways* at Watford, Birmingham and Leeds.

BY AIR. The main centers of England, Ireland, Scotland and Wales are now covered by frequent air services which often cost little more than first class rail fares. The outlying islands are equally accessible by air and flying is often preferable to the choppy and longer sea crossing. Companies with widespread domestic routes are: *BEA*, Dorland House, Lower Regent Street, London S.W.1 (WHI 9044). *British United Airways*, Portland House, Stag Place, London S.W.1 (VIC 8121), whose air terminal is above Victoria Station. *BKS Air Transport Ltd.*, Hodford House, 17 High Street, Hounslow, Middlesex. *British Midlands Airways*, 78 Buckingham Gate, London S.W.1 (ABB 2345). *Cambrian Airways*, Wood Street, Cardiff, S. Wales (Cardiff 22555). *Aer Lingus*, 43 Upper O'Connell Street, Dublin (Dublin 42921), and 174 Regent Street, London W.1 (REG 1212). Full information can be obtained from any of these companies. *BEA* baggage allowance on domestic flights: one large and one small suitcase, regardless of weight. (The latter must fit under your seat).

You can hire a helicopter (1 passenger only) for £25 per flying hour ($60), as well as executive jets, hot-air balloons, etc., from *D. Kay*, Holbrook, Horsham, Sussex.

LEAVING BRITAIN

CUSTOMS GOING HOME. If you propose to take on your holiday any *foreign-made* articles, such as cameras, binoculars, expensive timepieces and the like, it is wise to put with your travel documents the receipt from the retailer or some other evidence that the item was bought in your home country. If you bought the article on a previous holiday abroad and have already paid duty on it, carry with you the receipt for this. Otherwise, on returning home, you may be charged duty.

Americans who are out of the United States at least 48 hours and have claimed no exemption during the previous 30 days are entitled to bring in duty-free up to $100 worth of articles for bona fide gifts or for their own personal use. The value of each item is determined by the price actually paid (so save your receipts). Every member of a family is entitled to this same exemption, regardless of age, and the allowance can be pooled.

Small, duty-free gifts to friends may be mailed (but not more than one to any one address and none to your own home) with a written notation on the package, "Gift, value less than $10". These packages, however, may not include perfumes, tobacco or liquor.

If your purchases exceed your exemption, list the items that are subject to the highest rates of duty under your exemption and pay duty on the items with the lowest rates. Any article you fail to declare cannot later be claimed under your exemption. To facilitate the actual customs examination, it's convenient to pack all your purchases in one suitcase.

Not more than 100 cigars may be imported duty-free per person, nor more than a quart of wine or liquor (none at all if your passport indicates you are from a "dry" state, or if you are under 21 years of age). Only one bottle of perfume that is trademarked in the United States may be brought in, plus a reasonable quantity of other brands.

Antiques are defined, for customs purposes, as articles manufactured more than 100 years ago and are admitted duty free. If there's any question of age, you may be asked to supply proof.

A foreign-made automobile that was ordered before your departure is subject to tax (10% of its "dutiable value"), even though delivered abroad. This same rule applies to any purchase initiated in advance of your trip.

Major purchases such as furniture, sets of china, and the like have to be shipped separately, of course, and are liable to duty. Before you do this, however, consider the pros and cons carefully. Deal with a thoroughly reliable and experienced store and find out exactly what the shipping charges will amount to. In many cases, shipments such as these are handed over to customs brokers and freight forwarders in your country whose charges may be in addition to what you have already paid. Americans in particular sometimes find themselves having to pay $30 to $50 in supplemental charges, such as those on shipments whose value may actually be little more. Make sure, too, that your shipment is insured and that the proper customs documents are attached.

Canada. A person returning from abroad after an absense of not less than 48 hours may take back into Canada any class of goods valued at not more than $25 free of all duty and taxes, *on condition that such goods are included in the baggage accompanying him*, and that they are for his personal or household use, or are intended as souvenirs or gifts. This exemption will not be granted within four months from the date of the last exemption, and is not allowed on alcoholic beverages in excess of 40 ounces, or on tobacco in excess of 50 cigars, 200 cigarettes and 2 lb. of manufactured tobacco. Full particulars are given in the pamphlet, "Customs Hints for Canadian Residents".

NUISANCE TAXES. London Airport does not ask you to pay a ransom to leave the country, but for some reason, the airports at the following do: Birmingham, Abbotsinch at Glasgow, Liverpool and Manchester, 7s 6d (90¢) each.

THE BRITISH SCENE

BRITAIN TODAY

A Fascinating Blend of "Swinging" and Sensible

by

KARL E. MEYER

(*London correspondent of the* Washington Post, *Mr. Meyer is a familiar figure around Whitehall, where he keeps a keen eye on the British political scene. His early book,* Fulbright of Arkansas, *has now been followed by one concerning the pleasures of archeology,* A Visa to Yesterday.)

Suddenly the reputation of everything British seems to be changing. A decade ago, the fashionable certitudes about Great Britain were few and firmly held. It was a nation with an insular people, lovers of tradition and propriety. The working class was stolid and beer-drinking, the middle-class, fusty and the aristocracy, snobbish. One went to Paris for an uninhibited good time; one went to London to photograph Beefeaters. In a previous edition of the Fodor *Guide to Britain*, Sir Compton Mackenzie warned travelers that the British were "excessively, even maddeningly, conservative."

Conservative? Hardly the word that leaps to mind today to describe this switched-on realm, whose capital has been earnestly anointed (by *Time*) as "The Swinging City". Once, Britain seemed indissolubly associated with stately homes, deferential footmen and The Queen. But ask the man next to you what instantly comes to *his* mind when you mention England now! The odds are overwhelming that he will refer to miniskirts, Carnaby Street and The Beatles. Small wonder that not long ago, both the Rev. Billy Graham and Hugh Heffner of *Playboy* simultaneously descended on London to proffer their contrasting therapies.

To a degree, things British are palpably changing. What, for example, could have seemed more unshakably conservative than those three unique institutions, the House of Lords, the BBC and *The Times*? Yet, consider the altered character of each:

Item. For nearly ten centuries, the House of Lords has nobly resisted change of all sorts, but since 1958, the ancient chamber's blue blood has been freshened by the creation of several hundred life peers, including women. Recently, their lordships have actually led the way in proposing liberal reforms of laws dealing with homosexuality, divorce and abortion. In 1965, the house startled everybody, including itself, by voting to abolish capital punishment.

Item. The British Broadcasting Corporation was long regarded as the genteel voice of the Establishment, one critic (Henry Fairlie) fuming in 1959 that no other body had done more to "perpetuate reverence for the mysteries of a conservative society". But now hardly a month goes by without someone making the reverse complaint—that the BBC is too daring, its satirical programmes too impudent, its dramas too earthy. The BBC cannot even produce Lewis Carroll without causing a scandal—some viewers were outraged when Jonathan Miller's television version of *Alice in Wonderland* was deemed too frightening for childish eyes.

Item. No less interesting has been the change in *The Times* (never called *The London Times*, except by foreigners). A century ago, Emerson wrote of *The Times:* "No power in England is more felt, more feared or more obeyed." Not long ago, the paper loftily advertised that it was intended for "Top People". Its front page consisted of grey and uncompromising layers of classified ads, and the news was scattered casually on inside pages. But *The Times* changed its format and proprietor in 1966. Now owned by Lord Thomson, the paper carries front-page news, and ordinary by-lines have supplanted the inscrutable credits to "Our Diplomatic Correspondent". Today the paper advertises that it is read by more people under 35 than any other national daily.

What Hasn't Changed?

If not portents of revolution, these are surely winds of change in a country once obsessed by tradition. Still, the point can be overdrawn. I have been living in London for nearly three years, contentedly sharing the British way of life. What has impressed me most, and what I suspect will most fascinate the discerning visitor, are those enduring British traits that remain so relevant to the world (and particularly to America).

First of all, there is the abhorrence of violence. Britain retains its unique distinction as the only major nation in which policemen carry no firearms. There are more murders every year in Dallas (pop.: 679,684) than in the whole of Britain (pop.: 55,068,000). When the Queen, or the prime minister, appears in public, there are no platoons of armed guards. In three centuries, only one prime minister has been assassinated (Spencer Perceval in 1812; killed by a madman). Possibly one reason for this pacific tradition is that the sale of firearms is subject to rigorous controls—try to purchase a pistol and see for yourself.

Secondly, I would list the courtesy and fair-play that seem almost instinctive. The queue at the bus stop is an emblem of national manners, and in no country are words like "please" and "sorry" more frequently used. The habit is quickly imitated by strangers, but, alas, not easily exported.

Next: the tolerance for eccentricity. It is true that England remains a class-haunted country, a place where one's pedigree, accent and schooling can assume undue importance. Generations of Americans have rightfully, and often righteously, made this reproach. But Alexis de Tocqueville observed a century ago that Americans tend to value equality more than liberty; in England, the reverse is the case.

This devotion to liberty can be illustrated in a hundred ways. There is Speakers' Corner at Hyde Park, where each weekend Britons gather to hear their country eloquently abused by apostles of everything from anarchism to Zoroastrianism. There is the custom of heckling at political meetings—and in parliament. There is the proliferation of curious cult groups, ranging from the Druids and the Jacobites (who still support the Stuart claim to the throne) to the International Flat Earth Society, which believes just what the name suggests. Above all, there is the respect accorded to the gifted non-conformist who insists on being incorrigibly himself: Bertrand Russell, Sir Francis Chichester and Malcolm Muggeridge are as much a part of the national landscape as Trafalgar Square.

Finally, the cultural amenities. Here we encounter an interesting contrast. Though Britain pioneered in the industrial revolution, she has since fallen badly behind. Her factories are often ill-equipped, ill-managed and bedeviled by strikes. Exasperated foreign residents delight in exchanging stories about the sometimes absurd inefficiencies of British life. My own apartment, for example, contains four (4) kinds of electric plugs; merely to move a lamp across the floor requires advanced electrical surgery.

Livable—and Lovable—Cities

The British themselves admit that such perplexities are hard to explain and impossible to defend. Still, though Britain has been outstripped by Americans in technology, she has managed somehow to make her cities livable, likable, even navigable. In London, the visitor is quickly impressed by the admirable transportation system. The homely taxis can zip like hares through the maze of streets; the bus stops are so clearly marked that a stranger can grope his way around after two days; and the Underground makes the New York subway look like an artifact of mesolithic times. No less impressive are the countless parks and squares, with their emerald lawns and bountiful flowerbeds. Indeed, everywhere one finds flowerboxes—on police stations, on banks and office buildings, and in Underground depots. It can be said that Britain rivals Japan in its passion for horticulture.

Britain's rise as a world cultural power is by now familiar, but still a little startling to those accustomed to believe that a nation of shopkeepers must be insensible to the arts. In fact, the British have long been devoted to music, and this addiction has helped London to acquire four major symphonies, two opera companies and an extraordinarily rich diet of concerts. (Covent Garden, by the way, is the only opera company in a non-German-speaking country that produces Wagner's *Ring* cycle every year.) The theater is in danger of being overpraised, but only the perverse would deny the excellence of the two state-aided repertory companies, the *Royal Shakespeare* and the *National Theatre*. Every year, films made in Britain seem to win more Academy Awards, though this may be a fallible gauge of merit. Less well-known elsewhere is the superlative quality of British television; it is generally conceded that the public benefits from competition between the Independent Television Authority, which takes commercials, and BBC, which doesn't. The important point is that on both networks, producers genuinely care about program *content* as well as ratings. Advertisers have no control of ITV, and politicians cannot dictate to BBC. British television comes as close as possible to being truly independent, and more often than any other service, it actually caters to grown-ups.

In my own field of journalism, a splendid competitiveness prevails. There are ten national dailies, and seven national Sunday papers—enough to give the visiting American a severe case of cultural shock. Moreover, the "quality" dailies (*The Times, Guardian, Telegraph, Financial Times*), together with the three best Sunday papers (*Sunday Times, Observer, Sunday Telegraph*) and the opinion weeklies (*Economist, New Statesman, Spectator*), collectively comprise the most literate press in the world. The British, in fact, are compulsive readers. They buy more newspapers, per capita, than any other nation, and more book titles are published each year than in the United States, despite the difference in population. (A notable British invention, incidentally, is the paperback of high quality and low price—the *Penguin* has proved a highly migratory bird.)

In all of this there is a salient common feature: what is best is highly accessible. Except for newly-opened hit plays and the National Theatre, theater tickets can usually be obtained the day of performance. There are bookstalls everywhere, more per capita than anywhere but Denmark. In warmer months, music can be heard free in the parks (the Greater London Parks Department puts out an admirable seasonal program, *Open-Air Entertainment*, for a shilling). To be sure, opera tickets can be scarce and dear, but outstanding productions are broadcast or televised. Seldom has so much been so available to so many for so little.

Still, any discussion of the quality of British life must sooner or later confront the unpalatable topic of food. It must be freely confessed: eating is a gamble that the patron too often loses. But there has been measurable improvement. There are enough acceptable restaurants to justify a thick and useful *Good Food Guide*. And there is sufficient candor about the infirmities of British gastronomy to warrant publication (in 1967) of the necessary companion volume, a *Bad Food Guide*. If and when Britain joins the European Common Market, perhaps France can be persuaded to send a Peace Corps unit to improve still further an underdeveloped native cuisine!

And in turn, the United States might benefit from a British Peace Corps, to make our cities more fit for human habitation —and to make our newstands a less depressing display of the monopoly mentality.

The Decline and Fall of Nobody

The visitor to these isles can be usefully forewarned of two things. First: don't dwell solemnly on "swinging London", because it is something of a national joke, like James Bond. It is strictly for the tourist trade; tellingly, Madame Tussaud's Waxworks has installed a special exhibition on the "Swinging Scene" (but in very temporary cardboard, not in expensive wax!). Cars have been barred from Carnaby Street during the daytime hours—the throng of gawking foreigners simply choked off traffic.

Second: don't expect the British to be in a despondent, tragic mood about the decline-and-fall theme. As long ago as 1758, an Irishman (Arthur Murphy) remarked: "The people of England are never so happy as when you tell them they are ruined."

There are persuasive explanations for the very casual, almost nonchalant, national response to adversity. One is based on the fact that Britain was the only major European country that did not endure the humiliation of defeat and occupation in World War II. The memory of 1940, therefore, survives as a comforting national legend which can be read to mean that, in the end, St. George always slays the dragon.

Geography, too, provides a clue; it has been decisive in shaping the British character. The country's position as an offshore island meant that Britain was able to develop its institutions without periodic invasions, unlike France, Germany and Italy. Indeed, the English commemorated the only recent military invasion—the Norman Conquest of 1066—as if it were a victory instead of a defeat! This insular security helped Britain to make a fetish of gradualness. Since 1789, France has lived under at least two dozen different constitutions, while the British have existed under only one—and an unwritten one at that. The gradualist temper that has evolved in Britain is in striking contrast to the apocalyptic mood that has encouraged recurrent wars and revolution on the continent.

But there are points of stress and tension in British life that the traveler can hardly fail to notice, because the country is coping with the perplexities of two nations, three roles and four (non-English) cultures. Let us look deeper into each.

The Young, "Swinging" and Sober

The Two Nations. Disraeli coined the phrase a century ago to describe the country's rich and poor. Sir Denis Brogan, earlier in this book, uses it to describe the South of England as opposed to other parts of Britain. Today, the phrase also can be applied to the young and old, who have seldom had so little in common. In graphic terms, the age distribution of the British population is not a pyramid but a dumb-bell. Improvement in health standards has markedly reduced the death rate, while the birth-rate has continued to remain high since the wartime baby-boom. Between now and 1980, the number of old people (over 65) will increase by 25 per cent, the number of people between 20 and 39 will increase by 15 per cent—while the middle-group, between 40 and 64, will *decrease* by six per cent. By 1984, half the population will be under 35.

The Welfare State has levelled out the old distinctions that marked the rich and poor. An excellent system of free medical care has eliminated the wretched teeth that were once the most visible badge of poverty. Relative full employment has banished all but the memory of the dole. So, as one walks down the streets today, the most obvious difference between people that one notices is not determined by income—it is determined by age.

The youngsters of Britain dress differently, behave differently and think differently than their sometimes dismayed elders. Their plumage is bright and individualistic; hair and dress styles serve to blur the differences between the sexes. Their outlook tends to be more classless, their tastes more impulsive, their sexual mores more relaxed than those of their disapproving parents. They think far less about Britain's role in the world, than their own role in a diminished country. They are as different as chalk and cheese from the generations that preceded them.

On almost every level of British life, the pressure of this rising generation is a powerful force for change in Britain, affecting everything from BBC programs and the format of *The Times*, to the legislation passed by the House of Lords. For better or worse, Britain is moving from a duty-centered to a pleasure-centered psychology, thanks to youngsters who have far more in common with each other than any among them—rich or poor—has with the dour oldsters of their own class and kind.

Eyes East, Eyes West?

The three roles. If the conflict of generations is remoulding British life at home, the choice of world obligations is reshaping the external attitudes of an island kingdom. Ever since the end of World War II, Britain has sought to accommodate to its three conflicting international roles, as the head of the commonwealth, as the Anglo-American partner, and as the good European.

The commonwealth (the word was minted, ironically, by Jan Christian Smuts of South Africa, which no longer belongs), has come to be a kind of emotional substitute for the British Empire, which once coated a quarter of the map in scarlet. In actual terms, Britain now has direct responsibility for 22 territories with 6,500,000 inhabitants, the biggest of which is Hong Kong (pop. 3,785,000). The rest of the commonwealth comprises 26 wholly independent countries with some 700 million inhabitants, white, black, brown and yellow.

In fact, as successive British governments have come to realize, the commonwealth is more an expression of sentiment than a geopolitical reality, since individual members not illogically give higher priority to their own national interests than to British needs.

Much more immediately relevant is the Anglo-American alliance, formed in two world wars and tested in recurrent crises. The Atlantic partnership is grounded in a common heritage, and finds expression in a variety of fields: financial, diplomatic and defence. There is little doubt that without American support, Britain long ago would have been compelled to devalue sterling—nor is there much doubt that without British support in Asia, the United States would be far more lonely in its rigorous prosecution of the Vietnam war.

But both the commonwealth and the Anglo-American tie complicate Britain's attempt to become the seventh member of the European Common Market. The American visitor will find far more concern with the continent than he is likely to expect—he will hear more than he anticipates about those cryptic initials "EEC" (European Economic Community, an alternate name for the Common Market). For the British, the EEC poses an uncomfortable dilemma.

Successive governments—the Tories in 1961, and the Labour Party in 1967—have decided that membership in EEC offers the best solution to this trading country's needs for a market, and for a diplomatic arena in which to play a significant role in the world. But former Pesident Charles de Gaulle of France made it no less evident that he felt Britain's ties with the commonwealth and the United States are incompatible with British membership in the EEC.

Hence Britain today is still debating where her ultimate interests lie, whether in becoming a full-fledged European country, or whether as an Atlantic and commonwealth power, prudently hedging her bets in a cruelly uncertain world.

England's "Other Ten Million"

The Four-Cultures Problem. However this dilemma is resolved, another is certain to continue, namely, the question of assuring peaceful co-existence between the English and the four non-English cultures of the United Kingdom: the Welsh, Scottish, Irish and non-white commonwealth immigrants.

In prosaic statistical terms, the four cultures can be measured like this:

Wales: 2,709,900 inhabitants.

Scotland: 5,186,600 inhabitants.

Northern Ireland: 1,425,000 inhabitants (the Republic of Ireland has 2,818,000).

Non-white immigrants: about 1,000,000 inhabitants.

In this breakdown, I have not included the English, the roughly 44 million inhabitants who constitute the overwhelming majority of the population. That, indeed, is the chief problem—there are so many English, and so few of the other four peoples, who have each developed a siege mentality. The English are so certain of their predominance that they cannot be troubled to take seriously the complaints of the minorities— or so it seems to those non-English peoples who must live with so overwhelming a majority. The fierce resentments of the Irish ultimately brought about the creation of an independent republic, though predominantly Protestant Northern Ireland remains under the Crown. In Wales (1966) and Scotland (1967), for the first times ever, nationalists were elected to parliament in by-elections. In both areas, the demand for home rule is growing. (In Scotland, the Queen is not universally recognized as Elizabeth II, since the first Elizabeth was the sovereign only of England—post boxes which contained the offending *II* were decapitated by zealous patriots, and now a noncommittal crown is appended to the Queen's name.)

The non-white immigrants constitute a more difficult, and contemporary problem. Some came from India and Pakistan, some from Africa, and many from the West Indies, but all came before Britain in 1964 tightened up the laws controlling commonwealth immigration. But the colored subjects who are already here have not been given an altogether laudable welcome. Official bodies have frankly admitted that blatant discrimination has been practiced against non-white Britons, and the country is coping with a problem alike in kind, if not in degree, with the civil rights problem in the United States.

Nevertheless, in the fullness of time, British fair play is sure to prevail over bigotry. In the classic phrase, the English "muddle through". Though this tradition provides grounds neither for complacency nor self-congratulation, it is still an accurate measure of the staying-power of a nation. It cannot be forgotten that a country which some observers decried as "decadent" in the 1960's, took stringent legislative medicine,

Trooping the Colour is an annual event

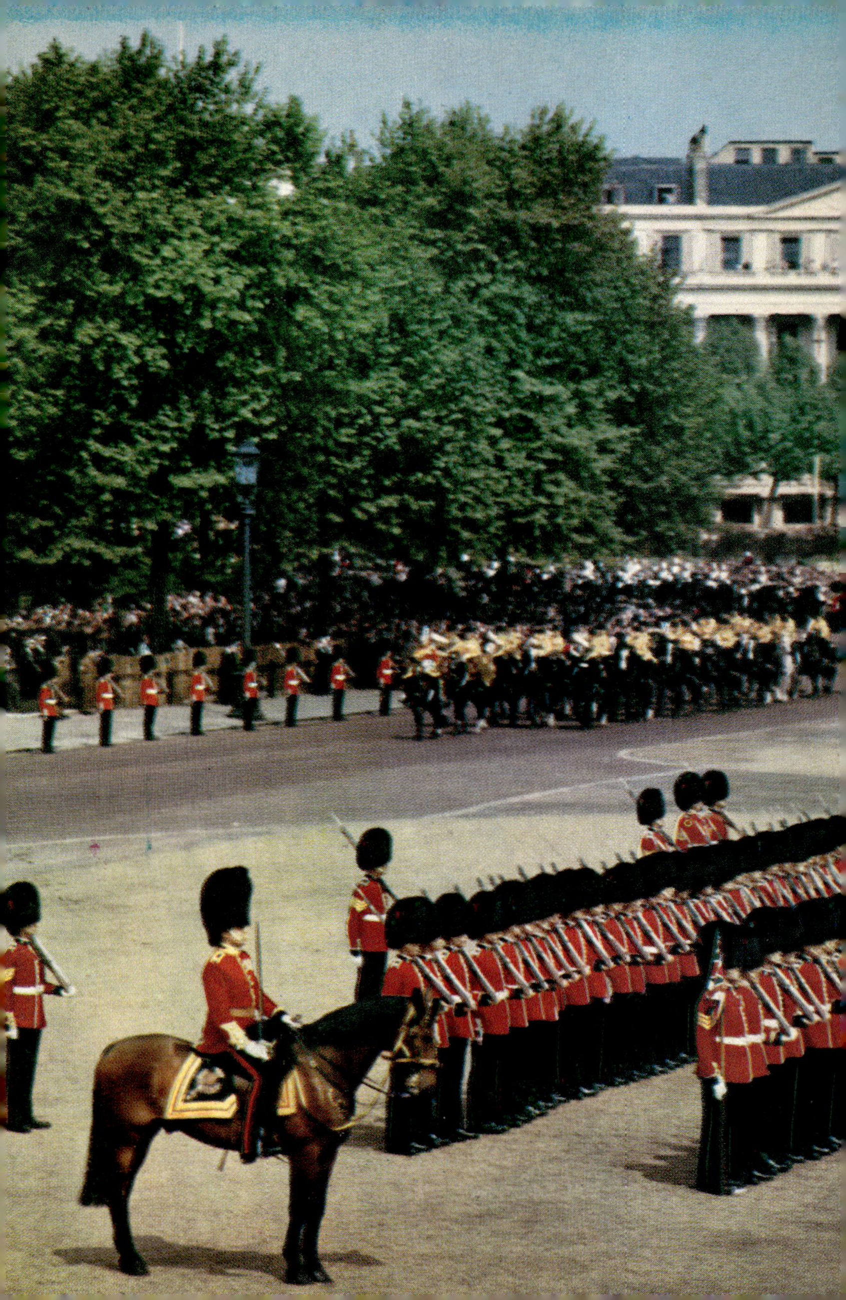

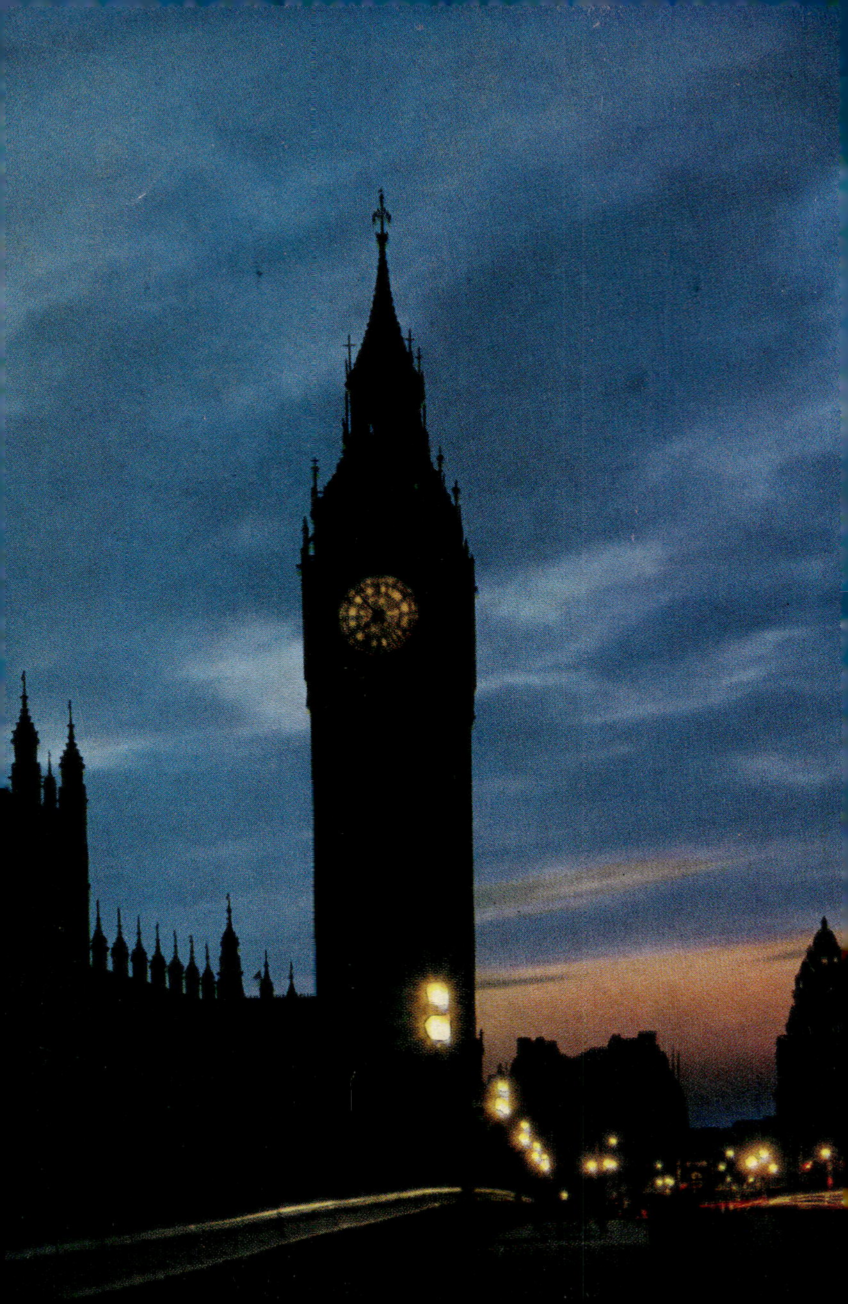

without precedent in any other free country, by freezing wages and prices for an entire year. The fact that so little enforcement was required for so sweeping a decree provides the best refutation to those who too easily count Britain out. Whatever the stresses in British society, the ability to muddle through remains.

In truth, Britain is a more complicated place than either its detractors or uncritical admirers usually suggest. There is no better summation of the complexity of the English traits than this fine passage from Emerson, which provides the aptest of conclusions:

"Everything English is a fusion of distant and antagonistic elements. The language is mixed; the names of men are of different nations ... the currents of thought are counter; contemplation and practical skill; active intellect and dead conservatism; world-wide enterprise, and devoted use and want; aggressive freedom and hospitable law, with bitter class legislation: a people scattered by their wars and affairs over the face of the earth, and homesick to a man ... nothing can be praised in it without damning exceptions, and nothing denounced without salvos of cordial praise."

Big Ben, one of the world's most famous landmarks.

THE BRITISH

Portrait of an Island People

by

JOHN BARR and J. P. MARTIN

(*Mr. Barr is the author of our* What's On in Britain *chapter, later in this book. J. P. Martin, an English author who lives in France, has written many books, including* The Silver Key *and* L'Ile Inconnue.)

Coming to Britain from the United States or from the continent of Europe, you will realize immediately that you have come to a strange little world. Britain is an island—and not only in the geographical sense of the word. The sea around this "green and pleasant land"—especially that blade of water, the Channel, which snips Britain off from the fabric of Europe—has created much more than a 93,000-square-mile lump on its own. The geographical separation has contrived a distinctively *British* quality in the people and in their institutions, manners and attitudes.

You will soon find that a deep distinction exists between *Us* (The British) and *Them* (everyone else). This does not mean that the British are unfriendly towards strangers, though suspicion of foreigners *is* a traditional British trait—a trait which, however, is fast vanishing in an age when London office girls spend their vacations on the Costa Brava and housewives in Liverpool concoct *spaghetti con carne* for menfolk more accustomed to Lancashire Hot Pot.

Even though outright suspicion of foreigners is dying, that distinction between *Us* and *Them* remains, and you will be conscious of it the moment you arrive and pass through the customs at the airport or seaport. Most probably you will encounter, first of all, that British institution-of-a-man, the bobby in elongated helmet (or, in these days of a shortage of policemen, perhaps a "bobbette" in a modified mini-skirt). After the bobby, the next thing that will strike you is the segregation into "British" and "non-British" entrances for passport stamping. You will find yourself in the more exotic line, alongside Neapolitan bricklayers coming to work in Bedfordshire or Egyptian bellydancers about to wriggle in a Soho strip club. When you reach the passport men and then the customs officers, you will be treated just as civilly as any Briton returning from a weekend in Paris. But you will have been subtly impressed by the fact that you are one of *Them*.

One caution at this point: it is easy—and sometimes socially perilous—for the foreign visitor to forget that not all Britons are English, that the United Kingdom of Great Britain and Northern Ireland (to give it its grand and proper name) is a marriage (and occasionally a *Who's Afraid of Virginia Woolf?* kind of marriage) of English, Scottish, Welsh and Ulstermen, each with their jealously-protected and -proclaimed national dignities. More of this later: what follows applies with few exceptions (but with the limitations common to any attempt to generalize about a nation) to all the British from John O'Groats in northern Scotland to Land's End on England's southwest tip.

Manners and Self-Discipline

In the first few days, before you get to know the British better, you will be struck only by the strangeness of their manners. They are a well-disciplined people, and it is probably no exaggeration to say that they have the best manners in the world. You will find fifty-four million gentlemen—if one may also include women in this heading (and why not?). You will find here banker-gentlemen, industrialist-gentlemen tobacconist-gentlemen, many road-sweeper-gentlemen, and fishmonger-gentlemen. They are all polite in their reserved and curt way; they all know how to hold their knives and forks and how to behave in society. But it is not so much a superficial layer of indoctrinated behaviour as inborn self-discipline that is so striking. During the first days of your stay, you will see some of the famous British queues at bus-stops and outside theatres. The idea of queueing—or standing in line as the Americans call it—is a British idea. The full acceptance of the idea of "first come, first served," the faithful observance and cheerful acceptance of the necessary drawbacks of communal life and, particularly, the realization of these thoughts in practical life, are of British origin.

On the continent, even in Western Europe, you will sometimes see two people run into each other in the street and then start a violent quarrel, calling each other names, usually of a zoological character. Such a thing is almost unimaginable in Britain. Should such an event occur, the two people concerned will say, "Sorry," to each other and proceed on their way. If there develops any argument at all, it will be to establish whose fault it was—each party stoutly maintaining that "it was my fault".

This is not to say that Britons are never rude. They are sometimes. But even rudeness is expressed only in undertones. That is why visitors often do not even realize that they have, in fact, been told off and roughly treated. Coarse expressions are hardly ever used. British discourtesy is, as a rule, phrased in brief, acid, or incredulous questions.

At least this gentlemanliness and gentleness, self-discipline and disguised rudeness is what you will *probably* encounter. But things are changing in Britain as elsewhere. For example, it is just possible these days that your first taxi ride will be with a cabbie far removed from the British stereotype of the self-effacing, taciturn, ever-polite chap who doffs his cap in gratitude (or tugs his forelock if he has one) when you grandly thrust a one shilling (12-cent) tip in his palm. He may instead be as boisterous and bellowing as the archetypal Brooklyn cabbie, full to the brim with sidewalk philosophy and ready with a devastating stream of contempt if you undertip. Or you may find, as you wait for your first red doubledecker bus in London, that the queue system is not quite so disciplined as expected: some thrusting, elbow-flagging dear little old lady from the very back of the queue may suddenly appear at your side, and as you massage your jabbed ribs slip in before you. And when she does, you may well hear oaths hissed by others in the queue that would hold their own in any knock-down verbal warfare.

But if traditional British politeness is suffering slightly in these days of faster, more impatient living, British understatement is still pretty much intact at most times and still impresses anyone accustomed to more obvious and often hyperbolic expressions. Only the fans of the Beatles or the Rolling Stones are likely to use overstatements like "fabulous". The more usual expression of glee is "rather nice". You will notice this when you first read the editorials ("leaders") in one of the "quality" newspapers—especially that one which is as much an institution as a newspaper, *The Times*. If a continental newspaper wishes to attack a politician it must use the most violent epithets in its vocabulary, or the most killing sarcasm to make the attack really effective. Should *The Times*, on the other hand, remark that "we are astonished", or, "it is rather surprising"—it counts as an outspoken expression of disapproval. (Whether this low-key approach will gradually change as a result of the takeover of *The Times* recently by the bluff Canadian press baron, Lord Thomson, remains to be seen.)

The result, naturally, is that *The Times*—and the everyday English language—has many more shades of disapproval and praise than any other language in the world, including the American. And so you may well be generally impressed by the "eloquence" of the British, especially the university graduates you meet. There is something about their fluency of speech, their verbal self-confidence, their "English accent" itself, which makes the most trivial statement appear somehow profound. This may not, however, be your reaction when you meet a less-educated Briton: then, instead of understatement and articulateness, you may be surprised by the informality and even apparent intimacy of the words they use. Many a foreign visitor has spilled his tea in astonishment when the waitress addressed him as "dearie" or even "darling". It isn't flirting and it isn't improper, but in fact a kind of politeness, a habit of working-class speech which no Briton would find offensive.

Dislike of Theories

The visitor is bound to notice that life in England is glorified village life. London, with its many small houses with comparatively large gardens, is not only the world's second largest town, it is also its largest village. London was built as a village, or rather as many villages. It was not planned, like Washington; it grew like a mushroom. Houses were built next to each other, and the result was a number of villages; these villages grew till they touched each other's frontiers, and the result is London.

It is, by the way, in London that you will meet most dramatically the changes and the contradictions in British manners and "life attitudes" that have been wrought in recent years. *Time* magazine has written about the "swinging London" of pop singers, fashion photographers and casino addicts—all far removed from the conventional picture of a somewhat staid city of people who don't display their emotions or seek their pleasures in quite so uninhibited a way as most other Europeans. Other commentators have called London "the new vice (or sex) capital of the world", bursting with heroin pushers, prostitutes and transplanted Mafia men. These are exaggerations, but there has been, throughout Britain and in London especially, a certain loosening of the high moral standards (in *public* at least) which characterized the Briton of Victorian days and even up to the Second World War. The younger Britons are certainly more carefree and less respectful of institutions than were their fathers and grandfathers.

But all this is pretty much on the surface; in the essentials, certain British attitudes and life-styles are so ingrained that they remain virtually unchanged. Take the people's optimistic ingenuity in times of crisis, their genius for improvisation, and their obsession with compromise in all things at all times. At times like Dunkirk and the Battle of Britain (and more recently during the country's economic difficulties), the Briton's quality of "a stiff upper lip" and of optimism in moments of possible disaster shows itself. "It's funny, but it works" is a popular national saying that tells a lot about the people: things may be unplanned or ill-planned, they may appear or in fact *be* inefficient, they may be laughable but if they work, then that is okay with everyone. This feeling contributes to (or is the result of) the national faith in the amateur as opposed to the professional, the gentleman rather than the player. And improvisation as a virtue is entangled with the love of compromise, which—in this highly democratic nation—often results in a lot of talk and very little action. When there is a problem, the typical British response to it is "set up a committee". This postpones difficult decisions and, when decisions finally drag their slow way to a conclusion, leads to compromise.

Fair Play and a Fair Hearing

The "love of fair play" is rather a worn-out phrase but, all the same, a true one. And the British love of fair play is much stronger than group, party, or even self-interest. Some time ago an anti-socialist play was banned on television (rather by mistake, as it turned out later), and a general loud outcry followed this decision. Socialists, Conservatives, and Liberals all protested. Almost everyone believed that freedom of speech and criticism was much more important than the question of whether a certain play made unfair and sarcastic remarks about a political party.

This tolerance of other people's views means that Britain probably has more eccentrics per head of population than any other nation in the world. Odd philosophies, crankish outbursts, unconventional behaviour are not viewed with alarm, nor is the conventional Briton's first inclination to pack such people off to the nearest asylum: they may be "nutty", but they are entitled to a fair hearing.

Curiouser and Curiouser?

Of course, when you first come to Britain, you may well decide that practically *all* the people are odd. Not true, of course, but it is true that there are many British traits which strike the foreigner as curious. There is their sentimentality and passion for animals: charities devoted to protecting dogs and cats from human cruelty receive far more money every year than charities devoted to the protection of children. "The animal cult", the late George Orwell called it in outrage.

Then there is the curious British taste for sex and violence—

but at second or third-hand, not at first-hand. Compared to the United States, Britain is a tame, law-abiding nation, with respected legal processes and unarmed bobbies; you may not be able to walk alone in Central Park in New York City after dark, but you can in London's Hyde Park. Violence is comparatively rare in real life, and that may explain why Britons so adore reading about it—or watching it on their television screens, usually in the shape of imported American gangster films and westerns. For in addition to the aforementioned *Times* of London, you should buy one of the morning tabloid newspapers or the sensational Sunday papers that sell anything up to seven million copies of a single issue. Their doses of sex and violence make the yellowest American tabloid look positively prim.

And finally, of course, there is the Britons' tenacious respect for traditions and for the authorities who exercise those traditions—an old-fashioned attitude which often surprises and amuses Americans. The young and irreverent minority, the swinging jet set which has appeared on the British scene in the 1960's, may suggest that this acceptance of tradition and authority is breaking down. Even so, for example, the vast majority of Britons (even British Communists) are fascinated by the panoply and persons of their largely impotent monarchy. Thousands of people will stand in the rain just to catch a quick glimpse of the Queen (or even Princess Margaret) passing by in a parade. The Queen, despite her lack of real power, is the ultimate expression of national tradition and authority. She is Britain, she *is* the British people.

Is this to say that the British are servile and worship authority? Certainly not. They do not worship authority but accept it willingly—with one important qualification. They, themselves, must be the source of this authority.

Hypocritical and Humourless Snobs?

Three common criticisms of the British should be touched on briefly. The first is this: are the British hypocrites? Well—what is hypocrisy? One dictionary defines the word as, "feigning to be what one is not". In that sense the British are not hypocrites because they are not liars. But they certainly think the world of themselves, not as individuals but as a nation, although they will not say so. Generally speaking, they often let the other fellow speak while they themselves keep silent. They are unwilling to speak their mind; when a clear statement or a forthright declaration is asked for, they puff their pipes and bring up another subject. They may not be hypocrites but are they sincere? "The English hardly ever lie, but they would not dream of telling you the truth."

The second common criticism of the British is that they lack a sense of humour—or that if they have one, it is so slow-motion as to be useless. Everyone is familiar with the stories, probably apocryphal, of the Englishman in the audience at a comedy show who laughs five minutes after the joke has been told. The truth is that the British *do* have a sense of humour, but that it is exclusive to them, a national "in-groupish" humour: dry, understated, frequently difficult for the stranger to perceive. Rollicking, red-faced, Teutonic humour—of the pulling-a-chair-out-from-under-someone sort—is almost unknown in Britain. But the Britons' ultimate and decisive answer to the charge of humourlessness is that they are, almost to a man, capable of what is surely the highest mark of humour: they can and do constantly laugh at themselves. (Just look at the cartoons in *Punch* for proof.) They see the preposterous side of British character and manners. Indeed, in recent years—as Britain's empire and her world importance have shrunk and her domestic economic troubles have grown—this poking-fun-at-ourselves game has reached such proportions that some sociologists and psychologists are contending that Britain is suffering from a national inferiority complex, infatuated with the notion of how awful everything in Britain is. You'll encounter this rather bitter attitude everywhere you go in Britain these days.

Lastly, are many British stuffy snobs, and is British society as class-ridden as often imagined? Only twenty-five or so years ago, the answer to both questions might well have been "Yes". But in postwar years, Britain has moved rapidly towards a "meritocracy", in which success depends not, as before, on birth and breeding, inherited wealth and exclusive education, but on natural talent, drive and ambition. By American standards, Britain is still a long way from being a meritocracy; class barriers are coming down, but they have not been abolished. For the Briton, if not for the foreigner, it is still possible to tell by a person's accent whether he has been to "Oxbridge" (Oxford or Cambridge universities.) By his or her manner of dress, you can tell a lot about "breeding" and wealth. (The working-class person wears his best clothes on Sundays; the upper-class person wears baggy old tweeds and a battered deerstalker cap, for example—but old and battered though his clothes may be, they are made of the very best quality cloth.) The "Old Boy Net" still operates in Britain—the best jobs, the highest pay, the social prominence, the positions of power go more often than not to the person who attended the right school, knows the right people, moves in the "Old Boy Net" circles. But in another fifty years, British class-consciousness, at the rate it is now disappearing, may be a sociological dodo.

Those Other Britons

In so far as any generalizations about national character mean anything, most of these things apply to all the British people—Scottish, Welsh and Northern Irish, as well as English. But there are distinct differences that you will notice if you travel to those other parts of the United Kingdom. You begin to feel the difference if you move north from London into Yorkshire and the counties that border on Scotland: the people are perhaps more like Americans—franker and, you may feel, friendlier than the people in the south of England. (Fewer snobs about too, you may say!) The tougher climate and, by British standards at least, the wide open spaces of northern England contribute to a more rugged, outspoken, no-nonsense kind of people.

When you reach Scotland, you will feel these changes even more abruptly: the Scotsman's slower and softer speech and his informality and lack of effeteness may well make you feel he is more akin to an American than to an Englishman. In Scotland, although education is considered every bit as important as in England, *exclusive* education at, say, a "public school" (what Americans would call a private school) is less valued and the Scots admire more the self-made man and the practical man. He may not know his ancient Greek, they'll say, but he is practical and efficient, hard-working and hard-headed. It is not, then, surprising that for centuries, the world has been populated by practical-minded Scottish inventors and engineers who have emigrated from their mother country to seek their fortunes. (Alexander Graham Bell and Andrew Carnegie are but two of an army.)

The Scots, it should be said, often consider themselves superior to the English. James Barrie wrote, "A young Scotsman let loose on the world . . . what could he not do? It's almost appalling to think of; especially if he went among the English!" (Many Scotsmen do still bear historical grudges against the English and nearly all Scotsmen are fiercely patriotic about Scotland—sometimes they can carry this patriotism to considerable extremes.) In any event, you will also find that Scotsmen consider themselves superior not only to the English but to their fellow Scotsmen from other parts: people from Edinburgh (the cultural capital of Scotland) look down on people from Glasgow (the industrial capital) as boors; Scottish Highlanders consider Scottish Lowlanders to be soft and spoiled by civilization; Scottish islanders have similar views about Scottish mainlanders!

The Scots are commonly considered to be a dour, even lugubrious people, except perhaps twice a year—on the anniversary of their beloved Robert Burns (January 25th) and at New Year, when practically every Scotsman takes at least one too many "wee drops" of his home-grown whisky.

There isn't, however, much more truth in this dour stereotype than there is in the common ideas about those other people of Britain, the Welsh. They are all imagined to be natural-born singers strumming away on harps or natural-born poets insistently writing away in their odd, dying Cymraeg, a Celtic language. All the men work as sheep-shearers or miners; all the women wear tall funny black hats—according to this description of the Welsh. It is, however, true that, like the Scottish, the Welsh are often fiercely patriotic and suspicious of those Englishmen across the border. In 1966, a Welsh Nationalist Party candidate was elected for the first time in history to a seat in the House of Commons. He ran on a platform that included separate nationhood for Wales and a seat for Wales in the United Nations. These aims will never be realized, and it should be said that most Welshmen don't want them to be, but the example does suggest that if you visit Wales, you will find a proud people who are clinging to old Welsh traditions and speech—and they won't appreciate it if you just lump them with the English. They like to consider themselves different, even if their traditions, like the language, are dying out.

The average Ulsterman, however, one of the 1.5 million inhabitants of Northern Ireland, is more likely to be vigorously loyal to England and the Queen. The stereotype of the Irishman, loud-lunged and rowdily roaming from pub to pub, with a brogue as thick as cheese, usually falls apart when you come to Northern Ireland. It is not just a matter of religion, that the Irishman from Ireland is usually a Roman Catholic and the Ulsterman usually a Protestant—although that religious divide, which caused the severance of Ireland nearly 50 years ago, still exists and still causes pain and tensions. It is just that the Ulsterman tends to be less outgoing by nature, less gregarious and garrulous than Irishmen from south of the border. In fact, if you visit Belfast, you may find the people only marginally distinguishable in their manners and attitudes and dress (bowler hats and umbrellas abound) from the people of any large English city.

Less British But Still British

For the fact is, all Britons—Scots and Welsh included—are getting more alike every year. And Britons as a whole are getting less "British" and more like people of other countries. This is the irreversible trend caused by jet air travel, international contacts, a shrinking world. The British sometimes complain that they are getting too Americanized, that American jazz and hamburgers and materialistic ideas are corrupting them. In may not be corruption, but it is happening —at least on the surface. But below the surface you will still find the British to be a distinct and appealingly different species—which is just as well. For that, after all, is one of the reasons you come to Britain, isn't it?

THE ROLE OF TRADITION

Living Links with the Past

There is no other nation that clings to the past with the tenacity of the British. The Briton has a sense of the continuity of history. He loves to go through his ancient ceremonies as he has always performed them, with the consciousness that he is keeping faith with his ancestors, that he is maintaining the community they created. He does not often change his manner of carrying out official acts, and if ever he does, the new method at once becomes the tradition.

Queen Elizabeth the First provided one of these examples of discarding the old and supplanting it with the new. She was knitting when the list of nominees for sheriff was brought to her. Tradition decreed that she should take up her quill and make a check in ink against the name of each person whom it was her pleasure to appoint. There was no pen handy. So Elizabeth the First, with one of her knitting needles, pricked a little hole in the parchment beside each favoured name. That is the reason why today Queen Elizabeth the Second appoints sheriffs of England by pricking holes in the paper listing their names.

Queen Elizabeth the First started another tradition, a ceremony participated in to this day by British barristers who are members of the Middle Temple. As a student, the aspiring lawyer goes into chambers, which is to say that he takes up a desk in one of the Four Inns of Court to read law, and among the requirements which he must fulfill is to take a certain number of meals at the commons of his Inn, an immense hall with long tables stretching down its length at right angles to that of the "benchers" at the head—the benchers being those fortunate chiefs of the Inn's hierarchy whose perquisites include a stated daily allowance of beer and port.

Of the four Inns, the Middle Temple had, for some reason, been the favourite of Elizabeth I. On one occasion she had done it the honour of preparing a pudding with her own hands, and since that day generations of barristers have been eating pieces of that same pudding. You might expect it to be a trifle musty after some three and a half centuries. Not a bit. For when Queen Elizabeth made the original pudding, part of it was carefully saved. The next week a new pudding was made, into which the original morsel was incorporated. A portion of the second pudding was saved also, and mixed, on the third week, into still another pudding. And so, for 350 years, the lawyers of the Middle Temple have continued to eat Queen Elizabeth's pudding. The dosage of the original confection must be extremely small by now, but no one can deny that it exists.

You are not likely to have a chance to take part in such ceremonies yourself unless you have English friends, but even the casual visitor to London can view without effort many of the brilliant parades and spectacles in which the colour of medieval times has been preserved for ours. And if you wish, you can also enter the visitors' gallery of the House of Commons and participate in the ceremony that has ruled the Commons as long as it has existed. If a speaker steps across the line on the floor that marks the point at which he would be within sword's length of his adversaries on the opposite side of the chamber, the session is automatically suspended. If a rebellious member should seize the great mace, the symbol of authority that rests on the table before the Speaker's chair, and make off with it (this has happened at least once), no legal business can be transacted until the mace has been restored to its position. You can also go into the House of Lords, where the glitter is more pronounced, the royal scarlet more in evidence, and where your own back will begin to ache sympathetically at the spectacle of the Lord Chancellor, so uncomfortably seated on the edge of the enormous woolsack.

Opening of Parliament

If you want to see the spectacle of the third oldest parliament in the world in action (it was preceded by the Althing of Iceland and the Parliament of the Isle of Man), ask your consulate to get you a ticket admitting you to the visitors' galleries. On the opening day of parliament the sovereign delivers the address from the throne, a speech worded as though it emanated from the crown, though actually it is written by the prime minister. This is a day when ceremony rules every gesture, and when officials appear to perform their appointed functions, whose exact role is not clear even to most Britons themselves —like Black Rod, who leads the parliamentarians into the hall to attend their ruler's address. The titles and functions of such officials, mysterious even to the British, are naturally doubly so to Americans. For example, no one is able to define the precise functions of Lord Privy Seal, for he has none. He is one of several members of the government who give it great flexibility since, having no stated department under their control, they are available for assignment by the prime minister to such special and unusual problems as may arise in the course of his term of office.

Although it is unlikely that you will be able to get inside the Houses of Parliament on the day of its opening, you can enjoy some of the spectacle in the street. The Queen and the Duke of Edinburgh ride in state to Westminster. The famous gilded coach of which you heard so much at the time of the Coronation parades from Buckingham Palace to the Houses of Parliament, escorted by the brilliantly uniformed and superbly mounted Household Cavalry—on a clear day, it is to be hoped, for this ceremony takes place in late October or early November, depending on the exigencies of parliament. As the Queen enters the Houses of Parliament the air shakes with the booming of heavy guns, and all London knows that the democratic processes that have so long protected England from oppression have once again been renewed with all their age-old ceremony.

Military Spectacles

The Household Cavalry just mentioned forms part of the

private escort of the sovereign. They are perhaps the best trained parade troops in the world, but they are not soldiers for show only. On the contrary, the guards regiments have distinguished themselves in every war Britain has fought. They are crack troops, but in time of peace the visitor can be excused if he thinks of them rather as perfectly drilled participants in a ballet, for the meticulous precision of their movements on parade seems oddly at variance with their role as fighting men. You will see this demonstrated at the Changing of the Guard any morning. To the music of a band, the relieving guards take over the duties of those who have mounted guard the day before, during a ceremony in which the ordinary soldiers parade with the slow-time two-movement stylized pace that is their trademark, behind an officer whose sword, held before him, points rigidly straight up into the air. (See *London Practical Information* for time.)

But to see the guards at their best, you should be in London in June. Trooping the Colour is the spectacle, the place is the Horse Guards' Parade, and the occasion is the Queen's birthday —her official birthday, that is, for the sovereign's birthday is always assigned to some day in June, in order to afford the celebration at least some chance of hitting a good day in the unfortunately dubious weather of London. Queen Elizabeth's birthday, officially, is June 10. This is not invariable, for often it takes place on days preceding or subsequent to that date.

The long lines of scarlet-clad soldiers in their tremendous bearskin headgear will amaze you by the precision of their marching, but the highlights of this performance are musical— the massed pipers who swing by with bagpipes skirling, and the mounted band, preceded by the drum horse with kettle-drums suspended on either side of his neck who moves forward undisturbed by the whirling drumsticks leaping from one side of his head to the other. The drum horse is a part of British military tradition, too. You will meet him in Kipling. He is fast disappearing, along with the cavalry.

It is an open question whether the Yeoman Warders of the Tower of London (popularly but erroneously called "Beefeaters") are to be classified with military spectacles or not. They were soldiers once, but the halberds they carry on ceremonious occasions would hardly serve them in battle

The notable double cube room, Wilton House, Wiltshire

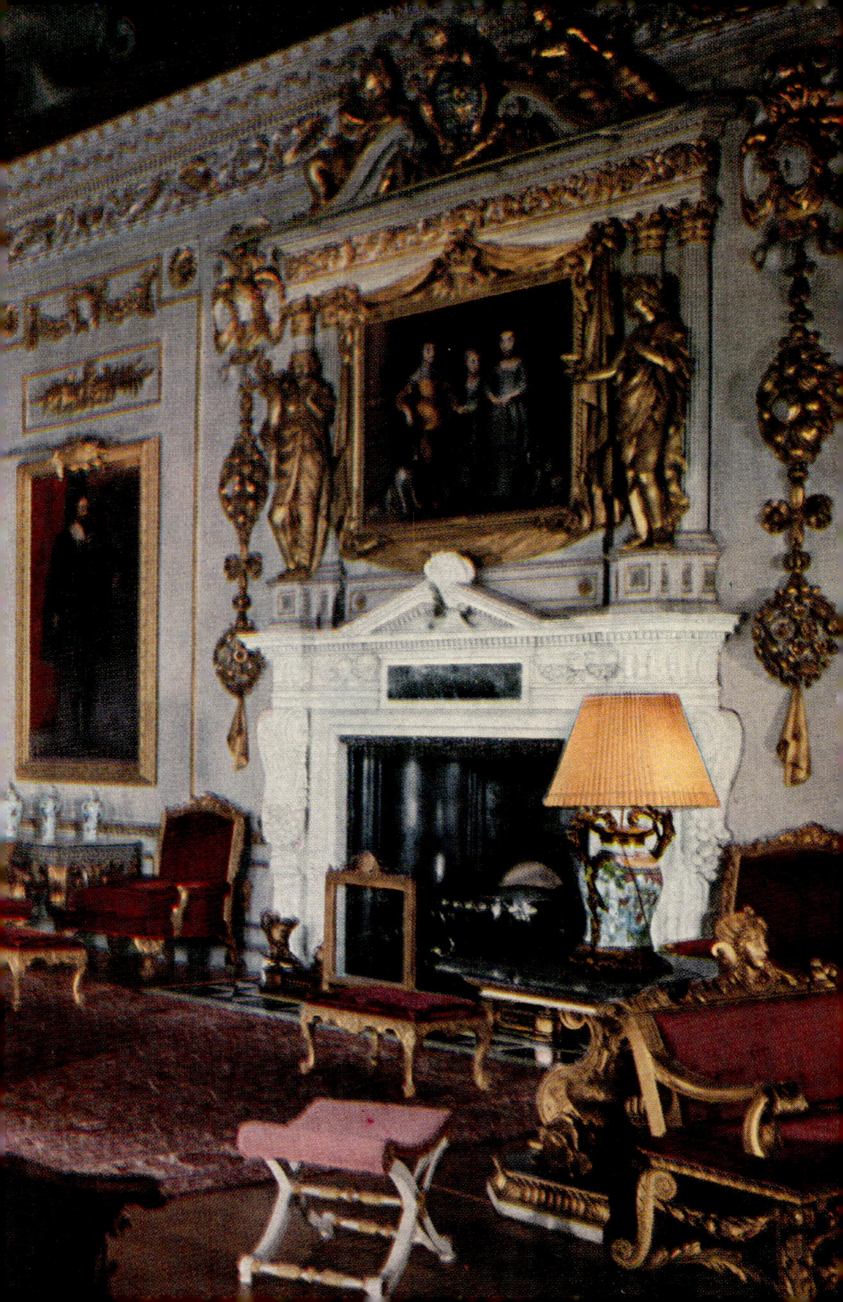

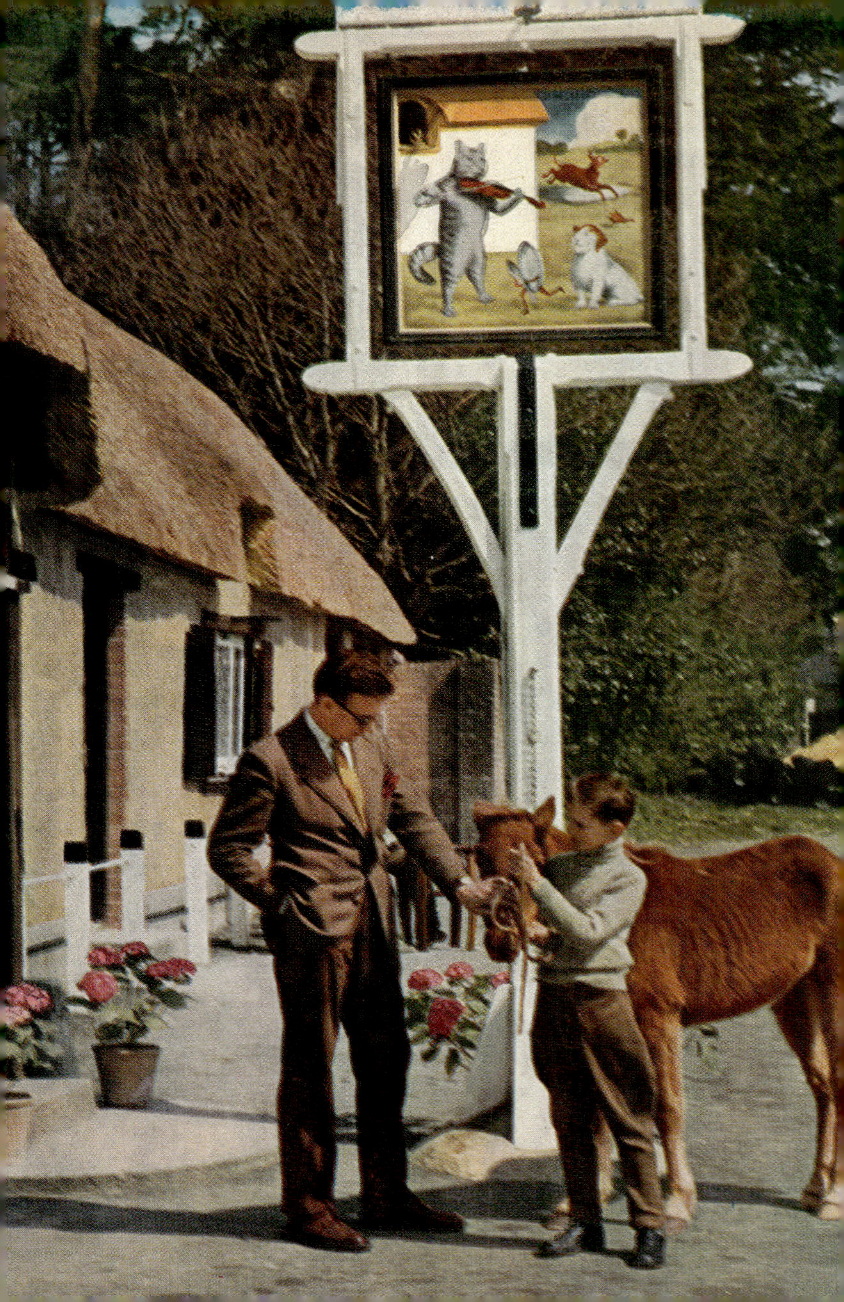

today. You will see them on duty in their colourful uniform when you visit the Tower.

Worth seeing is the "Ceremony of the Keys", the nightly locking of the main Tower by the "Beefeaters", just before 10 p.m. For tickets, write to the Resident Governor, H.M. Tower of London, E.C.3, enclosing international mail coupons for return postage. Another daily ritual: at 4 p.m., 15 elegant guards leave Wellington Barracks, London, with drummer and piper to march to the Bank of England in "The City" (the banking center) for their nightly guard duties. Leap out of bed and be at the Bank by 7 the next morning and you can see them marching back to the barracks. (Trucks have been used to carry the men on occasions, so this custom may be on the way out.)

The Lord Mayor's Show

A spectacular event occurs annually on an early Saturday in November, when the Lord Mayor's Show, really a parade, passes through the streets of the City from the Guildhall to the Law Courts for the swearing in of the new lord mayor. He has his gilded coach also, and he wears his robes of office and the chain that signifies his mayoralty. Accompanying the coach are escorts in the brilliant costumes of the period when this spectacle began, more than 700 years ago, and also modern paraders—cavalry, soldiers, dignitaries—and a procession of decorated floats. The lord mayor is of necessity a wealthy man, for he pays out of his own pocket for this display, and to some extent he is judged by the people in accordance with its magnificence. It *is* magnificent, and you should not miss it.

It is over three and a half centuries ago that Guy Fawkes was discovered in the cellars of the Houses of Parliament with enough kegs of gunpowder to blow the place up, but all over the country 5 November is still celebrated by burning the "guy" on a bonfire and letting off firecrackers, and a ritual inspection of the cellars is made by the Yeomen of the Guard each year just before the arrival of the sovereign at the state opening of parliament in November.

The Cat & Fiddle Inn at Hinton Admiral, Hampshire

A MINI HISTORY OF BRITAIN

Kings and Queens and All That

Reigning Monarch	Dates	Important Events
	50 B.C.	Julius Caesar arrives with expedition
	43 B.C.	Emperor Claudius invades Britain
	412	Romans withdraw from Britain to help defend Rome
	5th cent.	Angles and Jutes arrive
	597	St. Augustine arrives at Canterbury to Christianize Britain
Egbert, *followed by other Saxons and Danes* 827-39	9th cent.	Invasions of Vikings at peak
Ethelwulf 839-58		
Ethelbald and Ethelbert 858 860/866		
Ethelred 866-71		
Alfred the Great 871-901		
Edward the Elder 901-25		
Athelstan 925-40		
Edmund 940-46		

A MINI HISTORY OF BRITAIN

Reigning Monarch	Dates	Important Events
Edred 946-55		
Edwy 955-59		
Edgar 959-75		
Edward the Martyr 975-78		
Ethelred II 978-1016		
Edmund Ironside 1016		
Canute the Dane 1017-35		
Harold I 1035-40		
Hardicanute 1040-42		
Edward the Confessor 1042-66		
Harold II 1066		
William I, *House of Normandy* 1066-87	1066	William of Normandy invades, defeating Harold at Battle of Hastings
William II 1087-1100 (probably murdered)		
Henry I 1100-35		
Stephen 1135-54		
Henry II, *House of Plantagenet* 1154-89	1170	Archbishop Thomas à Becket murdered
Richard I 1189-99 (killed in battle)	1189	Richard The Lionheart embarks on Third Crusade
John 1199-1216	1215	King John forced to sign Magna Carta at Runnymede
Henry III 1216-72	1265	Summoning of the first parliament
Edward I 1272-1307		
Edward II 1307-27 (murdered)	1314	Robert the Bruce routes English under Edward II at Bannockburn
Edward III 1327-77	1337	Edward III claims French throne, starting Hundred Years' War
Richard II 1377-99 (deposed, then murdered)	1348–49	The Black Death (plague) sweeps Europe, killing one-third of population

THE BRITISH SCENE

Reigning Monarch	Dates	Important Events
	c.1362	John Ball preaches scriptural equalitarianism
	c.1376	John Wycliffe presages Reformation with his preaching
Henry IV 1399-1413	1381	The Peasants' Revolt, defused by 14-year-old Richard II
Henry V 1413-22	1415	Henry V's victory at Agincourt
Henry VI 1422-61 (deposed)	1431	Joan of Arc burned
	1455-85	Wars of the Roses
	1460	Lancaster defeats York at Wakefield
Edward IV, *House of York* 1461-83	1461	York wins with victory at Towton, biggest battle yet on English soil
Edward V 1483 (probably murdered)	1485	Henry Tudor defeats Richard III at Battle of Bosworth Field
Richard III 1483-85 (killed in battle)		
Henry VII, *Tudor Dynasty* 1485-1509	1530's	Reformation and dissolution of the monasteries by Henry VIII
Henry VIII 1509-47	1534	Henry VIII divorces Katherine of Aragon
	1536	Anne Boleyn executed at Tower of London
	1537	Jane Seymour dies in childbirth giving birth to Edward VI
	1540	Henry VIII marries Anne of Cleves
Edward VI 1547-53	1542	Katherine Howard executed in Tower
Jane 1553-54 (beheaded)	1543	Henry VIII marries Katherine Parr, who outlives him
Mary I 1553-58	1558	"Bloody Mary", daughter of Henry VIII by Katherine of Aragon, dies
Elizabeth I 1558-1603	1588	Spanish Armada fails to launch invasion
		Mary, Queen of Scots, flees to England (later executed)
James I (James VI of Scotland) *House of Stuart* 1603-25	1605	Guy Fawkes tries to blow up Parliament
	1620	Pilgrim Fathers sail from Plymouth on the "Mayflower" and settle in New England.
Charles I 1625-49 (beheaded)	1640's	Civil War between royalists and parliament

A MINI HISTORY OF BRITAIN

Reigning Monarch	Dates	Important Events
Commonwealth 1649-1660		
Charles II 1660-85	1665	Plague sweeps London
	1666	The Great Fire of London
James II (VII of Scotland) 1685-88 (deposed and exiled)		
William III and Mary II 1689-1702	1690	William defeats James II at the Battle of Boyne
Anne 1702-14	1707	Act of Union united England and Scotland as Great Britain
George I, *House of Hanover* 1714-27	1721-42	Robert Walpole, Prime Minister
George II 1727-60	1745	Bonnie Prince Charlie lands in Scotland and tries to regain his throne, but is defeated and flees again to France
	1755-63	Seven Years' War
George III 1760-1820	1776	Americans declare their independence
	1783-1801	William Pitt, Prime Minister (and again, 1804-06)
George IV 1820-30	1805	Nelson killed at victorious Battle of Trafalgar
	1815	Wellington defeats Napoleon at Waterloo
William IV 1830-37	1832	Reform Bill extends the franchise, ending rule of great landowners
Victoria 1837-1901		
	1861	Prince Albert dies
	1868-86	Disraeli and Gladstone, Prime Ministers (latter also 1892-94)
Edward VII, *House of Saxe-Coburg* 1901-10	1899-1902	Boer War
	1902	Anglo-Japanese Alliance signed
	1904	Anglo-French Alliance
	1907	Anglo-Russo Alliance
George V, *House of Windsor* 1910-36	1914-18	First World War
	1926	The General Strike
Edward VIII 1936 (abdicated)	1939-45	Second World War; Churchill, Prime Minister (also 1951-55)
George VI 1936-52	1945	Labour Party wins election
	1947	India becomes independent, followed by nearly all of the Empire
Elizabeth II 1952-	1951	Conservatives regain government
	1964	Labour party back in power

CREATIVE BRITAIN

The Sceptred Isle's Poetry in Word and Form

by

JOHN LEHMANN

(*John Lehmann, C.B.E., the founder and editor of two literary journals,* New Writing *and* Orpheus, *is a leading figure in the Britain of arts and letters. Among his later books are the autobiographical* I Am My Brother *and* And Ancestors and Friends.)

The creative genius of the inhabitants of the British Isles has manifested itself in many forms. When we think of the novel, painting, sculpture, architecture, the applied arts, music, opera and ballet, we find that the British have made a notable contribution to all these arts at one period or another in their history; but in no arts have they made a greater, more continuous and more variously inspired contribution than in poetry and the poetic drama.

English poetry has flourished from the 14th century to our own times. Though the fires burnt low in the 15th century, an age of prolonged civil and foreign wars, they were never extinguished. In the previous century, the English language had emerged from its long submersion under the French that the Norman conquerors had brought with them: it was a new language, to which the mixture of the original Anglo-Saxon and Teutonic forms with Latinate Romance gave an immense subtlety, flexibility and range of expressive power.

The first great English poet was Geoffrey Chaucer (1340–1400), though a large body of anonymous religious and secular poems, often of captivating beauty, precedes him. Chaucer is chiefly remembered for his love romance of the Trojan wars, *Troilus and Criseyde*, and for his supreme masterpiece, *The Canterbury Tales*, a collection of stories, serious, romantic and humorous, which he puts into the mouths of a group of pilgrims on their way to visit the shrine of St. Thomas in Canterbury. Chaucer is a skilful and absorbing story-teller, witty, shrewd, sensuous, a remarkable psychologist with a tender sense of joy and sorrow in earthly life. It is not too fanciful to see in *The Canterbury Tales* the seeds of Shakespeare's comedies and romances and the psychological novel of the 18th century.

During the 15th century a series of remarkable poets appear in Scotland: King James I (died 1437), William Dunbar (1465–1520?) and Gavin Douglas (died 1522). At the beginning of the 16th century, individual English poets become prominent, notably Wyatt and Surrey, who modelled themselves on classical and contemporary Italian poetry; but the great flowering began in the reign of Queen Elizabeth I. It was an age of national self-confidence and expansion, both material and intellectual. Poets abounded—poets who are remembered for a few lyrics and songs, and poets of greater ambition and achievement such as Sir Walter Raleigh, Sir Philip Sidney, and Edmund Spenser (1552–99), whose long poem, *The Faerie Queene*, a fabulous romance written in honour of Queen Elizabeth, was to have a lasting influence on English poetry, above all in the dreamy, imaginative intensity that suffuses it and its extremely skilful, mellifluous verse-making.

Poetic Drama

A more brilliant and extraordinary flowering of this great age was in the poetic drama. Its roots lay far back in the past, in the medieval Mystery and Morality plays and the learned attempt to reproduce the effects of the Latin dramatists Seneca and Plautus in the English language. When Christopher

Marlowe (1564–1593) appeared, however, a radical change took place. This young genius, who died all too early, gave the drama of his age the medium it needed, the unrhymed iambic line of five feet (blank verse), and, chaotic though his production was, expressed the passionate dreams of the Renaissance soul in such plays as *Dr. Faustus*.

The fire Marlowe kindled set alight the vastly more abundant powers of William Shakespeare (1564–1616), the greatest figure in English literature and one of the supreme geniuses of the world. He began as a humble actor and ended—paradoxically enough to our way of thinking—as a rich, retired theatrical businessman. He would be remembered as a sublime poet for his *Sonnets* alone, if he had never written a play; and a large number of speeches and songs in his plays would remain as great poetry even if the dramatic context had been lost. For a quarter of a century, the plays poured out in dazzling profusion: dramas of English and Roman history, such as *Richard III*, *Henry V*, *Julius Caesar* and *Anthony and Cleopatra*, comedies such as *A Midsummer Night's Dream* and *Twelfth Night*, tragedies such as *Romeo and Juliet*, *Hamlet*, *Macbeth*, *Othello* and *King Lear*, and the half-magical romances of his last period, such as *The Tempest*, where reconciliation and happy-ever-after endings take the place of the apparent triumph of evil, unrecompensed suffering and death. All the time, he was developing the new instrument of blank verse, while at the same time introducing prose to vary tempo and mood. It is not only for sheer poetry that the plays are remarkable, but also for the amazing range of psychological understanding they display, for intellectual wit as well as bawdy humour, the depiction of unbridled passion and transcending love, realistic common sense and ethereal imaginative invention. It is a measure of Shakespeare's greatness that every age has found some new facet of his work that has profoundly illuminated their own experience.

Outstanding among the many writers of the most diverse accomplishment who complete the dramatic glory of the Elizabethan age and the Jacobean age which followed it (and into which Shakespeare himself lived), are Thomas Dekker, Ben Jonson (the one excellent satiric comedy writer of the period), John Ford, John Webster and Philip Massinger. One may say that they would appear a far more notable company if it were not for Shakespeare's colossal presence in their midst.

At the time when Shakespeare was reaching his triumphant maturity, roughly at the turn of the century, a young, non-dramatic poet appeared, whose stature, admired though he certainly was in his own day, has enormously increased in the modern age. John Donne (1573–1631), the greatest of the so-called "metaphysical" poets, is famous not only for the love poems of his youth and his later religious poems, both of a passionate intensity, but also for the sermons he preached as Dean of St. Paul's. The complexity of his powerful, questioning intelligence, and the ingenious daring of his imagery, allied to an unconventionally colloquial manner of expression, have made him a powerful influence on his successors of the 20th century.

Milton and the Puritans

Other striking poets between the death of Shakespeare and the Restoration were Herbert, Vaughan, Crashaw, all three religious in their inspiration, Herrick and Marvell, the last-named author of two of the most famous lyrics in the English language, *To His Coy Mistress* and *Bermudas*. The middle 17th century is, however, undoubtedly the age of John Milton (1608–74), scholar of immense learning, puritan partisan of Cromwell's side in the Civil War, and author of the most memorable epic in the English language, *Paradise Lost*. Milton showed himself from the beginning of his career a fastidious, conscious artist, almost the exact opposite, it may be said, of Shakespeare the dramatist. The poems of his youth, *Lycidas*, *L'Allegro* and *Il Penseroso*, have nevertheless an unequalled lyrical charm and freshness.

After the collapse of the Puritan regime, the literary scene shows a radical change. England, after the Civil War, the Restoration and the Revolution of 1688, was a country interested primarily in the settled life and civilized manners. The poetry that became the fashion was above all social poetry, in which wit, elegance of expression and correct attitudes were valued above the soul-searching and the questioning of the universe in the mighty past. John Dryden (1631–1700), critic as well as poet and dramatist, was the dominant figure in this period until the end of the century. His successor, Alexander Pope (1688–1744), polished the iambic couplet to the utmost point of refinement. In his hands it became the deadliest of rapiers for satire against the vices of his time (and his personal enemies), and a medium for the airiest gaiety in his comedy of fashionable life, *The Rape of the Lock*.

After Dryden, the outstanding names were Otway, Vanbrugh (a man of many parts who was also a distinguished architect), Farquhar, Wycherley and William Congreve (1670–1729), whose *The Way of the World* is not only the peak of his achievement but also one of the peaks of English comedy. As the 18th century advanced, though the fundamental difference from the earlier drama remained, a change of tone occurred: sentiment took the place of cynical raillery, and witty bawdy was no longer fashionable for an increasingly bourgeois audience. Two Irish-born playwrights dominated the London scene, Richard Brinsley Sheridan (1751–1816) and Oliver Goldsmith (1728–94). After their triumphs, the drama went into a long decline, from which, in spite of many poets' plays essentially intended for reading, it did not revive until the later 19th century.

After Pope's death, as in his lifetime, poetry remained under his enormous shadow. Even so forceful a character as Doctor Johnson (1709–84), greater perhaps as lexicographer, critic and conversationalist (and subject of one of the great English biographies by James Boswell) than poet, took him as the inescapable model. Nevertheless, William Cowper (1731–1800), Thomas Gray (1716–71) and William Collins (1721–59) represent a turning away from city life and society to country life and quiet contemplation out of the hum and bustle. The last outstanding poet to use the style that had been fashioned by Dryden and Pope was George Crabbe (1784–1832) in his poetic narratives of rural life.

Meanwhile, two great figures had appeared in Scotland: Robert Burns (1759–96) and Sir Walter Scott (1771–1832). Burns was of Scottish peasant stock: his poetry, based on the folksongs and ballads of the Lowlands, has a natural freshness, human warmth and humour, qualities that combine in his lyrical genius to make an imperishable whole. Sir Walter Scott more properly belongs to the history of the novel, but his ballad tales are incomparable in their field.

A predecessor of the Romantic movement in England, William Blake (1757-1827) was a mystical poet who could write the most poignantly lovely lyrics and the most arcane prophetic rhapsodies. It is with William Wordsworth (1771–1850) and Samuel Taylor Coleridge (1772-1834) that 18th-century attitudes (and 18th-century versification) finally crumble and are swept away in new visions of man's destiny and man's place in the scheme of creation. Coleridge is remembered above all for *The Ancient Mariner*, and Wordsworth for a series of sublime poems in which he expounded his faith in nature and an indwelling spirit of the universe that will transform our existence if we live in harmony with it.

The Romantic Movement

The outstanding poets in the second generation of the Romantic movement were Lord Bryon (1788-1824), Percy Bysshe Shelley (1792-1822) and John Keats (1795-1821). All three died young, Shelley and Keats scarcely known outside the circle of their intimates, Byron a gigantic presence in European literature. Yet the admiration for Byron grew less and less during the remainder of the century, while the reputations of Shelley and Keats steadily increased until they were recognized as two of our greatest poets. In his day Byron, always a writer of dazzling fluency and virtuosity, was chiefly admired for such highly-charged narrative poems as *Childe Harold;* today, his reputation, partially restored, rests rather on *Don Juan*, in which romantic feeling is brilliantly mixed with witty and cynical worldly observation.

In the next phase, again three poets claim the highest places: Alfred Lord Tennyson (1809-1892), Robert Browning (1812-89), and Matthew Arnold (1822-88). They were writers of very diverse gifts, though the currents of romanticism still ran strongly through the poetic veins of all three. Tennyson, the inheritor of Keats's mantle, became, as it were, the official poet of the Victorian age, a role that obliged him to write a great deal of morally didactic verse that threatened to eclipse his natural lyric genius. Browning took a totally different line: though capable of writing passionate love lyrics, the majority of his poems are complex, often extremely elliptical and obscure explorations of men's motives in dramatic situations. Arnold, critic and scholar, is above all the poet of the melancholy and doubt that lay beneath the optimism of the Victorian age. It is important to remember that these three giants were surrounded by a host of other poets only slightly less worthy of remembrance.

When we come to the present century, what strikes one at once is the variety of the poetry written, the fact that most of the great figures were distinguished in other fields of literature as well, and the more curious fact that many of them, though assimilated to the British literary tradition, were of non-British origin. Kipling, Hardy and Lawrence are remembered primarily as novelists, though in each case the poetry would have been important if they had written no prose. W. B. Yeats (1865–1939) was Irish-born and became a senator of Éire; T. S. Eliot (born 1888) was of American origin, and like his compatriot, Henry James, took British citizenship. Yeats and Eliot are undoubtedly the dominant figures in this period, though a special place must be reserved for the only highly gifted woman poet, Dame Edith Sitwell (1887–1964). A surprising thing happened at the end of the First World War: the poet Robert Bridges published the poems of the friend of his youth, G. M. Hopkins, a tortured Catholic recluse: though written long before, their passion and daring technical experimentation made an overwhelming impression.

The Revival of Drama

In the later years of Queen Victoria's reign, British drama began to show life again. The two leading playwrights were Oscar Wilde (1854–1900), whose play *The Importance of Being Earnest* is one of the greatest of English comedies, and Bernard Shaw, born two years later (like Wilde, in Dublin), who reintroduced intellectual discussion to the stage, and was a master of paradox and comic situation. His first play was produced in London in 1892; *Saint Joan*, widely acknowledged as his masterpiece, was written in 1923. The stage in the early years of the century was, apart from Shaw, dominated by three writers in the strictest realistic convention: Sir Arthur Pinero, John Galsworthy, and William Somerset Maugham, and by the more whimsical Scot, Sir James Barrie. Two other Irishmen, though less completely identified with the London theatre than Shaw, must be mentioned: J. M. Synge and Sean

O'Casey. If O'Casey was a master of broad comedy with a hint of tragedy in it, Noël Coward, whose plays took London by storm in the twenties, was a master of comic bathos and witty absurdity—with a dash of sentimentality.

From the First World War, four poets who died or were killed in action are especially remembered: Rupert Brooke, Wilfred Owen, Isaac Rosenberg and Edward Thomas. Two other remarkable soldier-poets survived: Siegfried Sassoon, famous for his bitterly satiric anti-war poems, and Robert Graves, who has lived on to become the most highly regarded love poet of our time. The so-called Georgian poets dominated the scene until the thirties; it is unlikely, in spite of radical changes of taste since that time, that John Masefield, Edmund Blunden or Walter de la Mare will be forgotten. In the thirties, a new group of poets in revolt—against moral conventions, unemployment and political conservatism, as well as outworn poetic usages—emerged: W. H. Auden (who has since become an American citizen), Cecil Day Lewis and Stephen Spender are still alive, but Louis MacNeice (who was born in Northern Ireland) died in 1963. Auden also collaborated with the novelist Christopher Isherwood in an original form of play, part verse, part prose, part cabaret-turn, of which *The Ascent of F-6* is the high water mark. In the forties, one must particularly note the work of George Barker, David Gascoyne, Roy Fuller, Alun Lewis and Keith Douglas, both the last-named killed in the Second World War.

In the fifties, a number of interesting poets appeared who are still young and vigorously at work today. Among the foremost are Charles Causley, who has re-invigorated the ballad form, Thom Gunn and Ted Hughes.

The outstanding literary development of the fifties was, however, the revival in the drama associated with the Royal Court Theatre, which occurred when the new verse drama of T. S. Eliot, Ronald Duncan, Christopher Fry and others appeared to be running out of steam. John Osborne's *Look Back in Anger* set the new style, and a large number of young writers who might otherwise have been occupied with fiction turned to the theatre.

The Novel

The novel, as we understand the art-form, scarcely existed

in Britain before the 18th century, when a tremendous flowering began, a flowering which is still going on today. There were, however, remarkable works of prose fiction before that time which can be considered ancestors of the novel.

Outstanding are: *The Pilgrim's Progress* by John Bunyan, in reality a religious allegory which has held the imagination of the English-speaking peoples ever since it was published in 1678; *Robinson Crusoe* (1719) and *Moll Flanders* (1722) by a failed haberdasher and journalist, Daniel Defoe, who was undoubtedly a literary genius; and *Gulliver's Travels* (1726) by Jonathan Swift, a towering figure, poet, satirist and pamphleteer, whose life was as extraordinary as his work.

The first great English novel in the accepted sense of the word was *Pamela*, by Samuel Richardson (1689–1761), published in 1740. With Henry Fielding (1707–54), Tobias Smollett (1721–71) and Laurence Sterne (1713–68), Richardson is one of the supreme quartet of English novelists in the 18th century.

During his lifetime, Sir Walter Scott dominated the European novel as Byron dominated European poetry, while Jane Austen's work was known only to a far more restricted public. It is one of the ironies of literary history that the position is reversed today: Scott has fallen into neglect, while Miss Austen is seen as the first modern novelist in England.

The 19th-Century Novel

The giants of the 19th-century novel in its first phase were all born between 1810 and 1820: William Makepeace Thackeray in 1811, Charles Dickens in 1812, Anthony Trollope in 1815. As with the men, so with the leading women novelists of the period: Mrs. Gaskell was born in 1810, Charlotte Brontë and her sister Emily in 1816 and 1818 respectively, and George Eliot (Mary Ann Evans) in 1819.

Charles Dickens (1812–70) is the greatest imaginative creator in English literature after Chaucer and Shakespeare. He is a master of both affectionate and satiric comedy, of cutting, mirthless satire and tragic pathos. His power of creating memorable characters in a few lines is unequalled, and he exposed the social injustices of his time with crushing innuendo and rhetoric. He is grotesquely unequal: his shallow judgements and his Victorian sentimentality (particularly in his female characters) appals our modern taste at times; and yet his greatest novels, *Oliver Twist*, *Nicholas Nickleby*, *David Copperfield*, *Great Expectations*, *Little Dorrit*, *Bleak House* and *Our Mutual Friend*, live by their superb imaginative grasp of the swirling undercurrents of human existence in society.

William Makepeace Thackeray (1811–1863) owed as much to his 18th-century predecessors as did Dickens. It has been customary to pit him as a rival against his great contemporary; and yet, magnificent though his masterpiece *Vanity Fair* still appears, his range of sympathies, his creative involvement with his characters, cannot ultimately stand the comparison. Anthony Trollope (1815–1882) is at the same time more efficient and of much narrower range and power as a novelist. A commonplace stylist, without any remarkable ingenuity of plot, avoiding the profound issues of his time, he had great skill as a creator of character in his rendering of the upper middle-class life of the Victorian age.

Wilkie Collins, father of the modern detective story, close friend of Dickens and collaborator with him in plays, is remembered chiefly for *The Woman in White* (1860) and *The Moonstone* (1868). Mrs. Gaskell is remembered not only for her penetrating life of Charlotte Brontë, but also for the novels in which she expressed the social conscience that inspired the best of her class and generation. The Brontës have proved more popular: Charlotte's *Jane Eyre* is a profoundly romantic work, a young woman's dream, but intensely realized and based on a searching truth to feeling, while Emily's *Wuthering Heights* stands alone in the whole range of the 19th-century novel, flawlessly developed, as completely personal in feeling as it is poetic in expression, an epic vision of man in the universe.

George Eliot (1819–1880) is in many ways, to modern taste, the greatest of the four. She has not Emily Brontë's soaring poetic vision, but her formidable learning and her seriousness of outlook add a weight to her work that is rarely out of balance with human feeling, as can be seen in her early triumphs, *The Mill on the Floss* and *Silas Marner*. Her profound moral preoccupation finds its richest expression in her long masterpiece, *Middlemarch*. With George Meredith (1828–1909), author of *The Ordeal of Richard Feverel* and *The Egoist*, as well as many remarkable poems, she represents a change in the whole tone and direction of English fiction.

Thomas Hardy, who was born in 1840, stands between these two and the impressive group of novelists who began to make their mark in the 1880's. He wrote fiction for twenty-five years after publishing *Desperate Remedies* in 1871, but after *Jude the Obscure*, turned to poetry until his death in 1928. Looked at from one aspect, he is naïve and a provincial, but his genius transcended these limits to give him the stature of a master.

In the eighties, the change in the aims and fundamental philosophy of novel writing which Eliot and Meredith heralded, was developed by R. L. Stevenson (1850–94), a Scot; George Moore (1853–1933), an Irishman by birth; Henry James, an American who took British citizenship before his death in 1916; and Joseph Conrad (1857–1925), a Pole who adopted England and the English language, all highly conscious and dedicated artists. The last two in particular have lost nothing in reputation as the 20th century has advanced. Samuel Butler was born in 1825, but it was not until 1903 that his novel *The Way of All Flesh*, a scathing denunciation of Victorian hypocrisy, was published. Rudyard Kipling, of the same generation, was a greater writer of short stories than of novels. He has been thought of as the apologist of the British Raj in India, but his finest work is far more complex in thought, feeling and moral judgement than such a label might suggest.

Recent Novelists

In the later sixties and early seventies of the 19th century were born the novelists who were to be outstanding until the outbreak of the First World War: H. G. Wells in 1866, Arnold Bennett and John Galsworthy in 1867, Ford Madox Ford in 1873 and W. Somerset Maugham in 1874. Three of the five, Wells, Bennett, and Maugham, achieved great popular reputations in their lives, but successful journalistic activities (and in the case of Maugham, playwriting) were as much responsible for this as fiction. Another novelist of great repute and with quite different aims from these five, E. M. Forster, produced four novels between 1905 and 1910, and then his last to be published, *A Passage to India*, in 1924. He is, fundamentally, a moralist who has questioned the ethos of his fellow-countrymen with devastating though affectionate analysis, and mixes fantasy and symbolism with shrewd perception.

Southwest England's coastal towns are noted for their beauty, here exemplified by Clovelly, in Devon.

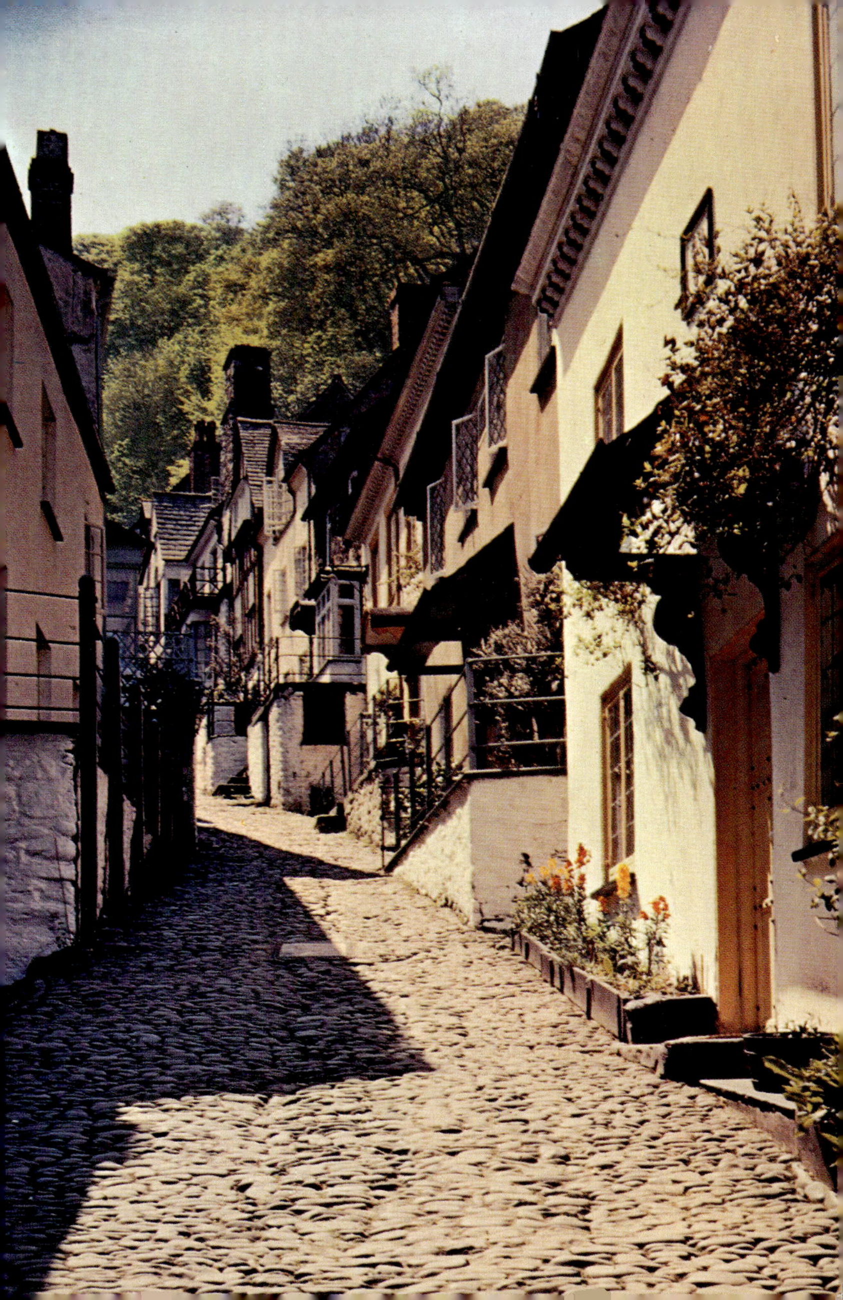

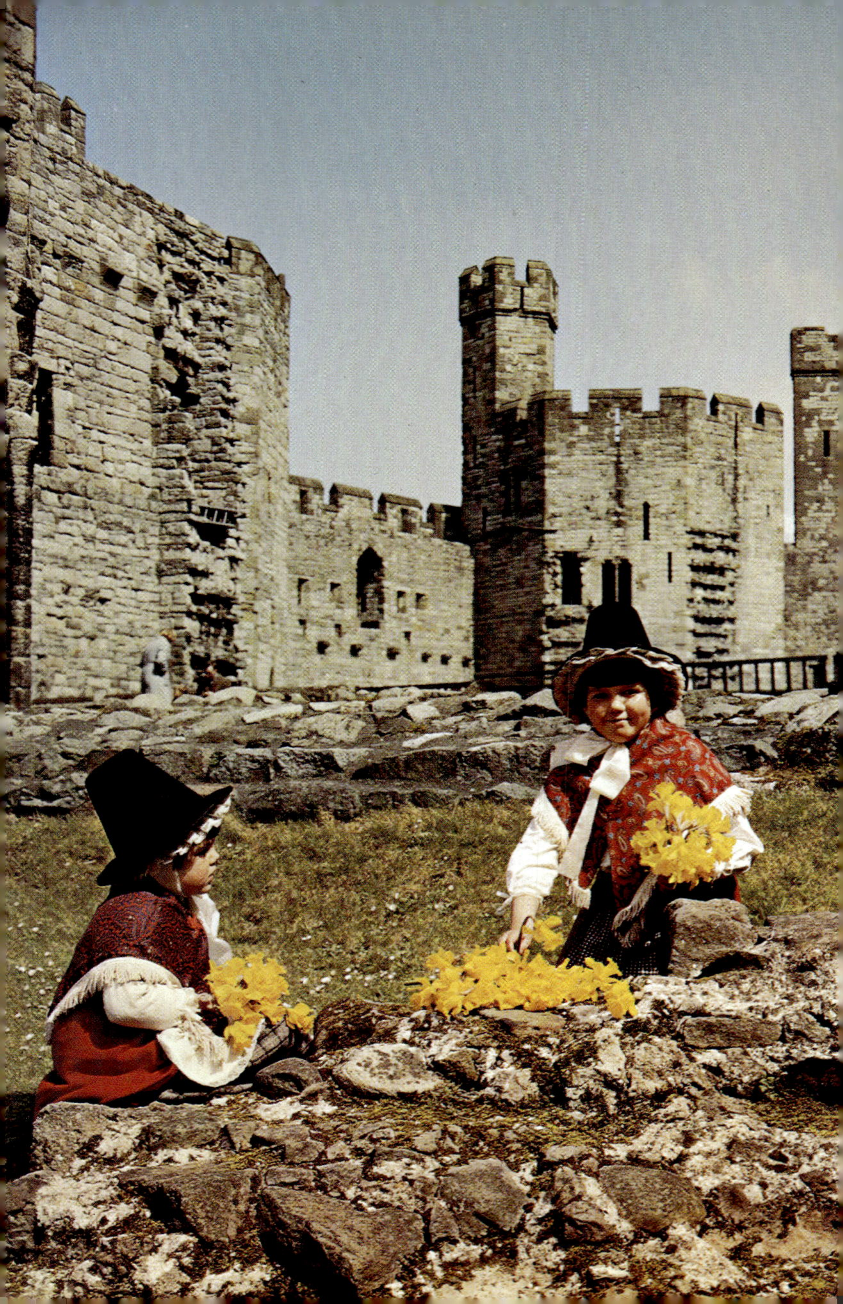

A revolt against naturalism, and an emphasis on individual sensibility can be seen in the novelists who began to write in that changed aesthetic atmosphere heralding the modern movement in all the arts, which one can roughly date from 1910. D. H. Lawrence, Virginia Woolf and James Joyce were all born in the eighties. James Joyce, though an Irishman, must be mentioned here, because his novel *Ulysses* has been an overwhelmingly powerful influence not only on English and American but also on world literature in our time. Virginia Woolf, a daring innovator in novel technique, was also a critic of rare perception. Of the same "Bloomsbury" generation, Aldous Huxley, polymath, superbly elegant stylist, brilliant and original essayist on literary, artistic and philosophical questions, belongs as novelist to the tradition of Peacock.

It is early to estimate the relative importance of the novelists of our own time, but two who are now dead stand out: George Orwell, satirist and prophet, author of *Animal Farm* and *1984*, and Evelyn Waugh, a brilliant entertainer whose farcical comedy is stiffened with mordant satire. Among those who are still writing, mention should be made of Dame Ivy Compton-Burnett, Graham Greene, Elizabeth Bowen, L. P. Hartley, Nigel Dennis, Christopher Isherwood, Anthony Powell, Angus Wilson and Kingsley Amis: a personal list which may suffer from the short-sightedness of those who are too close to their material.

Painting, Sculpture and Architecture

British art may be said to begin with the sacred drawings and illuminated books of the 10th century, which emerged in England (particularly at Winchester) after the break-up of the Empire of Charlemagne. In this early period, the English were also pre-eminent in the art of embroidery. The English style was remarkable for the free and vigorous lyricism of its compositions. The Norman Conquest (1066) only temporarily submerged this native tradition, which recovered to become famous throughout Europe in the 13th and early 14th centuries. The end of the 14th century saw the rise of the characteristically English variation of Gothic, the Perpendicular style, seen at its most impressive in Winchester Cathedral and the roof of Westminster Hall in London.

Daffodils, the Welsh national flower, bloom before Caernarvon Castle, seat of the Princes of Wales.

In Elizabethan times, a school of miniature portrait painters emerged, the most remarkable being Nicholas Hillyard, whose excelling qualities as an artist are clearly evident in spite of the tiny scope of his medium. Otherwise, the 16th and early 17th centuries in Britain are dominated by foreigners who made their home here, chief among them Hans Holbein the Younger. Van Dyck (born 1599), who came to live in England in 1632, brought the rhetorical continental style of Rubens and Titian to Britain, but his magnificent series of portraits had little to do with the English genius.

One man alone stands out as a native genius in the first half of the 17th century—Inigo Jones, architect and stage designer. Deeply influenced by contemporary Italian developments, he nevertheless showed a characteristically British spontaneity and lyrical freedom in his designs. He died in 1652. His masterpiece in interior design is the Banqueting Hall in Whitehall.

Another solitary genius in architecture dominates the second half of the 17th century, Sir Christopher Wren, born in 1632. It was the Great Fire of London in 1666 that gave Wren his opportunity. Though his complete plans were not adopted, he designed more than fifty new churches, many of which can be seen on a walk through the City of London, as can his masterpiece, St. Paul's Cathedral, newly cleaned.

After the long eclipse of native painting, a renaissance began in the second quarter of the 18th century, with the satiric genius of William Hogarth (born in 1697). Within twenty years, Scotland had produced Allan Ramsay, and Wales Richard Wilson, both painters of outstanding accomplishment—Ramsay (son of the poet of the same name) in portraiture, Wilson in landscape painting, deriving from Claude Lorrain. By 1760–70, the increasing wealth and power of Britain favoured art patronage, and fashionable portrait painters were much in demand. Sir Joshua Reynolds (born 1723) and Thomas Gainsborough (born 1727) were the dominant figures: both had superlative gifts, but modern taste today awards the palm to Gainsborough. At the same time, a number of exceptionally gifted architects and interior decorators appeared, the most brilliant of whom were Robert Adam and John Nash—the latter the creator of the superb terraces of houses in Regent's Park.

In this period, English furniture was also of outstanding excellence, being mainly the work of three inspired cabinet-makers, Thomas Chippendale, George Hepplewhite and Thomas Sheraton. During the Regency, a classical style, reflecting developments in France but skilfully anglicized, produced tables, chairs and desks of the utmost elegance, much in demand today.

The Later Artists

Thomas Rowlandson and William Blake are generally considered as early 19th-century artists, but in fact, they were born in 1756 and 1757, respectively. Rowlandson was the most famous caricaturist after Hogarth, but he was also a sensitive lyrical artist in water colour. Blake's visionary genius was made apparent in his drawings only less emphatically than in his poems. The Regency and post-Napoleonic period was, however, increasingly dominated by two of the greatest artists Britain ever produced, both of the highest international stature: John Constable, who transformed landscape painting and deeply influenced the French Impressionists; and J. M. W. Turner (born 1775), whose increasingly visionary paintings, in which fleeting effects of light and storm play an essential part, seem to anticipate the whole of modern painting.

No such masterly geniuses appeared in Victorian times; but the school of the Pre-Raphaelites, which deliberately defied the conventional painting of the time, based upon the precepts of Reynolds, is remembered for the highly individual work of Sir John Millais (especially in his earlier period), Holman Hunt and the young Dante Gabriel Rossetti (also a remarkable poet). It was the example of Rossetti which inspired the work of Sir Edward Burne-Jones and William Morris, the latter a man of the most extraordinarily varied gifts, poet, painter, architect, interior designer, printer, and socialist propagandist, who has been called the greatest pattern designer of all time.

The later years of the century produced two remarkable draughtsmen: Aubrey Beardsley, an illustrator of genius, who died (at the age of 26 in 1898) too young to show all that he could have achieved, and Max Beerbohm, a satirist with an elfin sense of humour and highly sophisticated style. The turn of the century saw the rise of a number of artists, deeply influenced by continental example, such as Augustus John, Philip Wilson Steer, Walter Sickert and Charles Conder.

It is probably too soon to evaluate the work of the artists who came to prominence during and directly after the First World War, such as Paul and John Nash, Stanley Spencer, Christopher Wood, Wyndham Lewis and Duncan Grant; or of that group which emerged during the Second World War, frankly owing its central inspiration to the romantic art of Blake and his followers. One can nevertheless say that out of these various movements and tendencies have arisen three artists who have a high European, indeed world, reputation today: Graham Sutherland, creator of the great Christ in the re-built Cathedral of Coventry (with its superb stained glass windows by John Piper), Francis Bacon, and Henry Moore, the greatest sculptor to appear in Britain since the Middle Ages.

Music, Opera and Ballet

English music, like Scottish and Welsh music, began with folk songs and folk dance tunes. Composition proper only began in the 11th century, but it was not until the 15th century that England possessed, in John Dunstable, a composer of high European renown. The 16th century saw the rise of unaccompanied choral music, and music for the earliest type of keyboard instruments. In both these branches of music, England was the equal of any continental nation (in fact, in the latter, she led Europe). Later in the century, William Byrd, one of the founders of the English madrigal school, composer of choral, keyboard and string music, dominated the international scene: his associates and pupils were much in demand in many foreign courts.

Much of the earliest Scottish music, in folk song and folk dance, has been lost, though a great deal has been recovered in recent years. The Highland and Hebridean songs in particular stand out for their range of expression and haunting pathos. The traditional Scottish musical instrument, the bagpipe, does not appear to have been developed until the 15th century. It is not known how far back the two characteristic Scottish dances, the Reel (with its offshoot, the Highland Fling) and the Strathspey go, but written records begin to appear in the 17th century.

The Welsh have always been noted as a musical race, and have produced some of the finest singers in the British Isles. The ancient bards seem to have been closely associated with the Druid religion. The folk music of Wales, in which the harp always played a prominent part, is partly harmonic and partly melodic, the latter tradition giving birth to the popular hymn tunes sung everywhere in the chapels after the Methodist revival.

The Civil War, and the triumph of the Puritan faction in England in the middle of the 17th century, checked the development of English music. With the restoration of the monarchy, however, in 1660, a revival occurred, associated mainly with the genius of Henry Purcell, who died in London at the early age of 36. He was one of the greatest composers in English history, and was pre-eminent in almost every branch of music practised at the time.

The first half of the 18th century is dominated by a naturalized Englishman, George Frederic Handel (born in Saxony in 1685), a prolific musician of enormous accomplishment, who excelled in opera and oratorio. His position was seriously challenged by the sudden emergence of ballad opera. Its chief example, *The Beggar's Opera* (1728), with words by the poet John Gay and music—from popular airs—arranged by Dr. Pepusch, was immensely popular, because of its roots in the life of the people, and the sly fun it poked at fashionable fads and the more serious satire on corruption in high places.

In the latter half of the 19th century, England undoubtedly showed a tremendous appetite for music, and foreign singers and instrumental players were in continuous demand at concert halls all over the country. Native composers of interest were, however, rare. The period was chiefly notable for the Gilbert and Sullivan comic operas, with music by the precocious Arthur Sullivan (1842–1900), which still find appreciative audiences today.

Into the 20th Century

Towards the end of the century, and at the beginning of the 20th century, a British revival began, associated with the names of Edward Elgar, Edward German, Frederick Delius (of German extraction), Gustav Holst, the Scottish William

Wallace and John McEwen, and perhaps the most influential of all, Ralph Vaughan Williams (born 1872).

In the period between the wars, an altogether outstanding composer emerged in the person of Sir William Walton. It was during the Second World War, however, that a number of composers attained maturity who have once more raised British music to high international status. Foremost among them are Michael Tippett, Malcolm Williamson, Humphrey Searle and Benjamin Britten, the last-named a many-sided musical genius whose *Peter Grimes* started a revival in native British opera that flowers every summer at the Aldeburgh Festival, in Suffolk.

Most of the composers of the avant garde music which is flourishing today are still too young to judge what stature they will achieve.

The revival of interest in the art of ballet in Britain in our time, which has made the Royal Ballet Company (originally Vic-Wells and then Sadler's Wells) one of the half dozen great ballet ensembles of the world, can be traced back to the overwhelming impact that Diaghileff's Russian ballet made in its visits to London beginning just before the First World War, and the dance recitals of Anna Pavlova, who broke away from Diaghileff. In the twenties and early thirties, the seeds were sown by two small groups of enthusiastic pioneers, the Camargo Society and the Ballet Club. With the inspired teaching of Dame Marie Rambert and Dame Ninette de Valois (Miss Edris Stannus) behind them, a school of dancer-choreographers emerged, the most notable among whom have been Sir Frederick Ashton, Anthony Tudor, Andrèe Howard, Robert Helpmann and Kenneth MacMillan, in addition to Dame Ninette herself. The Royal Ballet has mounted not only original English ballets by these choreographers, but also full-scale productions of the classics, such as *Giselle*, *The Sleeping Beauty*, *Swan Lake* and *Coppelia*. It has in addition given birth to a second, touring company of almost equal distinction.

WHAT'S ON IN BRITAIN

Sports and Special Interests for the Connoisseur

by

JOHN BARR

(*A globe-trotting American journalist who has worked and taught in such diverse countries as Japan and Bolivia, the author is now on the staff of the weekly journal,* New Society. *His self-proclaimed Anglophilia is confirmed by marriage to a Norfolk girl and ownership of a 17th-century thatched cottage, surrounded by brussels sprouts fields, in Bedfordshire.*)

Just wearing out shoe leather is sport enough for most visitors to Britain, The whole country may be smaller than Wyoming, but—with trembling apologies to any Cheyenne reader about to dust off his scalping hatchet—there is a lot more to see per square mile: sights are jammed into this little island almost as tightly as people. Even so, there comes a time in most sightseers' lives when one more ancient monument is, well, just one more ancient monument, or when the prospect of yet another museum raises secret, perhaps unspoken, prayers for a sudden national strike of museum attendants. When, or if, this time comes for you, it may be time for something more active than plodding along the tourist furrows—

or maybe something *less* active, but with the illusion of being active: sitting and watching *other* people leaping about, throwing or hitting or kicking things around.

(Although details of many activities appear in the following description, the reader should note that information about many more sports will be found in the various regional chapters of the book. Scottish specialties, such as curling, the Highland Games and all that, will be found in *Scotland*, Lakeland Games information in *The Lake District*, boating on the Broads in *East Anglia*, and so forth.)

Sports for Spectators

At this point you'll encounter that particularly British concept of Fair Play, its roots not only in the nation's history but, more obviously, in the British passion for playing games. A passion, certainly, but more amateur than professional, with the participants usually falling into one of two categories: the never totally reputable "players" (the pros) and the always reputable "gentlemen" (amateurs). The gentlemen can be as viciously competitive as the players—even more so—but for them, the game's the thing, not the rewards of victory or prestige or money. To lose or to win—it matters little, so long as the game is played with elegance and *panache*, the verdict accepted with grace and good manners. Nowhere is this philosophy of sport more evident than on the immaculate and gracious greens where the British national sport-cum-passion-cum-ritual is acted out.

Cricket on the Heath

The British equivalent of baseball—cricket—dates back to the 16th century, and since 1744, has been played under an unchanging set of rules—or perhaps "laws" more than rules. In 1787, the Marylebone Cricket Club—today the king of all cricket clubs—was founded by a Yorkshireman named Thomas Lord. The club's playing ground near Regent's Park, London, is still called Lord's, after its founder, and it is at Lord's that you can see—if it is not too crude a description for so graceful a sport—"big-league" cricket.

The season begins in May, ends in September, and if you are lucky you could be in Britain during one of the Test

Matches, when the best cricketers from commonwealth countries—Australia, India, the West Indies and others—take on England in a kind of World Series of cricket. (You'll know if there's a Test Match on—wars and world political crises will be pushed into the background and the BBC and newspapers will talk of little else except "wickets" (something like baseball's home bases) and "pitches" (not throwing a ball, but the field on which the game is played) and "bowlers" (not the hats that Englishmen wear, but the men who hurl the cricket balls—the pitchers).)

The intricacies of cricket are beyond description in a few paragraphs, but one warning is in order: if you think baseball has become a slow sport, wait till you've been to your first cricket match! A Test Match, for instance, lasts no less than 30 hours—with frequent recesses for the inevitable cups of tea and is spread over five or even six days. Even so, cricket is worth seeing—at Lord's or at the other famous grounds such as the Oval, also in London, Old Trafford in Manchester—or simply on practically any village green in the summer. The manicured turf, the ritual, the players (all in spotless white) make an attractive and very British spectacle, even if you don't have a clue as to what they're doing. Joining in yourself is not recommended—it wouldn't be cricket!

Football Without Space Suits

During all those often gray and drizzly months—autumn, winter and early spring—when cricket bats are packed away in the attic, Britons turn to their second addiction: football (or soccer). No Buck Rogers helmets and shoulder pads for the eleven stalwarts who make up a soccer side, however: no matter a quagmire or snow drift or two on the playing field— out they go *in shorts*. Soccer is faster than American football —none of those seemingly interminable huddles—and many U.S. visitors find it more exciting. You'll see the stars if you attend one of the First Division professional matches staged during the season every Saturday (admission from 4s, 48¢) and sometimes one other day (or evening) as well. You may become such a fan that you also get hooked on the Pools— filling in coupons predicting how you think all the soccer matches will turn out. You can join in the Pools for a matter of pennies and you could win up to one million dollars—but don't count on it, as the odds are infinitesimal.

The other British brand of football—more like American football, with lots of tackling and rolling about in the mud—is rugby football. There are 15 players a side and it's a rough-and-tough game. The best rugby can be seen at Twickenham, London, when England meets teams from Scotland, Wales. Ireland, and—for some odd reason—France, in international matches. To confuse things further, there is a professional Rugby League in the north, where there are only 13 players a side.

For Kings and Suckers

The 17th-century writer, Robert Burton, claimed that "England is a paradise for women and hell for horses." If anything, the opposite is true, so revered are horses—at least if they're racing thoroughbreds. There are two seasons for horse racing: flat racing from late March till November and steeplechasing from September to May. In all, about 70 racecourses with 700 days of racing a year—enough to satisfy the most obsessed racegoer. There is betting either at the windows of the "Tote" (as little as 4s, 48¢) or at the stands set up by the gravel-voiced bookies—who will usually accept a bet as small as 1s (12¢). The two biggest flat races of the season are the Derby at Epsom Downs in early June and the Royal Ascot at Ascot Heath in late June. Take your wife to this one—at least if she has a fantastic hat in tow. Ascot is as famous for its flamboyant ladies' fashions as for its horses. Chances are you'll see some of the Queen's horses running—and you might well see the Queen herself.

Also, there are more than 1,000 show-jumping competitions every year—it's not only a Texan, but many an upper-class British girl, who is brought up in the saddle. The biggest shows are the Royal International Horse Show at White City, London, in late July and the Horse of the Year Show at Wembley, London, in early October. There are also major jumping events at Hickstead near Brighton in July, August and September.

And how about the night trots? For something different, try Prestatyn Raceway in North Wales, where every Tuesday and Saturday night from Easter to October, there are trotting races under the lights.

How to be Foxed

Despite organized campaigns by opponents of blood sports, the gentry still ride to the hounds. There are more than 200 packs of hounds in the country, some of them so large that as many as one hundred mounted followers go out after a puny, but sly, fox. If this sort of thing is to your taste, you'll find it expensive. But if those old fox-hunting prints have made you want to see a real hunt, you can do what the less wealthy Britons do—follow a hunt in your car. The hunting season is from early November until April. Or, if it's a real hunting and shooting safari you're looking for, this can be arranged—for deer, grouse or pheasant—with *Tippett's Safaris*, Overdown House, Odiham, Hampshire.

Sports for Participants—Anyone for Tennis?

The *Lawn Tennis Association*, Barons Court, London W.14, will supply the addresses of tennis clubs where you can become a temporary member—but remember to leave your lavender pedal pushers or Hawaiian sports shirt in your hotel room: the strict rule at all respectable British tennis clubs is to play in all-white outfits. For just viewing the top amateur players in action, of course, Wimbledon—held near London in late June and early July—is the tournament of tournaments. Lots of elegant spectators, and strawberries and cream, too. But it is practically as difficult to get a ticket for Wimbledon as it would be for you to win the singles title there. The best bet is to contact your local lawn tennis club a long time before you come to Britain. Sometimes, however, *Alfred Hays, Ltd.*, 100 St. Martin's Lane, London W.C.2, has a few of the precious tickets. If you fail, there is always a pleasant tournament the week immediately before Wimbledon at the Queens Club, London, where most of the Wimbledon entrants tune up—and no problem about tickets.

Playing at Robin Hood

Archery is an ancient British sport, dignified and disciplined, pursued by some 10,000 eager archers. You could become a temporary member of many of the country's 700 clubs, or just go along and watch the archers in action. (It is not advised to chew an apple while watching.) Full details: *Grand National Archery Society*, 20 Broomfield Road, Chelmsford, Essex, enclosing a self-addressed stamped envelope or an international mail coupon for a reply.

Putting About

Obsessed golfers will want to try out their talents on a course in Scotland, the home of golf, where there are more than 300 links. The most celebrated ones are Gleneagles, where there is an equally famous and swank hotel, and, of course, St. Andrews, the golf capital of the world. The old St. Andrews course, a real test of skill, has broken the heart of many an over-confident player—especially those enormous double greens which, if an approach shot is not accurate, can leave you with a 60-yard putt. And the bunkers look about as big as the White Cliffs of Dover. For a complete list of courses and fees, the *Scottish Tourist Board*, 2 Rutland Place, West End, Edinburgh 1, Scotland, publishes a booklet, *Scotland—Home of Golf*. Price 1s (12¢).

For a golf weekend or week in Scotland, with all arrangements made for you, there are air tours from London, Birmingham and Manchester, arranged by *British European Airways,* to courses at North Berwick and Nairn. Full board in first-class hotels and air fares are included and prices range from about £27 ($65) for a weekend and £65 ($156) for a full week. Details from BEA or any travel agent.

Holidays on Horseback

Cook's have pony-trekking holidays in Scotland at Aberfoyle and Glendevon. The weekly charges, which include full board at country hotels and your very own pony for the week (a guide and instruction for beginners, too) range from about £21 ($51). This could be the ideal solution for a restless teenager. Details from any Cook's office.

If you want to try your skill in the saddle on something more challenging than a pony, a full list of approved riding establishments is available from the *British Horse Society,* 35 Belgrave Square, London S.W.1. The fashionable thing to do on a Sunday morning is to ride in Rotten Row, London. This could be arranged by contacting the *Knightsbridge Riding School,* 11 Elvaston Mews, London S.W.7.

Is it Angling or Fishing?

For the enthusiastic fisherman—the British would call you an "angler"—there are so many possibilities that it would require a book to talk about them. But certainly Scotland, especially for trout in roaring streams and sea fish along rocky coasts, is a paradise. The Scottish Tourist Board publishes a guide book, *Scotland for Fishing*, price 4s. (48¢). If you want to try your luck in a competition, one of the biggest seashore fishing contests of the year is along the Causeway Coast at Portrush, Northern Ireland (a part of Britain which rivals Scotland as a fisherman's mecca). This is a four-day festival in early September. The daily entrance fee is £2 ($4.80) and there are prizes galore, including something called The

Leprechaun Irish Whiskey Trophy. *Details:* 61 Castle Street, Ballycastle, County Antrim, Northern Ireland.

For a really big catch, travel down to Cornwall and try your luck at shark fishing. The principal center is Looe, headquarters of the *Shark Angling Club of Great Britain.* Thousands of sharks are landed at Looe each season (May through September). To hire a boat for a day, plus all tackle and experienced skipper, costs about £3 ($7.20) each for four persons.

Fishing Areas: You'll find good salmon and wet-fly trout fishing in the southwest, coarse fishing along the southern coast's rivers, trout in Yorkshire, Derbyshire and the Lake District. Salmon and trout in Wales, and in Scotland, salmon, sea trout and brown trout. Northern Ireland is best for the same three fish, wet-fly fishing.

Face First in the Snow

By the standards of the Rockies, Britain's mountains may seem like little more than bumps unworthy of respect—and until a few years ago, it is true that skiing in Britain was something of a bad joke. Even so, if you visit Scotland in the winter or spring now, you'll find a well-developed winter sports set-up in the Cairngorm Mountains, north of Edinburgh. The best-developed area is around the village of Aviemore, where there is now a $6,000,000 development including hotels, ice-rink, heated swimming pool, sauna baths, bowling, theater and lots of *après-ski* fun. All the hotels and ski shops in the village rent out ski equipment and offer lessons. The slopes are well equipped with lifts but tend to be crowded, with long waits, at weekends around Christmas and Easter. The season is from December to April, but a lot depends on the weather. So it's best to check on snow conditions before you go. (The daily newspapers publish details about snow depths and conditions.) Full details about Aviemore and other Scottish ski resorts can be found in a free booklet, *Winter Sports in Scotland,* available from the Scottish Tourist Board.

Sailing on Sand or on Water

The sportsman-adventurer determined to visit the northernmost tip of the British Isles—John O'Groats—in any season (but preferably summer) could try his hand at a new sport: sand yachting. This began on Dunnet Sands, east of Thurso, during the summer of 1967—and because in that far-north stretch of sandy coast, it is never really dark for weeks on end in summer, they even had sand yacht races at midnight. A club has been formed and visitors from overseas are welcomed. Full details from the *Scottish Tourist Board*.

Water sports are available everywhere—canoeing holidays in Wales, lazy cruises up the Thames to Oxford, and canal touring holidays in many parts of the Midlands. The favourite area for sailing and motor cruising inland is the Norfolk Broads. Among the leading operators are *Blakes Ltd.*, Wroxham, Norwich, NCR 41Z. Blakes have a vast fleet of sailing craft and U-drive cabin cruisers for hire. They are comfortable and fully equipped, and prices for hiring a 4-berth cabin cruiser for 1 week start around $24, may be nearly double in the August high season. If you can, go in May, when prices are cheap and the Broads are at their quietest and prettiest.

Barge-ing Around

Just about the laziest way of all to get around Britain is to float off on a holiday on board a canal barge. Known as "narrowboats", these colourful old canal craft have been cunningly converted into comfortable mobile hotels in which you can explore part of Britain's network of 3,000 miles of peaceful inland waterways. To tell you more about canal cruising, there's a colourful booklet, *Leisure and the Waterways*, price 6s (72¢), available from the Stationery Office in London. Also useful is *Holidays on Inland Waterways*, price 2s 6d (30¢), published by British Travel.

Cruising on Dry Land

Promoted unashamedly as "the most expensive tour of England, Scotland and Wales ever devised", the *Landcruise* is a 15-day all-inclusive luxury tour around Britain by streamline coach, stopping at top hotels such as *Gleneagles* and the *London Hilton*. The route lies through Winchester, the West Country, Bath, Wales, Chester, Lakeland, Edinburgh, York, Lincoln, Stratford-upon-Avon, Oxford and the Cotswolds. Also included: tea at an English country vicarage, a Welsh medieval banquet, a visit to a Scotch whisky distillery and best seats at the Royal Shakespeare Theatre. The cost? $600 per person. Details from *Evan Evans Tours Ltd.*, 72-73 Russell Square, London W.C.1.

Tramp, Tramp, Tramp

Is walking a sport or just a way of getting from A to B? Some U.S. physiologists have long warned that Americans of future generations may be born with legs as useless as an appendix—if everyone continues to go everywhere by automobile. So if you want to toughen up those auto-softened leg muscles, and see some of Britain on foot, you could trudge along one of the beautiful Nature Trails which were set up by Shell Oil in 1967 in Northumberland, the region just north of Newcastle. Each of five different Nature Trails is marked by numbered posts, the numbers cross referenced to leaflets which describe the wild flora and fauna along the way. Leaflets and trail maps are available free from *Shell-Mex and B.P. Ltd.*, Shell-Mex House, Strand, London W.C.2 or the *Hancock Museum*, Newcastle (the museum is cooperating in the project). The *British Travel Association* has a 20-page booklet listing 143 different nature trails, with maps. Available for 1s 6d (22¢) plus postage.

Special Interests for the Non-Sporting

If some master census of the world's population ever managed to single out the eccentrics from the conformists, chances are that Britain would rank high on the international eccentric's list. Tolerance of zany dress, curious habits and oddball activities is part of Britain's interpretation of freedom. At a level below eccentricity—simply the pursuit of minority interests—this tolerance also shows itself. And more than tolerance—a positive plethora of clubs, societies and associations devoted to the special interests of a small band of addicts. This means that Britain is well equipped for the visitor who doesn't want to follow the conventional tourist tracks. Everyone from Dickens-scholars to ancestor-hunters is catered for—either in groups or individually.

Coach Tours for Connoisseurs

By becoming a member of the *Hellenic Travellers Club* (entrance fee $3), you can join one of the 97-guinea ($232.80) tours organised by *W. F. & R. K. Swan (Hellenic) Ltd.*, 260 Tottenham Court Road, London W.1. There is a choice of two 10-day guided tours of Britain's great country houses and gardens, and also a 12-day guided tour of Roman Britain, planned by leading British archeologist Sir Mortimer Wheeler.

Adventure for Youngsters

If you come to Britain encumbered with a brood of teenage and sub-teenage kids, they could find the sightseeing round of cathedrals and castles that may fascinate you something of a bore. To entertain them (and incidentally, get them off your hands into other safe hands), you could sign them up for one of the seven-day "Adventure Holidays" organized by, and thoroughly supervised by, Britain's *Youth Hostels Association*. These cost as little as £8 5s ($19.80)—a real bargain—and include canoe-cruising, skin-diving, birdwatching, horseback-riding and mountaincraft. There is a registration fee of £2 ($4.80), which makes your youngster (ages 11–15 eligible) a member of the YHA. Details: *Youth Hostels Association*, Home Tours Dept., 6 Buckingham Street, London W.C.2.

By Carriage or by Double-decker Bus

If a little jogging is your desire, try a half-day horse-drawn carriage ride through Richmond Royal Park and Hampton Court near London. Departures daily in summer from London, price about £3 ($7.20), including a large bowl of traditional hot punch en route. The name of the firm running these tours is *Bartlett's*. Details from any travel agent.

Or if you want to drive a horse-drawn carriage yourself, you could try *Langston Carriage Stables*, at Kingham, Oxford, half-way between Oxford and Stratford. This company, which advertises itself as "purveyors of horse-drawn carriages to the nobility and gentry since 1781", will even sell you a carriage if you fall in love with it!

More up to date, but still great fun, is a one-week tour through the English countryside on a double-decker bus, stopping at old pubs and tourist highspots such as Windsor, Stratford-upon-Avon and York. The price is $99 and the people to contact are *Grand Omnibus Tours Ltd.*, Suite 1013A, Statler Office Building, Boston, Mass.

Floating Around

One way to escape the tourist mob is to go to sea. *Bells of Oxford*, Ship Street, Oxford, operate a 140-ton luxury yacht which cruises frequently to the Channel Island of Guernsey. The yacht sleeps eight, so if you have a large family in tow or a lot of pals, you could make it a private party. The yacht cruises for a week and you spend one week in a first-class hotel on Guernsey.

On Your Own—Getting Tartaned Up

Even if your surname doesn't start with a "Mc", you may like a glimpse of the clans in full array, ancient Highland games and the blare of bagpipes and whirl of Scottish reels. During 1968, there are clan gatherings at Galashiels in June, Strathdon and Oban in August, and Braemar in September. There will be Highland Games (with special events like Tossing the Caber

The tattoo on Edinburgh Castle's ramparts highlights the city's International Festival.

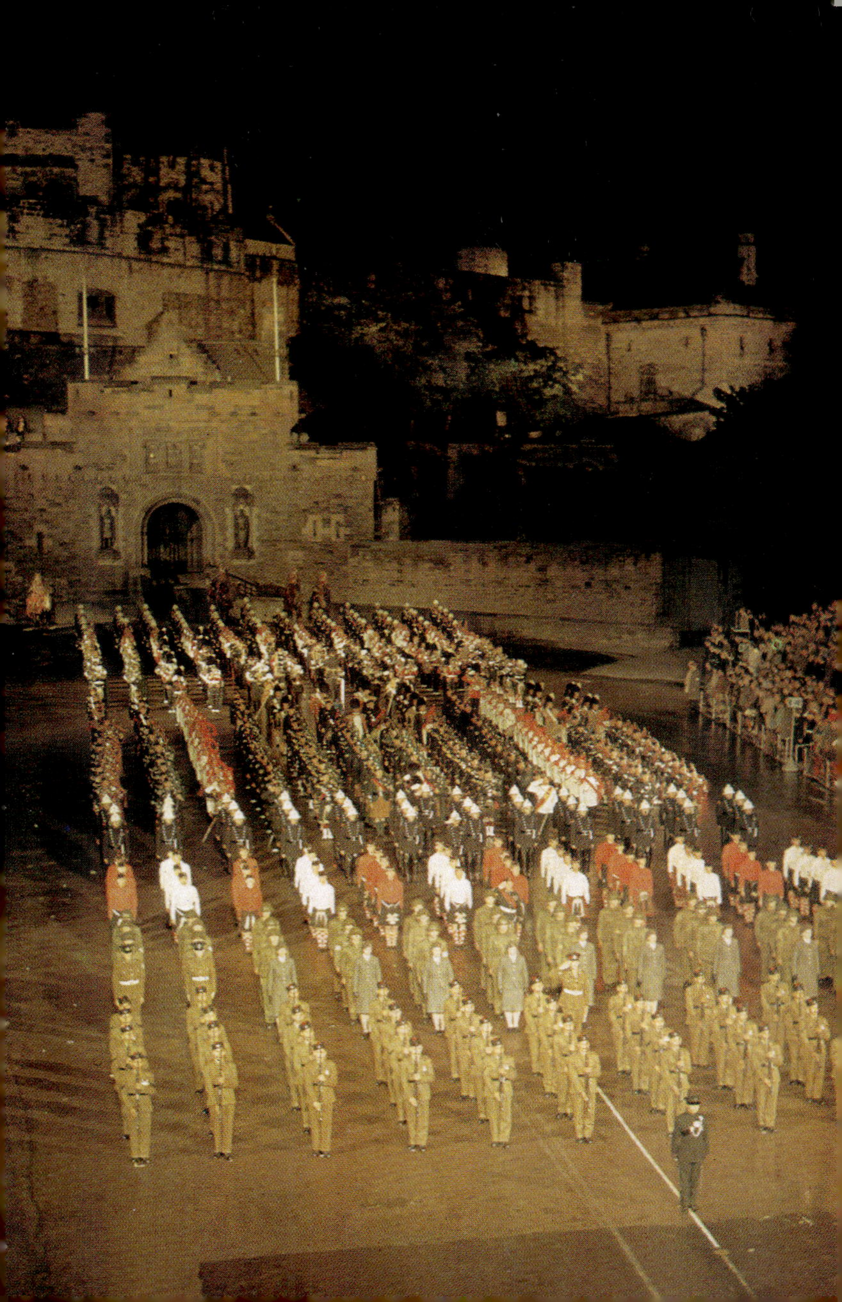

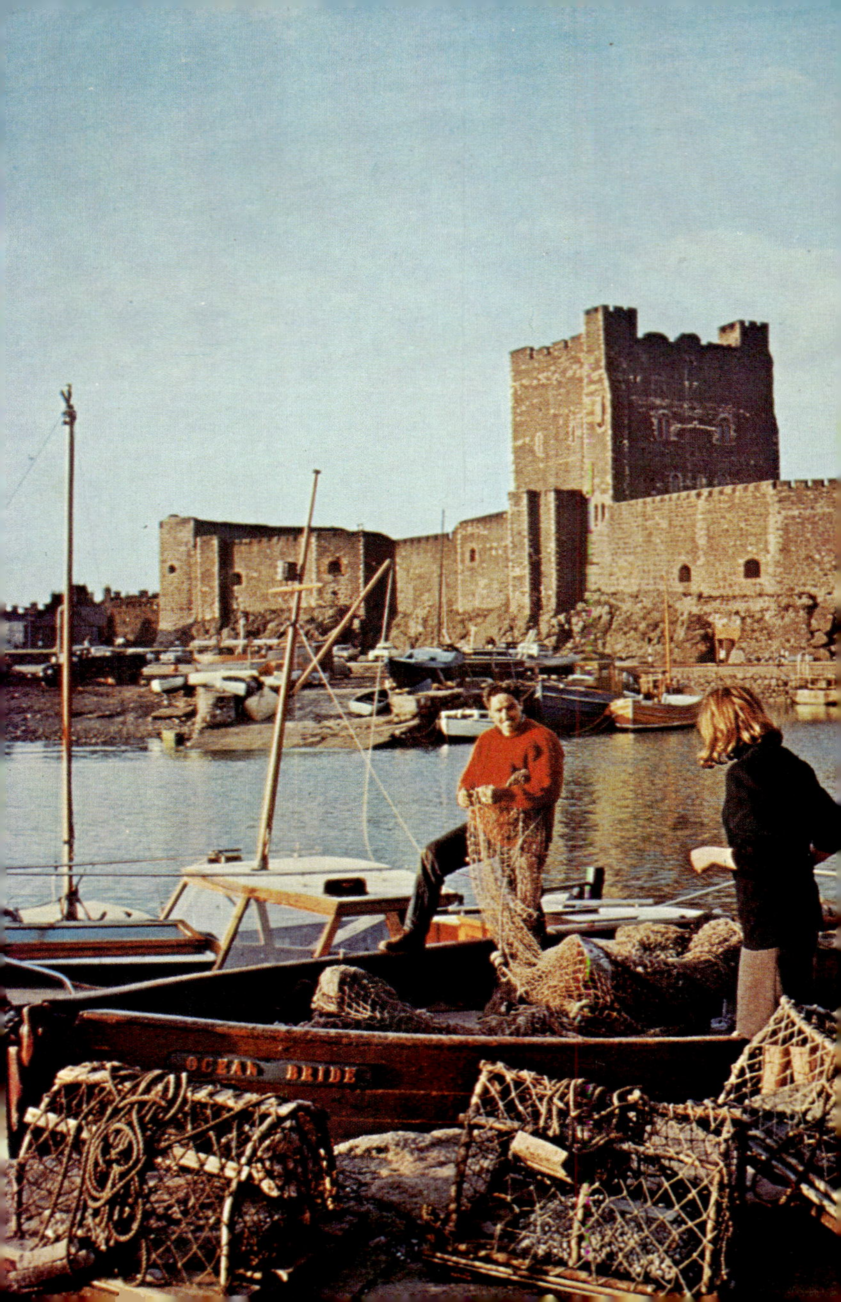
OCEAN BRIDE

and Putting the Weight) in Edinburgh and Aberdeen in August. This isn't a complete list: the *Scottish Tourist Board* can supply that.

Macgregors from Minnesota and Macphees from Mississippi who want to know all about their clan tartans can find the full story at the *Scottish Tartans Society* in the historic Tolbooth in Stirling, Scotland. Expert information on any and all of Scotland's 1,000 tartans and a large library about tartans. Identification of a particular tartan costs 5s (60¢) search fee, and you can join the society for a year for 11s ($1.32).

Living with the Natives

If you are as eager to know the British as to know Britain, you can arrange to stay with British families in their own homes. *Tourist Hospitality Service*, Suite 3, 119 Oxford Street, London W.1, has two arrangements which make it possible for you to meet the people. For only $5 a day, meals and accommodation included, you can stay with British hosts who are screened so that they have interests similar to yours.

Live Like a Lord

Paying a half-crown to stroll around a stately home is one thing. But staying as a guest of the owner is something else! This novel experience is offered by *Oakleaf Enterprises Ltd.*, 15 Pall Mall, London S.W.1. who have more than 300 houses and castles on their books. You choose an elegant country mansion or ancestral castle. You sleep, maybe, in a fourposter bed. A butler is at your service. And in the evening you dine with your hosts. (So as not to spoil the feeling of being a personal house guest, no money passes between you and your host. All the financial details are taken care of by Oakleaf.) It is the most enjoyable way to experience that unique pleasure, English country life, and to meet the English themselves, at home, which, magnificent or not, is always a castle.

Digging up Your Roots

About one in every ten American visitors to Britain spends some of his time searching for records of his Anglo-Saxon ancestors. But come to Britain armed with as much informa-

Carrickfergus Castle in County Antrim has seen many battles, but is now only a backdrop for water sports.

tion about your forebears as possible—names, birth- and death-dates, place of birth, and anything else you can glean from family records at home. Once in Britain, if your ancestor came from England or Wales, the places which may be able to help you are the *Society of Genealogists*, the *College of Arms* (if you imagine that some blue blood flows through your veins), the *General Register Office*, and the *Public Record Office*—all in London. For Scottish ancestors, try the *Scots Ancestry Research Society* in Edinburgh; and for some relative long gone from Northern Ireland, the *Public Record Office* in Belfast. If your ancestor was born, married or died since 1837, the General Register Office (Somerset House, Strand, London W.C.2) can produce a certificate of those milestones for about 7s (84¢) each. For pre-1837 ancestors, the best course is to consult the register in the ancestor's local parish. Thanks to the old British habit of never throwing away ancient documents, you stand a chance of tracing someone back as far as 1538. But if do-it-yourself ancestor-tracing proves unsuccessful or just too tiring, the British Travel Association has a list of professional searchers who charge between 14s and 21s ($1.68 and $2.52) an hour for the job, plus expenses. These are all reputable firms. Beware of unrecommended ones—they may be disreputable and so ready to satisfy, say, a cherished desire to boast of a distinguished pedigree that they will use their imagination much more than their shoe leather—and you'll end up paying dearly for a purely fictional family tree.

Ancient Haunts

The British Travel Association, 64 St. James's Street, London S.W.1, receives so many requests for the names and addresses of haunted houses in Britain that the association has produced a leaflet, *A Ghost Hunter's Guide to Britain*. If the obvious ghostly hang-outs such as the Tower of London and Windsor Castle are too tourist-haunted for your tastes, the guidebook will soon lead you to some Victorian nerve-racking mansion on the Yorkshire moors or remote Scottish castle, where dragging chains attached to nothing much may keep you awake all night chewing on your fingernails.

Valliant Cronshaw Ltd., 331 Pinner Road, Harrow, Middlesex, operate special ghost-hunting visits to Salisbury Hall, Hertfordshire, said to be haunted by Nell Gwynne.

FOOD AND DRINK

Stamping out the Bad Food Myth

by

KATO FRANK

(*In addition to raising her children on good British food, Mrs. Frank has written extensively about its merits, one of her works being a directory of regional foods.*)

So much mud has been thrown at British food that its defenders almost feel a crusading fire in their veins. The best advice to the visitor is to forget the stories; the myth of bad food in Britain is outdated and is very far removed from the present reality. If you avoid certain pitfalls, and they will all be mentioned here, you can eat in Britain almost as well as anywhere else in the world. As with all myths, this one on British food is just limping several steps behind the real world, which is ever-changing in food as in fashion, art and politics, for that matter.

It is not very difficult (and quite amusing) to trace the origin of the legend, which must stem less from the quality of food than the British attitude to eating. "I eat because I have to live, not because I enjoy my food," is a state of mind which is clearly a hangover of 19th-century Victorian primness. This disdainful attitude towards the pleasures of eating was still present in certain age groups and strata of society in Britain before the Second World War. With the war and its food shortages, the non-caring attitude became a necessity, a cover-up for the inevitably poor food. So the myth was fully grown, and after bouncing about for some twenty years, is obviously lurking in the subconscious of most visitors to Britain. Although it may take another twenty years to destroy the myth, let's make a start here and now!

It is no longer shameful or sinful to enjoy good food, so the ethical aspect has been cleared up for British moralists. Further the yearly mass emigration on vacation to the sunny parts of the continent has successfully eliminated the insular attitude about "that greasy foreign mess", so small restaurants and even unsophisticated private homes might easily today serve guests *paella*. Finally, the sophisticated *avant-garde* has long passed the *paella* stage and is now happily feasting on Basic British Perennials, like steak-and-kidney pie or boiled silverside of beef.

The Historic National Cuisine

The outstanding feature of all British cooking is that it is straightforward, unfussy, good food, entirely dependent on top quality and *fresh* raw materials. Nothing could be simpler than a large hunk of roast beef—juicy, succulent and tender—served with crisp and light Yorkshire pudding and a bit of horseradish sauce. Yorkshire pudding is a baked pancake mixture, originally meant for serving before the meal to take the edge off your appetite. Now it is generally served with the meat, except in private homes in the north of England. The roast "joints" are excellent and always served with two or three vegetables and gravy. Roast young English lamb with mint sauce is a culinary feat in itself. The quality of the home-produced meat is very high, so if the meat you are going to eat is either English or Scotch, you can be sure it will be the best you have ever had.

Other three-star British dishes are steak-and-kidney pie and steak-and-kidney pudding. Both of them are disastrous for the waistline, but who wants to diet on a holiday, anyhow?

FOOD AND DRINK

To compensate for these delicious, but high-calORied, joys, choose grilled Dover sole, the larger the better, for your next meal. In good restaurants, specialized fish restaurants and hotels, you usually find Dover soles prepared in three or four different ways—stick to the plain grilled one; its taste is so delicately perfect that anything added would be gilding the lily.

Other popular British dishes include: smoked Scotch salmon, cockie leekie soup, poached salmon with cucumber sauce, and for dessert, Somerset syllabub, perhaps served with Gloucester gingerbread. Whitebait, a small fish cooked whole, is good, too. The famous grouse is expensive, and should hang at least a week before eating.

Veal-and-ham pie is a widely known and popular cold buffet dish, but it is the game pie which brings a welcome whiff of Elizabethan England to the table, though they can usually only be found in high-priced and specialized restaurants. Specialties like jugged hare and potted shrimp are usually expensive.

The country's long association with India left its mark on the national cuisine. You will find all kinds of curries on the menu, led by a soup called mulligatawny, part of the established British cooking. It is a highly-spiced, rich vegetable broth. Kedgeree is another dish adopted from India; it contains rice with flaked smoked fish and hard-boiled eggs, and is usually served for lunch or even breakfast. The above are most of the national dishes, which you will find in good hotels and good restaurants throughout the country.

Added to the national dishes there are any number of regional specialties, many of which are available everywhere. Most of the south of England specialties seem to be tea-time delicacies: Chelsea buns, brandy snaps filled with fresh cream and cream darioles (small custard tarts topped with red currant jelly and whipped cream). Similar to the English muffin in America, but with holes drilled through, are crumpets—luscious, round tea breads, toasted and soaked with lashings of butter. They are a winter-time food, traditionally meant to be toasted on a long toasting fork by the open fire, so they tend to disappear during the summer months.

The other regional specialty, which you can get wherever you go, is a savoury pie called Cornish pasty. These are individual, half-moon-shaped pies filled with meat, onions and other vegetables; you will find them in pubs and snack bars, or you can buy them freshly-baked at small baker's shops in the suburbs or provinces.

Cheesecake, which many think is a typical Austrian or German specialty, is a long-time favourite in Yorkshire, where it is a traditional family treat. Unfortunately, it is less often found in restaurants than in private houses. The other contribution from Yorkshire to the national cuisine is a scone which goes by the delightful name of Yorkshire Fat Rascal.

As a wild generalization, one can say that the further north you go in England, the more the cooking and general overall interest in food improves. In the Midlands and the north of England, and in Scotland, you can often find farmhouses serving teas of such quality and quantity that you will have no thought of food till next breakfast time. In these regions, the term "tea" really means "supper". If you don't want a big meal, ask for "afternoon tea".

The greatest of all British sauces comes from a county called Cumberland, in the extreme north of England. This sauce alone should give British cooking a better reputation than it has. Made of a piquant mixture of lemon and orange peel and juice mixed with port wine and red currant jelly, it is usually served with either game or ham.

Crossing the border into Scotland, you should taste the famous Celtic *wurst*, the haggis, of course. The most likely other national specialties you are bound to encounter are girdle scones (a featherlight delicacy) and the richest of fruit cakes, called Dundee cake. All are well worth trying. The other Celtic inhabitants of the British Isles are the Welsh, who also have a national cuisine, but who find their music and poetry favoured more by visitors than their food.

The Urban National Dish

Your gastronomic education in the British Isles would be incomplete without tasting that famous grab-and-gulp dish called fish and chips. You are unlikely to find a fish-and-chip shop in Knightsbridge or Princes Street—you will have to go a short distance from the smart shops and restaurants, into less elegant residential districts (or places like Soho) to find them. There are a few dotted along the shopping parades of middle-income group districts, but the bulk of them flourish in "working-class" areas. They are called fish bars, or fish restaurants, and are enveloped in an oily haze and smell of frying, which must be deliberate, as it puts you off wanting to sit down and eat there. The drill is to make your choice of fish (there are always at least five different ones chalked up on their blackboard), ask for it and sixpennyworth of chips to take out, and, exiting hurriedly, to rush to your car or taxi, where you consume it elegantly with your fingers. You may not believe it, but fish and chips taste best from a newspaper.

Cheeses

With a few exceptions, the British have the same self-deprecating attitude towards their cheese as towards their entire national cuisine. Don't let them feed you on foreign cheeses all the time, however, because you will miss a real treat if you don't taste the home-produced ones. Wensleydale looks pale and wan, but has a subtle, delicate taste, with a slightly honeyed aftertaste. It comes from Yorkshire, where they say "An apple pie wi-owt tha cheese is like a kiss wi'owt a squeeze". Double Gloucester is the thing to have with a pint of ale. Cheddar, Leicester, Lancashire and Caerphilly are all subtly different in taste and all excellent. The king of them all is blue Stilton. It is truly a connoisseur's cheese, which should be scooped out of the centre of a big round half, wrapped in a table napkin. Sip a glass of port with your Stilton.

Meal times ought to be engrained on your memory firmly if you go anywhere outside the big towns and large seaside resorts. Generally, they are: Breakfast: 8:30 to 9:30; lunch: noon to 2 p.m.; tea: 3 to 4:30 p.m ; and dinner, 7 to 8:30 p.m.

Imbibing, Bitterly or Otherwise

Licensing hours vary from district to district, by half an hour to an hour, and from weekdays to Sundays and public holidays, but roughly speaking, they are from 10:30 a.m. to 3 p.m. and 5:30 to 11 p.m. You get longer drinking hours in hotels, restaurants and coffee bars, if you are consuming food with your drink. You have yet more privileges to carry on drinking if you are resident at an hotel. The intricacies of the licensing laws could fill a volume on its own, so let us just say that if you are keen on your drink carry your own bottle and you need never go thirsty in Britain!

If your cup of tea is alcohol, you should look into the uniquely British drinking scene. Guzzling in this land means mostly beer, whether it be called "bitter", "ale", "brown ale", "lager", "porter" or "stout". Anything written on the subject of British beer leads to endless controversy, as the distinctions between some of the drinks mentioned above are blurred (and some think deliberately so) by the general drinking public. In theory, the generic term "beer" is not used in a British pub. If you ask the man behind the counter for "a bottle of beer", you will likely get lager, which is rather similar to American beer (unless it's Danish or German).

The majority of drinkers ask for "a pint of bitter" or "a half of bitter" (half pint, that is.) (Ale, brown ale, lager and stout usually come in bottles only.) The term originally came from the phrase "bitter beer". It tastes like what it says. Ale in Britain usually means any light-coloured beer, not so strongly hopped as American ale. Brown ale is *dark* brown, and some think it's a cross between bitter and stout. Porter is an even stronger, darker ale, with more malt. Stout, finally, is the darkest, the strongest and the maltiest of the lot. Learning to drink it takes time. It is said to be marvellous for the health, full of iron, and death to the diet-watcher.

In any event, draught beer in Britain is better than the bottled stuff, and if you taste around a bit, you'll undoubtedly come up with a flavour you like. The old tale about "hot beer" is no longer always true—the British like it cool, but not iced—and you'll find that you can actually *taste* the beer when it's served in the British manner, not paralysing your tongue with coldness as so often happens when drinking beer in North America. Variations on beer-drinking include "lager and lime", a mixture of lime juice with lager, especially refreshing on hot summer days, as is "a shandy", a mixture of ginger beer and real beer or lemonade and beer.

Cocktails are still regarded as but an amusing diversion to the British, and you should specify the exact ingredients if you want one in a bar or restaurant. "A martini" will get you a glass of nothing but sweet vermouth, so beware! A "dry martini" will get you a glass of dry vermouth. Minor aberrations of British drinking include a fondness for spoiling brandy by putting ginger ale in it and the idea that a manhattan should be made with Scotch whisky, not with bourbon.

There are British wines, but forget we ever told you. Good French and German wines are available at prices similar to those in America (because of very high taxes here) or sometimes a bit lower. Many of the labels are different from those North Americans are accustomed to, so don't hesitate to ask the wine steward to recommend something.

Britain's crowning glories (spiritually speaking) are Scotch whisky and English gin. Of the latter, little can be said except that the aroma differs from one brand to the other, but of the former, books and poems could be written (and have been). Although North Americans have boosted the sales of the very light Scotch whiskies (which were especially distilled for the U.S. market) to amazing heights, your stay in Britain should be a good opportunity to sample the wide variety of whiskies. Though a bottle of whisky costs from £2 10s ($6) up, the usual single shot in an ordinary pub will cost but 3s (36¢). You therefore have no economic excuse to avoid sampling the heavy, tangy Scotches as well as the light ones (and all those in between). When ordering, try at least to drink one each of the two basic types, *malt* whisky and *grain* whisky. The former is made only from malted barley. Grain whisky, however, is made from malted barley, unmalted barley and maize (corn). About 100 different firms produce malt whisky, about one dozen manufacture grain whisky. The more you sample, the more you'll appreciate the delicate differences and the fanaticism various brands or blends have engendered.

In the *Anglo-American Vocabulary* (or Glossary of Misunderstood English Words), at the back of this book, you will find a few more terms relating to the pub and drinking in general.

When these are all sorted out, as the British would say, pop off to a pub and order a pint in your very best man-of-the-world manner. Turn to your neighbour, raise the glass and utter that most pleasant of toasts, "cheers". Your drinking in Britain, with a little bit of luck, will then undoubtedly be a series of "cheers" all the way.

For a good guide to British restaurants, supplementing our own lists in this book, get The Good Food Guide, *produced by the Consumers' Association. Cost: 25s ($3).*

COMING OF AGE

A Satirical Glance at Cuisine, Manners and Class

by

GEORGE MIKES

(*Mr. Mikes is the author of those fabulous best sellers:* How to be an Alien, How to Scrape Skies *and* Milk and Honey, *among others. He is a merciless humorist who has polished off the English, the Americans, the Israelis, the French, and last but not least, himself. He is of Hungarian origin, but the British were magnanimous enough to disregard this and to consider him as one of their own.*)

It was nearly thirty years ago that England and I first set foot on each other. I came for a fortnight; I have stayed ever since. In these thirty years England has gained me and lost an empire. The net gain was small. Many things have changed in the last three decades. The Britain of the 1960's is vastly different from the Britain of 1938.

When I first came here, Englishmen were slim and taciturn, while today they are slim and taciturn. Then, they were grunting and inscrutable; today they are grunting and inscrutable. Then, they were honest, likeable but not too quick on the uptake; today, they are honest, likeable but not quicker on the uptake. Then, they kept discussing the weather rather dully; today they keep discussing the weather much more dully. Then, their main interests were cricket, horses and dogs, while today their main interests are dogs, horses and cricket. Then, the main newspaper topics were sex, crime and money, while today it is money, money, money and crime with a little sex somewhat perfunctorily thrown in. Then, Britain was being inundated by blooming foreigners and she did not like it. Today foreigners are called *visitors, tourists* and other fancy names—and in extreme emergency, when shortage of foreign currency is too pressing—even Distinguished Europeans. We must all exercise the greatest care, because the resemblance between a Distinguished European and a bloody foreigner is most misleading.

Then, Britons travelled to the continent, drank tea with milk in Paris, ate roast beef and Yorkshire pudding in Monte Carlo, kept to one another's company everywhere and were proud of their insularity; today, they drink tea with milk in Paris, eat roast beef with Yorkshire pudding in Monte Carlo, keep to one another's company everywhere and are proud of how cosmopolitan they have become.

In those happy days, Munich crisis or no Munich crisis, no one really knew where Czechoslovakia was: the problem was too *small*. Today we have the Bomb of Damocles hanging over our heads, but nobody cares: the problem is too *big*. In those days "reaching for the moon" was still a metaphor and not a short-term programme.

A Thoroughly Modern "Limey"

If you want to be a modern Englishman, you must be what an Englishman has always been, throughout the ages, except that you have to be a shade more class-conscious. Here are some brief clues on how to be class-conscious:

(1.) If you belong to the so-called higher spheres of society, you will, of course, never be flagrant about this. You simply look down (not with a superior, simply with a pitying, smile) upon those miserable and ridiculous creatures who do not know the conventions of your world. Nothing can possibly amuse you more than hearing someone address the third son of a marquess in the style due to the second daughter of an earl.

I must admit that I still often find these rules confusing. The other day I received an invitation to a party from a friend of mine who is a baronet. The invitation was signed by his wife and was R.S.V.P. From my reference books, I sought advice on how to address an envelope to a baronet's second wife. "If the daughter of a commoner . . .", I read, then I stopped, picked up the telephone, rang the lady in question and asked her: "I say, Eileen, are you the daughter of a commoner?"

She said: "What the hell do you mean?"

I told her: "That will do. You are a commoner. And getting commoner and commoner every day."

That solved one problem. Many other problems, however, still remain. One of the most exasperating cases you may come across is how to address a Dame of the Order of the British Empire married to a baronet or a peer. Skill, ingenuity and determination may solve even that. But if you hear of the third daughter of a marchioness married to an archbishop, you should carefully avoid the combination. Nobody knows what to call her.

(2.) Another excellent device of the British aristocracy to drive poor foreigners—primarily Americans—crazy, is the changing of names. The fact that Lord Upperstone's elder son is called Lord Ipswich, while his younger son is Mr. Hinch, does not mean that they are both bastards. The elder daughter of the noble lord may be the Hon. Mrs. Cynthia Cunliffe-Green and his younger daughter the Hon. Mary Cumberland, just for good measure. And if even that does not drive the poor onlooker raving mad, then the "as he then was" business comes in. You find such passages in field-marshals' memoirs:

"I then went to the Viceroy's Lodge and asked to see Lord Irwin (as he then was) without delay. I shook Lord Halifax (as he then was not yet) by the hand in the friendliest manner but spoke to him sternly: 'Mr. Wood' (as he no longer was), I began, 'I've just had a message from Mr. Churchill (as he then was) about 2nd Lieutenant Birch (as he still is),' etc., etc."

(3.) In the old days, people used to aspire to higher classes. Since the angry-young-man literature has made its impact, quite a few people proudly assert that they are of lower origin than, in fact, they are. (I am using here the word "lower" in the worst snobbish sense.) The place of the upstart is being taken by the downstart. I know people who secretly visit evening elocution classes in order to pick up a cockney accent. Others are practising the Wigan brogue. And I know others again who would be deeply ashamed if the general public learnt that their fathers were, in fact, book-keepers and not dustmen, village grocers and not swine-herds, solicitors and not pickpockets.

Equality and the Telly

The English talk, and talk a great deal, of upper, middle, and working classes. They also talk of upper-middle and lower-middle classes, and more recently, they have started mentioning a top-working class—just to fit in between the middle-working class and the lower-middle class. This, of course, makes them fully conscious of how pitifully inadequate their language is to describe the other 120 clearly defined castes and 413 sub-castes of English society. What about the lower-middle-upper layer of the lower-upper-middle class? What about the middle-middle of the middle-middle class? And how can you really clearly distinguish between the upper-upper-middle people who by no means qualify yet for the bottom-upper?

While all this goes on, the English remain staunch believers in equality. Equality is a notion the English have given to humanity. Equality means that you are just as good as the next man but the next man is not half as good as you are. But then, you both own a "telly".

When I first came to England, television was still a kind of entertainment and not a national disease. During the happy war years, it was off the air altogether, but afterwards, it returned with a vengeance.

The main and most glorious achievement of television is that it is killing the art of conversation. If we think of the type of conversation television is helping to kill, our gratitude must be undying. Not that British conversation was shrill, or anything of the sort. English people sit down in comfortable armchairs and keep silent for a couple of hours. This is considered normal or even animated conversation in England. If you are courting an English girl, don't say a single word to her during the first five days. If you *must* talk (to her or others), do not discuss anything that might possibly interest you. The weather is always a safe subject, and you will find out soon enough that English weather is something worth wasting a few remarks upon. The trouble is, really, that television has not yet killed enough of this kind of conversation. Easily the best part of television, of course, is the advertisements, but they are not perfect, either.

All advertisements are utterly and hopelessly un-English. They are too outspoken, too definite, too boastful. Why not evolve a national British style in television advertising instead of slavishly imitating the American style of breathless superlatives, with all their silly implications (buy our shampoo and you'll get a husband; buy our perfume and you are sure to be attacked by hungry males in Bond Street; smoke our pipe-tobacco and you will become a sun-tanned Adonis)? I feel sure that the effect of these advertisements could be vastly improved if they were made more English. Some ads, for example, could be given an undertone of gambling:

"Try your luck on Bumpex Fruit Juice. Most people detest it. You may be an exception."

Or appeal to the Englishman's sense of fairness. A beautiful, half-nude girl (you cannot do without them in any advertisement, British, American or anything else), might call to the public:

"S.O.S. We are doing badly. Business is rotten. Buy Edgeless Razor Blades and give us a sporting chance. Honestly, they're not much worse than other makes."

Or, just moderate your language. Make no extravagant claims; be vague and incoherent; in other words natural:

"Drink Danford's beer. It's dirt cheap and you *can* get used to it."

Getting the Puritans Out of the Kitchen

Food, too, is a matter of growing importance in England. It used to be said, with full justice, that continental people had good food, the British had good table manners. This is not quite true any more: the table manners of continentals have improved.

But, let's be fair, so has the food of the English. Until the end of the war, a puritanic notion reigned in Britain that food had to be consumed in order to hold body and soul together but certainly not to be enjoyed. To enjoy food was a French habit, consequently despicable.

But after the war, Englishmen started travelling abroad and discovered the joys of French restaurants, Spanish *paëlla*, *Wiener schnitzel* and other tricky alien devices. What was even more important, foreign restaurateurs started travelling, too, and they came to London in large numbers, opening admirable restaurants. Add to all this the wonderful (but now departed) habit of expense accounts. Businessmen were not too slow to discover that if you have to spend the same amount on good food as on bad, you might as well have the good food and to hell with the puritans. As a result of all this, food in Britain improved beyond recognition. Today, if you know where to go, you can eat as well in London as in Paris or in any other capital of the world. But *if you know where to go* are the operative words. In Paris, you may chance it and, unless you are awfully unlucky, you cannot really go wrong; in London—and particularly in the provinces—you *can* go wrong easily. But if you do know where to go, I repeat, you just cannot recognize the Britain of yesteryear and you must acknowledge —with joy or with a regretful sigh (it depends on your temperament)—that even Britain is changing.

But more important than food is tea. You must really pay a great deal of attention to tea. The trouble with tea is that it must be drunk; this was easier many years ago, for originally, it was quite a good drink. As soon as it was "discovered", a group of the most eminent British scientists put their heads together and made complicated experiments to find a way of spoiling it.

To the eternal glory of British science, their labour bore fruit. They suggested that if you do not drink it clear, or with rum or lemon or sugar, but pour a few drops of cold milk in it and no sugar, the desired object is achieved. Once this refreshing, aromatic, oriental beverage was successfully transformed into colourless and tasteless gargling-water, it suddenly became the national drink of Great Britain—still retaining, indeed usurping, the name of "tea".

There are some occasions when you must not refuse a cup of tea, lest you be judged a barbarian. If you are invited to an English home to stay, at five o'clock in the morning you get a cup of tea. It is either brought in by a heartily-smiling hostess, or—this is still possible at some places—by a malevolently-smiling maid or valet. When you are disturbed in your sweetest morning sleep, you must not say: "Madame, (or Mabel or Brown), I think you are a cruel and spiteful person who deserves to be shot." On the contrary, you have to declare with your best five o'clock smile: "Thank you so much. I *do* adore a cup of early morning tea, especially *early* in the morning." If they leave you alone with the liquid, you may pour it down the wash-basin.

Then you have tea for breakfast; then you have tea at eleven o'clock in the morning; then after lunch; then you have tea for tea; then after supper; and again at eleven o'clock at night.

You must not refuse additional cups of tea under *any* of the following circumstances: if it is hot; if it is cold; if you are tired; if anybody thinks you might be tired; if you are nervous; if you are gay; before you go out; if you are out; if you have just returned home; if you feel like it; if you don't feel like it; if you have had no tea for some time; if you have just had a cup. You'll be considered rude if you do.

Minding One's Own Business

This is one of the basic English virtues. It is not to be interpreted as really minding your own business (getting on with your job, keeping your promises, etc.); it simply means that you are not to interfere with others. If a man happens to be standing on your foot in the bus, you must not ask him to get off, since it is clearly his business where he chooses to stand; if your neighbour's television or radio is blaring military marches till midnight, you may not remonstrate with him because it is his business what he pleases to listen to and at what time; if you are walking peacefully in the street and someone pours two gallons of boiling water over your best bowler through his bathroom overflow (the pipe of which is aimed at the street), you should proceed without uttering a word—however short—because it is obviously the other fellow's business when he has his bath and how hot he likes it.

In the late 1950's, a man committed a murder in the Midlands, splashing himself with blood in the process. Afterwards, near the scene of the crime, he was seen to board a bus with about 50 people on it. Yet when he got off, leaving a pool of blood on the floor, not one single passenger bothered to ask him what he had been doing lately. They were true Britons, minding their own business.

COMING OF AGE

If another man had been carrying some victim's decapitated head under his arm, that would not make the slightest difference. The parcel you carry is your own business.

I remember an old story from my childhood which ought to be one of the basic ideological parables of English life.

A man bends down in a London street to tie his shoelace. While he's at it, someone kicks him in the behind with such force that he falls on his nose. He gets up somewhat bewildered and looks at his assailant questioningly. The latter explains:

"I *am* sorry. I seem to have made a mistake. I thought you were my friend, Harry Higgins. I meant this as a joke".

The man (presumably of foreign origin) is not altogether satisfied with this explanation and remarks plaintively:

"But even if I had been Harry Higgins . . . must you kick him quite so hard?"

The other man replies coolly and pointedly:

"What has it got to do with you, *how* hard I choose to kick my friend, Harry Higgins?"

For this reason, a few hints on manners for the tourist may be in order:

Etiquette in Reverse

For Americans: If you meet an archbishop, an earl of the realm, or a roadsweeper, do not pat him on the back, and call him by his first name in the first five minutes. Do not ask him whether he has a love affair and how much he earns. (He might be so astounded that he would tell you everything.) Keep your American hat, tie, and accent; the English will recognize you immediately and will treat you with leniency.

If you have a business lunch, do not discuss business under any circumstances. Do not cut up your meat and do not put the knife on the edge of your plate. The English will consider it childish and will believe that you are your own nanny. If you eat soup, do not tilt the plate towards yourself, always tilt it away. This is both important and eminently sensible, because if you happen to spill the soup, you won't pour it on yourself but on your neighbour.

At the table never use your fork in the natural way, always hold it with its points downwards It will take some time before you learn how to eat peas in this way as the naughty little things have a tendency to roll away, but learning is always hard and in this case you might have the gratifying feeling that it is not worth the trouble. Never put a teaspoon in your mouth. This is considered an unforgivable sin. There is one simple way of finding out whether the tea or coffee is too hot. Lift the cup to your mouth and taste it; if it burns your tongue, it *is* too hot.

You may criticize everything and everybody in England; they are very good in accepting criticism, because they do not take it in the least seriously. Do pretend, however, that you love queueing and adore cats. All cats, irrespective of colour and creed. The cat is a sacred animal in England, just as in ancient Egypt. As for the queue, it is formed for everything from a seat at the theatre to a bench in the park.

The Art of Tacit Conversation

For Europeans: If an Englishman invites you for dinner at eight, he does not mean half past nine, he means eight. Do not bow, do not click your heels, and never shake hands with anyone. If you are introduced to somebody, do not announce your name but enquire after his health. On the other hand, if somebody enquires after *your* health, do not tell him how you are, because he is not in the least interested. Do not try to learn the English monetary system, it is quite hopeless, and they won't cheat you with your change in any case. (Besides, the English, who need a bookkeeper or a ready-reckoner to calculate ten per cent of £237 8s. 10d., believe that their system is engagingly simple and that yours, although you can perform the corresponding calculation in one second, is stupid and insuperably complicated.)

Don't forget that the English think all foreigners frightfully funny. In their eyes it is irresistibly comical that people talk foreign languages and shake hands. They will never say so, but that is what they think. In the zoo, I often thought that we human beings must seem just as entertaining to the monkeys and lions, as they seem to us. We, too, are behind bars—from their point of view—and behave curiously. They have the advantage of being able to stay at home without having to pay anything for the pleasure of seeing us. Do not deceive yourself in the British Zoo, called England. You have come to watch and study strange beings. But it is primarily the British Lion (and often the British Monkey) who is amused.

THE FACE OF BRITAIN

LONDON

"Swinging", but Satisfyingly Static

by

ROGER BAKER

(*A freelance journalist, the author has been on the staff of* The Tatler, *Features Editor of* London Life, *and the producer of special supplements for the* Illustrated London News. *Editor of* The Book of London, *he is always right on the scene in his favourite city.*)

Suddenly the long, careful years of building and re-planning have brought results: London has changed. Not since the war years has the capital altered as it has in the years between 1960 and 1970. And, at the same time, a vital post-war generation has been busy growing up—an unprecedented number of young adults, imaginative and eager, have burst in on the scene. The coincidence of these things has helped to create the pervasive image of London as a "swinging" city; an adjective which has worked results temperamental as well as visual.

The great open spaces of central London are still green and filled with flowers; there are still wild fowl in St. James's Park and boats on the Serpentine. But behind them, the skyline has assumed a new profile, with familiar shapes set in a new perspective of towering office blocks. Some of these changes set the reactionary ablaze with horror, but the majority have enough grace and elegance to satisfy any discerning eye. At the end of every street, it seems, the high Post Office Tower (opened in 1966) looms as a constant reminder of the technological age.

The enforcement of smokeless zones across the middle of London during this period has had a double effect. The deadly autumn fogs have been minimized, and a sweeter atmosphere has inspired a wholesale cleaning of the city's older, more remarkable buildings. The visitor will see St. Paul's Cathedral riding high and white over the rooftops of the City of London, just as it does in Canaletto's 18th-century views of the Thames. The great cathedral, cleaned, glows honey-gold, breathtakingly floodlit by night, making Wren's detail and proportion evident once again.

And St. Paul's is being nudged by new, taller buildings as the war-devastated City nears the end of its redevelopment programme. With the older buildings relieved of their layers of grime (the Mansion House and the Royal Exchange have clean faces, too), glass and steel tower blocks march two abreast the length of London Wall, with shopping precincts and linking pedestrian walks ("pedways") high above the road. The whole scheme is expected to be completed this year, making the City of London spectacularly modern and helping to ensure that it retains its financial supremacy. The few remaining fragments of Roman London and the famous City churches have been carefully repaired as integral parts of the new architectural scheme.

The celebration of London as a "swinging" city reached its first climax during the summers of 1966 and 1967. Superficially, "swinging" meant that London had acquired the sort of nightlife that young people could enjoy. They organized new kinds of entertainment for themselves; never before have club, discothèque and bistro owners been so youthful. To have a pleasant evening out, it was no longer necessary for youngsters to choose between dressing up and spending more money than they could afford, or merely drifting into the local cinema and having a coffee on the way home.

And in many other areas of living, the young took a decisive hand, given at last the opportunity and encouragement to do things for themselves. Boutiques sprang up, design groups emerged; this and other activities conspired to create a free-and-easy, but always youthful, image for London. The new atmosphere was catching, permeating most cultural and leisure activity. Ultimately, it meant that people were enjoying themselves more.

All this means, naturally, that the visitor, too, will enjoy himself more. There are more than 50 theatres, all comparatively easy and inexpensive to attend, always offering a cross-section of the best in British (and American) drama from Shakespeare to the latest in experimental attempts. The traveller will find elegant gambling casinos (government strictures towards the end of 1968 meant that only the most successful survived). He will find many excellent restaurants, representing most of the cuisines of the world (he will wonder what happened to that old tag about the British not caring much for food!).

On the other hand, while the outward shapes may alter and the inner spirit may be a touch gayer, underneath, the base-rocks of London's character and tradition remain the same. The biggest city in Europe, London sprawls over more than 600 square miles. Through its centre curls the River Thames bending and twisting from beyond Richmond and greener fields, past the seat of government, and alongside the docks towards Greenwich and the sea. Sometimes London is criticized for not making more of its river; a strong and beautiful attraction, it is the most spectacular throw-away in the country, and the further one moves away from it, the less interesting London becomes. Yet you can enjoy its drama, real and potential, anywhere from London Bridge itself up to Chelsea, by walking alongside it.

But before you go dashing off on your voyage of discovery to Carnaby Street, the Tower or King's Road, you'd better get settled and plan a bit ahead. Which leads us, not surprisingly, to the next section of this chapter, *Practical Information for London*.

Practical Information for London

To help make your visit to London more pleasant, a few of the most important practical details have been gathered together here to facilitate ready reference when you reach the plan-making stage.

HOTELS. Several new hotels have been built in recent years, and many more are in the planning stage, but London is still short of rooms in the tourist "season", from late April until late September. During popular shows, such as the International Motor Show, or the Cruft's Dog Show, they can be jammed out of "season", too! The international hotels and a great many of the smaller ones in the capital are equipped, like most of their counterparts all over the world, with hot and cold running water, comfortable public rooms, and an increasing number of private baths.

If you have difficulty finding a vacant room, get in touch with London Hotels Information Service, 20 Upper Brook Street, London W.1 (MAYfair 5414). They can usually help. Similar organizations are: Hotel Booking Service, 5 Coventry Street, W.1 (437 5052); Hotel Booking and Information, 47 Charing Cross Road, W.C.2 (734 7560); Hotel Accommodation Service (HOTAC) at 93 Baker Street, W.1 (935 2555).

Lists of London hotels can be obtained from the British Travel Association offices in the United States, Canada and on the continent (see *Facts At Your Fingertips*), as well as in London.

Alternatively, if you would like to live at home with a London family, contact the *London Private Accommodation Bureau*, London Tourist Board, 170 Piccadilly, London W.1. Weekly charges range from $18 per person for bed and breakfast in the suburbs, and from $20 in central London. Minimum stay is a week, maximum 3 months.

The general custom in London is for rates to be quoted including "bed and breakfast". What Americans call "European Plan" is rare in Europe and rarer still in Britain. But a few London hotels, especially the top-class ones, have begun to quote rates for room only. Rates charged in June, July, and August may be up to 30 per cent higher than those at slacker seasons. The categories reflect average rates (see "Hotels" section in *Facts At Your Fingertips*).

"Welcome Television" is a special daily TV programme screening travel features and films of interest to visitors to London staying at the following hotels: *Bedford, Carlton Tower, Cumberland, Europa, May Fair, National, Piccadilly, President, Royal, Royal Garden, Royal Lancaster* and *Tavistock*.

SUPER DELUXE

CLARIDGE'S, Brook Street, W.1 (MAY 8860). Long regarded as Britain's most exclusive hotel and the best address in London. Haunt of visiting royalty and acme of expensive comfort. All its 250 rooms have private bath.

CONNAUGHT, Carlos Place, W.1 (GRO 7070). Quietly luxurious, catering to established county clientele. The type of hotel where you don't have to dress for dinner, yet are surrounded by about 10 serving waiters. All its 81 rooms have private bath.

RITZ, Piccadilly, W.1 (HYD 8181). Most famous hotel name in the world, the London Ritz

LONDON

enjoyed its greatest days in the Edwardian Era, but it is still a fabulous old rendezvous, with chandelier-hung elegance to delight guests. All 120 rooms have bath.

SAVOY, Strand, W.C.2 (TEM 4343). One of London's largest, famous for impeccable service and location overlooking Thames Embankment. 500 rooms (all with bath). Popular with celebrities from many fields, stages excellent cabarets.

LUXURIOUS

CARLTON TOWER, Cadogan Place, S.W.1 (BEL 5411). Has 307 rooms (256 with bath), gold and pewter decor, television. Executive suite on the 18th floor. Excellent cuisine and service, international atmosphere in famed *Rib Room* (best beef in London) and elegant *Chelsea Room* (international menu).

CHURCHILL, a Loew's Hotel, is to open in May 1970 on Portman Square, W.1. 500 rooms with bath, colour TV. All imaginable amenities.

CAVENDISH, Jermyn Street, S.W.1 (WHI 2111), opened in 1966 on site of old Cavendish. 24-hr. restaurant. 252 quiet rooms in heart of London.

DORCHESTER, Park Lane, W.1 (MAY 8888). One of London's best-known hotels, facing Hyde Park. Center for many glamorous functions and chosen by world-famous celebrities. All 275 rooms have bath.

EUROPA, Grosvenor Square, W.1 (HYD 1232) has 300 rooms with bath; ballroom, *Etruscan* bar, *Grosvenor* bar Underground garage. Roof garden.

GROSVENOR HOUSE, Park Lane, W.1 (GRO 6363). Palatial, with Grecian columns and luxurious spaciousness, 500 rooms with bath.

HILTON, Park Lane, W.1 (HYD 8000). Opened in 1963, this 510-room (all with bath) skyscraper has the usual galaxy of luxury suites, grill rooms, restaurants and amenities associated with Hilton Hotels.

HYDE PARK, Knightsbridge, S.W.1 (BEL 2000), 192 rooms (most with bath). Comfortable, spacious, near Hyde Park Corner.

INTERCONTINENTAL, 290 rooms, to open during 1970 on Portman Square, W.1. Should be up to usual chain standards.

MAY FAIR, Berkeley Street, W.1 (MAY 7777). Gay and fashionable in quiet, exclusive surroundings on fringe of Mayfair. 452 rooms (all with bath).

ROYAL LANCASTER, Lancaster Gate, W.2 (PAD 9830). London's newest, with 6 bars, roof-top restaurant, 24-hr. grill, full international conference facilities. Overlooking Hyde Park, perched on top of a subway entrance; very convenient, with perfect location. 392 rooms (all with bath).

WESTBURY, Bond Street, W.1 (MAY 7755). One of the Knott Hotel Corp. of U.S. chain. All 255 rooms have bath and shower. Elegant comfort, fine continental (Belgian-inspired) cuisine, excellent service. Attractive *Polo* bar. Garage.

FIRST CLASS SUPERIOR

BERKELEY, a fashionable rendezvous for years, closed in late 1969 but will open at a new site, in Knightsbridge, in 1971.

BRITANNIA, Grosvenor Square, opened in 1969; 440 rooms with bath.

BROWN'S, Dover Street, W.1 (HYD 6020). This one-time favorite, centrally situated and yielding nothing in its traditional furnishings to modern fancies, is still favored by overseas visitors who like atmosphere. 165 rooms, most with bath. Trust House hotel.

CLIVE. Primrose Hill Road, N.W.3. Clean and modern, with 60 rooms (51 have bath). Not central, but excellent value.

CUMBERLAND, Marble Arch, W.1 (AMB 1234). All 900 rooms have bath. Popular with overseas visitors. Leading hotel of the Lyons combine.

DE VERE, 60 Hyde Park Gate, W.8. Faces Kensington Gardens. Victorian exterior, modernized interior with 80 rooms (68 have bath).

GORE HOTEL, 189-191 Queen's Gate, S.W.7 (KNI 6601), 43 rooms (all with bath). Small but elegant Kensington hotel, famous for its food and *Elizabethan* and *Star Chamber* rooms serving exotic Tudor candlelight feasts.

GORING, Grosvenor Gardens, S.W.1 (VIC 8211), 100 rooms (all with bath—the first hotel in the world to be so equipped). Well-established, quiet, near Victoria Station.

INTERNATIONAL, Lancaster Gate, W.2. Has 70 rooms (all with bath), 4 luxury suites and one of London's finest views over Kensington Gardens.

KENSINGTON PALACE, De Vere Gardens, W.8 (WES 8121). 300 rooms with bath.

KINGSHILL, 55 Westbourne Terrace, W.2 (723 3434), opened in 1968, 139 rooms (all with bath).

KENNEDY, Cardington Street, N.W.1 (387 9533), opened in 1968, 410 rooms (all with bath).

LONDON INTERNATIONAL, Cromwell Rd., opp. West London Air Terminal, should have about 100 of its 300 rooms ready by 1970.

LONDONDERRY HOUSE, Park Lane, W.1 (493 7292). Luxury newcomer (1967) next to the Hilton. French-operated, 24-hour restaurant with French cuisine. 170 rooms (all with bath).

THE LONDONER, Welbeck Street, W.1 (WEL 4422). 120 rooms with bath.

MEURICE, 16 Bury Street, S.W.1 (WHI 6767), is a charmingly elegant establishment above Quaglino's nightclub. 54 rooms with bath.

MOUNT ROYAL, Marble Arch, W.1 (MAY 8040), 700 rooms (all with bath). Large apartment-block style, with full service, club on premises.

OLD ST. JAMES'S HOUSE, Park Place, S.W.1 (HYD 2412), 40 rooms (all with bath). Exclusive.

PARK LANE, Piccadilly, W.1 (GRO 6321). Large and fashionable, faces Piccadilly (not Park Lane). 360 rooms and 40 suites (all with bath).

PICCADILLY, Piccadilly, W.1 (REG 8000). Busy, popular, close to Piccadilly Circus. 222 rooms (all with bath).

ROYAL GARDEN, Kensington High Street (WES 8000), overlooking Kensington Palace, 445 rooms with bath, suites; garage. 4 restaurants.

ST. GEORGE'S, Langham Place, W.1 (LAN 0111), near Oxford Circus. Trust House, new in 1963.

ST. JAMES'S, Buckingham Gate, S.W.1 (VIC 2360), 500 rooms and suites (300 with bath). Elegant and tasteful, recently modernized, with a view to the Green Park.

STAFFORD, St. James's Place, S.W.1 (HYD 0111). Small, traditional *pied à terre* in London's Clubland. All 47 rooms have bath.

21 CLUB, 8 Chesterfield Gardens, W.1 (GRO 3233). Much favored by American businessmen. 25 rooms with bath.

LONDON

VISCOUNT, Prince of Wales Terrace, W.8 (937 0752), 40 rooms (8 with bath, rest with shower). New (1967).

WALDORF, Aldwych, W.C.2 (TEM 2400). Located between two of London's best theaters and convenient for businessmen. 300 rooms (250 with bath).

WASHINGTON, Curzon Street, W.1 (GRO 7030), 148 rooms (all with bath). In the heart of Mayfair; modernized.

WHITE'S, 90/92 Lancaster Gate. W.2 (AMB 2711), 70 rooms with bath.

FIRST CLASS REASONABLE

BEDFORD, Southampton Row, W.C.1 (MUS 7822). Good location near British Museum. Commercial hotel atmosphere, 181 rooms (all with bath). Stereo and TV.

BLOOMSBURY CENTRE, Coram Street, W.C.1. New (1969), 250 rooms (all with bath). Excellent conference facilities.

BONNINGTON, Southampton Row, W.C.1 (CHA 2828). 270 rooms (69 with bath).

CHARING CROSS, Strand, W.C.2 (TRA 7282). Although above a rail station, 219 rooms (81 with bath) are quiet.

CLIFTON-FORD, Welbeck Street, W.C.2 (HUN 6600). 218 rooms (all with bath). Quiet and homelike atmosphere.

FLEMINGS, Half Moon Street, W.C.2 (GRO 2964). 104 rooms (65 with bath).

GREAT EASTERN, on Liverpool Street, E.C.2 (AVE 4363). 187 rooms (47 with bath).

GREAT NORTHERN, at King's Cross, N.1 (TER 5454). 70 rooms (28 with bath).

GREAT WESTERN ROYAL, Paddington, W.2 (PAD 8064). 181 rooms (144 with bath).

GROSVENOR, Buckingham Palace Road, S.W.1 (VIC 9494). 240 rooms (50 with bath).

IMPERIAL, Russell Square, W.C.1. New (1969), with 465 rooms (all with bath).

KENSINGTON CLOSE, Wright's Lane, W.8 (WES 8170). 503 rooms (all with bath). Swimming pool and most other facilities.

KINGSLEY, Bloomsbury Way, W.C.1 (CHA 5881). 175 rooms (98 with bath). Helpful staff.

MANDEVILLE, Mandeville Place, W.1 (WEL 5599). 90 of its 165 rooms have bath attached. Close to Oxford Street shops.

MILESTONE, Kensington Court, W.8 (WES 0991). 100 rooms (52 with bath).

NORFOLK, Harrington Road, S.W.7 (KEN 8191). 93 rooms (49 with bath).

PARKWAY, Inverness Terrace, W.2 (BAY 9222). 85 rooms (15 with bath).

POST HOUSE, a motor inn, should open in summer of 1970, conveniently located in Hampstead near Belsize Park underground station. 140 rooms with bath, TV.

PRESIDENT, Russell Square, W.C.1 (TER 8844). 447 rooms with bath. Restaurant, bar, quick grill.

PRINCE OF WALES, De Vere Gardens, W.8. 350 rooms (50 with bath). Adjacent to the Royal Albert Hall.

QUEENSWAY, Princes Square, W.2 (PARK 8621). 122 rooms (5 with bath).

REGENT PALACE, Piccadilly Circus, W.1 (REG 7000), 1143 rooms (none with bath). London's largest, built close to the West End's busiest point. Glitter and efficiency. One of the Lyons group.

REMBRANDT, Thurloe Place, S.W.7 (KEN 8100). 168 rooms (152 with bath).

RUBENS, Buckingham Palace Road, S.W.1 (VIC 6600). 137 rooms (87 with bath). Unpretentious, recently modernized.

RUSSELL, Russell Square, W.C.1 (TER 6470). 300 rooms (290 with bath). Rooms recently modernized.

ST. ERMIN'S, Caxton Street, S.W.1 (ABB 7888). 252 rooms (all with bath). Between Westminster Abbey and Victoria Station.

STRAND PALACE, Strand, W.C.2 (TEM 8080), 776 rooms (all with bath). Under the same ownership as Regent Palace, and with similar popular modern amenities.

TAVISTOCK, Tavistock Square, W.C.1 (MUS 8383). 301 rooms (all with bath).

MODERATE

ALEXANDER NATIONAL, Finsbury Park, N.4 (Stamford Hill 8090). 200 rooms (100 with bath). Opened 1965.

BLAIR HOUSE, 34 Draycott Place, S.W.3 (FRE 3785). 17 rooms. Near London's "swinging" King's Road.

CULFORD HALL, Culford Gardens, S.W.3 (KNI 7231). 18 rooms. In Chelsea.

GRAND, Southampton Row, W.C.2 (HOL. 2006). 77 rooms (46 with bath). Nicely located between the British Museum and the City.

KENILWORTH, Bloomsbury Street, W.C.1 (MUS 7632). 170 rooms (many with bath). Practically next door to the British Museum.

NATIONAL, Bedford Way, Russell Square, W.C.1 (LAN 0051). 327 rooms. Close to London University.

ROYAL, Upper Woburn Place, W.C.1 (MUS 8401). 774 rooms. A bit far out, but good value.

STANTON COURT, 32 Nottingham Place, W.1 (WEL 5441). Near Regent's Park and Mme. Tussaud's Wax Museum.

WAVERLEY, Southampton Row, W.C.1 (TER 6292). Is situated at pedestrian entrance to Queen Square, quiet hospital and publishing center.

INEXPENSIVE

If really inexpensive accommodation is required, consult the list published by the British Travel Association and check personally before booking. There are any number of inexpensive, clean, unlicensed hotels and pensions, but it is not wise to book without personal inspection, as conditions vary so much.

OUTER LONDON

See *Environs of London* chapter.

LONDON AIRPORT

Four hotels near London Airport are a boon to air travelers arriving late or delayed at the airport.

ARIEL (SKY 2552), circular, has 184 rooms (all with bath and television). Also first-class superior.

CENTRE AIRPORT (759 2400), newest: opened 1968, in Bath Road adjacent to airport. 300 rooms (all with bath).

FORTE'S AIRPORT (SKY 6611), located at the north entrance to the airport. Opened in 1964. 300 rooms (all with bath and television). First-class superior.

MASTER ROBERT (HOU 6261), a motel on the Great West Road at Osterley, 3 miles from London

LONDON

Airport, on the road to London. 30 units (all with bath); restaurant. First-class superior.

SKYWAY (SKY 6311), 320 rooms (all with bath and television). First-class superior.

THE LONDON SEASON. This is a social season, during which the Royal Family is in residence at Buckingham Palace. It opens with the Royal Academy Summer Exhibition at Burlington House and closes with the end of the Goodwood Races. It lasts from about early May until late July. Royal garden parties, racing at Royal Ascot, balls, coming-out parties, and many other lavish spectacles brighten the season, although debutantes are no longer presented at Court. The London weather during this period is usually quite dry, with a good deal of sunshine. When August starts, London is deserted by the social set: the Court goes to Balmoral, in the highlands of Scotland, and London swelters in humid, sticky conditions.

Nevertheless, London is more crowded in August than at any other time of the year, and the month's calendar is crowded with popular—if not exclusive—events for visitors from all over the world.

SIGHTSEEING. London Transport issue *Red Rover* tickets for weekends and summer use, which entitle the holder to travel on all red central buses (routes 1-298) for an inclusive fee of 6s or 7s per day. *Twin Rovers* at 10s or 12s cover the same facilities, plus travel on the underground. Children under 14, half price. *Green Rover* tickets give a day's unlimited travel on the country bus routes (300-499, 801-809 and 852-854a—with a few excepted, special, routes) for 6s or 7s any day in the week. Full details and free bus and coach maps can be obtained from all railroad stations, most underground stations, and from London Transport head office, 55 Broadway S.W.1 (ABB 1234).

The Southern Region of *British Railways* has a weekend Rover ticket (choice of three) issued for 8s 6d entitling the holder to unlimited travel on trains running to inner and outer suburbs, including such beauty spots as Virginia Water, Ascot, and Knockholt during Saturday *and* Sunday.

London Transport also offers a sightseeing tour of London by bus (2 hours), covering 20 miles of the West End and City for 5s, and conducted coach tours to outlying points of interest.

Bloomfield Cars (London) Ltd., 90 Camberwell Road, S.E.5 (ROD 6121) run *London After Dark* tours which take in visits to night clubs, at prices ranging from £4 10s ($12.50).

Complete tours of London by coach are offered by *Thos. Cook's* Head Office from their Berkeley Street building. Morning and afternoon drives with a guide cost 11s 6d. Both drives and lunch are provided for 28s 6d. Evening drives to London's East End are arranged for 10s. Other tours are organized by *Charles Rickards,* 13 Spring Street, W.2, and by *Frames' Tours, Ltd.,* 25 Tavistock Place, W.C.1.

Personal sight-seeing services are operated by *Take-A-Guide Ltd.,* 11 Old Bond Street (HYD 1688). The city tour by car is £3 ($8.40) for three passengers.

The *American Express* office at 6 Haymarket is a departure point for a variety of tours every weekday at 9:30 a.m.

TRANSPORTATION. London is well served by fleets of doubledecker buses, single-deck buses, and underground trains (subways), known as 'The Tube'. Bus travel is easy and cheap. Just wait at the bus stop, joining the inevitable queue. When the bus comes, just get on and sit down. The conductor will ask you where you want to go, collect your fare and give you a ticket. You simply state your destination. "Oxford Circus. please" or "Two to Trafalgar Square." The cheapest fare is 6d (6¢). All this applies to all buses except the red single-decker *Red Arrow* buses, which operate a fast, almost non-stop service on some busy routes. On the Red Arrow there is a fixed fare of 6d (6¢) and you obtain your ticket by putting a 6d piece into the automatic machine on entering the bus. On the red buses you can make journeys of up to 12 miles out of town. For longer suburban or country trips, take the green double-deckers from bases reached at the end of the red routes, or else take speedy Green Line single-deckers which maintain services within a 30-miles radius of London, cutting across town.

UNDERGROUND. Londoners sometimes differentiate between the *underground* and the *tube*. This may confuse you at first. but you'll get used to it. All trains running in "cut-and-cover" subways (like New York's) are underground; those running in deep level tubes, sometimes 80 or more feet below the surface of the city. are tube trains.

Underground and tube routes cover all inner London, and you'll often find it's the quickest way to get about. Most stations have ticket issuing machines that make change and save a lot of time.

You buy your ticket at the station before starting your journey. Fares vary with length of journey. Cheapest is 6d (6¢). Tickets can be bought from the ticket offices, or from automatic slot machines. A few stations, notably on the new Victoria Line, have automatic entry and exit barriers which operate on the insertion of your ticket. *Be sure to get it back after insertion!*

Colored lights indicate the various lines, and if you follow these carefully, you can't go wrong. Just the same, it's always a good idea to study a subway map of London (ask at any subway station or see the one on page 200).

RAILWAY. If you want to visit suburbs not served by the underground, try the electric services of *British Railways*. To places like Croydon (10 miles in 15 minutes), Richmond (9 miles in 14 minutes), Ilford (7 miles in 12 minutes), Wembley (9 miles in 18 minutes), Woolwich (9 miles in 13 minutes), this is the quickest way. For round trip, ask for "return ticket"; or for the cheaper "day return" if you're coming back on the same day out of rush hours.

WATER BUSES. In recent years, London's River Thames has come back into its own as a transport highway. Water buses operate from April to October downstream as far as Greenwich and upstream to Richmond and Hampton Court. You can join them at Tower Pier, Charing Cross Pier, Westminster Pier, Battersea Fun Fair, or at any floating landing-stage on the central section of the river.

TAXIS. These unmistakable vehicles, with square bodies and the driver in a separate forward compartment, are liberally scattered throughout

LONDON

the streets of central and west London. If their flags are up, or a "for hire" sign lighted, just hail them. But you can rarely find an empty one between 5 p.m. and 7 p.m.—which is when you so often want one. Best bet at this busy time is to phone LOR 1133 and have a radio-cab contacted for you.

Taxi fares start at 2s when the flag falls. This covers you for about three-quarters of a mile, after which the meter clicks up 6d about every one-quarter mile (6d extra is charged for luggage carried in the driver's compartment, and 6d per extra passenger). Tip the driver 1s if the total fare comes to less than 5s, and 2s for fares up to 8s. Above that (which means quite a long ride), give about 15 percent (3s per £). These are generous tips, but not overdoing it.

PARKS AND PLEASURE GARDENS. *Hyde Park,* most famous of the Royal Parks, 360 acres stretching from Park Lane to Kensington Gardens. Contains the Serpentine lake, Rotten Row, the Ladies Mile, and the Achilles Statue, and is famous for its "Speakers' Corner" near Marble Arch.

Kensington Gardens, a 275-acre Royal Park adjoining Hyde Park and extending to Kensington Palace. Contains the Albert Memorial and Round Pond (famous for model yacht sailing), and part of the Serpentine.

St. James's Park, small (93 acres), but most attractive of the Royal Parks. Lake with many ducks and other wild life. Fine views of Buckingham Palace and the towers and spires of Whitehall from the bridge over the lake.

Regent's Park, a Royal Park stretching from the Marylebone Road to Primrose Hill, covers 427 acres, and dates from the days of the Prince Regent. Surrounded by lovely and classic houses in famous architectural styles. Adjoined by the Zoological Gardens.

Green Park, smallest (53 acres) of the Royal Parks, bounded by Piccadilly and the Mall.

Kew, Royal Botanic Gardens, 288 acres, about 10 miles west of the center of London. Many fine examples of rare plants. Gorgeous grounds best seen in May. Admission costs 3d.

Battersea Park, owned by the London County Council, covers 200 acres, contains Fun Fair and Pleasure Gardens created for the 1951 Festival of Britain. From April to October, Londoners and others have riotous fun here beside the river, especially on the Big Dipper. Entry to the park is free, but the Fair levies a charge.

Blackheath, a big sweep of open common covering 268 acres, is an LCC open space where fairs are staged, also cricket matches. Near the southeast corner is Morden College, founded in 1695 for "decayed Turkey merchants".

Holland Park, Kensington. (Off the High Street). Private grounds of old Holland House until after the war, this lovely area contains part of the Elizabethan mansion, now a youth hostel, charming conventional and wild gardens, open-air restaurant and concerts in summer.

Hampstead Heath, an LCC park, North London's favorite Bank Holiday spot, covers 494 acres, with fun fairs and open-air displays. Here you will find Kenwood House and the old Spaniards Inn.

Greenwich Park, a Royal Park of 185 acres, beside the river, contains Royal Naval College, the former Royal Observatory, and National Maritime Museum.

Clapham Common, a big LCC open space covering 205 acres, southwest of London, mainly devoted to sports. The British Transport Museum is nearby.

Waterloo Park, a small LCC park of 26 acres on the southern slopes of Highgate Hill, containing Lauderdale House, formerly occupied by Nell Gwynn.

Parliament Hill, 271 acres of LCC parkland adjoining Hampstead Heath.

Highgate Wood, 70 acres of woodland owned by the Corporation of London and maintained as it was in Dick Whittington's time.

Richmond Park, largest (2,358 acres) of the Royal Parks, houses many semi-wild deer as well as fine trees and mansions.

Syon Park, opposite Kew Gardens, contains Syon House, historic home of the Duke of Northumberland, who created in 1968 a national *Gardening Centre*. Its 55 acres include 10,000 roses and a lake area with the largest collection of water lilies in the country. Excellent restaurant on grounds.

POST OFFICE TOWER, Maple Street, W.1 (off Tottenham Court Road). Panoramic view from the observation gallery 580 feet up: on a clear day you can see to London's outskirts and beyond. Open daily from 9:30 a.m. to 8 p.m. Adults 4s, children 2s. Above the gallery is Butlin's rotating restaurant—very expensive.

PUBLIC SPECTACLES. *Changing the Guard:* This colorful ritual takes place in two ceremonies: *Queen's Life Guard,* daily at 11 a.m. (10 on Sun.), (20 min.), Horse Guards, Whitehall. *Queen's Guard,* daily at app. 11:30 a.m. (30 min.) except in very bad weather, Buckingham Palace. Tube for Whitehall: Strand or Trafalgar Square; bus: 3, 12, 53, 77, 88, 159. Tube for the palace: Victoria or Green Park.

WHAT TO SEE? Sightseeing which is mandatory includes, in a nut shell, the following: the Changing of the Guard ceremonies (see above); the Guildhall, 15th-century council hall of the City, restored after the great fire of 1666, and again after German bombs ruined it in 1940; the legal enclave called the Temple at the entrance to Fleet Street, comprising the Inns of Court or Courts of Law. The whole area forming the Law Courts across the Middle Temple and down to the Thames is worth your careful contemplation on a tranquil afternoon, for this is Old London at its most charming. Finally, you will not want to neglect imposing Buckingham Palace. With its background, St. James's Park, and the wide sweep of the square in front of it (dominated by a statue of Queen Victoria), this symbol of the continuing tradition of British monarchy is a notable exception to the rule that Londoners do not know how to set their monuments and public buildings off to maximum advantage.

OTHER PLACES OF INTEREST. *Houses of Parliament:* House of Commons may be visited between 10 a.m. and 4:30 p.m. Saturdays (also Mondays and Tuesdays in August), admission free; to hear debates admission to gallery after 4:15 p.m. (11:30 a.m. Fridays) on application

LONDON

to Admission Order Office in St. Stephen's Hall (but foreign visitors are advised to apply to their embassies or high commissioners in London). House of Lords (to hear debates in Strangers' Gallery apply as for House of Commons), Tuesdays and Wednesdays 2:40 p.m. and Thursdays 4:10 p.m. Tube: Westminster; bus: 3, 11, 12, 24, 29, 39, 53, 59a, 77, 88, 159.

Law Courts, Strand, W.C.2. Public galleries open during sessions, 10-4, Monday-Friday. Tube: Aldwych; bus: 6, 9, 11, 13, 15.

Madame Tussaud's, Marylebone Road, N.W.1. World's most famous waxworks of famous and infamous. Latest: a Battle of Trafalgar spectacular! Open daily 10-6 (7 weekends and summer). Admission 7s 6d. Tube: Baker Street; bus: 2, 13, 23, 59a, 159.

Old Bailey, Newgate Street, E.C.4. Central criminal court. When not in session, conducted parties daily, 11 a.m. and 3 p.m. To attend sessions: Public Gallery open 10:15 a.m. and 1:45 p.m.; queue at door in Newgate Street. Tube: St. Paul's; bus: 7, 8, 22, 23, 25.

Planetarium, Marylebone Road, N.W.1. Next to Madame Tussaud's. Study of night sky with explanatory talks and displays. Open daily, admission 4s 6d (children 2s 6d).

Roman Bath, Strand Lane, W.C.2. Open 10 a.m.-12:30 p.m., weekdays. Tube: Aldwych; bus: 6, 9, 13, 15.

Royal Hospital, Chelsea, S.W.3. Charming home for old soldiers ("pensioners"), founded by Charles II and designed by Wren. Open weekdays, 10-12 and 2-5, Sunday, 12-1 and 2-5. Tube: Sloane Square; bus: 11, 39, 137.

St. Paul's Cathedral, E.C.4. The masterpiece of Sir Christopher Wren, built after the Great Fire of London. Contains memorial chapel to the American forces in Britain. *Son et lumiere* from June to Sept. at dusk. Open daily. Tube: St. Paul's; bus: 6, 9, 11, 13, 15, 18, 22, 25.

The Commonwealth Institute, Kensington High Street, W.8. Open daily, 10-5:30. Sundays, 2:30-6. Admission free. Modern exhibition hall with permanent displays for all Commonwealth countries. Films, restaurant. Tube: High Street, Kensington; bus: 9, 49, 73.

Westminster Abbey, Parliament Square, S.W.1. Open daily 8-6 winter, 8-7 April-Sept. Royal Chapels open weekdays, 9:45-4 (Tues. and Fri. from 10:45, closed Sats. at 5). Admission 2s. Tube: Westminster; bus: 3, 11, 12, 24, 29, 39, 53, 59, 59a, 76, 88, 159, 159a.

Cockneyland, housed on Middlesex Street in a converted five-storey warehouse, is a living museum of London life complete with jellied eels and barrel-organ music.

THE LONDON DOCKS. These stretch down-Thames from the Pool of London (between London Bridge and Tower Bridge) for 22 miles to Tilbury. They include London Docks, St. Katherine's, East and West India Docks, Millwall Docks, and Surrey Commercial Docks (the only ones on the south bank of the Thames). The Port of London Authority, which owns and manages them, arranges steamer trips through the docks on Wednesday, Thursday and Saturday afternoons in high summer (mid-July through August). These commence from Tower Pier at 2:30 p.m. (4 hour trip). Book well in advance. Apply: Chief Information Officer, P.O. Box 242 or tel. ROY 2000.

CANAL TRIPS. Departures every day during the summer from Canaletto Gallery, 20 Blomfield Road, W.9 (tube to Warwick Avenue, or buses Nos. 1, 6, 8, 16, and 60). Usually three return trips every afternoon along Regent's Canal, an ancient waterway in the heart of London. Phone CUN 3428 for bookings.

SHIPS OPEN TO THE PUBLIC ON THE THAMES. *H.M.S. Discovery*, in which Captain Scott made his 1902 Antarctic voyage, is moored at King's Reach, Victoria Embankment. Admission free, daily 1-4:45. *Cutty Sark*, the great tea clipper of the '60s, is in permanent drydock at Greenwich. Open 11-5, weekdays, 2:30-5 Sundays (later in summer; admission 2s).

ZOO. Situated in Regent's Park, N.W.1, the huge London Zoo contains one of the world's largest collections of animals, reptiles, and birds. Children's Corner affords camel, elephant, and pony rides. Open daily from 9 a.m. to 7 p.m. in summer, 10 to sunset in winter. Closed on Christmas Day. Admission 7s 6d except Mondays, when it's 5s. Feeding times are: *Penguins*, 4 p.m. in summer, 12:30 in winter, Mappin Pavilion Pond; *Pelicans*, 2:30 p.m., Pelican Enclosure; *Eagles*, 3:30 p.m., except Wednesdays (2:15 in winter), Birds of Prey Aviaries; *Lions and Tigers*, 3 p.m. in summer, an hour earlier in winter (except Wednesdays), Lionhouse; *Small Cats*, 11 a.m., Small Cats' House; *Sea Lions*, noon and 3:30 p.m. in summer, 2:30 in winter, Sea Lion Pond; *Seals*, 4:30 in summer, 3 in winter; *Wolves and Foxes*, 11:30 a.m.; *Chimpanzees' Tea Party*, 4 p.m. in summer (weather permitting), except Sundays. Don't miss Lord Snowdon's beautiful Aviary and *Chichi*, the giant panda.

MOTORING IN LONDON. As in every big city, there are unofficial and unwritten rules for drivers which can only be learned by experience, but in general, the speed limits are: 20 m.p.h. through the parks, 30 m.p.h. on all other roads, streets and avenues, unless you see the huge 40 m.p.h. limit signs. Pedestrians have priority on "zebra" crossings, those with black and white stripes across the road between two striped beacon poles with orange bowls on top (that flash off and on at night). On any other crossings, except those governed by traffic lights, pedestrians must give way, and the way London drivers behave, the pedestrian should give way always. (The great London specialty is to drive through pedestrians who are trying to cross the street where the motorist wishes to go). Traffic lights are all 3-color (red, amber, green), but many have arrow-style filter lights attached for controlling the left- or right-hand turns. At night the use of horns is theoretically prohibited in London or any built-up areas between 11:30 p.m. and 7 a.m. Parking at night only requires lights on bus routes, but it is desirable to park as near as possible to a street lamp.

London's parking problem increases monthly. Parking meters are being progressively installed, and at about the same rate, traffic wardens are handing out fine tickets for "illegal" parking (which may involve only a very short unattended car stop.) Since receipt of such a

LONDON

ticket may mean a court case (and at worst your car will be towed away by the police), best play safe and use public or taxi transport. You can waste plenty of time and gas just *trying* to find a legal available place to park.

CAR HIRE. Among the leading firms in the London area supplying both chauffeur-driven and self-drive cars are: *Avis Rent a Car*, 12a Berkeley Street, W.1, tel. 499-4881; *J. Davy*, behind the Ritz Hotel, Piccadilly, S.W.1, tel. HYD 3141; *Hertz Rent-a-Car*, 243 Knightsbridge, S.W.7, tel. KNI 5050; *Godfrey Davis*, Wilton Road, S.W.1, tel. VIC 8484. (For information on rates and terms, see *Traveling in Britain* section of *Facts At Your Fingertips*.) *Patrick Barthropp, Ltd.*, Colebrook Court, Sloane Ave., S.W.3, tel. 589-4585, operates exclusively chauffeur-driven Rolls Royces and Bentleys, starting at about £8 ($19) per day. A useful London feature is evening hire, which gives you use of a car from around 6:30 p.m. until early morning.

SPORTS

HORSE AND DOG RACING. Several horse and greyhound racing tracks are to be found in the London area, where you'll find both tote and bookmaker betting. Visitors can usually obtain introductions to reputable bookmakers (listed as Turf Accountants) through their hall porters, friends, or advertisements in glossy magazines.

Horse Racing

Alexandra Park. Flat racing only. Reached by underground to Wood Green station, about 9 miles from Piccadilly on that line. Stages about six meetings each season.

Ascot. Flat racing only. Reached by Southern Region electric trains from Waterloo (28 miles) or by Green Line bus. Royal Ascot is the very fashionable meeting attended by the Queen during the third week in June. Apart from that, Ascot course stages one 1-day, two 2-day, and one 3-day meeting each season.

Epsom. Flat racing only. Scene of the Derby, held first week in June. Reached by electric trains from Victoria to Epsom Downs or Charing Cross to Tattenham Corner in about 35 minutes (21 miles). One 3-day and one 2-day meeting staged as well as 4-day Derby and Oaks meeting.

Kempton Park. Steeplechasing and flat racing. At Sunbury-on-Thames, railway station is Kempton Park, reached by electric train from Waterloo in 35 minutes. Four winter 2-day steeplechase meetings; five summer 2-day flat meetings.

Sandown Park. Steeplechasing and flat racing. Train to Esher station, Surrey, from Waterloo, in 21 minutes. Six winter 2-day steeplechase meetings; five summer flat meetings of 1-2 days.

Royal Windsor. Steeplechasing and flat racing. A mile west of Windsor. Four steeplechase and six flat meetings each year.

Dog Tracks

Most tracks stage meetings twice weekly, not conflicting with each other if possible, such as Tuesday and Friday, Wednesday and Saturday. On Saturdays, when tracks in various parts of London hold meetings, some will start at 2:45 p.m., others at 5 p.m., or 7:30 p.m.

Main tracks are: *White City, Wimbledon, Charlton, Catford, Stamford Bridge, New Cross, Wembley, Park Royal, Hendon, Hackney Wick, Dagenham, Romford, West Ham, Walthamstow, Clapton, Crayford.*

GOLF COURSES. Although most golf clubs in the Greater London area are the private membership type, visitors are often able to play on them by payment of a "green fee". This varies widely according to the course, but an average is 10s per round of 18 holes weekdays, 15s per day, and 20s-30s for Saturdays, Sundays or public holidays. Since many clubs have tournaments at busy weekends, it is desirable for visitors who wish to play a round to telephone in advance. In mid-week, it is usually merely a matter of paying the green fee to the secretary, or the professional, but some clubs require that you be a member of some club at home. At weekends, visitors must usually be accompanied by a member.

Here are some clubs near to London with first-class 18-hole links on which you may play on payment of a green fee:

Royal Blackheath, tel. ELT 1041. Nearest station Mottingham, 11 miles from Charing Cross.

Chigwell, tel. Hainault 59. Nearest station Chigwell Underground (Central Line).

Moor Park, tel. Rickmansworth 3146. Moor Park station, Metropolitan Line from Baker Street.

South Herts, tel. HIL 0117. Nearest station Totteridge and Whetstone, Northern Line underground.

Hendon, tel. Sunnyhill 1008 and 8344. The 125 and 240 buses from Golders Green underground station (Northern Line) pass the gates.

Addington Palace, tel. ADD 3061. Train to East Croydon from Victoria, thence 130 bus or taxi.

Addington Court. Public Golf Course. Tel. SAN 2690. Nearest mainline station East Croydon.

Royal Mid-Surrey, tel. Richmond 1894. Visitors should bring a letter of introduction from a recognized golf club. Reached from Richmond station, 9 miles from Waterloo.

OTHER SPORTS. The popular American sports of basketball and baseball are played in the London area, though facilities for watching them or taking part are few and far between.

Bowling, to the British, is "lawn bowls", and many hundreds of bowling greens will be found in use outdoors from May to September, white-coated figures of middle age and beyond eagerly sending down their "woods" to the "jack". But American-style bowling is presently enjoying a great vogue and you will find bowling alleys all around, often in converted movie theaters. They are equally popular in the provinces. Most convenient for tourists is *Excel Tenpin Bowling Centre*, Shaftesbury Ave., W.1 (near Piccadilly Circus).

Baseball is played during the summer season on various recreation grounds, usually on Sundays, and the teams tend to have a stiffening of Americans living in London. The most famous is that played nearly every Sunday in Hyde Park by Americans from the movie colony.

Details of forthcoming games can be found in the Sports Diary of the weekly *What's On In London*, but not, as a rule, in the daily newspapers. The same applies to **basketball**, which is usually played in some drill hall, or at a Y.M.C.A.

Ice and roller skating. Many rinks cater for these popular indoor sports. They usually have two sessions, beginning at 2:30 p.m. and 7:30 p.m. daily, including Sundays. *Queens Ice Club*, Queensway, W.2 and *Silver Blade*, Streatham, S.W.16, are among the leading ice skating centers. *Alexandra Palace*, north London, has a large roller rink.

Tennis headquarters for not only London but the world is Wimbledon. This is a large suburban center reached by train from Waterloo in 12-15 minutes or by District Line underground from Kensington and Earls Court. Many tennis clubs exist all over London, and thousands of public courts are available in the parks which can be played on by the hour for modest fees (about 3s 6d). The tennis tournament season in Britain starts early in April on hard courts, changes to grass towards the end of May. The Surrey Championships are held at Surbiton, 12 miles from Waterloo, and the Kent Championships at Beckenham, 10 miles from Victoria. The London Championships are held at Queen's Club, West Kensington, immediately before the All-England Championships at Wimbledon in late June. Admission to the Wimbledon events is only 5s (or 2s 6d after 4 p.m.), but this does not provide reserved seating. Unless you apply for Center Court tickets as early as February (for application blank write to the Secretary, *All England Lawn Tennis Club*, Church Road, Wimbledon, S.W.19, enclosing self-addressed envelope), it's a matter of luck or standing in line very early whether or not you can get one of the 300 tickets sold daily at the turnstiles during the championships for 15s. Subscribers wishing to sell their tickets often advertise in the newspaper columns of *The Times* or *Daily Telegraph*.

Swimming. London's Lido is the Serpentine, in Hyde Park. Water-skiing and swimming may be enjoyed at the Ruislip Lido, in Middlesex, reached from Paddington by train, or by the Central Line tube to West Ruislip.

Association football is the leading British winter game. Best first-class matches, held on Saturday afternoons in the London area, are to be seen at Stamford Bridge (Chelsea), West Ham, Tottenham, and Highbury (Arsenal). The daily newspapers will give details of forthcoming matches. On the first Saturday of May the Cup Final is played at Wembley Stadium, when 100,000 fans watch the last two survivors of an 8-month-long knock-out competition battle for honors. Tickets for this highly popular event are virtually unobtainable at short notice, but it is fully televised on British networks.

Cricket is the traditional British summer game, played daily all over the country. The first class matches in the London area are those played at the Oval ground, where Surrey have their headquarters, and at Lord's, St. John's Wood, the Middlesex ground. Except when Test matches are played against visiting Australian, South African, West Indies, and other Commonwealth teams, it is easy to enter these grounds on payment of a few shillings at the gate.

Rugby football is played between October and the end of March. Big matches are staged at the Twickenham ground, within easy reach from

Waterloo station, about six times during the season. Otherwise, rugby matches are amateur ones in the London area.

Ice hockey is played by leagues, at Empire Pool, Wembley, reached by Metropolitan Line from Baker Street in 15 minutes.

Boxing tournaments are staged frequently, all year round, usually in town halls or big arenas. Details are given in the daily newspapers.

Miscellaneous sports. You can watch speedway racing at Wimbledon Stadium on occasion, cycle racing at Herne Hill Stadium, field and track events at White City Stadium, and swimming and wrestling at Crystal Palace.

CHURCH SERVICES. There are hundreds of churches in London. Here are just a few of the famous, or conveniently-located ones: Church of England centers, with Holy Communion service at 8 or 8:30 a.m., morning service at 10:30 or 11 a.m., and evening service at 6 or 6:30 p.m. are: *St. Paul's Cathedral*, City, E.C.4. *Westminster Abbey*, S.W.1. *St. Martins-in-the-Fields*, Trafalgar Square, W.C.2. *St. George's*, Hanover Square, W.1. *Southwark Cathedral*, S.E.1.

Leading Roman Catholic churches, with weekday and Sunday Mass, are: *Westminster Cathedral*, Ashley Gardens, Victoria Street, S.W.1. *Brompton Oratory*, Brompton Road, S.W.3.

TURKISH BATHS, ETC. The baths are uncommon in Britain, but cosmopolitan London has one famous spot—*Savoy Baths* (Men), 92 Jermyn Street, S.W.1.

Finnish Bath (Sauna), at the Finnish Travel Information Center, Finland House, 56 Haymarket, S.W.1. and *Strand Sauna* (men only), 396 Strand, W.C.2.

On topics of health, nudists will be pleased to know there is a nudist resort, *Spiel Platz*, at St. Albans, for long or short holidays.

LONDON AIRPORT. You can reach Heathrow Airport by Green Line bus, from Victoria, or by Piccadilly Line underground to Hounslow West thence 81b or 91 bus routes.

HOW TO GET TO LONDON FROM THE AIRPORT. *Heathrow:* Cheapest method is to board one of the airport buses which will take you to the central London terminals (see below). The one-way fare is 7s 6d (90¢), and the journey usually takes about 40 minutes, depending upon traffic conditions. If you decide to go by taxi, check first with the driver as to the fare, which should not be more than about £2 10s or £3 ($6 to $7.20) to central London. Most London taxi drivers adhere to this, but there are always a few unscrupulous characters (as in every city) who prey on unsuspecting tourists. *Avis* and *Hertz* cars also available (*Avis* also at Gatwick Airport).

A 40-minute train ride on the Brighton line from Victoria takes you to *Gatwick Airport*, 30 miles south of London. One of the world's most modern airports, it is designed to take the overflow from London Airport.

AIR TERMINALS IN LONDON. *British European Airway's* West London terminal is in Cromwell Road, Kensington, S.W.7. Most domestic and continental departures by bus for London Airport leave from here, including those operated by foreign airlines. *British United Airways,* Victoria Station, S.W.1.; *Aer Lingus* at 249 Brompton Road, S.W.3.

Airways House, Buckingham Palace Road, near Victoria Station, is where all long-distance departures are concentrated. *BOAC* and *Pan American* use this terminal. *TWA* terminal is on Kensington High Street.

ALL-NIGHT POSTAL SERVICE. For after-hours stamp purchases, telegrams and all services, the St. Martin's Place, Trafalgar Square, post office is worth seeing for the decor alone. A feature is the panel of hand-drawn postage stamps on glass, coloured and illuminated.

LOST AND FOUND. Anything found in the street should be handed to the police. Items lost in tubes and buses should be enquired for at the London Transport Lost Property Office, 200-202, Baker Street, London N.W.1. Office hours are 10-6 Mondays through Fridays, 10-1 on Saturdays. For property lost in taxicabs, apply to Lost Property Office of Metropolitan Police District, 109 Lambeth Road, London S.E.1. Hours are 10-4, Mondays through Fridays, 10-1 on Saturdays.

HAIRDRESSERS. The ladies will want to try *Vidal Sassoon,* New Bond Street, who will cut it short, or *Raphael,* Upper Grosvenor Street. For beauty treatments, *Katherine Corbett,* 21 South Molton St.

It is a myth that all Englishmen are wearing their hair round their shoulders these days; barber shops to remember are *Stone and Cane* (Park Close, opposite Knightsbridge underground station), *Trumper* (Curzon Street), *Truefitt and Hill* (Old Bond Street). Of the newer set, approach *Vidal Sassoon* or *Lino Taboas* (George Street), who has a brisk, non-camp, salon.

HELP—on Weekends and at Night. Real emergencies are taken care of by dialing 999 (fire, police or ambulance). But what about other situations which seem like emergencies—when you run out of cash on a weekend, or want a meal at 5 a.m. or to buy aspirin at midnight? Well, here's a little list of helpful miscellany to get you out of that panicky, or depressing, mood:

Cash. You can cash personal cheques every day of the year (365 of them), from 10 a.m. to 8 p.m. at the *National Export Bank,* 6 Berkeley Street (just off Piccadilly), W.1. You should make prior arrangements *before* you need the money, by filing for the right to do this.

Meals. All-night restaurants include the *Cavendish Hotel Restaurant,* Jermyn St., S.W.1. (again off Piccadilly) and the coffee shop of the *Royal Garden Hotel,* Kensington High Street, W.8.

EMERGENCIES. If you need drugs in a hurry after normal hours, ask your hall porter for the address of the nearest chemist shop (equivalent to a drug dispensing counter in an American drug store) which remains open for emergencies; *Boots,* the chemists, Piccadilly Circus, is open all night. If in need of a doctor or dentist, the best thing to do is to call your embassy for the name of one. Failing that, your hotel will know the addresses of doctors on call. In a case of vital emergency, go to any telephone and dial 999, immediately telling the operator who replies: "Ambulance". The 999 emergency number also applies to police and fire brigade.

CHILDREN. *Universal Aunts*, 36 Walpole Street, King's Road, S.W.3 should be able to find you a baby sitter at any time. *Baby Ward Laundry Service Ltd.,* 169 Millbank, S.W.1 have a daily diaper (nappy) service.

WHAT?...WHEN?...WHERE? The useful weekly publication, *What's On In London* (sold at bookstalls, 1s 3d), supplies information on theatre and cinema programmes, nightclub floor shows, soloists appearing at dining clubs, and sports events (including those not usually announced in the daily newspapers, such as baseball and basketball). Brief columns listing the shows appear also in the evening papers.

Between the hours of 7 a.m. and 11 p.m. you may pick up the telephone and dial the "Teletourist" number 246—8041 for recorded information on the day's events, such as Changing of the Guard, art exhibitions, theatrical first nights, etc.

LONDON TOURIST BOARD. This organization provides information on all you may want to know about London. Head office is at 29/30 St. James's St., S.W.1. (WHI 0878), but this is for letters and telephone calls only. There is an information bureau at West London Air Terminal, Cromwell Rd. (373 4933); BOAC's terminal, Buckingham Palace Road (834-3750); and at Victoria Station, opposite platform 9.

BRITISH TRAVEL ASSOCIATION maintains a *Tourist Information Centre* at 64-65 St. James's St., S.W.1, conveniently located and very helpful (629-9191).

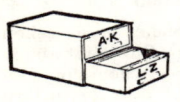

USEFUL ADDRESSES. *United States Embassy*, Grosvenor Square, W.1. (GRO 9000). *American Express* has offices at: 6 Haymarket, S.W.1. (WHI 4411) and 89 Mount Street, W.1. (GRO 4436). *Diners Club/Fugazy* at 214 Oxford Street, W.1; *Thomas Cook,* offices at: 45 Berkeley Street, Piccadilly, W.1.; Australia House, 170b Strand; 103 Cheapside, E.C.2; St. Pancras Station, N.W.1; 98 Gracechurch Street, E.C.3; 104 Kensington High Street, W.8; 100 Leadenhall Street, E.C.3; 108 Fleet Street, E.C.4; 125 Pall Mall S.W.1; 378 Strand, W.C.2; and many others.

For a temporary secretary, ring *Secretarial Services*, 28 Watling Street, E.C.4 (CIT 1033), or *Secretarial Assistance Service*, 140 Sloane Street, S.W.1 (SLO 5564). *Universal Aunts* also provides all sorts of services from finding hotel rooms and flats, getting domestic servants, shopping, etc.

Young Men's Christian Association, 112 Great Russell Street, W.C.1. *Young Women's Christian Association*, 16 Great Russell Street, W.C.1.

American Chamber of Commerce in London, 75 Brook Street, W.1.

London Airport, Heathrow, Middlesex (SKY 4321), (extension 286 for general inquiries); *American Automobile Club Service*, 15 Pall Mall, S.W.1.

LONDON'S ARTISTIC ATTRACTIONS

Museums, Theatre, Music and Cinema

by

JULIAN ASTON

(*A freelance travel writer who at present is working for B.B.C television, Mr. Aston has travelled widely in England and has a special knowledge of the Thames country.*)

In the sphere of visual art, London can fulfil the demands of almost any visitor. The British Museum is an almost incomparable introduction to Egyptian, Greek, and Roman arts in all their branches, from pottery to sculpture; and it can hold its own with the antiquity department of the Louvre or the pre-war Pergamon Museum in Berlin. The collection has been arranged with great care, and the layout is clear and easy to grasp.

The National Gallery in Trafalgar Square has one of the best balanced picture collections in the world. It can show the progress of Italian painting from the medieval to the mature masters of the Renaissance; some outstanding pictures of the old German masters; an excellent choice of Spanish painters, with El Greco, Velasquez, and Ribera leading; a great variety of unsurpassed Dutch and Flemish masters; a most valuable display of French paintings from the early days to the Impressionists; and, of course, the bulk of the finest English painting, with Gainsborough, Turner, Constable, and Reynolds.

The Tate Gallery in Millbank has a collection complementary to that of the National Gallery, for it presents modern masters of England and France. Its collection of French Impressionists is outstanding and there are some fine examples of modern sculpture. The Victoria and Albert Museum in Brompton Road has a splendid collection, mainly of the applied arts from all countries and periods, as well as a Costume Court, and many exhibits of interest to any student of the visual arts.

There are great art treasures dispersed in private collections throughout the country; the Queen's collection is the most valuable among them (some items are to be seen in Windsor Castle and at the Queen's Gallery, adjoining Buckingham Palace). While in London, don't forget to pay a visit to the charming Wallace Collection in Manchester Square, one of the finest in Europe for Venetian painters (like Guardi and Canaletto), for French masters of the art of *intimité* (like Watteau and Fragonard) and for some magnificent specimens of English painting.

For contemporary art, the Royal Academy in Piccadilly still provides the most imposing show, although many artists regard it as more of a snobbish social centre than as an abode of real inspiration. The Summer Exhibition at the Royal Academy can still give a good idea of the standard of average English painting, with its predilection for portraiture and its rather puritanical abhorrence of the nude (Paris exhibitions are just the reverse). In the immediate vicinity of the Royal Academy, there are several art galleries where exhibitions of modern painting are arranged, especially in Burlington Street and Bond Street (Marlborough, ICA, Gimpel Fils, etc.). One can see there both contemporary English and continental artists; but these art galleries also arrange from time to time shows of past English, French, German, and other artists. One never experiences a shortage of exhibitions in London. Both the Tate Gallery and the Royal Academy have shown in recent years some truly magnificent exhibitions of art treasures; and obviously will continue to do so. London is one of the best places in the world for seeing continental paintings, mainly French. Art galleries in Suffolk Street and in Leicester Square also arrange interesting shows of modern painting.

MUSEUMS AND ART GALLERIES. London is one of the two or three most important centres of western civilization, and many of its museums are incomparable in their scope, variety, and imaginative presentation. Here is a brief selection of the more specialized collections. Admission is free and museums are open daily including Bank Holidays, except where otherwise stated. The best times to visit are between 10 a.m. and 4 p.m., or Sunday afternoon. Information about public transport is included.

British Museum, Great Russell St., W.C.1. The single most important institution of its kind in the world. Among the various departments are prints and drawings; coins and medals; Egyptian and Assyrian antiquities; Greek, Roman, British, Medieval, Oriental antiquities; ethnography. Lecture tours begin at 11:30 a.m. and 3 p.m. daily, except Sundays from the main entrance hall. If you're limited for time, go straight to the King Edward VII gallery, where a representative sampling from all the collections has been gathered together. Highlights: the Elgin Marbles, the Raphael cartoons, the Rosetta Stone, 2 of the 4 original copies of *Magna Carta*, the Portland Vase, the Sutton Hoo Treasure, and first editions of Chaucer and Shakespeare, to mention only a few. Tubes: Russell Square, Tottenham Court Road, Holborn (Kingsway). Buses: 7, 8, 19, 22, 25 to Museum St.

Carlyle's House, 24 Cheyne Row, S.W.3. (Closed Tuesdays.) Letters, manuscripts, furniture, portraits, and other family mementos are displayed in the house that was Carlyle's home from 1834 until his death in 1881. Admission 2s. Buses: 19, 39, 45, 49.

Courtauld Institute Galleries, Woburn Square, W.C.1. Italian paintings of 14-16th century, French Impressionists, also varying modern collection. Private collection of the Courtauld family.

Dickens' House, 48 Doughty St., W.C.1. Closed Sundays and Bank Holidays. Occupied by the author from 1837 to 1839. On display are portraits, letters, first editions, furniture, and autographs. Admission 1s 6d. Tube: Russell Square. Buses: 5, 19, 38.

Geffrye Museum, Kingsland Rd., Shoreditch, E.2. Furniture and furnishings arranged chronologically from 1600 on. Closed Mondays. Tube: Liverpool Street, then bus 22 or 35.

Guildhall Museum, the Royal Exchange, E.C.3. (Closed Sundays.) Portrays the history of the City of London from Roman times to the present. Also an outstanding collection of watches and clocks. Tube: Bank or Mansion House.

Hogarth's House, Hogarth Lane, W.4. (Open weekdays 11-4 in winter, 11-6 in summer; Sundays 2-4 and 2-6.) Drawings, engravings, and paintings of the artist in the home occupied by him for 15 years. Admission 1s. Tube to Hammersmith, then bus 71, 90c.

Horniman Museum, in London Road, Forest Hill, S.E.23. Open daily except Mondays, 10:30-6, Sundays 2-6. The museum's three departments deal with ethnology, musical instruments and zoology. The last is noted for its aquarium. Station: Forest Hill, from London Bridge. Bus: 12.

Imperial War Museum, Lambeth Road, S.E.1. Comprehensive collection of the Commonwealth during two world wars, including an art collection and a library of films, photographs, and books. Highlights: Epstein's head of *Churchill* and bust of *Lord Fisher*. Tube: Lambeth North, Elephant & Castle. Buses: 3, 10, 12, 53.

Dr. Johnson's House, 17 Gough Square, E.C.4. Closed Sundays and Bank Holidays. Home of the great lexicographer from 1748-1759. Admission 2s. Buses: 6, 9, 11, 13, 15 to Fleet Street.

Keats' House and Museum, Keats Grove, N.W.3. (Open weekdays 10-6, closed Sundays.) The home of the poet during the most creative years of his brief life. Tube: Belsize Park. Bus: 24 from Charing Cross Road.

London Museum, Kensington Palace, W.8. Illustrates the life, history, and memorabilia of London from its beginnings to the early 20th century. Outstanding collection of royal robes and Victoriana. Tube: Queensway. Buses: 9, 27 49, 52, 73.

National Gallery, on Trafalgar Square, W.C.2. (Open weekdays 10-6, Sundays 2-6.) Collection of Italian, Dutch, Flemish, Spanish, German, and French painting up to 1900, plus British painters from Hogarth to Turner. Highlights: Botticelli's *Nativity*, the Leonardo Cartoon and his *Madonna of the Rocks*, the Rembrandt Room, the Constable and Turner Room, Van Gogh's *Sunflower*, to mention only a very few. Tube: Trafalgar Square or Strand. Buses: 3, 6, 9, 12, 13, 15, 60, 88.

National Maritime Museum, Romney Road, Greenwich. S.E.10. (Open weekdays 10-6, Sundays 2:30-6.) Superlative collection of ship models, navigational instruments, charts, uniforms, medals, portraits, and paintings of naval scenes. Train: Charing Cross to Maze Hill. Buses: 70, 163, 177; see also Water Buses.

National Portrait Gallery, at St. Martin's Place, Trafalgar Square, W.C.2. Paintings, drawings, busts of famous British men and women over the last 450 years. (Also George Washington and Benjamin Franklin, who were British *before* 1776.) Same hours as National Gallery except closes at 5, Mon.-Fri.

National Postal Museum, King Edward Street. $7 million collection of British stamps dating from 1840.

Natural History Museum, Cromwell Road, S.W.7. Animals, plants, minerals, fossils, and insects (nearly 15,000,000 specimens). Tube: South Kensington. Buses: 14, 30, 45, 49.

Queen's Gallery, adjoining Buckingham Palace. Selection of paintings and other masterpieces from the Royal Collection. Weekdays (exc. Mon.) 11-6, Sunday 2-5. Admission 2s 6d.

Old Curiosity Shop, 13-14 Portsmouth Street (Kingsway), W.C.2. A 16-cent. building worth inspection, though any connection with Dickens' novel is doubtful. Mostly an antique and gift shop. Open 9-5:30, weekdays, Sunday 9:30-5.

Percival David Foundation of Chinese Art, 52 Gordon Square, W.C.1. Administered by the School of Oriental and African studies, London University. Open Mon. 2-5, Tues.-Fri. 10:30-5, Sat.

LONDON'S ARTISTIC ATTRACTIONS

10:30-1. Closed Bank Holidays, the first two weeks in September and Dec. 24-31. Tube: Russell Square, Euston Square or Goodge Street. Buses: 14, 68, 73, 77.

Pollock's Toy Museum and Toy Theatres, 1 Scala Street, W.1. Collection of amusing antique toys, dolls, games. Historical toy theatres. Monday to Saturday, 10-5. Tube: Leicester Square. Buses: 14, 19, 22, 38.

Public Record Office Museum, Chancery Lane, W.C.2. Historical documents include Domesday Book, two examples of Magna Carta, many rare items of Americana. 1-4 p.m. Mon.-Fri. Tube: Chancery Lane. Buses: 6, 9, 11, 13, 15.

Science Museum, Exhibition Road, S.W.7. Illustrates the development of mathematics, physics, chemistry, engineering, transport, mining, communications (an operating radio station), and industry as a whole. Originals of many famous locomotives, aircraft and cars. Many working displays. Tube: South Kensington. Buses: 9, 30, 45, 49, 52, 73, 74.

Soane Museum, 13 Lincolns Inn Fields, W.C.2. Open Tuesdays to Saturdays, 10-5. Contains the collections of Sir John Soane (1753-1837) including the sarcophagus of Seti (1370 B.C.) and many classic vases. Tube: Holborn. Buses: 7, 8, 22, 23, 25, 77.

Tate Gallery, Millbank, S.W.1. Despite some modern foreign painting and sculpture, primarily dedicated to British artists, especially Turner, Blake, and the Pre-Raphaelites. Highlights: the Turner Collection, Epstein's *Einstein*, Henry Moore's *King and Queen*, and Rodin's *Le Baiser*, among others. Bus 88.

Theatre Museum, Leighton House, Holland Park Road. Exhibits of the British theatre. Open Tu., Th., Sa. only.

Tower of London, Tower Hill, E.C.3. (Closes at 4 p.m. from October to mid-March.) Outstanding collection of armour, uniforms, historic relics (admission 2s.). On show in the Jewel House are the Crown Jewels, including the 530-carat Great Star of Africa and the Koh-i-Noor diamonds. St. Edward's Crown, the Imperial Crown of State (set with 3,093 precious jewels), and other treasures (admission 2s extra). Tube: Tower Hill. Bus 13 to Monument; then walk.

Victoria and Albert Museum, Cromwell Road, S.W.7. Illustrates fine and applied arts of all countries and styles, British, European, and Oriental; a magnificent collection. Highlights: Raphael's cartoons and Gainsborough's *Queen Charlotte*, among others. Tube: South Kensington. Buses: 9, 14, 30, 45, 49, 52, 73, 74.

Wallace Collection, in Hertford House, Manchester Square, W.1. Exceptionally fine works of Dutch, Flemish, French, Spanish, Italian, and British painters together with sculpture, furniture, china, armour, and work in gold. Highlights: Limoges enamels and Hals' *The Laughing Cavalier*, among others. Tube: Bond Street. Buses: 2, 13, 23, 30, 159.

Wellington Museum, Hyde Park Corner, W.1. The London home of the famous duke containing uniforms, decorations, trophies, and some paintings. Admission 1s. Tube: Hyde Park Corner. Buses: 9, 14, 19, 22, 25, 30, 52, 73.

Wesley's House and Museum, 47 City Road, E.C.1. Closed Sundays. The home of the evangelist and founder of Methodism containing many items associated with him and his family. Admission 1s. Tube: Old Street. Buses: 43, 76.

ART FOR SALE

These galleries are usually open from about 10 to 5, and on Saturdays until noon or 1 p.m. (Many close altogether on summer Saturdays.) This is just a partial list of the many fine galleries in London:

A I A Gallery, 15 Lisle Street, W.C.2.
Alwin Gallery, 56 Brook Street, W.1.
Art Federation Galleries, 6½ Suffolk Street, S.W.1.
Arts Council Gallery, 4 St. James's Square, S.W.1.
Canaletto Gallery, Blomfield Road, W.9.
Cooling Galleries, 92 New Bond Street, W.1.
Drian Galleries, 5-7 Porchester Place, Marble Arch, W.2.
Ewan Phillips Gallery, 22a Maddox Street, W.1.
Gimpel Fils, 50 South Molton Street, W.1.
Grabowski Gallery, 84 Sloane Avenue, S.W.3.
Grosvenor Gallery, 30 Davies Street, W.1.
Guildhall Art Gallery, E.C.2.
Heim Gallery, 59 Jermyn Street, S.W.1.
ICA Gallery, Nash House, Carlton House Terrace, S.W.1.
Leicester Galleries, 4 Audley Square, South Audley Street, W.1.
Madden Gallery, 77 Duke Street, Grosvenor Square, W.1.
Marlborough Fine Art, 39 Old Bond Street, W.1.
Marlborough — New London Gallery, 17-18 Old Bond Street, W.1.
O'Hana Gallery, 13 Carlos Square, Grosvenor Square, W.1.
Roland, Browse & Delbanco, 19 Cork Street, W.1.
Royal Academy of Art, Burlington House, Piccadilly, W.1.
Royal Institute Gallery, 195 Piccadilly, W.1.
Tooth's, 31 Bruton Street, W.1.
Trafford Gallery, 119 Mount Street, W.1.
Tryon Gallery, 41 Dover Street, W.1.
Upper Grosvenor Gallery, 19 Upper Grosvenor Street, W.1.
Woodstock Gallery, 16 Woodstock Street, W.1.
Wright Hepburn Gallery, 10 Halkin Arcade, Motcomb Street, S.W.1.

Theatre in London

"Kitchen Sink", "Theatre of the Absurd", "Theatre of Cruelty", "Happenings", "Theatre of Fact". These are just a few of the epithets that have been bandied about in the press during the last few years, whenever there has been a discussion of the theatrical scene in London. Each season witnesses fresh taboos and conventions smashed to the ground by angry young iconoclasts. From a distance, it must look as if the theatre in London is in a state of continual ferment. In fact, nothing could be further from the truth. The longest running play in London, for example, is still Agatha Christie's *The Mousetrap* (in its 18th year in 1970), and the most consistently successful from the point of view of the box office are still

LONDON'S ARTISTIC ATTRACTIONS

those "sweet" mixtures of wit, music and titillation known as "light entertainment".

Of the fifty or so theatres in London, the number of managements consistently presenting avant garde or experimental plays can be counted on the fingers of one hand. Broadly speaking, the London theatres can be divided into three main camps: the strictly commercial West End managements, the repertory and experimental companies and the theatre clubs. Needless to say, the managers of the latter two are not exactly averse to making a profit, but this is not their only criterion of success.

Most of the theatres are to be found within walking distance of one another, between Piccadilly Circus in the west, Aldwych in the east and Tottenham Court Road in the north. The oldest of present-day theatres is the *Theatre Royal*, at Drury Lane, which was opened in 1663 and has been reconstructed several times since. The existing theatre was finished in 1812, and although the auditorium was completely reconstructed in 1922, the foyer, rotunda and staircase are original and are the only remaining example of Georgian theatre architecture left in London. Drury Lane, as the theatre is generally known (when it isn't called "Shaftesbury Avenue"), was long the home of spectacular dramas and pantomimes, but in recent years it has housed long-run musical shows like *My Fair Lady* and *Hello Dolly*. In fact though, most theatres usually maintain a tradition as to the type of production staged.

You can expect, therefore, to see elaborate musicals at *Drury Lane*, *Her Majesty's*, the *Saville* and the *Palace*, while the *Phoenix*, *Wyndhams*, *Haymarket*, *Globe*, *Lyric*, *Queens*, *Apollo* and the *New* show straight plays and comedies. The *Garrick*, *Criterion* and *Whitehall* specialize in farce and light comedy, while variety is firmly established at the famous *London Palladium* and the *Prince of Wales*.

Productions of serious classical drama, both English and foreign, are generally limited to the two main repertory companies: the National Theatre Company at the *Old Vic*, and the Royal Shakespeare Company at the *Aldwych* Theatre. Both these companies spill out during the summer months and run productions at other theatres. The National is, of course, waiting patiently for a home of its own, to be completed on the South Bank site adjacent to the Royal Festival Hall. (They hope to be installed in 1970.) It is often extremely difficult at present to obtain tickets for the National, partly because the *Old Vic* is rather small, but mainly because of the popularity of their productions. While new plays are rarely performed, the company almost never fails to inject new life into established works. Since its inception in 1963, the National has produced several stars, such as Robert Stephens and Maggie Smith, and has attracted a number of established stars, who enjoy playing in the repertory system.

The *Aldwych* company also runs a repertory system, but the artistic policy is considerably different. Under the general direction of Peter Hall, the RSC is consistently producing new and exciting plays by contemporary playwrights as well as staging the more successful of the company's Stratford Shakespeare productions. There is a large company, and although occasionally established names are used, there is increasingly less and less need for them, as stars are made within the group. The *Aldwych* has been the centre of a lot of the criticism concerning the "new" approaches to the theatre, and in any one week there is bound to be at least one production of a controversial piece. (Another Aldwych contribution to London is its annual International Theatre Festival, featuring companies from as far away as Greece, Japan and Russia, as well as those nearer to home.)

Perhaps the real home of avant garde drama in England is the *Royal Court Theatre*, at Sloane Square. This is the home of the English Stage Company, who, since their production of *Look Back in Anger* in 1966, have been in the vanguard of the struggle to revive the British theatre. Formerly under the direction of George Devine, the *Court* is now run by William Gaskill, who is continuing with the old policy of innovation and revolution with even more fervour. Hardly a production goes by these days without some attendant scandal and or crisis!

While there is nothing strictly comparable to "off-Broadway" theatres in London, there are outside the West End a number of theatres well worth visiting. Perhaps one of the most interesting is the *Mermaid Theatre,* near Blackfriars Bridge. The *Mermaid* has no proscenium arch, offering unrivalled sight lines from every seat in the house. It is run by the actor Bernard Miles, who has very strong views on what sort of place a theatre should be. There is a spacious foyer, several very pleasant bars and a coffee bar, as well as an excellent restaurant that overlooks the River Thames (ideal for dinner before or after the show). Another good theatre is the *Jeannetta Cochrane,* on Southampton Row.

If you feel more adventurous still, there are several excellent theatre clubs, which produce plays on almost any subject. Most important of these clubs is the *Hampstead Theatre Club,* at Swiss Cottage. You must, however, be a member, but this is easily arranged over the telephone and for a low cost. Indeed membership of the *Hampstead Club* now includes membership of the long-established *New Arts Theatre Club* in Leicester Square. Both theatres have exciting productions of new and off-beat plays. Newer, and much more experimental, are the "cellar theatres", the three leading of which are run by Americans: *Open Space,* 32 Tottenham Court Road; the *Arts Laboratory,* Drury Lane; and the *Ambiance Restaurant Theatre,* Queensway.

Theatre-going in London is generally much less difficult than in New York. Seats are much cheaper and there is not always the necessity to book months in advance. There was a time when a seat in the dress circle implied formal dress, but today, almost anything goes as far as clothes are concerned, although first-night audiences still tend to wear tuxedos. All London theatres have bars, but if you want to enjoy your drink it is advisable to order beforehand or leave your seat a minute or so before the interval curtain. Indeed, many seasoned playgoers always book the end of the row seats so that they can enjoy both the play and the interval! Coffee is served too, in your seats, but it must be ordered beforehand, and is not recommended.

There is something for everyone in the London theatre, which in recent years has once more become the center of theatrical influence.

LONDON'S ARTISTIC ATTRACTIONS

For scope and variety of productions, if not in lavishness, it beats Broadway hands down.

There is such an abundance of creative entertainment in London that the newly arrived visitor with limited time at his disposal might find it difficult to reap its full benefit. There is an excellent weekly publication to help you out of this predicament—it is called *What's On in London*; it gives you a complete break-down of everything that is happening in London, week by week. It also contains useful synopses of plays and films, together with times, venues, etc. The evening papers also carry comprehensive listings of theatres and cinemas.

Most of the theatres have a matinee twice a week (Wed. and Sat., usually) and an evening performance, which begins between 7:30 and 8:30. Prices for seats vary between theatres, but in general, expect to pay 8s 6d to 10s 6d for the upper circle ($1.02 to $1.26), 12s 6d to 25s ($1.50 to $3) for the dress circle and about the same for the stalls. Most theatres have boxes; these range in price from £2 to £7 ($4.80 to $16.80), dependent on the number of people it holds.

There are many theatrical ticket agencies where you can book a seat and save yourself the trouble of queuing at the theatre itself. Their service charge is about 2s 6d (35¢) and you will find the assistants extremely up-to-date with exactly what is on at the moment. Leading agents: *Ashton & Mitchell*, New Bond Street, and *Keith Prowse*, New Bond Street. Both have branches.

Theatre Clubs: There are a number of these clubs, whose object is to present serious plays that otherwise might not be seen on the West End stage. Overseas visitors can easily become temporary members of these on application to the box office. (Telephone ahead.) The best of them are the *Hampstead Theatre Club* (PRI 9301) and the *New Arts* (TEM 3334) and membership of one includes the other. If you would like to spend an evening at a real Edwardian music hall, then you should apply for temporary membership of the *Players* (TRA 1134). With all clubs there is a statutory 48-hour period before membership becomes valid.

Music

There is only one really first-class concert hall in London: the *Royal Festival Hall*, which was built for the Festival of Britain in 1951. And even this has a relatively smallish auditorium. The principal alternative is the *Royal Albert Hall*, with its wedding-cake architecture and positively Victorian acoustics (it is far better suited for wrestling and conventions than concerts). Despite this seemingly glaring handicap, London supports six major orchestras, a host of chamber-music ensembles and countless soloists. In addition, rarely a month goes by without some world ranking conductor or instrumentalist appearing in town. The new *Queen Elizabeth II Hall*, while very smart, is too small for really important concerts.

L

The Festival Hall has recently been renovated and the already excellent acoustics are now superlative. There is also a selection of attractive bars and restaurants overlooking the river, where you may dine, drink or simply reflect.

Wigmore Hall, in Wigmore Street, in the heart of the West End, is comparable to New York's Town Hall. Here, virtually every new soloist or singer makes his professional debut. An appearance at the Wigmore Hall is a sort of visiting card, almost an audition, for London's severe and powerful music critics.

The best place to discover who is playing what and where is in the "weekend review" sections of the quality Sunday newspapers, like the *Observer* and the *Sunday Times*.

During the spring and summer, various London boroughs hold arts festivals, the largest of which is the St. Pancras Arts Festival, whose music programme always embraces a wide range, from way-out operas to top-rank soloists.

An essential part of the London music curriculum are the *Promenade Concerts* at the Albert Hall. Founded over 70 years ago by Sir Henry Wood, they are called promenade because it is possible to stand in the large arena and listen to the music. The cost of the "prom" ticket is low and, as you would expect, most of the promenaders are young students. The last night of the proms in September, if you are lucky enough to obtain a ticket, is a unique spectacle, in which patriotism frequently ousts satire.

London's best concert hall is the *Royal Festival Hall*, South Bank, S.E.1 (WAT 3191), but there are regular concerts at the *Royal Albert Hall*, Kensington, S.W.7 (KEN 8212), the *Wigmore Hall*, Wigmore Street; and slightly further afield, the *Fairfield Hall* at Croydon.

During the year, *Residence Recitals,* 34 Hillgate Place, London W.8., organise concerts, readings and exhibitions in London houses where famous musicians, poets and painters once lived.

During the summer there are frequent open-air concerts at Kenwood House and Holland Park, details of which can be obtained from County Hall (WAT 5000).

Opera

Opera is to be found at the *Royal Opera House*, Covent Garden. A splendid building with a massive Corinthian portico, it is situated, somewhat surprisingly, in the middle of London's flower and vegetable market. Perhaps because the auditorium is somewhat smaller than the Metropolitan, it is a far more intimate house. The standard of singing and playing is international, and the productions are nearly always superlative. Under the artistic direction of Georgi Solti, the repertory is being gradually overhauled and interesting new works are being introduced. World-famous singers like Tito Gobi and Maria Callas make frequent appearances, and directors such as Zeffirelli and Visconti are invited to direct at least one major production each year. Indeed, Visconti's production of *Don Carlos* is widely acclaimed as the best in the world. Each summer, there is a special treat for lovers of Wagner, as the entire "Ring" cycle is performed. An evening at Covent Garden is always something of an event, and although there is much less formality than before the war, tuxedos are still not out of place in the best seats, although conservative lounge suits are equally in keeping. If you are fortunate to obtain tickets for a first night, then this will be an evening you will never forget.

Far less formal and somewhat less impressive is the *Sadlers Wells Theatre,* at the London Coliseum, W.C.2. Opera is sung here only in English, and the repertory is much broader and more experimental than at the Garden. As the theatre is under the control of the Arts Council, it can only hire British singers. But what it lacks in vocal resources or financial freedom, it more than compensates for in the inventiveness and scope of productions. It is most popular with younger opera-goers as it is considerably cheaper, and easier to book, than the Royal Opera House.

Unique in the world is the *Glyndebourne Festival Opera,* which is also one of the highlights of the English summer season. Evening dress is absolutely essential, and the operas are given in two parts, with a long interval, during which the audience walks in the superb grounds of the house and picnics by the cool lakes and woodland pools on cold chicken and champagne. (You should bring your own hamper and wines.) It is perhaps worth mentioning that Glyndebourne is very much a social occasion and many of the audience attend no other opera performances. Although the car park is always packed with Rolls Royces and Bentleys, do not be deterred as there is an excellent train service that leaves Victoria Station as 3:45 p.m., connecting with a bus at Lewes; the return to London is accomplished by midnight. Also good: *Evan Evans* bus.

Ballet

Of all the performing arts, perhaps the hardest to see in London is the ballet. This is partly attributed to the generally low level of interest and support afforded to the ballet by the public in general (and the Arts Council in particular). There is virtually only one major ballet company and that is the *Royal Ballet*. A few years ago, it looked as if even this great company was grinding to a creative halt, but since Sir Frederick Ashton has taken over the artistic direction of the company, the future looks very much brighter. Under his aegis, choreographers such as Kenneth Macmillan and Michael Soames have been given a remarkably free hand to devise new and exciting productions. The influence of Rudolph Nureyev cannot be ignored, either, and many people claim that he is one of the most important influences in the revival of British ballet. The Royal Ballet has two companies, one of which is continually on tour.

Although ballet is a minority interest, it is frequently difficult to obtain seats, and on the rare occasions when Nureyev and Dame Margot Fonteyn are dancing, there is a veritable black market for tickets.

Another large, but less potent, company is the *Festival Ballet,* who give occasional seasons at the Royal Festival Hall (or whatever London theatre is available). Their productions are always big and spectacular and, in the best sense of the word, "popular".

The Ballet Rambert, which has been one of the real roots of British ballet over the last 30 years, has suffered many setbacks and there is always talk of it disbanding, but last year it reappeared in a pared-down form, with a small, flexible and technically-expert team dedicated to experiment and able to present it as its best.

Opera and Ballet are principally performed at the *Royal Opera House,* Covent Garden (COV 1022) and the *Sadlers Wells* at the London Coliseum, St. Martin's Lane (836-3161). At the Opera House, ticket prices depend on what is playing, but generally range from 11s to £4 ($1.32 to $9.60). Sadlers Wells is cheaper, with prices comparable to the ordinary theatre. For the cheaper seats, there is always great competition, and they are frequently sold out on the first day of the booking period.

Glyndebourne Festival Opera at Lewes, in Sussex, presents unrivalled productions of opera in a magnificent country setting. Tickets are only available direct, and are difficult to obtain. Evening dress is compulsory. Write months ahead if you want to get tickets.

Jazz

American jazz musicians visiting England, either on tour or while passing through on vacation, nearly always make a point of mentioning how alive and interesting the current British jazz scene is. There are a great number of highly-talented jazz musicians in London, but it is comparatively difficult to hear them play, as there are so few real jazz clubs. By far the best of them all is *Ronnie Scotts,* in Frith Street, Soho. Here you can hear all that is best in British modern jazz, and eat and drink in relative comfort until three in the morning. The club is owned and personally-run by a doyen of jazzmen, Ronnie Scott, and he frequently takes the stand himself, especially when visiting American musicians drop in late at night for a jam session.

If your taste is more inclined towards New Orleans style jazz, then a visit to the rather hot and sweaty cellars of *100 Oxford Street,* or *Ken Colyers Club* in Leicester Square is a must. Be prepared, however, for a rather young and very informal crowd.

There are countless small clubs, usually in pubs, just out of town, and many of them feature top line performers, and are well worth the trouble of hunting up. One of the best of these is situated at Barnes, on the Thames, and is called the *Bulls Head.* Don't forget that if the club is in a public house, it will close at 10:30 or 11 p.m.

There are so many small jazz clubs in London, that apart from *Ronnie Scotts* at 47 Frith Street, W.1, and the *100 Club* at 100 Oxford Street, the best place to find out who is playing, and where, is to buy the weekly music newspaper, the *Melody Maker.*

Cinema

Although the general state of the British film industry is never extremely healthy, and although the number of suburban cinemas is declining each year, the West End first-run cinemas are doing better business than ever. Unless you buy or book the most expensive seats, usually about £1 ($2.40), be prepared to stand in line. This is not always quite as deadly as it may sound, as the cinema queues are entertained by London's famous street buskers, who will sing, dance or perhaps even escape from chains for you, in return for a small "donation".

In most London cinemas only the most expensive seats are bookable in advance. If you should book, be certain to arrive well in time, as most performances are continuous, with only a five-minute interval between screenings. Generally, the price of tickets in the West End ranges from 7s 6d up to £1 (90¢ to $2.40). In the suburbs, the local or second-release cinemas rarely charge more than 7s 6d.

The West End cinemas and their suburban brothers generally show popular entertainment films, the type of which is denoted, approximately, by the censors' rating. This appears in small print alongside the title of the film. If it has a *U* rating (Unrestricted), it is considered fit for all ages; if the film carries an *A* (Adult) certificate, then children under the age of 16 are not admitted to the cinema unless in the company of an adult. Finally, if there is an *X* rating (eXtra-special?), then no person under 16 is admitted at all, and the film can be assumed to be of an extremely adult nature.

In addition to the art houses, there are two important cinema clubs, which can be easily joined, the *National Film Theatre* WAT 3232, and *Academy Cinema Club,* GER 8819.

There are no all-night cinemas in London, most performances ending around 11 o'clock. However, on Saturday nights, an increasing number of cinemas are presenting a late show, which starts at 11.

WINING AND DINING IN LONDON

International Choices and Very Varying Standards

Curiously, Britain still retains a reputation for indifferent food. Eminent gastronomes still continue pompous arguments, but today they are unable to apply a general pejorative to everything; their standards of discussion have risen to the finer points of the exact texture of smoked salmon or *when* the cream should be added to spaghetti carbonara. Standards have risen enormously during the 1960's; the tourist will find, for example, much more home-made mayonnaise about, more ice in drinks, a greater variety of bread, more cream for coffee and puddings. He will find decent meals, well-cooked and efficiently served with an air of distinction.

Of course, there are nasty restaurants, hundreds of them, with soggy vegetables, dirty table coverings and indifferent service; but the eye and nose will warn you off. The general rise in standards is probably due to a new maturing generation, who have traveled abroad and thus broadened their gastronomic education. New restaurants, largely foreign-oriented, have set standards that others must emulate, or fall by the way. Another phenomenon you will find is the rash of bistros that have appeared, mostly in the Chelsea and Kensington area. Catering basically for the younger generation, they generally provide good food in simple, even spartan surroundings, but always with a lively and colorful atmosphere.

What is still lacking, however, is good *English* food, as opposed to French, Italian, Spanish or what-not. Britain has always possessed the finest raw materials, meat and vegetables, and this is reflected in normal domestic cookery. But this cool expertise rarely extends to the restaurants serving "typical English fare" (with exceptions noted in the list following).

London does possess many fine restaurants of every nationality, with the accent on France and Italy, Chinese following on closely. The newer ones are modish and highly competitive, which means the owners keep a constant eye on standards and price. Eating in London is certainly more expensive in 1970 than it was in, say, 1963, but still compares favourably with Paris for price, if not quality.

In the following lists, the restaurants have been divided according to price, along these lines:

Very Expensive: where you can expect little change out of £10 ($24) for two, including wine and a drink, and it may come to more. Food, decor and service of the highest standard, with elegant fellow-diners for company.

Expensive: where the bill will range between £6 and £10 ($14.40-$24) for two, including wine and a drink. Restaurants with individuality and high reputations.

Reasonable: under £5 ($12) for two, including wine and a drink. The food is likely to be simpler, but still good.

Cheap: where you could get away for less than 30s ($3.60) per person, and some for well under £1 ($2.40) each. Prices include a modest wine or beer. Nice, bright places which will never rate with gastronomes, but are worth remembering for an economical moment.

There are also sections of restaurants that specialize in seafood, Indian and Chinese food, not listed in any price category—the latter are usually *reasonable*, while seafood places vary from reasonable to expensive.

All restaurants are *closed* on Sunday unless otherwise specified.

VERY EXPENSIVE

LE BOUDOIR. 257 Fulham Road, S.W.3. An experience in sumptuous decor and presentation. Waiters with *jabots*, plush and gold everywhere, lace tablecloths, silver cutlery. French cuisine equally extravagant and very, very rich, but undeniably excellent. An air-conditioner would be useful in summer.

CAPRICE. Arlington St., S.W.1. Still the favoured haunt of show business people, still superb French cooking, still a fine wine list, still that opulent decor. Always crowded, reservations essential. The waiters are among the most helpful and sophisticated in London.

CONNAUGHT GRILL. Connaught Hotel, Carlos Place, W.1. For many, the best hotel and the best restaurant in town. The bar is an elegant meeting place. The Grill maintains the same feeling. Open Sunday.

COQ D'OR. Stratton St., W.1. Ex-patron Henri Sartori still presides from time to time; good, expensive wine list. Cuisine is *haute* but not so *haute* as before, and French in name.

L'ECU DE FRANCE. Jermyn St., S.W.1. The atmosphere is Parisian, with a lunchtime overtone of expense accounts. More relaxed in the evenings. Useful for after the theatre, but the food needs a bit more attention.

INIGO JONES, 14 Garrick Street, W.C.2. Very good food with some English specialties in elegantly-rustic surroundings. Convenient to Covent Garden.

THE IVY. West St., W.C.2. Theatre people flock at lunch and after the show. International cooking, but a reliable spot to try something essentially English—such as tripe and onions.

MIRABELLE. Curzon St., W.1. Perhaps the most exclusive and fashionable restaurant in town. Cuisine is *haute* impressive and expensive, ambiance luxurious, and their pampering does wonders for the self-esteem.

LA NAPOULE. N. Audley Street, W.1 Opulent modern setting for excellent French-only menu, fabulous wine list. New in 1969, already promises to be a pacesetter.

PARKES. Beauchamp Place, S.W.3. There is joy in food here, reflected in the decor, the service, and the often really original dishes, finely cooked.

LES PIES QUI RIENT. Abingdon Road, W.8. French cooking with an interesting line in oriental specialties. Pleasant to sit in, good service, well-selected but rather highly-priced wine list.

PRUNIER'S. St. James's Street, S.W.1. Politicians have lost top secret documents here, probably diverted by the amazing and unconventional menu, which is French, and with the accent on, naturally, seafood. Special pre-theatre dinner served between 5:45 and 7 p.m. is worth noting. Open Sundays.

RIB ROOM. Carlton Tower Hotel, Cadogan Place, S.W.1. Enormous plates of roast rib of beef and other goodies. The room is large but well-designed (to avoid agoraphobia), and extremely elegant.

RULE'S. Maiden Lane, W.C.2. Tucked away in Covent Garden, Rule's has been here since the 18th century, and has a plushy

Edwardian atmosphere. A different English main dish appears each day (apart from the wide *à la carte* menu) and is worth trying—steak and kidney pudding, jugged hare, etc.

SAVOY GRILL ROOM. Savoy Hotel, Strand, W.C.2. The decor is slightly less diffident than in the past, and the food retains its classic brilliance. A top place, it demands the compliment of being dressed up for, after the show or for a leisurely evening. Open Sunday.

TOP OF THE TOWER. Post Office Tower, Howland St., W.1. View spectacular, less so the food, which can be ludicrously expensive. Times and bookings are rigid, so book well in advance.

VILLA DEI CESARI. Grosvenor Rd., S.W.1. Riverside restaurant attempting to convince one that the Thames is the Tiber. Lots of Roman trappings and an off-beat Lucullan cuisine. Dancing in the evening. Strictly for fun.

WHITE HOUSE, Albany St., N.W.1, is considered by some gourmets the best in London. *Haute cuisine*, marvellous wine list. Excellent service in ultra-modern surroundings. Book far ahead.

WHITE TOWER. Percy St., W.1. Here you eat Greek (though there are dishes of other nationalities): *avgolemono* soup, *taramasalata* and *moussaka*. Glamorous people turn up to add to the sophisticated atmosphere. Take your time— you'll need it.

EXPENSIVE TO MODERATE

L'AIGLON. 44 Old Church Street, S.W.3. Run by two actors, has a theatrical decor and clientele. Service is friendly and good, the menu is French and English. A quiet, pleasing place in a pretty part of Chelsea.

ALVARO. 124 King's Road, S.W.3. Immediately on opening in 1966, became the most "in" restaurant for the new, young swinging set. Noisy, crowded; the waiters tend to get a touch harassed, and it's no longer the most. Try their *piccatine di vitello Francesca*. Food rather good. So popular, the telephone number is ex-directory (unlisted). It is KEN. 6296.

ANDREA'S. 8 Blacklands Terrace, S.W.3. More romantic Chelsea atmosphere, with a wide menu, good cooking, pleasant service.

L'APERITIF GRILL. 102 Jermyn St., S.W.1. In fashionable St. James's, a modish luncheon spot. French cooking, reliable service.

AU PERE DE NICO. 10 Lincoln St., S.W.3. In a narrow street off King's Road; walls lined with signatures of everyone in show business. Charming atmosphere with a patio, which is nice in fine weather. The menu does not range far, but is quite satisfactory. Open Sunday evening.

AU SAVARIN. 8 Charlotte St., W.1. Attractive French atmosphere, continental cuisine, with *steak Diane* as a specialty. But other dishes well worth trying.

LA BICYCLETTE. 61 Elizabeth St., S.W.1. Intimate and perhaps over-decorated; food is French and pleasant.

BROMPTON GRILL. 243 Brompton Road, S.W.3. Enjoys a high, and well-deserved, reputation for fresh vegetables and good service. Continental food, well-prepared and presented. Open Sunday (dinner).

BUCKINGHAM. 62 Petty France, S.W.1. Good place to bear in mind, when in the area of St. James's Park. Specializes in good meat;

you may choose your own steak and watch it being cooked. Lunch is reasonably priced, dinner more expensive. Open Sunday, closed Sat.

CARRIER'S. Camden Passage N.1. Well out of central London, in Islington, and surrounded by antique shops. Run by Robert Carrier, noted cookery journalist, it has a chic and colourful decor. The food is remarkably good with a taste of cream, eggs and fresh herbs about it, the pastry fresh, the meat excellent. Highly recommended for lunch, can be difficult and overcrowded in the evening. Set prices for a four-course lunch and dinner.

LE CARROSSE. 19 Elystan St. S.W.3. A large and faithful following ensures the continuing high standard of cuisine and presentation. Rather suave atmosphere.

CAFE ROYAL. 68 Regent St., W.1. *Fin de siècle* memories linger in the elaborate, glittering decor of the grill room. There's a feel of opulence and the food is good, but ranges towards the expensive. *Grill Room* much better than other rooms. Open Sunday.

CELLIER DU MIDI. 28 Church Row, N.W.3. Open evenings only, and worth travelling out to Hampstead, a delightful part of London. Provençal cooking with slightly more variety of menu than one comes to expect. Not licensed; but take your own bottle or send out for one.

CHANTERELLE. 119 Old Brompton Road. The atmosphere can turn a pleasant evening into something like an occasion. Good menu and, with care, you can remain on the reasonably-priced side.

CHARCO'S. 1 Bray Place, S.W.3. Slightly restrained atmosphere due to upper-middle class type clientele. Charcoal grill and roasting spit. Out-of-door eating possible in fine weather.

CHEZ CLEO. 11 Harrington Gdns., S.W.7. More enlivening atmosphere, this time gay French, as is the cooking, which is satisfactory.

CHEZ KRISTOF. 12 St. Alban's Grove, W.8. In a secluded backwater, attractive possibility for an intimate dinner for two. The cooking is Polish and authentically good. Open Sunday.

CHEZ SOLANGE. 35 Cranbourne St., W.C.2. Just by Leicester Square underground, right in the middle of theatreland. Family-run, service is entirely in the hands of brisk French women. The food can be quite excellent, if too uniformly rich (careful selection can avoid this) but try *coq au vin*, which is luscious. Small bar, discreet piano in the evenings, good wine list.

THE SINGING CHEF. 41 Connaught St., W.2. Sometimes the chef will, if not too pressed, show you the food before it is cooked. Friendly and reliable.

COPPER GRILL. 60 Wigmore St., W.1. Open-grill restaurant specializing in Scottish steaks. Elegant feeling, attractive decorations, featuring 400-year-old oak panelling, Royal Copenhagen porcelain and antique copper pots. Open Sunday.

EMPRESS. 15-16 Berkeley St., Large, opulent room (looks like 1st class lounge on the *Queen Mary*) with a superb table of cold food at the entrance. Menu wide and international with some interestingly unusual thoughts. A specifically luncheon section is useful when shopping around Piccadilly. Open Sunday.

WINING AND DINING IN LONDON

ETOILE. 30 Charlotte St., W.1. Excellent French cuisine in quasi-provincial surroundings. Expensive.

GALLIPOLI. 7-8 Bishopsgate Church Yard, E.C.2. One of the newer additions to the usually dead City of London. Cuisine is Turkish and interesting. Belly-dancers appear twice nightly for cabaret.

THE GARDEN. 9 Henrietta Street, W.C.2. Ideal for after-theatre dining among café society and occasional royalty. Possible to enjoy two courses of good English food for £1.

LE GAVROCHE. 61 Lower Sloane St., S.W.1. Very fashionable, very hard to get reservations. *Haute cuisine* and even more *haute* prices.

GAY HUSSAR. 2 Greek St., W.1. Considered to have the best Hungarian cuisine in town; atmosphere and service pleasant.

GENEVIEVE. 13 Thayer St., W.1. Popular with the U.S. Embassy crowd. Really distinguished French cuisine. Wise to book a table.

GUINEA GRILL. 30 Bruton Place, off Berkeley Square, W.1. Well-established steak house where you can choose your own meat and watch it being cooked. The pub is 500 years old and the atmosphere is pervasive. In the miniscule dining area, customers sit along a corridor, but there is a larger dining room out back, garden patio style. Sadden the waiter with a credit card, not cash.

HUNGARIAN CSARDA. 77 Dean St., W.1. A high standard of traditional Hungarian cooking, reflected in the decor. A refreshing change from the usual Soho range of continental flavours.

ISOW'S 10 Brewer St., W.1. International menu, but with the accent on Jewish cooking, which could be much better. Wise to book a table. Open Sunday.

JASPER'S EATING HOUSE. 4 Bourne St., S.W.1. Edwardian decor and high-backed pews for eating in privacy. One of the few restaurants with emphasis on good English cooking—steak and kidney pudding, suckling pig, boiled beef, etc. Filling and fun.

KEATS. 3-4 Downshire Hill, N.W.3. Another memorable restaurant in Hampstead; expensive, high-quality food well presented. Decor mostly concerned with the poet, who lived near here.

KETTNER'S. Romilly St., W.1. Good Soho after-theatre spot; good food, reasonable wine list. Comfortable, efficient service. Open Sunday (dinners).

L'OPERA. Great Queen St., W.C.2. Close to the Royal Opera House and the Theatre Royal, Drury Lane; its decor continues the opulent feeling of those two theatres—all plush and gilt. So-called French cuisine, attractive wine-list. Don't sit near noisy kitchen.

LA POPOTE. 3 Walton St., S.W.3. Food here—which is continental in approach—can vary, but the atmosphere is elegantly Chelsea.

LA SPERANZA. 179 Brompton Rd., S.W.3. Being Knightsbridge, the atmosphere is peaceful and well-bred. The food is Italian, the decor plushy. Try the *canneloni* as a warm-up, followed by a *tournedos Rossini*. The wine-by-the-glass is quite respectable. All this and elegant Venetian mirrors.

LE P'TIT MONTMARTRE. 15 Marylebone Lane, Wigmore St., W.1. Well-favoured, typically French, restaurant. Music in the evenings.

MASSEY'S CHOP HOUSE. 38 Beauchamp Place, S.W.3. Typically English meat-eating atmosphere; charcoal grill and spit.

MARTINEZ. 25 Swallow St., W.1. Down an easily-missable side-turn off Regent Street, where the bend straightens out. Authentic Spanish decor and cuisine—big, cool, tiled. Excellent food. Open Sunday (dinner).

NICK'S DINER. Ifield Road, S.W.10. Fashionable, crowded, little eating-place. Everything on Nick's adventurous and tantalising menu is good. Booking essential, so 'phone.

OLD VIENNA. 94 New Bond St., W.1. Austrian cooking in a sometimes slightly overwhelming Viennese atmosphere (lederhosen and aprons), but pleasant.

OMAR KHAYYAM. 50 Cannon St., E.C.4. Another oriental restaurant in the City of London. Persian accent and really excellent cuisine, the decor evocative of Arabian nights.

PETIT SAVOYARD. 36 Greek St., W.1. Friendly French restaurant, quiet and comfortable. Food good.

PLANTERS' GROVE, Syon Park Gardening Centre, is a 20-min. drive westward and worth it for good food in splendid surroundings.

POOR MILLIONAIRE. 158 Bishopsgate. E.C.2. Slightly sophisticated modern restaurant in the City. Steaks and crustaceans a specialty. Watch city gents at lunch; in the evening, there's a cabaret.

QUO VADIS. 26-29 Dean St., W.1. Italian, heart-of-Soho, old-fashioned, reliable and good cooking. Nothing spectacular. Karl Marx lived upstairs. Open Sunday (dinner).

LA RECOLTE. 67 Duke St., Grosvenor Square, W.1. A fairly high standard of French cooking is maintained right through the menu, but nobody's perfect.

RISTORANTE PIZZALA. 125 Chancery Lane, W.C.2. Just off the Strand, near the law courts, a big, elegantly-tiled restaurant with primrose napery and an impressive cold table of starters. International cuisine, but Italian specialties predominate.

RITZ. Piccadilly, W.1. Sparkles impressively at the edge of Green Park. Both restaurant and Grill Room are elegant and offer some fine eating.

ROYAL GARDEN HOTEL. Kensington High St., W.8. *Garden Grill* offers spectacular view of the Kensington Gardens and Palace, and a good, but fairly expensive, meal. Downstairs is the *Bulldog Chophouse*, with the emphasis on traditional English dishes.

SCOTT'S. Now at 20 Mount St., W.1. One of the best restaurants, with a fine tradition. Mirrors and gilt, seafood specialties.

SIMPSON'S. Strand, W.C.2. Stronghold of first-class meat (you must tip the carver 1 shilling per person) and basically British. The vegetables have been known to disappoint, but the beef and lamb are superb.

STONE'S CHOP HOUSE. Panton St., Haymarket, S.W.1. Good meat and fine steaks particularly. Claims to serve English specialties. Service can vary from good to otherwise.

LA TERRAZA. 19 Romilly St., W.1. A vastly popular Italian restaurant in Soho, highly favoured by show-business and advertizing clientele. If you can get a table downstairs, then count yourself "in". Food sets new Italian standards for many follow-

WINING AND DINING IN LONDON

ing trattorias. Decor cool and clean. We suggest *petto di pollo* (breast of chicken rolled in breadcrumbs, fried and injected with garlic butter), followed by the specialty of the house, delicious "mystery pancakes" with their unique, nut-like flavour. Open Sunday.

TIBERIO. 22 Queen Street, W.1. Outstanding Italian food and service—possibly the best of its kind in Town. Expensive.

TIDDY-DOL'S EATING HOUSE. Hertford Street, W.1. Set in the Mayfair village of Shepherd Market. Named after an eccentric 18th-century gingerbread vendor. Decorated with prints by Hogarth and Gillray. Serves unusual old English fare, including *Tiddy Dol's Gingerbread*.

VERREY'S. 233 Regent St., W.1. Well-established restaurant with an international menu and good service.

TRADER VIC'S, in the London Hilton, Park Lane, W.1. Polynesian decor and food, plus Indian, Hawaiian and other specialties. Open for lunch and dinner; moderately expensive. Open Sunday.

REASONABLE

THE ARK. 122 Palace Gardens Terrace, W.8. Opened in 1962 and instantly popular among the young people of Notting Hill Gate, it is not misnamed—the small restaurant looks like a chic hut. The food is rather good; high value for money rating.

BERTORELLI'S. 70-72 Queensway, W.2. Only remarkable thing about the decor is the contented look on the diners' faces. Friendly, unobtrusive service.

BLOOM'S. 90 Whitechapel High St., E.1. "The most famous kosher restaurant in Britain", it says across the front, and quite right, too. Noisy, crowded, friendly, huge servings of excellent food. Open Sunday.

BIANCHI'S. 21a Frith St., Soho, W.1. This has been the quiet prize of good-food lovers for a number of years. The rather dismal entrance doesn't look a bit enticing, but upstairs there is pleasant service and some fine cooking. Good *coq au vin*.

BUZZY'S BISTRO. 11 King's Road, Chelsea, S.W.1. A candlelit basement, eccentrically decorated, and a gay atmosphere. Food not outstanding, but good value for money.

THE CARVERY. Cumberland Hotel, Marble Arch, W.1. Roasts are the specialty here. You carve as much as you wish from huge joints of beef, pork or lamb. There's another *Carvery* at the Regent Palace Hotel, Piccadilly Circus, and a *Carving Room* at the Strand Corner House, Charing Cross. All belong to the Lyons group.

CHANTICLEER TAVERNA. Roebuck House, S.W.1. Delicious Greek food, with Greek music and dancing. Open to 3 a.m. "A little bit of Athens", well worth the trip. (Near Victoria Station.)

CASSEROLE. 331 King's Road, Chelsea, S.W.3. A favorite with young people. Try the chicken casserole or *veal Chulo*. The desserts, which are lip-smacking, are rather expensive, but the espresso coffee is truly great. Wine from a nearby pub. Open Sunday.

CHEZ VICTOR. 45 Wardour St., Soho, W.1. Another old Soho favourite that goes on. French decor and food.

COMEDY. 33 Panton St., S.W.1. English cooking; the decor perhaps a little too self-conscious.

CORDON BLEU. 31 Marylebone Lane, W.1. Food cooked by young lady Cordon Bleu cooking school graduates. Very popular.

FLANAGAN'S, Baker Street, W.1. Food. surroundings, singing pianist—all in the Victorian idiom. Very amusing and informal.

HOSTARIA ROMANA. 70 Dean St., Soho, W.1. Bustling, friendly atmosphere, good basic Italian menu. Not the place for intimate discussion. Insist on a table on the ground floor, as the upstairs section is quite different in mood. Open Sunday.

MAGGIE JONES'S. 6 Old Court Place, W.8. Just off Kensington Church St., English food and country dishes. Guess why it has this very famous name—ask the waiter if you don't have the answer by dessert.

LUBA'S BISTRO. 6 Yeomen's Row, S.W.3. Inexpensive Russian food; popular, noisy, lots of pretty girls, great fun.

MAURER'S. Greek Street, W.1. A small, modest restaurant whose undistinguished exterior hides some of the best home cooking in Soho. Huge helpings. Try Madame Maurer's own *paté, bratwurst fruit flans* and *ice cream*. Not licenced, but there's a wine shop next door.

LA PARRA. Draycott Avenue, S.W.3. A colorful dash of Spain in a Chelsea cellar. Dine by candlelight on authentic Spanish cooking. Cheap wines, and refreshing *sangria*.

MON PLAISIR. 21 Monmouth St., W.1. A difficult place; once you are in and seated, the food is excellent and served with the carelessness of affection. But the bistro is always packed, tables must be booked and if you are late—you've had it. Try the *paté maison* and the *tournedos*, both truly superb.

NORWAY FOOD CENTRE. Brompton Road, S.W.3. A little bit of Scandinavia in London complete with pretty waitresses in national costume. Help yourself from the famous cold table. You can eat as much as you want for a guinea ($2.52).

LA POULE AU POT. 231 Ebury St., S.W.1. Where the bright young things go for good (and moderately-priced) French cuisine.

TRATTORIA SANTA LUCIA. 20 Rupert St., W.1. Clean, summery decor—tiles and pink napery; excellent *al dente* spaghetti, good range of chicken, veal and fish dishes. Angelo will tell you if there is anything special on today. Adequate wine list, though the house wine is excellent. Crowded at lunchtime. Of its kind, the best in London. Basic prices reasonable, but the bill can mount to the next higher level. Open Sunday.

TRATTORIA DA OTELLO. 41 Dean St., Soho, W.1. One of the first trats, and still crowded, though its style has been outdated by the cooler newcomers.

"235". 235 King's Road, S.W.3. Warns all "peasants" to keep out, but all our readers can enter to enjoy simple, but excellent, French cooking.

VENEZIA. 21 Great Chapel St., off Oxford St., W.1. Modest family restaurant which serves a three-course meal (including meat) for about 15s. Classical Italian dishes, excellent food and service.

VERBENELLA. 145 Notting Hill Gate, W.11. There are lots of Alpine-styled Italian restaurants in London, usually as inadequate as their phoney decors. This is an exception, with pleasing food well presented.

LA ZIA TERESA. 6 Hans Road, S.W.3. Basic Italian food and service, with a strong-following.

WINING AND DINING IN LONDON

SEAFOOD

BENTLEY'S. 11 Swallow St., W.1. A delightfully atmospheric place, with a fine restaurant on the first floor serving classic treatments of seafood. Downstairs, sit at the long counter or in booths. Can be fairly expensive. The fish restaurant on the first floor has superb *lobster bisque* and their *sole Bentley* is cooked in wine with oysters, lobsters and mushrooms—a gastronomic experience.

BRAGANZA. 50 Frith St., Soho, W.1. Oyster bar on the ground floor, also restaurant. A member of the Wheeler's group, therefore reliable.

CONTENTED SOLE. 19 Exhibition Rd., S.W.7. Mock-up of a Victorian fish parlour—marble-topped tables, posters, boaters and long black skirts. Popular with the younger set. Sometimes the helpings can be too much.

OVERTON'S. (Opposite Victoria Station.) Its façade intermittently obscured by the massive upheavals connected with building the new underground line, this popular restaurant continues to give good service, good food. Try crab salad or oysters with a glass of stout.

PRUNIER'S and **SCOTT'S**; see "Expensive" listings.

WHEELER'S. 19 Old Compton St., Soho, W.1. One of the best. The ground floor is smartest (there's a tiny bar at the back) and has a long counter for cold food. There are three floors in this narrow Dickensian house, comfortable and full of atmosphere. Expensive. (Also branch at 12a Duke of York St., S.W.1.)

VENDOME. 20 Dover St., W.1. Another member of the Wheeler's group. Fish is the basis of the menu, but there is a range of French dishes, too. Rather opulent, can be expensive. Open Sunday.

WILTON'S. 27 Bury St., S.W.1. Excellent for sea food, and very expensive. Intimate and elegant decor, select clientele, authoritative wine steward and waiters. Smoked salmon, oysters get first priority. Magnificent wine list.

CHINESE

KUO YUAN. 259 High Road, Willesden Green, N.W.10. Far away, but go, anyway. The best Chinese restaurant in Europe. Their *table d'hôte* dinner is magnificent: hot and sour soup, shrimps on crackling rice, etc. Peking duck is a specialty. Fine service.

New (1968) branch at 2 Princes St., W.1, near Oxford Circus, not as good.

FU TONG. 29 Kensington High St., W.8. One of the best-known and smartest; though the menu sticks pretty closely to the familiar, food is well cooked and served. Open Sunday.

GOOD EARTH. 316-318 King's Road, S.W.3. Chinese in Chelsea; smart, elegant, mouth-watering food, and better than usual service. Open Sunday.

GOOD FRIENDS. 139 Salmon Lane, W.14. Down in the east end of London; ideal starting place for a tour of dockland pubs. Food attracts connoisseurs from all over town, so book in advance. (Note: at the time of writing the area is being rebuilt, so check before leaving, anyway). There is a twin, the *New Friends*, just down the lane. Equally good is a third member of the chain, the *City Friends*, 11 Creed Lane, E.C.4. Open Sundays.

RICE BOWL. 27 Pelham St., S.W.7. As with all the top Chinese restaurants it is a good idea to give the chef a day or so notice if you want his best work. First class. Open Sunday.

GOLD FISH. 12 Sutton Parade, Church Rd., Hendon, N.W.4. Rather far from center, but worth the trip for excellent Peking-style food and marvelous service. Ask for manager Eddie.

MR. CHOW'S. 151 Knightsbridge, S.W.1. Trendy and exciting crowd, but food very westernized and *very* expensive.

INDIAN

VEERASWAMY'S. Corner of Regent St. and Swallow St. Spectacular decor, with turbaned waiters and lots of Indian leitmotifs. Enjoys a massive reputation, largely well-earned. Every known curry and Birani dish from tepid to blast-furnace. Open Sunday (dinner).

SHAFI'S. 18 Gerrard St., Soho, W.1. London's oldest-established Indian restaurant. Reliable for decent food at a reasonable price. Open Sunday.

TANDOORI. Fulham Road, S.W.3. Indian restaurants have mushroomed in London, but few are as outstanding as this one. Dishes from the Northwest Frontier region are the specialty, notably Tandoori chicken, cooked in a clay oven.

JAPANESE

HIROKO. 6 St. Christopher's Place, W.1 (off Wigmore St., near Marylebone Lane). Strictly authentic Japanese cuisine, from tempura to sushi, served in great style by beautifully-gowned girls flown in from Tokyo. Ground-floor theatrical elegance or downstairs *tatami*-floored private rooms. Reserve ahead for latter. Expensive, but worth it.

INEXPENSIVE

As with most places, in London "cheap" too frequently equates with "nasty"; but good cheap meals do exist. It is possible to make not unpleasant economies, particularly at lunchtime. Most public houses (pubs) serve food at the bar, ranging from freshly-cut sandwiches with a variety of fillings, to pies, sausages and baked potatoes from the hot plate. Some have tolerable salad selections (see page 178 for a brief list). Here is a short list of coffee bars and restaurants, mostly small, which have kept prices down and give you eatable food in pleasant surroundings:

ANDREA'S. 22 Charlotte St., W.1. Greek restaurant with main dishes well under 10s ($1.20) and large helpings. Licensed.

AS YOU LIKE IT. 18 Monmouth St., W.C.2. Tiny coffee house with a theatrical flavour. Mainly salads and sandwiches.

SCHMIDT'S. 14 Charlotte St., W.1. You will like it, or loathe it: really heavy German food of excellent quality, German beer. Service sometimes a little slow.

GUYS 'N' DOLLS. 74 King's Rd., S.W.3. Not a place for the rather staid, but an ideal spot for watching the Chelsea mod parade. Sandwiches and hot dishes.

GRUMBLES. 35 Churton St., S.W.1. Bistro-type (bring your own wine), informal atmosphere, pleasant food.

SPAGHETTI HOUSE. Sicilian Arcade, W.C.1. Basic Italian food, large helpings served with a smile. Branches, too, at 15 Goodge St., W.1 and in Blenheim St., W.1, though prices vary.

WINING AND DINING IN LONDON

CHAINS

Series of restaurants, usually with the same outward appearance, scattered across London serving inexpensive to moderately-priced meals, usually very standardized.

PETER EVANS EATING HOUSE. 65 King's Road, S.W.3; 1 Kingly St., W.1; 225 Brompton Road, S.W.3.; 78 Kensington High St., W.8; 115 Finchley Road, N.W.3; 60 Fleet St., E.C.4.

Each comfortably decorated according to the atmosphere (real or imagined) of its area. Steak and scampi the specialties; usual starters—corn on the cob, paté, avocado pear, etc.

LONDON STEAK HOUSE. There are 13 branches, including a welcome one in Lincoln's Inn Fields, W.C.2, and at 7 South Grove, Highgate, N.6. Both areas worth exploring. Steaks, grills, fish.

ANGUS STEAK HOUSE. 12 branches. Steaks, chops, the main items. Service can be a little off-hand occasionally, but the restaurants are comfortable.

LYONS CORNER HOUSE. A demonstration of the mastery of mass catering for the British. Four or five restaurants under one roof, ranging from a quick hamburger bar to what is almost a night club. There's the *Egg & Bacon*, the *Grill and Cheese*, the *Chicken Fayre*, the *Salad Bowl*—all of which speak for themselves. The *Seven Stars* offers English specialties, including hefty slices of roast beef. Service fast and helpful; decor is basic. Some oddities, such as ice in the butter but none in the gin; ancient parmesan for a tolerable minestrone and too much cream for the baked potato. Carafe wine very good.

Strand, W.C.2; Coventry St., W.1. (open Sunday); Marble Arch, W.1; Oxford Circus, W.C.2.

QUALITY INN. 8 branches; popular food, popular prices.

LUNCH AND SNACKS

Many of the big department stores have good restaurants. The atmosphere is predominantly feminine—often there's a fashion parade at the same time—and they are usually busy. Try *Fortnum & Mason's*, Piccadilly, W.1 (see below); *Simpson's*, Piccadilly, W.1 (Clover Room downstairs); *Harrod's*, Knightsbridge, S.W.1; *Selfridge's*, Oxford St., W.1; *Derry & Toms*, Kensington High St., W.8 (for its wonderful roof garden).

BOULEVARD. 56 Wigmore St., W.1. As with almost every other place at lunch-time, crammed. Viennese in flavour, right down to the delicious pastries and magazine-cum-newspaper rack. Austrian dishes are usually starred as the *plat du jour*.

CAUSERIE. (Claridge's Hotel). Brook St., W.1. Excellent smörgåsbord vies with chic chapeaux in this citadel of class as the prime attraction. The perfect luncheon spot. Eat as much as you want for 15s. Reservations essential.

DANISH CENTRE. Conduit St., W.1. In their effort to promote the virtues of Danish farm produce in Britain, the Danes have set up a tiny restaurant just off Regent Street featuring, quite naturally, their delicious open-faced smørrebrød sandwiches. The centre closes at 5:30, 1 on Sat.

FLORIS. 24 Brewer St., Soho, W.1. Best-known (deservedly) patisserie in London—they make royal wedding cakes and all that. The little restaurant upstairs caters for typically feminine tastes.

GERMAN FOOD CENTRE. Knightsbridge S.W.1. You'll find Upstairs a lunch bar, downstairs a restaurant (also open in the evening). Good German dishes and wine. Ideal after a shopping spree in this big-store area.

GLORIETTE. 128 Brompton Road S.W.3. This is our very favorite London pastry shop. The true genius of Vienna brought to Knightsbridge: *Sacher* and *Dobosch torte*, etc. Expensive, but they only use the best ingredients. Delicious little luncheon snacks, too, and good espresso coffee. Make a note of this address.

MERMAID THEATRE RESTAURANT. Puddle Dock, Blackfriars Bridge, E.C.4. If by chance you've been touring the City or St. Paul's, try lunch here. Splendid river view. It is open for dinner, but apt to be crowded with theatre-goers. Moderate.

THE VINE. 3 Piccadilly Place, W.1. First floor, over a delightful little pub standing mid-way between Piccadilly and Regent Street you will find a restaurant of quality. Much frequented by discerning businessmen who appreciate the very fine steaks. Reservations a must. Moderately expensive.

FORTNUM & MASON'S. Piccadilly, W.1. Eating in one of London's most exclusive stores is an experience—if you're a man, you'll probably be the only male in the room. While you down little calory-saving nothings (quite delicious, by the way), beautiful models parade through the room, looking haughty. Great fun. Expensive, of course. Also *Fortnum's Fountain*, very quiet and refined, but an unusual idea for after-theatre suppers. Grills, sandwiches, lavish ice-cream sundaes. Licensed.

CRANK'S. Marshall Street, W.1. (off Carnaby Street). You may feel like something slightly more substantial after viewing this heart of the swinging young mod world, but this is a first-rate vegetarian restaurant.

SIMPSON'S. Piccadilly, W.1. Has a popular luncheon room downstairs and a roof garden lunch club. As good a department store restaurant as you will find.

HARRODS. Knightsbridge, S.W.1. Everyone has lunch or tea here at least once. Fairly expensive.

SELFRIDGE'S. Oxford St., W.1. Restaurant on the top floor, also soda fountain and small ground floor eatery where you can get excellent light meals. Popular and not expensive.

DERRY & TOMS. Kensington High St., W.8. Has a spectacular roof garden restaurant.

PUBS. You can get simple lunches at most pubs, more elaborate meals at a few. See *London by Night* chapter, following.

LONDON BY NIGHT

Dancing, Dining and Afterwards

London's night life has undergone a radical change in the mid-1960's, due to the great take-over by young people with a little money to spend. They demanded and ultimately devised their own style of evening entertainment, which has brought about a rash of discothèques. These follow a simple and predictable pattern of opening with glitter and a smart following, followed by a slow decline as the trend-setters move elsewhere. A handful remain forever sparkling. They are youthful, dark, noisy, interestingly decorated and some are alarmingly expensive.

The hard core of older, famous nightclubs (in the old sense of the word) remain, building the evening round a good international cabaret, with dancing in between. Food is often indifferent, so if you must eat, stick to the simplest items, which can hardly go wrong. Wine is expensive and spirits are frequently served from a marked bottle set on the table.

Nearly all clubs demand that you join. For visitors, this requires a preliminary telephone call and production of the passport on arrival. (In some cases, an internationally-recognized credit card will serve the purpose.)

All in the following list are closed Sundays unless otherwise specified:

HOTEL DINING & DANCING is a popular pastime in London. Among the very best are the restaurants at the *Berkeley*, *Dorchester* and *May Fair*. The *Hilton* has its Roof-top and the *007*. The *Savoy* still leads them all, of course, with elegant dancing and cabaret in its restaurant.

ANNABEL'S. (Sub.). 44 Berkeley Square, W.1. Very elegant *boîte* below the *Clermont Club*, London's most posh gambling den. Hard to get in at times. Discothèque.

ASTOR. (Sub.). Lansdowne Pl., Berkeley Square, W.1. Intimate; French cuisine; dancing to two bands from 9:30 p.m. to 4 a.m. Vaudeville-style floor show at 1 a.m.

BEACHCOMBER. (May Fair Hotel). Berkeley St., W.1. If you go in for witty South Seas decor (with real alligators!) and Polynesian-type cuisine, this might be right up your alley. Very expensive, exotically-named drinks served at the bar. Dancing on a tiny dance floor.

BIRDLAND. (Sub.). Duke St., St. James's, S.W.1. Where boy meets girl for discothèque dancing.

BLAISE'S. (Sub.) 121 Queens Gate, S.W.7. Another discothèque, low entrance and membership fee.

BLUE ANGEL. (Sub.). Berkeley St., W.1. Our particular favourite. Top-notch floor show, on the clever, sophisticated level of its New York counterpart. Usually jammed with smartly-dressed teenagers or under-25's, who find it the least expensive nightclub in town. Top calypso band, small dance floor. Reservations a must.

CARAVANSARAI. Kensington High Street, W.1. A newcomer in Arabian Nights style, with discothèque, late-night eating, floor-show in the Emir's Tent!

CAROUSEL. 190 Piccadilly, W.1. Bright spot for dinner in gay surroundings. Two bands and lavish cabarets help it into the top category rather than the food and drink, which are just fair.

CHURCHILLS. 160 New Bond Street, W.1. Cozy traditional spot with dim lights and hostesses. Waiters use torches to find your table. Star-studded floor shows. Open 6 p.m. to dawn, with free breakfast. Most people dress here.

DANNY LA RUE'S. (Sub.). 17 Hanover Square, W.1. Fast, witty revue at 1 a.m. Food above average. Chic place for top show-biz strata—Coward, Garland, Fonteyn, etc. The "lady" m.c. is Mr. La Rue.

DIDI'S. (Sub.). 57 Jermyn St., S.W.1. Another popular trend spot, no live music, *demands* membership. Noisy discothèque.

EDMUNDO ROS' CLUB. (Sub.). 177 Regent Street, W.1. Gay, lavish, this boasts two orchestras and cabaret. Open 8:30 p.m. to 3 a.m., but you can dine and dance before 11 p.m. The master of Latin-American rhythm presides amiably. The food is good.

EMBASSY. (Sub.). 6 Old Bond St., W.1. Plush and roomy. Star floor show, and often televised. Open till 4 a.m. with two bands for dancing.

EVE. (Sub.). 189 Regent Street, W.1. Exotic floor shows. Open 9 p.m. to 4 a.m. but you can have a five-course dinner up to 11 p.m.

GALLIPOLI. Bishopsgate Churchyard, E.C.2. A 1967 newcomer. The City with belly dancers!

GARGOYLE. 69 Dean Street, Soho, W.1. Roof gardens, a

LONDON BY NIGHT

superb floor show and cabaret. There's a Nell Gwynn Room—she used to live on this site. And a Matisse Room, decor by Henri himself.

HATCHETT'S. Piccadilly, W.1. Restaurant, 2 bars, downstairs discothèque with psychedelic lighting (entrance £1, $2.40). Won 1968 International Academy Award for Interior Design, awarded by American hotel & catering industry.

MURRAY'S CLUB. (Sub.). 16 Beak Street, W.1. Is famed for its floor shows.

MURRAY'S CABARET CLUB. (Sub.). 16 Beak St., W.1. Well-established favourite, well-dressed floor shows.

OMAR KHAYYAM. 50 Cannon St., E.C.4. Claims to be the only Persian restaurant in London, complete with hubble-bubble smoking and belly dancers, and quite a diversion. Two floor shows.

PLAYBOY CLUB. (Sub.). 45 Park Lane, W.1. London's branch opened with flourishes in mid-1966; usual ambiance but all-English bunnies (some of aristocratic vintage), closed circuit TV on entrance. Prices high. Membership 5 gns. ($12.60). Initiation. 3 gns. ($7.56). Open Sundays. Cabaret, etc.

QUAGLINO'S. 16-17 Bury St., S.W.1. For decades Quag's has seen pomaded swains pushing pampered debutantes around the dance floor during the season (May-July); still much the same.

RAFFLE'S. King's Road, S.W.3. Dance and dine with the Chelsea set. Really good food.

REVOLUTION. 14 Bruton Place, W.1. Upstairs action, downstairs peace and quiet for dining. Bright young things and jet-set types.

SAN FREDIANO. 62 Fulham Rd., S.W.3. A swinging discotheque with cool music.

SAN LORENZO. 22 Beauchamp Place, S.W.3. The girls may be starving, but they're all looking their best and in their best. Discotheque, loud.

SAVOY RESTAURANT. Savoy Hotel, Strand, W.C.2. For the grand evening. Expensive, but good value. Top floor show and good dancing.

SCOTCH OF ST. JAMES'S. 13 Masons Yard, Duke St., S.W.1. Live groups, not as trendy as it has been, but can give you a good evening. Discothèque.

LA SEINE A LONDRES. (Sub.) 129 Grosvenor Rd., S.W.1. The former River Club, this is now Harry Satlzman's "hobby". The producer of James Bond films has gathered a French chef and *maitre d'hotel* and some gorgeous Chinese girls together to serve food from the Touraine. Luscious and expensive.

SHOWBOAT. Lyons Corner House, Strand, W.C.2. Dancing and floor show.

SPEAKEASY. 48 Margaret St., W.1. Discothèque and restaurant with an attempt to recreate the atmosphere of gangsters, Chicago and the 1930's. Live groups and discs. Very popular.

SYBILLA'S. (Sub.). 9 Swallow St., W.1. Celebrated new discothèque, with a steady support from the "in" crowd. Beatle George Harrison is a part-owner. Food good but expensive. Membership (7 gns.) is closed as of press time.

TALK OF THE TOWN. Near Leicester Square underground station. W.C.2. An extraordinary event; a vast room, vast floor show, top-liner cabaret star as well, two dance bands, better-than-average food, all for an inclusive price.

THE POOR MILLIONAIRE. 158 Bishopsgate, E.C.2. An event. In the City since 1965, with good food and cabaret. Still going strong.

GAMING

A short list of the leading casinos and gaming clubs, now more-or-less legal in the U.K.:

Charlie Chester Casino, 12 Archer St., W.1.
Crockford's, 16 Carlton House Terrace, S.W.1. Long-established, exclusive.
Curzon House, 20 Curzon St., W.1.
Knightsbridge Sporting Club, 163 Knightsbridge, S.W.7.
Pair of Shoes, 21 Hereford St., W.1.
Palm Beach Club, May Fair Hotel, Berkeley St., W.1.
Victoria Sporting Club, 150 Edgware Rd., W.2, London's biggest.
Le Cercle, a gambling room in a restaurant, *Les Ambassadeurs* (Sub.), 5 Hamilton Pl., W.1. The famous House of Rothschild converted into a lush restaurant. Summer dining in terraced garden. Expensive.

STRIP TEASE

There are a number of strip clubs in Soho, the majority of them not worth the money. There are two exceptions we know of:

Casino de Paris, 5-7 Denman St., just off Shaftesbury Ave. by Piccadilly Circus, W.1. Continuous show from 2:30 p.m. Drinks, no food. Tasteful, amusing show.

Raymond Revuebar. Brewer St., Soho, W.1. Well-presented strip shows, featuring a number of international acts in the theatre; also bars, dancing.

PUBLIC HOUSES

There are at least 4,000 pubs in London ranging from tiny, back-street bars to loud, noisy places; from the unutterably squalid to the suavely opulent. Opening times are 11 a.m. to 3 p.m. and 5:30 p.m. to 11 p.m. with slight local differences of half an hour. (Sundays, noon to 2:30 p.m. and 7 to 10 p.m.) All serve beer (draught bitter up to 3s—36¢—a pint), most offer spirits, wine and soft drinks. Simple food at most bars, hefty meals in an attached restaurant. A short list of key pubs, of various types:

Music and Entertainment

City Arms, West Ferry Rd., E.14 (in the docks). Amateur singers.

Crown and Anchor, Crown St., Islington. Jazz on Thur. night and Sun. at noon.

Iron Bridge, East India Dock Rd., E.14. Good jazz.

Waterman's Arms, Glengarnock Ave., Millwall, E.14 (far into dockland).

Sir Christopher Wren, Paternoster Row. City pub with entertainment some nights by the talented "Barrow Poets".

Windsor Castle, 309 Harrow Rd., W.9. Music hall flavour.

Theatrical

Nag's Head, James St., Covent Garden, W.C.2. Next to the Opera House; food at the bar or restaurant upstairs. Ballerinas, stage hands.

The Opera, Catherine St., W.C.2. Bar food, actors, dancers.

The Salisbury, St. Martin's Lane. W.C.2. Fine Victoriana, more actors, good cold food.

Young Smart Set

Antelope, Eaton Terrace, S.W.1. Good food, too.

Grenadier, Wilton Row, S.W.1.
Shepherds Tavern, Hertford St., W.1. (A royal sedan-chair is the phone booth.)

Press

Falstaff, Fleet St., E.C.4.
El Vino, Fleet St., E.C.4. Wine and spirits, sandwiches, press chat.
Printer's Devil, Fetter Lane, E.C.4.

Country and River

The Doves, Upper Mall, Hammersmith, W.6. Old and oak-beamy, with Thames views painted by Turner and Brangwyn.
Flask, Flask Walk, Hampstead.
The Spaniards, Spaniards Row, Hampstead Heath, N.W.3.
Star Tavern. St. John's Wood Terrace, N.W.8.

Historical

Anchor, Bankside, S.E.1. Shakespeare drank in the original, destroyed in the Great Fire. Also excellent restaurant. 7 different bars!
Angel. Rotherhithe St., S.E.16. Overlooks the river. Pepys liked this one.
Cheshire Cheese, Crutched Friars, E.C.3.
Cock Tavern, Fleet St., E.C.4. Dickens and Thackeray liked this one.
George Inn, Borough High St., S.E.1. Only galleried inn, where Shakespeare's plays are still performed in summer.
Mayflower, Rotherhithe St., S.E.16. Where the Pilgrims allegedly stepped on to the boat for Holland; a new pub on site of an old one, blitzed during the war. (Passenger manifest on the walls.)
The Mitre, Ely Place, E.C.1. On the site of palace of the bishop of Ely.
Ye Olde Cheshire Cheese, Fleet St., E.C.4. Dr. Johnson's favourite. Steak-and-Kidney Pudding a specialty here.

Strictly for the Tourist, but Fun

Dirty Dick's, Bishopsgate, E.C.2. Filled with cobwebs and mummified cats, to illustrate an old, sad legend.
Gilbert and Sullivan, John Adams St., W.C.2. Models of G & S stage settings, and music by you-know-whom.
Prospect of Whitby, Wapping Wall, E.1. Right on the riverside and named after an old sailing ship. The sandwich was said to have been invented here, by the Earl of Sandwich; Pepys and Whistler were habitués. But today, it is jammed with tourists.
Sherlock Holmes, Northumberland St., W.C.2. Replica of Baker St. rooms, models, etc.. Very pleasant.

Pubs of Character

Chelsea Potter. King's Road, Chelsea S.W.3. Rub shoulders with the Chelsea trendies!
George and Vulture, Castle Court, Cornhill E.C.3. Famous City pub and chophouse. Dickens would still feel at home here. Closed weekends.
Victoria, Strathearn Place, W.2. Authentic Victoriana plus good pub fare.
York Minster. Dean Street, W.1. Soho rendezvous for homesick Frenchmen.

Note: Every Londoner has his local. Ask and be directed to out-of-the-way pubs, where, if you initiate the conversation, you *may* find warm, friendly and alarmingly intense conversation. If you don't speak first, no one else is likely to!

SHOPPING IN LONDON

The Hallmark is Quality and Style

Shopping is exciting in London. Apart from the realistic touch of certain concessions for visitors from overseas (see *Purchase Tax*, below) the new spirit abroad in the 1960's has been reflected in the addition of many brilliant and adventurous new young shops to the hard core of elegant and well-established traditional houses. There is little unobtainable in London from anywhere in the world, and nothing unobtainable that is produced within the British Isles.

The serious shopper will call first of all at the *Design Centre* at 28 Haymarket, S.W.1. Here there is a constantly changing exhibition of consumer goods that have reached a high standard of design—furniture, textiles, glass, cutlery and pottery, just to mention a few things. Exhibitions of British products can also be found at the *Tea Centre* in Lower Regent Street from time to time.

The London street without at least one interesting shop (if only a second-hand bookstore) is rare, but the main shopping areas are concentrated westwards. Oxford Street, Regent Street, Bond Street and Piccadilly bind an area of high-class, and often exclusive, shops. Further west, there are Kensington,

SHOPPING IN LONDON

Knightsbridge, Brompton Road, Beauchamp Place and Sloane Street. Chelsea has its good shops, too.

Prices vary from area to area and obviously, the more exclusive the area, the higher the price. A common article bought in Bond Street is likely to be more expensive than the same article bought in another part of London. This does not apply to exclusive goods, of course, which set their own price wherever they are sold.

Many shops display signs that say "By Appointment". This means that they supply goods to a royal household; it is the highest honour a British shopkeeper can achieve. The signs usually specify to whom they are attached: "By Appointment to Her Majesty the Queen", or to another member of the royal family, who has approved of their goods and service. This means of course, that their standards of quality and service are totally reliable, as far as the casual shopper is concerned.

Purchase Tax

The purchase tax on goods in England—particularly cameras—is sometimes most alarming. The visitor from overseas, however, has the advantage of being exempted from paying it. This represents a considerable saving.

Some large stores can deliver goods free of tax direct to an overseas address. Other shops participate in a personal export scheme that enables purchases to be sent tax-free directly to the plane or boat.

The chief formality required is presentation of your passport, but regulations vary, so always talk first to the manager of the shop if it is fairly small, or go direct to the information section of larger stores. The goods must usually be delivered to the port or airport for shipment as accompanied or unaccompanied passengers' baggage, or else they must be exported as freight or by post.

The Commissioners of Customs and Excise are most helpful, and publish a special leaflet explaining the complete system, obtainable from them (call in person or write) at *King's Beam House,* Mark Lane, London E.C.3.

Department Stores

The most famous department store in London—if not in the world—is *Harrods,* in Knightsbridge. The vast store began as a simple grocery shop in 1849, and just expanded. Harrods can supply anything, it is said, and anything bought there has the natural cachet of being the best.

Then there is *Fortnum & Mason,* on Piccadilly, again, a very old-established firm which began as a grocery store. Today the accent is still on groceries, with its soft-carpeted food hall staffed by immaculate gentlemen in morning suits (and floor-walkers in 18th-century robes!). There is a feeling of ease and luxury, and also of gluttony barely kept at bay by the enticing array of food. Look for the best English goods—jam, marmalade, honey, jars of cheese.

On a more popular level, and with a much wider price range, is *Selfridges*, in Oxford Street, another very famous store. All types of goods are found here, and there is a useful food hall at the back. *Barker's* has similar influence in the Kensington area, with *Derry & Toms* (famous for its amazing roof garden) nearby. The *Army and Navy Stores* in Victoria Street has an odd name. This is because it originally catered specifically for the needs of the British serviceman and his family. The range is much wider now and it has a particularly reputable wine and spirits department.

Every major area has its department store. *Harvey Nichols* in Knightsbridge has a good fashion section; *Peter Jones* in Sloane Square also has clothing, but is perhaps more sought after for household equipment, furniture and home decoration. *John Lewis,* in Oxford Street, has a good domestic section as well as a wide selection of dress materials. *Liberty* in Regent Street has an international reputation for printed silks, and their gift section always produces the unexpected—a most gracious shop. *Marshall and Snelgrove, Dickens and Jones* and *Debenham and Freebody* make their strongest appeal to women.

Swan and Edgar, in Piccadilly Circus, is a conveniently central meeting spot and a varied store; *Peter Robinson* have just revamped their Oxford Circus store, using the most up-to-date methods of display (they have another branch in the Strand); and *D. H. Evans* is notable for gloves and clothing.

Fashion

Since the leaders of world fashion started the habit of much-publicized diving into obscure boutiques or chain stores for some of their clothes, the world of high fashion has inevitably become slightly more ramified. But *haute couture* remains, and its London stronghold is the Mayfair district where that expert in tailoring, *Michael,* and *Norman Hartnell,* dressmaker to the Queen, have their salons. Others of importance include *Hardy Amies, Lachasse, Digby Morton,* and *Clive.* (The *House of Worth* reopened in 1968, but deals in *avant-garde,* not *haute couture.*)

British *haute couture* is noted for something called "understated elegance"—suits, coats and dresses of utmost simplicity, only achieved by perfect tailoring in superb materials. The clothes made by the great fashion houses are extremely expensive and demand time and trouble with parades and fittings. But good model clothes are now stocked in most quality department stores like *Debenhams* (Valentino copies) and *Fortnum and Mason* (Ungaro models). *Lachasse* retains its high reputation for tailored suits and beautiful evening dresses.

Ready-made clothes from the top stores are generally excellent.

SHOPPING IN LONDON

Harrods (Courreges copies) and *Harvey Nichols* have superb dress departments. In the Bond Street and Knightsbridge neighbourhoods, there are many exclusive smaller dress shops worth investigation.

Jaeger, in Regent Street, made their reputation with wool and still hold pre-eminence with their camelhair coats and inexpensive jersey dresses. Like many other established houses, Jaeger have made massive strides towards attracting the younger woman with beautifully-cut and -designed dresses and suits. *Burberry* and *Aquascutum* remain the places for rainwear. *N. Peal,* at the corner of Burlington Arcade, is an important shop for cashmere items and woollen fabrics. Always look for Harris and Shetland tweeds. *Lilleywhites* and *Wetheralls* are specialists in sports wear.

Many people prefer to buy material by the length and take it home to be made up (fabrics also make a superb present). The fabric counters of the big stores have good selections. *Gasmey,* 33 Brook Street, W.1, has possibly the widest selection, from delicate chiffons to tough tweeds, and *John G. Hardy,* 4 New Burlington Street, W.1, offers a complete display of traditional British tweeds, woollens and worsteds.

A wide selection can also be seen at several shops in Bond Street: *Hunt and Winterbottom* have a wide range of fabrics from tweed made in the north of Scotland to suitings made in their own mills in western England. *Racson, Ltd.,* in Jermyn Street, also feature tweeds and knitwear. *Scott Adie* in Clifford Street and the *Scotch House* in Knightsbridge will supply authentic Scottish tartans and clothes. For something quite different, try the Welsh tweeds and other materials from *Welsh Wool Shop,* Whitehorse St., off Shepherd's Market.

There are many London tailors and dressmakers who will be delighted to make up customers' materials to their own designs, or to make alternative suggestions and sketches. The advertisements in London's leading fashion magazines, *Vogue* and *Queen,* or an information bureau can usually help in this direction. An inquiry from an English friend can frequently elicit the address of the little women round the corner who can produce the equivalent of a model dress at far from model price.

Younger English women are increasingly reluctant to wear hats, but in town, hats are always correct, and frequently *de rigueur,* as at weddings, garden parties and all events that smack of slight formality. French models can be found in many of the larger stores and also in small exclusive milliners. But London designers can compete very well—Otto Lucas, Vernier, James Wedge and Aage Thaarup are names to look for in London.

Department stores have model and inexpensive departments for hats; go to *Harrods, Ltd., Debenham & Freebody,* and *Liberty.* For exclusivity, try *Rudolf.* 56 Grosvenor Street; *Reed Crawford,* Studio Place, Kinnerton Street; *Vernier,* 82 George Street and *Simone Mirman,* 9 Chesham Place.

Should you wish to hire clothes for a special occasion, go to *Moss Bros.,* in Covent Garden. Dress clothes for men are their specialty, but women are catered for, too. A Hartnell gown can be hired for $37, a mink cape for $25.

Lingerie, Furs and Jewellery

Rigby and Peller, in South Molton Street, hold the Royal Warrant for corsets, and have a long, well-established reputation. So has *Illa Knina*, at 30 Bruton Street, an excellent *corsetière* with original ideas, colours and materials. *Selfridges, Harrods* and *D. H. Evans* keep a good selection of well-known makes. *Lydia Moss, Honore*, in South Audley Street, and *Elizabeth Arden,* in Old Bond Street, have delicate hand-made lingerie, and most department stores have exquisite stocks ranging from fine silk to the sort of woollies required in draughty country houses.

Fur of some sort—gloves, boots, coats, stoles—is recommended in the English climate, and a necessity in the winter. The best makes of fur-lined boots are those by *Morlands* of Glastonbury, found at most of the bigger shoe shops. For fur coats, *Bradleys* keep their established reputation, and the *National Fur Company* offers a wide selection. Also try *S. London* in Sloane Street, *Calman Links* in Margaret Street and *Maxwell Croft*, in New Bond Street.

Most of the great names in world jewellery can be found in London. In Bond Street, there are *Cartier, Boucheron, Benson and Drayson. Garrard & Co.* are in Regent Street; *Kickman and Newman* in Hatton Garden, E.C. 1, and *Asprey* in Bond Street; all are leading shops in this field. With a little money and time, it is worth visiting *John Donald's* shop at 120 Cheapside in the City. He is a young designer and craftsman who will produce something elegant, modern and original, either from your own stones or from his own large stock. His shop is in the exact area where the jewellers were established in medieval times. Another name to remember in the field of modern jewellery is *Andrew Grima*, whose work is sold all over the world.

The great names in cosmetics—like *Elizabeth Arden* and *Helena Rubenstein*—are in the West End, as is *Carita*. And the women whose hair looks smartest go to *Rene, Vidal Sassoon*, the *House of Leonard* in Grosvenor Square and to *Carita. Raymond, Steiner* and *Richard Henry* retain their eminence as well. For English scents, try *Yardley*, in Bond Street.

The only amber shop in the world is *Sac Frères*, Old Bond Street, a 300-year-old business (125 of those in England).

Leather Goods and Accessories

Leatherwork has been a British specialty for centuries and London still offers the best, as well as the unusual and adventurous. Starting feet first, one old-established, mainly theatrical firm that has acquired a sudden wider fame in the 1960's is *Anello and Davide* in Drury Lane. They supply boots and shoes for motion pictures and stage productions. In 1965, they were suddenly discovered by the younger generation, who wanted high boots (partly Beatle-inspired, partly Spanish) and queues formed every Saturday outside the shop. They will make boots to any requirement, beautifully.

Most of the leading shoe shops are clustered around the Bond Street area, with *Pinet, Raynes, Delmans* and the *London Shoe Company*. The

SHOPPING IN LONDON

main shop of *Bally* is found in New Bond Street; they have several other branches including a boutique in the King's Road, S.W.3. All the better makes of shoe come in American sizes, and *Elliotts* specialize in narrow fittings. *Charles Jourdan* in Old Bond Street attracts a discriminating clientele.

Shoes for all occasions, and at popular prices, are found at the big stores of *Dolcis, Saxone* and *Lilley & Skinner*—all of whom have their main branches in Oxford Street.

Raynes and *Delmans* also sell handbags to match some of their shoes. Leather goods are excellent, too, at *Fortnums, Finnigans* and *Aspreys*. The currently "in" shop for super, but expensive, handbags and shoes is called *Medway Bagagerie*, at 77 Knightsbridge, S.W. 1. *Lederer* and *John Pound* in Regent Street show good leatherwork and *Revelation* in Piccadilly have a superb range of all sorts of luggage and accessories. Also good for all kinds of luxurious accessories are *Gucci, Hermes* and *Loewe's*, the latter two in Jermyn Street, the former in Old Bond Street.

Boutiques

Perhaps the most significant change in London's shopping scene during the last five years has been the mushrooming of *boutiques*. They are little shops, gay and informal, usually run by the proprietors themselves, and selling exclusive clothes and accessories. Naturally, their appeal is directed towards the young and the goods offered by some are extraordinarily way-out. It is quite easy for a girl or young man to set up a boutique, and even easier for it to fail and disappear. A number, however, have established themselves as an integral part of the fashion scene. They should be seen, and older women need not be put off by the youthful flavour of these shops as many of the accessories—from shoes to hats—have an appeal that has nothing to do with age groups.

At the last count, there were well over 100 boutiques in full operation: they have strange names, such as *The Gas Banana, Granny Takes a Trip* and *The Carrot on Wheels*. The common denominator is that the clothes are genuinely inexpensive, partly due to the fact that the young fashion scene changes rapidly and the clothes are not really expected to last for very long. Instead, one gets something bright, interesting and, often, original.

Leader in the field was *Mary Quant,* who opened *Bazaar* in King's Road, Chelsea (since closed), in 1955. Now her shop is at 46 Brompton Road, S.W.3. Mary Quant prefers to call her shops "minature fashion stores", and since her name has a world-wide fame, her contribution really transcends the term "boutique". The range of clothes and accessories seems limitless, the shops are comfortable (music in the background—a frequent concomitant of boutique shopping), and dresses start around the £5 mark. **Stop press.** All Quant shops now closed.

One of the best boutiques is called *Biba,* and is at 19-21 Kensington Church Street, W.8. Proprietress is the striking Barbara Hulanicki, once a model and a fashion artist. Her clothes are instantly recognizable for their style and cut; the shop has a modish Victorian feeling with *art nouveau* designs on the windows, polished furniture inside. Stock includes wigs and feather boas. Service is from ravishingly beautiful girls in the ultimate in mini-skirts. Prices are extremely low, with dresses from around 3 gns. ($7.56) and trouser suits from about £8 ($19.20). Almost next door is another trendy boutique called *Bus Stop*. Prices again unbelievably low.

There are many boutiques for men (see *Men's Clothing*) and for children (see *Children's Clothing*), and a number specializing in second-hand clothes, whose value to the serious shopper is low, but to the sightseer quite high. Of the many others, worth looking out for are *Countdown* and *Top Gear* (135a-137 King's Road, S.W.3), run by hatter James Wedge and model Pat Booth; *Tony Armstrong* (109 Walton Street, S.W.3), who is a leading designer of both fabrics and clothes; *Bally Boutique* (132 King's Road, S.W.3); *Annacat & Co.* (23 Pelham Street, S.W.7), which is a little more pricey than the rest; and *Victoria & Albert* (28-29 Victoria Grove, off Gloucester Road, W.8), which is half for boys and half for girls.

Finally, *Harrods*, the greatest of London's stores, opened a boutique, *The Way In*, in 1967. Discothèque decor, music in the background (classics and pops), youthful staff and the widest range of merchandise: clothes for boys and girls, records, books, greeting cards. (Closed Mondays).

Men's Clothing

The hard core of quality tailoring remains under the all-embracing banner of Savile Row, for generations synonymous with all that is best in British cloth, cut and style. Not perhaps in the Row itself, but in the immediate neighbourhood, are the aristocrats of tailoring—catering for aristocrats, publicity-shy, and immensely civilized. *Henry Poole & Company* (10 Cork Street) take on new customers only by recommendation; *H. Huntsman and Sons* (11 Savile Row) are alleged to be the most expensive tailors in London; *Hawes and Curtis* (43 Dover Street) numbers the Duke of Edinburgh among their customers; *Hawkes* (1 Savile Row) first opened in 1771 and dresses many public figures, as does *Kilgour, French and Stanbury* (33a Dover Street). For men looking for something that combines elements of tradition with something of the new dandyism, *Blades* (25 Dover Street) has created a special place. Prices are high, but the styles and materials (corduroy and velvet included) are superb. Famous mobile tailor is *Douglas Hayward*, who travels among the sharpest men in his Bentley ('phone FUL 6179). In the same exclusive category, and slightly more expensive, is *"Mr. Terry"* (44a High St., Harrow-on-Hill, tel. 864-1589), who comes to you and creates suits and slacks exactly the way you want them. The Beatles' tailor is *Dougie Millings* (41 Great Putney Street), who is great on light-weights.

This new awareness in clothes has hit London males hard, and most of the leading, established men's stores discovered they had to keep in line: most have responded by opening genuine boutiques (i.e., shops within a shop). The results have been spectacular. *Simpsons* in Piccadilly, in addition to the restrained elegance of their clothes and fine sportswear, have a *Trends* department, featuring superb jackets, shirts and interesting accessories; *Moss Brothers* in Covent Garden have their *One Up* shop (on the first floor), offering similarly modish clothes. Moss

Brothers, incidentally, specializes in immaculate sporting clothes, and from here can be hired the correct clothes for any occasion you care to imagine, bearing in mind the Englishman's subtle deviations in dress between, say, a country wedding and Ascot, a Royal Garden party and a dance.

Austin Reed, in Regent Street, has its *Cue* shop within the store (which already caters for every possible requirement, including haircutting); it is full of wild ties and sweet shirts. *Aquascutum* has its trendy department called *Club 92,* and *Jaeger,* in Regent Street, has refined its youthful man's department to answer the need for good ready-to-wear suits as well as bathing trunks, ties and interesting shirts. The *John Michael* chain of shops (18 Savile Row) offers excellent clothes for the smart younger man as well as an amazing range of super accessories and even magnificent toys, such as a massively elegant executive's yo-yo in polished wood. All the big department stores have reliable men's tailoring departments—*Harrods, Fortnum & Mason* and *Selfridges* among them.

The sporting man will go to *Moss Brothers* or *Simpson's* to be rigged, or perhaps to *E. Tautz and Sons* (16 Stratton Street), most famous for riding breeches and golf clothes. He may go to *Lillywhites* (Piccadilly Circus) for his gear; there's everything from aqualungs to golf bags. For shoes and riding boots, the experts are *Peals* in Oxford Street and *Lobbs* in St. James's. The world's leading makers of equipment for hunting, shooting and fishing are to be found in London. *Swaine Adeney Brigg and Sons, Ltd.* (185 Piccadilly) are best for saddlery, whips and leatherwork of all kinds (umbrellas, too); *James Purdey & Sons* (57 South Audley Street) are the leading gunsmiths and *Hardy Brothers* (61 Pall Mall) make everything for the fisherman.

Having bought his umbrella from *Swaine Adeney,* his shoes from *Peals,* the complete city man will look for a hat, and go at once to *James Lock & Co.* (6 St. James's Street), with its elegantly Dickensian front and atmosphere of impeccable tradition. London's best haberdasher is generally agreed to be *Turnbull and Asser* (71 Jermyn Street, St. James's). They supplied Sir Winston Churchill with ties and dressing gowns, and their shirts, socks and silk handkerchiefs are seen on quite the best-dressed males around town. This shop's modern outlook has been attributed to *Michael Fish,* who was a stylist there, and who has now opened his own shop, selling magnificent custom-tailored shirts. More superb haberdashery at *Hilditch and Key* (Jermyn Street) and *Budd Ltd.* (Piccadilly Arcade). Worth looking in at is *Douglas Hayward's* shop at 95 Mount Street, which is very grand, with some lovely Italian shirts and ties. It is no myth about the vagaries of the English weather so to cover all, a raincoat from *Burberrys* (Haymarket) is recommended.

Carnaby Street should be mentioned, no doubt, but more as a sight to see than as a place to actually shop. Clothes here have a built-in obsolescence and have been so copied that their originality has tended to be lost. However, narrow girls like to buy trousers here and narrow men could find some natty knockabout slacks as well. Some alarming psychedelic ties may catch the eye. Many items are cheap—most appear to be cheaply-made.

> *Here's a tip for the male traveler who left his dinner jacket at home to help conform with the baggage allowance:* Moss Brothers *of London will rent you at reasonable cost anything from a complete outfit for the Ascot Races to immaculate evening dress for a society ball. Everything correct to the last detail. A godsend in case of an unexpected invitation.*

Children's Clothing and Toys

Children are still rather formally dressed in England, largely due to the universal insistence by schools of the adoption of a socially-levelling uniform. But the last five years or so has seen a much more broad-minded approach to the dressing of children, particularly for leisure activity and especially among the tiny tots. New designers tend to take the intelligent approach that since little girls have no waists, why pretend they have? The result has been a new freedom, a more decisive use of color (the blue for a boy, pink for a girl, school of thinking is dying slowly), and an attempt to lower prices. Consequently, just like the young adults, the children have their *boutiques* as well. There is *Colts* (31 South End Road, Hampstead, N.W.3), which caters solely for boys with casual wear from Sweden, Austria and America; *Pelisse* (240 Brompton Road, S.W.3), which is for girls from 7 to 15, and *Small Wonder* (296 King's Road, S.W.3).

As the boy grows up, he will most likely be dressed by one of the big department stores, which have remarkably efficient children's departments. *Harrods* of Knightsbridge (which crops up here in every section devoted to shopping), *The Scotch House* (also in Knightsbridge), *Liberty* in Regent Street, *Barkers* in Kensington and *Debenham and Freebody* all have famous customers and dress children impeccably. *Rowes* in Bond Street is an old-established firm, makes short trousers and shirts for little boys, also produces a miniature sailor suit for party-going. *Billings and Edmonds* (4 Princes Street, W.1) specialize in made-to-measure clothes for schoolboys.

London's most famous toyshop is *Hamley's*, in Regent Street, several floors of fascination for children and—naturally enough—adults. For the more intellectually minded, there is *Galts*, in New Marlborough Street (which runs out of Carnaby Street behind *Liberty's*), which specializes in elegantly simple, functional toys such as plain, polished building blocks, educational toys and games. *Hamley's* has the color, noise and excitement of remembered childhood; *Galts* is cool and sharp.

One further toy shop must be included: *Pollock's Toy Museum*, in Scala Street, W.1. It has a tiny rather Victorian front, and inside, it is a wonderland of penny black and tuppence coloured. Specialty is cut-out models of Regency and Victorian theatres, ranging from inexpensive, small ones to big, elaborate ones, with lighting systems and lots of scenery. You can buy complete scenarios for traditional pantomime, and cut-out characters that slide on to the stage on wires. Lots of other

One of England's greatest charms lies in the contrast between its tranquil countryside and its dynamic urban conglomoration. Time stands still in the lovely village of Castle Combe, Wiltshire, while even London's busy Regent Street can settle down to a between-rush-hours calm.

Love of sports, love of pageantry: these are two components of the British soul. The royal game of golf spread from the land of its birth to the four corners of the world, and from the four corners thousands come each year to see such pageants as the Scots Guards parading at Windsor Castle.

things as well, 19th-century and modern. It should be possible to get a present here for anyone with style and imagination.

For the Connoisseur

Sotheby's and *Christie's* are the famous auction rooms; there is no need to get involved with a sale, but the showrooms provide hours of pleasing study and often afford opportunities of seeing rare objects as they move from one private collection to another via the hammer.

Spinks in St. James's is one of London's most outstanding antique shops—they have a particularly superb Japanese collection. To look at the massed displays of antique silver, drop in at the *Silver Vaults* in Chancery Lane. There are 70 vaults in all, containing something like $7 million's worth of silver treasures, making this the world's richest street market. Silver is also gleaming at *Tessier's*, New Bond Street.

Charing Cross Road is the centre of the London book trade; on both sides of the street there are many bookshops selling all kinds of publications, from old volumes to the most recent issues. Many have second-hand shelves. *Foyles*, in Charing Cross Road, is a many-floored shop stocking virtually everything a reader could require, including music. *Her Majesty's Stationery Office* (High Holborn and also in Oxford Street) publishes for the British Government and official bodies like museums. There is an amazing variety of subject matter, of course, from pamphlets to big volumes. In the British Museum area, look at *Dillon's* (Malet Street), which caters for university students; also *Hamilton Blumer*, 109 Southampton Row, where good London prints can be obtained as well as fine bindings and antiquarian books. *Hatchards* in Piccadilly is a famous, old-established store with an elegant facade and an air of quiet charm inside. A fine rare-book binding department upstairs.

Not everyone wants to go home loaded down with portraits of the Queen, Dickensian toby jugs and washable plastic street signs ("Carnaby Street," "Piccadilly," etc.). For the collector of rare things, London has a wide choice of connoisseurs' shops to satisfy the most exacting tastes. Collectors of military and marine paintings and ship models should try the *Parker Gallery*, 2 Albemarle Street. For English sporting prints and watercolors of birds, try the *Tryon Gallery*, 41 Dover Street. If a suit of genuine old armor appeals to you, try *Peter Dale*, 12 Royal Opera Arcade. Antique cufflinks and earrings are found at *The Button Queen*, 5 Marlborough Court, while antique clocks and barometers are sold by *Aubrey Brocklehurst*, 124 Cromwell Road. Or how about some Victorian greeting cards from *John Hall Antique Prints*, 17 Harrington Road, or 18th-century glass paperweights from *Alan Tillman Antiques*, 469 Fulham Road? For these and a hundred other shops, a very useful booklet is *A Connoisseur's Guide*, available free from Richard Gainsborough Periodicals, 8 Wyndham Place, London W.1.

If it's the unusual you're looking for, you could buy old books at many shops around the British Museum or at *Maggs Brothers*, Berkeley Square; blazer badges at *Viceroy*, 118 Euston Road; skeletons at *Educational and Scientific Plastics*, Holmethorpe Avenue, Redhill, Surrey; ceremonial swords at *Wilkinson Sword*, 16 Pall Mall; snuff boxes at *Smith's Snuff Shop*, 74 Charing Cross Road; antique and unusual pipes at *Inderwick*, 45 Carnaby Street; very British-gentleman umbrellas at *James Smith & Sons*, 53 New Oxford Street; china door handles at *Charles Harden*, 9b New Cavendish Street; horse brasses at the *Curio Shop* in Shepherd Market (near the Hilton Hotel); toy soldiers at *Hummel's* in Burlington Arcade; and chess sets at *Mackett Beeson*, 22 Lansdowne Row.

Fabergé is the specialty of *Wartski*, 138 Regent Street, W.1, arms and armour of *P. C. German*, 125 Edgware Road, W.2. Pewter specialists include the two *Casimir* shops at 142 and 194 Brompton Road, S.W.3. Victoriana can be had at *Bayly's Galleries*, Princes Arcade, Piccadilly, W.1.

Markets

Antique Hypermarket 26-40 Kensington High Street, W.8. Shop front decorated with 8 ft. high Caryatides. Inside are more than 100 top antique dealers' stalls, with over a million pounds' worth of treasures for sale.

Antique Supermarket, Barrett St., W.1. Variety of reasonably-priced items. Near Selfridges.

Billingsgate, Lower Thames St., E.C.3. This is the world's most colourful fish market and it has been thriving since the 17th century. Quaint caps of the porters are modelled after Henry V's archers who fought at Agincourt. Open daily, 4 a.m. and 7 a.m.

Camden Passage, Islington (Tube or buses 19, 30, 73 to "The Angel"). Open-air antique market, Saturdays. Fascinating antique shops in Camden Passage and Pierrepont Arcade, particularly for silverware.

Chelsea Antique Market, 253 Kings Rd., S.W.3. A collection of stalls, with wide range of prices.

Covent Garden, W.C.2. Opposite Opera House. Fruit, flowers, and vegetables on Tuesdays, Thursdays, and Saturdays from 6 a.m. to 8 a.m.

Petticoat Lane, in Middlesex Street, E.1. Open on Sunday mornings only, for pets, clothes, fabrics and curios of all descriptions. (Watch your wallets!)

Portobello Market, Portobello Rd., W.11. (Take 52 bus or tube to Ladbroke Grove.) Best day is Saturday, from 9 a.m. to 6 p.m. for all kinds of curios, silverware, antiques, etc. Several dealers with shops in other parts of London have booths here.

Smithfield, E.C.1. London's main meat market and one of the biggest in the world. Best days are Mondays and Thursdays.

Miscellany

It is possible to buy practically anything from any part of the world in London and while the visitor is probably looking for something with a specifically British flavor, it is worth while noting some of the more interesting foreign shops.

There is, for example, *Mexicana* (89 Lower Sloane Street, S.W.1), with peasant shifts and shirts, also lovely paper flowers and colorful toys. At the *Venetian Glass Galleries* (5 William Street, S.W.1), there is everything you can find around the Piazza San Marco, in beautiful glass.

Mitsukiku (73a Lower Sloane Street, S.W.1) is a Japanese shop (name means "three chrysanthemums") with wooden clogs (geta), kimonos, books on *karate,* delicate wind chimes.

The *Russian Shop* (278 High Holborn), is a treasure house of exotic items from the Soviet Union. There is an array of fine amber jewelery, handicrafts in woods, bone and stone, ceramics, exquisite hand-painted boxes, dolls and puppets galore, wooden toys, and perfumes from the gardens of Kiev and Samarkand. In addition there are long playing records, vodkas, foods and wines from Georgia and a host of original gifts.

The *Israeli Shop* (New Oxford Street eastwards from Tottenham Court Road) has national products and some arresting chess sets.

Latest unbelievable addition to London's galaxy of shops is *Glints* (South Moulton Street, just off Oxford Street near Selfridge's), a beauty shop for men. Everything from after-shave lotion to false eye-lashes!

Getting it Home

U.S.-bound air travelers who find their luggage disastrously overweight can arrange to have it picked up and shipped to anywhere in the U.S. and Canada (cars picked up anywhere in the British Isles, cleaned to meet U.S. Agriculture inspection, etc., and delivered to any place in the U.S.) with: *Robert Fisher (Shipping) Ltd.,* 32 Lexington Street, W.1. (REG 6901).

Take Britain Home

One last thought: if souvenirs and memories and photographs are not reminders enough of your pleasant stay in Britain, you can now do more than that. *Wissel Ltd.,* of 18 Seymour Street, London, has come up with the ingenious idea of selling Americans plots of land in southern England. Each plot is one square foot in area and you have rights of way to it across the 43,559 other one-foot plots owned by others. You can stand on your plot (only just), stiff as a guardsman, all day if you wish—or until you faint. An official certificate of ownership is included in the purchase price of $3.60 (£1 10s).

EXPLORING LONDON

Yesterday's Charm and Today's Clever Chaos

Whether for good or bad (opinions are divided), Piccadilly Circus is generally regarded as the centre of London and the hub of the universe (though Boston also lays claim to the latter title). If you stand here long enough, it is said, you will meet everyone you know. The same, no doubt, applies to Times Square and the Piazza San Marco. Raffish, noisy, crowded (sometimes with very dubious-looking characters), the circus attracts everyone. On Boat Race Night, New Year's Eve, on the evenings of big football matches, national events and Bonfire Night, here is where the crowds are, singing, rioting, having fun. The Angel of Christian Charity, designed in 1893 and known erroneously as Eros (the God of Love), is then boarded up, and the fountains switched off, to prevent climbing to the top of this statue, a favourite pastime.

On the corner of Piccadilly in 1612, there was a shop owned by Robert Baker, a tailor, selling pickadills or lace collars. These collars gave their name to the now famous thoroughfare. Residences, palaces, and villas that used to grace streets and avenues near Piccadilly and Pall Mall have mostly disappeared.

Select whatever area of Central London you want to explore, go to Piccadilly Circus, there face in the appropriate direction and start. To the north runs Regent Street, curving up one side of Mayfair and the fine shops. To the south is Lower Regent Street, leading towards Whitehall, the parks and the palaces. To the east are Shaftesbury Avenue and Coventry Street, for theatres and Soho; to the west is Piccadilly itself, heading off for Hyde Park and Knightsbridge.

St. James's

Looking south from Piccadilly Circus, down the wide stretch of Lower Regent Street, you will see the Duke of York on his column, and beyond, the towers and spires of Whitehall. The area bounded on the north by Piccadilly, on the east by Lower Regent Street, on the south by The Mall and on the west by St. James's Street, is known as St. James's. It is one of the very few areas of London whose plan has barely changed from the time it was laid out in the late 17th century—though visually, it has altered a lot.

Pall Mall has a dignity and elegance brought about by the presence of many important clubs; it ends by St. James's Palace, which many consider ugly, being squat and made of brick. It has a delightful Tudor gatehouse, however, facing up St. James's Street, which itself emerges on Piccadilly near the great, newly-cleaned *Ritz* hotel. On St. James's Street are Boodles Club—a graceful 18th-century house—and next to it the *Economist* building (built by Alison and Peter Smithson in 1964), creating quite a reactionary stir with its trio of hexagonal towers, spaced out on a public court. Opposite is the *Tourist Information Centre* of the British Travel Association. Further along, just before Piccadilly, are White's Club on the right and the Devonshire and Naval and Military Club on the left.

St. James's is an essentially masculine area; Jermyn Street cuts across, parallel to Piccadilly, and contains splendid shops, many for men's clothing and accessories, and the sole "men-only" Turkish Baths in central London. There is little enough to attract the explorer's particular attention here, but the area is historically interesting in a general way and exudes a slightly pompous elegance.

St. James's fringes Green Park, while Piccadilly forms another side of this triangular piece of greenery. Green Park is just what it says—a park, and very green; in the summer it is peaceful and shady; in the winter the bare trees make a striking frame for the towers of Westminster and Victoria. St. James's Park, across The Mall, has a lake, wild birds and gardens, and is much prettier than Green Park.

A triumphal way from Buckingham Palace to Trafalgar Square is The Mall, where commercial vehicles are not allowed nor are cabs permitted to pick up fares (as in all the royal parks). It is the site of several great houses occupied by various members of the Royal Family. The most important of these is Clarence House, occupied by the Queen Mother on Stable Yard Road. At the eastern end of The Mall is Carlton House Terrace, a fine row of Georgian houses with colonnades, now mostly offices. On summer Sundays between 8 a.m. and 8 p.m. all traffic is banned from the Mall, and for 12 blissful hours it is given over entirely to strolling sightseers. (The practice also extends to Constitution Hill and the area before the palace.)

Buckingham Palace itself is so fixed as a symbol in England that one rarely pauses to think how dull it is. (It won't be dull trying to cross the street to see it, however; the authorities refuse to put traffic signals or marked crosswalks in front of the palace as they don't want to "spoil the beauty of the place"—so lots of luck en route!) The palace was built in the 18th century for the Duke of Buckingham, who sold it to George II for £21,000. Initially it stood on three sides of a courtyard, the east-facing end open to St. James's Park. The heavy façade of the "east front", which the tourist sees through the iron fence, was added later (the present one in 1912) and is considered less pleasing than the "west front", which the public cannot see. The interior and the gardens are never open to the public, though the Queen's Gallery (adjoining the palace on its south side) is, and regular exhibitions drawn from the vast and spectacular royal collections are on display. The royal standard flying above the "east front" indicates that the Queen is in residence. The Changing of the Guard is one of London's most important tourist attractions. Since a guardsman had an unfortunate altercation with an importunate tourist a few years ago, the sentries have been moved inside the palace railings.

On the site where Buckingham Palace stands there once stretched a mulberry garden—planted at the time when James I wanted to encourage the making of silk in England.

The large monument outside the palace is the Queen Victoria Memorial, an epic recapitulation of Victorian ideals, with Motherhood, Truth, Justice, Peace and Progress all represented, *inter alia*. From the palace, a street named Constitution Hill leads alongside Green Park, back to Hyde Park Corner.

Cross St. James's Park, entering from The Mall, pausing on the bridge across the lake to look at the unexpected and vaguely oriental profile of Whitehall through the trees. Leave the park on Birdcage Walk, which leads directly into Parliament Square, with the Houses of Parliament and Westminster Abbey. To the left, Whitehall leads up to Trafalgar Square, to the right, Millbank leads south towards the Tate Gallery and Chelsea.

The Houses of Parliament

Seen across Parliament Square, the Houses of Parliament seem at first an incoherent complex of elaborate spires, towers and crenellations. Many people are surprised to discover that they were built only just over a century ago, between 1840 and 1860. Most of the older building was razed in 1834 and the designer of the New Palace of Westminster, Sir Charles Barry, selected the richly-decorated Perpendicular style, probably in order to harmonize with Henry VII's chapel opposite. Seen from across the river, it is clear that the Houses of Parliament are basically planned with classical simplicity, the towers and roofs just giving an impression of confusion from some viewing angles.

Westminster was the first major settlement outside the City of London; Roman remains have been found and Edward the Confessor between 1050 and 1065 built a palace here in order to be close to the abbey which he refounded. William Rufus in 1099 completed the vast Westminster Hall, and his medieval successors made many further additions. The present Houses of Parliament, therefore, occupy the site of a palace and so still rank as such (hence the term, the "Palace of Westminster", in occasional references to Parliamentary news). English kings resided here up to the time of Henry VIII, but from the mass of buildings, only a few survived. Westminster Hall stands in the center, facing across Parliament Square; it has a fine hammerbeam oak roof, put there by Richard II in 1399, and to its east, the crypt of St. Stephen's Chapel (14th-

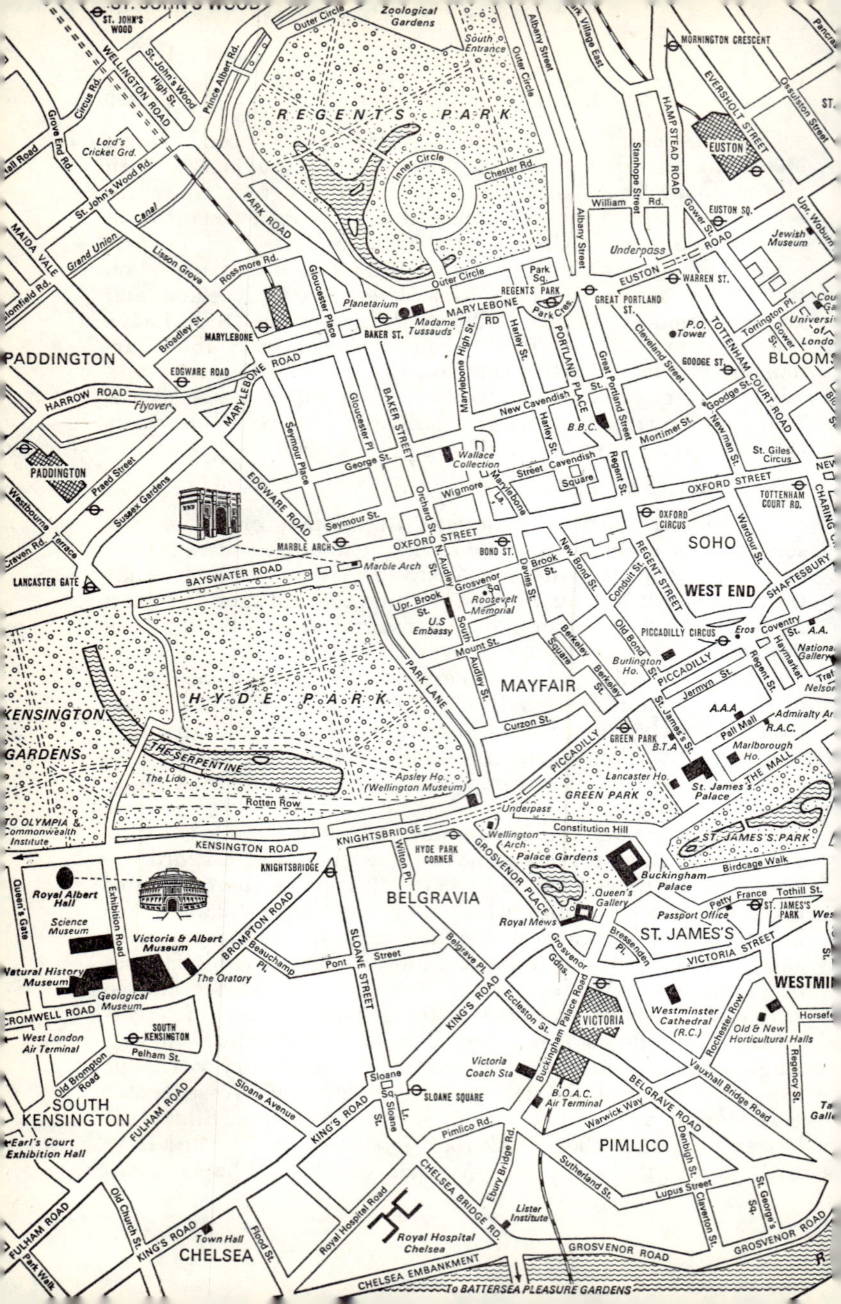
ST. JOHN'S WOOD
ST. JOHN'S WOOD
Outer Circle
Zoological Gardens
South Entrance
Albany Street
Park Village East
MORNINGTON CRESCENT
Pancras
WELLINGTON ROAD
St. John's Wood High St.
Prince Albert Rd.
Outer Circle
Circus Rd.
Grove End Rd.
REGENTS PARK
EVERSHOLT STREET
Ossulston Street
ST.
Lord's Cricket Grd.
HAMPSTEAD ROAD
Stanhope Street
EUSTON
Hall Road
St. John's Wood Rd.
Inner Circle
Chester Rd.
William Rd.
Gower St.
EUSTON SQ.
Upr. Woburn
Canal
PARK ROAD
Albany Street
Jewish Museum
MAIDA VALE
Grand Union
Lisson Grove
Rossmore Rd.
Underpass
ROAD
EUSTON
WARREN ST.
Park Sq.
Outer Circle
REGENTS PARK
Bloomfield Rd.
Gloucester Place
Planetarium
MARYLEBONE
Park Cres.
GREAT PORTLAND ST.
Torrington Pl.
Broadley St.
MARYLEBONE
BAKER ST.
Madame Tussauds'
RD
Harley St.
PORTLAND PLACE
Cleveland Street
P.O. Tower
TOTTENHAM
Gower St.
University of London
PADDINGTON
EDGWARE ROAD
ROAD
Marylebone High St.
GOODGE ST.
BLOOMS
Gloucester Pl
BAKER STREET
St.
Great Portland Street
COURT ROAD
Goodge St.
HARROW ROAD
MARYLEBONE
Flyover
New Cavendish
B.B.C.
Harley St.
Mortimer St.
Newman St.
Seymour Place
PADDINGTON
Praed Street
George St.
Wallace Collection
Cavendish Square
Regent St.
St. Giles Circus
Westbourne
Sussex Gardens
EDGWARE ROAD
Wigmore
Street
Marylebone La.
Orchard St.
OXFORD STREET
TOTTENHAM COURT RD.
CHARING
Seymour St.
OXFORD CIRCUS
SOHO
Craven Rd.
Terrace
MARBLE ARCH
OXFORD STREET
BOND ST.
New Bond St.
REGENT STREET
Wardour St.
LANCASTER GATE
BAYSWATER ROAD
Marble Arch
N. Audley St.
Brook St.
Davies St.
Grosvenor Sq
Roosevelt Memorial
Conduit St.
WEST END
SHAFTESBURY
Upr. Brook St.
U.S. Embassy
South Audley St.
Old Bond St.
PICCADILLY CIRCUS
Eros
Coventry St.
Haymarket
A.A.
National Gallery
Berkeley Square
Mount St.
Burlington Ho.
PICCADILLY
Regent St.
Trafalgar
Nelson
HYDE PARK
PARK LANE
Audley St.
MAYFAIR
Berkeley St.
Jermyn St.
KENSINGTON
A.A.A.
Admiralty Arch
Curzon St.
St. James's St.
Pall Mall
R.A.C.
GARDENS
THE SERPENTINE
GREEN PARK
B.T.A.
Marlborough Ho.
PICCADILLY
THE MALL
The Lido
Apsley Ho. (Wellington Museum)
Lancaster Ho.
GREEN PARK
St. James's Palace
Rotten Row
Underpass
TO OLYMPIA & Commonwealth Institute
KNIGHTSBRIDGE
Wellington Arch
Constitution Hill
ST. JAMES'S PARK
KENSINGTON ROAD
HYDE PARK CORNER
Wilton Pl.
GROSVENOR PLACE
Palace Gardens
Birdcage Walk
KNIGHTSBRIDGE
Buckingham Palace
Queen's Gate
Royal Albert Hall
Exhibition Road
BELGRAVIA
Queen's Gallery
Petty France
Tothill St.
ST. JAMES'S PARK
Science Museum
BROMPTON ROAD
Royal Mews
Passport Office
ST. JAMES'S
Victoria & Albert Museum
Beauchamp Pl.
SLOANE STREET
Belgrave Pl.
Grosvenor Gdns.
Bressenden Pl.
VICTORIA STREET
Pont Street
Natural History Museum
The Oratory
KING'S ROAD
Eccleston St.
Buckingham Palace Road
VICTORIA
WESTMIN
Geological Museum
Westminster Cathedral (R.C.)
Rochester Row
Horseferry
CROMWELL ROAD
SOUTH KENSINGTON
Old & New Horticultural Halls
West London Air Terminal
Pelham St.
Victoria Coach Sta
Regency St.
Old Brompton Road
Sloane Avenue
Sloane Sq.
SLOANE SQUARE
B.O.A.C. Air Terminal
BELGRAVE ROAD
Vauxhall Bridge Road
Tate Gallery
SOUTH KENSINGTON
FULHAM ROAD
KING'S ROAD
Sloane St.
Lr. Sloane
Pimlico Rd.
Warwick Way
Denbigh St.
Earl's Court Exhibition Hall
Ebury Bridge Rd.
PIMLICO
CHELSEA BRIDGE RD.
Sutherland St.
Lupus Street
St. George's Sq.
FULHAM ROAD
Old Church St.
Royal Hospital Road
Lister Institute
Claverton St.
KING'S ROAD
Town Hall
Flood St.
Royal Hospital Chelsea
GROSVENOR ROAD
GROSVENOR ROAD
Park Walk
CHELSEA
CHELSEA EMBANKMENT
To BATTERSEA PLEASURE GARDENS

CENTRAL LONDON

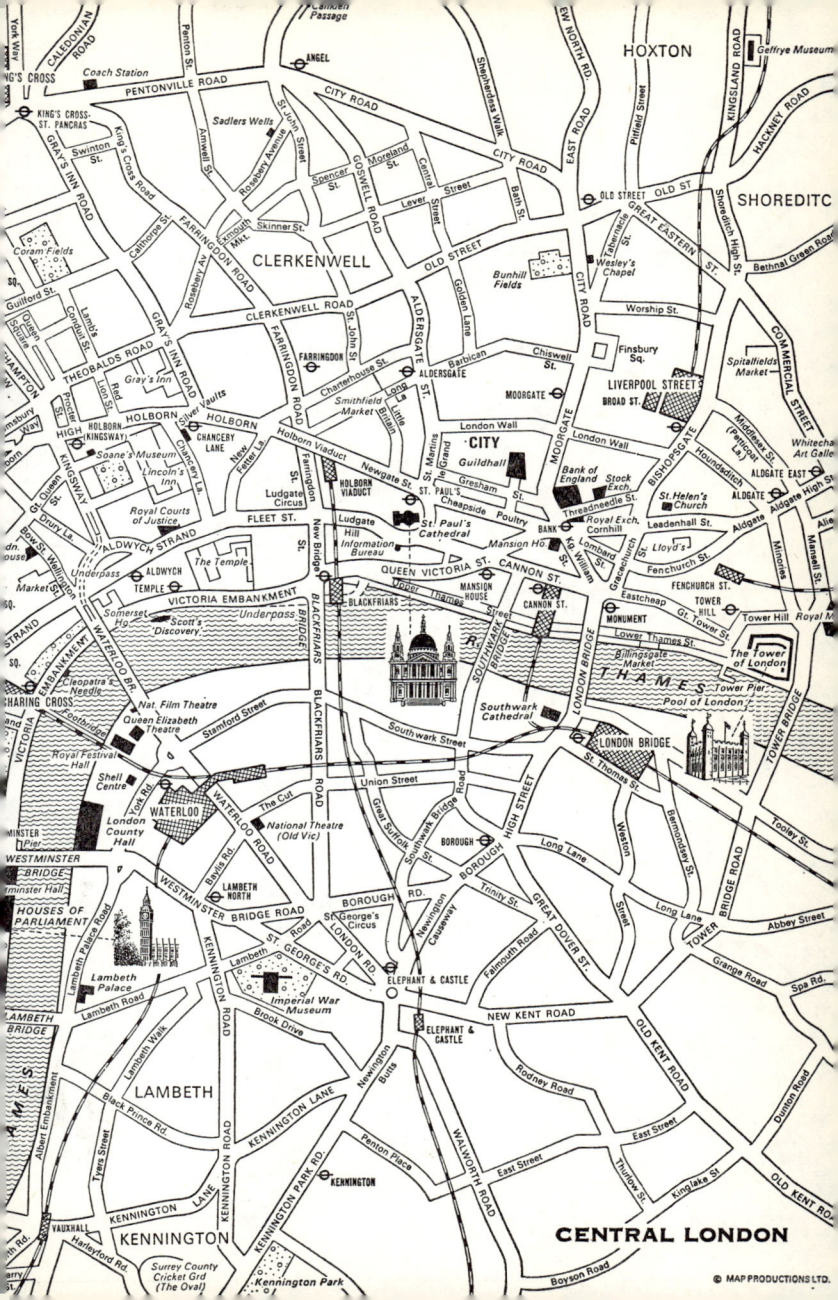

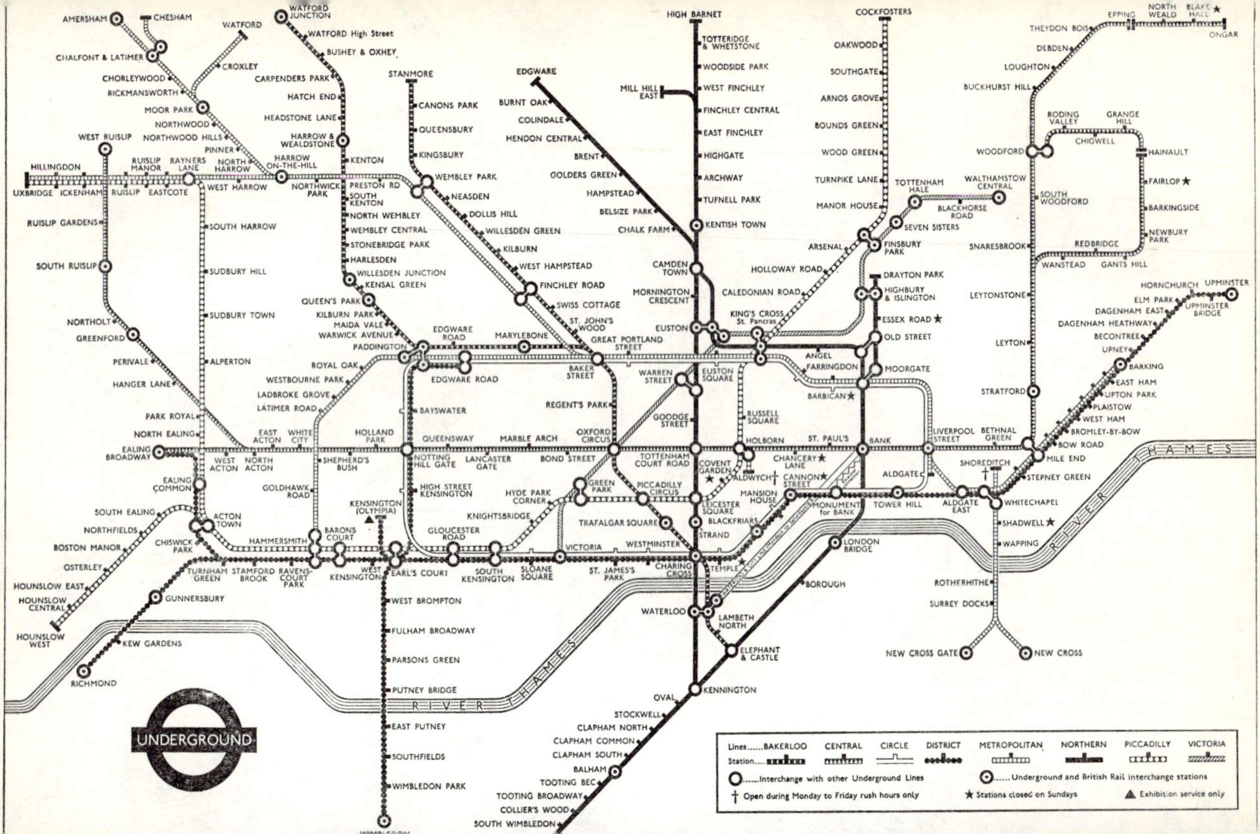

AMERSHAM
CHESHAM
CHALFONT & LATIMER
CHORLEYWOOD
RICKMANSWORTH
MOOR PARK
NORTHWOOD
NORTHWOOD HILLS
PINNER
NORTH HARROW
WATFORD
CROXLEY
WATFORD JUNCTION
WATFORD High Street
BUSHEY & OXHEY
CARPENDERS PARK
HATCH END
HEADSTONE LANE
HARROW & WEALDSTONE
KENTON
NORTHWICK PARK
PRESTON RD
SOUTH KENTON
NORTH WEMBLEY
WEMBLEY CENTRAL
STONEBRIDGE PARK
HARLESDEN
WILLESDEN JUNCTION
KENSAL GREEN
QUEEN'S PARK
KILBURN PARK
MAIDA VALE
WARWICK AVENUE
PADDINGTON
WEST RUISLIP
HILLINGDON
UXBRIDGE
ICKENHAM
RUISLIP
RUISLIP MANOR
EASTCOTE
RAYNERS LANE
WEST HARROW
HARROW ON-THE-HILL
RUISLIP GARDENS
SOUTH RUISLIP
NORTHOLT
GREENFORD
PERIVALE
HANGER LANE
PARK ROYAL
NORTH EALING
EALING BROADWAY
EALING COMMON
SOUTH EALING
NORTHFIELDS
BOSTON MANOR
OSTERLEY
HOUNSLOW EAST
HOUNSLOW CENTRAL
HOUNSLOW WEST
SOUTH HARROW
SUDBURY HILL
SUDBURY TOWN
ALPERTON
STANMORE
CANONS PARK
QUEENSBURY
KINGSBURY
WEMBLEY PARK
NEASDEN
DOLLIS HILL
WILLESDEN GREEN
KILBURN
WEST HAMPSTEAD
FINCHLEY ROAD
SWISS COTTAGE
ST. JOHN'S WOOD
EDGWARE
BURNT OAK
COLINDALE
HENDON CENTRAL
BRENT
GOLDERS GREEN
HAMPSTEAD
BELSIZE PARK
CHALK FARM
HIGH BARNET
TOTTERIDGE & WHETSTONE
WOODSIDE PARK
MILL HILL EAST
WEST FINCHLEY
FINCHLEY CENTRAL
EAST FINCHLEY
HIGHGATE
ARCHWAY
TUFNELL PARK
KENTISH TOWN
CAMDEN TOWN
MORNINGTON CRESCENT
EUSTON
KING'S CROSS St. Pancras
CALEDONIAN ROAD
HOLLOWAY ROAD
COCKFOSTERS
OAKWOOD
SOUTHGATE
ARNOS GROVE
BOUNDS GREEN
WOOD GREEN
TURNPIKE LANE
MANOR HOUSE
ARSENAL
FINSBURY PARK
TOTTENHAM HALE
SEVEN SISTERS
BLACKHORSE ROAD
WALTHAMSTOW CENTRAL
DRAYTON PARK
HIGHBURY & ISLINGTON
ESSEX ROAD ★
OLD STREET
ANGEL
FARRINGDON
MOORGATE
BARBICAN ★
EDGWARE ROAD
MARYLEBONE
GREAT PORTLAND STREET
BAKER STREET
WARREN STREET
EUSTON SQUARE
ROYAL OAK
WESTBOURNE PARK
LADBROKE GROVE
LATIMER ROAD
BAYSWATER
REGENT'S PARK
GOODGE STREET
RUSSELL SQUARE
EAST ACTON
WHITE CITY
HOLLAND PARK
QUEENSWAY
MARBLE ARCH
OXFORD CIRCUS
HOLBORN
ST. PAUL'S
BANK
LIVERPOOL STREET
BETHNAL GREEN
WEST ACTON
NORTH ACTON
SHEPHERD'S BUSH
NOTTING HILL GATE
LANCASTER GATE
BOND STREET
TOTTENHAM COURT ROAD
COVENT GARDEN ★
ALDWYCH †
CHANCERY LANE ★
CANNON STREET ★
ALDGATE
SHOREDITCH †
GOLDHAWK ROAD
HIGH STREET KENSINGTON
GREEN PARK
PICCADILLY CIRCUS
HYDE PARK CORNER
KNIGHTSBRIDGE
LEICESTER SQUARE
MANSION HOUSE
MONUMENT for BANK
TOWER HILL
ALDGATE EAST
WHITECHAPEL
STEPNEY GREEN
ACTON TOWN
KENSINGTON (OLYMPIA)
BARONS COURT
GLOUCESTER ROAD
TRAFALGAR SQUARE
BLACKFRIARS
STRAND
CHISWICK PARK
HAMMERSMITH
VICTORIA
WESTMINSTER
SHADWELL ★
WAPPING
TURNHAM GREEN
STAMFORD BROOK
RAVENS-COURT PARK
WEST KENSINGTON
EARL'S COURT
SOUTH KENSINGTON
SLOANE SQUARE
ST. JAMES'S PARK
CHARING CROSS
TEMPLE ★
LONDON BRIDGE
BOROUGH
GUNNERSBURY
KEW GARDENS
RICHMOND
WEST BROMPTON
FULHAM BROADWAY
PARSONS GREEN
PUTNEY BRIDGE
EAST PUTNEY
SOUTHFIELDS
WIMBLEDON PARK
WATERLOO
LAMBETH NORTH
ELEPHANT & CASTLE
KENNINGTON
OVAL
STOCKWELL
CLAPHAM NORTH
CLAPHAM COMMON
CLAPHAM SOUTH
BALHAM
TOOTING BEC
TOOTING BROADWAY
COLLIER'S WOOD
SOUTH WIMBLEDON
ROTHERHITHE
SURREY DOCKS
NEW CROSS GATE
NEW CROSS
EPPING
NORTH WEALD
BLAKE HALL ★
ONGAR
THEYDON BOIS
DEBDEN
LOUGHTON
BUCKHURST HILL
RODING VALLEY
GRANGE HILL
CHIGWELL
HAINAULT
FAIRLOP ★
BARKINGSIDE
NEWBURY PARK
WOODFORD
SOUTH WOODFORD
SNARESBROOK
REDBRIDGE
WANSTEAD
GANTS HILL
LEYTONSTONE
LEYTON
STRATFORD
MILE END
BOW ROAD
BROMLEY-BY-BOW
WEST HAM
PLAISTOW
UPTON PARK
EAST HAM
BARKING
UPNEY
BECONTREE
DAGENHAM HEATHWAY
DAGENHAM EAST
ELM PARK
HORNCHURCH
UPMINSTER BRIDGE
UPMINSTER
RIVER THAMES
UNDERGROUND
Lines......BAKERLOO
CENTRAL
CIRCLE
DISTRICT
METROPOLITAN
NORTHERN
PICCADILLY
VICTORIA
Station....
......Interchange with other Underground Lines
......Underground and British Rail interchange stations
† Open during Monday to Friday rush hours only
★ Stations closed on Sundays
▲ Exhibition service only

century), still used occasionally for weddings and christenings by members of parliament and their families. Across Old Palace Yard is the moated 14th-century Jewel Tower.

The Houses of Parliament and Westminster Hall are open to the public on Saturdays; the tour takes up to an hour. If you are fortunate enough to know, or to meet, a tame MP, persuade him to take you around and see places not shown to the general public. Tea on the terrace with a member is most prestigious. The palace covers eight acres, has two miles of corridors and more than 1,000 rooms. The large, square Victoria Tower is supposed to be the tallest square tower in existence, while the 320-foot clock tower is the universally-accepted symbol of London known as "Big Ben". (Actually, this is the name of the 13½-ton bell on which the hours are struck, named after Sir Benjamin Hall, First Commissioner of Works when it was hung.) That parliament is sitting is indicated by a flag flying from the Victoria Tower during the day and by a light on the clock tower by night.

Several statues stand around the Houses of Parliament and Parliament Square. Oliver Cromwell stands outside Westminster Hall and also around are Richard Coeur de Lion, George Canning and Abraham Lincoln.

Westminster Abbey

Across Parliament Square stands Westminster Abbey, officially called the Collegiate Church of St. Peter in Westminster. As with most Christian edifices that attempt to contain the whole history of all their respective nations, the abbey is packed (some say stuffed) with monuments to the great and famous. Not all the memorials are aesthetically interesting and the effect can be bewildering. But visitors should not be put off by this, nor should they allow a constant search for inscribed great names to blind them to the sheer overall beauty of the place, which is a fine example of Early English architecture.

The first authenticated church on this site was a Benedictine abbey, established by 970, dedicated to St. Peter. West Minster means "western monastery", indicative of its geographical relation to the City of London. Here, every British monarch since William the Conqueror has been crowned with the exceptions of Edward V and Edward VIII. A focal point inside the abbey is, therefore, the Coronation Chair, made by the order of Edward I, which has been used ever since. The chair encloses the Stone of Scone (pronounced *skoon*), or Stone of Destiny, which has long been a source of friction between England and Scotland. The kings of Scotland were crowned on it and it was used for the coronation of Macbeth's stepson at Scone in 1057. It was carried away from Scotland by Edward I in 1297 but has, over the centuries, become a symbol of Scottish independence. It has been removed from the abbey only three times—once to Westminster Hall for the installation of Oliver Cromwell as Lord Protector; once for safety from German bombers in 1940; and finally, by Scottish nationalists in 1950, who took it far north. (It was returned six months later.)

The finest architectural aspects of the abbey, and most impressive views, can be obtained from outside by wandering through the cloisters, which are full of atmosphere. The Chapter House dates from the 13th century but the oldest relic is the 11th-century Chapel of the Pyx, a stern Norman place contrasting with the bright courtyard beyond. The abbey has been much altered and enlarged over the centuries; some additions are recent, such as the western towers, built in 1740, and the north porch, of 1884.

Edward the Confessor did a great deal of rebuilding and Henry III carried on this work. Reconstruction was finished in 1528. Edward the Confessor's Chapel is the centre of the abbey, round which Henry III built a series of chapels. Many kings and queens are buried here: Henry III, Edward I, Edward III with his queen, Richard II and his first consort, Henry V, and Anne of Cleves, one of the wives of Henry VIII. There are some fine tombs near the sanctuary, and the finest chapel in the abbey is undoubtedly Henry VII's, where several kings and queens are buried. Nearby is the Battle of Britain Chapel, with its impressive stained-glass windows.

Westminster Abbey has been the scene of many splendid coronation ceremonies as well as royal weddings. It is also the burial place of famous statesmen and literary men—Benjamin Disraeli, Palmerston, Gladstone, Robert Peel, are all buried here together with scientists such as Newton and Darwin, and poets from Chaucer and Byron to Kipling and T. S. Eliot. There are also memorials to Henry Wadsworth Longfellow,

James Russell Lowell and Franklin Delano Roosevelt.

Nestling near the abbey is the church of St. Margaret, originally erected by William the Conqueror and attaining its present appearance in the 15th century. (Extensive restoration was carried out in later centuries, however.) The east window, made in Flanders in 1509, was a gift from Ferdinand and Isabella of Spain. The church has an intimate atmosphere and is the scene of many smart weddings; Samuel Pepys, Milton and Sir Winston Churchill were all married here.

A thorough study of both Westminster Abbey and the Houses of Parliament takes time and is exhausting. But if you have the energy, or on another day, take a side trip to Westminster Cathedral near Victoria Station, approached down Victoria Street from Westminster Abbey. This is the premier Roman Catholic church in England; quite enormous, it was built between 1895 and 1903. Its exterior is striking, as it is designed in a Byzantine style with alternating stripes of red brick and grey stone. Inside, some of the brick walls are bare, while others are covered with sumptuous mosaic. The tower is 284 feet high and, naturally, there is a marvellous view from the top, which is accessible by lift.

Whitehall

From the parliament-abbey complex, our walk goes along Whitehall, passing the end of Westminster Bridge. Once, this whole area from the river to about where Trafalgar Square now is, was an extensive and fascinating palace, which has simply disappeared, most of the buildings being destroyed by fire in 1695. It was a series of courts, lawns, walks and buildings wonderful in conception, but never fully completed. According to a historian it was: "A glorious city of rose-tinted Tudor brick, green lawns, and shining marble statues". Today Whitehall is a rather dull, not quite straight, street.

The big government buildings that line the first part of the street are slightly brutal, but impressive. On the left is Downing Street, a pleasant row of 18th-century houses, where Boswell lodged when he made his famous visit to London. No. 10 is the official residence of the prime minister. To the right on Whitehall is New Scotland Yard, its rather quaint brick exterior familiar from a thousand detective and police films set in London. (The headquarters of the Metropolitan police, however, were moved in 1967 to a vast modern block in Victoria.)

In the middle of the road stands the Cenotaph, a simple memorial to the dead of two wars; here, every year on Armistice Day, the sovereign lays the first tribute of poppies. The next item of interest on our path is the Banqueting Hall on the right; this was designed by Inigo Jones as part of the extensive Palace of Whitehall in 1622, to replace one burned down in 1619. In front of the hall, Charles I was beheaded in 1649. The whole building has been newly cleaned to reveal the Palladian beauty of its form. Opposite is William Kent's Horse Guards, a not very tall, but beautifully proportioned, building with a clock tower. Here, the Changing of the Queen's Life Guard takes place every morning, and in the Horse Guards Parade beyond the forecourt, the ceremony of Trooping the Colour is held annually on the Queen's official birthday in June. It is one of London's most spectacular military pageants, with the Queen taking the salute on horseback.

At the north end of Whitehall is Trafalgar Square, which may rival Piccadilly Circus as the tourist's centre of London. Laid out in 1829, it was finished in 1841. In the centre is another celebrated London landmark, Nelson's Column, erected in the 1840's to celebrate the victory of Nelson at the Battle of Trafalgar in 1805. At the base are four vast lions. There are pigeons everywhere, and also many photographers, equipped with birdseed to entice the semi-tame birds to settle on snap-happy tourists. Trafalgar Square is a focal point for rallies, marches and political meetings; on evenings of high jinks and celebrations, crowds throng the square, and even on cold winter nights—like Bonfire Night or New Year's Eve—some students will certainly strip and climb on top of the still-flowing fountains. At the northeast corner of the square is a 1921 statue of George Washington.

North of the square is the long, low National Gallery, housing the national collection of art and containing much that is priceless and magnificent. To its right is the delicate spire of the church of St. Martin's-in-the-Fields, the work of James Gibbs. Beyond the church is the interesting St. Martin's Lane, with its theatres, Victorian pubs and historical associations. Watch for a very narrow opening on the right into Goodwin's Court, with a row of bow-fronted shops.

The Strand runs off Trafalgar Square to the east and on the other side is The Mall, approached through Admiralty Arch or Pall Mall. From the latter, Haymarket—once a social centre in the 18th century—leads back to Piccadilly Circus. The other major road out of Trafalgar Square is Northumberland Avenue, a wide street of government offices leading to the embankment on the Thames.

The Embankment is probably at its best by night, when the lights twinkle on the water, but there is much of interest around here in the day, including the gardens, where bands play in the summer. Cleopatra's Needle, downstream towards Waterloo Bridge, first erected about 1450 B.C. in Egypt, was given to Britain in 1875. It resembles the obelisk in Paris' Place de la Concorde. Captain Scott's ship *Discovery*, in which he voyaged to the South Pole, is moored here along with other training ships. Across the river stands the Royal Festival Hall, built for the Festival of Britain in 1951, and a fine auditorium for concerts. Next to it are the new (1967) Queen Elizabeth II concert halls, a strange-looking block from the outside (just featureless concrete), but an imaginatively designed complex on the inside. On a fine evening, walk to the Festival Hall by the footbridge that runs along Hungerford Bridge—it takes you straight onto the esplanade on the first floor of the Festival Hall. Or cross Waterloo Bridge, and look eastwards for one of London's finest views—the City, dominated by St. Paul's, sparkling in the evening sun. Across Waterloo Bridge, too, is the Old Vic Theatre, at the moment the home of the National Theatre Company.

Soho

Soho is conveniently regarded as being bounded by Shaftesbury Avenue, Charing Cross Road, Oxford Street and Regent Street, making a small, nearly square area, its geometry emphasized by the way in which the streets run east to west or north to south, crossing each other neatly. It is associated with food, foreigners and sin. But sin in its widest sense, which means that the area's reputation is vastly inflated, helped by sensational headlines in the London papers.

This development of Soho as a place of specific reputation came late. The food aspect arrived only early in the present century, the sin label even later. Originally, the district was developed (residentially) after the Great Fire of London in 1666, when many people wanted new homes. The parish of St. Anne was formed out of St. Martin's in 1686, and splendid streets and squares of great houses rose. Earlier it had been a hunting spot, which is where the name derives from, *So! Ho!* being a call of the field. Historically and architecturally, it should be one of London's glories, but it isn't. Most of the original houses have been demolished over the centuries, many going when Shaftesbury Avenue was laid out.

But the atmosphere is amusing. There is a high density of continental residents, which means excellent food shops, delicatessens and, naturally, many of London's best foreign restaurants. There is, too, a continental feeling, with cosmopolitan newspaper shops, a freedom about the pubs and a general air of happy drifting. At night come the neon, the painted smiles from an upper window, the slouching figures in doorways suggesting a trip inside for a strip show. There are many such dives and clubs, most of them squalid and unattractive. There are seamy characters and dubious types lurking about, as Soho has for long been a haunt of the underworld. There's little enough to be afraid of, though; the police have the place well supervised.

Curiously, the east-west streets are more interesting than the north-south ones. The latter, though boasting a few clubs and restaurants, are dull, full of offices and the headquarters of film companies. The lateral streets, however, are lined with shops, cafés and restaurants. Old Compton Street is fascinating, with some excellent restaurants and shops.

Just off the Regent Street side of the area is Golden Square, architecturally dull, but with perhaps one house indicating its 18th-century grace. Here, too, is Carnaby Street, which has risen from dingy ordinariness to being a world-wide synonym for swinging young attire. It is a sight—particularly on a Saturday morning, when the lads turn up on their scooters to scour the boutiques for new gear. The street has started to lose its magic, though, and the days when one might spot the odd Beatle buying a new shirt are long past.

The other main square is Soho Square, near the Oxford Street side—again fairly dull. Elsewhere, the main part of the church of St. Anne, on Wardour Street, was destroyed by

Symbol of postwar reconstruction, the modernistic Cathedral at Coventry is now one of Britain's places of pilgrimage, both for worship and for sight-seeing. (Courtesy, Thompson, Coventry.)

The Thames, London's historic highway, flows quietly beside the Neo-Gothic buildings of Parliament, then moves into the teaming London docks, Britain's gigantic gateway to the world.

bombing in 1940, but the tower remains. There are some interesting pubs—especially *The York Minster*, known as the "French House" since it was associated with the French Resistance during the Second World War; here, poets, writers and actors mingle with even more unconventional types. There are also daytime street markets of picturesque interest.

Shaftesbury Avenue cuts through the southern part of Soho; this is the main street for theatres. Between this street and Coventry Street, Soho still runs on, but with less flavour, to Leicester Square, another centre of entertainment where most of the major cinemas are. This square, once the place for duels, has a statue of Shakespeare in the middle.

Mayfair

Broadly speaking, the confines of Mayfair are represented by Regent Street, Oxford Street, Park Lane and Piccadilly. The main interest of this area lies in its fine shops, beautiful residential houses and squares. As it represents all that is gracious in London living and shopping, there is an air of wealthy leisure, even on the busiest days.

Regent Street is perhaps London's most impressive shopping strip, running wide and straight after the initial bend out of Piccadilly Circus. The street was originally planned to run in a direct, triumphal line from Pall Mall to Portland Place, but as with most of the great planning schemes attempted in London, bends and deviations were forced on the builders. Running parallel to Regent Street further west are New Bond Street and Old Bond Street, equally famous for their even more luxurious and expensive shops.

In the 17th century, Mayfair was a quiet country spot, popular as a residential area away from the bustle of Westminster and the City. Old Bond Street was created in 1686 and New Bond Street followed on some 14 years later, forming a neat snobbish distinction between residents of both streets.

In Mayfair is Grosvenor Square and the American Embassy. The large, graceful square, laid out in 1695, has in its centre Sir W. Reid Dick's memorial statue to President Franklin D. Roosevelt, erected in 1948. Eero Saarinen designed the embassy, which takes up the entire west side of the square, often called "Little America" by Londoners. John Adams, first American ambassador to Britain and second president of the United States, lived in the house at the corner of Brook and Duke streets here.

Another spot of considerable charm within this area is Shepherd Market (off Piccadilly and behind the *Hilton* hotel), a network of narrow streets with some charming houses and fascinating shops. There are no sheep here, but a couple of rousing pubs and a few of London's most expensive lady "French-teachers". There is also Berkeley Square, where the nightingale sang, some of the better hotels, and many distinguished night spots. Berkeley Square, still beautiful with its fine trees and gardens, was once one of London's most distinguished residential centres. Robert Walpole and his son Horace, Charles James Fox, and Clive of India lived here.

Piccadilly

Walking westward from the Circus along Piccadilly itself, you will see, again, famous shops, and on the north side, Burlington House, home of the Royal Academy of Arts, where the celebrated summer exhibition is held. A statue of Sir Joshua Reynolds stands in the courtyard. Before you reach Burlington House, watch out for a narrow turning on the right, next to *Meakers*, in which stands Albany, a fine Georgian house divided into "sets" (not "flats") where some highly distinguished people live (including J. B. Priestley and Edward Heath, leader of the Conservative Party). On the left is St. James's Church, severely damaged in the Blitz. The last house on Piccadilly—address No. 1, London—is Aspley House, built by Robert Adam in 1771 and the residence of the Duke of Wellington. (Opened in 1952 as the Wellington Museum.) It faces Hyde Park Corner, a busy traffic roundabout with a central green space on which stands the Wellington Arch.

The western limit of Mayfair is Park Lane, which faces Hyde Park, and which once was synonymous with high living and beautiful houses. Most have now been demolished to be replaced by hotels. Here are the *Hilton*, the *Dorchester*, *Londonderry House*, *Grosvenor House* and the *Playboy Club*. At the north end of Park Lane is Marble Arch, another traffic whirlpool, where you will find, on the park side, Speakers' Corner, a space specially reserved for anyone with anything to say that they *must* say publicly. Great entertainment for a Sunday afternoon.

Marble Arch itself is not particularly impressive; it used to stand in the forecourt of Buckingham Palace, until brought to this spot in 1850, near the place where once stood the public gallows known as Tyburn Tree.

The north limit of Mayfair is Oxford Street, a long straight shopping thoroughfare containing many department stores and shops of all kinds. It begins on the east at Tottenham Court Road, and continues to Marble Arch. Turn right at the westerly corner of *Selfridge's*, one of the department stores on Oxford Street, and you come shortly to Baker Street, a place of pilgrimage for admirers of the greatest detective of all, though you'll look in vain for the house where Sherlock Holmes "lived". The post office, however, still deals with many letters every year addressed to Holmes from all over the world.

In Manchester Square, off Baker Street to the east, was the town house of the Marquis of Hertford, now home of the Wallace Collection.

Turn back down to Wigmore Street and, a few streets east, you'll come to Harley Street, which is entirely devoted to medicine; most of Britain's greatest specialists have their consulting rooms there. It's a place of reassuring, rather expensive calm, fine houses, and costly automobiles. A few streets north of Oxford Street, where it nears Soho Square, is the Post Office Tower, at 620 feet, London's tallest building. There is an observation platform and a revolving restaurant.

Chelsea

Begin your exploration in Sloane Square, where stands the Royal Court Theatre. Behind it are the quiet, rich residential streets of Belgravia; ahead lies the King's Road—colourful, bohemian, packed with boutiques, bistros and antique shops. This is the road to visit on Saturdays, from about noon until 3 p.m., when the pavement is crowded with trendy young men and their dollies, every one of them trying to wear something more stunning and/or outrageous than the other. If there is a "swinging London", this is its center. Don't miss the pubs, *Chelsea Potter* and *Six Bells*, or the coffee house, *Guys 'n' Dolls*. Streets leading south from the King's Road bring you to the Chelsea Embankment; those to the north lead to Kensington. This is traditionally the artists' quarter; it is clean, sweet and, nowadays, very chic.

There have been many eminent residents in Chelsea (there still are), beginning in 1524 when Sir Thomas More, that man for all seasons, settled here with his large family. In 1523, More bought Crosby Hall in Bishopsgate (in the City of London), from where it was moved in 1910 to Chelsea; it stands on the corner of Danvers Street, on the Embankment, on land which was once part of More's garden. There are a number of More associations in Chelsea, and a movement is afoot to erect, possibly in 1968, a statue to him outside Chelsea Old Church, where he worshipped; this was badly damaged by a bomb in 1941 but has been well restored.

Other distinguished residents have included Thomas Carlyle, Leigh Hunt, George Eliot, Count d'Orsay and Dante Gabriel Rossetti, Whistler, Sargent, Augustus John, Ellen Terry, Henry James and Smollett.

The most notable building in the area is the Chelsea Royal Hospital, designed by Sir Christopher Wren in 1682. Visitors are admitted daily and may attend services in the chapel, which is still practically as Wren left it. The hospital houses old or disabled warriors who are familiar figures in the area, wearing their scarlet or blue coats.

Along the river are some lovely houses, and houseboats moored on the water. The bridges are characteristic but not very interesting; the famous bridge Whistler painted was replaced in 1890. Just across the river is Battersea, with its large park in which south Londoners play. There is an enormous fun fair with roller-coasters and water-splash, and during the summer an exhibition of sculpture in the open air—which is always fascinating, as modern works seen outside the confines of a museum take on a completely new relevance.

Kensington

Even in these democratic days, one occasionally hears someone say that the *only* area where one could *possibly* live in London is "north of the river and south of the park". The park is Hyde Park, the area, the Royal Borough of Kensington. Though the district has many contrasting facets, this really sums up the basic tone: it is a grand residential area. Unfortunately many of the rather pompous houses have been broken up into flats, but the feeling of stuccoed wealth

EXPLORING LONDON

remains, the pillared porches and tree-filled squares exuding a sense of well-being.

It was King William III who, socially speaking, really put Kensington on the map. "The Smoak of the Coal Fires of London much incommoded his Majesty," wrote a contemporary, "who was always troubled with Asthma and could not bear lying in town." The king found the Thames mists that frequently veiled Whitehall particularly trying. So for 18,000 guineas he bought Nottingham House, conveniently situated in the village of Kensington. Renamed Kensington Palace, and enlarged from time to time, it was a royal residence until recent times.

With the arrival of royalty the village "flourished almost beyond belief", according to a chronicler writing in 1705. Court personages hastened to follow the royal example, and Kensington Square (look for Thackeray's house in Young Street close by) was built to accommodate them. In the reign of Anne, the demand for lodging became so pressing that at one time an ambassador, a bishop, and a physician occupied apartments in the same house in the square. With the court and society came the wits and the men of letters. Walk along Knightsbridge, just south of Hyde Park, and you come into Kensington Gore, with the vast, domed Royal Albert Hall, scene of the summer's series of Promenade Concerts. Opposite is Albert, sitting in his Memorial, regarded with horror when reaction to Victoriana set in, but now discovered to have charm.

Continue west, past Hyde Park Gate, where Sir Winston Churchill lived, and died, and reach Kensington High Street, with its famous department stores. The road bends in a pretty fashion and to the right is Kensington Church Street, which has great charm, antique shops, the best boutique in town and a few rather smart (debby) pubs.

Edwardes Square, one of London's loveliest, is also in Kensington. It was developed around 1802 by a Frenchman named Changier—in perfect taste, though entirely English in atmosphere and architecture. The story goes that Changier was really one of Napoleon's agents and as such built the square to house the Corsican's civil servants after England had been successfully invaded!

Kensington has a magical quality of surprise. It has houses and antique shops that seem to belong to a cathedral city. It has a delighful pub—the *Windsor Castle*—on the top of Campden Hill, with a charming arboured garden, and another in Edwardes Square, with tables in the open air, a fine collection of Hogarth etchings, and a good kitchen.

Further down Kensington High Street, you turn into Earls Court Road, a rather gay quarter with a slightly foreign and a slightly raffish ambiance. This crosses Cromwell Road, where the West London Air Terminal is located, several streets to the east.

The Parks

London has developed, over the centuries, an awareness of the importance of having wide, green spaces in the centre of the city. St. James's Park, Green Park and Buckingham Palace Gardens make a large open swathe in the middle of central London; this is continued westwards by Hyde Park and Kensington Gardens, which together make more than 600 acres of space to play in, walk babies and dogs, lie in the sun, boat, swim, make discreet love and generally romp about. London takes advantage of this opportunity and Hyde Park is a focal point for relaxation.

The main gate to Hyde Park is Decimus Burton's screen at the south end of Park Lane. To the left is Rotten Row, a sand track for horse riders who use it daily. The paths either side of the Row have always been a fashionable strolling place, particularly on Sundays after church.

Today you will find the park rather less fashionable than of old—mostly because elegant lounging is out of fashion. But there are still riders on the Row on a fine morning, and you may row on and swim in the Serpentine, and take open-air refreshment in the cafés you'll find amongst the trees.

Kensington Gardens, once the private territory of Kensington Palace, has lovely walks and trees. Cutting across both parks is a crescent of water called in Hyde Park, The Serpentine and in Kensington Gardens, Long Water. It was in this lake that Harriet Westbrook, who was married to the poet Shelley, committed suicide in 1816. Peter Pan, the hero of J. M. Barrie's play annually revived at Christmas, lived on an island in the Serpentine, and on the bank of Long Water is the famous statue of him.

Kensington Palace was the residence of the reigning sovereign until 1760, when George II died. It has been

EXPLORING LONDON

altered by two great architects, Wren and William Kent. Queen Victoria was born here and also Queen Mary. Present residents include Princess Margaret and Lord Snowdon. The state apartments are open, and the London Museum is housed here too.

A less famous, but no less delightful, space is Holland Park, at the north end of Earl's Court Road and just off Kensington High Street. Holland House, a Tudor mansion, was a brilliant centre for artists and wits during the residence of the third Baron Holland between 1773 and 1840. The grounds are pleasant and wooded, and have peacocks strolling about. Just by the entrance is an interesting modern building with a copper-sheathed roof; this is the Commonwealth Institute, which frequently advertises exhibitions and recitals

Serving north London is Regent's Park, to the north of Oxford Street, generally considered the most splendid park in London. It contains the Zoological Gardens, an open-air theatre and the Regent's Canal and is surrounded by terraces and town houses of great distinction. The zoo is gradually being redeveloped on a long-term plan which is expected to be finished by the early 1970's. At the moment, however, the various animal houses offer a fascinating cross-section of architectural styles, of which perhaps the most famous piece is the Aviary, designed by Lord Snowdon. The open-air theatre is a favourite summer place with fine productions of Shakespeare in a magical setting. No matter how warm the day, take a blanket, for as night falls, while the stage may look invitingly warm, the breeze will make you cold enough. There is a supper tent offering food and wine.

To the south of Regent's Park is Marylebone, containing Harley Street, Wigmore Street and Wimpole Street and, in Manchester Square, the Wallace Collection. To the north lies St. John's Wood, a select residential area, but of little interest to the explorer.

It is possible to take a barge trip along the Regent's Canal, which goes through the Zoo; apart from being pleasant, it offers charming views of this part of London.

Holborn

Two major highways link central London with the City: the Strand and Holborn. Strand here means "beach", as it was originally a riverside road along the Thames. Holborn derives from Hole Bourne, or "stream in the hollow", as it lies along the route of the little Fleet River (now obliterated). Between these two arteries lie the great Inns of Court, and round them, the first urban development outside the cities of London and Westminster took place; so while much ugly rebuilding has been done, there are still quiet and charming streets of genuine historical charm.

Begin at Holborn underground station, at the north end of Kingsway, a wide, tree-lined street linking Holborn with the Strand, and walk eastwards. At first, the street is unexciting: shops, big office blocks, a pompous insurance company building. Soon, on the right, comes Chancery Lane, and just after is Staple Inn, a romantic-looking, half-timbered block. It is not original (having been blown up by a V-bomb in 1944), but has been rebuilt so that it does in fact look exactly as it did in Elizabeth I's London; the original dated from 1586. Inside are two pleasant courtyards, on one of which Dr. Johnson lived for a while. Here, too, in the street, are Holborn Bars, two small obelisks that mark the western limits of the City of London. On the left is Gray's Inn Road, a depressing street.

Further along is *Gamages*, a big department store, full of surprising bargains, and opposite, the offices of the *Daily Mirror*. This junction is Holborn Circus, in the centre of which is an equestrian statue of Prince Albert. On the left is Hatton Garden, occupied by diamond merchants. A little way along Hatton Garden, on the right, is *The Mitre*, a small historical pub hidden away down a narrow alley (well-posted on the pavement). Just off Holborn Circus, too, is Ely Place, built in 1772. Here was the town house of the bishops of Ely; the place is guarded by night watchmen who used to call the hours in traditional manner. In Ely Place is Ely Chapel (St. Etheldreda's), a noted example of 13th-century Gothic, which has a vaulted crypt standing on Roman foundations.

But let us continue along Holborn. On the right is Wren's church of St. Andrew, whose tower interior dates from 1446. Wren did not alter it; nor did the restorers of 1960, while repairing bomb damage.

The street now becomes a viaduct, constructed in 1867 to take the road across the Fleet valley. It is an impressive construction with elaborate bridges. To the right are the offices of the *Evening Standard*, to the left is Smithfield Market. At the end of the viaduct is the 12th-century church of St. Sepulchre, (tomb of Virginia's Capt. John Smith), which had its bells rung when there was an execution at Newgate. Newgate Prison stood opposite, on the site now occupied by the Central Criminal Court (the "Old Bailey"), topped by the symbolic statue of justice. There are five courts, open to the public and usually crowded, especially when a sensational case is in progress.

To the left of this corner is St. Bartholomew's Hospital, built by James Gibbs in 1730, though founded in 1123. Just past the hospital (Smithfield Meat Market on the left), is the church of St. Bartholomew the Great, well worth visiting. Apart from the chapel in the White Tower, it is the oldest church in London, being part of the priory founded in 1123. It is approached through a charming gateway with an Elizabethan, timbered façade, revealed when a bomb explosion in 1915 shattered its covering. The interior is beautiful; the heavy roundness of authentic Norman architecture fully evident.

At the junction by the Old Bailey, Holborn becomes Newgate Street, leading to St. Paul's Cathedral and Cheapside.

Bloomsbury

Before the redivision of London into the Greater London Council's new areas, Holborn was a borough. It is now joined with others into the much bigger area called Camden. An important part of Holborn, to the west of Holborn underground station, is called Bloomsbury, associated with students, the university and the literary set of the twenties (of which Virginia Woolf was the leading light). Bloomsbury lies north of the street called Holborn and consists mainly of a series of beautiful, linked squares and fine streets of 18th-century origin. Much ugly rebuilding has been done during the past 50 years or so, but a lot of the charm remains. It is all rather restrained and though containing London University, the British Museum and the Courtauld Institute Galleries (which contain a fine collection of Impressionist paintings), the area has none of the *rive gauche* atmosphere one might expect.

It is a district of neat squares, and Bloomsbury Square,

planned by the Earl of Southampton, is the oldest. Macaulay reports that foreign princes were taken to see it as one of the wonders of England, a veritable "little town". Here Herbert Spencer wrote his *First Principles*, and Sir Hans Sloane started the collection that was to be the nucleus of the British Museum. Steele, the writer, entertained his friends in one of the prim houses—using the bailiffs as waiters. In his youth Disraeli was a resident. And other Bloomsbury squares—Russell, Bedford, Woburn, for example—have had almost equally distinguished pasts.

A suggested itinerary for a walk around Bloomsbury: Starting again from Holborn underground station, cut north through Red Lion Square (not so pretty, but Dante Gabriel Rossetti lived there) into Theobalds Road, a wide, noisy, boring thoroughfare. Walk east, past Great James Street (a narrow street built in 1722 and a fine example of domestic Georgian architecture—many of the original glazing bars and fan lights remain) until you reach the pleasant greenness of Gray's Inn. Opposite, turn north on John Street, which also contains some good 18th-century houses. In John Street's continuation, Doughty Street, is Dickens' House, where the writer lived from 1837 to 1839. It contains a good library and museum. In the basement is a mock-up of the kitchen at Dingley Dell. (The house is not open on Sundays.)

At the end of Doughty Street, turn left along Guilford Street past Coram's Fields, a children's playground on the site of the Foundling Hospital. Turn left into Lamb's Conduit Street, in which is a pub called *The Lamb*, usually full of students and writers and interestingly decorated. From Lamb's Conduit Street, turn right into Great Ormond Street, with its famous Hospital for Sick Children, through Queen Square (surrounded by hospitals), and through a little walk westward into Southampton Row. A few yards south, reached through Bloomsbury Place, is Bloomsbury Square, not particularly attractive architecturally, but one of the oldest squares in London, dating from the mid-17th century. Up Bedford Place from this square is Russell Square, very large and full of trees, lawns and fountains. Dominating it is the central tower of the University of London. In Montagu Place, on the west side, is the entrance to the King Edward VII Gallery of the British Museum.

EXPLORING LONDON

North of Russell Square are Woburn Square (where the Courtauld Galleries are), Gordon Square and Tavistock Square, pretty, green places with some attractive town houses. To the west is Tottenham Court Road, and to the north, Euston Road, where there are three railway stations, Euston, St. Pancras and King's Cross. Southampton Row becomes Woburn Place, at the top of which is St. Pancras church, a strange mixture of styles and with a copy of the Athenian Erectheum attached. Watch, too, for Woburn Walk, a narrow alley with some pretty shops.

The Strand

The Strand runs from Trafalgar Square eastward to Temple Bar—main gate to the City of London—where it becomes Fleet Street, finally ascending to St. Paul's under the name of Ludgate Hill.

Between Trafalgar Square and St. Mary le Strand—a Gibbs church islanded by traffic—the Strand is little more than a reasonably-interesting shopping street with two theatres, the *Adelphi* and the *Vaudeville*. Off to the north, however, up Southampton Street, is Covent Garden, the central fruit, flower and vegetable market, quiet during the afternoon, but a hive of activity in the early hours of the morning. In its centre are the plaza and St. Paul's church by Inigo Jones (where Shaw set the first scene of *Pygmalion*, father of *My Fair Lady*). There are lots of crates and dead lettuces knocking about, but the network of streets, containing the Royal Opera House, Drury Lane, many theatres, some good restaurants and clubs, is fascinating and full of history.

To the south of the Strand lies the Adelphi complex, built by the Adam brothers, now demolished and, sadly, rebuilt. Some examples of fine 18th-century architecture remain in John Adam Street, where there is a pub called *The Gilbert & Sullivan*, decorated with models of the operas, where you can hear piped selections from *The Mikado* and so on. Further along the Strand are the famous *Savoy Hotel* and its theatre, where most of the Gilbert & Sullivan operas were first performed. Many turnings south from the Strand lead down to the river and the Victoria Embankment.

By Lancaster Place (leading to Waterloo Bridge) is the Aldwych, a crescent containing the theatre of that name, the

London home of the Royal Shakespeare Company. Beyond is St. Clement Danes, a Wren church with a Gibbs tower and a statue of one of its regular worshippers, Dr. Johnson, outside the choir. The original "oranges and lemons, bells of St. Clement's" church, it is now dedicated to the R.A.F. To the south is Somerset House, whose long, low, spectacular façade is best seen from the river, built in 1776. The huge house now contains government offices and the office of the Registrar-General of Births, Deaths and Marriages, where wills may be checked for a small fee. Outside is a second "church in the road", St. Mary's. Next door, under King's College, are the so-called Roman Baths.

Just before Temple Bar (now marked by a rather uninteresting memorial with statues of Queen Victoria and Edward VII) are the Royal Courts of Justice or Law Courts, amazingly Gothic in the Victorian style.

It is possible to listen to cases in the courts, but, as they are mainly civil actions, they quickly become tedious to the inexpert. To get a better idea of how British justice deals with the man in the street, drop in at a Magistrates' Court, the main central one being in Bow Street.

On the other side of the road is The Temple, approached by many unlikely-looking alleys. This is the legal quarter, very beautiful, with linked courtyards and a quiet, easeful atmosphere.

The name derives from the Knights Templar, a powerful medieval order created during the Crusades. It was dissolved in 1312, and in 1346, the ground belonging to the Knights Templar was leased to law students; it has been, ever since, the home of lawyers. The Temple Church dates from the 12th century and was badly damaged during the Second World War but has now been restored. The Middle Temple Hall is one of those rare glimpses of Elizabethan times remaining just as it was when built. Explore this area on a quiet afternoon, using Wren's gatehouse in Middle Temple Lane (off Fleet Street) to enter.

The Strand becomes Fleet Street at Temple Bar, where traditionally, the Lord Mayor of London must challenge the reigning monarch when she (or he) enters the City. Sir Christopher Wren designed the old gate that stood here, but it was removed in 1878.

Fleet Street is, of course, the artery of the press; on and around this famous street are the offices of most of the major newspapers. You will see the rather restrained *Daily Telegraph*, the shiny black *Daily Express* and many provincial papers' headquarters in London.

Just off Fleet Street, in Gough Square, is Dr. Johnson's house, where he lived and where he compiled his amazing dictionary. At Ludgate Circus, Ludgate Hill rises to St. Paul's Cathedral. To the right is Blackfriars Bridge, and next to that, the little *Mermaid Theatre*, at Puddle Dock. Here, too, are the modern offices of *The Times*. The great cathedral was cleaned completely in 1965-66 and now looks even more spectacular from this approach, though as one gets nearer, a new (and highly controversial) office block masks part of the façade. Illuminated at night, the cathedral is at its most splendid.

The area immediately around St. Paul's was devastated during the blitz over London. Now, years of careful planning and rebuilding are just beginning to yield results. To the left of the cathedral is Paternoster Square, a new pedestrian complex of plazas with shops, restaurants and pubs. It has been cunningly designed to afford unexpected views of Wren's cathedral, which stands moored like a vast ship among the smooth surfaces of concrete and glass. Just behind the cathedral is the new Choir School, but to the southwest, much still remains to be done. The scheme for St. Paul's precinct was devised by William Holford, with the intention of framing the cathedral from various angles, with paved courts, flights of steps and lawns. Some voices urged for wide open spaces around the cathedral, but a stroll round the new developments quickly indicates today how wrong this would have been. Moreover, any Londoner will say at once that it is his *right* to be able to go close by St. Paul's on a bus!

St. Paul's Cathedral

In the crypt of this great monument is the tomb of Sir Christopher Wren, bearing the epitaph: *Lector, si monumentum requiris, circumspice*. ("Reader, if you want a memorial, look around you.") Perhaps the most potent comment on London's largest and most famous church, this boast refers to a living church, the cathedral of the Bishop of London. It was begun in 1675 and completed during the reign of Queen Anne, in 1710, when Wren was almost 80. The Renaissance-style building is 520 feet long (the nave is 125 feet long), and the marvellous dome is 112 feet across; the top of the cross is 365 feet above the pavement of the church.

It is an enormous and impressive church and crowded with memorials, some indifferent, some good, most of them large and elaborate. Dr. Johnson, John Donne (the dean here as well as being the metaphysical poet, who died in 1631), the painters Reynolds and Turner and even George Washington are commemorated here. In the crypt, too, is a commemorative tablet to one of the American pilots who "died that England might live". (The Jesus Chapel, in the Apse, is dedicated to the 28,000 Americans who fell in operations based on Britain during World War II.) The Whispering Gallery around the base of the dome is a source of fascination; it is 112 feet across but words whispered on one side can be distinctly heard on the other, similar to the dome of the Capitol in Washington, D.C.

The enormous church is crowded with memorials, some of them on a truly gigantic scale. This applies to the monument of the Duke of Wellington, who defeated Napoleon at Waterloo in 1815 and became a national hero. The funeral of the Iron Duke, in 1852, was, with that of Sir Winston Churchill's in 1964, the most impressive ever staged in London for anyone outside the royal family. The huge funeral car, made largely out of captured guns and weighing about 11 tons, can still be seen in the crypt. The memorial itself was erected in 1875. Lord Nelson, the victor of Trafalgar, was given a statue, as was Lord Kitchener, drowned off the Orkney Islands in 1916.

During the summer months of the annual Festival of the City of London, St. Paul's is used for concerts. To hear the requiems of Berlioz or Verdi in this setting is truly awe-inspiring.

While you are here, it is well worth having a look at the Barbican, an area just to the north of St. Paul's, which after 1940 was reduced to 35 acres of continuous devastation. Slowly it is being re-built along the most modern lines. Tower blocks march two abreast down London Wall (a street so called because it follows the route of the old Roman Wall, remains of which are incorporated into the new scheme) and are connected by pedways, above traffic level. There are plans for flats, hotels, swimming pools and a permanent home for the Royal Shakespeare Company—in fact a completely new residential area within the City of London.

The City

Known as "The Square Mile", the City of London is an irregularly defined crescent stretching from Temple Bar to the Tower of London. Its heartbeat is at the giant crossroads, a meeting of seven streets, where stand the Bank of England, the Royal Exchange and the Mansion House, official residence of the Lord Mayor.

From behind St. Paul's, the most immediate approach is a walk along Cheapside, past the Cockney's church of St. Mary-le-Bow to the big seven-way intersection. Memories of Saxon times haunt the streets near Cheapside; indeed, the very name Cheapside is of Saxon origin; *ceap* meaning barter. The earliest Saxon (if not Roman) relic in the City is claimed to be the famous London Stone. The stone was formerly embedded in the wall of St. Swithin's Church, in Cannon Street, but the church, damaged by bombing, was demolished in 1958. The stone is incorporated in a new office building on its old site. All round Cheapside and east of St. Paul's Cathedral, street names (Bread Street, Ironmonger Lane, Wood Street) indicate that busy markets flourished there in medieval times.

Off Cheapside to the left, down King Street, is the Guildhall, the centre of the City Corporation and the City guilds. Only the porch and one 15th-century window survive; otherwise, it is a mass of replacements. It was destroyed by the Great Fire of 1666 and again by German bombs in 1940. Behind the Mansion House is the church of St. Stephen Walbrook, considered to be one of Wren's finest works. The Royal Exchange is an impressive building, but no transactions are performed there now. Its courtyard houses the Guildhall Museum and there are Roman and medieval objects displayed.

The Bank of England, another citadel of Britain's financial power, faces the Royal Exchange. Although the old building was erected in 1743, it has been extensively reconstructed; it is an imposing block, with some dubious additions derived from an Italian pattern, but it lacks architectural unity and clarity. Farther east, near London Bridge, stands a towering 200-foot monument built as a memorial to the Great Fire of 1666. Pay 6d (6¢) and you can climb its 311 steps for a fine view of London's most historic area.

The City is full of noise and bustle during the day, and at night becomes quiet and deserted. To the east of Mansion House are London Bridge and Billingsgate fish market—famous for its colourful language.

The Tower of London

The Tower is the root of London and of England's history; for this reason, we are fortunate its Norman and medieval fabric has been well-preserved. See it at night when floodlit and it becomes a setting more magical than any designer could create; in the summer, *son et lumière* performances can be viewed from boats here; sometimes floodlit performances of Gilbert & Sullivan operas are held, too—an interesting experience, weather permitting.

The White Tower, in the centre, is the oldest part of the fortress, having been built for William the Conqueror. Wren, who had a hand in many of London's buildings, made some alterations to the exterior, but inside, the Norman origins are still self-evident. The White Tower is the most infamous, for here most of the important prisoners in bygone days were confined and tortured. One particularly nasty cell was called Little Ease. The unfortunate inmate couldn't stand, sit, or lie down. The authorities also made themselves unpleasant by use of the rack, which was kept in the lower part of the White Tower. It's said that in 1546 a woman called Anne Askew was tortured with it so greatly to the delight and interest of the Lord Chancellor, who attended the proceedings, that he himself pressed on the levers and almost tore the woman's body apart. Some years ago a well was found in the lower part of the tower—filled almost to the top with human bones!

This main tower is surrounded by fifteen others, each individually named, the whole complex resting across the ancient wall of the City of London. A Roman fortress certainly occupied the site, and later a Saxon castle stood there. Since it was built (William the Conqueror wanted to frighten the

Londoners), the Tower has never been besieged or seriously attacked. It has therefore been more of a state prison than a fortress as such, and innumerable famous people have been immured here and many have lost their heads on the block.

A good afternoon is needed to do the Tower full justice (there are a café and restaurant here), and it is closed at 5 p.m. Things to see are the Gun Floor, St. John's Chapel—the oldest church in London—the armouries, with a collection begun by Henry VIII, and the site of the scaffold on Tower Green. Hopping about on the Green you may see the Tower's tame ravens. There have been ravens here since time immemorial, and legend says the Tower will crumble if they should ever leave.

The Beauchamp Tower has had a most distinguished list of prisoners—from Sir John Oldcastle, who was executed on Tottenham Court Road in 1418 for his religious beliefs, to Robert Dudley, a favourite of Queen Elizabeth I. Inscriptions on the walls of the tower total nearly a hundred. The list does not, of course, comprise all the victims, most of whom were buried in the Chapel of St. Peter ad Vincula, or in the burial ground close by (now part of the green). The great English historian, Macaulay, said of the Tower that "in truth there is no sadder spot on earth".

Among the famous people who were beheaded in the Tower at least four should be mentioned: the philosopher, creator of Utopia, saint, and statesman, Sir Thomas More; the two wives of Henry VIII, Anne Boleyn and Catherine Howard, and that versatile courtier and mysterious lover of Queen Elizabeth, the Earl of Essex. When the axe fell for the last time in 1747, it was upon a rebel's head. The axe, execution block and instruments of torture can still be seen in the White Tower.

Elizabeth I (while still Princess) knew something about the Tower from personal experience. Queen Mary imprisoned her in the Bell Tower. She arrived by water at Traitors' Gate. It was raining, but she sat on the steps and refused to budge. Looking at the grim place, you'll scarcely blame her.

Perhaps the most famous part is the Bloody Tower—the name seems to sum up the history of the place. Some inmates, however, must have found it tolerably comfortable, as jails go. Sir Walter Raleigh spent thirteen years there—for seven of them his wife was permitted to be with him, and his son, Carew, was actually born there. He received visitors and worked on his *History of the World*.

Of course, you'll want to see the Crown Jewels, and doubtless you'll be impressed by the elaborate precautions taken to ensure their safety. Formerly they were kept in the Martin Tower, and while they were there a Colonel Thomas Blood made a determined effort to steal them, actually getting as far as Traitors' Gate before he was stopped. Instead of being punished, he received a royal pension. Understandable perhaps, when rumour said that Charles II, being short of ready cash, had connived with Blood over the attempted theft. Since most of these jewels were scattered during Cromwell's Commonwealth, the ones you see today are largely post-Restoration (after Charles I). Since 1967, the jewels have been kept in a depository below the Wakefield Tower.

The Tower is a peaceful enough place today, and it is pleasant to sit in the gardens near the ancient cannon and watch the Thames roll by. Remember, however, that the Tower is still a military fortress. You'll see the troops of crack regiments as well as the Yeoman Warders in their picturesque Tudor-style uniforms.

Tower Bridge, nearby, is frequently mistaken for London Bridge, upstream. Tower Bridge is new, having opened to traffic only in 1894.

Near the Tower is All Hallows church, important to American visitors as it was the site both of William Penn's baptism in 1644 and the marriage of John Quincy Adams, sixth president of the U.S.A.

The East End

The Tower of London and Tower Bridge, being on the eastern edge of the City of London, mark about the farthest east that the visitor generally goes. Beyond these two great landmarks lies the East End, slightly forbidding, both through its looks and its reputation. The districts have evocative names like Limehouse, Wapping and Isle of Dogs; the area contains the vast concentration of the docks, some notorious streets, and hundreds of thousands of Londoners who are never seen in the more sophisticated haunts of the West End.

EXPLORING LONDON

To be a Cockney, one has to be born within the sound of the church bells of St. Mary le Bow, on Cheapside. The Cockney is a quintessential Londoner who may suddenly begin using the local slang, which operates on a rhyming system: thus "apples and pears" means "stairs", "trouble and strife" means "wife", and so on. Quite fun, but it is not used extensively.

The East End really starts at Aldgate, a dull-looking area, but rich in history. The two main thoroughfares—Whitechapel High Street and Commercial Road—are wide and monotonous, but the area has many delights. There are, for example, some superb churches by the great 18th-century architect, Nicholas Hawksmoor, such as St. Anne's (at the junction of Commercial Road and West Ferry Road), and also, in Cannon Street Road, St. George-in-the-East, which was badly damaged in 1914, but has been cleverly rebuilt with a modern church inside the old walls. There are a number of pretty Georgian squares and rows in this area, hardly worth seeking out for their individual value, but lending incidental pleasures to exploration.

Perhaps the best plan is to spend a whole summer evening down here, to catch the full flavour of the atmosphere as well as to see the churches and dock landscapes at their magical best. Begin by eating in one of the restaurants in the City of London, or in the East End. Afterwards, call in at one or two (or more) pubs. The pubs are the East End's nightlife—they are big, noisy, inexpensive and always have an amazing variety of entertainment. Towards the end of the East India Dock Road is the *Iron Bridge Tavern*, which has a reputation for good jazz. Or go down the Commercial Road and turn off down West India Dock Road and then West Ferry Road. Here the Thames makes a big loop, containing within it many docks; the area is called the Isle of Dogs. Down West Ferry Road, there are many pubs, all with rows of motorcars parked outside (a sure sign that a pub is worth going to). There is amateur entertainment at the *City Arms*, just by a swing bridge and usually with a vast ship towering over it. Further along, be on the lookout for Glengarnock Avenue and the *Waterman's Arms*, a beautiful recreation of an Edwardian pub, always offering singing and entertainment.

Just along Whitechapel High Street is the Whitechapel Art Gallery, which now has an international reputation for its major exhibitions of modern art. Also running out of the same street is Middlesex Street—known everywhere as Petticoat Lane—the huge, crowded, noisy bustling street market which is at its height on Sunday mornings. Along Commercial Road is the London Opera Centre, once the *Roxy*, the biggest cinema in the East End, now converted to contain a stage like that of the Royal Opera House, where much rehearsal and training is done.

The London Docks are the biggest in the world, though they are curiously hard to find on foot; the most one usually sees is a tantalizing row of cranes on the sky-line, or more sensationally, an ocean-going boat at anchor, apparently at the end of a quiet little street. The wharves are screened from the roads by characteristic high walls, a feature of dockland. Cable Street was once notorious as an area full of drinking-dens and worse; it is now being demolished.

It is no good pretending that this area makes a charming afternoon visit. The high spots are far apart and getting about is difficult unless you know the bus routes and numbers. But it should not be missed, for here is the lifeblood of London.

Behind the *Wa'erman's* is a little public park. Walk in there and you are by the river, directly opposite Christopher Wren's superb Royal Naval College at Greenwich, with Inigo Jones' Queen's House central in the perspective—an unexpected and splendid view. When you reel out of the pub at closing time, it will be dark. Walk a little by the river, or wander down an alley between warehouses to the water's edge—the river is wide and silky, and London glows in the distance, silhouetting the profile of the docks. (There is a pedestrian tunnel under the river here to Greenwich if you want to walk *under* water.)

The docks can be seen from the river on the usual boat trips from Westminster Bridge to Greenwich, and further detailed explorations are also possible. For information about tours and cruises contact the Public Relations Officer, Port of London Authority, Trinity Square, E.C.3.

Conclude the evening by stopping off at Aldgate and eating at Tubby Isaacs' stall in the street; he sells prawns, whelks, jellied eels and cockles. Lots of interesting characters to talk to. You will be exhausted and exhilarated; you will have felt like a tourist (which is unavoidable), but you will at least have seen the East End at its most glamorous.

Greenwich and South London

After Tower Bridge, the banks of the Thames take on a new workman-like character. Massive warehouses and cranes loom over a bewildering variety of ships flying the flags of every nation in the world. The best way to see the thriving industry of the Port of London is to take an afternoon's excursion from Tower Hill on a small motor launch which chugs round the bewildering collections of docks that go up to make the Port of London. It is sometimes hard to remember that the source of this river is, at the most, three hours' drive away in a tiny Cotswold village, with trout leaping in its infant stream.

By far the most interesting place on this side of London is Greenwich, with its Royal Naval Hospital, maritime museum and the famous *Cutty Sark*. It is also the site of the original Greenwich Observatory, on a hill behind the college, through which runs the zero meridian of longitude. You can stand at the very line, one foot east, one foot west. (The observatory today is housed at Herstmonceux, near the Sussex coast.)

The Royal Naval College is the work of Christopher Wren, who built St. Paul's Cathedral, its architectural splendour ranking second in all of his masterpieces. It was first built as a royal palace for Henry VIII, and it was here that Queen Elizabeth and her ill-fated sister, Mary, were born. Since the time of William III, it has been the home of old naval pensioners.

Close by the hospital is the *Cutty Sark*, preserved in a dry dock. This is the most famous of the tea clippers that used to sail around the world during the last century. The ship is open daily to visitors and is an excellent reminder of the days when clippers like the *Cutty Sark* would sail from Australia to England in 100 days. On view in a special dry dock near the *Cutty Sark* is the yacht *Gipsy Moth IV*, in which Sir Francis Chichester made his historic single-handed voyage around the world in 1967.

The south bank of the Thames in London is hardly ever seen by visitors, except as they pass through, detrain at Waterloo Station, or attend performances at the Old Vic or the cultural complex around the Royal Festival Hall. However, there are plenty of intriguing reminders of Old London here for the seeking, provided you can put up with the generally drab atmosphere of the South Bank.

Pride of place is shared between Southwark Cathedral, a proud 13th-century Gothic building with a chapel honoring John Harvard, and the Pilgrim Fathers' Memorial Church in Great Dover Street. Not far from Southwark Cathedral, in St. Thomas Street, you can visit the operating theatre of old St. Thomas's Hospital, complete with bare wooden operating table and a box of sawdust underneath to catch the unfortunate patient's blood!

If you feel in need of a drink after this experience, the place to make for is the *George*, in the Borough High Street, the only galleried inn left in London. At No. 103 in the same street is a Georgian House on the site of John Harvard's family tavern. Or you could try the *Anchor*, another interesting tavern at the corner of Clink Street, which not only serves good food, but also affords fine views across the Thames to St. Paul's Cathedral. The name "Clink Street" recalls the notorious old Clink Prison, now thankfully long vanished, along with the bear pits and the Globe Theatre of Shakespeare's day.

Westward, beyond the Royal Festival Hall complex, stands the Shell Centre, a rather characterless building which nevertheless offers magnificent riverscapes from the public viewing gallery on the 26th floor. West again sprawls the massive bulk of County Hall, leading to the Tudor brick walls of Lambeth Palace and the adjoining church of St. Mary's, in whose churchyard is the tomb of Captain Bligh of "Mutiny on the Bounty" fame. Away to the south, down Lambeth Road, is the Imperial War Museum, filled with the relics of two world wars.

One other South Bank highspot remains to be visited. This is Battersea Park and its Pleasure Gardens, dwarfed by the four giant smoking towers of Battersea Power Station. The gardens are filled with funfair attractions of the Coney Island kind, including a hair-raising Big Dipper ride, but there are also some notable sculptures by Henry Moore to admire.

Hampstead

This is an area that should be visited for many reasons. Hampstead lies to the northwest of central London, high on a hill; it has a clean, refreshing, countrified atmosphere (rather like a particularly charming English county town); it has literary associations, some beautiful houses, good shops, interesting pubs and several first-class restaurants.

If you go by underground, you will emerge at Hampstead tube station in the middle of Old Hampstead, half way up the hill. This is the most picturesque part, with delightful streets like Flask Walk and Well Walk, where the poet Keats lived. Down the hill is Church Row, with some grand Georgian houses; the streets behind the main roads also offer many architectural delights.

Hampstead is dominated by its Heath, a vast stretch of parkland, mainly rough (that is, not divided into formal walks), from which there are spectacular views over all London; this is where kites are flown, barrels are rolled, swimming is done and where, on bank holidays, a fair is held.

By the Heath, at the top of the hill, is *Jack Straw's Castle*, a big, recently-modernized pub; further along is the 18th-century inn called *The Spaniards*, which contains, among other literary and historical associations, the pistols that Dick Turpin used—or so they say.

A little farther along to the east is Kenwood, a house built by Robert Adam, set in a fine park and possessing a fine collection of paintings and furniture. In the summer, open-air concerts are held by the lake. Near Hampstead, also topping a hill, is Highgate, again retaining a village atmosphere and some pretty houses. Highgate Cemetery is famous as much for its elaboration of memorial and tombstone as for the famous buried here—the latter including Herbert Spencer, George Eliot, Karl Marx and Michael Faraday.

LONDON'S OUTSKIRTS

Pastoral Beauty in the Capital's Environs

The immediate environment of London offers the visitor many refreshing contrasts which are comparatively easy of access. Good transport, one of the most important advances made in England during the past decade, will get you in and out of the centre quickly. Trains are swifter—especially the electric services to the midlands, and two major motorways, the M1 and the M4, extend almost into central London, which makes it far easier for the motorist to get out of the city. *See pp. 141-2 for details of underground, bus and rail services.*

There is much to see just outside London, whichever direction is taken. Instant countryside, with well-manicured charm, is best found to the west of the capital, going towards Windsor, where the River Thames becomes a pleasant, winding stream with villages and the great houses built by nobles who wanted to live well outside the centre of things.

Practical Information for Environs of London

HOTELS. While all the places mentioned in this chapter are within easy reach of central London on either day- or half-day trips, there are a number of good reasons to stay outside the metropolis and run into London by bus or train. Moreover, a quick visit to certain districts may entice the visitor to extend his tour to more than a day. This list contains selected hotels and inns in the prettier areas, or at places central to a number of beauty spots. They vary in standard; some of the smaller ones have no private bathrooms, but have adequate public ones. But all are comfortable, with acceptable standards of service and comfort. Mileage from London is indicated in brackets.

ASCOT (Berks.). (26.) *Berystede*, a country house hotel. 49 rooms (17 with bath). Swimming pool.

BLETCHINGLEY (Surrey). (22.) Charming village with ancient inn, the *Whyte Harte*, 8 rooms. Originally built in 1388.

BOX HILL (Surrey). (21.) Celebrated beauty spot. *Burford Bridge*, 25 rooms (all with bath) (Trust House). Heated swimming pool; large, beautiful gardens. Dancing nightly in *Burgundy Room* (exc. Sun.), Sat. night dinner dance and cabaret in 15th-century *Tithe Barn*.

CHERTSEY (Surrey). (21.) Thames-side. *Bridge*, 10 rooms (Trust House).

CROYDON (Surrey). (11.) Residential town absorbed by Greater London. New civic centre. Fairfield Halls cultural centre. Convenient springboard for spots south. *Elgin*, 61 rooms; *Queens*, 70 rooms.

DORKING (Surrey). (25.) Good walking centre. *White Horse*, 43 rooms (14 with bath) (Trust House); *Star & Garter*, 12 rooms. Restaurant: *Little Dudley House*.

EGHAM (Surrey). (19.) Thames-side; *Great Fosters*, a 16th-century manor, once home of Anne Boleyn and a hunting lodge of Queen Elizabeth I. 25 rooms (9 with bath). First-class. *Angler's Hotel*, 112 rooms (2 with bath); next to Runnymede on the A-30. Good restaurant and bar.

EPPING (Essex). (23.) London's forest and archeological relics. *Epping Forest Motel*, 28 units (all with bath); *Bell Motor Hotel*, 10 units (all with bath).

EPSOM (Surrey). (16.) Packed during racing weeks. *Drift Bridge*, 19 rooms; *Linden House*, 39 rooms.

CRAWLEY (Sussex). (30). Modern industrial town. Gatwick, London's second airport is here. So is new (1967) *Airport Hotel*, 100 rooms (all with bath).

GODSTONE (Surrey). (20.) Pretty village with cricket green. *White Hart*, 8 rooms, in a very old inn; *Wonham House*, 14 rooms.

GRAVESEND (Kent). (25.) Shipping town on the Thames. *Clarendon Royal*, 32 rooms (3 with bath). Best place to eat is the hotel's *Chop House*.

HADLEY WOOD (Herts.). (12.) Golfing centre. *West Lodge Park*, 30 rooms (10 with bath). Beautifully decorated.

HAMPTON COURT (Middx.). (12.) Riverside resort, historic palace. On the river, 300-years-old. *Mitre*, 6 rooms (2 with bath); *Greyhound*, 16 rooms (Trust House), built for Henry VIII.

HARROW-ON-THE-HILL (Middx.) (11.) Charming town on the hill, famous school. *King's Head*, 20 rooms (1 with bath).

HAYES (Middx.). See *London Airport* in London hotel listings.

HEMEL HEMPSTEAD (Herts.). (25.) A "new town". *Breakspear*, Trust House motel, 28 rooms (all with bath). Very comfortable.

LEATHERHEAD (Surrey). (19.) Riverside town; theatre, golf. *New Bull*, 9 rooms (2 with bath).

LETCHWORTH (Herts.). (37.) *Letchworth Hall*, 16th-century house, with adjoining golf course. 18 rooms (7 with bath).

OXTED (Surrey). (22.) Country village. *Hoskins Arms*, 18 rooms, (2 with bath).

REIGATE (Surrey). (22.) At the foot of the North Downs. *Monks Court*, 34 rooms (2 with bath); *Bridge House Motel*, Reigate Hill, 12 suites, all well-equipped and overlooking heated swimming pool; also excellent restaurant.

RICHMOND (Surrey). (10.) Beauty spot on the Thames. *Richmond Hill*, 85 rooms (7 with bath) *King's Head*, 20 rooms, an old-fashioned hotel.

ROEHAMPTON (Surrey). (15.) *Golden Egg Motel*, 85 rooms with bath. First class. New.

ST. ALBANS (Herts.). (21.) Cathedral city, Roman capital of Britain, major remains. *White Hart*, 10 rooms, good food; an ancient inn. Also *Great Red Lion*, 15 rooms; *Peahen*, 14 rooms; and *The Pré*, 14 rooms, outside the city.

SANDERSTEAD (Surrey). (14.) Quiet spot, good for points south. *Selsdon Park Hotel*, 156 rooms (most with bath). Set in park with golf, tennis, riding, swimming available.

SEVENOAKS (Kent). (25.) Near Knole House. *Royal Oak*, 28 rooms (2 with bath).

SHEPPERTON (Middx.). (17.) On the river. *Thames Court*, 12 rooms. *Ship*, 12 rooms with showers.

SOUTH MIMMS (Herts.). (15.) *Esso Motor Hotel*, 74 rooms (all with bath). Very modern and comfortable. Good restaurant.

STAINES (Surrey). (17.) Thames-side resort. *Angel*, 10 rooms; *Pack Horse*, 16 rooms with river views and *Windjammer Bar*. Both have restaurants.

STEVENAGE. (Herts.) (32) Modern motel attached to old inn: *Roebuck Post House*, 40 rooms with bath.

SUNNINGDALE (Berks.). (24.) Noted golf centre. *Sunningdale*, 5 rooms, good food.

WALTON-ON-THAMES (Surrey). (17.) *Ashley Park*, 9 rooms, restuarant: *Weir Hotel*, on the river.

WATFORD (Herts.). (18.) Good golf. New (1968): *Caledonian*, 90 rooms with bath. *Rose & Crown*, 21 rooms.

WESTERHAM (Kent). (23.) Lovely countryside, near Sir Winston Churchill's home. *King's Arms*, 12 rooms.

WEYBRIDGE (Surrey). (19.) Ancient Thames side town. *Oatlands Park*, 160 rooms (46 with bath). Swimming pool in large grounds. River-side pub: *Lincoln Arms*.

WINDSOR (Berks.). (23.) *Old House*, a country hotel. Built by Sir C. Wren in 1675. On the Thames, 40 rooms (16 with bath). Next: *Castle* or *White Hart*, about same size and facilities.

LONDON'S OUTSKIRTS

INNS AND RESTAURANTS. One of the great pleasures of touring England is sitting, on a summer evening, in a pleasant pub, chatting amiably to the locals or just watching the tranquil world ease by. There are many small inns and pubs on the roads of England, and the immediate environment of London is no exception. Perhaps you are likely to come across a higher proportion of roadhouses with several bars, restaurants and sometimes swimming pools and dancing. This short list consists of places where you can get a drink and a snack under pleasantly traditional conditions. Where a hotel restaurant is best the fact has been so indicated under *Hotel* listings.

CHIGWELL (Essex). *The King's Head*, where Dickens was living when he wrote *Barnaby Rudge*; *Two Brewers*, another pub with historical interest.

DORKING. *Star Inn*, renowned for snacks and sandwiches.

EGHAM. *Bailiwick*, by Windsor Great Park, serves good Spanish and French dishes.

EPSOM. *Spread Eagle*. Near the race course, so lots of horsey chat. Also good, the *Epsom Grill*.

GUILDFORD (Surrey). *Angel Hotel, Bull's Head, The Horse & Groom, Merrow*.

HAMPTON WICK (Surrey). *Old King's Head*.

OXTED. *The Old Bell*, a timbered country pub.

RICHMOND. *Three Pigeons, Castle Hotel, White Cross Hotel*—by the river; *White Swan Hotel; Richmond Rendezvous*, excellent Chinese food (attracts regular clients from London).

WESTERHAM. *Grasshopper*. Haunt of local youth for dancing; pleasant bar, good food.

WINDSOR. *Knight's Tavern*, with King Arthur decor, is good.

ENTERTAINMENT. Every suburb of London is well-equipped with cinemas, often two or three belonging to the major groups. Some have independent "art houses", showing better-quality foreign films. Releases from the West End go to north London and then south London. It is worth-while knowing that a quick bus ride can bring you to a cinema where you can see last week's West End hit at a fraction of its West End price.

There are fewer out-of-town theatres, but the Golder's Green *Hippodrome* has West End hits (before or after). Other notable theatres are: *Ashcroft*, Croydon; the *Palace*, Watford; *Richmond Theatre; New Theatre* at Bromley (in Kent); *Queens'* at Hornchurch; *Leatherhead Repertory Theatre* and the *Yvonne Arnaud Theatre* at Guildford. The *Theatre Royal*, Angel Lane, Stratford East, is a charming house and has a reputation for experimental and off-beat work.

Historic Houses Open to the Public

For opening dates, see p. 44.

BEDFORDSHIRE. *Woburn Abbey*. Home of the Duke of Bedford. 18th-century treasure house, deer park and only herd of European bison. Also a bevy of giraffes installed in 1969. Open daily in afternoons, throughout the year.

Luton Hoo. Home of Sir H. Wernher. Open Mons., Weds.. Thurs., Sats., Bank Holidays and Sunday afternoons, spring, summer, autumn.

BERKSHIRE. *Windsor Castle.* Royal residence. The world's largest inhabited castle. Open daily except when the Court is in residence.

BUCKINGHAMSHIRE. *Hughenden Manor*, High Wycombe. National Trust. Home of Disraeli. Open Tuesday to Friday, February to December.

ESSEX. *Ingatestone Hall.* Dates from 1540. Open April to early October. Admission free.

HERTFORDSHIRE. *Hatfield House.* Home of the Marquess of Salisbury. Queen Elizabeth I lived here. Open April to early October.

Knebworth House. near Stevenage. Fine Tudor mansion. Open weekends, May to September.

Salisbury Hall, near St. Albans. Moated 17th century house associated with Nell Gwynne. Open Sundays, April to September, also Thursdays from July to September.

KENT. *Knole.* Home of Lord Sackville. Built in 1456. Open March through December, Wed. through Saturday.

Penshurst Place. Home of Rt. Hon. Viscount De L'Isle. Dates from 1340. Open Weds., Thurs., Sats. and Sundays, April through September.

Chartwell. Home of the late Sir Winston Churchill, now owned by the National Trust as a permanent memorial. Open Weds. and Thurs., March to November.

Chiddingstone Castle, near Edenbridge. Royal Stuart and Jacobite relics. Open daily (not Mondays), Easter through October.

Hever Castle, near Edenbridge. Home of Henry VIII's second wife, Anne Boleyn. Splendid gardens. Open Wednesday and Sunday afternoons. Easter through September.

MIDDLESEX. *Hampton Court Palace.* Former residence of Cardinal Wolsey and Henry VIII. Fantastic maze. Open all year.

Syon House (Brentford). Home of the Duke of Northumberland. New (1968) national *Garden Centre* in park. Open April through September. Weds. through Sats., also Bank Holidays and each Sunday from July on.

SURREY. *Kew Palace.* Built in Dutch style, 1631. Maintained by Ministry of Works. Open April through September, weekdays and Sun. afternoons.

Exploring London's Environs

Just to get out of the built-up conglomeration of London for a few hours, and as a specific trip, try the Royal Botanic Gardens (known as Kew Gardens) which are especially popular during the spring and summer. The gardens cover 288 acres and contain more than 25,000 varieties of plants. There are strong Hanoverian associations here, as the gardens were actually begun (in 1759) by Princess Augusta, George III's mother. The Georges and their queens spent much time here and Kew House contains plenty of their memorabilia. The gardens have beautiful walks and the plants are housed in a series of sometimes spectacular buildings, such as the Orangery, the Palm House, built by Decimus Burton, and various hothouses. A feature is the pagoda, built in 1761 by Sir William Chambers—a delicious folly. Kew itself is on the river, with a village green fringed with 18th-century houses; the painters Gainsborough and Zoffany are buried in the church yard.

Richmond

Just up river is Richmond, which has been a favourite residential town since Henry VII (at the time, Duke of Richmond, in Yorkshire) changed its name from "Sheen". It is picturesquely sited on the slope of a hill, at the top of which is Richmond Park. The hill commands a celebrated and fine view of the Thames and the park (2,350 acres), which is stocked with deer. There are several private (and originally, royal) residences in the park, some open for inspection. Richmond also contains a number of pleasant pubs and the *Richmond Theatre,* an elegant and well-known repertory house.

Richmond is particularly rich in fine houses and literary associations. On the southwest side of Richmond Green is all that remains of the Richmond Palace and on its site is now a series of interesting houses. The side streets of Richmond well merit exploring for their quaint alleyways, largely given over to antique and curio shops.

An extension of Richmond Park is Ham Common, and just outside Richmond is Petersham, a delightful riverside village with more 17th- and 18th-century houses, including Ham House, with souvenirs of Elizabeth I (including a touching earring that has a lock of the ill-starred Earl of Essex's hair).

Following the course of the river, Kingston-upon-Thames is now reached. This is a busy market town and a royal borough,

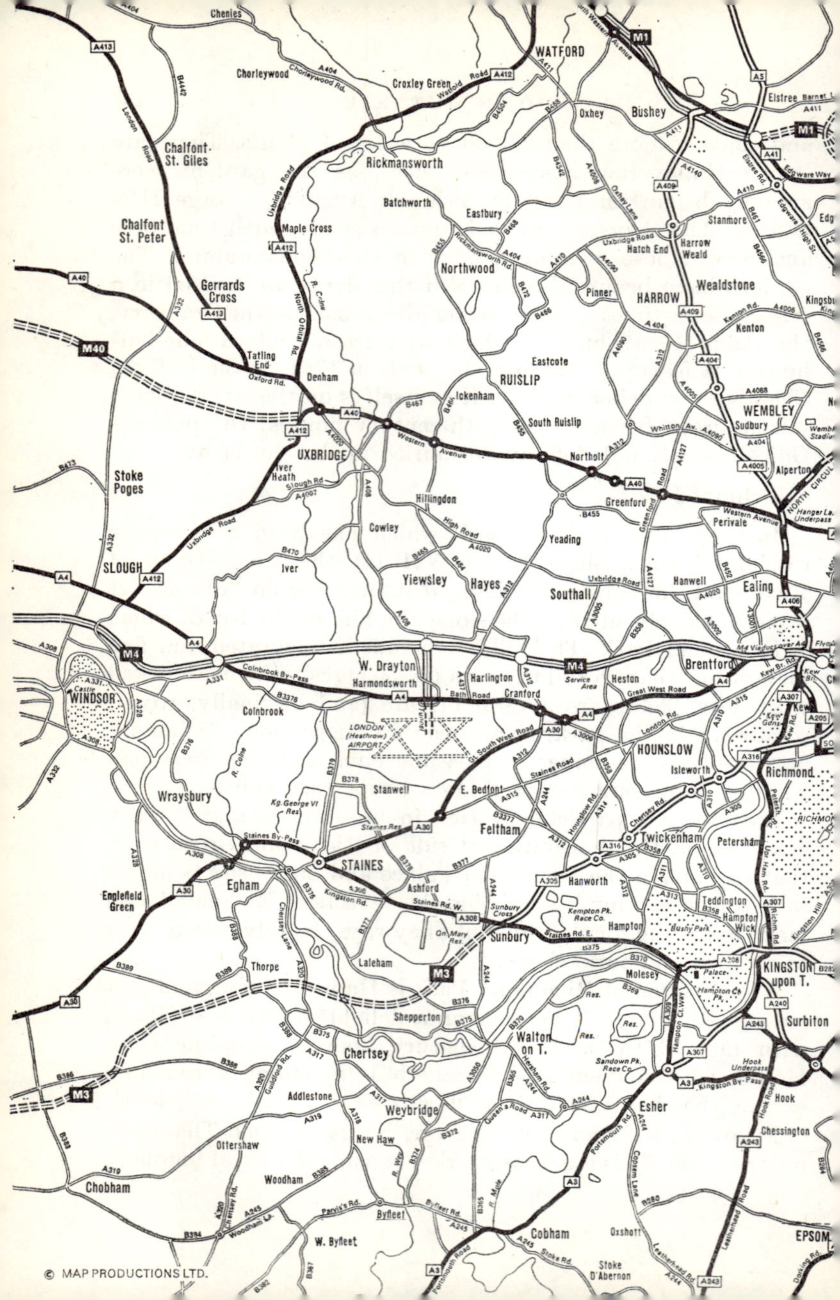
Chenies
WATFORD
M1
Chorleywood
Chorleywood Rd.
Croxley Green
Watford Road
A412
A413
Oxhey
Bushey
Elstree
Barnet L.
A411
A5
London Road
Chalfont St. Giles
Rickmansworth
Uxbridge Road
Batchworth
Eastbury
Edgware Way
Stanmore
Edgware High St.
Chalfont St. Peter
Maple Cross
Northwood
Rickmansworth Rd.
Uxbridge Road
Hatch End
Harrow Weald
Pinner
HARROW
Wealdstone
A40
Gerrards Cross
North Orbital Rd.
R. Colne
Kenton Rd.
Kenton
M40
Tatling End
Oxford Rd.
Denham
Eastcote
RUISLIP
Ickenham
WEMBLEY
Sudbury
Whitton Av.
South Ruislip
Wembley Stadium
UXBRIDGE
Western Avenue
Northolt
Alperton
Iver Heath
Slough Rd.
Stoke Poges
Greenford Road
Greenford
NORTH CIRCULAR
Hanger La. Underpass
Hillingdon
Perivale
Cowley
High Road
Yeading
Iver
SLOUGH
Yiewsley
Hayes
Uxbridge Road
Hanwell
Ealing
Southall
M4
A4
A308
M4 Viaduct over A4
W. Drayton
Harmondsworth
Harlington
Service Area
Heston
Brentford
Kew Br. Rd.
Kew
Colnbrook By-Pass
Castle
WINDSOR
Bath Road
Cranford
Great West Road
Colnbrook
LONDON (Heathrow) AIRPORT
Gt. South West Road
London Rd.
Kew Gdns.
Kew Rd.
HOUNSLOW
Richmond
Staines Road
Isleworth
Wraysbury
R. Colne
Stanwell
E. Bedfont
Kg. George VI Res.
Staines Res.
Feltham
Chertsey Rd.
Hounslow Rd.
Twickenham
Petersham
RICHMOND
Staines By-Pass
STAINES
Egham
Englefield Green
Kingston Rd.
Ashford
Hanworth
Staines Rd. W.
Sunbury Cross
Kempton Pk. Race Co.
Teddington
Hampton
Hampton Wick
Bushy Park
Qn. Mary Res.
Sunbury
Staines Rd. E.
Richm. Rd.
Kingston Hill
Chertsey Lane
M3
Thorpe
Laleham
Molesey
Palace
Hampton Ct. Pk.
KINGSTON upon T.
Shepperton
Res.
Surbiton
Chertsey
Walton on T.
Hampton Ct. Way
Sandown Pk. Race Co.
Hook Underpass
Kingston By-Pass
Hook
Addlestone
Guildford Rd.
Weybridge
Hersham Rd.
Queen's Road
Esher
Hook Road
Chessington
Ottershaw
New Haw
R. Wey
Portsmouth Rd.
Copsem Lane
Chobham
Woodham
R. Mole
Byfleet
Parvis's Rd.
Byfleet Rd.
Chertsey Rd.
Woodham La.
Cobham
Oxshott
Leatherhead Road
EPSOM
W. Byfleet
Stoke Rd.
Stoke D'Abernon
Portsmouth Road
Leatherhead Rd.
Dorking Rd.
© MAP PRODUCTIONS LTD.

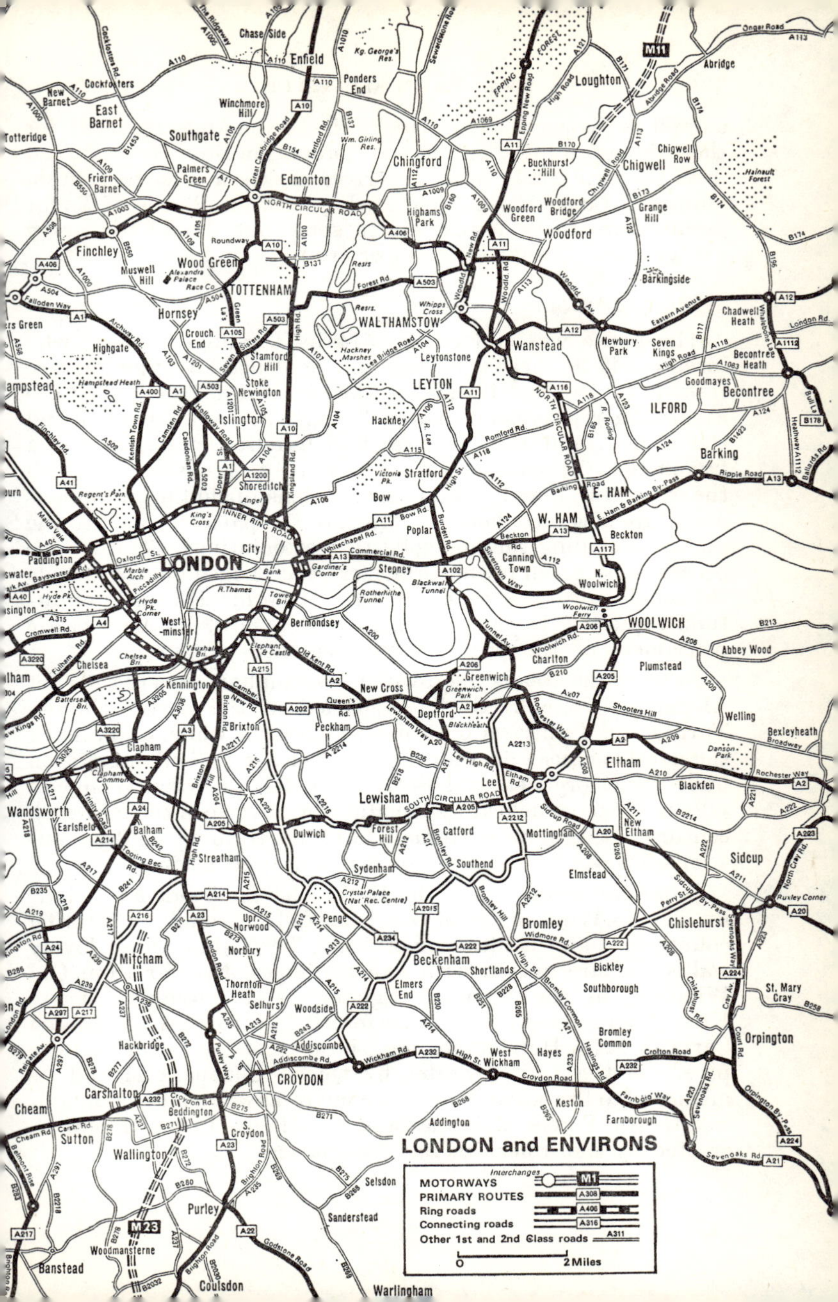
LONDON and ENVIRONS
Interchanges
MOTORWAYS
M1
PRIMARY ROUTES
A308
Ring roads
A406
Connecting roads
A316
Other 1st and 2nd Class roads
A311
0
2 Miles
Enfield
Chase Side
Ponders End
Kg. George's Res.
Loughton
Abridge
Onger Road
EPPING FOREST
Epping New Road
M11
Cockfosters
New Barnet
East Barnet
Winchmore Hill
Southgate
Totteridge
Edmonton
Chingford
Buckhurst Hill
Chigwell
Chigwell Row
Hainault Forest
Palmers Green
Friern Barnet
NORTH CIRCULAR ROAD
Highams Park
Woodford Green
Woodford Bridge
Grange Hill
Woodford
Finchley
Muswell Hill
Wood Green
Alexandra Palace
TOTTENHAM
WALTHAMSTOW
Whipps Cross
Barkingside
Hornsey
Crouch End
Stamford Hill
Stoke Newington
Hackney Marshes
Leytonstone
Wanstead
Newbury Park
Seven Kings
Chadwell Heath
Becontree Heath
Highgate
Hampstead Heath
LEYTON
Goodmayes
Becontree
ILFORD
Islington
Hackney
Barking
Regent's Park
Shoreditch
Victoria Pk.
Stratford
E. HAM
Bow
W. HAM
Beckton
Paddington
King's Cross
INNER RING ROAD
City
Poplar
LONDON
Marble Arch
Bank
Gardiner's Corner
Stepney
Canning Town
N. Woolwich
Hyde Pk.
R. Thames
Tower Bri.
Rotherhithe Tunnel
Blackwall Tunnel
Hyde Pk. Corner
West-minster
Bermondsey
Woolwich Ferry
WOOLWICH
Elephant & Castle
Old Kent Rd.
Charlton
Abbey Wood
Chelsea
Vauxhall Bri.
Kennington
New Cross
Greenwich
Greenwich Park
Plumstead
Battersea Bri.
Brixton
Peckham
Deptford
Blackheath
Shooters Hill
Welling
Clapham
Bexleyheath Broadway
Clapham Common
Eltham
Danson Park
Rochester Way
Wandsworth
Lewisham
SOUTH CIRCULAR ROAD
Lee
Blackfen
Earlsfield
Balham
Dulwich
Forest Hill
Catford
Mottingham
New Eltham
Streatham
Sydenham
Southend
Elmstead
Sidcup
Crystal Palace (Nat. Rec. Centre)
Penge
Upr. Norwood
Bromley
Chislehurst
Ruxley Corner
Mitcham
Norbury
Beckenham
Shortlands
Bickley
Thornton Heath
Elmers End
Southborough
St. Mary Cray
Selhurst
Woodside
Addiscombe
West Wickham
Hayes
Bromley Common
Orpington
Hackbridge
CROYDON
Croydon Road
Crofton Road
Carshalton
Beddington
Keston
Farnborough
Cheam
Sutton
S. Croydon
Addington
Wallington
Orpington By-Pass
Sevenoaks Rd.
Selsdon
Purley
Sanderstead
M23
Woodmansterne
Banstead
Coulsdon
Warlingham
Godstone Road

as well as the coronation-place of the Saxon kings from 910 (or thereabouts) to 978. The Saxon Coronation Stone is preserved near the Guildhall. Here, the river makes a loop to contain Hampton Court Palace, one of the finest specimens of Tudor architecture to be found, and a spot that should top every visitor's list of what to see in or around London.

Hampton Court

The house was started in 1514 by Cardinal Wolsey, who intended it to surpass in size and opulence all other private residences. Henry VIII rather liked it, and in 1529 forced the cardinal to relinquish it to him. The king added a great hall and the chapel, and for the next two hundred years, it was a favourite royal residence. With reason—its site is perfect, with the river running by, and the gardens, including a famous maze, are elegantly laid out. Much of the palace is open to the public, including the fine collection of paintings. Concerts are occasionally given in the Orangery, and alleged ghosts include the shades of Jane Seymour and Catherine Howard (unfortunate queens). Royalty doesn't live here now, but aristocratic pensioners of the crown have residence.

In the same area is the town of Twickenham, where the poet Alexander Pope lived—he is buried in the parish church. Turner and Tennyson both lived here for a while, and among the notable houses are Marble Hill House, a Palladian mansion built for George II, and Strawberry Hill, Horace Walpole's villa in the most delicately fanciful Gothic style of the mid-18th century. It is now a Roman Catholic training college, but admission can be obtained on written application.

From Hampton Court, the River Thames bends and winds its way to Windsor. It moves peacefully through enchanting countryside and is ideal for cruising. The banks afford lovely walks and are dotted with sweet villages. Not far from Old Windsor, in the town of Egham, is Runnymede where King John's rebellious barons forced him to sign the Magna Carta in 1215. Here stand, too, the acre of land ceded to the people of the United States by Queen Elizabeth II and its memorial to President John F. Kennedy, as well as the Commonwealth Air Forces Memorial and the Magna Carta Memorial, erected by the American Bar Association.

The Burlington Arcade, sporting a distinctively dressed "beadle," is among London's best known and most fashionable shopping centers. Tradition decrees that you may not enter it carrying an opened umbrella.

A timeless reminder of England's stormy past, the monumental ramparts of Arundel Castle in Sussex. "Let nature be your teacher" ... Wordsworth's ideal comes true in this lovely mixture of nature and learning at Cambridge, second oldest University in Britain.

Windsor

Lying in the extreme east of the county of Berkshire, almost on the Surrey and Buckinghamshire borders, is the historic town of Windsor, the home of English kings, at least since the times of Henry I, and possibly before. The grey stone castle dominates the town and looks out over the Thames, but this is not simply a show-piece town—there is a great deal of light industry in its environs, and anyone who arrives by train will see that not all the streets have the gracefulness of Park Street and High Street. Naturally, the Royal Castle and the surrounding parks are the chief focus of interest, but the town round the castle has its own special charm and it is well worth wandering in the narrow streets.

The first king recorded as living in the Windsor area was Edward the Confessor, who gave his palace at Old Windsor to Westminster Abbey before he died. William the Conqueror, realizing the military importance of the site, built himself a fortress. Timber fortifications were replaced with stone by Henry II and Henry III, who built the three drum towers overlooking Thames Street. Most medieval kings resided in Windsor, some for two or three weeks at a time. Edward I lived here and gave the town its royal charter, while Edward III transformed the old castle, building new apartments, the great round tower, the Norman gateway and the two other towers, all of which still stand today. Edward IV began St. George's Chapel, Henry VII completed the nave and Henry VIII set the vault over the choir, and built the castle gateway. Elizabeth I built the north terrace and Charles II restored the state apartments. But it was George IV who transformed the essentially medieval castle into the royal palace you can visit today. Later William IV built the Waterloo Chamber and Queen Victoria decorated the Albert Memorial Chapel.

Despite the multiplicity of hands that have gone into the making of Windsor, the palace has managed to retain a unity of style and a very marked character of its own. It is, in fact, the largest inhabited castle in the world. The Round Tower, which is, of course, not round, rises above the walls to the height of 230 feet, dividing the structure of the castle into two wards—the upper ward with the royal apartments and the lower ward, containing St. George's Chapel, the deanery and cloisters.

It is difficult to think of many Englishmen who have not walked along the castle terraces. Chaucer, for one, is said to have lived here while he was in charge of building improvements. It is from the North Terrace that entry is gained into the State Apartments, which can be visited by the public when the Queen is not in residence. The present queen, in fact, uses the castle far more than any of her predecessors. It has become over the last decade a sort of country weekend residence, which allows the royal family a few days of relaxation and informality away, as much as possible, from the public eye. On these occasions, Prince Philip often captains his polo team against local groups in Windsor Great Park. Apart from the splendour and grandeur of the various rooms that go to make up the State Apartments, a visit to the Queen's Doll House should not be missed. Given to Queen Mary in 1924, it is a perfect, fully-working palace within a palace. Electric lights work, the doors all have keys, the lifts are practical and there is running water. There is even a miniature library, with over two hundred tiny books.

St. George's Chapel, in the lower ward, is one of the noblest buildings in England. Over 230 feet from end to end, with two tiers of great windows and hundreds of gargoyles, buttresses and pinnacles, it is quite grand. The exterior of the chapel is only rivalled by the interior. Light floods in from the stained glass windows, and above the dark oak of the stalls hang the banners, swords and helmets of the Knights of the Order of the Garter. Here lie some of the most famous kings of England, beginning with Henry VI, and including Charles I, Henry VIII (Jane Seymour, the mother of his only son, is also here) and many others, up to the late King George VI.

The beauty of the church in the lower ward is matched by the exquisite reception rooms, a guard room, and a picture gallery. The Gobelins tapestries in the reception room are splendid and so is the collection of pictures, with a Rubens and a Van Dyck room. The royal library contains a fine collection of Da Vinci's drawings and 87 portraits by Holbein.

The walls of the castle itself include only 13 acres of land, but below the battlements are nearly 1,800 acres of Windsor Great Park. Charles II planted an avenue of elm trees, the Love Walk, to join castle and park. On the southeast side of the castle is the smaller Home Park, filled with great oaks, some of which were planted in the time of the first Queen Elizabeth. It was here at Frogmore that Queen Victoria liked to spend her days.

The River from Greenwich to the Sea

The Thames to the west of London is often referred to as the country's second coastline, with its pleasant hotels, boating facilities and scenery, and during the summer months Londoners regularly flock to Maidenhead, Henley and Marlow, to escape the city for a few hours. But there are very few Londoners who regularly visit the Thames east of London, and if they do so, it is to travel abroad or to visit the capital's closest seaside resort, Southend-on-Sea.

Beyond Greenwich and the charming Blackheath, lies Woolwich, on the south bank of the river, with its arsenal (where more than 40,000 people were employed during the Second World War) and military establishments and the interesting museum of the Royal Artillery. At nearby Abbey Wood can be found the ruins of Lessness Abbey, now cleared to reveal the complete plan of the 12th-century monastery (including the domestic buildings). In Dartford, Wat Tyler's rebellion may have started; it is a market town with a good church that has some interesting tombs. Horns Cross and Greenhithe, further on, are pleasant places with naval and historical associations.

Gravesend is the port from which Leonard Calvert (whose father, Lord Baltimore, founded Maryland) set sail in 1633, and from where George Fox and the Wesleys began their American journeys. It is the pilot station for vessels using the Port of London and has a characteristic atmosphere of the sea and ships with pubs and old houses. The Indian princess Pocahontas is buried in St. George's church here.

Across the river (steam ferry) lie Tilbury Docks, which, though some 26 miles below London Bridge, are the last in the series of the London docks. It is a place with strong historical associations. The original rights for the ferry were granted by Henry IV to Gravesend as recompense for the assaults of a French pirate and the Fort was built by Henry VIII in 1539. It was the major position of defence for London in the 16th century and a garrison was assembled there in 1588 in preparation to welcome the Spanish Armada. To this great army Queen Elizabeth I addressed her famous speech from horseback: "I know I have the body of a weak and feeble woman, but I have the heart and stomach of a king, and of a king of England, too".

From Gravesend onwards, the river rapidly broadens out, the smell of the sea becomes more distinct, and the now rare Thames sailing barges are sometimes to be seen carrying cargoes to the coastal towns of Essex and Suffolk. Occasionally, there are races of these old craft, and if you are fortunate enough to witness one, you will be filled with admiration for the skill with which their crews handle the vast amount of sail.

River estuaries are favourite sites for oil refineries and the Thames estuary is no exception. The vast almost spacelike constructions, at Thameshaven and Shellhaven, dominate the river landscape for miles. They soon give way to the cottages of Canvey Island, a favourite summer resort for people living in nearby counties. Practically the last site before the Thames finally enters the North Sea is the longest pleasure pier in the world, at Southend-on-Sea. This is the very epitome of the popular seaside resort, with its golden mile of amusements, pleasure pier, hot dog stands, circuses, funfairs and cockle-and-whelk stalls.

Epping Forest

To the northeast lies Epping Forest, often referred to as "the Londoner's forest", 6,000 acres of woodland which, though almost 12 miles long, is rarely more than two miles wide and often less. By leaving the paths, it is possible to immerse oneself completely in the forest glades, where the atmosphere is remarkably similar to that of Robin Hood's Sherwood Forest, in Nottinghamshire. There are a number of varieties of wild life in Epping Forest (including poisonous adders), the present piece of which is all that remains of the royal hunting forest of Waltham.

Waltham Abbey is worth looking at. Harold, who was killed at the Battle of Hastings, is buried here and the architecture is a blend of 11th, 12th, 15th and 19th centuries. The entire area has great archeological interest, including a big earthwork, Ambersbury Banks, where Boadicea is traditionally supposed to have been defeated by Suetonius. Beyond Waltham Cross sits the old Temple Bar, removed from its position in the Strand in 1888 and erected as an entrance to the Theobalds Park estate.

St. Albans and the North

St. Albans lies just over 20 miles to the north of London and is swiftly accessible by train and easily by bus. It is the successor to the capital of Roman Britain called Verulamium, built beside the little river called the Ver. The site of the Roman *municipium* (which lasted from A.D. 43 to about 410, surviving a sacking by the irrepressible Boadicea) is now occupied by a park and school playing fields, but much remains, including the major Roman finds of Britain. Part of the city wall stands and archeological work is continuing at the site of the Amphitheatre. Visit the Verulamium Museum, in which most of the finds are collected.

Major feature of the modern city is the 11th-century cathedral, which has the longest medieval nave in existence as well as a fine Norman tower; its west front is an unhappy 19th-century addition. St. Albans has considerable historical associations and was the site of two important battles during the Wars of the Roses. Its name derives from St. Alban, a Roman soldier who was the first Christian martyr in England; he was beheaded here in 303 and his tomb is in the cathedral. Verulamium, the ancient Roman City, contains the Roman theatre (the only one to be open to view in Britain) and the Hypercaust, a Roman heating system of a private suite of baths, which has been excavated and preserved.

Between this ancient place and London lie the wealthy outer suburbs, large houses along wide, tree-lined roads or hidden behind secluded gardens. At Elstree and Boreham Wood stand the film studios of British and American companies; Stanmore has two churches; Watford is swamped with industry, and the nearer London one gets, the less interesting the suburbs become, until the fringes of Hampstead and Highgate are reached.

One spot of particular interest, however, is Harrow-on-the-Hill, which possesses one of England's great public schools.

The hill rises about 200 feet from the surrounding plain. The school can be seen by arrangement with the School Custodian if one wishes to examine the physical structure of the most famous side of England's educational system. The museum contains many Greek and Egyptian antiquities.

Sir William Gilbert lived at Harrow Weald in "Grims Dyke", a large and beautiful house built for Frederick Goodhall, the Victorian painter. Gilbert wrote many of the lyrics for the famed Gilbert and Sullivan operas while living in "Grims Dyke" and still to be seen, in what was once the music room, are the minstrels' gallery and a huge 15-foot-high carved alabaster fireplace designed by Sir William himself. After Gilbert's death many pictures of various characters from the operas were found in the house in addition to the block and headsman's axe used in the original production of the *Yeomen of the Guard*.

South of London

Curiously, there is little of interest immediately south of the Thames in central London. Two celebrated beauty spots, however, are easy of access. Dulwich, five miles south of the City of London, is a sought-after residential area that has successfully retained the qualities of a village. Its interest to the visitor (apart from the charming feel of the place) lies in the Dulwich College Picture Gallery, built by Sir John Soane and opened in 1814. Its collection is particularly brilliant (and acquired unusual fame in 1966, when thieves made off with some of its treasures, since recovered), with Dutch masters including Rembrandt, pictures by Raphael, Veronese, Velazquez, Murillo and Poussin, plus much British portraiture of the 17th and 18th centuries. Here, too, are Dulwich College and the last surviving toll gate in London. There are also Dulwich Park and the Horniman Museum, with its collection of musical instruments. Nearby is Crystal Palace—not, unfortunately, the original, but a reconstruction of the palace of glass and iron built in Hyde Park for the Great Exhibition of 1851—that was rebuilt here in 1854 and burned down in 1936. The site is used for a television centre and a National Youth and Sports Centre.

Wimbledon is internationally famous for being the site of

the All-England Lawn Tennis Courts, but possesses, too, a superb common, joining up with Richmond Park to the west and Putney Heath to the north. There is a windmill in the centre, and some fine landscape views, with the tall new flats of south London a distant profile. At the top of Wimbledon Hill, there is a pond on the fringe of the common, and some charming houses, plus one or two good pubs and eating houses.

Sevenoaks, in Kent, is a green, neat place that should be seen in May or early June, but Knole Park, nearby, may be (and, in fact, should be) seen by anybody interested in the old way of life in England. In the time of King John this house belonged to the Earl of Pembroke, and it is open to the public. There are few houses that can compare with Knole House and a visit will bring to anybody a closer and clearer vision of old England.

Churchill's Chartwell

In the summer of 1966, a new focal point for visitors emerged; Chartwell, the home of Sir Winston Churchill, was opened to the public. It is 21 miles south of London in the pleasant county of Kent and just outside the town of Westerham, which is famous as the birthplace of General Wolfe (the victor at Quebec in the French and Indian War). One mile south of the town, one crosses a beautiful wooded ridge of the South Downs; at the end of the ridge is Churchill's country house.

He first inspected it in 1923 and was to live there for 40 years. The National Trust bought the house from the Churchill family in 1946 to preserve it for the nation on the understanding that Sir Winston would have possession for life.

Henry VIII once spent the night there on his way to nearby Hever Castle, where he had Anne Boleyn imprisoned. But Churchill didn't buy the house for its history—he bought it for its setting, which is rapturous, with fine views over lovely orchard country to the south and to the Weald of Kent. Over the years of his residence here, Churchill made many alterations, most important being his total rejection of much Victorian nonsense and the stripping down of the house to its original medeval beams and bricks. For its opening to the public, advice was taken from Lady Churchill and other members of the family to restore as much of the condition and atmosphere of the thirties as possible.

The rooms are full of Churchilliana; here he wrote his epic historical books, *The History of the English Speaking People* and *The Second World War*. There is a large painting of Blenheim Palace, where Sir Winston was born to a beautiful American mother, and an autographed photograph of President Franklin D. Roosevelt. The studio is stacked with paintings, the library is packed with books.

The grounds are virtually Churchill's own creation. In the centre of the 82 acres is a chain of lakes, for which he made the dams himself. He also built the 350-yard-long, seven-foot-high wall around the kitchen garden between 1925 and 1932.

While in the area, see Westerham, already mentioned; it has a nice feel of history about it and Quebec House is open to the public. Hever Castle, at Edenbridge, built at the end of the 13th century, is a moated castle and well worth a visit, not only for its historic associations as the home of Henry VIII's second wife, Anne Boleyn, but also for the beauty of its planned gardens.

Epsom should be seen as it is the most famous place in the racing world, and if you happen to stay in London at the end of May or at the beginning of June when the Derby is run, you should go to Epsom Downs to witness the racing. The Victorian artist Frith made a celebrated painting of Derby Day, when all manner of sideshows, fairground rides, gypsies and tumblers descended on the course. It is still a boisterous and gay occasion, with the fairground fringe very evident, if slightly less picturesque than in Victorian days. Any illusions that the English are placid and undemonstrative will be totally shattered here.

Epsom became established as a fashionable watering place in the mid-18th century, though mineral springs had been discovered there much earlier, in 1620. Horseracing was introduced here by James I as a courtly diversion, but assumed a permanent establishment in 1780 when the Derby and the Oaks were run. These races are named after the 12th Earl of Derby and his seat, The Oaks, which is nearby. The grandstand (in Frith's picture) was built in 1829 but rebuilt later.

This is a particularly beautiful part of the country, with pleasant towns and superb countryside.

To the south, between Epsom and Dorking, is Box Hill, a celebrated beauty spot now preserved by the National Trust and created where the River Mole has carved a deep valley through the wooded chalk escarpment of the North Downs. (Jane Austin lovers will know this as the scene of the dramatic cllmax of *Emma*.) The hill is named after its acres of box-tree woods, and on its western slope is Flint Cottage, where George Meredith lived for 30 years until his death in 1909. Near the station is the late 12th-century West Humble Chapel. In fact there is so much of interest in this pleasant part of Surrey that you may wish to spend a day or two here. A good choice would be the *Burford Bridge Hotel*, beside the River Mole, where Keats wrote the last stanzas of *Endymion*, and Horatio Nelson stayed on his way to fame and death at the Battle of Trafalgar. Or you could stay at the busy market town of Dorking, with its tall church spire, expensive antique shops and old houses. In the wide High Street stands *The White House*, an ancient coaching inn, and there is another very old inn, *The King's Arms*, in West Street.

With Dorking as your base you can explore on foot the ancient Pilgrims' Way, which runs along the southern slopes of Boxhill, or visit Mickleham, where two famous Canadians, the late Lord Beaverbrook and Lord Bennett, a former premier, lie buried in the churchyard, But above all, be sure to visit Polesden Lacey, a National Trust house standing in its own magnificent grounds at Great Bookham, above the valley that links Leatherhead with Dorking. The house was rebuilt in the Regency style in 1824 and houses the Greville collection of pictures, some good furniture and fine porcelain. In summer the local dramatic society stage open-air performances of Shakespeare's plays in the grounds.

THE THAMES COUNTRY

From the Cotswolds to London

by

JULIAN ASTON

Liquid history, that's Old Father Thames. The very name is often synonymous with London and even with Britain itself. As far as size goes, it is hardly in the world-league, being barely 210 miles from source to mouth, and a major part of it is little more than a stream when compared with the mighty continental rivers like the Danube and the Rhine. The Thames is not even the longest river in Britain, as the Bristol-Severn has that honour. But with rivers, as with men, size is no criteria of greatness, and the celebrity of the Thames is well deserved. On its banks grew the city of London, and historically, it has been the cradle of the country's mercantile and naval strength. The same river flows past Windsor Castle, Hampton Court Palace, and the Royal Palace at Greenwich. Prisoners incarcerated in the Tower of London watched its flowing freedom enviously, as perhaps some members of parliament might when trapped in the House on a fresh spring afternoon. Students at Oxford and schoolboys at Eton row or swim or just laze by its banks and, during the summer,

Londoners by the thousand resort to its charms for a few idyllic hours.

The River Thames rises in the county of Gloucestershire, and flows through Oxfordshire, Berkshire and Buckinghamshire before reaching London. It then cuts through the capital and on to the counties of Essex and Kent, finally emerging into the North Sea.

A tour through the Thames country is one of the most richly rewarding that can be made by a visitor to Britain. Not only is the countryside quite beautiful, but there is a veritable surfeit of history at hand. If you tend to suffer from historical indigestion, then the best prescription is to ignore the hundreds of old churches, thatched villages, stately homes and other places of interest, and to simply concentrate on the unrivalled scenic beauty of the river and its surrounding countryside.

Most of the places mentioned in the following section can be visited with comparative ease from London.

Practical Information for the Thames Country

GETTING THERE BY RIVER BOAT. Apart from the river buses that operate in the London area, steamers serve the upper and lower Thames throughout the summer. In the upstream direction, *Salters Steamers* run services from mid-May to mid-September. Their vessels leave Kingston daily, one of them going right through to Oxford and taking three days on the cruise. Nights are spent at Marlow and Reading. Local trips are run periodically between Kingston and Windsor, Windsor and Marlow, Abingdon and Oxford. Teas and light refreshments can be obtained on board. Combined railway and steamer tickets are issued from many *British Rail* stations, but for details of the longer steamer trips, you should contact *Salter Bros. Ltd.*, 11 Folly Bridge, Oxford, *Boat Enquiries Ltd.*, 12 Western Road, Oxford, or any office of *Thomas Cook's* or *American Express*.

Every day from mid-May to mid-September, *British Rail* (Western Region) run a combined rail and steamer trip to Henley and Reading. The river cruise covers nine miles of the loveliest reaches. Ring Paddington Station (PAD 7000) for details.

For those who would like to spend longer on the river, *European Yacht Cruises Ltd.*, 36 Edgware Road, London W.2, operate a one-week cruise, Hampton Court to Oxford and back for a little under $75. Alternatively, if you would rather be your own skipper, you can hire a cosy 4-berth U-drive cabin cruiser, fully equipped, for around $60 per week from *Bushnell's of Maidenhead*, Ray Mead Road, Maidenhead, Berkshire. If the cost is split four ways, this becomes an inexpensive and very enjoyable way of exploring the Thames.

HOTELS AND RESTAURANTS

ABINGDON. Buildings dating back to 15th-century. *Crown & Thistle*, 20 rooms (4 with bath).

AMERSHAM. Charming old town tucked away in the Misbourne Valley, with beautiful 17th-century main street. *Kings Arms Hotel*, 8 rooms (2 with bath); an old coaching inn.

ASTON CLINTON. Buckinghamshire village famed for good food served at *The Bell*.

AYLESBURY. Once famous for its ducks: today, it's a busy county town with an interesting market on Wednesdays and Saturdays. The *King's Head*, a charming old inn, has 14 rooms (2 with bath).

BANBURY. The home of Banbury cakes and Banbury Cross. Helicopter service is available (24 hrs. notice) from *Whately Hall*, 60 rooms (35 with bath), a most pleasant hotel. Also good, smaller *Cromwell Lodge* and *Crown*, 32 and 21 rooms, respectively.

BIBURY. Among the loveliest of Cotswold villages. Try *Bibury Court*, 17th-century manor house, 15 rooms (some with fourposter beds), and trout fishing.

BRAY. For outstanding food, try *Hind's Head Hotel* restaurant.

BOURTON-ON-THE-WATER. The River Windrush flows through this delightful country town; an interesting aviary and model village. *Old New Inn*, 26 rooms (7 with bath).

BROADWAY. Elizabethan Cotswold village. *Lygon Arms*, 52 rooms (32 with bath). Magnificent Tudor dining room. One of the most famous inns in Britain. Booking essential. Best eat here (*demand* table in Great Hall). Expensive, but worth it. *Farncombe House*, 19 rooms (4 with bath). Smaller, but still excellent value. The *Swan* has a good dining room and a fine wine list.

BURFORD. Typical ancient wool town with many grey stone houses. The renowned *Lamb Inn*, 15 rooms (2 with bath), a 15th-century inn; *Bull*, 14 rooms (4 with bath), built in 1397, but modernized recently; *Bay Tree*, 23 rooms (12 with bath), an old Tudor house.

BURGHFIELD. Try lunch at highly-recommended *Knight's Farm*, in an old farmhouse.

CHELTENHAM. An excellent centre for the Cotswolds, this is an old-fashioned, but popular, spa town. *Carlton*, 32 rooms (all with bath), first-class; as is *Queens*, 71 rooms (26 with bath); *Park*, 26 rooms (14 with bath), quiet chalet type. *Rossley Manor Country Club*, at Andoversford, is a pleasant place with pool, tennis, etc. 14 rooms (5 with bath).

CHIPPING CAMPDEN. The home of many medieval wool merchants, rich in historical connections. *Noel Arms*, 15 rooms (4 with bath). 2 rooms have four-poster beds. *Cotswold House*, 13 rooms (2 with bath). Moderate. *Kings Arm*, 15 rooms (2 with bath).

CHIPPING NORTON. Highest town in Oxfordshire. *White Hart*, 16 rooms, moderate. *Fox Inn*, 10 rooms (1 bath).

CIRENCESTER. Roman town near the source of the Thames. *Kings Head*, 43 rooms (10 with bath), *Stratton House*, 19 rooms (5 with bath), *Fleece* (Trust House). 26 rooms (1 with bath), *Crown*, 18 rooms.

DRAKES BROUGHTON. A charming inn, filled with curiosities to amuse the visitor, is *The Plough and Harrow*. Very interesting menu, too.

THE THAMES COUNTRY

GLOUCESTER. Situated at the lowest crossing point of the Severn and the routes into Wales. A touring headquarters rather than a town to stay in. *New Inn*, 32 rooms (6 with bath); *Lemon and Parker*, a modern inn; *Spread Eagle*, 20 rooms (3 with bath). Restaurant: *Don Pasquale*.

HORTON-CUM-STUDLEY. Near Oxford. *Studley Priory Hotel*, 14 rooms (5 with bath). romantic Elizabethan country house hotel.

LECHLADE. Lovely Upper Thames village. For good food, *The Trout*, famous fishing inn. Trout on the menu!

LITTLE WASHBOURNE. North of Cheltenham. The *Hobnails Inn*, in the same family for over 200 years.

MAIDENHEAD. Very busy residential town and boating centre. *Skindles*, 13 rooms (10 with bath), very famous, with excellent dining rooms and terraces; *Bull*, 6 rooms (3 with bath), *Thames*, 29 rooms. New (1968) *Esso Motor Hotel*, 100 rooms (all with bath); At nearby Hurley, *Ye Olde Bell* is good, as is a fine restaurant, the *East Arms*.

MALVERN. *The Unicorn* is a pleasant watering spot here.

MARLOW. Beautiful Thames-side town. The home of the poet Shelley. *Compleat Angler*, 45 rooms (35 with bath). Idyllic riverside setting and good food. Dinner: Try the *Hare and Hounds*.

MINSTER LOVELL. Cotswold village on the River Windrush. Dinner at the medieval *Old Swan* inn is well worth the half-hour drive from Oxford.

MORETON-IN-MARSH. Market town off the beaten track. *Manor House*, 31 rooms (15 with bath), *White Hart Royal*, 23 rooms (2 with bath), *Redesdale Arms*, 15 rooms (3 with bath). All are good English hotels.

NEWBURY. Old coaching town on a natural crossroads from London to the west, south and midlands. Ideal stopping place. *Chequers*, 58 rooms (15 with bath). *Bacon Arms*, 9 rooms (2 baths). Restaurant: *La Riviera*. Queen's pub has Civil War theme.

OXFORD. University town. *Excelsior Motor Lodge*, 60 rooms (all with bath); *Randolph*, 117 rooms (60 with bath), a Victorian edifice. Also *Oxford Motel*, 60 rooms (all with bath); *Eastgate*, 68 rooms (half with bath). Restaurants: *Luna Caprese*; *Elizabeth*; *La Sorbonne* and *Royal Oxford*. Pub with cartoons of "fops and dandies": the *Roebuck*.

QUINTON. Formerly owned by Magdalen College, Oxford (for nearly four centuries), the *College Arms* still boasts the same arms as the college. Very good, but simple, dining here.

STOW-ON-THE-WOLD. Small town perched on a hilltop, a meeting place of eight roads. Enormous market square, used in the middle ages as a sheep market. *Talbot*, 30 rooms (16 baths); *Unicorn*, 11 rooms. Both moderate.

TEWKESBURY. Historic Norman abbey church. *Cupshill Manor*, a 14th-century inn, is nearby.

THORNBURY. 12 miles north of Bristol. Dine in style amid sumptuous baronial decor of genuine Tudor *Thornbury Castle*. Booking essential.

WINCHCOMBE. Tomb of St. Kenelm. *The George*, an old

pilgrim's inn, offers a soft bed and a very good dining room.

WESTON-ON-THE-GREEN. *Weston Manor* is highly praised by many readers who have stayed in this very comfortable spot when visiting Oxford. 18 rooms.

WOODSTOCK. Ancient village next to Blenheim Palace. *Bear Inn*, 15 rooms (5 with bath), good for dinner, a rambling Cotswold inn; *Marlborough Arms*, 12 rooms (all with bath). Moderate. *Dorchester*, 8 rooms, also moderate.

Historic Houses Open to the Public

Abingdon. (Berks.) *Milton Manor*, 17th-century house. Open on Sat. and Sun. afternoons, May through September.

Banbury. (Oxon.) *Broughton Castle*. A little-known, but very interesting 14th-century castle, complete with moat. Still inhabited. Open Weds. only, 2-6. April to September.

Bath. (Glos.) *Dyrham Park*, on the Cotswolds north of Bath. National Trust. Unaltered 17th-century house. Open daily (except Mon. and Tues.), Easter through September (Sat. and Sun. in winter).

Berkeley Castle. (Glos.) One of England's most historic homes, the scene of the murder of Edward II. Open April to September.

Broadway. (Glos.) *Snowshill Manor*, with an important collection of musical instruments, clocks and toys, interesting for children. Open Easter to October, Saturdays and Sundays, and Bank Holidays. May-October, Weds., Thurs., 2-6.

Charney Bassett (Berks.) *Charney Manor*. Unique manor house dating from 1260. Open Thursday and Sunday afternoons, all year round.

Chipping Sodbury. (Glos.) *Dodington House*. Fine Regency house on the slope of the Cotswolds. Play area for children. Open daily May through Sept.

Great Badminton (Glos.) *Badminton House*. Palatial 17th-, 18th-century mansion of the Duke of Beaufort. Open Wed., June to early Sept.

Greenwich. See chapter, *Environs of London*.

Maidenhead (Bucks.) *Cliveden*, ex-home of the Astor family, now National Trust. Open afternoons, Wed., Sat. and Sun. April through October.

Mapledurham. (Oxon.) *Mapledurham House*. Elizabethan house, setting for Galsworthy's *Forsyte Saga*. Open weekend afternoons, Easter to September.

Moreton-in-Marsh. (Oxon.) *Chastletown House*, built 1603; the box garden is said to be the oldest in England. Open throughout the year, except Wednesdays.

Windsor Castle. (Berks.) See *Environs of London*.

Wing. (Bucks.) *Ascott*. Unusual house containing important collection of Chippendale furniture and 18th-century paintings. Open Wednesday-Saturday, afternoon; April to September and Bank Holiday Mondays.

Woodstock. (Oxon.) *Blenheim Palace*. Birthplace of Sir Winston Churchill (who is buried nearby at Bladon). Built by Vanbrugh for Duke of Marlborough. Magnificent planned gardens. Open most weekday afternoons, April to October. Son et lumière performances, July-September.

THE THAMES COUNTRY

MUSEUMS in the Thames Country can be found in nearly every town of importance, but a few are top-notch. Here are some of them: Abingdon: *Borough Museum* (Saxon pottery), *Guildhall Art Gallery* (silver plate); Broadway: *Snowshill Manor* (Tudor house with clocks, toys, etc.); Burford: *Tolsey Museum* (doll's house, costumes); Chalfont St. Giles: *Milton's Cottage* (first editions of *Paradise Lost* and *Paradise Regained*); Chedworth: *Chedworth Roman Villa and Museum* (mosaic pavements); Cheltenham: *Cheltenham Art Gallery & Museum* (paintings, pottery and porcelain); Cirencester: *Corinium Museum* (Roman antiquities).

Gloucester: *Folk Museum* (arts and crafts), *Gloucestershire Regiment Museum* (from 17th-century to present); High Wycombe: *Art Gallery & Museum* (Windsor chairs), *Disraeli Museum* (home of the great prime minister).

Oxford: *Ashmolean Museum of Art & Archaeology* (one of the best Oriental collections in the world, plus a treasure trove of paintings, sculpture, ceramics and nearly everything else), *Christ Church Old Master Collection* (old paintings in new gallery), *Museum of the History of Science* (early instruments), *Oxford University Museum* (zoology and geology), *Pitt Rivers Museum* (ethnology), *The Rotunda* (dolls' houses).

Reading: *Museum & Art Gallery* (Delft ware), *English Rural Life Museum* (village life), *Museum of Greek Archaeology* (antiquities); Winslow: *Florence Nightingale Museum* (the Crimean War, etc.).

Exploring the Thames Country

The actual source of the Thames has in the past been a point of controversy. In 1958, the august body of the Thames Conservatory Board definitely marked the source as a spring which flows out of a meadow called Tewkesbury Mead near the village of Coates. There is now a statue at the spot where the stream comes to light. If you make the journey to Coates, don't expect to find a rushing mountain stream, as this is the most infantile of rivers and it has several miles to flow before you can even take a boat out on it. Only once in recent years has the water flowed so copiously that it was possible to float a canoe on the stream here. Then, and only then, could it be said that the river was navigable from source to mouth. The first village on the baby Thames is Ewen, followed by Ashton Keynes, but Cricklade is the first real town on the banks of the river. Below Cricklade, the river slowly meanders through an almost undisturbed part of the English countryside. This is the stripling Thames, which the poet Matthew Arnold extolled. At Castle Eaton, there is the first of the countless riverside pubs and the first bridge of any size. All these quiet little villages in the upper reaches of the river look almost undisturbed by the bustle of the twentieth century, and it is hard to remember that London is only three hours' drive away. Just above Lechlade, which is the last Thames town in the county, the river is joined by the first of its tributaries, the Lech, famous for its trout. Here, too, is the first of the 45 locks which ease navigation on the upper reaches. As the river flows out of this first lock and on through Oxfordshire, it has at last become recognizable as the Thames.

The Thames is probably the most important river that starts its life in Gloucestershire, but it is by no means the only one. The county is noted for its deep valleys and grassy slopes, with their rushing young rivers. The most singular geographical feature of Gloucestershire are the rolling Cotswold Hills, that rise from the Severn Vale in the West and slope eastwards into Oxfordshire and Wiltshire. They are part of the band of oolitic limestone which runs across England from Dorset to Lincoln. It is from these hills that the coloured stone is quarried that you will see everywhere in the county. Indeed, the greystone walls, the honey-coloured cottages and austere grey churches are so common that the county can justly claim the most unified architecture in the country. The art of the mason and the quarryman is to be seen everywhere, in the heavy stone walls supporting the angular slate roofs of the houses and mills, and in the numerous churches (many of which were built or endowed by rich medieval wool merchants and clothiers).

Starting at Gloucester

The best starting point for a tour of Gloucestershire is Gloucester itself, the county town. There are plenty of comfortable hotels and inns in which to spend the night. Before setting out in the morning, pay a visit to the famous cathedral. There is little else in the town of interest, as traces of antiquity have been skilfully removed, leaving the cathedral as a monument of the city's ancient and distinguished past. Within the elegant exterior of the church, there is an almost complete Norman carcass; the massive pillars of the nave have been left untouched since their completion in 1100. It is a shame that this is all that is left of a town which has witnessed so much of England's history. Even in Roman times Gloucester was an important *colonia*, its name being Colonia Glevum, founded by Nerva in A.D. 96. Before the Norman conquest,

Boating enthusiasts and birdwatchers relax on the "Broads", Norfolk's natural network of waterways, while fun-seekers at Brighton cheer on their favorite horseless carriage in the sputtering finish of the Old Crocks' Race on the annual London to Brighton run.

Chester, in the north-west of England, retains its medieval charm in narrow streets of half-timbered houses, while fox hunting is still the chief preoccupation of the Midland rural gentry during the greater part of the year.

Gloucester was a borough with a royal residence and a mint, a sign of its highly privileged position.

Leave the town by the western routes and travel down into the Severn Vale and across the river. Very shortly, you will be in the Forest of Dean. In pre-industrial England, this was a thriving area, from which much of the oak came to build the British "hearts of oak". This was also the principal source of coal, and there are still one or two open-cast mines left to this day. But the general air of the Forest of Dean is one of complete disrepair and decay, and the remaining villages are mere skeletons of their former glories.

Cheltenham

Bypass Gloucester on your return and follow the signs for Cheltenham and the North Cotswolds. Cheltenham has managed to obtain for itself an undeserved reputation for Victorian stuffiness, but in fact, it is one of the country's most beautiful towns. It rivals Bath in its Georgian elegance, with wide, tree-lined streets, graceful secluded villas, plentiful gardens, crescents and squares. Unfortunately, many visitors see only the High Street, which ironically, is the only street not worth stopping in. Take any turning off the High Street and you will be amazed at the difference. Nearly every house is an almost unsurpassed example of Victorian elegance, an elegance that is frequently eclipsed by the architectural monstrosities that were produced later in the century.

Until the 18th century, Cheltenham was simply another Cotswold village, but in 1715, a mineral spring was discovered, and by 1740, the first spa had been built. Over the following 200 years, it became a favourite retiring place for colonial civil servants, who found the waters most effective in relieving the liver and digestive troubles that afflict Europeans living in hot climates. Hence, the distinctly colonial air of the town.

The Proper Cotswolds

After leaving Cheltenham on A46 for Broadway, you begin to enter the Cotswolds proper, with the rolling green landscape deeply incised by rushing clear streams, and its little grey villages and mills lying quietly at rest in the arms of the hills. This is the old wool country, and here are the famous wool towns. The most spectacular of these is Chipping Campden, east of Broadway, which though it has buildings from the 17th century to the 18th century, has a striking air of unity, thanks to the continuity of the stonemason's craft. The "wool" church dominates all else, and here you can see, possibly for the first time, the commemorative brasses that were used in medieval times to cover burial places.

Turning south now, pass through Moreton, Stow-on-the Wold, and Bourton-on-the-Water, all of them with their roots deep in history. Grey stone churches, honey-coloured cottages, peaceful lawns and commons predominate in each. In each of their churches you will find countless monuments to the region's past importance. Of all the wool churches, the one at Northleach is perhaps the best. Like so many in the county, it owes its very existence to the wool merchants who are buried within. They never forgot the source of their wealth, even in death—in their memorial statues, they are invariably depicted with their feet resting on a young lamb. At Sapperton, near Cirencester, is one of the loveliest houses in England, Daneway House, a pleasant mixture of 14th- and 18th-century styles.

Cirencester

Gloucestershire as a county was well-known to the Romans and at Cirencester, further south, there is a reconstructed Roman villa, which will give you a good idea of how much the Romans valued their creature comforts. In the town (pron. *Sisiter*) there is a museum which houses many of the antiquities that have been found on the site. To the west of the town is Cirencester Park, owned by Earl Bathurst, but open daily to walkers who can explore its 3,000 acres and five-mile avenues of chestnut trees. There is an excellent museum in Park Street. Many of the streets in the town are unchanged from the 16th and 17th centuries; and the parish church, the largest in Gloucestershire, dates from Norman times, but most of the structure was built in the 13th to 15th centuries.

Before leaving Gloucestershire, stop at Fairford, east of Cirencester, if only to visit the church and examine its stained-glass windows. They were donated to the church by one John Tame, a wealthy wool merchant, and they are reputed to be the best in England. The damned are all depicted as women!

Oxfordshire

The River Thames takes on a new graciousness as it flows along the borders of Oxfordshire for 71 miles, and with each new mile it increases in size and importance. Four tributaries swell the river as it passes through the county: the Thame, the Isis, the Windrush and the Evenlode. Just after Lechlade, which is east of Cirencester on A417, there is the first of the 45 locks which make the upper reaches of the river navigable. Each of these locks is carefully maintained by devoted lock-keepers, many of whose families have done nothing else for centuries. In between opening and closing the gates of the lock, the keepers all take great pride in tending their neatly-kept gardens and flower beds, and should you want to know anything about the surrounding countryside, these are the men to ask. Be careful, if you are in a hurry, as they can delay you for hours with their stories and reminiscences of "the good old days".

The Thames Conservancy Board has the overall responsibility for the locks, as it does for the towpaths which border the river. These narrow, dusty paths were originally used by barge horses pulling their heavy loads; today, they provide excellent riverside walks, far away from the reach of the traffic and bustle of the main roads. The stretch of the river between Lechdale and Oxford is intensely rural, frequently winding out of reach of even the smallest road. This is *Wind in the Willows* country. At almost any moment, you expect to find Ratty and Mole sunning themselves on a grassy bank with remnants from a lunch hamper by their sides. After Oxford, the river is sufficiently large for "steamers"; for the last century, *Salter Brothers* have been running a daily service to Kingston. Leaving Folley Bridge in Oxford at 9:30 in the morning, the boat trip takes two days, and is an excellent, if somewhat leisurely, way of seeing perhaps the most interesting section of the river.

Cruising Down the Thames

At first the river is so narrow that you might as well be on the towpath; it is quite easy to start a conversation with any of the people strolling along there. This is the Thames at its most intimate and most inviting, either for boating or fishing or just simply walking. The river winds on through lush meadows and then, as it widens out, the banks become gradually more wooded. There are occasional glimpses of thatched cottages and distant spires, and the number of small craft seems to increase by the mile. This is the ideal "messing about in boats" country.

Although the river is so important to the county (it forms its southern boundary for one thing), Oxfordshire is not all meadows, willow trees, locks and boats. North of the river and the city of Oxford, there is some of the most fertile farming land in the country, and the dominant topography of both the western and eastern borders are undulating hills. In the west there are the Oxfordshire Cotswolds, with their grey stone villages like Burford, and in the east are the Chilterns, with the chalk soil so well suited for the growing of barley and the malting of hops. Indeed, if the county were famous for nothing else, it would be known for its local beers. There are not really many wooded areas, but there is a tiny remaining fragment of an ancient royal forest in Wychwood, which still possesses something of a magical air about it. There is a weird inland marsh at Otmoor, with no roads across it, that is now used by the army as a manoeuvring area.

On the Way East

Naturally, the centre of interest for any visitor to the county is Oxford and its university, but there are several other interesting places that should at least be seen before arriving at Oxford itself.

Following the course of the river as it enters the county after Lechdale, you will soon arrive at Kelmscott, the home of William Morris, and for a time, Rossetti. It was here at Kelmscott Manor that they established the revolution in artistic taste a century ago. Even the most perfunctory look at the surrounding countryside will reveal the principal source of Morris' inspiration. Some of the clusters of the trees look as if they have stepped straight from one of his wall-paper designs. The house itself is now owned by Oxford University, and is a unique monument to the "Brotherhood". Morris died at Kelmscott and is buried here in the simple village church.

Journey north from here into the Cotswolds once more and

stop at Burford. A model English town built on the slopes of the Windrush, it is still in much the same state of preservation as it was two centuries ago, when it was a popular horse-racing town. Most of the buildings are set at right angles to the main street and must be approached on foot up narrow alleys and yards. Look for the 16th-century *Crown Inn*, the 15th-century Grammar School, and the 17th-century Great House, in Witney Street. Witney itself, famous the world over for its wool blankets, is a few miles' drive to the east on A40: you will have to pass through it to reach Woodstock and Blenheim Palace (take A4095 at Witney).

This imposing palace was granted to the Duke of Marlborough after his victories in the low countries in 1704, which included the battle at the town of Blenheim—hence the name. The palace was designed by Vanbrugh, and the impressive gardens and lakes are mainly the fruits of 20 years of work by Capability Brown. This most famous of English landscape gardeners declared that his object at Blenheim was to "make the Thames look like a small stream compared with the winding Danube in Blenheim Park". At points, he almost succeeds—the scale of these grounds must be seen to be believed. The total cost of landscaping is reputed to have been in the region of £300,000. It was here that Winston Churchill was born, and in the nearby village of Bladon, in the simple churchyard, he lies buried. Due south of Woodstock and Bladon on A34 lies the city of Oxford.

Oxford

Whatever preconceived notions you may have about Oxford, your first sight of the city will doubtlessly confirm them all. Stop, before entering the city, and climb one of the low hills that surround it, to look at the sky line. If you are fortunate, and the sun is shining, the towers, spires, turrets and pinnacles will look like a scene from a medieval fairy story. Here, stretched out in front of you is Oxford, the home of erudition and scholarship of Oxford English and—of Oxford marmalade. From here, time appears to have passed by Oxford; from this distant viewpoint, the city must look much the same as it did 200 or even 500 years ago.

First appearances are deceptive, however. The last 50 years have seen changes in Oxford that have revolutionized not only the town, but the very basis of university life itself. It is, in fact, one of the fastest-growing manufacturing towns in England. Although the average undergraduate can spend his three years at Oxford and only once a year, perhaps, pass the two vast industrial concerns that are responsible for the changes, he cannot ignore them. BMC motor works and the equally enormous Pressed Steel factory that are situated in the outlying suburb of Cowley are behind the rapid growth of the city. This burgeoning of industry has brought changes to the city which might not be apparent to the visitor, but which are felt most keenly by the shopkeepers and various trades people, who 50 years ago were totally reliant on the university for trade. Today, they have a vast pool of customers from the outlying housing estates, providing them with business throughout the year.

The exact date of the origins of the city of Oxford is not clear. It was most likely an early Saxon town, that was part port, part fortress, and part market. No doubt the early Saxon chieftains were attracted to the centrality of its position, and it became a favourite venue for royal conferences, a kind of Saxon convention centre. During the early middle ages, the city thrived as a centre of the flourishing wool trade—the earliest records date back to 1147, and can still be inspected in the town hall.

The University

At some time during the 12th century, Oxford became a meeting place for scholars. There is no definite explanation of how and when the university began, but some theories claim that it was founded by English students who had been expelled from the University of Paris in 1167, while others hold that it is an offshoot of the various monastic institutions in the immediate neighbourhood. Whatever its origins, it is certain that by the end of the 12th century, the Royal Borough of Oxford was the home of the first established centre of learning in England.

The earliest colleges founded in Oxford were University College (1249), Balliol (1263), and Merton College (1264). From the 13th century onwards a succession of royal charters strengthened the position of the university at the expense of the city; in many instances it was the university that ruled the town and not the other way round. Oxford became a power in the kingdom, as Canterbury once was, and its splendour was enhanced by new colleges built during the reign of the Tudors and by magnificent buildings of the later era (Sheldonian Theatre, Radcliffe Camera, etc.). There was a good deal of reconstructing and rebuilding of the medieval and renaissance Oxford in the 18th century, which destroyed some of the old streets that used to run along the ancient city walls separating the fortified city itself from the "Latin Quarter" of the university. Many old almshouses, friaries, and houses inhabited in the Middle Ages by various religious bodies were sacrificed in the process, and the city that emerged from all those efforts was less compact, less uniform in its character than before. Nevertheless, even today a diligent visitor will find no difficulty in discovering the real Oxford after wading from the railway station across nondescript approaches of a rather commercial city towards the stern beauty of the colleges.

Touring Oxford

There is such a bewildering display of architecture in Oxford that the visitor at first frequently finds it difficult to look at the "right" buildings. You can, of course, just wander around the centre of the city and generally take in the atmosphere, but if you have the entire afternoon to spare, and feel fit, it is fairly easy to visit most of the more important buildings and to come away with a feeling for the university.

Start at the Carfax Tower, as this is the centre of the city. Walk south down St. Aldates Street, towards Folly Bridge, with the Town Hall (you can examine the ancient records of the city if you wish to, including its Royal Charter—1199) and the public library on the left. You will soon come to the impressive Christ Church, known to its members as "the house". Its chapel is the aristocrat of all college chapels and revels in the title, cathedral. There was a time when this enormous college only had 101 students—Great Tom, its huge bell, can still be heard tolling 101 strokes at five past nine every evening to summon them home. The inhabitants of the much smaller Pembroke College, opposite, hear these bells only too well, as its buildings lie in the shadow of Big Tom. (There are now *son et lumière* performances at Christ Church from June to September.)

Moving on from these two eastward, north of Christ Church meadows, you will find yourself in Corpus Christi, which introduced Latin and Greek to the university curriculum. Standing next door is Merton College, one of the richest and oldest. Henrietta Maria, the wife and queen of Charles I, was billeted at Merton during the Civil War, and a secret passage was cut to allow her access to the king, who was staying at Christ Church. Oriel is Merton's neighbour, and is famous for its sons, among others, Sir Walter Raleigh, Cecil Rhodes and Matthew Arnold.

Leaving Oriel, make your way up Bear Lane, past the *Bear Inn*, which boasts the lowest ceiling in Oxford, into the High Street, referred to as "the High". In fact, most streets in the town are known by their nicknames and abbreviations, so Turl Street is never referred to as anything but "the Turl", and then there are "the Corn" and "The Broad", etc. Crossing "the High" then, enter Brasenose College (or BNC for short), named from an ancient bronze nose-shaped knocker that used to hang on the front door. The fate of one BNC student is still vividly remembered—he was a leading light in the infamous 18th-century Hell Fire Club, whose objects were "blasphemy, obscenity and drinking". One night a don, hearing excessive revelry coming from one of the rooms in which the club was meeting, looked up and saw a horned and tailed devil dragging an agonised undergraduate through the bars of the window. When the don rather shakenly reported the incident at the Porter's Lodge, he was confronted with the news that the leader of the Hell Fire Club had a few minutes earlier died of apoplexy "in the midst of a blasphemous tirade".

All Souls and Magdalen

Across the road from BNC is All Souls, which is the only college that has no undergraduates. It consists almost entirely of appointed fellows, and is one of the most exclusive and erudite clubs in the world. Radcliffe Square (behind Brasenose), which is the heart of the university, boasts the third largest dome in England in its Radcliffe Camera. The building at the northern end of the square is the famous Bodleian Library, where a copy of every book published in England must be sent. It takes its name from Sir Thomas Bodley, who was in charge of restoring the building in 1602. The college closest to the

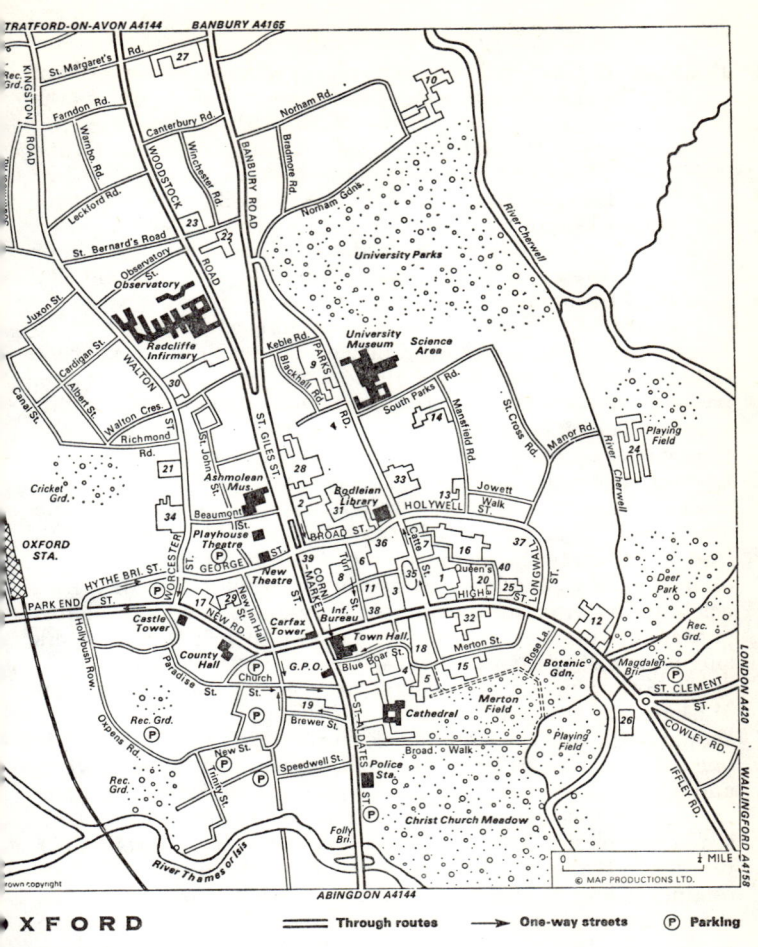

OXFORD

=== Through routes → One-way streets (P) Parking

COLLEGES

All Souls, 1437	9. Keble, 1870	17. Nuffield, 1937	25. St. Edmund Hall, 1220	33. Wadham, 1610–13
Balliol, 1260–6	10. Lady Margaret Hall, 1878	18. Oriel, 1324–26	26. St. Hilda's, 1893	34. Worcester, 1714
Brasenose, 1509	11. Lincoln, 1427	19. Pembroke, 1624	27. St. Hugh's,	35. Radcliffe Camera
Christchurch, 1525	12. Magdalen, 1448	20. Queen's, 1340	28. St. John's, 1555	36. Sheldonian
Corpus Christi, 1516	13. Manchester, 1891	21. Ruskin, 1899	29. St. Peter's, 1929	37. St. Mary the Virgin Ch.
Exeter, 1314	14. Mansfield, 1866	22. St. Anne's, 1952	30. Somerville, 1879	38. St. Martin & All Saints
Hertford, 1874	15. Merton, 1264	23. St. Anthony's, 1948	31. Trinity, 1554–5	39. St. Michael 'Northgate
Jesus, 1571	16. New, 1379	24. St. Catherine's, 1962	32. University, 1249	40. St. Peter's-in-the East

Bodleian is Hertford College, which claims to be one of the oldest and is probably one of the poorest. In fact, during the last century, it all but fell down, and was inhabited by gipsy squatters. Hertford also boasts a bridge modelled on the Bridge of Sighs in Venice. Thomas Hobbes was a Hertford graduate. Backing on to Hertford is New College, the home of the famous Doctor Spooner and his spoonerisms; he is reputed to have told one dilettante student "You have hissed your mystery lessons and tasted a whole work." Part of the old city wall runs through the gardens of the college.

No tour of Oxford would be complete without a visit to Magdalen (pron. *Maudlin*) College. To reach it from New College, walk down New College Lane into Queen's Lane, passing on your left St. Edmunds Hall, and on your right, Queens. Turn left at "the High," pass the Examination Halls (known as schools), opposite, and find Magdalen College, a few minutes' walk further on. This is one of the richest colleges, with a magnificent main quadrangle and a supremely monastic air. A walk round the Deer Park and along Addisons Walk will lead you to envy the members of the college for the experience of living here. Magdalen Bridge is famous for the May Day celebrations after an evening of May Balls. Undergraduates gather in punts under the bridge at dawn to hear the choristers singing the May Day anthem from the tower.

The other principal colleges, and the famous Ashmolean Museum all lie north of Carfax, so that after Magdalen, you should walk up "the High" back to the Carfax. "The High" is one of the last remaining Renaissance streets in Europe and if you close your eyes a moment, it is not difficult to imagine the same street 500 years ago. Without cars and bustling with students, clerics and wealthy guildsmen off to sell their produce at the market, it must have been marvellously quaint. When you reach Carfax, turn right up Cornmarket Street, through the new shopping centre and soon, the massive walls of St. Johns and Balliol loom into sight. It was opposite Balliol that Ridley, Latimer and Cranmer were burned by "Bloody Mary" in 1555 and 1556; there is a memorial statue marking the spot. St. Johns has colonnades and a garden front that was designed by Inigo Jones.

Beaumont Street, on the other side of Magdalen Street, opposite St. Johns, leads to Worcester College, and is a

Regency street, housing the Ashmolean Museum, with its famous collection of paintings, prints and scientific curios. The museum has, among other items, the Alfred Jewel, said to be connected with King Alfred.

There still remain two colleges of interest to be visited. The first is Keble College, unique for its monstrous Victorian architecture; it rivals the University Museum, opposite, for the title of the ugliest building in Oxford. Indeed, Ruskin used to alter the course of his daily walk in order to avoid seeing it. Keble was the only men's college founded in the 19th century. It will be interesting to see whether the second college, St. Catherine's, Oxford's newest, with its ultra space-age architecture, will be criticized as much as Keble 100 years from now.

Berkshire

On the southern bank of the Thames lies the Royal County of Berkshire—royal because of Windsor Castle, situated at its eastern border. If you look at a map of the county, you will see that, geographically, it is rather like an old, battered boot—the sole treading heavily into Hampshire, the heel digging into Wiltshire, with Oxfordshire hanging on its uppers. The toe of the boot points directly towards Surrey and London.

Because of its proximity to the capital, and also partly because of its loose topography, the county has always been something of a through route. As early as prehistoric times, men were wearing down the Ridgeway, as it crosses the North Downs, on their way to the great religious centre of Wiltshire at Avebury and Stonehenge. During the coaching days of the 18th and 19th centuries, wealthy passengers streaked through Berkshire on their way to the fashionable watering places of the west country. Today, every summer weekend, the main roads through this county have a heavy flow of traffic bound for Cornwall and Devon. This transitory mood is further emphasized by the number of commuters who leave their comfortable country homes every morning to work in London. Berkshire is commuter territory as far as Reading and Didcot, and with commuters have come housing estates, golf courses and all the attendant trappings of town life.

Another, rather more bizarre, consequence of being so near the capital has been the establishment of almost every kind of institution imaginable, from the scholastic and scientific to the military and the lunatic. What is more, the spread of light industry (especially in the eastern part of the county) is rapidly turning the county into a garden suburb of London itself.

Abingdon and the White Horse

After leaving Oxford, Abingdon is the first place of interest. It is one of the most ancient towns in the Thames Valley. Few towns of comparative size have retained so much of their heritage. Its spires and towers loom above the grassy meadows, so that the unsuspecting visitor might think he has come upon more Oxford colleges. But Abingdon is considerably older than Oxford—there was a Saxon abbey here as early as the sixth century (little of it remains today). The town that grew up around the abbey still has much to offer the visitor. There are beautiful medieval churches, St. Helens and St. Nicholas, bounded by their ancient alms houses and guest houses. The Poor House dates from the 13th century and has recently been restored, while the 17th-century County Hall still looks as impressive as it must have done when it was built in the times of Charles II.

If you still have a taste for more history, leave Abingdon by the A420 and make for the Vale of the White Horse, and the tiny village of Uffington that lies in the crook of the vale. It will only be a matter of minutes before you will see the gigantic white horse that gallops over the downs and from which the vale draws its name. This is the oldest and best-known of the animal figures that are cut into the chalk hills of England. It looks northwest into the Cotswolds, and is formed by trenches in the chalk two to three feet deep and ten feet wide. The head, neck and body are drawn in one line, as are the four legs. If you have the energy, climb up and inspect this creature closely—it is supposed to bring good luck if you stand on its eye. It takes three weeks for four men to scour and clean it of weeds. The origin of the horse is uncertain. Although there is some evidence that it was cut to mark the victory of Berkshire-born King Alfred over the Danes at Ashdown in 870, this strange chalk figure is probably much older, and some say it dates as early as the time of Christ.

On the summit of the hill, "ancient men" raised a massive earthwork which has been called Uffington Castle. Today, it provides a fine view into the neighbouring counties. The village of Uffington itself has a fine 13th-century church without a spire, which it lost in a storm some two centuries ago (it has never been replaced). Uffington was the birthplace of the author of *Tom Brown's Schooldays*, Thomas Hughes; there is a brass head to his memory in the church. The downs that surround Uffington and that go to make up North Berkshire present a refreshing and austere contrast to the lushness of the river valley. The road, the ancient Ridgeway, that runs along the northern crest is as old as any in Britain. It can still be followed, right across the county, and even the shortest walk will be enough to convince you of the beauty of the downs.

Newbury, on the southern border of the county, can be reached from Uffington by driving straight across the downs from Ashbury on B4000, past Castle Ashdown and through Lambourn. Newbury itself is today a bustling town of 20,000 inhabitants, but it owes its importance almost solely to one man, Jack of Newbury, an almost legendary figure cast in the Dick Whittington mould. Born John Smallwood, he was sent to Newbury by his father to make his way in the wool industry. According to the 17th-century historian, Thomas Fuller, Smallwood became the most important clothier in Tudor England. It is said that he kept a hundred looms fully employed throughout the year and was the "most considerate and benevolent of employers". The parish church of St. Nicholas was built by him and finished by his son in 1532.

Newbury is the natural crossroads of roads leading to Oxford, Winchester, Bath and London, and in the 18th century, it was a famous coaching stop. As a result, there are several fine inns and a long tradition of catering for hungry travellers. This is an excellent spot to taste real English cooking before restarting your journey. The River Kennet, which flows through the town, is shortly swallowed up by the ever-increasing Thames at Reading.

Home of Washington's Mother

Just south of Reading is a little-known village called Barkham, in whose churchyard lie several of George Washington's ancestors. His mother's maiden name was Mary Ball and there are records of that family owning land at Barkham in the

15th and 16th centuries. George Washington often said that it was to his mother of Berkshire origin that he owed the qualities which enabled him to do his special work for the United States.

Because of our detour over the downs, much of the Thames scenery has been missed. A very pleasant way of seeing it is to take a half-day steamer excursion from Reading to Wallingford. This will enable you to see the delightfully-wooded scenery that graces this part of the Thames Valley. On each bank there are fine wooded hills, with spacious houses, greenhouses, flower beds and clean lawns that stretch down to the water's edge. Once again we are reminded of *Wind in the Willows*, and indeed, it was to Pangbourne, along this stretch of the river, that Kenneth Graham retired to write that immortal book.

Downstream once more from Reading, there are a whole succession of Thames-side villages, each one more charming than the last. They all have attractive riverside inns and churches that look as if they have not been altered for centuries. If we must be selective, we can choose Sonning as the quintessence of them all. The old bridge spans the Thames with its 11 arches, and the Georgian-fronted houses, the ancient Mill that is mentioned in the *Domesday Book* and the black, white and yellow cottages make it all too perfect a Thames-side village.

Royal Henley

The river at Henley stops winding abruptly and for just over a mile downstream from Henley Bridge, it is almost dead straight. It is on this stretch of water that the famous Henley Royal Regatta is held in the first part of July every year. This is the premier river regatta in the world and attracts thousands of visitors, who watch the races from specially-erected stands or from punts and rowing boats that are permitted to be moored on the banks. Competition in this event is between the best oarsmen from all over the world, and many an overenthusiastic supporter who has forgotten he is standing in a rowing boat has found himself unwittingly in the water while cheering a favourite on. The regatta was started in 1838 by the local townspeople, who initiated the first and most famous of the cups, the Grand Challenge Cup. Very quickly, other awards were donated, such as the Diamond Challenge Plate and the Ladies Challenge Plate. Henley during Regatta Week is one of the high spots of the social summer, rating with Ascot and Wimbledon as a sports event and as a fashionable outing.

Later in the month of July, Henley sees the end of another occasion, hardly as popular as the regatta, but interesting nevertheless. This is the Swan Upping. All the swans on the Thames belong to the Queen, with the exception of those which, by Royal Charter, are the property of the Ancient Livery Companies. The process of Swan Upping is to determine "the ownership of all new cygnets encountered on the Thames between London and Henley". So, once a year, six skiffs set out from London, rowed by oarsmen in red, blue and white jerseys, under the command of the Queen's Swan Keeper, who stands, resplendent in his scarlet livery, while the oarsmen attempt to ascertain the ownership of the parent birds. (If they are unmarked, they are assumed to belong to the Queen.) They then brand the cygnets in the face of what is usually the fierce opposition of their parents.

Downstream from Henley lies Maidenhead, which is perhaps the busiest of the river resorts. It is only 27 miles from London and can now be reached extremely quickly by a new fast motorway, so it supports several excellent hotels and countless inns and tea shops where you can sample real English tea. Order it with fresh cream and scones, home-made cakes and wafer-thin brown bread. Close to the river bank is the village of Bray. Of its most famous vicar, Simon Alley, it was sung "That whosoever king may reign, I'll still be the Vicar of Bray, Sir". This remarkable man held the post from 1667 to 1709, one of the most changing and troubled times of English domestic history, but was able to adapt his political and religious views to coincide with those of each successive monarch, so enabling himself to keep his post. One visit to Bray will reveal why he was so enthusiastic to stay. Near the church is a well-known inn called the *Hinds Head*. A bridge here gives access to historic Monkey Island; this was built as a fishing lodge for the third Duke of Marlborough and derives its name from the monkey fresco that adorned the domed ceiling of what is known today as the Monkey Room.

Shortly after Bray, the river takes a sharp turn to the left, and in the distance, you will see the towers and battlements of the Royal Palace of Windsor. (If you can see the Royal Ensign flying from the flagpole, Her Majesty the Queen is in residence.)

Buckinghamshire

Buckinghamshire is not always thought of as a county connected with the Thames, but in fact the Thames forms its southern boundary, and the southern half of it is, geographically speaking, orientated towards the river valley. The rolling Chiltern Hills, which divide the county into two halves, are for many the most characteristic feature of the area. North of the Chilterns, there are many small rivers, streams and marshes that lead towards the sluggish, great Ouse, on the northern boundary of the county.

The southern escarpment is characterized by leafy forests of beech trees and silver birches, while to the north there are great rolling grass vales, that look from the distance like a chequer board. Because of the hills, there are many fine vantage points in the county, such as Coombe Hill near Wendover (over 850 feet) and Ivinghoe Beacon (811 feet). The sharp contrast in the land south and north of the Chilterns is the outward sign of the highly varied geological deposits that go to make up the soil, ranging from hard, dry and infertile chalkland to the rich, fertile alluvial deposits of the Thames Basin. Buckinghamshire is, in short, a geologist's paradise.

Like its neighbour, Berkshire, across the Thames, Buckinghamshire has also suffered as being something of a through route to the west and to the Midlands, the dry valleys of the southern slopes of the Chilterns offering perfect ready-made routes through the hills. (The oldest road in England, the Icknield Way, runs along the top of the Chilterns.) Buckinghamshire has been a centre of civilization from prehistoric times onwards. The county has raised more than its fair share of famous sons, and many distinguished people have adopted the county as their home. It was to Horton that Milton first came, going later to Chalfont St. Giles, in an attempt to escape from the plague in Cambridge. At Olney, William Cowper wrote nearly all the poems and letters that have made him remembered, and it was the churchyard at Stoke Poges that inspired Gray to write his famous *Elegy*. Three prime ministers have been born and raised here, the most famous, of course, being Disraeli, who was later to take the title Lord Beaconsfield, and whose home, Hughenden Manor, near High Wycombe, is open to visitors from February through December. William Penn, the founder of Pennsylvania, came from the village of Penn, and is buried there.

But for Englishmen, the real significance of Buckinghamshire stems from the stormy days of the Civil War, when Royalists and Republicans fought each other across the length and breadth of the land. It was in Buckinghamshire that John Hampden was born, and here he is buried. It was his action of refusing to pay the king the ship money that launched a wave of resentment that was soon to split the country, and even families, into two warring halves.

Buckinghamshire men will tell you that they may not have much of the Thames, but what they do have is probably the best. "The best" includes the great sweep of the river at Marlow Lock, with the wooded hills of Cliveden dipping down to the river bank, the incomparable view of Windsor Castle, and Eton College. Buckinghamshire claims an equal share of Boveney and Bray, Boulters Lock and Cliveden Reach. The lazy water meadows of Hambleden, which are so often crowded in the summer, are here, as is the equally enchanting village of Medmenham, where, incongruously, the Hell Fire Club held its meetings in the ruins of the abbey. At Cliveden, we remember George Villiers, the powerful and insolent Duke of Buckingham, who played such a large role in the country's affairs during the reign of Charles II. Formerly the home of the Astors, Cliveden is now in the hands of the National Trust.

Eton's Playing Fields

Eton College, opposite Windsor Castle, is probably England's most famous academic institution, next to Oxford and Cambridge. It is certainly the most famous "public" (fee-paying) school, although not the most expensive. It was founded in 1440; its architecture will remind you of Oxford. The school yard and cloisters can be visited in the afternoons and so may the School Chapel, which has a sung evensong every day during the school term except Wednesday, at 2:30 p.m. The best view of Eton and its famous playing fields is, in fact, from the battlements of Windsor Castle. The importance of Eton lies less in what it is than what it stands for. All over the English-speaking world, an Eton education is a visiting card that opens almost any door, or at least did at one time. Today, as social values are changing, there is frequent criticism of the Etonian method of education, which tends to place more emphasis on games and manners than on academic and in particular, scientific, training. But Eton is an ancient institution and the English are very attached to traditional things, so there is almost no fear of the school turning into a state-run affair. It is still necessary to put a child's name on the waiting list as soon as he is born to ensure a place in the school.

A few miles north of Eton, tucked away amidst tall birch trees, lies the Quaker village of Jordans, which for any American visitor is a mandatory stop. Here are preserved the original timbers of the *Mayflower*, which took the Pilgrim Fathers to America in search of religious freedom. The stout black beams of the ship form a great black barn, normally thronging with visitors during the summer months. Here also is buried William Penn, who founded the state of Pennsylvania, and the city of brotherly love, Philadelphia, in an attempt to create a state governed according to Quaker principles.

Surrounding Jordans and nearby Beaconsfield are the magnificent woods that formerly belonged to another well-known Quaker, George Cadbury, of chocolate fame, who generously donated them to the country. Beaconsfield itself is a charming place to wander in, with its broad-timbered inns and hotels. It is the ideal place to break for refreshment. In the large church, you can see the tomb of Edmund Burke and his two sons. Burke was one of England's leading political thinkers, and in the last decade of the 18th century, was one of the most important influences on political thinking in the western world.

High Wycombe

The road from Beaconsfield to High Wycombe (A40) is also the main London to Oxford road, and is often filled with heavy traffic. Nevertheless, the undulating green countryside on either side of the road makes an otherwise uninteresting drive very pleasant. High Wycombe is one of the busiest towns in the county, and the site of natural traffic jams every day of the week as the seemingly unceasing flow of cars and lorries is forced through its narrow streets. Many motorists are in such a hurry to get through the town that they miss the Norman arches of the 13th-century Knights Templar Hostel, and the 18th-century Guildhall at the end of the High Street, with its wooden cupola, on top of which stands a weathervane in the shape of a centaur firing an arrow into the wind.

The golden ball high on the hill that immediately strikes your eye as you leave High Wycombe is yet another meeting place of the Hell Fire Club. West Wycombe, lying below the hill, and strung out along the Oxford Road, is the only village in England completely owned by the National Trust. It is a perfect example of gabled roofs, thatched cottages and old beams. The famous Hell Fire Caves at West Wycombe are said to be the largest man-made chalk caverns in the world, complete with underground river (appropriately named the Styx).

After the rather sinister and magical atmosphere of the caves, the lushness of the surrounding countryside makes a refreshing contrast. Drive northwards through the famous gap at Princes Risborough to Stoke Mandeville, the home of John Hampden, of Civil War fame, and then on to Aylesbury. Famous for its succulent duckling, it lies at the very heart of the county. Unfortunately, many of the older inns, which in medieval times used to stand around the market square, have vanished. But there still remain two of interest: the *Bull's Head*, which boasts a 300-year-old barn for its garage and the *King's Head*, a medieval inn in an almost perfect state of restoration. The latter was originally the guest house of the adjoining monastery; its lounge was the old refectory. The leaded glass in the windows is more than 500 years old. Wander through Aylesbury's curious, winding streets, narrow alleys and crooked passages and feel the unique English atmosphere that has been preserved here almost effortlessly.

After Aylesbury, the visitor can roam through the villages and towns of northern Buckinghamshire, all of which possess some interest—none are devoid of charm. Try Stowe, for instance, with its famous public school housed in an extraordinarily beautiful building (almost one quarter of a mile long), or Boarstall, with its gatehouse, and the county town itself, Buckingham, with the house to which Catherine of Aragon came to be feasted and entertained while she was still queen.

But if time is limited, drive south on A413 from Aylesbury to Wendover, deep in the heart of the Chilterns, with the Roman Icknield Way as your highroad. There are excellent views from the top of Boddington and Coombe Hill, from which on a fine day you can see St. Paul's Cathedral in London. Then, drive on to Amersham. This town possesses a street that, once seen, you will never forget; it will probably epitomize the county in your memory long after you have forgotten everything else. At each end of the street are water-mills and in the very middle is a 17th-century market hall, with its wooden turret. The houses in the village, with their black and white fronts and dark sloping roofs, look as if they have been brought straight out of a history book.

In fact, Amersham is the perfect last stopping place in the county before returning to the capital—in an intangible way, it seems to suggest everything there is to say of the county.

THE SOUTHERN COUNTIES

History's Sweep from Canterbury to Stonehenge

by

PETER WHELPTON

(*Mr. Whelpton, Travel Editor of the* Daily Mail, *is a well-known journalist, author and broadcaster on travel subjects. Author of* An Innocent's Guide to Paris, *he has also written guide books to Portugal, Wales and the Isle of Man.*)

A great deal of British history has been forged in the "sunny south". Since the Norman invasion culminating in the Battle of Hastings, there have been alternating periods of rural peace and wars or threats of wars. The Cinque Ports stood guard, their ships, the "Wooden Walls" of England, setting sail on voyages of discovery and conquest. From Dover Castle and from the Martello towers of Romney Marsh, the soldiers stood watch, as Napoleon stood brooding over his invasion fleet at Boulogne only 21 miles away.

From Dover, Portsmouth and Southampton, the "old contemptibles" of 1914 embarked for the trenches of Flanders. A generation later, their sons were to do the same thing in the

Second World War. The beaches, accustomed to the happy laughter of children, became strangely silent. Barbed wire, concrete pill boxes and anti-aircraft guns scarred the promenades of Brighton, Bournemouth and Bognor. Across the Channel big guns threatened, and in the skies above the Weald of Kent took place the Battle of Britain. From a tiny airstrip at Biggin Hill, the gallant "few" once again made history in the south.

Now, happily, all is peaceful again. The big seaside resorts have repaired the scars of war. In spring, the bluebells and primroses brighten the woods and hedgerows, while in summer, the beaches are thronged with families.

In an era when it has become fashionable to have everything as small as possible; from minature transistor radios to mini-skirts, the southern counties will inevitably have great appeal to overseas visitors. From the air, the tiny fields, neatly hedged, look like a patchwork quilt. Motoring (once away from the new, fast motor-ways), one can drive through narrow lanes between the orchards and hop gardens of Kent. Turn west and you find the expanse of the Downs, starting at the white cliffs of Dover and terminating at the Hog's Back. In between, there are cathedral towns to be explored and sleepy villages discovered. It may be fun to conjecture, for instance, why the bell tower of the church at Brooklands on Romney Marsh stands on the ground apart from the main building. You may be lucky enough to watch the ancient game of stoolball, which still survives in parts of Sussex. It is great to discover for oneself a village inn, only 30 miles from London, where the old men gather on a Saturday night to sing the old country songs—passed down from father to son, but never written down. For those with eyes to see, there is history in every churchyard, every signpost, every place name in the southern counties.

Practical Information for Southern Counties

WHERE TO DINE AND STAY? *Resorts and Inland.* All round the coast of Kent, Sussex and Hampshire, resort towns stretch along beaches and bays, their hotels and guest houses cheek by jowl. Only a few of the hotels remain open throughout the year, as most of them do only seasonal business from Easter to September. Holiday

THE SOUTHERN COUNTIES

hotels usually quote all-inclusive rates for a week's stay, which works out cheaper than taking room and meals by the day. You can expect prices to go up in July and August, however. Hotels listed are all moderate to first-class reasonable unless otherwise stated. (Inland hotels are open year-round.)

AMESBURY (Wiltshire). A centre for tours of Salisbury Plain and Stonehenge. *George*, 22 rooms (1 with bath), garden restaurant; *Antrobus Arms*, 17 rooms (4 with bath).

ASHFORD (Kent). Pleasant centre for touring Kent. *Saracen's Head*, 16 rooms; *George*, 8 rooms. At nearby Boughton Aluph is the *Flying Horse*, a small 16th-century inn; excellent food.

AVEBURY (Wiltshire). *The Red Lion, The Ailesbury Arms*, High Street, Marlborough (about 7 miles from Avebury).

BARHAM (Kent). Lovely resting place: *Spinning Wheel*, on Dover-Canterbury road. 21 rooms, a few with bath.

BEXHILL-ON-SEA (Sussex). The *Granville* (Trust House), 40 rooms (2 with bath). Restaurant: *Café Royal*.

BOGNOR REGIS (Sussex). *Royal Norfolk Hotel*, 44 rooms (11 with bath); *Royal*, 30 rooms (3 with bath). Restaurant: *Aldwick*.

BOURNEMOUTH (Hampshire). An all-year resort, famous for its clear air. Many winter attractions, concerts, shows, ballets and theatre. *Adelphi*, 60 rooms (all with bath); *Palace Court*, 123 rooms (all with bath); *Norfolk*, 64 rooms (36 with bath); *Carlton*, 150 rooms (all with bath); *Highcliff*, 129 rooms (60 with bath); *Royal Bath*, 100 rooms (76 with bath); *Savoy*, 92 rooms (40 with bath); *Winter Gardens*, 45 rooms (5 with bath); *Marsham Court*, 120 rooms (26 with bath); *White Hermitage*, 97 rooms (17 with bath). New *Roundhouse*, scheduled to open by 1970, 102 rooms with bath.

Restaurants: *Cavalier, Czech, San Marco*, and, 10 miles north on A35, at the *Cat and Fiddle*, in Hinton Admiral (illustrated opp. p. 81).

BRIGHTON (Sussex). New (1967) *Bedford; Old Ship*, 171 rooms (70 with bath); *Grand*, 250 rooms (75 with bath); *Metropole*, 265 rooms (all with bath); *Royal Albion*, 115 rooms (42 with bath), excellent cuisine; *Royal Crescent*, good location, 64 rooms with bath.

For dining in Brighton, try *Antoine's, Edlin's, Mascotte, Sheridan Tavern, Pump House, English's Oyster Bar, Pickwick, Wheeler's* for seafood, or *Lotus House* (Chinese). A few miles west, stop for a drink at *Ye Olde Red Lion*, in Old Shoreham (A27).

BROADSTAIRS (Kent). *Royal Albion*, 26 rooms, Trust House, moderate; *Castle Keep*, 20 rooms (16 with bath); *Castlemere*, 42 rooms. Restaurant: *Marchesi*.

CANTERBURY (Kent). Ancient cathedral city. *Chaucer*, 53 rooms (5 with bath); *Slatters*, 31 rooms (25 with bath); *Abbots Barton*, 36 rooms (9 with bath); *County*, 46 rooms (7 with bath). At Barham, *Broome Park*, 17th-century country house, once home of Lord Kitchener, 25 rooms (5 with bath).

For dinner, try the *Falstaff*, a pub, *Trattoria Roma Antica*, the *Continental Grill*, or *Hop Kweng's*.

Have a cherry brandy (the only place it is on tap in Britain) at *The Crown*, a famous old place at Sarre, 8 miles east of town. Also called "Halfway House", it is the inn where Dickens wrote much of *Bleak House*.

CASTLE COMBE (Wiltshire). Has been acclaimed as England's prettiest village. Is now back to normal after being used as setting for filming of *Dr. Dolittle*. The place is crowded in summer, with parking sometimes impossible. Make a beeline for the *Manor House*, 15 rooms (10 with bath) or *Castle*, 6 rooms, excellent food and bar.

CHICHESTER (Sussex). Cathedral city with Roman Walls. *Dolphin and Anchor*, Trust House, 48 rooms (25 with bath); *Chichester Motel*, on the A27 (nr. Goodwood), 34 rooms (all with bath); *Ship*, 30 rooms. Restaurants: *Old Cross Inn* (excellent food and service), *Old Priory*.

CHILHAM (Kent). One of England's loveliest villages, just 5 miles west of Canterbury on A252. Eat at the *Woolpack Inn*.

CHRISTCHURCH (Hampshire). Near Bournemouth. The *King's Arms Inn*—a charming, half-timbered hostelry where the floors slant, the ceilings bend and the furnishings are Elizabethan.

CLIFTONVILLE (Near Margate, Kent). *Endcliffe*, 60 rooms; *Grosvenor Court*, 85 rooms (7 with bath); *Walpole Bay*, 64 rooms (3 with bath); *Ye Old Charles*, 16 rooms.

DEAL (Kent). *Royal*, 29 rooms (4 with bath); *Queens*, 62 rooms (39 with bath); *Black Horse*, 13 rooms (3 with bath).

DOVER (Kent). *White Cliffs*, 84 rooms (21 with bath); *Dover Stage*, Britain's first hotel designed for transit passengers, 42 rooms, many with balconies. Eat at *White Cliffs*.

DYMCHURCH (Kent). A modern motel, the *Neptune*.

EASTBOURNE (Sussex). This well laid-out resort is included in the estates of the Duke of Devonshire. A town of 60,000 people, it retains a good deal of elegance, especially in the spring. *Burlington*, 153 rooms (60 with bath); *Cavendish*, 120 rooms (95 with bath); *Grand*, 200 rooms (130 with bath); *Hydro*, 100 rooms (46 with bath); *Mansion*, 124 rooms (30 with bath); *Queen's*, 120 rooms (66 with bath); *Kings Motel*, 30 rooms (all with bath). The prize place to eat is the excellent *Chez Maurice*, closed Sundays. Also good: *Summer Palace* (Chinese).

FOLKESTONE (Kent). *Grand*, 122 rooms (49 with bath); *Burlington*, 50 rooms (40 with bath); *Princes*, 70 rooms (11 with bath or shower); *Clifton*, 60 rooms (7 with bath), Trust House.

Also: *Lyndhurst*, 85 rooms (13 with bath); *Continental Wampach*, 80 rooms (5 with bath); and *Garden House*, 52 rooms (7 with bath).

Between Hythe and the Sussex border lies the desolate Romney Marsh, with its fascinating history of smuggling and its ancient trading connections with France. The closeness of Lydd Airport and Lympne Airport with frequent flights to Le Touquet (about 20 minutes), makes this area almost bi-national.

Restaurant: *New Metropole*, or eat at the Burlington's *Grill Room*.

GODALMING (Surrey). Small country town. *Lake*, 12 rooms.

GOUDHURST (Kent). The half-timbered *Star and Eagle* has 6 rooms, and a famous grillroom.

Same size and pleasant are the *Goudhurst* and the *Vine*.

GUILDFORD (Surrey). *Angel*, 27 rooms (13 with bath). Noted for good food. Second best, and newer: *White Horse*, 23 rooms (15 with bath). Eat at the *Angel*.

HASTINGS and ST. LEONARDS (Sussex). *Queen's* (Hastings), 120 rooms (30 with bath); *Royal Victoria* (St. Leonards), 93 rooms (17 with bath); *Beauport Park*, Battle (nr. Hastings), 15 rooms (some with bath). Restaurant: *Le Chanticler*.

HINDHEAD (Surrey). Beauty spot near Devil's Punch Bowl. *Moor House*, 9 rooms.

HYTHE (Kent). *Imperial*, 65 rooms (all with bath); *Stade Court*, 29 rooms (2 with bath). Eat at the *Imperial*.

LACOCK (Wilts.). In this charming village, looking more like a medieval dream than anything else, stay at the *Sign of the Angel*, 7 rooms (1 with bath). Excellent home-cooked meals.

LIPHOOK (Hampshire). Excellent golf. *Royal Anchor*, 19 rooms (1 with bath). Eat here, if anywhere in town.

LYNDHURST (Hampshire). In the heart of the New Forest. *Crown*, 28 rooms (4 with bath); *Grand*, 60 rooms (14 with bath).

MAIDSTONE (Kent). At Hollingbourne, near Maidstone, on the M20 London-Dover-Channel route, is Rank Hotel's *Great Danes*, a luxurious establishment boasting 81 rooms (all with bath or shower), heated swimming pool and restaurant, grill room and bar. Also: *Veglio's Motel*, 12 rooms (all with bath) and *Royal Star*, 40 rooms (10 with bath).

MERE (Wiltshire). *The Old Ship*, 10 rooms, is famous for its superb hospitality and quiet charm.

MIDHURST (Sussex). Pleasant country town, good golf, polo, and fishing. The *Spread Eagle*, an ancient showplace inn, has 27 rooms (8 with bath) and excellent cuisine. Also, *Angel*, an ancient posting inn, 18 rooms. Restaurant: *Old Manor House*.

NEWENDEN (Kent). The *White Hart*, an old inn here, was chosen English "country pub of the year" in a 1967 newspaper contest.

PETWORTH (Sussex). Ancient small town. *Swan*, 15 rooms (1 with bath).

ROCHESTER (Kent). *Royal Victoria and Bull*, 35 rooms (10 with bath). Dickens associations.

ROYAL TUNBRIDGE WELLS (Kent). For dining, try the *Spotted Dog*.

RYE (Sussex). French fishermen visit the Rye inns for Kentish cider and the Marsh folk feel quite at home with wine. The best places to stay in Rye: *Rumpel's Motel*, 4 rooms (all with bath), or the ancient and beautiful *Mermaid* or the *George* (Trust House), both small, first class, and reasonable. Eat at *Flushing Inn*.

SALISBURY (Wiltshire). Cathedral city, touring centre. *King's Arms*, 16 rooms (3 with bath), lovely old inn, modern amenities; *Red Lion*, same category, 35 rooms (6 with bath); *White Hart* (Trust House), 54 rooms (12 with bath), renovated in 1968. *Haunch of Venison* is a good chop house to remember, as well as the *New House* or the *Old Inn*. The *House of Steps* is a quaint lunchroom near the old town gate. In old Sarum, *Old Castle Inn* for dining.

SEAFORD (Sussex). New (1967), the *Newhaven Mercury Motor Inn*, 70 rooms (all with bath).

SOUTHSEA (Near Portsmouth, Hampshire). *Queens*, 80 rooms (23 with bath); *Pendragon*, 56 rooms

(25 with bath), *Royal Beach*, 125 rooms (51 with bath); *Solent*, 61 rooms. Restaurant: *Belshazzar*.

SOUTHAMPTON (Hampshire). Hardly a seaside resort, but listed because many visitors from the U.S.A. land here. *Botleigh Grange*, 36 rooms (10 with bath); *Dolphin*, 76 rooms (20 with bath); *Polygon*, 125 rooms (66 with bath); *Royal*, 100 rooms (20 with bath); *Skyway*, 125 rooms (all with bath). Also: *Cotswold*, 50 rooms (7 with bath). At nearby Hamble, the *Hamble Manor* is good for bed *and* board. 25 rooms (half with bath), heated pool, games. Eat at the *Botleigh Grange* and *Polygon* hotels.

WEST STOKE (near Chichester, Sussex). *Wooded House*, 13 rooms (1 with bath). A country mansion once home of Lily Langtry, the actress, and Captain Hardy (Nelson's aide).

WINCHESTER (Hampshire). Old city, once England's capital. *Wessex*, new Trust House, 91 rooms with bath; *Royal*, 31 rooms; *Southgate*, 17 rooms; *Abbey Hill Manor of God Begot*, 10 rooms. Restaurant: *The Elizabethan*.

WORTHING (Sussex). *Beach*, 90 rooms (54 with bath); *Warnes*, 120 rooms (13 with bath); *Eardley*, 73 rooms (14 with bath).

WYE (Kent). Dine at the charming *Wife of Bath*, whose owner's wife comes from Bath.

HOW TO GET AROUND? Southern Region of *British Rail* operate fast services throughout Surrey, Sussex, Kent and parts of Hampshire. For £6 15s (10 guineas first-class) ($14-$25), you can buy a 7-day ticket entitling you to unrestricted travel within the region. Regional *bus* services are frequent and economical, and there is also a consortium of fast long-distance coaches (*London Coastal Coaches*), operating from London's Victoria Coach Station. There are reservation facilities in all large towns and many small villages.

In the past few years, the number of 24-hour filling stations has increased considerably. Check with the R.A.C. or A.A. handbook if you are planning to do any night driving in the area, however.

For rent-a-car services, if arriving from France at Dover, try *Avis*, 83 High St.

Historic Houses Open to the Public

HAMPSHIRE. *Beaulieu Abbey*, New Forest, home of Lord Montagu of Beaulieu. Cistercian abbey founded in 1204. Remarkable veteran car museum. Both open daily (winter, Sundays only).

Jane Austen's House, Chawton. Open daily throughout the year, by Memorial Trust.

Breamore House, near Fordingbridge. Fine Elizabethan Manor House. Open daily except Monday and Friday, April to September.

The Pilgrims Hall, Winchester Cathedral. 14th-century hall. Open daily.

KENT. *Smallhythe Place*, Tenterden. National Trust. Timbered 15th-century yeoman's home. Relics of Dame Ellen Terry, Mrs. Siddons. Open daily except Tuesday, March to October.

Chilham Castle, near Canterbury. Norman keep. Garden open Thursday and Sunday, May to October (also Wednesday from June). By appointment at other times.

THE SOUTHERN COUNTIES

Chartwell, near Westerham. Home of the late Sir Winston Churchill. Open Wednesday and Thursday afternoons, Saturday and Sunday, March to November.

Ightham Mote, near Ightham. Medieval moated manor house. Open Fridays all year.

Quebec House, Westerham. National Trust. Early 16th-century in origin, but now mainly 17th-century. Relics of General Wolfe. Open March to October, Tues., Wed. and Sunday afternoons.

Sissinghurst Castle, near Cranbrook. National Trust. Tudor buildings and glorious gardens. Open daily, April to October.

SURREY. *Clandon Park,* near Guildford. National Trust. Beautiful 16th-century Palladian House. Open Easter to September. Monday, Wednesday, Saturday and Sunday afternoons.

Polesden Lacey, near Dorking, National Trust. Regency House (altered in Edwardian period) in charming surroundings. Open Wednesday afternoons, Saturday and Sunday. (Closed most of December to February).

Puttenden Manor, near Lingfield. Plantagenet manor house with superb collection of antique furniture. Open end of March to October, Wednesday, Saturday, Sunday afternoons.

Loseley House, near Guildford. Noble Elizabethan mansion, built 1562. Open Friday and Saturday afternoons, June to September.

SUSSEX. *Arundel Castle.* Home of the Duke of Norfolk. Ancient castle rebuilt in the 18th-century and altered at the end of the 19th-century. Open from Easter to September, most weekdays.

Brede Place, near Rye. A wonderful 14th-century manor house with 16th-century additions, open every Wednesday and Saturday afternoon in summer.

Goodwood House, near Chichester. Built by Wyatt. Fine collection of pictures, and Louis XV furniture. Open Wednesday and Sunday afternoons, May to September.

Petworth House, Petworth. National Trust. Palatial mansion rebuilt in 1696 by the 6th Duke of Somerset. Fine collection of paintings. Open Wednesday, Thursday, Saturday afternoons, April to October.

Bateman's, near Burwash, National Trust. Built 1634. Delightful house of Rudyard Kipling. Open afternoons daily except Friday, March to October.

Charleston Manor, near Seaford. Mellow house with famous Norman wing. Open Wednesday afternoons (by appointment only—telephone Alfriston 267), mid-May to September.

Firle Place, near Lewes. Has important collection of pictures and many items of particular interest to visitors from the U.S.A. Open Sunday afternoons in June, Wed., Thur. and Sun. afternoons from July to September.

Great Dixter, Northiam. Medieval half-timbered manor house with fine gardens. Open daily (not Mondays), Easter through September.

Michelham Priory, near Hailsham. Tudor farmhouse, originally an Augustinian Priory. Surrounded by medieval moat. Open daily, Easter through October.

Parham, Pulborough. Magnificent Elizabethan house. Open Sun., Wed. and Thur. afternoons, Easter to early October.

WILTSHIRE. *Longleat House,* near Warminster. Home of the Marquis of Bath, built in 1566. Many lions in the grounds, not to mention hippopotami, monkeys, a children's zoo, etc. Titian, Raphael, Holbein paintings. Open daily all year.

Wilton House, Salisbury. Home of the Earl of Pembroke. Noted for its "double cube" room, and ancient lawns and cedars of Lebanon. Open April to September, Tuesday to Saturday.

Corsham Court, near Chippenham, Elizabethan and Georgian House of the Lord Methuen, with many paintings. Open Wednesday, Thursday, Sunday and certain other days, April to September.

Lacock Abbey, near Chippenham. National Trust. 13th-century abbey, converted into a house in 1540, with later alterations in Georgian "Gothick". In one of the most beautiful villages in England. Open Wed., Thur. and Sat. afternoons. April to September.

Stourhead, Stourton, near Mere. 18th-century house and magnificent gardens, built for Henry Hoare, the banker. Owned by the National Trust. Open all year, gardens on most days, house on Wednesday, Saturday and Sunday.

Avebury Manor, Avebury. Romantic Elizabethan house and gardens ringed by giant prehistoric circle. Open daily (not Tuesdays) in May, June, July, August. Also weekends in September.

Littlecote House, near Hungerford. Historic Tudor manor house with famous Cromwellian Armoury. Open Mon., Tue., Wed., Sat. and Sun. afternoons, April to mid-October.

SHOPPING. Try in *Canterbury:* Antiques along *Palace Street*, pottery at *Northgate Studio* (the pilgrims' Canterbury Bell is a specialty) or *Canterbury Potters,* Christ Church Gate. Elsewhere: the usual souvenir shops abound, but no local specialties of interest to the visitor.

COUNTRY WORKSHOPS. Hampshire. Handmade pottery: *Patty Elwood,* Meon Pottery, 1 Doctor's Lane, West Meon, nr. Petersfield. Handmade stoneware: *Godshill Pottery,* Godshill Ridge, nr. Fordingbridge. Saddlery, riding equipment: *M. E. Howitt,* Saddlers, 4 Turk Street, Alton.

Kent. All hand-thrown pottery: *Ursula and Tony Benham,* Mill Pottery, Mill Lane, Wateringbury, nr. Maidstone. Handmade stoneware: *Langton Green,* Tunbridge Wells. Slipware and high-fired earthenware: *John Solly Pottery,* 36 London Road, Maidstone. Cabinet makers, restorers of fine antiques: *E. R. Truphet,* Forge Antiques, Station Road, Borough Green, Sevenoaks.

Surrey. Saddlers: *D. Q. Field* (Saddlers), 2 Ewhurst Road, Cranleigh. Wood sculptures: *Ian Frazer,* Bachelors, Ockham,

Ripley. Custom-made furniture: *R. J. Minnitt*, Knigh, Heath End, Petworth. Plain and decorated fancy pottery: *Surrey Ceramic Co. Ltd.*, Kingwood Pottery, School Road, Grayshott, Hindhead.

Sussex. "Pycombe crooks" for secular or sacred herding: *Sean Black*, the Forge, Pyecombe, near Brighton. Traditional Sussex black metallic pottery and various red earthenware: *Brickhurst Pottery*, Laughton, nr. Lewes (Keith & Fiona Richardson). Stoneware individual pieces: *Derek David*, Duff Gallery, Tarrant Street, Arundel. Handwoven furnishings: *Gospel Weavers Ltd.*, Ditchling. Coffee sets, tea sets: *Iden Pottery*, 115 Winchelsea Road, Rye. Potter-stoneware: *Eric J. Mellon*, 5 Parkfield Avenue, Aldwick, Bognor Regis. Hand-thrown tableware: *Milland Pottery & Gallery*, Milland, Liphook. Sussex trug baskets: *R. W. Rich & Sons Ltd.*, South Street, East Hoathly, Lewes.

Wiltshire tweeds and ties at *John Battye's*, The Old Post Office, No. 4 Latton, Swindon. Sculpture by *David L. J. Bridges*, 16 Lowbourne, Melksham. Saddlery by *Frederick J. Chandler Ltd.*, London Road, Marlborough. Falconry furniture, fishing tackle, suedes, etc. at *Leathercraft*, 78 High Street, Marlborough. Traditional English pottery by *Ivan Martin*, Cricklade Pottery, Cricklade, near Swindon. Hunting and racing equipment by *H. Till & Son*, 15 Brown Street, 19 Milford Street, Salisbury. Door knockers and lamps at *Lucien Varwell*, Bounds Forge, Ebbesbourne Wake, Salisbury. Rugs, tweeds, sweaters at *White Horse Spinners & Weavers*, Beech Bank, Bratton, near Westbury.

MUSEUMS. Among the many, a few of the best: Basingstoke: *Basing House Ruins & Museum* (Roman coins, Norman and Tudor gargoyles, Dutch and Tudor pottery, Cromwellian swords). Beaulieu: *Montagu Motor Museum* (veteran and vintage motor car and motor cycle collection). Bodiam: *Bodiam Castle Museum* (medieval architecture). Bignor: *Bignor Roman Villa Collection* (coins, women's jewellery, models of villa). Bournemouth: *Russell-Cotes Art Gallery & Museum* (oil paintings, Japanese arts, theatrical). *Rothesay Museum* (Lucas collection of early Italian paintings and pottery). Bramber: *Potter's Museum* (animal tableaux and the illustration of nursery rhymes). Brighton: *Brighton Art Gallery & Museum* (old-master paintings and modern English water-colours). *The Booth Museum of British Birds* (birds mounted in their natural habitats). The *Grange Art Gallery & Museum* (collections of Kipling's books, letters, documents and illustrations). *Brighton Motor Museum* (veteran and vintage cars, motor cycles). *Thomas-Stanford Museum* (period furniture, silver, etc.). Buckler's Hard: *Maritime Museum* (exhibits of ships of bygone days). Burwash: *Bateman's,* Rudyard Kipling's Home (home of Rudyard Kipling from 1902 until 1936, his study as he used it).

Camberley: *National Army Museum* (former Irish regiments). Canterbury: *Canterbury Royal Museum* (local archeological material). *The Westgate* (museum of arms and armour). The *Roman Pavement* (foundations of Roman villa). *St. Augustine's Abbey Museum* (collection from ruins of abbey). Chawton: *Jane Austen's Home* (personal relics of herself and her family). Christchurch: *Red House Museum & Art Gallery* (19th-century fashion plates, dolls and bygones).

Eastbourne: *The Towner Art Gallery* (British painters of 19th and 20th centuries). *Royal National Lifeboat Institution Museum* (all types of lifeboats). Faversham: *Maison Dieu* (finds from a Roman cemetery). Godalming: *Charterhouse School Museum* (Carthusiana). Guildford: *Guildford Museum & Muniment Room* (needlework collection of general interest).

Haslemere: *Haslemere Educational Museum* (fine collection of British birds). Hastings: *Public Museum & Art Gallery* (Sussex and Kent pottery). *Museum of Local History* (Cinque Ports relics, ships models). Horsham: *Horsham Museum* (Sussex iron and pottery). Hove: *Hove Museum of Art* (English fine art). Lewes: *Barbican House Museum* (prehistoric, Romano-British and medieval antiquities). *Anne of Cleves House* (furniture, costumes, household equipment). Maidstone: *Museum & Art Gallery* (archeological, William Hazlitt relics, Dutch and Italian oil paintings). *Maidstone Museum of Carriages* (the history of horse-transport and coach building).

Portsmouth: *Cumberland House Museum & Art Gallery* (local history and archeology). *Dickens' Birthplace Museum* (Dickensiana). *The Victory Museum* (relics of Nelson, his officers and men). Richborough: *Richborough Castle* (objects found during excavation of the site). Rochester: *Rochester*

Public Museum (fine collection of clocks). Rye: *Rye Museum* (Victoriana). Silchester: *Calleva Museum* (Roman objects from site of Calleva). Southampton: *Southampton Art Gallery* (British painting, particularly contemporary). *Tudor House Museum* (Tudor mansion). *God's House Tower Museum* (local archeology). *Maritime Museum* (a museum of shipping).

Tenterden: *Ellen Terry Museum* (relics of her, of Irving, Mrs. Siddons and David Garrick). Tunbridge Wells: *Royal Tunbridge Wells Museum & Art Gallery* (permanent collection of Victorian paintings). Westerham: *Quebec House* (childhood home of General Wolfe). West Hoathly: *The Priest's House* (old furniture, dolls and embroideries). Wilmington: *Wilmington Museum* (old agricultural implements and farmhouse utensils). Winchelsea: *Winchelsea Museum* (the history of the Cinque Ports). Winchester: *Winchester City Museum* (archeology and geology). *Winchester College Museum* (Greek pottery, English water-colours). *The Westgate Museum* (the civic history of Winchester). Wonersh: *The Sharp Collection* (old English village). Wye: *Agricultural Museum* (implements, machinery, hand tools).

ENTERTAINMENT. Most of the coastal resorts will be found to have some form of shows, staged either on the pier or in municipal theatres. Larger resorts will also have a municipal orchestra and often a good legitimate theatre. The *Bournemouth Symphony Orchestra* is well known and the town has, in addition, several good theatres. *Brighton*, too, has a beautiful old theatre, where plays are frequently produced prior to production in London.

All the major resorts have facilities for *tennis*, *golf*, *swimming*, etc., and many other entertainments and sports are available during the season. In Sussex, the *Glyndebourne Open Air Opera Festival* has become famous (formal dress required), and there are modern theatres presenting well-known artists at *Chichester*, *Croydon*, *Guildford* and *East Grinstead*.

Gambling. The *Metropole Hotel* at Brighton has a modern casino, where most games of chance may be played. Stakes may be modest or high according to your pocket. Also: *Curzon Club* and *Domingo* at Bournemouth, *Norfolk Club* at Brighton, *Hunter's Lodge* at Chichester, *Clifford* and *Sundowners* at Eastbourne, the *Regency* at Salisbury, *Celebrity*, *Magnum* and *Silhouette* at Southampton, and the *Grenadier Casino* at St. Leonard's.

Night Life. The new relaxation of legislation has meant that small clubs are springing up in most large centres. In principle, you have to be a member to gain admittance but overseas visitors can often be granted temporary membership on producing their passports.

A few choice clubs: *18 Club* at Bournemouth, *Edwarde* and *New Hove Albany* at Brighton, *Rayners Beach Club* at Folkestone, *Ivy House* at Hastings, *Brown Derby Country Club* at Lyndhurst, *Carousel* at Southampton, *Golden Apple* at Southsea, and *Oak Lodge Country Club* at Westerham.

Practical Information for Isle of Wight

HOW TO GET THERE? By *British Railways* ferry services from Portsmouth Harbour to Ryde. The journey takes about half an hour and the service frequency is about once an hour in the winter and twice an hour in summer. Alternative routes are *Red Funnel Steamers* from Southampton to East and West Cowes (55 min.), and *British Railways* service from Lymington to Yarmouth (though this is least frequent and most subject to alteration). On both these routes there are facilities for carrying cars on the drive on-drive off system. For cars and their passengers, one of the best routes is another British Railways ferry from Portsmouth Harbour to Fishbourne.

If you are taking your car to the Isle of Wight during the summer months, early reservations are absolutely essential as the ferries are heavily booked months ahead at the weekends.

Seasonal *air services* exist from Portsmouth and Shoreham to Ryde and Bembridge.

In 1966, *Hovercraft* services started between Southsea and Ryde (6 min.), and Southampton and Cowes (20 min.). They are fast and comfortable, but do not operate in inclement weather.

WHERE TO STAY AND DINE? *Bembridge.* Family resort, popular with the sailing fraternity. Good sands and intimate atmosphere. First-class reasonable: *Royal Spithead*, 34 rooms (15 with bath). Restaurant: *Birdham*, pub. *Cowes.* Famous yachting resort and home of the International Power Boat Race and of the Royal Yacht Squadron. Really good beaches are some distance away. Reserve early for Cowes Week. Moderate: *Gloster*, 19 rooms, *Grantham*, 21 rooms (1 with bath). Eat at the *Gloster*.

Freshwater. Pretty rocky and pebble bay with a little sand at low tide. Good sea fishing and golf nearby. Moderate: *Farringford*, 37 rooms (30 with bath). Inexpensive: *Osborne*, 13 rooms.

Ryde. Port of entry and popular resort with good communications, making it a good touring centre. Sandy beaches overlooking the Solent. First-class reasonable: *Royal Squadron*, 13 rooms. Moderate: *Ryde Castle*, 18 rooms; *Spencer's Inn*, 14 rooms; *Yelf's*, 26 rooms. Eat at the *Royal Squadron*.

Sandown. Family seaside resort with good sandy beaches. Entertainments, children's zoo and usual facilities. First-class reasonable: *Ocean*, 100 rooms (20 with bath). Moderate: *Royal Cliff*, 32 rooms (3 with bath); *Sandringham*, 84 rooms (20 with bath); *Trouville*, 84 rooms (16 with bath).

Shanklin. Family seaside resort with good sands and cliff walks. Historical association with Keats. First-class reasonable: *Cliff Tops*,

70 rooms (31 with bath). Moderate: *Holliers*, 27 rooms (1 with bath); *Shanklin Towers*, 53 rooms (4 with bath). Eat at *Holliers*.

Ventnor. Beautifully terraced gardens and an attractive promenade. Sea fishing and golf available. First-class reasonable: *Royal*, 61 rooms (11 with bath); *Metropole*, 37 rooms; *Ventnor Towers*, 40 rooms (7 with bath). Restaurant: *Peacock Vane*, near town at Bonchurch.

Yarmouth. Haven of small-boat enthusiasts with busy yacht basin. Small sandy beach and good communications. First-class reasonable: *George*, 25 rooms (1 with bath).

Historic Houses Open to the Public

Arreton Manor, near Newport. 17th-century manor house with early and late Stuart furniture. Fine pictures and a good Folk Collection. Open April to November, weekdays, 10 a.m. to 6 p.m.; Sundays 2.30 p.m. to 6.30 p.m.

Carisbrooke Castle, near Newport. Fine example of a medieval castle, where Charles I was imprisoned. Interesting small museum and donkey-powered well pump. Open daily all the year. Weekdays 9:30 a.m. to 7 p.m. (closes 4 p.m. or 5:30 p.m. in winter). Sundays 2 p.m. to 5:30 p.m. (winter, 4 p.m.).

Osborne House. Near East Cowes. One-time residence of Queen Victoria. Open 11 a.m. to 5 p.m. Easter to Spring Bank Holiday, Mondays, Wednesdays and Fridays. Spring Bank Holiday to September 29, Monday to Friday, 11 a.m. to 5 p.m.

Exploring the Southern Counties

It was through the gently rolling countryside of Kent that the early pilgrims went on their way to Canterbury and caught their first sight of the cathedral. The mother church of England, the seat of the primate, it is a magnificent achievement of Gothic architecture (with remains of an earlier Norman structure), some rare early stained-glass and a wonderfully serene crypt.

The history of Canterbury Cathedral goes back to the days of Ethelbert, King of Kent, who in 597 granted the site now occupied by the cathedral to St. Augustine, the Christian missionary from Rome. St. Augustine's church, despoiled by the Danes in 1011, was destroyed by fire in 1067. The oldest stones in the existing fabric of the cathedral belong to the church built by Lanfranc, who in 1070 became the first Norman archbishop of Canterbury. In 1175, William of Sens, a renowned French architect, was called in to design a splendid new choir and presbytery to house the tomb of Archbishop

T

Thomas à Becket, who was murdered in the church in 1170. Stone was shipped from Caen, Normandy, and brought up the River Stour, at that time navigable as far as Fordwich. The shrine was destroyed by Henry VIII.

Behind the high altar in the Trinity Chapel is the tomb of the Black Prince, that redoubtable fighter who won his spurs at the Battle of Crécy in 1346. The high vaulted nave and beautiful choir, one of the longest in England, are among the most striking features. The whole of the cathedral is open free and the cathedral authorities rely on the visitors contributing voluntary offerings in the boxes placed at different points in the cathedral. (No official permission is needed to photograph or sketch in the cathedral or the precincts except in the case of commercial usage.)

The city still retains much of its medieval character with the famous West Gateway, part of the ancient walls, old churches, houses and inns. It is also a modern town with plenty of diversion for the holiday-maker; excellent shops, cinemas and the *Marlowe Theatre*, which produces plays of a high standard and even a week of good ballet. Also if you are interested in cricket, you can certainly watch it here. The students of the newly-founded university also help give colour to the snack bars and pubs of the town. For the authentic atmosphere of medieval Canterbury, there are such inns as the 15th-century *Falstaff*, or the 16th-century *Beverlie*, originally the parish clerk's house. The *Olive Branch*, close to the cathedral, has a charming courtyard to sit in on summer evenings.

Canterbury contains many other ancient and lovely buildings: the Norman keep; the Church of St. Martin, one of the historic gems of British Christianity, which claims an unbroken pattern of worship lasting nearly 1,500 years; Christ Church Gateway, a lovely Tudor structure with 17th-century gates, and the Weavers' House, where the Huguenots plied their trade at the end of the 17th century; and many other buildings of great historic interest.

Canterbury is rich in literary associations, Chaucer's *Canterbury Tales* (c. 1380) being the most famous. Elizabethan poet Christopher Marlowe was born in Canterbury and Joseph Conrad (1857–1924), writer of stirring sea tales, is buried in Canterbury Cemetery.

THE SOUTHERN COUNTIES

There are endless excursions to be made through the varied countryside of Kent, pink and white with apple blossom in the spring, the woodlands pale with primroses and wood anemones and, later, deep in a mist of bluebells. It is a county of orchards, market gardens and the typical, round, red-roofed *oast* houses (for drying the hops), now often transformed into unusual dwelling houses. Scattered over this varied landscape are some of the loveliest villages and small towns in England.

Chilham, to the west of Canterbury on A28, with its castle set in a park and gardens designed by Capability Brown, overlooks the valley of the Stour; a crown cut into the Downs near here commemorates the coronation of Edward VII in 1902.

Further south, and towards the market town of Ashford, but off A28, lies Wye. Here you can combine a day on the race course near the station, with lunch or dinner at the *Wife of Bath*, frequented by members of the agricultural college, where you will have an excellent meal cooked with French subtlety.

For those who want to stray into the depths of rural England and seek out unfamiliar places, Barfreston, well to the south-east (off the A2 midway between Canterbury and Dover), and difficult to find in a maze of secondary roads (it is also spelt in a variety of ways), has one of the finest examples of a Norman village church in England. It has a wealth of carvings, a rose window and a bell oddly hanging in an old yew tree.

The residential town of Tunbridge Wells, reached from London on A21 and A26, has for its main attraction the charmingly laid-out parade called the Pantiles, paved and free from traffic, with fascinating antique shops and the gaiety of a band playing on summer evenings. Here you can not only visit some cheerful pubs, but you can drink from the "chalybeate spring". It has its own extensive common, and is a good centre for walks and excursions as well. Nearby Penshurst Place retains its Great Hall dating from the 14th century, but is mainly Elizabethan, with gardens laid out in the 16th century. Here you may like to have a meal at the *Spotted Dog* or go on to Groombridge, with its attractive cottages on the village green, and try the *Crown*.

To the east, along A263 and 262, is the lovely garden at Sissinghurst Castle, at its best in spring. Created by the authoress, the late Victoria Sackville West, and her husband,

Sir Harold Nicholson, it is now maintained by the National Trust. Nearby, at Sissinghurst Place, there are fine rhododendrons on great sweeping lawns. For a splendid view, climb the tower of the fine old church at Tenterden and, if you are interested, go on to 15th-century Smallhythe Place, with its relics of Dame Ellen Terry.

Any number of enchanting villages can be explored in the region: Biddenden, further east, with the great red roof of the Weaver's House and the local sign of the famous Biddenden Maids whom, legend tells us, were Siamese twins who lived for 34 years; or tucked away, picture-book Smarden; or villages with romantic sounding names like Appledore, St. Mary-in-the-Marsh, Stone-cum-Ebony, Ivychurch, the latter scattered over Romney Marsh, which spreads into Sussex.

On the marsh, too, are many splendid churches. Some are almost cathedrals, as at Lydd and New Romney, but others are small and reached only on foot across fields. At Stone, you can see an old Mithraic altar, in the pewter-coloured church which stands on a rise, surrounded by golden daffodils in spring and looking out across the marsh to the sea.

The coast is as varied as the inland region; the desolate pebble stretch of Dungeness, with its great atomic station and new "pencil" lighthouse, in contrast to its strange little fishermen's shacks, has the smallest passenger railway in the world over the thirteen miles to Hythe; the sandy beach of Littlestone, with New Romney church in the background; Dymchurch and, round the bay, the seaside resort and port of Folkestone, a cheerful place with a lovely cliff walk (from which you can see the French coast), some good restaurants and shops.

Dover

Dover, the channel port, and chief of the ancient Cinque Ports, with its welcoming white cliffs, its impressive castle dominating the harbour, has the liveliness and movement of shipping to compensate for its pebble beach, and Deal (north of it and opposite the Goodwin Sands), has many Georgian houses which give it a rather forlorn charm. Sandwich, also a Cinque Port, but now two miles from the sea, still keeps the atmosphere of its past importance in its Barbican and gateway, its old houses and inns and the Pilgrim's Guest House of the 15th century.

Further north, and beyond the wide sands of Pegwell Bay, lies the fishing port and popular resort of Ramsgate. Here you can fish, bathe, play golf and explore round this most interesting and relatively unfrequented stretch of coast. Hengist and Horsa are reputed to have landed at Ebbsfleet in 449 and a cross to St. Augustine records that he landed here in 597. There is also a 20th-century replica of a Viking longship which crossed the North Sea in 1949.

In the inn at Kingsgate you can have snacks and step outside to watch the waves dashing against the rocks below. Margate has much the same amenities as Ramsgate but also has the restored *Theatre Royal*. In August you can attend a gymkhana and carnival at adjoining Westgate. There is an amusement park, dancing and all the general evening entertainments of a popular resort.

Whitstable, north of Canterbury, has been famous for its oysters, "Whitstable Natives", since the days of the Romans; you can watch the beds being dredged by a fleet of yawls and, in early September, see the waters blessed at the beginning of the oyster season, at an open-air service. The bay of this quiet little fishing port and resort is often full of activity, with boating and yacht racing. Here the River Swale cuts off from the mainland the area known as the Isle of Sheppey.

Rochester, on the Medway, and back toward London, is renowned for its fine cathedral and massive Norman castle keep. There are many fine buildings, but the general atmosphere is of a busy town, without the peace associated with a cathedral city. The "illustrious larder" described by Dickens still stands off the hall of the *Bull* here. Indeed, Kent is Dickens' country, for he not only lived here for many years at Gad's Hill on the outskirts of Rochester), but several of the inns keep his memory alive. At the *Leather Bottle* at Cobham, the landlord carefully preserves the armchair in which he wrote the last chapters of *The Pickwick Papers*.

Dickens spent many summers in Broadstairs (1837-1851) and a number of houses record the fact that he lived in them. *Bleak House* is not the setting for the novel of that title, but is open to the public in summer, and each year in July a Dickens' Festival is organized in the town.

Sussex

Sussex lies next to Kent, and in parts closely resembles its neighbour, for Romney Marsh links the two counties in the south and both can claim some of the Cinque Ports, of which, incidentally (and in case you've been counting), there are more than five. Sussex, too, has its delightful villages, but its shores and old inns are more closely associated with smuggling, particularly at the Cinque Port of Rye, high on its hill above the marsh, deserted by the sea and now patterned with dykes and innumerable sheep. This once fully-walled and even today, gated town, with its lovely old church, still has some cobbled streets and almost all its houses are either half-timbered or 18th-century. Henry James lived here for several years. Some distance towards Winchelsea Beach lies the 16th-century Camber Castle and, to the east, are the broad Camber Sands, overlooked by the famous golf course. Nearer at hand, most of the Rye fishing fleet moor near the town saltflats in the Rother.

A few miles away, Winchelsea, standing on a wooded rise, is also entered through a fortified gateway, and has a splendid church built, like Canterbury, with stone from Normandy.

Hastings, on the coast further to the west, has a charming old fishing harbour and some fine streets, but they are rather overwhelmed by the shopping centre and the more modern holiday resort linked to St. Leonards. First-class concerts are given at the White Rock Pavilion, and some good continental films come to the repertory cinema; there is also a varied choice of restaurants. On the sandstone cliff above the Old Town are the ruins of England's first Norman castle. The victory of William the Conqueror over the Saxons is commemorated in the name of the town of Battle, where William erected an abbey (a stone in the grounds marks the spot where the Saxon King, Harold, was killed), but most people will find it more interesting to visit the complete shell of the 14th-century Bodiam Castle, built to protect the approaches up the Rother and now standing reflected in a moat half-covered with water lilies and surrounded by trees.

There is little enough of old Bexhill left, but for elderly people who like their entertainments close at hand and sheltered, the De La Warr Pavilion provides varied entertainments and an inexpensive glassed-in cafeteria overlooking the sea; plays of the "family" type are also produced by a resident repertory company and there is old-time dancing on a terrace in summer as well as more modern dancing for younger people. An annual July Festival of Music with morning lectures, wine and cheese tastings, afternoon coach tours to historic castles, evening concerts, supper parties and dancing, after the concerts, is centred round the world-famous Hallé Orchestra, led by Sir John Barbirolli.

The silver grey stones of Pevensey Castle turn the main road to Eastbourne into a narrow lane for a few yards before it approaches this attractive and popular resort with its great cliffs and Beachy Head rivalling those of Dover. It naturally has all the diversions of a popular seaside town and, if you like French food, carefully served and good wine at a very reasonable cost, stop at *Chez Maurice* for lunch. The climate along this part of the coast through Seaford and the Channel port of Newhaven to Brighton is very good, with a large share of the English sunshine and little of its cold and rain, although it cannot claim to be always free from gales.

For anyone who does not mind a busy, lively resort, now developed into a big town with a broad coast road, Brighton can provide a delightful holiday for, quite apart from the obvious attractions of good shops, restaurants and entertainment, there is the maze of alleys full of antique shops referred to as "The Lanes" and the fanciful Pavilion built in the late 18th century (mainly by John Nash) for George IV when he was Prince Regent, with domes and pinnacles in oriental style. Furthermore, there is a well stocked aquarium by the Palace Pier and even a branch of the Montagu Motor Museum, not to mention racing at Kemp Town. If you are interested in Regency architecture, there are also many fine squares and terraces, and a short distance away, Rottingdean, which has retained its village character. One of the liveliest and most successful of the new universities, founded in 1961 in Stanmer Park, brings plenty of young people into the town. Wonderful walks are provided by the South Downs, those low, rolling hills so characteristic of southern England and so highly praised by Kipling, Chesterton and Belloc.

The ancient county town of Lewes, northeast of Brighton on A27, has very old churches and side streets almost too steep for a car to manage. Try to see the narrow but beautiful High Street here. For music lovers, Lewes is a good stepping-off place for Glyndebourne, which, in the summer season, offers some of the finest opera productions in the world, in a beautiful rustic setting.

Beyond Brighton, a number of resorts, Worthing, Littlehampton, Bognor Regis) enjoy equally good weather. Inland lies Chichester, with its Norman cathedral, fine old 18th-century houses and beautiful 16th-century market cross. The waters of Chichester harbour are always animated with small boats and yachts, all making a perfect setting for the excellent Festival Theatre, which has an open stage on which are performed outstanding productions of advanced plays. Like Glyndebourne, it has an international reputation. Essential short side-trips from Chichester are to Bosham, a yachting village with a church depicted in the *Bayeux Tapestry*, and the excavated Roman Palace of King Cogidubnus at Fishbourne (open daily March through October, (normal admission charge).

Arundel Castle, near Chichester, has been much restored and the great park with its attractive lake is always open to the public, though no cars are allowed in. Racing enthusiasts may like to visit Goodwood Park and racecourse, where the fashionable meetings take place at the end of July (usually attended by the royal family).

Inland too, along the South Downs, there are villages and small towns every bit as attractive as those of Kent, such as Alfriston, with its "Cathedral of the Downs", a church of the 14th century, and its delightful *Star Inn*. You can have an unpretentious meal at the *George* with its 16th-century frescoes and, a mile or so away at Lullington, is the smallest church in Sussex, which scarcely holds a dozen worshippers. Further north, near the old town of Midhurst, you can watch polo in the summer in Cowdray Park or, further east, visit the lovely little town of Petworth, with its 17th- and 18th-century houses. South of Petworth, at Bignor, is a Roman Villa Museum, with fine mosaics.

Great areas of forest distinguish Sussex from Kent, such as Ashdown Forest, stretching north of the South Downs behind Brighton on A27 and 26, where you can drive and ride and walk for miles overlooking splendid landscape and finish up at one of the friendly little pubs in any of the villages such as Sharpethorne, Wych Cross or Coleman's Hatch.

To the east of the forest, on A265, you will find Kipling's village of Burwash, where you can get an excellent midday traditional meal at the *Bell*, with steak-and-kidney pie or roast meat and potatoes, before visiting the author's house, *Bateman's*. Here, you can linger in the attractive garden and perhaps explore the region he writes of in *Puck of Pook's Hill*.

Surrey

The landscape of Surrey is distinguished by its countless heaths and commons, many of which link up and provide a chain of wild free country which can never be built on. It is easily accessible from London by excellent roads, by train or by bus. The hill known as "The Hog's Back" is one of the best-known stretches, commanding magnificent views but apt to be crowded at week-ends. It runs to the west of Guildford, which is Surrey's county town and its most interesting centre.

Above the town of Guildford stands the modern cathedral designed by Sir Edward Maufe. This structure is built of rose-coloured brick and the architect relied more on the skilful disposition of the masses and the simple grace of Gothic lines than on elaborate decoration. The statue of St. John the Baptist, in the transept, is by Eric Gill, a modern sculptor whose fame is likely to endure.

Guildford is an ancient city which has suddenly become an important centre. The Royal Grammar School, in the High Street, was founded in the early 16th century, but the actual structure was built in the reign of Queen Elizabeth I. Bibliophiles should visit the library to inspect the 80 chained books that include the original version of Sir Walter Raleigh's *History of the World*. Other historical buildings in this beautiful thoroughfare include the Abbott's Hospital, founded in 1619 by George Abbott, Archbishop of Canterbury, who collaborated in the translation of the Authorised Version of the Bible.

Also built in the 17th century, but fifty years later, the timber-faced Guildhall is easily discernible from afar because of the clock that projects out over the street. The courtroom, with its Georgian panelling, is worth visiting if only because of the 17th-century portraits of monarchs and the superb silver plate used by the town corporation on state occasions.

To the south of the Guildhall, the ruins of a Norman castle stand on a mound not far from the museum, which exhibits objects found in burial grounds of all periods in the vicinity of the city. Lewis Carroll, (C. L. Dodgson), author of *Alice in Wonderland*, died at The Chestnuts, a house near to the main entrance to the castle.

Despite the flood of traffic that surges up and down the steep, cobbled High Street, it is still possible to find pleasure in the 17th- and 18th-century houses, as well as the ancient inns, such as the *Angel* and the *White Horse*.

Since it has become a satellite city (to London), Guildford has developed in the modern manner, but with its own individuality. The *Yvonne Arnaud Theatre*, by the river, presents good plays, both classical and avant garde. The university transferred and recreated here in 1965 is growing rapidly and combines scientific studies with modern languages as its specialties.

Farnham, due west of Guildford, is also in the process of becoming a satellite town, but it has a castle inhabited for centuries by the bishops of Winchester. The streets of the centre are still filled with splendid examples of English architecture of most periods. There are 18th-century mansions with doorways in the Adam style, as well as one or two Tudor inns and Tudor houses, though all around Farnham new streets of houses are being built for the commuters.

Godalming, to the south of Guildford, is yet another of these country towns, growing rapidly because it is on the famous Portsmouth road, and within easy distance of London by rail. It was the birthplace of James Oglethorpe, founder of the state of Georgia. The High Street still has some fine old houses —some of them half-timbered—and a church with a Saxon chancel and a Norman tower. To the west of Godalming lies Frensham Common, with its expanses of heather and pine-woods, and its broad pond, in which you may sail or bathe in the summer time.

However, the best of Surrey is to be found in the villages and commons away from the main roads. Further south on A3 from Hindhead Beacon (nearly 900 feet high), there are views of this green countryside in every direction. Still further south again is Shottermill Common (near to Haslemere), where George Eliot lived in a small cottage. Haslemere is an elegant little town to which people come to hear old English music during the yearly Dolmetsch Festival.

To the north of Haslemere is the village of Chiddingfold, the centre of glass-making in the early Middle Ages. One maker, Lawrence by name, was responsible for making many of the stained glass windows in Westminster Abbey. Since this industry prospered, there are many old houses round the broad village green. About the year 1281, Cistercian monks here began to build a traveller's rest house, laying the foundations of the 13th-century building which is now the oldest inn in Surrey, the *Crown*, where you can still enjoy good food. The *Crown* was already thriving in the 14th century and it was here that King Edward VI stayed on one of his royal progresses.

Though the population of Surrey is growing quickly, a lovely stretch of countryside with a number of ancient villages has been preserved in the area that lies to the southeast of Guildford, and to the southwest of Dorking. There are beechwoods thick with bluebells in May, there are heathery commons, there are meadows with Hammer Ponds, used by the blacksmiths who forged the guns for Elizabeth's fleet. Friday Street, Holmbury St. Mary, Abinger Hammer—their names ring out like a poem. Possibly the loveliest of the Surrey villages is Shere, on the banks of the Tillingbourne stream. Then there is Wootton, where the diarist John Evelyn spent most of his life, laying out the garden round his house, which is still standing. And there is Gomshall, where you can eat a real English country tea in a converted watermill that once belonged to King Harold.

Hampshire

Hampshire has a greater variety of attractions to offer the holiday-maker than any other southern county. Southampton Water gives it the excitement of a great port connecting with all parts of the world; the New Forest is still wild, free country, and the Isle of Wight in itself provides even greater variety, with its ever-changing coastline. Bournemouth adds a large seaside resort with stretches of sand and pine woods; and Winchester with its magnificent cathedral, was once the capital of England. A fine array of distinctions!

The county boundary between Hampshire and Sussex is just

west of Chichester at Emsworth on A27, which, despite P.G. Wodehouse's fertile imagination, really does exist. From here, the coast is indented, with the great landlocked naval base of Portsmouth, the stretch of the Solent dividing the mainland from the Isle of Wight, and Southampton Water, which cuts deep into the county to the port. The latter then narrows to the River Test, which flows by the splendid Norman abbey of Romsey, founded in the 10th century; here, the carved abbess's doorway is Norman and, beside it, is a most moving crucifix, believed to be Saxon. From here, anglers can follow the Test north to the famous little fishing town of Stockbridge, where the *Grosvenor Hotel* keeps its built-out porch, originally designed to give travellers shelter when descending from their coaches. The main street here is so broad that it was once used as a racecourse. Westwards, the three Wallops, Middle, Nether and Over, lie close together and, quite apart from their fascinating shared name (the origin of which is unknown), they are very attractive. Nether Wallop has early wall paintings in the church, and Over Wallop has a 15th-century font.

Southampton, from whence the *Mayflower* sailed for Plymouth, England, is primarily a shipping and commercial center, but there are a number of rustic riverside walks in the region once you get out of the built-up area. Into Southampton Water's east shore flows the River Hamble and, near Bursledon in the dip of Hungerford Bottom, just southeast of Southampton, you will find a vine-covered pub, *The Fox and Hounds*. If it amuses you to sample English cheeses as well as mead, cowslip and the less familiar strawberry wine, you may want to linger here some time.

Hampshire has many associations with the national game of cricket. It was at Hambledon, just north of Portsmouth, that the first county cricket match was played in silk stockings, knee breeches and top hats. This is commemorated by a memorial stone set up, aptly enough, opposite the *Bat and Ball Inn*, one of the most famous hostelries in England and a place where you are likely to meet noted players. At Hambledon, if you like seeking out early architectural details, you will find, with a little difficulty, some Saxon remains in the church.

The city of Winchester, easily reached from Southampton on A33, is famous for its beautiful medieval cathedral, its public school and the reputed burial place of Alfred the Great.

Winchester, besides being one of the most ancient is also one of the most graceful and unspoilt of English cities. It reflects the history of England from earliest times, and was a capital city before London assumed that dignity. It was from Winchester that King Alfred, the first great king of England, and its saviour from the Danes, reigned from 871 to 899. Under Alfred, Winchester became a great centre of learning, and in late Saxon times Winchester was the home of the finest school of calligraphy and manuscript illumination in Europe. It was from here that William the Conqueror compiled the *Domesday Book*.

The cathedral, set in a peaceful close with a partly 13th-century deanery, the Pilgrim's School and the Tudor Cheyney Court, has early Norman Perpendicular features, the Gothic roof being supported by clusters of pillars. There are seven richly carved chantry chapels as well as carved choir stalls and a Norman font. It has the longest Gothic nave in Europe.

Of the nearby castle, the birthplace and abode of many kings, all that remains is the Great Hall, finished in 1235. In it hangs the famous Round Table of the legendary King Arthur. It was the meeting place of many medieval parliaments and the scene of many notable trials, including that of Sir Walter Raleigh who was there sentenced to death, and the "Bloody Assize" held by Judge Jeffreys in 1685. Today it is open to visitors when not in use as a court.

A walk of about a mile to the south of the cathedral will bring you to the ancient charitable institution of St. Cross Hospital, where the Wayfarer's Dole of a horn of beer and a portion of bread has been handed to travellers through the porter's doorway for more than six centuries. (It must be given on request.)

The large seaside town of Bournemouth (take A31 southeast from Winchester) has everything to offer in the way of good bathing from a sandy beach, all kinds of sport and entertainment with, close-by, Christchurch Priory, providing a splendid example of Norman to Perpendicular ecclesiastical architecture. It is also a centre for visiting the New Forest, to the east, which is one of the largest unenclosed areas in England, spreading over much of the county; though accessible by car, its remoter regions are best explored on foot. Lyndhurst, the "capital" of the New Forest is an even better centre. At

Stoney Cross in Canterton Glen, near the Cadnam-Ringwood road (A31), a stone commemorates the death of William Rufus, mysteriously killed by an arrow when out hunting. It is not very likely that you will see many deer here, however, but there are still large numbers of semi-wild ponies. Great care is needed when driving as, being free, they are very vulnerable and many are killed every year. At Balmer Lawn on the Lyndhurst to Brockenhurst road (A337), pony races and sales are held during August. One of the most famous places in the forest is Buckler's Hard, a hamlet which was formerly a shipyard, where some of Nelson's three-deckers were built. It now has a maritime museum. The village is situated on the river some two miles from Beaulieu. Nearby is Beaulieu Abbey, founded in the early 13th century, and Palace House, originally the abbey's great gate house. Here lives Lord Montagu of Beaulieu, whose famous Montagu Motor Museum, with its collection of over 200 vintage cars, has helped to make this one of England's most-visited stately homes.

To complete a visit to Hampshire, a short crossing can be made to the Isle of Wight from Portsmouth, where, while waiting for the ferry, you can have a drink and a snack at the *Union Tavern* and watch the movement of shipping. This is the home port of the royal yacht *Britannia* and the place where Nelson's famous flagship, *H.M.S. Victory*, is on view.

If you sail from Portsmouth, you will arrive at Ryde in the east of the island, but if you prefer to cross from Lymington, you will land at Yarmouth in the west. This island, sheltered by the mainland to the north, is a small county in itself and its inhabitants still talk contemptuously of people on the mainland. Cowes, famous all over the world for its regattas, lies on the north coast opposite Southampton, while the Needles—the lovely white monoliths rising out of the sea to the extreme west—are seen by many travellers arriving in England from distant ports. The changing coastline combines semi-tropical vegetation to the east with sheltered coves and dramatic ravines called "chines" and, on the west coast, the strange, coloured sand of Alum Bay can still be collected beneath the four hundred feet high cliffs. Inland, you will find many typical Hampshire villages and small towns. The whole history of the Isle of Wight centres round Carisbrooke Castle,

THE SOUTHERN COUNTIES

which has a fine church and which was once the chief Roman settlement in the island. The well-preserved fortress has a museum, where the exhibits include old maps, coins and paintings, as well as relics of Charles I, who was a prisoner in the castle in 1647 and 1648.

Nearly 150 square miles of undulating country, criss-crossed with narrow winding lanes, the Isle of Wight is separated from the mainland of Hampshire by the Solent, known all over the world as a yachting centre.

Although a very small island, the Isle of Wight crams into its circumference a dozen or so towns and some considerable industry. One major source of employment is a company manufacturing a large percentage of the world's greeting cards and picture postcards. In spite of all this, the countryside is unspoiled, with great stretches of moorland and downs, and even in the height of the holiday season of July and August, there is never a feeling of being crowded.

The Isle of Wight started to become a tourist centre when Queen Victoria came to live at Osborne House, near Cowes. Tennyson, too, was an inhabitant of the isle, living at Farringford, near Freshwater. In those days, Cowes in particular, was the centre of high society during the summer months, especially during the Cowes Regatta, when millionaires' yachts jostled for moorings and the fashionable ladies strolled on the lawns of the Royal Yacht Squadron. Cowes Week is still patronised by royalty, the Duke of Edinburgh being a regular participant. The doyen of British yachtsmen, Uffa Fox, and press tycoon, Sir Max Aitken, own houses on the Sound.

But yachting in the 20th century is no longer the prerogative of millionaires. Small boat enthusiasts from all walks of life throng the yacht harbours of Cowes, Bembridge and Yarmouth. The beaches, too, are a great attraction. The major resorts of Ryde, Ventnor, Shanklin and Sandown bustle with families and the bucket-and-spade brigade during the summer months. Quieter spots are Bembridge and Seaview, and for the real away-from-it-all holiday, there are some lovely secluded beaches on the stretch of coast between Ventnor and Freshwater. Particularly good sands can be found at Chilton Chine, Compton and Brook.

With modern transportation, the Isle of Wight can be

reached from London in under two hours. Fast hovercraft scuttle across the Solent in a matter of minutes and drive on-drive off car ferries make it a simple matter for the visitor to take his car. But the charm of the island is its rich vegetation, narrow lanes, thatched cottages and above all, its people. One elderly resident of Brighstone confessed that he had never been to the sea, and constantly referred to his son's trip to the mainland as "going abroad"!

Wiltshire, Salisbury and Stonehenge

Lately Lord Nelson, great grand-nephew of the hero of Trafalgar, presented the National Trust with a pepperbox—the weird, red-brick structure that caps Pepperbox Hill, on his estate "Trafalgar", five miles from Salisbury. This "folly" was built about 1606 by old Giles Eyre, a man with eccentric notions on architecture but admirable ones as to views. No doubt the rounded hills of Wiltshire were once largely covered with forest. Today they form a high breezy plateau called Salisbury Plain.

The 404-foot stone spire of Salisbury Cathedral, often painted by Constable, dominates the entire valley. Inside this Early English-style edifice are lancet windows, a 14th-century clock of wrought iron, tombs of Crusaders and of those who died at Agincourt. Don't overlook the beautiful octagonal chapter house with sixty wondrously carved 13th-century friezes upheld by a single pillar and a fan-span to the roof. One of the four existing copies of the Magna Carta is kept here, where it was brought for safekeeping shortly after its signing in 1265.

Close to Salisbury is Wilton House, the splendid home of the Earls of Pembroke with an incomparable art collection—including 16 Van Dyck canvases hung in the famous double cube room where General Eisenhower planned the Normandy invasion. Old Sarum is the site of a fascinating Saxon and Norman town with prehistoric fortifications on a ledged green hillside.

At a point about 3 miles west of Amesbury on the Shrewton road where the plain starts to climb, stands the lone, eerie collection of boulders called Stonehenge. Stonehenge is the best example in Britain of that group of ancient stone remainders known as Druids' circles, confidently thought to be the sun-worshipping temples of a people in whose lives sun and stones played the biggest parts. Despite its intense and ancient significance, Stonehenge disappoints many sightseers who arrive in coaches, expecting to see monoliths the height of factory chimneys. Believed to be even older than Stonehenge is a similar circle at Avebury, west of Marlborough. A mile from it is an enormous prehistoric mound called Silbury Hill, an example of the tumuli that are scattered all over Wiltshire. Silbury, however, is unique in that it's the largest artificial mound in Europe, being 450 yards round at the base, and 120 feet high. It is thought to be associated in some way with Avebury.

South of Marlborough is Pewsey, sporting an annual national congress of Town Criers who, gorgeously garbed in robes that almost rival those of London's Lord Mayor, parade and compete for a prize awarded for the loudest and clearest voice. Circuiting the county west and northward, we come to Swindon, a busy rail centre, and not far away Wanborough and its 400-year-old *Harrow Inn*, in which is an ancient wooden pulley allegedly used to string up customers who misconducted themselves. A more likely use was to hoist contraband to the attic. Exhibit No. 2 is an old "dog grate", a relic of days when the housewife put a dog in a cage in the chimney to drive a fan. Some venerable inns are linked with a past even older than themselves. *The Angel*, Chippenham, was built on part of the site of the ancient palace of King Alfred; it still exhibits a sentry lookout.

Four miles south of Chippenham is one of the most beautiful villages in southwest England—Lacock—where in 1839 Fox Talbot invented the photographic process named after him. Another dream village is Castle Combe, also near Chippenham, though it has been slightly spoiled by American film-makers, who "redecorated" it for *The Story of Dr. Dolittle*. (A baronet was accused of sabotaging the film set when residents protested about the use of the village.) Bradford-on-Avon not only has one of the most perfect small Saxon churches in England, but also an interesting example of a type of bridge that the medieval monasteries used to build, erecting a chapel at its end to remind wayfarers of the industry of these religious foundations. Like the Wilmington Long Man, the representation of a horse cut out of the chalk on a hillside near Westbury is of assured vintage. Measuring 180 feet from head to tail, this equestrian giant is thought to mark the spot where King Alfred scored one of his biggest successes against the Danes, historically pinpointed as Ethandune, or Edington—in 878.

A little farther on—beyond Warminster, itself lying astride a scattered miscellany of ancient battlegrounds—rise the noble outlines of Longleat House, home of the Marquis of Bath, with a name all to itself on the map. The house is the country's prize gem of Jacobean architecture and is approached by a long, leafy drive of towering rhododendrons. Started in 1368, it was completed during Elizabethan times. Its leather-lined library contains one of the largest private collections in Europe. Good Queen Bess was served in its banquet hall where a Sèvres dining service stands ready for another royal visit. A costume museum displays breakfast bonnets, wedding garments, and other rare period robes. More recently, Longleat has been making a name for itself as the stately home where lions roam free in the grounds — a brilliant stroke of showmanship by the Marquis of Bath which has attracted thousands of extra visitors to the house.

THE SOUTHWEST

A Sunny Corner of England

England is not often thought of as having distinct regions, as on the continent or in the U.S.A., but this is because so many visitors do not travel outside London. If you do have time to leave the capital for more than a few days, the southwest is one of the most rewarding and relaxing places to visit. The four counties that make up the long, southern peninsula are Somerset, Dorset, Devon and Cornwall, and they all have a distinct individuality. You'll be surprised to discover a regionalism that almost amounts to patriotism. Each county has a distinct patois and even a distinct cuisine, although these are often limited to the older inhabitants.

Somerset is noted for its rolling green countryside; Dorset has deep valleys and high chalk downs together with an unusual and fascinating coastline. Devon's wild and dramatic moors contrast with the restfulness of its many sandy beaches and coves. And Cornwall has still managed to retain something of its old insularity, despite the annual invasion of thousands of holidaymakers.

The southwest is one of England's largest agricultural areas, and although industry is by no means absent, the skyline is nowhere ruined by smoking chimneys and factory architecture. The predominant atmosphere is rural. Dairy and sheep farming are common to all four counties. As all the counties, particularly Devon and Cornwall, have long coastlines, they have always had strong connections with the sea. Indeed, many of England's most famous sailors were born in the Southwest.

As with most places in England, the southwest can be delightful in the warm months when the sun shines, but when it's overcast and raining, it can be gloomy and depressing in the extreme. Because of the distance from London, not many foreign tourists venture further than Bath in Somerset, so one should not expect to find the comforts of first-class hotels and restaurants everywhere throughout the region.

Practical Information for the Southwest

HOTELS. Any visit to the southwest must include a stay on the coast *and* a stay inland. Many of the hotels and restaurants listed here are not open in the winter months and it is advisable to check through the *British Travel Association*, 64 St. James's Street, London, S.W.1 (629-9191) if you are traveling out of season.

COASTAL RESORTS

BUDE (Cornwall). Excellent large sandy beach—but rather desolate in poor weather. *Falcon*, 58 rooms; *Grenville*, 86 rooms (15 with bath), and private pool.

CLOVELLY (Devon). Old cobbled fishing village, no cars allowed. *New Inn*, 20 rooms.

DARTMOUTH (Devon). Old sea port. *Dart Marina*, 22 rooms (4 with bath), *Royal Castle*, 23 rooms (1 with bath).

FALMOUTH (Cornwall). Yachting centre and old port. Subtropical gardens. *Falmouth*, 85 rooms, *Green Bank*, 50 rooms (10 with bath), *Royal Duchy*, 41 rooms. *Budock Vean*, a manor house on the river, has own golf course, tennis, boats, etc. 40 rooms (most with bath). At Mawnan Smith, nearby, the *Meudon* is beautifully-sited. 37 rooms, most with bath.

FOWEY (Cornwall). Good yachting centre, delightful in June and early July. *Riverside*, 14 rooms, *Fowey*, 40 rooms.

ILFRACOMBE (Devon). Popular resort among giant cliffs. *Runnacleave*, 120 rooms, *Imperial*, 88 rooms (8 with bath).

LOOE (Cornwall). Quaint old town with tidal river. *Boscarn*, 25 rooms, *Alexandra*, 25 rooms, *Tregertha Court Motor Inn*, 24 rooms with bath.

LYME REGIS (Dorset). Old fishing town with a town crier who still does the daily rounds. *Highcliff*, 12 rooms, *Alexandra*, 25 rooms.

LYNTON & LYNMOUTH (Devon). Twin towns at the top and bottom of a lovely cleft. *Tors* (Lynmouth), 43 rooms, *Crown*, 18 rooms (3 with bath).

MEVAGISSEY (Cornwall). Colourful fishing village resort, dominated by a hugh cliff. *Travalsa Court*, 10 rooms (2 with bath).

NEWQUAY (Cornwall). Centre of English "surfing" on nine large beaches. *Atlantic*, 62 rooms (24 with bath), *Glendorgal*, 33

THE SOUTHWEST

rooms (11 with bath), *Headland,* 120 rooms (45 with bath), *St. Rummons,* 66 rooms. *Bristol,* 120 rooms (half with bath).

PAIGNTON (Devon). Family resort—good, long, sandy beaches. *Redcliffe,* 75 rooms (35 with bath).

PENZANCE (Cornwall). Fishing port, sand and shingle beach. *Queens,* 66 rooms (9 with bath).

PLYMOUTH (Devon). Famous for the *Mayflower* sailing and Francis Drake. *Continental,* 78 rooms (10 with bath). *Berni Grand,* 80 rooms (2 with bath). New in 1970 is the *Mayflower,* 102 rooms (all with bath), swimming pool and two restaurants.

POLPERRO (Cornwall). Very artistic little colony, small harbour. *Noughts & Crosses,* 8 rooms. No cars allowed.

SALCOMBE (Devon). The county's most popular sailing resort. *Marine,* 52 rooms (30 with bath), *Tides Reach,* 30 rooms (5 with bath), *Bolthead,* 25 rooms (2 with bath).

SIDMOUTH (Devon). Good bathing, but generally a rather quiet place. *Belmont,* 50 rooms (30 with bath), *Victoria,* 67 rooms (18 with bath).

ST. IVES (Cornwall). Busy holiday centre and artist colony. *Garrack,* 23 rooms (4 with bath), *St. Ives Bay,* 54 rooms (5 with bath), *Treganna Castle,* 90 rooms (40 with bath), *Porthminster,* 50 rooms (12 with bath).

ST. MAWES (Cornwall). Yachting centre with Mediterranean atmosphere. *Tresanton,* 28 rooms, *Rising Sun,* 19 rooms (7 with bath). Both hotels have excellent restaurants

SWANAGE (Dorset) Family resort with sandy beaches. *Royal Victoria,* 45 rooms, *Grosvenor,* 150 rooms (70 with bath).

TORQUAY (Devon). An all-year resort with a Mediterranean-type climate. Several really first-class hotels. *Imperial,* real luxury class, 150 rooms (all with bath). "Gastronomic Weekends", held throughout the year, are a dining treat. *Livermead House,* 73 rooms, *Astra House,* 21 rooms, *Palace,* 150 rooms (82 with bath), and *Victoria,* 70 rooms (40 with bath). *St. Ives Motel,* 12 rooms (9 with bath), *Grand,* 132 rooms (half with bath).

WAREHAM (Dorset). *Woolbridge Manor,* at Wool, 5 rooms. Scene of Hardy's *Tess of the D' Urbervilles.*

WESTON-SUPER-MARE (Somerset). Popular family holiday spot. *Salisbury,* 50 rooms; *Grand Atlantic,* Trust House, 81 rooms (15 with bath).

IN THE COUNTRY

BATH (Somerset). Oldest (Roman) spa in Britain. Best book ahead for the festival. *Francis,* 86 rooms (26 with bath), *Lansdown Grove,* 50 rooms (12 with bath), *Royal York,* 54 rooms (7 with bath). Also: *Pratt's,* 56 rooms (9 with bath).

BIDEFORD (Devon). *Weare Gifford Hall,* 9 rooms. Small, newly renovated. Has minstrel's gallery, hammerbeam roof, and a mile of salmon fishing on River Torridge.

BLANDFORD FORUM (Dorset). An 18th-century town. *Crown,* 27 rooms, *King's Arms,* 15 rooms.

BRISTOL. Important port, 7 miles up the Avon river. Best is *Unicorn,* 200 rooms (all with bath). Then the *Grand,* 206 rooms (101 with baths), *Grosvenor,* 70 rooms (14 with bath), and *Royal,* 164 rooms (25 with bath). Excellent motel: *Ship Post House,* on M4. 50 rooms with bath, TV.

At Clifton, *Grand Spa,* 67 rooms with TV (32 with bath).

CHAGFORD (Devon). *Easton Court* is a fine hotel with an excellent reputation for service and comfort. *Gidleigh Park* and *Mill End* are equally fine.

CHEDDAR (Somerset). Picturesque village in Cheddar Gorge. Pot-holing, stalactite caves, cheese. *Cliff*, 20 rooms, *Valley*, 10 rooms, *Bath Arms*, 6 rooms.

DORCHESTER (Dorset). Ancient town connected with Thomas Hardy. *Antelope*, 23 rooms, *King's Arms*, 28 rooms.

DUNSTER (Somerset). Village with castle. (Centre for Exmoor.) *Luttrell Arms*, 21 rooms (3 with bath).

EXETER (Devon). County town. *Rougemont*, 61 rooms (12 with bath), *Royal Clarence*, 107 rooms (62 with bath), *White Hart*, 20 rooms (1 with bath).

On the by-pass. *Devon Motel*, 27 rooms (all with bath), and *Exeter Motel*, 31 rooms (all with bath).

FROME (Somerset). Old steep-streeted market town. *George*, 12 rooms (pleasant bar), *Portway*, 20 rooms (3 with bath), *Mendip Motel*, 20 rooms (all with bath).

GLASTONBURY (Somerset). Old pilgrimage town, good touring centre. *George & Pilgrim's Inn*, 13 rooms, a famous 15th-century inn for pilgrims. Best to book ahead. *Copper Beech*, 25 rooms (8 with bath).

ILMINSTER. (Somerset). New *Horton Cross Motel*, 23 rooms with bath, is good.

MORETON HAMPSTEAD (Devon). Small town on edge of Dartmoor. *Manor House*, 68 rooms (40 with bath). also golf and trout fishing.

SHAFTESBURY (Dorset). Market town overlooking Blackmore Vale. Nearby is a huge U.S. Air Force rest and recreation centre. *Grosvenor*, 44 rooms (5 with bath).

SHERBORNE (Dorset). Ancient town with beautiful Abbey Church and two castles. *Post House*, 60 rooms (all with bath), TV, opened in 1969.

TAUNTON (Somerset). Old town, good touring centre. *Castle*, 53 rooms (12 with bath), *County*, 80 rooms (10 with bath).

TAVISTOCK (Devon). Centre for Dartmoor. *Bedford*, 27 rooms. *The Moorland*, 33 rooms, at Shaugh Prior, is good for dining. *Endsleigh* is a fine 19th-century country house with pool, 14 rooms (5 with bath).

TIVERTON (Devon). *Hartnoll Country House*, 12 rooms (2 with bath).

TOTNES (Devon). Picturesque old town. *Seymour*, 28 rooms (4 with bath), *Royal Seven Stars*, 20 rooms. *Gabriel Court* is a 15th-century manor 4 miles from town.

TRURO (Cornwall). Cathedral and county town. *Red Lion*, 35 rooms (2 with bath).

WELLS (Somerset). Beautiful cathedral city. *Crown*, 10 rooms (4 with bath), *Swan*, 25 rooms (1 with bath).

WIMBORNE MINSTER (Dorset). Has a fine minster. *King's Head*, 27 rooms (12 with bath). *The Dormy*, just outside, is delightful.

ISLES OF SCILLY. There are 4 good hotels on the island of St. Mary's: the *Atlantic*, *Fernleigh*, *Star Castle* and *Tregarthens*, and one on Tresco: *The Island*.

RESTAURANTS. On the whole, the area lacks an abundance of decent restaurants and the best places to eat are invariably the large hotels. However, Truro, the county town of Cornwall, does boast one of the finest French restaurants outside of London in its *Rendezvous des Gourmets;* booking is essential. Perhaps the most lasting gastronomic memories of Cornwall are the lavish Cornish cream teas and the piping hot Cornish pasties served in almost all the numerous inns and pubs in the county. Crabs and lobsters are good, too. The "Gastronomic Weekends" at Torquay's *Imperial Hotel* are magnificent—superb cooking, fine wines, beautiful service.

ON THE COAST

DARTMOUTH. *Glenie's Buttery*. Excellent views of the River Dart. Good fish and shell-fish.

FOWEY. *Cordon Bleu*. Good comprehensive menu, certainly above-average cooking.

PLYMOUTH. *Quo Vadis*. Good all-round value. *Gennonis*. Almost luxurious. *Octogan*. For sea-food.

PORTLOE. *The Lugger*. Set in tiny Cornish fishing hamlet. Lobsters a specialty.

SALCOMBE. *The Galley*. Comfortable and efficient restaurant.

SIDMOUTH. *Victoria Hotel Restaurant*. English food attractively served and very tasty. Dancing twice a week.

ST. IVES. *Hart's* is not a restaurant, but an ice cream parlour that serves the best ice cream in Britain.

INLAND

BATH. *The Hole in the Wall*. Varied cold buffet table, and an extensive menu of nearly 25 items. One of England's best restaurants.

BRISTOL. Fine French cuisine at *Gourmet*, open until 1 a.m. Cold buffet table (a converted dinghy) is good at *Dunlop's* pub.

GUNNISLAKE. In the Tamar Valley, west of Dartmoor on the Devon/Cornwall border. The *Tavistock Hotel* for superb French cuisine and fresh Tamar salmon in season.

LYDFORD. *Dartmoor Inn*. Good food and hospitality.

PRIDDY. Lost in the Mendip Hills, the *Miners' Arms* has home-grown Mendip snails on a gourmet's menu.

TAVISTOCK. At nearby Gulworthy is the *Horn of Plenty*, with excellent French food and wine.

TRURO. *Rendezvous des Gourmets*. In the middle of Cornwall one of England's finest restaurants. Well worth a detour.

TRANSPORTATION. *British Railways* serve the area with fast and frequent trains from Waterloo (Southern Region) and Paddington (Western Region). Plymouth is 225 miles from Paddington and 232 miles from Waterloo, the trains using completely different routes but both serving Exeter on the way. Penzance, the farthest point that can be reached by the Western Region, is 305 miles from Paddington. Pullman Diesel expresses run from London (Paddington) to Bath (1 hr. 35 mins.) and Bristol (1 hr. 55 mins.). *BEA* operate a helicopter service between Penzance and the Isles of Scilly, a 20-minute trip which gives a fascinating bird's eye view of the Land's End cliffs.

ENTERTAINMENT. The southwest region of Britain abounds in entertainment of all kinds from the sophisticated to the simple. Torquay, most elegant of resorts, has a *Gastronomic Festival* in April, the *European Bridge Championships* in September. Age-old fairs and festivals are held all round. Bath has a *Festival of the Arts* in May or June. At Looe you can hire boat and tackle for shark fishing from June through September. Bristol has an important repertory theater, the *Theatre Royal*, where the Bristol Old Vic performs, and dancing at *The Heartbeat*. There is a dramatically sited theatre, the *Miracle,* at Porthcurno, near Penzance.

Historic Houses Open to the Public

DEVON AND CORNWALL. *Buckland Abbey,* Tavistock. The National Trust. 13th-century Cistercian monastery, later home of Sir Francis Drake. Open daily in summer. *Compton Castle,* near Torquay. The National Trust. Fortified manor house. Open Mon., Wed., and Thurs., April through October. *St. Michael's Mount,* Penzance. National Trust, but home of Lord St. Levan. Open all year Wed. and Frid., also Mon., June through September. *Cotehele House,* Calstock. Romantic medieval house and gardens. Open daily, April to September. Also Wed., Sat. and Sun. afternoons from October to March. *Penfound Manor,* Poundstock. Historic house mentioned in Domesday Book. Open weekdays, Easter to end of September. *Powderham Castle,* near Exeter. Medieval home of Earl of Devon. Open daily, summer afternoon (not Sats.).

DORSET. *Creech Grange,* Wareham. Home of the Bond family. Open mid-July to mid-September, Wed. Thurs., Sun. afternoons. *St. Giles House,* Wimborne St. Giles. Seventeenth-century mansion of the Earl of Shaftesbury. Open mid-May to early October. Wednesday and Sunday afternoons. *Athelhampton,* near Puddlestown. Splendid stone-built medieval house with enchanted gardens. Open Wed. and Thur. afternoons, April to September. Also Sundays and Mondays, June to July. *Clouds Hill,* near Wareham. National Trust. Home of Lawrence of Arabia after World War I. Open Wed., Thur. and Sun. afternoons, all year round. *Forde Abbey,* near Chard. Former 12th-century Cistercian monastery with beautiful gardens. Open on Wednesdays, May through September. Also open on a number of Sundays. *Purse Caundle Manor,* near Sherborne. Mellow Tudor house. Open Weds., Thursday and Sunday afternoons, all year round.

SOMERSET. *Dunster Castle,* Dunster, near Minehead. Home of the Luttrells. Open June through September. Wed. Thurs. *Montacute House,* Yeovil. Open from March through October. The National Trust. Elizabethan house open daily, except Tues. *Claverton Manor,* 2 miles out of Bath, contains the only American Museum in Britain. Open summer afternoons, ex. Mondays. *Barrington Court,* near Ilminster. Beautiful 16th century house and gardens. National Trust. Open all year.

MUSEUMS in the southwest region are plentiful, but we list only a few of the best, together with one or two comments on items of special interest therein. (Many contain thousands of different objects, but we cannot, obviously, list them all.) Ashburton: *Ashburton Museum* (local objects, American Indian items); Bath: *The American Museum in Britain* (a magnificent display of Americana from 17th to 19th centuries, as well as a garden, etc.—well worth a trip), *Holburne of Menstrie Museum of Art* (general collection), *Bath Roman Museum* (next to the baths, many early artifacts), *Museum of Costume* (fashion from the 17th century to the present). Bristol: *City Museum* (archeology and natural history), *Blaise Castle Folk Museum* (including reconstructed farm buildings),

Georgian House (period furnishings), *The Red Lodge* (Elizabethan and later decor). Cheddar: *Motor Museum* (vintage cars).

Dorchester: *Dorset County Museum* (Thomas Hardy memorabilia), *Dorset Military Museum* (Hitler's desk); Glastonbury: *Glastonbury Lake Village Museum* (prehistoric antiquities); Looe: *The Cornish Museum* (Cornwall arts and crafts, witchcraft items); Plymouth: *City Museum & Art Gallery* (ship models and Plymouth china), *Buckland Abbey* (Sir Francis Drake relics); Poole: *Poole Museum* (Roman antiquities).

Totnes: *Elizabethan House* (general furnishings); Tresco: *Valhalla Maritime Museum* (figureheads from old shipwrecks); Truro: *County Museum & Art Gallery* (Cornish minerals); Wareham: *Royal Armoured Corps Tank Museum* (from first to latest in warfare); Weston-Super-Mare: *Yieldingtree Railway Museum* (Irish choo-choos); Wookey Hole: cave relics of earliest man in Britain; Yeovil: *Wyndham Museum* (firearms); Yeovilton: *Fleet Air Arm Museum* (naval aviation).

Exploring the Southwest

Somerset, like the whole of the Southwest, is intensely rural in character, but nowhere else does the countryside appear so rich and well-tended as in this serenely beautiful county. The secret of exploring Somerset is to ignore the main highways and just follow the signposts through the leafy narrow country roads that lead through miles of buttercup meadows and cider apple orchards to countless mellow villages of stone and thatch. The village names are music to the ears. There's Tintinhull, Midsomer Norton, Huish Episcopi, Bower Hinton, and dozens more, each with its architectural treasure, maybe an ancient tithe barn, or one of the noble perpendicular churches for which Somerset is renowned.

In the centre of Somerset is the strange, secretive lowland region known as Sedge Moor, where King Alfred once hid from the marauding Danish armies of the ninth century. To the east lie the Mendip Hills, slashed through at one point by the Cheddar Gorge, a miniature Grand Canyon of grey limestone riddled with miles of spectacular caverns. To the west rise the lovely wooded Quantocks, and beyond, finest of all, are the heathery heights of Exmoor, bounded by great hog-backed cliffs that tumble headlong into the sea between Minehead and Porlock.

Plunging into Bath

Bath is a delight to the eye—it rightly boasts of being the best-planned town in England. The layout of the city is clear and noble, its river, the Avon, having been woven into the fabric of the town. The present Georgian air of Bath is a result of a tremendous planning scheme envisaged and carried out by the 18th-century architect, John Woods. If you climb the hill past the terraced white-pillared houses that surround the famous Pump Room, you will reach the famed Royal Crescent, and be able to admire the sheer unity of Woods' scheme.

But the pedigree of Bath reaches back to Roman times. The Romans called the place *Aquae Sulis*, after a little-known deity, Sul, and the mineral springs they discovered here. The Romans, coming from a mild climate, suffered badly from rheumatism, and treated their various complaints at springs and baths. When in Bath, you must visit the Roman baths, which are still going strong and are among the most striking Roman relics in Europe.

Visit the Pump Room upstairs, with its Chippendale furnishings, where Beau Nash entertained in the 18th century and made Bath the most fashionable resort of his day. Gainsborough, Queen Victoria, Lord Nelson and Jane Austen, among others, have travelled here to sip the waters, which Dickens described as tasting like "warm flat irons". See the beautiful abbey church and browse around the Abbey Green amongst the myriad of antique shops, and don't forget the remarkable Costume Museum, in the elegant Assembly Rooms.

Bath is not merely a place for people groaning in the grip of rheumatism. In recent years, a very successful summer musical festival has been launched, where opera (Mozart in particular), symphonies and chamber music are presented together with other cultural attractions.

Nearby, in Claverton Manor, there is an American Museum, where each room is arranged by region and by period. The Georgian house is set in a splendid 55-acre estate.

North of Bath a few miles is Castle Combe, one of the prettiest villages in all England. Set on the banks of a little river, it remains beautiful in spite of the sightseers that crowd the place in summer.

Bristol, proud port and city, with a population of nearly half a million, can be called "the birthplace of America" with some confidence, for it was from the old city docks of Bristol that John Cabot and his son Sebastian sailed in 1497 to the discovery of the American continent. Furthermore, Bristol was the home of William Penn, developer of Pennsylvania, and haven for John Wesley, whose Methodist movement played such a large part in the settling of Georgia. If you visit Bristol, west of Bath on A4, seek out the Church of St. Mary Redcliffe, described by Queen Elizabeth I as "the fairest, goodliest and most famous parish church in England".

Brunel's famous Suspension Bridge spans the beautiful Avon Gorge and is only a short bus-ride from the city centre. Besides being a treasure-house of great historic interest, entertainment of all kinds is available. The famous *Theatre Royal*, the oldest theatre in the country, is the home of the Bristol Old Vic.

Wells and Glastonbury

Wells provides in her glorious cathedral, south of Bristol on A37 and 39, the body and bone structure which other edifices often lack. The cathedral derives its beauty from a perfect harmony of all its component parts, from the gamut of colours of its splendid stained-glass windows to the peaceful setting among aged trees and glistening lawns. Its great glory is the west front. Wells is one of those places where time seems to stand still and where eternal calm seems to permeate everybody who enters the precincts of its cathedral. Although it has the status of a city, the atmosphere is more like that of a small country town. When you have seen the cathedral, make your way from the market square through the curiously-named Penniless Porch to the moated Bishop's Palace and its famous bell-ringing swans. Hanging from the wall beside the moat is a rope attached to a bell, which the swans ring when they want to be fed.

Two miles from Wells are the Mendip Hills and Wookey Hole Caves, with their strange stalagmite-stalactite formations. Visit also the three-mile-long Cheddar Gorge, with the fantastic Gough's and Cox's caves. All these caverns were once the home of Prehistoric Man.

Glastonbury, south of Wells on A39, is a little and unimportant place today, but a visit to its antiquarian museum and a walk round its abbey (the Benedictine Abbey of St. Mary) and its strange Tor (or hill), a conical height of some 500 feet crowned by ruins of a chapel, would convince one that it wasn't always so. The very soil of Glastonbury is drenched with legends—of Joseph of Arimathea, of the Holy Grail, and of King Arthur, whose reputed grave lies among the Abbey's sombre ruins. The Abbey was destroyed by Henry VIII in 1539 during the Dissolution of the Monasteries.

Taunton, southwest of Glastonbury on A361, and the county town of Somerset, is a pleasant market town, with a fine shopping centre. As a centre for touring, Taunton is ideal, as it is set in the pleasant Vale of Taunton Deane, enclosed by the Quantock and Blackdown hills, and within easy reach of the Somerset, Devon and Dorset coasts, and Exmoor. This part of Somerset is an area of exceptional scenic beauty, and also has many historical associations. Taunton offers excellent facilities for sport, and there are first-class hotels and restaurants, a number of which remain open until midnight.

People who come to Somerset by car will find the county's roads excellent. In autumn, when the beaches are deserted and the trees turning to golden brown, you should go to Exmoor and ride the lonely paths, catching glimpses of deer silhouetted on the crest against the timid blue of the sky, or go to the Quantocks and watch the sun setting towards the sea.

Visit Muchelney Abbey, a medieval Benedictine abbey with lovely 15th-century cloisters and a carved stone fireplace, beside the foundations of a seventh-century Saxon church. (Until lately, the cloisters were used by a local farmer as a cider cellar.) If Druids and prehistoric circles fascinate you, see Stanton Drew Circles and cove.

Old Cleeve, near the charming village of Washford, is an example of a noble building becoming derelict after being ravaged by fires and the hostility of men. But even in its dilapidation, this sunny skeleton of Cistercian cloisters, surrounded by ancient trees, bears witness to the enormous labours of old monks who settled here not only to praise God but also to teach the art of cultivating the land. Those zealous monks have left a legacy of patient love for the good earth, of pruning orchard trees, of an ingenious system of irrigation; and they probably had some part in the manufacture of decent cider, for which Somerset is still justly famous all over England.

Dunster and the Coast

Dunster is a market town that has lost much of its old importance as English history shifted from both western and eastern counties towards the centre, to concentrate more and more on London. Only some 1,000 people live there now, but visitors are fond of the place, for it has preserved in its lovely mellowed walls a warmth and an intimacy that some towns of south Germany and Provence have kept. In the market you are greeted by a picturesque, octagonal building with a deep sloping roof, built about 1600, that looks like a creation of Scandinavian architecture. The streets of the little town rise sharply towards the castle, built between the 13th and the 15th centuries. The castle, the residence and seat of the Luttrell family, gives Dunster a great house of rare distinction. The view from its ramparts is grand, the eye having room to play on the spacious polo field beneath, where deer are lazily wandering, or upon the beige sandy heights of the moor, or to repose on the cornflower blue of the sea near Blue Anchor. The southern, sun-exposed wall of the castle is a brief version of Sicily, with its lemon and orange trees, and the layout of the grounds and building has a generosity matched only by such magnificent residences as Warwick Castle, near Stratford-upon-Avon.

Dunster Castle still belongs to the class of English residences that have been inhabited continuously for centuries. This continuity is one of the charms of the noble houses of England, one not found often on the continent. Its soundness and gentle robustness of shape are beautiful and its view truly glorious.

If, after visiting Dunster, you feel like a trip to the sea, go to nearby Minehead, centre for Exmoor National Park. Beaches are good here, and the sea is bracing and refreshing. There is a very pretty little bay at Porlock, dwarfed almost by the heights of the hills that surround the town. Indeed, Porlock Hill is one of England's steepest, with a gradient of 1 in 3. So be warned, if you intend to drive up Porlock Hill—be sure your car will make it, and be sure to have enough gas in the tank.

The coast of Somerset, except for the short section between Porlock and Minehead, is generally disappointing. If you want an Atlantic City-type experience, try Weston-super-Mare, down the coast from Bristol. But you will probably find it more rewarding to turn away from the coast and explore the soft green hinterland. Nether Stowey, at the foot of the

Quantock Hills, has many memories of the poets Wordsworth and Coleridge, and you can visit the cottage in which Coleridge lived. Also well worth a visit are the cluster of picture-book villages that lie to the southwest of Minehead. Selworthy, Luccombe and Allerford are the loveliest. Not far from here is Dunkery Beacon (1705 feet), the highest point on Exmoor, which can be reached on foot by way of a beautiful walk through Horner Woods.

Dorset

Dorset is a county that the visitor to Britain frequently passes through or even overlooks; indeed, many Englishmen who have never been to Dorset tend to dismiss it as well. Consequently this green and hilly county has remained quite unspoilt, and is, in fact, one of the last remaining corners of the old, rural England. Many of the finest stretches of the Dorset coast are preserved by the National Trust, and most of the countryside has been officially declared an "Area of Outstanding Natural Beauty" by the government.

If you have a chance to read some of Thomas Hardy's novels before visiting Dorset, you'll already have a feeling for it, and indeed, you'll recognize some places immediately from his descriptions. The countryside surrounding Dorchester, in particular, is lovingly described in *Far from the Madding Crowd*.

The coast of Dorset is blessed by long southward-facing beaches. Bright white chalk intermingles with darker rocks and innumerable small bays and inlets provide ideal natural harbours for fishermen and sailors. Poole, Dorset's largest town, has always been an important port from medieval times onwards. Its enormous natural harbour, almost 100 miles around, has no less than seven islands and a multitude of channels through shallow flats that dry out at low tide.

Today, Poole has become part of neighbouring Bournemouth (in next-door Hampshire) and the town has lost much of the individual charm it possessed when it was a separate entity. There are still streets in the centre, however, such as Blue Boar Lane, Malet Street, West Street and New Street, where you can see the proud 18th-century homes of the prosperous merchants and shippers of Poole.

Dorchester

Dorchester, west of Poole on A35, is the county town and is basically a quiet place, with only 15,000 inhabitants. It only comes alive on market days, Wednesdays and Saturdays. On these days the streets are thronged with ruddy-faced country farmers and people from the outlying villages all around. The centre of the town is basically Georgian, interspersed with Victorian churches and modern shop fronts. But the modern intrusions are not as blatant as in other similar places; old inns, tea rooms and antique shops abound, and St. Peter's Church, built in the Perpendicular style and possessing a fine tower, is worth seeing. Archeologists will tell you that Dorchester is situated at the intersection of a number of Roman roads and that its Roman name was Durnovaria. To support that claim, remains of a Roman amphitheatre are shown near the town; the place where the remains were excavated is known by the strange name of Maumbury Rings. Evidence of a pre-Roman settlement can be seen at the fortified earthwork called Maiden Castle, as spectacular in its way as the Pyramids of Egypt, and at the vast entrenchment known as Poundbury. Relics from these and many other ancient sites are on view in the County Museum, near St. Peter's Church, which also has a Hardy Memorial Room.

It is difficult to imagine this cheerful little town as the place of the infamous Bloody Assizes, presided over by the sadistic Judge Jeffreys. It's even harder to think of these gruesome connections when one takes tea and scones in *Judge Jeffreys' Lodgings*, which today is both a tea shop and a restaurant. The actual trials, at which men were sentenced to hang for taking part in the ill-fated Monmouth Rebellion, were held in the oak-panelled back room of the *Antelope Inn*. The room can still be seen by the curious today.

Dorchester and other little towns of Dorset have some excellent antique shops, and prospective buyers of good furniture are advised to make a tour of those places.

Thomas Hardy actually lived about two and a half miles from Dorchester at Higher Bockhampton, where his home, Max Gate, is open to visitors; it includes a reconstruction of his study, along with various other memorabilia. A little farther away, at Clouds Hill, the adventurer and novelist, **T.**

E. Lawrence (Lawrence of Arabia, as he is better known) spent several years writing his *Seven Pillars of Wisdom*. Lawrence considered Clouds Hill as "one of the most English and most wonderful places in the country".

The chalk hills that run southeast through the county from Shaftesbury contain some of the most perfect prehistoric earthworks in the world. Maiden Castle near Dorchester is the most famous, but the most spectacular site is Eggardon Hill, crowning an 800-ft. chalk escarpment between Dorchester and Beaminster. From its ancient banks you can see far across Dorset and into Devon. Equally extraordinary is the enormous 180-foot hill drawing known as the Cerne Giant, which stares down on you from miles around. (North of Dorchester on A352.)

Another Dorset curiosity is the Swannery at Abbotsbury, where the sea has flung up a great bank of pebbles called the Chesil Beach, trapping behind it a broad lagoon on which hundreds of swans live and breed. Before the Dissolution, Abbotsbury was the home of one of the most important monasteries in England. Today virtually all that remains is the great medieval tithe barn.

To the east of Dorchester the Purbeck Hills stretch away towards Wareham, in whose Saxon church there is a fine marble effigy of Lawrence of Arabia. The Purbeck coast is magnificent, with soaring white cliffs and unusual rock formations at Lulworth Cove and Durdle Door, but some of the grandest stretches are out of bounds to the public as they are used by the Army as a gunnery range.

However it was not the Army's guns that created the spectacular ruins of Corfe Castle, whose thick grey walls have guarded a strategic gap through the Purbecks since Saxon times. The damage was done by the cannons of Cromwell's soldiers during the Civil War. But even in its ruinous state, Corfe Castle is a place of heady romance.

Wimborne Minster, in the eastern corner of the county, is a small market town whose glory is its ancient Norman Minster, or church. From Wimborne, B3082 follows the placid River Stour northwest to Blandford Forum, which, despite its Roman-sounding name, is very much an 18th-century town, with a wealth of Georgian architecture.

In North Dorset, buried among the lush foxhunting landscapes of Cranborne Chase and the Blackmoor Vale, are two more venerable towns, Shaftesbury (the 'Shaston' of Hardy's novels) and Sherborne. In Sherborne there are two castles, one founded in 1107, the other begun by Sir Walter Raleigh, but the town's most imposing building is the Abbey Church. Built of honey-hued local stone, it contains within its weathered walls the tombs of ancient Saxon kings of Wessex.

Just outside Sherborne, at Over Compton, is one of the only two butterfly farms in the world. (The other one is also in England, in Kent.) The farm belongs to *Worldwide Butterflies Ltd.*, who stage a summer exhibition of their specimens on the Marine Parade at Lyme Regis, on the Dorset coast, as well as on the farm.

Devon

Devon is one of England's biggest counties, exceeded in size only by Yorkshire and Lincolnshire. But the total population is only just under a million, with most people living in or near the few large towns, such as Plymouth and Exeter. Consequently there are great tracts of Devon that are relatively empty and utterly peaceful. Dartmoor, whose bare heathery hills fill the southern half of the county, is one of the loneliest places in Britain, seemingly inhabited only by hill sheep and shaggy wild ponies.

Once you leave the Moor, however, the countryside is unbelievably green and luxuriant, and the rich red soil adds to the colour of the Devon scene. Devon is fortunate in having two holiday coasts. The north coast faces the Atlantic and is rugged and invigorating. The south coast is the complete opposite, soft and languid, with red cliffs and south-facing bays that enjoy a mild, almost Mediterranean climate in spring and summer. Because of its close connections with the sea, many of Devon's most famous sons have been sailors and adventurers. Not only was Drake a Devon man, but so was Sir Walter Raleigh. In literature, too, Devon has a place, for it was at Ottery St. Mary that Samuel Taylor Coleridge was born and spent a good deal of his life. And from Plympton came the master of English painters, Sir Joshua Reynolds.

Today Devon is reached in under five hours from London, and although it is far enough from the capital to avoid the curse of "day-trippers", it is an extremely popular and crowded holiday area during the summer months. Booking, therefore, is essential between July and September.

Exeter

Devon, in contrast to Somerset and Cornwall, has comparatively few sites of historic interest, and monastic remains (with the exception of Tavistock Abbey) are rather rare. Exeter undoubtedly is the principal historic city here—it has managed to preserve some medieval and Tudor character. Roman foundations can be found alongside fragments of Roman mosaics and pavements, and the city, situated on a broad ridge of land overlooking the River Exe, must have been tempting from time immemorial for those who wanted to build a fortress here. Rougemont Castle was a valiant bastion for many generations and held a record in sieges, some of them prolonged and bloody. Today, this menacing citadel, which was considered a key position for the south Devon coast, looks quite domesticated. The mound of the castle is laid out as a promenade lined with trees, and the knights exercising their mounts have been replaced by nannies pushing prams. Only part of the gate tower remains.

Exeter Grammar School (founded by Walter de Stapledon, Bishop of Exeter and founder of Exeter College, Oxford), is one of the chief showplaces of the city. (The grammar school dates from 1332 and was re-founded 300 years later.) Now, Exeter also has a university that is gaining esteem in the academic world.

Exeter Cathedral, built in the so-called Decorated Gothic style, is an architectural rarity, as there is only one other church in this country that has a similar design, that is, the use of transeptal towers. This is a Norman survival in the realm of the Gothic; the cathedral took about 90 years to build (1280-1370), and its west front is covered with statues. There is no central tower, or lantern, above the long nave of the church. The window tracery is elaborate.

Other buildings of note are the Guildhall, rebuilt in 1330, with a stone colonnaded facade straddling the pavement in the High Street; the Cathedral Library containing the *Exeter Book of Anglo-Saxon Poems*, c. A.D. 950, and the *Exeter Domesday*, 1085-1087; the Priory of St. Nicholas, founded in 1080—good undercroft and kitchens; Tuckers' Hall, the craft guild hall of the weavers, incorporated in 1489, with a fine oak-panelled chamber and timbered roof.

Exeter abounds with ancient churches and a fascinating feature of the city is the system of underground passages, certainly dating before the 14th century. Visitors should not miss the ancient inns, particularly the *White Hart* (14th-century), the *Turks Head* (possibly earlier), and the *Ship Inn*, which, partly reconditioned, is notable for its connections with Elizabethan admirals, particularly Sir Francis Drake.

South Devon

The most important resort area in South Devon is Torbay, which is an amalgamation of three resorts, Torquay, Paignton and Brixham, all spread around a sheltered south-facing bay. The biggest of the three is Torquay (pron. *Tor-key*), which is probably the most elegant and fashionable of all the British seaside towns. Modern hotels, luxury villas and apartments climb the hillsides above the harbour. Palm trees and other exotic semi-tropical plants flourish in the seafront gardens. The sea is a clear and intense blue, and the whole place in summer has an unmistakable continental atmosphere. There are a number of delightful coves tucked away among the red sandstone cliffs, including Anstey's Cove, a favourite spot for scuba-divers, with more beaches farther along at neighbouring Babbacombe. Before leaving Torquay you should find time to visit Cockington, on the outskirts of the town, where there is a cluster of old-world cottages, a blacksmith's forge and a beautiful village church, surrounded in springtime by carpets of daffodils.

Paignton has broad sands, a harbour, a zoo, and unusual grotto gardens at Oldway Mansion, a miniature version of Versailles.

Much more interesting is Brixham, a bustling fishing port on the southern rim of Tor Bay. Here, with the gulls clamouring and baskets of crabs and lobsters being unloaded from the fishing boats, you can savour the true flavour of Devon. The statue on the quay is of William of Orange, who landed here in 1688 to assume the throne of England.

Salcombe, a town honeycombing a green mount overlooking the Kingsbridge Estuary, sits surrounded by fjord-like scenery. It's a favourite with the nautical crowd—you'll like scenery. Ils a favourite with the nautical crowd—you'll find them in the *Ferry Inn*, a three-storied house of bars, or at *Fortescieu's Buttery*. For greater seclusion, there's nearby Bolt Head and Hope Cove.

There are some marvellous isolated holiday spots on this part of the coast, such as Torcross, a tiny village on a lagoon south of Dartmouth, commanding a causeway and a wide and lonely stretch of beach.

Plymouth, known the world over for its great seafaring traditions, is a proud West Country city with a unique setting on the beautiful south coast of Devon. Plymouth Sound, on whose shores the city has grown, is one of the finest natural harbours in the world. Although badly damaged during the war, Plymouth has been rebuilt and is a pleasant blend of ancient and modern. On the Barbican is the Mayflower Stone, commemorating the spot from which the Pilgrim Fathers sailed to the New World, and it was on Plymouth Hoe that Sir Francis Drake lingered to finish his game of bowls before dealing with the Armada. Plymouth is very popular as a holiday resort, and ideal as a touring centre for Devon and the neighbouring county of Cornwall, which can be reached by the splendid new road-bridge over the River Tamar. Throughout 1970, Plymouth will be the focal point of nation-wide celebrations to mark the 350th anniversary of the sailing of the Pilgrim Fathers on board the *Mayflower* in 1620.

Dartmouth and the Dart

The 12-mile trip by steamer down the River Dart to Dartmouth is one of the most enjoyable experiences to be found in the Southwest. It starts at Totnes, a fascinating old town which has managed to preserve its medieval gateways, 17th-century colonnaded Guildhall and Norman Castle keep. Situated at the highest navigable point of the Dart, it is an excellent centre for exploring South Devon, for Dartmoor, Plymouth and Exeter are all within easy reach. The Dart winds its way down to the sea through thick oak woods, cider apple orchards and plunging meadows, passing some of the most peaceful hamlets in England. The whole district along the Dart seems to belong to the loveliest relics of old rural England. This vision of peace and timeless charm should stay long in your memory.

THE SOUTHWEST

To reach Dartmouth by car, leave the main highway after Paignton. Cut across green fields to Kingswear for the little ferry and a four-minute push by tug across the Dart.

Dartmouth is a small port visited by the Pilgrim Fathers in *Mayflower* and *Speedwell* for repairs prior to their journey to America. The town is steeped in history and has recorded associations with Raleigh, the Gilberts and John Davis, all of whom lived in the area.

Overlooking the town is the Britannia Royal Naval College, famous as the training ground of officers of the navies of Great Britain and the Commonwealth, where tradition is still preserved and where the walls breathe stories of the time when Britain "ruled the waves".

Dartmouth itself is a cross between an English and a Dutch town, where Dutch architecture intrudes itself pleasantly into a mixture of Georgian and Tudor black and white buildings. The whole place is quiet in an almost Dutch way and some of its tea rooms are among the cosiest and best furnished in the country. To add to the architectural interest are Dartmouth Castle and Kingswear Castle, facing each other like sentinels across the mouth of the river. The former is open to visitors during normal daylight hours.

North Devon

Between the two coasts of Devonshire lies the massive expanse of Dartmoor, one of the most romantic and impressive sights in England. Dartmoor consists of 300 square miles of wild moorland, desolate and without a tree, the biggest mass of granite in the country. On the average, it is 1,200 feet above sea level, with numerous hills, some of which rise to over 2,200 feet.

In contrast to the southern coast, the beaches of the north of Devon, facing Wales, are half-rocky, half-sandy, while the promontories between Lynmouth and Ilfracombe are dangerously precipitous. The sea here is the Atlantic, of course, far less friendly than the warmer Channel. However, Combe Martin, situated in a sheltered creek near Ilfracombe, affords the maximum amount of shelter from the cold currents. The surrounding vegetation is rich with geraniums, myrtles and abundant heliotropes. Ilfracombe is the largest town on the northern coast, which doesn't mean it is the best kind of holiday resort, but it could make a nice base for excursions to various parts of the coast. Further south, Lynmouth and Lynton still manage to retain their natural beauty despite being scarred by countless fish-and-chip shops, and some ungainly hotels and boarding houses. There are some interesting walks here up the valleys of the East and West Lyn, two rivers that come bounding down from the lonely heights of Exmoor, the *Lorna Doone* country of R.D. Blackmore's romantic novel.

Clovelly, a village to the west of Bideford, always seems to have the sun shining on its cobbled streets. The car is no use in Clovelly as the village tumbles down for almost half a mile to the sea at such an angle that the donkey is the only sensible form of transport. It was in this timeless village that Charles Kingsley was brought up, and it was the fishermen of Clovelly that inspired his great book, *Westward Ho!*

Cornwall

The last 50 years have produced a remarkable change in this southernmost county of England. There was a time in the not-too-distant past when the inhabitants of Cornwall spoke their own language. Indeed, Cornishmen have always considered themselves something of a separate entity to the rest of the country, and almost anyone who lives on the other side of the Tamar River is a "foreigner". This parochialism still exists today, despite the fact that Cornwall is perhaps the country's most visited county.

A mild climate coupled with long stretches of sandy beaches (which at points stretch almost to two miles) are Cornwall's principal attraction. The coast line is, however, remarkably varied. It's much rockier and far more precipitous than the rest of England's coast. The cold blue Atlantic pounds the northern coast, while the warmer and more gentle English Channel laps the southern.

Cornwall's history has always been bound up with the sea, and the coastline, indented with hundreds of coves and bays of all sorts, was a natural favourite for smugglers and pirates. The pirates of Cornwall were, of course, immortalized in Gilbert and Sullivan's *The Pirates of Penzance*.

The building of the Tamar Bridge and the extension of the railway line down to Penzance in the early part of this century brought the greatest changes. Today, Cornwall can be reached in under six hours by a fast express train from London, or in about eight hours by car. There is a great deal to see and enjoy in Cornwall and it's the ideal place to head for if you need a rest or a break from London.

The best months in which to visit the county are, without doubt, May and June, for not only is the weather better than anywhere else in England at that time of the year, but the countryside looks its loveliest, and the tourist season has not yet really got under way. If you want to go in July or August, it is imperative to book both accommodation and train seats in advance.

The Farthest West

The most interesting part of Cornwall is to the west of Truro. Nowhere are you more than seven miles from the sea in this part of Cornwall, with the Atlantic in the north and the Channel in the south. But both coastlines have totally different characteristics. The Atlantic coast is forever being battered with large breakers that have eroded the coastline into a wrecked age of abrupt headlands, high granite cliffs and sheltered, difficult harbours.

Make a trip along this northern coastline from Morwenstow, not far south from Clovelly (about 15 miles), with its lonely church perched on the very top of a cliff, to Land's End. It can be a most spectacular and rewarding experience if the weather is good. If it's raining, however, the journey can take on an almost sinister air as the high cliffs frequently cut out whatever natural light might be coming from an overcast sky.

Tintagel, further south along A39 and B3263, is reputed to have been the birthplace of King Arthur; the remains of his great castle stand for all to see. All that is left is the outline of the walls, moats and towers, but it only requires the smallest amount of imagination to conjure up a picture of Sir Lancelot and Sir Galahad riding out in search of the Holy Grail over the narrow causeway above the seething breakers. The ruins themselves are in rather poor shape, with lush green turf growing where rushes probably once covered the floors of the halls and corridors of the castle. A westerly Atlantic wind seems always to be sweeping through Tintagel and the thunder of the breakers is forever in your ears. Even on a summer's day, when visitors swarm all over the battlements, one cannot help being awed with the proximity of the past. (Whether it was Arthur's castle or not, it is a most impressive place.)

It's about 40 miles from Tintagel to Land's End, a journey through some of the most remarkable scenery in England. Newquay, Cornwall's busiest resort, is along this coast. There are a number of good hotels here, set on the cliff-tops overlooking nine of the finest beaches in Europe, thronged with summer visitors who come to swim, sunbathe and enjoy the surfing. Still farther west lies the old fishing port of St. Ives. Leave your car in one of the municipal car parks and then proceed on foot to explore what is probably the most popular holiday resort in Cornwall.

St. Ives and Land's End

Once an ancient and quiet fishing village, St. Ives today finds its narrow streets always tightly packed with young holiday-makers. Because it acts as a magnet for young people, it is often compared with St. Tropez, in the south of France. The main centre of attraction in the evenings is a harbour-front pub called the *Sloop*. Almost any night of the week you'll find the place packed. For many years, an artists' colony has lived in St. Ives, so there are several galleries where original paintings and sculptures can be bought very reasonably. The hand-thrown pottery of master potter Bernard Leach is world-famous.

Although the Atlantic breakers in Cornwall are nowhere like the size of those off the Californian coast, surfing (in rubber suits, naturally) has recently become a very popular sport. The favourite centres for the English surfing community are Newquay, St. Ives and Bude.

The road from St. Ives to Land's End runs through a barren and severe landscape, in which there is little habitation; the dominant colour is the cold steel grey of exposed granite. Land's End, as the title suggests, is the most westerly point of the mainland of England, and it offers an unrivalled view of the seas that surround the British Isles. Here, the cliffs come to an abrupt and craggy halt. One lonely hotel stands here, baring its face to the seemingly ever-present winds, while seagulls swoop overhead.

Not far from this remote spot, to the south, is Porthcurno, where, during the summer, there are regular performances of classical and Shakespearean drama in a tiny open-air theatre known as the *Minack Theatre*. Nearby is a delightful cove, Porth Chapel, and in the very opposite direction, the strange natural phenomena of the Logan Rock, which is an enormous mass of stone balanced on a natural pedestal.

A little further east, at Lamorna, skin-divers are frequently to be seen. Then there is the curious little fishing village of Mousehole (pron. *Muzzle*), with narrow winding streets and harbourside restaurants, reminiscent of St. Ives, but much smaller. At Mousehole there is an excellent hotel and restaurant, *The Lobster Pot*, which is an ideal base from which to explore the region.

Penzance, just round the headland north from Mousehole, is southern Cornwall's principal town and main shopping centre. There are regular helicopter and boat services from here to the Isles of Scilly. Beyond Penzance at Marazion, which was a Jewish settlement in the Middle Ages, is St. Michael's Mount, which rises out of the sea to the height of 230 feet. At low tide you can walk across to the island, as you can to its "sister" of the same name in France. According to legend, it was here that the child Christ was brought by Joseph of Arimathea on their way to Glastonbury.

Between the two sea coasts are networks of flower-bordered lanes, green valleys and granite-capped moors. The countryside is rich in prehistoric remains, stone circles, burial chambers and Iron-age settlements such as Chysauster, near Penzance.

Middle Cornwall and the Coast

Bodmin, the assize and county town of Cornwall, is situated almost exactly at the geographical centre of the county, providing an ideal centre for touring. The town has free car parks, an attractive central park with children's playgrounds, tennis courts, an indoor heated swimming pool and other recreational facilities.

The parish church of St. Petroc is the largest church in Cornwall and contains the battle honours of the old county regiment. The Duke of Cornwall Light Infantry's Museum is situated at The Keep, Victoria Barracks, Bodmin.

Inland Cornwall between Penzance and the Tamar River is

comparatively uninteresting, but along the coast there are fine beaches, especially near the few small fishing villages-cum-holiday resorts, such as St. Mawes, Mevagissey, Fowey, Polruan and the shark fishing centre of Looe. But if you want to discover what Cornwall was like before the 20th century, tour the area around *Jamaica Inn,* made famous by Daphne Du Maurier's novel of the same name.

The Isles of Scilly

The Isles of Scilly (or the Scillies, as they're known by their inhabitants), are about 30 miles from Land's End; they are a cluster of about 100 tiny islands, of which the five largest are inhabited. The islanders will tell you that however cold and wet England may be, you'll always find the sun here. The Scillies are the last link with land before North America and stand at the entrance of the English Channel with the warm Gulf Stream washing their shores. They are easily reached either by boat or helicopter from Penzance, and the difference in climate is noticeable immediately. It's mild and temperate, a fact borne out by the principal industry of the islands, which is horticulture. In early spring almost everywhere you look, the fields are covered with the narcissi known as Scilly Whites. These flowers are harvested in December each year, and during that month, the quays are stacked with boxes for export.

Communications between the islands are well organized, so the visitor will have no difficulty in reaching any of them, even the uninhabited ones where only puffins, seals and porpoises bask in the sun. As most of the regular boat trips leave from St. Marys, the largest island, this is the obvious place to stay, especially as there are more hotels than on any of the other islands. Booking, in any case, is absolutely necessary.

The ideal time to visit the Scillies is in April and May in order to avoid the crowds, and to reap the maximum advantages of the mildness of the climate.

The discovery of the wreck of Admiral Sir Cloudesley Shovel's flagship, *Association,* lost in 1707, has focussed additional interest on the Scillies, where divers are still busy recovering the admiral's treasure, reputed to be worth £5 million.

EAST ANGLIA

Rural Beauty and Pleasant Towns

by

PAT BARR

(*Author of the successful book,* The Coming of the Barbarians —*a tale of Japan's opening to western visitors, Mrs. Barr is a native of Norfolk, and as much in love with her own part of England as she is with the exotic lands about which she writes. She is presently working on her third book, a novel.*)

In East Anglia one is never very far from water—sea, inland lake, wide, slow-moving rivers and fen canals; one is never far from the countryside—acres of cornfields, stretches of marsh and heath, farmlands of potatoes and sugar-beet, woods of beech, oak and pine; and in the towns one is never far from the past—Norman castles, medieval churches, 18th-century mansions and, always, here and there, the lovely timber-and-plaster houses of the 15th and 16th centuries.

These last-mentioned centuries were the period of East Anglia's greatest prosperity and importance. Nearly all the finest of Cambridge's colleges were either founded or generously endowed then; many of the region's most celebrated manor houses and grammar schools were built; in the numerous thatch-roofed, oak-panelled inns, the sturdy market crosses, the solid stone guildhalls lives the memory of an age when merchants, corn-traders and landed gentry spent their money here freely and well.

North of Ely the fens of Cambridgeshire merge without break into the fens of Lincolnshire, discussed under our *Midlands* chapter.

Practical Information for East Anglia

HOTELS & RESTAURANTS

ALDEBURGH (Suffolk). Noted for June music festival. *Brudenell*, 48 rooms (27 with bath); *Wentworth*, 32 rooms (10 with bath). Both first-class reasonable.

BLAKENEY (Norfolk). Sailing centre and bird sanctuary. *Blakeney*, 55 rooms (14 with bath); *Manor*, 26 rooms, moderate.

BRAINTREE (Essex). Pleasant town, good touring centre. *White Hart*, 38 rooms (24 with bath).

BURNHAM-ON-CROUCH (Essex). Sailing centre on the River Crouch. *Ye Olde White Harte*, 10 rooms, moderate.

BURY ST. EDMUNDS (Suffolk). Georgian town with medieval remains. *Suffolk*, 32 rooms (13 with bath). *Angel*, 50 rooms (8 with bath); faces the Abbey Gardens. Good English dining. *Everards*, 30 rooms. All moderate.

CAMBRIDGE. University city, ancient buildings. *University Arms*, 126 rooms (80 with bath), first-class superior; *Blue Boar*, 47 rooms (6 with bath); *Garden House*, 84 rooms (18 with bath). Both first-class reasonable. Also *Royal Cambridge*, 101 rooms (18 with bath). Advisable to book well ahead.

Restaurants: *Arts Theatre*, *Le Jardin*, *Bath Hotel* and *Miller's*, all excellent.

COLCHESTER (Essex). Centre for the Constable country. Historic Oyster Feast is held at the Moot Hall in October. *George*, 32 rooms (12 with bath); *Red Lion*, 35 rooms (some with bath), a 15th-century hostelry, excellent cuisine. Both moderate.

CROMER (Norfolk). Popular seaside resort and centre for excursions to the Norfolk Broads; good sands, sports facilities. *Albany*, 67 rooms (15 with bath); *Hotel de Paris*, 62 rooms (4 with bath). Both first-class reasonable.

DEDHAM (Essex). On the River Stour and often painted by Constable. *Dedham Vale*, 12 rooms (4 with bath), moderate. Restaurant: *Le Talbooth*.

ELY (Cambs.). Cathedral city dating from Saxon times. *Lamb*, an old hostelry, 26 rooms.

FAKENHAM (Norfolk). Delightful market town dating from Saxon times. *Crown*, 11 rooms; *Red Lion*, 14 rooms. Both moderate.

FELIXSTOWE (Suffolk). Popular seaside resort, golf, yachting. Passenger ferry to Harwich. *Ordnance*, 20 rooms; *Orwell*, 33 rooms. Both moderate.

FRAMLINGHAM (Suffolk). Quiet town with interesting remains of moated castle. *Crown*, 8 rooms (4 with bath).

FRESSINGFIELD (Suffolk). Some reports indicate the *Fox and Goose* here is best place to eat in all East Anglia.

EAST ANGLIA

GREAT YARMOUTH (Norfolk). Large, extremely popular seaside resort; good sands, all sports amenities, race-course. Easily accessible to Norfolk Broads. *Carlton*, 125 rooms (19 with bath); *Queen's*, 90 rooms (12 with bath). Both first-class reasonable. *Showboat*, new, 39 rooms (all with bath); *Royal*, 60 rooms, moderate.

HARLOW (Essex). *Saxon Inn Motel*, on A11, 40 rooms with bath. The *Old Mill* restaurant, fairly expensive, in a pleasant setting.

HARWICH & PARKESTON (Essex). Harbour for continental travel and ancient seaport. Dovercourt, the modern half of the borough, has good sands. *Cliff* (Dovercourt), 25 rooms, moderate.

HUNSTANTON (Norfolk). Small resort, good sands, sports amenities; has a lavender distilling industry. *Le Strange Arms*, 43 rooms (8 with bath); *Golden Lion*, 32 rooms (1 with bath). Both moderate.

IPSWICH (Suffolk). County town and inland port. *Great White Horse*, 58 rooms (6 with bath). Has a "Pickwick Room" with four-poster beds. *Crown and Anchor*, 48 rooms. Both first-class reasonable. *Belstead Brook*, 25 rooms (most with bath). Eat at *Belstead Brook*.

KING'S LYNN (Norfolk). Ancient town and seaport on River Ouse. *Globe*, 50 rooms (3 with bath); *Duke's Head*, 42 rooms (2 with bath). Both first-class reasonable.

LAVENHAM (Suffolk). A "showplace" of East Anglia. *Swan*, 13th-century inn, 9 rooms (all with bath). Duck and chicken specialties.

LONG MELFORD (Suffolk). Old wool town with magnificent church. *Bull,* medieval inn, 21 rooms (11 with bath). Eat here, or at *La Vieille Maison*.

LOWESTOFT (Suffolk). Large seaside resort, good sands; golf, sea and river fishing; large fishing industry and harbour. *Hatfield*, 43 rooms (5 with bath); *Victoria*, 67 rooms; *Suffolk*, 40 rooms. All first-class reasonable. At Oulton Broad, the modern *Golden Egg Motel*, 28 rooms with bath.

NEWMARKET (Suffolk). Famous racing centre; all accommodation booked solid during big racing meetings. *Bedford Lodge*, 12 rooms (4 with bath); *Rutland Arms*, 34 rooms (6 with bath); *White Hart*, 23 rooms (10 with bath). All first-class reasonable.

NORWICH (Norfolk). Historic county town of Norfolk. *Maid's Head,* over 600 years old. Elizabeth I slept here. 95 rooms (45 with bath); good cuisine; *Lansdowne*, 47 rooms (8 with bath); *Town House*, 20 rooms. Eat at the last-named. *Bell* (Trust House), 54 rooms, *Royal, Castle,* moderate.

SAFFRON WALDEN (Essex). Busy, pleasant market town. *Rose and Crown*, 18 rooms, moderate.

THAXTED (Essex). Old wool centre; timbered Town Hall. *Swan*, 8 rooms, moderate. Elegantly furnished 15th-century house, the *Recorder's Restaurant*, is expensive, but has a moderate *table d'hôte*.

THETFORD (Norfolk). Old market town being expanded under an agreement with the Greater London Council. Good golf. *Bell*, 29 rooms; *Central*, 17 rooms.

WOODBRIDGE (Suffolk). Lovely old town and yachting centre. On River Deben. *Crown*, 14 rooms; *Seckford Hall*, 12 rooms (1 with bath). Both first-class reasonable.

Historic Houses Open to the Public

ESSEX. *Audley End House*, Saffron Walden. Jacobean mansion. Open daily April through October. *Hedingham Castle*, Castle Hedingham. Norman keep and Tudor bridge. Open Tues., Thurs. and Sat. afternoons, May to September. *Paycocke's*, Coggeshall. Richly ornamented merchant's house, 16th-cent. Open Weds., Thursday and Sunday, April to September.

SUFFOLK. *Ickworth House*, near Bury St. Edmunds. Late Regency. Open most weekday afternoons, mid-April to October. *Somerleyton Hall*, near Lowestoft. Ancient mansion, mentioned in the Domesday Book. Open Thurs. afternoons May through September.

NORFOLK. *Blickling Hall*, Aylsham. Jacobean house. Open Weds., Thurs., Sat. and Sun. afternoons, Easter Sat. to September. *Holkham Hall*, Wells. Palladian mansion. Open Thurs. afternoons, June to September. *Sandringham House*, home of H.M. the Queen. Gardens only. Open Weds. and Thurs. June to September, except when the royal family is in residence. *Walsingham Abbey*, between Wells and Fakenham. 11th-cent. Shrine of Our Lady, later Augustinian Priory. Open all year, Weds., (Sundays in summer).

CAMBRIDGESHIRE. *Anglesey Abbey*, near Cambridge. National Trust owned Elizabethan manor and 100-acre gardens. Open afternoons, Wed., Thur., Sat. and Sun., April to October.

MUSEUMS. A few of the best in East Anglia: Cambridge: *Fitzwilliam Museum* (old masters); *Cambridge & County Folk Museum* (in an old inn); *Scott Polar Research Institute* (Arctic and Antarctic expedition memorabilia); *University Museum of Archeology & Ethnology* (items from prehistoric times); *University Museum of Classical Archeology* (Greek and Roman sculpture); *University Museum of Mineralogy & Petrology* (rocks); *University Archives* (manuscripts dating from 13th century to present); *Sedgwick Museum of Geology* (fossils); *Whipple Museum of the History of Science* (instruments from 16th century onwards).

Chelmsford: *Chelmsford and Essex Museum* (collections of

EAST ANGLIA

Roman Essex). Colchester: *Colchester and Essex Museum* (a castle, a house and finds from Roman Colchester).

Great Yarmouth: *The Elizabethan Museum* (a Tudor house); also *The Tolhouse* (local history). Ipswich: *Ipswich Museum* (Roman and Saxon artifacts); *Christchurch Mansion* (includes Wolsey Art Gallery). King's Lynn: *King's Lynn Museum & Art Gallery* (English drinking glasses and pottery).

Norwich: *Norwich Castle Museum* (dioramas); *Strangers' Hall* (medieval mansion); *St. Peter Hungate Church Museum* (ecclesiastical art). Sudbury: *Gainsborough's House* (his birthplace). Thetford: *Ancient House Museum* (Saxon pottery).

Exploring East Anglia

Like the rest of Great Britain, East Anglia is both older than the 15th century and a lot younger. Colchester, in northeastern Essex, for instance, is the site of the first official Roman colony in the country, founded in about A.D. 49. Coins were minted in Cambridge from the year 975 onwards and William the Conqueror built a castle there in 1086. Norwich, the seat of the county government of Norfolk, began life as a Saxon settlement a thousand years ago.

Today, Colchester's booming electrical engineering industry makes the town and its surrounding area flourishing and prosperous; the world-famous University of Cambridge is still founding new colleges, meeting new scientific challenges; Norwich is a thriving, ever-expanding social, market and shopping centre of over 160,000 people. Recently too, Colchester and Norwich have both become the homes of two of Britain's new universities.

Norfolk

The right of Norwich to call its university the one "of East Anglia" suggests, correctly, that it is the provincial capital of the region—that large, predominantly low-lying, still-rural region of four counties: expanding, southernmost Essex, "sleepy Suffolk", Norfolk, original home of the Angles from over the sea; and small, inland Cambridgeshire. "The Wash", that very wide, inward-thrusting estuary of the River Ouse, marks East Anglia's northern boundary; round its further shores and up to the much busier, but less attractive estuary of the River Humber, lies Lincolnshire.

To explore this part of eastern England one cannot do better than to go first to Norfolk—England's fourth largest county, extending over 2,000 square miles, a "dead-end" county, leading to nowhere but the sea, but from which the other East Anglian counties radiate, like spokes from a wheel.

Norfolk's coast juts out into the North Sea all the way from the ancient port of King's Lynn in the north (cargo boats from Copenhagan and the Baltic still call here regularly) to the seaside town of Gorleston in the south. This seaward-facing bulge of land gives its inhabitants 100 miles of shoreline to live near, its visitors an extensive and varied range of seaside towns and villages to investigate. And, incidentally, if it's summer holidays you have in mind, as so many visitors have, Norfolk can boast of an average annual rainfall that's well below the country's average. Largest, most popular of the resorts that burst with family-holiday entertainment throughout the season, are Yarmouth, Cromer and Hunstanton; quietest coastal villages are those that lie along the marsh-flats between Salthouse and Brancaster and among the sand-dunes around Hemsby and Winterton.

Blakeney is perhaps the quaintest of all the villages. Its narrow main street of fishermen's cottages slopes steeply down to a sudden, open view of the estuary, sailing boats, and distant Blakeney Point, now a bird sanctuary. Launch-trips to the point can easily be arranged during the summer months and the miles of marram-grass dunes and clean wide beaches to be found there give pleasure to all—not only to ornithologists.

A few miles inland from the Norfolk coast, the "Broads" begin—a name which caused much comment among GI's during the last war. In fact, these innocent Broads are a network of shallow, reed-bordered lakes, many of them linked by wide rivers, which cover about 5,000 acres of the eastern part of the county and offer about 200 miles of water for travelling on. As the Broads are nearly always calm, you can enjoy them as you wish: modern well-equipped cabin cruisers, motor boats and small sailing craft can be hired by the week from all the main Broadland centres, such as Beccles, Wroxham and Hickling and row-boats and small pleasure launches provide day or half-day excursions during the season. There are grassy, open spaces around the edges of most of the Broads that are pretty sites for ideal, lazy summer picnics.

Two of England's showplaces: Hampton Court, one of the finest specimens of Tudor architecture, was Henry VIII's sumptuous residence. St. Albans Cathedral is of early Norman origin, but much of the construction contains bricks and tiles taken from the site of Verulanium the Roman capital.

Bath, in Somerset, was noted as a spa centuries before Chaucer created his Good Wife in the Canterbury Tales. *Although the stately façade of the Camden Crescent, above, suggests a more recent origin, the Romans built the first baths about 44 A.D. whose remains, below, may still be seen.*

The lapping waters of the Broads, moreover, are well-stocked with most kinds of coarse fish to angle for from bank or boat. A leisurely week spent cruising through the quiet Broadland waterways, past stretches of marsh where snipe, moorhens and, sometimes, bitterns hide, with time to explore the round-towered, silent village churches, time to moor at riverside inns for beer, a meal and, perhaps, a night's rest . . . all this makes for a holiday, indeed.

Norwich

It is quite easy to sail from the Broads along the River Wensum and into the very heart of Norwich—though there are, of course, more conventional ways of arriving. Whichever way you go, one of the first sights of the city, if you are in a high position, may be the elegant, tapering spire of Norwich Cathedral, soaring 315 feet towards the sky. The cathedral itself is surrounded by a secluded "Close" of lovely old buildings, including the famous Norwich Grammar School, where Lord Nelson was once a pupil. Inside the cathedral, be sure to see the 15th-century choir stalls and the slender-columned clerestory, and stroll through the gracious monastic cloisters.

The second building which dominates the Norwich skyline is its castle, a square, stubborn-looking fortress on a steep, grassy mound. From the mound, you are supposed to be able to see most of the city's 50 or so churches and 300 or so pubs—as a local saying puts it, "a church for every week of the year and a pub for every day". Most of the castle's pleasant stone exterior was re-faced during the 19th century and to get some idea of its Norman origins one must go inside, where there are plans of the building's original structure and some pretty gruesome medieval-like dungeons. The Castle Museum also contains some exceptionally attractive panoramas of Norfolk wildlife and a comprehensive collection of the Norwich School of Painting. Other museums are The Strangers Hall, in a 16th-century merchant's house, The Bridewell, a square black flint building dating from 1360, and St. Peter Hungate, an ecclesiastical museum in a pre-Reformation church.

Try, too, to visit the city's Assembly House, which has an exquisite Georgian entrance hall, and wander down Elm Hill, a narrow, cobbled alley, deliberately preserved in its former condition and, in consequence, lined with curio shops—but charming, nevertheless. Not far from Elm Hill, down another of the city's narrow alleys, you will come across the famous Maddermarket Theatre, built about 40 years ago, with an Elizabethan-type apron stage and a gallery. Plays are performed with professional skill and feeling by amateurs who have proved that they are afraid of nothing. Shakespeare is a staple, of course, but Brecht, Chekov and Tennessee Williams all have their turns and, invariably, Restoration Comedy is performed, with the sparkle and finesse of any West End production.

Norwich is surrounded by amiable, orderly old villages and market towns. One of the prettiest is Wymondham (pronounced *Windham*), with its Market Cross and overhanging cottages. A few miles to the west lies the parish of Hingham, where Abraham Lincoln's family lived for many generations until they emigrated to America in 1637. A bronze bust of the president can be seen in the fine village church. Routes westward lead on across the rolling heath and forests of Norfolk's Breckland and to Thetford, birthplace (on White Hart Street) of Thomas Paine, author of *The Age of Reason*. Thetford is being jolted into the 20th century by large-scale, rapid development of housing and industry.

Lastly, while in Norfolk, don't forget that it is a "royal county" and contains the parish of Sandringham, where the Queen herself is "squire". The gardens and grounds of the royal estates, about 40 miles from Norwich, are surrounded by large areas of heath, rhododendron and pine plantations and parts of them are open to the public when the Queen is not in residence. Sandringham House, built in the 19th century in the style of an earlier period, is a favourite home for all the royal family and they sometimes spend Christmas there when they attend services in the Sandringham parish church.

Essex

Southernmost of East Anglia's counties is Essex. Because of its position—about 50 miles closer to London than Norfolk—the rate of its industrial and population growth has been extremely rapid during recent years. (The Ford Company, for example, now Britain's second-largest motor manufacturer, employs over 41,000 of the county's inhabitants.) Consequently, some Essex towns, such as Basildon and Brentwood, are very like any London suburb, with miles of new-brick housing estates, lots of supermarkets and hordes of commuters shuttling between home and office.

Nevertheless, Essex is much more than a hotbed for industrial expansion; it is also a long-established rural county, as old and, in parts, as beautiful as any other in East Anglia. Of its two most inviting areas for the tourist, one is the northwest where ploughed fields roll toward the horizon in spring, acres of wheat ripen in summer and cow-pastures are lush and green all the year round. Timber-frame and thatch cottages, which sheltered the purely rural lives of earlier inhabitants, still house both country people and many professional people from the cities, who like to combine old-world surroundings with modern conveniences.

Thaxted is, perhaps, the fairest of the many fair villages. There you will find a very fine church, built of soft, yellow-grey limestone, adorned with carved gargoyles, animals and birds, which is a permanent reminder of the days when the little place was a wealthy centre for the local wool and cutlery trades. West of Thaxted lies Finchingfield, best known of the charming group of "field" villages (others, Great and Little Bardfield, Toppesfield and Wethersfield, are all worth a visit). The immaculately-preserved houses and curving lanes of Finchingfield all centre upon a large green that slopes down to a pond, and one can well imagine the days when Maypole dancers with ribbons and pipes celebrated spring here.

The area's two principal market towns, Saffron Walden (once noted for its culture of saffron) and Braintree, are both of considerable interest. With their merry, haphazard jumbles of ancient, historic inns, modern shopping centres, Victorian public buildings and market stalls bursting with farm produce, they both are typical of the county—its today and its yesterday.

And after that, there is the second Essex world to explore: this lies south of Colchester, where marshes, estuaries and low meadows lie under the same delicate, pale seaward light that some of the earlier East Anglian artists depicted so surely in their paintings. Maldon, Tollesbury and Burnham-on-Crouch (the River Crouch!) are the main marshland villages, real boating centres where boats are made as well as used. They are haunts of fishermen in thigh-high boots who tell their fishermen's tales over a noonday pint in the "local" and of birds —black-headed gulls, lapwings and coots—who leave their trails of claw-prints on the muddy salt flats.

Those who find such quiet, flat spaces bleak and dull need only travel a few miles to find the bright lights. The beaches of the county's most popular resorts, Southend, Clacton and Walton-on-the-Naze, are packed with holiday-makers in the summer. Here there are amusement piers with miniature railways, Punch-and-Judy shows and donkey rides for the kiddies, and miniature golf greens, open-air theatres and lots of sand and sea for everyone.

Suffolk

Harwich lies just south of the River Stour; north of the river, Suffolk begins. Like the rest of the region, Suffolk has its full share of agricultural land, white or strawberry-wash plaster and timber cottages, high-hedged lanes, market towns, beaches and its full complement of East Anglians.

Living closer to London than their Norfolk neighbours, Suffolk's peace-loving inhabitants are, at present, feeling the effects of the capital's insatiable need for more space in which to build and grow. Ipswich (population about 120,000) is becoming East Anglia's largest city, now that its new development plan to house and provide work for some 70,000 of London's "overspill" (as the ex-Londoners are rather ungallantly called) is forging ahead.

New shopping centres contrast in Ipswich with older streets lined with attractive buildings of many periods, including the *Ancient House*, probably Britain's oldest and most picturesque bookshop. The *Great White Horse Hotel* is noted for the famous Pickwick episode of the "lady in the yellow curl papers". Christchurch Mansion (c. 1550), a fine period building in a beautiful park close to the Town Centre, houses a large collection of domestic antiquities and pictures in the Wolsey Gallery. (Cardinal Wolsey was born in Ipswich.)

Haverhill and Bury St. Edmunds, two of the county's most attractive market towns, are also accommodating their share of "overspill". And indeed, anyone wanting to look at the process of how British planners are—with varying degrees of success—fitting the new in with the old, will find all these places of special interest. There are also, of course, some very rewarding pieces of "the old" to see: the carefully-tended remains of the famous abbey in Bury St. Edmunds, surrounded by gardens; the "Ancient House" on the Ipswich Buttermarket, which has rich examples of pargeting, a form of decorating plaster walls much in vogue during the 16th and 17th centuries.

A fierce battle against the inroads of "overspill" has recently been fought and won (more or less) by residents of the Valley of the Stour on the Essex-Suffolk borders. And certainly, it is an area that deserves sympathetic preservation. For this is "Constable Country", named after the 18th-century artist, John Constable, who was born here in the village of East Bergholt. His paintings (*The Haywain* is perhaps the most famous of them) reflect the quiet pastoral loveliness of his home surroundings. Flatford Mill, subject of another of his best-known works, still stands here, much the same as in Constable's day and it, together with the Constable Memorial Hall in the village, helps to perpetuate the artist's memory.

The River Stour meanders to the sea near Felixstowe, one of those breezy, popular East Coast resorts which, like the larger town of Lowestoft to the north, provides lots of vacation-time fun for lovers of the summer seaside. Lowestoft can boast of several additional attractions into the bargain. On its outskirts lies Oulton Broad, a boat-busy stretch of water that forms a major gateway to the Norfolk Broads. It is also an active fishing-port and in early autumn, trawlers and drifters bring back huge catches of herring, mackerel and halibut which are auctioned, cleaned and packed on the bustling quay-side. Near Lowestoft too, is Somerleyton Hall, one of the county's finest brick mansions; tapestries and Grinling Gibbons carving adorn the main reception rooms, and there is a very puzzling maze in the beautiful gardens.

Aldeburgh, a coastal town midway between Felixstowe and Lowestoft, is also well worth a visit. Its history goes back to Saxon times. There is an exceptionally well-preserved 16th-century Moot Hall on the sea-front. Because it was the birthplace of the poet George Crabbe and also, for several years, the home of Benjamin Britten, one of England's leading composers, the Aldeburgh Festival of Music and Arts is held here every June. Since its foundation in 1948, this festival has gained world-wide renown; many famous musicians attend it and some of Britten's own works are invariably played. At Orford, just down the coast from Aldeburgh, there is a Norman castle keep, a bird sanctuary (Havergate Island), and a marvellous shop and restaurant, the *Butley-Orford Oysterage*, that sells delicious fresh oysters at unusually low prices.

From Aldeburgh, it is an excellent idea to drive unhurriedly west through the very heart of "sleepy Suffolk", with its comfortable villages, slow rivers and quiet country roads. If you do this, be sure to make a detour for the lake-reflected ruins of Framlingham Castle and, most particularly, for Lavenham. Lavenham, which can boast of its very own Preservation Society, is an almost-unspoilt, picture-postcard little place, whose wool-dealing forebears gave it a perpendicular-style church of great beauty, a wealth of timber-frame cottages built by weavers (with their top storeys bulging over the lower ones), two or three venerable inns and nice down-to-earth names, such as Shilling Street and Water Street. In Lavenham's medieval timber-framed *Swan Hotel* can be heard echoes of Aldeburgh, when the Trust House hotel group stage their regular monthly concerts here from September to March.

The most pleasant gateway out of Suffolk is Newmarket—and Newmarket, as everyone knows, means horses. And not only horses, but lithe little jockeys, courtyards of mellow-tiled, rambling stables, stablelads and girls, and smooth acres of rolling grasslands which almost encircle the town and over which, from dawn onwards of just about any fine day, you might see a string of elegant racehorses and their riders enjoying a practice trot. Race meetings are held from April to October; they include such famous classics as the Cambridgeshire and the Cesarewitch. The town has been horse-crazy since the days of James I and royal patronage has helped to maintain its prestige ever since.

Cambridgeshire

From Newmarket you have to go to Cambridgeshire, the county which almost surrounds it. The county boundary lines run right through the centre of the railway station, and by crossing to the up-platform one is in Cambridgeshire—and certainly, whether by waiting for the next train or getting into a car or coach, it's easy to reach Cambridge, 12 miles away.

EAST ANGLIA

CAMBRIDGE

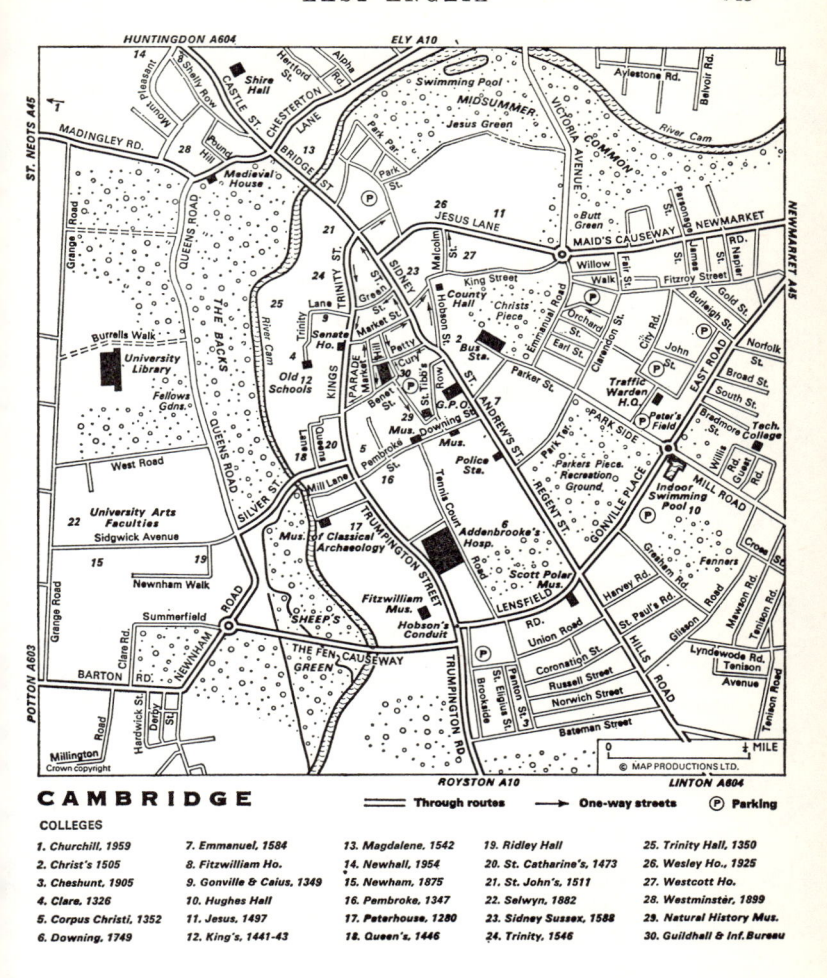

Through routes — One-way streets — ⓟ Parking

COLLEGES

1. Churchill, 1959
2. Christ's 1505
3. Cheshunt, 1905
4. Clare, 1326
5. Corpus Christi, 1352
6. Downing, 1749
7. Emmanuel, 1584
8. Fitzwilliam Ho.
9. Gonville & Caius, 1349
10. Hughes Hall
11. Jesus, 1497
12. King's, 1441-43
13. Magdalene, 1542
14. Newhall, 1954
15. Newnham, 1875
16. Pembroke, 1347
17. Peterhouse, 1280
18. Queen's, 1446
19. Ridley Hall
20. St. Catharine's, 1473
21. St. John's, 1511
22. Selwyn, 1882
23. Sidney Sussex, 1588
24. Trinity, 1546
25. Trinity Hall, 1350
26. Wesley Ho., 1925
27. Westcott Ho.
28. Westminster, 1899
29. Natural History Mus.
30. Guildhall & Inf. Bureau

It is now more than 700 years since the first scholars went to live in Cambridge; they had no university, no teachers, no endowments—they were just earnest young men seeking knowledge together. The oldest college, Peterhouse, was founded in 1284; lecturers and students, and the endowments to provide accommodation for them, have proliferated ever since. To tour the university buildings then, is to see evidence of practically every architectural style from the 13th century to the 20th. The magnificent colleges, each one a self-governing corporate body, spread through the heart of the city, dominating the banks of the River Cam, their lofty, old stone walls abutting on nearly every main thoroughfare. However, these walls suggest an inaccurate air of exclusiveness. Today's undergraduates are approachable, chatty people on the whole and, unless there is a notice expressly forbidding entrance to a particular area, visitors may wander at will through courtyards, gardens, college chapels and libraries.

Make, first of all, for the city's greatest glory, the "finest flower of Gothic in Europe", King's College Chapel. The great, vaulting stone ribs of this truly perfect building have, on many and many a Christmas Eve, echoed to the pure tones of angel-faced choir boys singing the Festival of the Nine Carols; during many a summer visitors have stood, in awed delight, and gazed at the delicate blues, greens and greys of the Flemish-made windows. The redecorating to house the new Rubens, *Adoration of the Virgin*, is disastrous, however.

After King's visit Queen's—the college founded in the 15th century "in honour of the sex feminine". Appropriately, Queen's is particularly beautiful, with secluded, mellow-brick courtyards dating from its earliest days and a quaint, narrow "Mathematical Bridge" humped over the river. Once you see that tree-shaded, slow-moving river, you will want to pole gently along it in a punt, as others are doing. These flat little boats (which can be rather wayward if you are not careful) can be hired from the Mill Bridge or the *Anchor Inn;* they provide the ideal way of seeing the "backs" of the colleges. The trip is one of sheer beauty—willow branches dangle to the water's surface, immaculate lawns sweep smoothly along the banks and, just beyond them, stand a series of gracious buildings—the proud, grey-white facade of Clare College, the garden-framed west end of King's, the towers of Trinity and the romantically-styled St. John's College, with its crenellated Bridge of Sighs to glide beneath.

Off-river, there is yet much more to see: the carved Wren library of Trinity College; the tapestries and manuscripts in the Fitzwilliam Museum; Emmanuel College, where John Harvard was educated and, for a change of pace perhaps, the exotic plants and trees in the well-stocked Botanical Gardens. Then there is Caius (pron. *keys*), with its pleasant courts. For those with time to explore further, there is Sawston Hall, just six miles from the city. This 400-year-old manor has its Long Gallery and its Secret Hiding Hole, as do many of the residences dating from a similar period; it also specializes in winter viewing programmes—by enchanting candlelight and log-fire—and is reputedly haunted!

One other pilgrimage which many visitors make while in Cambridge is to the American Cemetery, where lie the remains of 3,811 airmen of the U.S.A.A.F. In 1945, the freedom of the borough was conferred on the American Air Force in grateful recognition of the protection it had afforded to the area. The quiet cemetery is beautifully situated on a hill at Madingley, four miles from Cambridge. Its Memorial Chapel contains a large map which shows the airlanes flown by American aircraft during World War II. (Prominent Americans who have attended Cambridge besides John Harvard include John Winthrop and John Eliot).

Ely, chief city of the fens, is built on a patch of high ground above the morasses of the lower-lying marshes, one of a series of almost-islands, in fact, on which stand the towns of northern Cambridgeshire. It was here that Hereward the Wake, leader of the Saxons, made his last extended stand against the Norman invaders, led by William the Conqueror. Ely's handsome cathedral, which dominates the city and the surrounding countryside, was begun after the conquest was complete; today, it richly rewards the unhurried appreciative visitor who has time to see not only the cathedral itself but the buildings in the immediate vicinity—the Bishop's Palace, portions of the monastery walls and the Monks' Barn.

Up to now, at least, most of East Anglia has been allowed to remain a quieter, lovelier land. It is still a land where the sails of a few remaining windmills creak on a breezy day, where fishing boats still creep homeward in the evenings, where towns still contain the jumbled traces of 1,000 years of habitation, where crops of wheat, beans, tulips, barley and clover still thrive under the sun and people still, on occasions, have time to stand and stare.

SHAKESPEARE COUNTRY

The Bard as Dignified Tourist Magnet

by

SYDNEY MOORHOUSE

(*The author was brought up in the Midlands, about which he writes in a later chapter of this book. After five years with the R.A.F., he returned to live in the Morecambe Bay area. He has written* Walking Tours in England and Wales, *and several other outdoor books.*)

Although that section of Warwickshire which we call "Shakespeare country" is, in reality, no more than a continuation of the familiar Midlands scene of green fields, slow-moving, mirror-like rivers, quiet villages, and lovely old halls, castles, and churches, it becomes an area apart through its role as the homeland of England's greatest dramatist.

Born in a half-timbered, early 16th-century building in the town of Stratford-upon-Avon on April 23, 1564, Shakespeare was buried in Holy Trinity Church after he died (on his fifty-second birthday) in a more imposing house at New Place. Although he spent much of his all-too-short life in London, where, of course, he became the leading figure of the Elizabethan theatre, the world associates him with Stratford. Here, he played as a boy, attended the local grammar school, and married Anne Hathaway in the years between his birth and 1587, and here he returned a man of fame and prosperity, to the town with which his name is indelibly linked.

Today, over three and a half centuries after his passing, he still remains the magnet that draws thousands of tourists each year to this south Warwickshire town. They come to visit the places with which he will always be identified, and to attend some performances of his plays in the Royal Shakespeare Theatre, where a Shakespearean Festival runs for nearly eight months of the year.

Although the famous actor David Garrick instituted something in the way of a Shakespearean Festival in the town in 1769, and there were suitable commemorations on the occasion of the 300th anniversary of the poet's birth in 1864, it was not until 1874 that Charles Edward Flower formed the Shakespeare Memorial Association, with a view to establishing a permanent theatre; the forerunner of the present building was opened in 1879.

From that time onwards, the festival has grown in both size and prestige so that when, in 1926, the original Memorial Theatre was destroyed by fire, productions in the town continued while a replacement was being built. For this last, a great amount of money was subscribed by the people of the United States, and in 1932, the Royal Shakespeare Theatre, designed by Elizabeth Scott, was opened.

Practical Information for Shakespeare Country

WHERE TO STAY AND DINE? You'll almost certainly want to include a visit to Stratford-upon-Avon during a trip to England. If you're touring outside London to the west, or in the Midlands, it's a good idea to make the Stratford area a headquarters. Some of the hotels are pretty busy, especially during the season of plays, which lasts from April until November, at the famous Royal Shakespeare Theatre. During this season, too, most hotels will only accept minimum dinner, bed and breakfast bookings. Most hotels listed here are from first-class reasonable to moderate.

STRATFORD-UPON-AVON (Warwickshire). Over a dozen hotels, but among the most atmospheric: *Shakespeare*, older than the man himself, 80 rooms (27 with bath). A very satisfactory restaurant in the hotel. *Welcombe*, with 55 rooms (30 with bath) has a fine restaurant. *Falcon*, 74 rooms (67 with bath). *Swan's Nest*, 33 rooms (4 with bath), noted for its restaurant. *Alveston Manor*, 75 rooms (50 with bath), has a good restaurant, as does *Red Horse*, 52 rooms (21 with bath). The Alveston Manor dates from the 16th century.

Good restaurants also include the *Black Swan* (known as the *Dirty Duck*), the *Royal Shakespeare Theatre Restaurant*, overlooking the river, and *Marianne*.

ALCESTER (Warwickshire). A new (1966) motel, *The Cherry Trees Garden*, has 12 rooms (all with bath).

BARFORD (Warwickshire). The lovely old *Glebe* is a good bet. 14 rooms (2 with bath). Attractive garden.

BROADWAY (Worcs.). 15 miles south. See listings on p. 252.

ILMINGTON (Warwickshire). Food at the *Howard Arms* has a great local reputation.

KENILWORTH (Warwickshire). Stay at the *Queen and Castle*, across the road from the real castle, or at the new (1967) *De Montfort*, 73 rooms (all with bath).

LEAMINGTON SPA (Warwickshire). Popular resort and inland spa; fishing, golf. *Clarendon*, 50 rooms (8 with bath); *Manor House*, 54 rooms (35 with bath); *Regent*, 85 rooms (19 with bath).

Try the elegant *Royal Pump Room* for good food at moderate prices, and also the *Manor House* and *Regent* hotels. and the *Blackdown Pub*.

QUINTON (Warwickshire). Ask for ham at the *College Arms* here.

STUDLEY (Glos.). Good dining at the *Duke of Marlborough*.

WARWICK (Warwickshire). Historic town with castle and ancient buildings. *Lord Leycester*, 47 rooms (8 with bath); *Woolpack*, 28 rooms (2 with bath); *Warwick Arms*, 33 rooms. *The Crown*, 11 rooms (2 with bath), is pleasant. For food, the *Saxon Mill*, part of which dates back to 1420.

GETTING THERE. In addition to automobile, conducted tour, and train, via Leamington Spa (change), you can get to Stratford-upon-Avon by 18th-century stagecoach. Starting from Runnymede, near London, the coach takes you to Shakespeare's home town in a 3-day trip, stopping over at inns and tourist sites enroute. A horn-blowing postillion announces your arrival and departure, and it's all great fun. Cost is $150, all-inclusive. Details from *Evan Evans Tours Ltd.*, 73 Russell Square, London W.C.1.

The Shakespeare Birthplace Trust Properties, Stratford-upon-Avon

Inclusive ticket admitting you to all five properties costs 7s (84¢). Each of these properties can be visited for 2s or 2s 6d (24¢ or 30¢), Apr. to Oct.: *Shakespeare's Birthplace*, Henley Street. Open 9-6 or 7, Suns. 10-6. *Anne Hathaway's Cottage*, Shottery. Open weekdays, 9-6 or 7, Suns, 10-6. *Hall's Croft*, Old Town. Open weekdays 9-6, Suns. 2-6. *New*

Place, Chapel Street, and *Mary Arden's House* at Wilmcote, same opening times as Hall's Croft.

Nov. to Mar.: All are open on weekdays from 9-12:45 and 2-4. Only Shakespeare's Birthplace is open on Sundays, from 2-4 p.m.

Seats for performances at *The Royal Shakespeare Theatre* on the banks of the Avon can be reserved in advance at any office of *Keith Prowse,* London, or at the box office at Stratford. Reservable seats cost about 5s to 30s (60¢ to $3.60).

Historic Houses Open to the Public

Warwick Castle, stately home of the Earl of Warwick. Open daily in summer, Suns. in winter. *Kenilworth Castle,* ruined medieval fortress. Open daily, all year. *Compton Wynyates,* near Banbury. One of the finest Tudor houses in England. Romantic and unusual topiary gardens. Open weekends and Wed. afternoons, April to September. *Charlecote Park,* near Stratford-upon-Avon. National Trust. Elizabethan house and deer park with Shakesperian associations. Open daily (not Mondays), April to September. *Ragley Hall,* near Alcester. Stately home of the Marquis of Hertford, with rich art treasures. Open most afternoons, mid-April through September.

MUSEUMS. In addition to the Shakespeare properties (see above), the following may be of interest: In Stratford-upon-Avon: *Harvard House* (home of John Harvard's mother) and the *Royal Shakespeare Theatre Picture Gallery* (costumes, designs, portraits). In Leamington Spa: *Leamington Spa Art Gallery & Museum* (Dutch masters, 18th-century English glass, etc.). In Nuneaton: *Nuneaton Museum & Art Gallery* (George Eliot relics, etc.). In Warwick: *Warwick County Museum* (history of Warwickshire), *St. John's House* (costume and furniture) and the *Doll Museum* (antique dolls).

Exploring Shakespeare Country

Although a good deal of restoration has been inevitable in the four centuries that have elapsed since 1564, the Henley Street birthplace itself, perhaps the most popular of Shakespearean shrines, still contains a good deal of the original timber framing, and that section of the building used as a residence is furnished in appropriate style.

When Shakespeare was born, his father, John, used part of the premises for his work as glover and wool-dealer; this part has been turned into a museum, housing many interesting relics of the time. The garden contains a unique collection of plants and trees mentioned in the poet's works.

New Place, on the other hand, was demolished in 1759, and only the site and foundations remain of what is said to have once been the most imposing residence in town. The gardens here are well cared for by the trust and contain a mulberry tree alleged to have come from a cutting of the original one planted by Shakespeare; the original was destroyed by a later occupant said to have been annoyed by the number of visitors wishing to see it.

The approach to these gardens is through Nash's House, the home of the poet's grand-daughter and her first husband, Thomas Nash, which again contains many interesting relics. Adjoining is a replica of an Elizabethan garden of great beauty.

Also administered by the trust is Hall's Croft (in New Town), another fine old Tudor house, with an even lovelier garden, where the poet's daughter, Susanna, and her husband, Dr. John Hall, lived. Here, during the period of the festival, regular recitals of poetry and lectures take place.

Quite apart from the places directly associated with the poet, Stratford contains many other features well worth visiting. The Guild buildings at the corner of Church Street and Chapel Lane contain a chapel with a chancel dating from 1450 and incorporating part of the fabric of the original (built in 1269), the early 15th-century Guildhall, and the grammar school attended by the playwright.

There is a fascinating link with the United States in the lovely half-timbered Harvard House, for not only was it owned by the parents of John Harvard, who gave his name to the famous American university, but it was actually bought and presented to the university by Edward Morris of Chicago in 1909. Holy Trinity church, beautifully situated by the Avon, contains the grave of Shakespeare, and the town hall, built of the lovely Cotswold stone from the hills to the south, was dedicated to the memory of the poet by David Garrick on the occasion of the forerunner of the famous festivals in 1769.

As is only to be expected, Stratford is redolent with old inns and hostelries, including the *Red Horse*, where Washington Irving stayed when engaged in writing his well-known *Sketch Book;* the *Golden Lion*, which was known as the *Peacock* until early in the 17th century, and the *Shakespeare*, which, despite its name, was actually there when the poet was born and is said to have been built as a residence by Sir Hugh

SHAKESPEARE COUNTRY

Clopton, who later became Lord Mayor of London and who died in 1496.

It must never be forgotten that Shakespeare, although born in what was then a smallish town, was essentially a country lad at heart and his wanderings through the fields and woods so close to his boyhood home gave him a knowledge of nature and rural lore that so often reveals itself in his plays.

One place he must have visited fairly often was Shottery, where his wife-to-be, Anne Hathaway, lived in the thatched farmhouse that, quite understandably, is one of the most photographed houses in the whole of Britain. It is another of the possessions of the Birthplace Trust who, as in the case of all the places in their care, have taken great pains to preserve the atmosphere of the key years of its story.

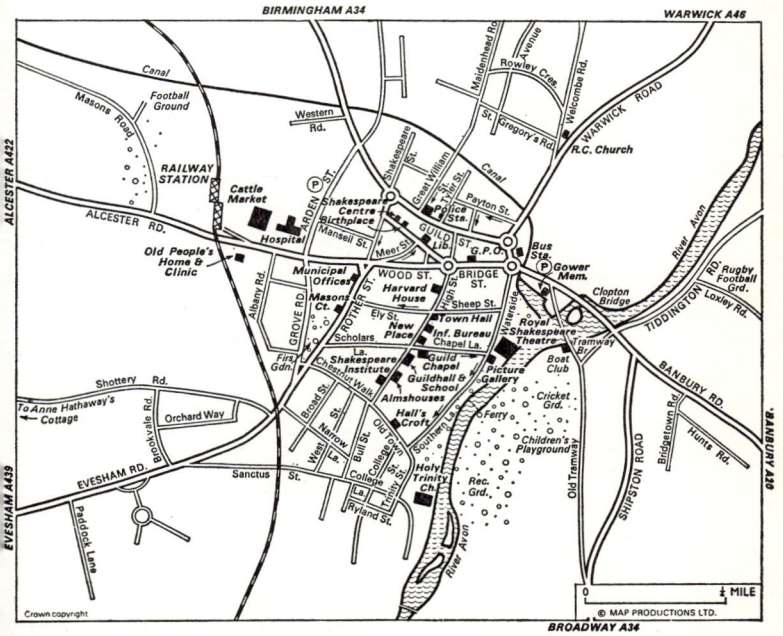

STRATFORD-UPON-AVON ═══ Through routes ⟶ One-way streets (P) Parking

There is a regular bus service from the town to Shottery, but many will prefer the mile-long walk through the field's which, most probably, is the way Shakespeare used on those courtship journeys (which do not seem to have ended in the manner he had hoped).

Outside Stratford

North of Stratford, what has long been known as "leafy Warwickshire" is at its best in the Forest of Arden, where the woodland glades and shady paths through the trees give little indication of the nearness of Birmingham and its suburbs.

Wilmcote, three miles from Stratford, contains another of the possessions of the Birthplace Trust, the Tudor farmhouse which was the home of Shakespeare's mother, Mary Arden, member of an old Warwickshire family whose earliest members lived at Aston (now a suburb of Birmingham). The family doubtless took its name from their woodland environment, the very word "Arden" being used by the Celts for such a district. In the adjoining parish of Aston Cantlow, Mary and John Shakespeare, the poet's father, are said to have been married in the church of St. John the Baptist.

The road from Stratford to Warwick passes just north of Charlecote Hall, with its magnificent manor house built on the site of an earlier mansion in 1558 by Sir Thomas Lucy, whose family owned the estate from the 12th century to 1945, when Sir Montgomerie Fairfax-Lucy presented it to the National Trust.

It was here that, according to the oft-quoted story, the young Shakespeare was caught poaching the deer in the park and was brought before Sir Thomas himself. It was an incident that seems to have left its mark on the mind of the poet-to-be, for there seems little doubt that the builder of the mansion was the prototype of Justice Shallow in the *Merry Wives of Windsor*.

History is certainly written over the face of Warwick, for even a great fire in 1694 failed to erase many of the medieval buildings. Its east and west gates piercing sections of walls that go back to the 12th century; its fine collection of half-timbered buildings, including Lord Leycester's Hospital (originally built as a guildhouse in the time of Henry VI but converted into a hospital by the Earl of Leicester in 1571);

Buxton, in Derbyshire, is another spa whose medicinal waters were discovered by the Romans. Its gentle, wooded countryside contrasts vividly with the dramatic skyline imposed by the fortress-castle of Mont Orgueil above Gorey harbour, Jersey, in the Channel Islands.

A world hub of shipping and commerce, Liverpool typifies the massive industry of Lancashire. However, rural areas still abound, such as the quaint village of Downham.

and the church of St. Mary's, largely destroyed by the fire but with parts of the older erection still to be seen, all remain to echo its historic past.

Warwick's crowning glory, however, is its great castle, perched conspicuously on a ledge of rock above the River Avon. The earls of Warwick, as indicated by the term "king-maker" applied to the holder of the title during the Wars of the Roses, were ever to the forefront in affairs of state; and throughout the castle's long history, it has withstood sieges by hostile armies, held prisoners of high rank, and been the scene of the trials of those who found themselves on the opposite side to the earls of Warwick.

Doubtless, the Saxons used the mound overlooking the Avon to house a fortification of sorts, and facing the present gatehouse, which is less than 200 years old, is an elevation known as Ethelfleada's Mound, in commemoration of the man who enclosed the town following its destruction by the Danes in A.D. 915.

The first Norman castle was erected soon after the Norman Conquest by Henry de Newburgh, henchman of William I, who was created first Earl of Warwick for his services. Only fragmentary evidence remains of the earliest building; the greater part of the present imposing collection of towers and domestic buildings is of later date.

Caesar's Tower, which rises to a height of nearly 150 feet from the river, was built in 1370 by the first Thomas Beauchamp, who carried out many structural alterations. His son, another Thomas, built the no-less-imposing Guy's Tower, nearly a quarter of a century afterwards.

Around Warwick

There are many other places of interest in the vicinity of the county town. At Guy's Cliffe, the grounds contain the cave used by the legendary Guy of Warwick who, tiring of the usual pastimes linked with love and war, retired to this beautiful spot to lead the life of a hermit. The nearby priory marks the site of a religious establishment created by the first Earl of Warwick and later converted into a mansion by one Thomas Hawkins. In 1926, however, the mansion was pulled down and shipped across the Atlantic, where it was re-built by its new owner.

Almost adjoining Warwick is Royal Leamington Spa, formerly a possession of the priory at Kenilworth, and now a fashionable watering place. It owes its popularity to the medicinal springs known to exist in the Middle Ages but which began to attract many visitors towards the close of the 18th century. It is a pleasing town, with many of its buildings going back to that period of increasing prosperity.

Some miles to the north is Kenilworth, where once more the Norman barons successfully used a site previously occupied by the Saxons to build a castle. This fortress, which still remains one of the most imposing in the land, was, of course, the one described by Sir Walter Scott in his novel of the same name.

Like nearby Warwick, Kenilworth has had as its owners men who were usually in the forefront of any trouble, including the all-powerful Simon de Montfort, Earl of Leicester, who led his barons in the civil wars of the 13th century.

The keep and some of the outer walls date from the early part of the 12th century, when the original castle was built by one Geoffrey de Clinton (in the time of Henry I); following the death of Edward II, it was one of the possessions of John of Gaunt, who built the Strong Tower, the Banqueting Hall, and other sections. Then, in the time of Queen Elizabeth I, Kenilworth became the possession of Robert Dudley, Earl of Leicester and strong favourite of the monarch, who showed much extravagance in adding new parts and who frequently entertained his royal mistress here.

The original builder of the castle also founded the Augustinan priory, to which Leamington Spa once belonged, but the greater part of this was demolished after the dissolution of the monasteries and only the gatehouse and some fragments of the original can be seen today.

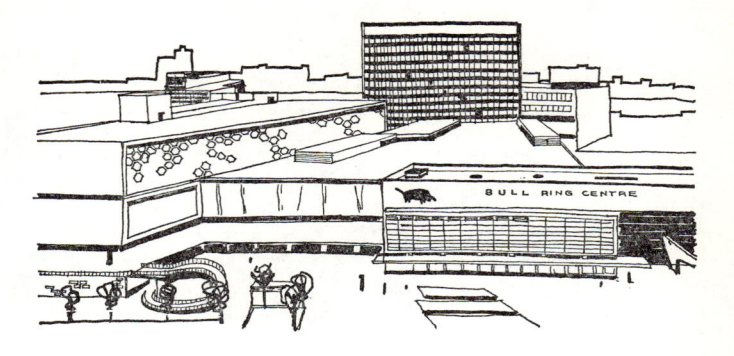

THE MIDLANDS

Hunting Shires and Industrial Heart

It is, perhaps, appropriate that the heart of England should be the area that most reflects its real spirit, for despite the existence of such thriving centres of commerce and industry as Birmingham, Coventry, and Rugby, much of it is not only rural but is the very essence of that rural scene which poets and painters have so often depicted as representing the typical, unspoilt English countryside.

Away from the towns, and, indeed, within a few miles of their outskirts, there is a sense of permanency not only about the natural landscape but about the works of man. The cottages, the country churches, the layout of the farms, all these and other manmade components seem to have been fashioned with one desire, that of fitting in so perfectly with their surroundings that time makes them essential features of the scene.

Practical Information for the Midlands

HOTELS AND RESTAURANTS. In so big an area it is, of course, impossible to suggest any one centre from which to visit the whole of the Midlands. Accommodation is reasonably plentiful in some of the smaller towns and larger villages, although in the more popular areas, it is often booked in advance. Most of the bigger cities and larger towns are close to the more interesting spots and in the majority of cases a complete list of accommodation can be obtained from the local town hall.

BIRMINGHAM (Warwickshire). One of the most up-to-date cities in Europe, with fine shopping centres, excellent theatres, and sporting amenities, including first-class football and cricket.

Principal hotels include the new (1968) *Excelsior Birmingham Airport*, 66 rooms (all with bath, air-conditioning and sound-proofing); new (1969) *Royal Angus*, 140 rooms (all with bath); *Albany*, 254 rooms (all with bath); *Midland*, 117 rooms (73 with bath); *Norfolk*, 132 rooms (15 with bath or shower). Also: *Cobden*, 175 rooms; *Arden*, 102 rooms; *Imperial Centre*, 102 rooms; *Garden House*, 17 rooms (all with bath) and at Sheldon, the new (1968) *Wheatsheaf Motel*, 29 rooms (all with bath).

Good restaurants include *Rackham's*, Corporation Street; *Savoy*, Hill St.; *Cardinal*, Grand Hotel; *Castillane*, Midland Hotel; *La Capanna*, Hurst St., and *Heaven Bridge*, Bull Ring (Chinese). Good curries at *Taj Mahal*, Smallbrook, Ringway.

BOSTON (Lincolnshire). Ancient port and fresh-water angling centre. Associated with the Pilgrim Fathers. *Peacock Royal*, 30 rooms (2 with bath); *White Hart*, 40 rooms (3 with bath); good cuisine; moderate. Newest (1969) is the *New England*, 11 rooms (5 with bath).

BRAMPTON (Hunts.). Midway between London and Nottingham. A new hotel, the *Brampton*, 17 rooms (all with bath) on the A1.

CHURCH STRETTON (Shropshire). Good centre for visiting Shropshire hills and Welsh border country. Hotels include *Longmynd* 60 rooms (9 with bath), and *The Hotel*, 34 rooms (4 with bath).

CORBY (Northamptonshire). En route to Lincoln, a convenient stopping place is the new (1966) *Strathclyde*, 40 rooms (all with bath).

COVENTRY (Warwickshire). Industrial city mainly rebuilt since the war and containing new cathedral which is interesting because of its modern ecclesiastical architecture. First-class theatre.

Principal hotels include *Leofric*, 98 rooms (70 with bath), and, on the outskirts, *Brandon Hall*, 35 rooms (3 with bath) and *Chase*, 20 rooms. Also, the *Godiva*, 50 rooms, near the centre.

CRAVEN ARMS (Shropshire). Interesting village with Stokesay Castle at hand. Good place for visiting Welsh borders. Big auction mart with fascinating sheep sales in the early autumn. There are two small hotels, *Craven Arms*, 9 rooms, and *Stokesay Castle*, 10 rooms.

DERBY (Derbyshire). Hotels include the new (1966) *Pennine*, 104 rooms, (60 with bath and the remainder with showers); the *Midland*, 64 rooms (27 with bath); the *Clarendon*, 46 rooms, and the *Gables*, 45 rooms (3 with bath).

Restaurant: the *San Remo*. There is a *John F. Kennedy Pub* (named with the family's permission) on the "American Estate". A nice "canal pub" is the *Green Dragon* at Willington, near Derby.

GRANTHAM (Lincolnshire). Fascinating town on Great North Road. Handy for Belvoir Castle and other interesting places. Two good hotels: *Angel and Royal*,

30 rooms (3 with bath), and *George*, 40 rooms.

GREAT MALVERN (Worcestershire). Inland holiday resort in the Malvern Hills. Possesses concert hall and festival theatre. Hotels include *Abbey*, 83 rooms (30 with bath); *Foley Arms*, 26 rooms (6 with bath); *Gold Hill*, 20 rooms (2 with bath) and *Mount Pleasant*, 20 rooms (3 with bath).

HEREFORD (Herefordshire). Cathedral city, on banks of the Wye, with many fine old buildings. Good salmon fishing close at hand. Hotels include: *Castle Pool*, 29 rooms (3 with bath); *City Arms*, 45 rooms; *Graftonbury*, 53 rooms (12 with bath and 2 showers), and *Green Dragon*, 77 rooms (20 with bath).

HORNCASTLE (Lincolnshire). Interesting market town at foot of Lincolnshire Wolds. One small hotel, *Bull*, 10 rooms.

KETTERING (Northamptonshire). Industrial town, but close to some interesting countryside and Rockingham Castle. Good hotels include *George*, 52 rooms (11 with bath), and *Royal*, 37 rooms (2 with bath).

LEICESTER (Leicestershire). Busy city, but with lovely country close at hand. Slated to open 1970: a *Post House*, off M1 at Exit 21, on A46. Meanwhile try the new (1967) *Abbey Motor Hotel*, 54 rooms (all with bath); *Bell*, 107 rooms (28 with bath); *Belmont*, 53 rooms (6 with bath); *Grand*, 142 rooms (27 with bath and 6 showers); *Midland*, 48 rooms (6 with bath), and *Royal*, 34 rooms (8 with showers). Nice "canal pub", the *North Bridge Inn*, Frog Island.

LEOMINSTER (Herefordshire). Quaint West Midlands town, with pleasing country and historic buildings close at hand. Hotels include *Royal Oak*, 20 rooms (1 with bath), and *Talbot*, 22 rooms (4 with bath).

LICHFIELD (Staffordshire). Fascinating cathedral city, with many associations with Dr. Samuel Johnson. Hotels include *George*, 30 rooms, and *Angel Croft*, 14 rooms. "Canal pub", *Swan,* at Whittington.

LINCOLN (Lincolnshire). Old cathedral city: golf, fishing. *Eastgate*, Trust House, 61 rooms (all with bath) and *White Hart*, 58 rooms (33 with bath). Both first-class superior. *Albion*, 26 rooms.

LOUGHBOROUGH (Leicestershire). Industrial and market town with bell foundry and tower with carillon of 45 bells—said to be largest in the world. *King's Head* has 30 rooms (3 with bath and 5 with shower). "Canal pub", the *Plough*, at Normanton-on-Soar.

LUDLOW (Shropshire). Beautiful old town with fine castle. Many lovely buildings. Hotels include *Angel*, 19 rooms (2 with bath), and *Feathers*, 25 rooms (8 with bath), this last one of the most beautiful half-timbered buildings in the town.

MANSFIELD (Nottinghamshire). Industrial and coal mining town on the edge of romantic Sherwood Forest. *The Swan* has 27 rooms (4 with bath).

MARKET HARBOROUGH (Leicestershire). Market town and one of the historic foxhunting centres of England. Hotels include *Angel*, 19 rooms; *Three Swans*, 11 rooms (5 with bath); *Grove*, 16 rooms (all with bath), and *Peacock*, 7 rooms. Nice "canal pub", the *Black Horse*, Foxton.

NEWARK (Nottinghamshire). Old town with castle and beautiful parish church. Hotels include

Clinton Arms, 21 rooms; *Ram*, 16 rooms, and *Robin Hood*, 13 rooms.

NEWCASTLE UNDER LYME (Staffs.). Just off M6, 53 rooms with bath: modern *Post House*.

NORTHAMPTON (Northamptonshire). Centre of boot and shoe industry and good place from which to visit interesting neighbourhood. Hotels include *Angel*, 41 rooms; *Grand*, 52 rooms (15 with bath); *Plough*, 29 rooms, and, on outskirts, *Westone*, 26 rooms (15 with bath).

NOTTINGHAM (Nottinghamshire). County town with castle and several interesting places. Close to Sherwood Forest. Outstanding theatre, which has a good restaurant.

Newest hotel (1969) is the *Albany*, 150 rooms (all with bath and air conditioning). Others include new (1968) *Post House* motel, 103 rooms with bath, off M1, at Exit 25; *Flying Horse*, 80 rooms (25 with bath); *Bridgeford*, 90 rooms (all with bath); *County*, 27 rooms (7 with bath); *Portland*, 50 rooms; *Victoria*, 110 rooms (23 with bath and 45 with shower), and *Black Boy*, 84 rooms (9 with bath). New *Strathdown*, 64 rooms with bath, scheduled to open by 1970.

For dancing, try *Eight Till Late* or *Hippo*.

OAKHAM (Rutland). Interesting county town, and close to good country. *George*, with only 5 rooms, and *Crown*, 30 rooms (5 with bath).

ROTHLEY (Leicestershire). *Rothley Court*, medieval country house hotel, birthplace of Lord Macaulay, 19 rooms (1 with bath).

SHREWSBURY (Shropshire). Fascinating county town with many old and interesting buildings. Has big flower show in August. Hotels include *Beauchamp*, 22 rooms (4 with bath); *Lion*, 72 rooms (32 with bath); *Lord Hill*, 26 rooms (4 with bath, 13 with shower); *Radbrook Hall*, 13 rooms (1 with bath) and *Prince Rupert*, 56 rooms (8 with bath).

SOUTHWELL (Nottinghamshire). Small cathedral town. Historic hotel, *Saracen's Head*, with very limited accommodation.

SPALDING (Lincolnshire). Centre of county's "tulipland". *White Hart*, 27 rooms, moderate. Book ahead for May Flower Festival.

STAFFORD (Staffordshire). Although there is a great deal of industry, the centre of the town contains many old buildings and is very picturesque. Handy for Cannock Chase. Hotels include *Swan*, 21 rooms, and *Tillington Hall*, 23 rooms (5 with bath).

TOWCESTER (Northamptonshire). Pleasant old town with reminders of its importance as a one-time coaching centre. Historic houses close at hand. The *Brave Old Oak* has 9 rooms.

WOLVERHAMPTON (Staffs.). Not far from Birmingham in this industrial city is the new-ish *Connaught*, 75 rooms (65 with bath, 10 with shower).

WOODHALL SPA (Lincolnshire). Health resort and golf centre. *Petwood*, 32 rooms (18 with bath), in delightful setting; first-class reasonable.

WORCESTER (Worcestershire). Interesting old city with fine cathedral and other old buildings. Has picturesque county cricket ground. The Three Choirs Festival, held every third year, is one of the big musical events in the country.

Hotels include new (1967) *Giffard* (Trust House), 104 rooms (all with bath); *Crown*, 27 rooms; *Diglis*, 13 rooms (2 with bath); *Loch Ryan*, 18 rooms, and *Star*, 33 rooms (6 with bath).

WORKSOP (Nottinghamshire). Country town from which to visit the Dukeries and Sherwood Forest. Small hotels include *Ashley*, 6 rooms; *Lion*, 13 rooms, and *Royal*, 10 rooms.

SEASIDE RESORTS.

There are two resorts on the Lincolnshire coast which offer the usual amenities and entertainments of the holiday town and are handily placed for visiting the inland countryside.

CLEETHORPES. Close to fishing port of Grimsby, but with beautiful sands, facilities for children, and entertainments. Hotels include *Kingsway*, 61 rooms (29 with bath) and *Lifeboat*, 25 rooms (2 with bath).

SKEGNESS. Extensive stretches of sand and plenty of amusement. Hotels include *County*, 46 rooms; *Links*, 29 rooms; *Lumley*, 18 rooms; *Seacroft*, 62 rooms (29 with bath) and *Vine*, 22 rooms (2 with bath).

Historic Houses Open to the Public

The entire Midland plain, especially the "shire" country and the "Dukeries", is liberally dotted with magnificent mansions, some still lived in, some derelict. Here are but a few:

HEREFORDSHIRE. *Croft Castle*, near Leominster. Continuously inhabited by the Croft family for 900 years, now National Trust. Open Easter through October, Wed., Thur., Sat., Sun. afternoons. *Dinmore Manor*, near Hereford, 14th century. Open daily, April through Sept. *Lower Brockhampton Hall*, near Bromyard. Small half-timbered manor house dating from about 1400. Open all year, Mons., Weds., Fris. and weekends.

LEICESTERSHIRE. *Belvoir Castle*, near Grantham. Seat of the Dukes of Rutland since Tudor times. Open April through September, Wed., Thurs., Sat., and Sun. afternoons. *Stapleford Park*, near Melton Mowbray; 16th-century home of Lord Gretton. Miniature passenger railway in grounds and lake with model passenger steamer. Open May through September, Thurs. and Sun. afternoons.

LINCOLNSHIRE. *Aubourn Hall*, near Lincoln. 16th-century house. Open May through August, Thursdays 2-6. *Fydell House*, Boston. Houses Pilgrim College. Open weekdays, all year. *Belton House*, Grantham. Built by Wren in the 15th century. Open daily Easter to September.

NORTHAMPTONSHIRE. *Rockingham Castle*, near Kettering. Medieval and Elizabethan house. Open Thurs., Easter through September. *Sulgrave Manor*, near Banbury. Home of ancestors of George Washington. Open daily, except Weds., all year.

Althorp, 16th-18th-century home of the Earl Spencer. Open May through September, Tues., Thurs., and Sun. afternoons. *Castle Ashby*, Elizabethan home of the Marquis of Northampton. Open Easter through September, Thurs., Sat. and Sun. afternoons. *Burghley House*, near Stamford. Elizabethan mansion of the Marquess of Exeter. Open Easter to early October, Tues., Wed., Thurs., Sat. and Sun.

NOTTINGHAMSHIRE. *Newstead Abbey*, north of Nottingham. Byron relics, Open Easter through September, afternoons. *Thoresby Hall*, one of the Dukeries houses. Open Easter through October, Wed., Thurs., Sat. and Sun. afternoons.

SHROPSHIRE. *Stokesay Castle*, Craven Arms. 13th-century moated manor house. Open daily, except Tuesdays, all year. *Coton Hall*, near Bridgnorth. Ancestral home of the Lees of Virginia. Open May through August, Sat. afternoons.

STAFFORDSHIRE. *Blithfield Hall*, near Rugeley. Elizabethan house with Georgian and Regency Gothic additions. Open Easter through September, Wed., Thurs., Sat., and Sunday afternoons.

WORCESTERSHIRE. *Harvington Hall*, near Kidderminster. Moated Tudor house containing priests' hiding places. Open daily except Mondays, all year.

MUSEUMS in the Midlands can be found, it would seem, in every village and town, but only a proportion of them are of interest to the traveller with a limited amount of time. Among the best are the following: Birchover: the *Heathcote Museum* (Bronze Age finds); Blithfield: *Museum of Childhood & Costume* (toys and uniforms); Burton-upon-Trent: *Burton-upon-Trent Museum & Art Gallery* (bird collections); Chesterfield: *Revolution House* (relics of 1688 revolution); Coalbrookdale: *Museum of Ironfounding* (anything made of iron); Coventry: *Herbert Art Gallery & Museum* (the Sutherland sketches for cathedral tapestry); Crich: the *Tramway Museum* (from horse to electric).

Derby: *Derby Museum & Art Gallery* (model railway); Grantham: *Grantham Museum* (Isaac Newton artifacts); Grimsby: *Doughty Museum* (model ships); Huntingdon: *The Cromwell Museum* (Cromwelliana); Leicester: *Museum & Art Gallery* (general collection), *Newarke Houses Museum* (the hosiery industry), *Belgrave Hall* (house, stables and gardens), *Jewry Wall Museum* (Roman Jewry Wall and baths); Lichfield: *Dr. Johnson's Birthplace* (relics of the great lexicographer); Lincoln: *City & County Museum* (Roman antiquities), *Usher Gallery* (collection of old watches), *Lincoln Cathedral Treasury* (one of four original copies of *Magna Carta*); Ludlow: *Ludlow Museum* (Roman objects and armour).

Northampton: *Central Museum & Art Gallery* (footwear), *Abington Museum* (Victoriana, Chinese ceramics); Nottingham; *City Museum & Art Gallery* (ceramics, more ceramics, and Wedgwood); Scunthorpe: *Borough Museum & Art Gallery* (John Wesley collection); Shrewsbury: *Rowley's House Museum* (Roman objects from Wroxeter); Shugborough: *Staffordshire County Museum & Mansion House* (industrial exhibits and general collection); Spalding: *Ayscoughfee Hall* (British birds); Stafford: *Izaak Walton Cottage and Museum* (his restored house); Stoke Bruerne: *Waterways Museum* (all about the canals, etc.); Stoke-on-Trent: *City Museum & Art Gallery* (Staffordshire pottery), *Ford Green Hall* (Izaak Walton and the Quakers), *Arnold Bennett Museum* (his early home), *Spode-Copeland Museum & Art Gallery* (Spode blue ware, bone china, etc.), *The Wedgwood Museum* (Josiah Wedgwood's prides and joys); Sulgrave: *Sulgrave Manor* (home of George Washington's ancestors).

Wall: *Letocetum Museum* (Roman finds); Wolverhampton: *Municipal Art Gallery & Museum* (enamels and Staffordshire pottery); Wroxeter: *Viroconium Museum* (Roman finds).

Exploring the Midlands

It is, of course, difficult to think of any one centre for exploring an area which stretches from the uplands of the Welsh borders on the west across England to the sandy shores of Lincolnshire by the North Sea, but for the central part of it, as well as the Shakespeare country (which is dealt with in the previous chapter), Birmingham, with its radiating network of road and rail communications, may well be chosen as typical of the great city that gives such easy access to the rural scene.

In recent years, the city centre has undergone so many structural alterations that, as the official guide book of the local authority says, "there is more of the future to be seen coming into being than there is of the past left to contemplate". Indeed, its £1,000,000,000 development schemes will result in it being a fitting monument to that late 20th-century outlook that is making it one of the most outstanding cities not only in Great Britain but in the whole of Europe.

No one can fail to be impressed with the 250-foot circular Rotunda building that rises above the tower of St. Martin's Church, itself severely damaged in an air raid of 1941, but restored through funds raised mainly by local industrialists and businessmen. Neither can one fail to admire that superb mixture of the old and new at the Bull Ring, where, in keeping with a tradition going back to the 12th century, an open-air market still exists, but with its stalls backed by a new centre opened by Prince Philip in 1964 and containing supermarkets and stores, restaurants, banks, and one of the busiest omnibus stations in the land.

Culture occupies an important place in the life of Birmingham. Its permanent symphony orchestra, which gives concerts in the Town Hall, is renowned throughout England, and its theatres, including the famous *Repertory Theatre* (established in 1913), put on first-class stage shows.

Among the many other facilities are the Museum and Art Gallery in Congreve Street which possesses one of the finest art collections in the provinces and also natural history, archeological and ethnographical collections; the branch Museum of Science and Industry in Newhall Street and the unique Aston Hall, one of the finest Jacobean houses in the country.

Coventry and Rugby

Eastwards are the other big industrial centres of Coventry and Rugby. In spite of Coventry's strong links with industry (and, particularly, motor-car construction), there is much evidence of culture in a city that has undergone important structural alterations since it was the victim of Nazi aggression from the air.

Despite the modern appearance, particularly of the cathedral (which was the object of a particularly foul air attack and was rebuilt in contemporary style and re-opened in 1962), Coventry is a place rich in history.

THE MIDLANDS

As long ago as 1043, Leofric, Earl of Chester, and his wife, Godiva, founded a Benedictine monastery which was to become one of the richest in the country, so that only sixty years later, the seat of the bishopric was transferred from Lichfield to Coventry.

Lady Godiva is, of course, always associated with Coventry on account of her riding through the streets of the town in a naked state, and while this incident, if it did take place at all, has often been made the subject of ridicule, it was in reality evidence of the lady's great piety and feeling for the poor. Time and time again she asked her husband to relax the taxations which were causing distress in the neighbourhood but he always refused, until one day he said in exasperation the request would be granted if she would ride through town naked, on a horse. This she did, and in all fairness to the Earl, it must be said, the taxations were relaxed. (Her ride also gave rise to a new expression in English, when a tailor named Tom peeped through a hole to watch her, in spite of the townspeople's pledge that all would remain behind shuttered windows during her ride. According to the legend, "Peeping Tom" was blinded for his trouble.)

Many have criticized the architecture of the new cathedral, but all who go to the city should see, behind the altar, the Graham Sutherland tapestry, said to be the largest in the world, as well as the brilliant abstract stained glass windows which rise from floor to roof, and the giant wall of engraved glass forming the front.

In the city, too, is the new *Belgrade Theatre*, which stages some of the finest productions in this part of the country.

Rugby is the site of engineering works and a famous public school founded in 1567, the scene of the well-known boys' favourite, *Tom Brown's Schooldays*, where in 1823, the game of Rugby football is said to have been born. A tablet in the wall of the school close recalls the last incident, the inscription reading: "This stone commemorates the exploit of William Webb Ellis, who, with a fine disregard for the rules of football as played in his time, first took the ball in his arms and ran with it, thus originating the distinctive feature of the Rugby game."

From Rugby we can leave Warwickshire and enter Northamptonshire, one of the loveliest of English counties.

whose charms are all too little known, even to discerning Britons.

Northampton and Kettering

Northampton, the county town, dates from pre-Christian times, an iron age fortification at Hunsbury Hill being the first evidence of settlement. There were several periods of Danish occupation in the 10th and 11th centuries. After the Norman Conquest, Simon de Senlis fortified the town. The castle which he built became famous for the holding of parliaments by Henry I and notable as the place of trial of Thomas à Becket, Primate of England in Henry II's reign. The castle was destroyed by Charles II following the town's support for the Republicans in the civil war.

The Battle of Northampton (1460), when the Yorkists captured Henry VI, was one of the most decisive in the Wars of the Roses. The town suffered plague (1637) and a devastating fire (1675), which virtually destroyed the whole town.

Around the county town, however, there has been more of the permanence usually associated with the Midlands. Althorp House, a few miles to the northwest, was partly remodelled in the 18th century, but so successfully as to make it one of the most imposing mansions in these parts. Even lovelier is the Elizabethan façade of Castle Ashby, east of Northampton, the home of the Marquesses of Northampton. Even older are the Saxon churches at Earls Barton and Brixworth.

Sulgrave Manor

Americans may want to detour from Northampton to Sulgrave Manor, built about 1560 by Lawrence Washington, a direct ancestor of the first president of the United States. It's a modest Tudor house with a slate roof, about 8 miles northeast of Banbury on a secondary road. It is reached from Northampton on A45 and B4525. Besides various mementoes of the family, there's a portrait of George Washington by Gilbert Stuart over the fireplace in the great hall. The manor was purchased on British initiative, restored, and has been endowed by the Colonial Dames of America. At Little Brington, a few miles north, is another Washington home, and at Great Brington, several Washington brasses in the village church.

Northwards the road (A43) goes through Kettering, a

market town that boasts a charter dating from 1227, in Rockingham Forest, once one of the largest forests in the Midlands and still with trees in plenty scattered about the wide valley of the Welland. Above the old stone houses of Rockingham village stands Rockingham Castle, whose history stretches back to the reign of William the Conqueror, and Boughton House (home of the Dukes of Buccleuch), which has been described as one of the finest specimens of a 17th-century house in the country.

Uppingham, across the county boundary from Rockingham on A6003 is famed for its public school, founded in 1584. From here, the road continues through a land of waving corn and pasturage for sheep to Oakham, capital of the county and every bit as unpretentious as its surroundings. We would be wrong to imagine that an unobtrusive place is naturally one devoid of interest. Oakham possessed a castle in the 12th century and, if much of this has disappeared, the remaining great hall still serves a useful purpose in the affairs of the neighbourhood, for it houses the assizes and sessions. An interesting feature is that its interior walls are almost entirely covered with horseshoes, a survival of the ancient right whereby the Ferrers family, who are descended from the *ferrarius* (chief of the shoesmiths) in the invading army of William the Conqueror, have the right to claim toll of a horseshoe from every peer passing through Oakham for the first time. The collection contains a shoe presented by Queen Elizabeth I, as well as those from later occupants of the English throne, including Elizabeth II, who presented a horseshoe to the lord of the manor in 1967.

Leicestershire

Now we enter Leicestershire, after retracing our route south on A6003 to A427, near Corby, where we turn west. Once again we are not conscious of any great change. Agriculture still holds sway, and the talk in country inns during the appropriate season is of hounds and horsemen.

Market Harborough stands on the border of Leicestershire and Northamptonshire, and its atmosphere is that of both. Its expanding population of approximately 13,000 find employment in over 50 factories manufacturing corsets and swimsuits, suits, rubber products, batteries and many more varied products. Its weekly market attracts dealers and farmers from all over the Midland shires. The two main architectural treasures of the town are the 14th-century parish church, with its fine 161-foot crocketed broach spire and the 17th-century pillared grammar school, standing adjacent to the church. There is also a wealth of interest in the 17th- and 18th-century coaching inns, namely, *The Angel, The Peacock*, and the *Three Swans*.

Next, to Leicester, on the A6. Here, only the Norman hall of the castle remains—rather a pity, because it was from Leicester Castle that the great Simon de Montfort summoned the forerunner of the present British Parliament, the organization that gave birth to democratic government in the mid-13th century. In the vicinity can be seen Trinity Hospital, which was founded in the time of Edward III (parts of the original chapel remain), the Newarke gateway, the Church of St. Mary de Castro, and some surviving specimens of 17th-century domestic architecture. But all these buildings are mere youngsters when compared with the extensive Roman remains at the Jewry Wall site in the centre of the city.

Charnwood Forest and Nottinghamshire

A few miles to the northwest of Leicester is Charnwood Forest, a miniature mountain district, with its remnants of primeval forest and strange outcrops of the oldest rocks in the land. Newtown Linford, loveliest of all Leicestershire villages, where thatched roofs and half-timbered cottages line the sides of the road, is easily reached from Leicester on B5327, and bordering the village is Bradgate Park, once the estate of the Grey family. Bradgate Park is certainly unlike the average Midlands park of green pastures and close-cropped lawns. Rather it is a true remnant of ancient forest, abounding with rocky sloped miniature dales and clumps of hoary old oaks. The herds of deer that roam unfettered through the craggy valleys add to the appearance of an old-time hunting chase.

Of special interest to those in search of the historic are the ruins of Bradgate Hall, where the tragic Lady Jane Grey, the "Tudor Rose", was born in 1537 and lived until her ill-fated marriage to Lord Dudley, son of Warwick, the haughty king-maker, 16 years later. Only a few weeks afterwards the girl had finished her nine days' reign as Queen of England by being

THE MIDLANDS

brought to the scaffold by the vengeful hate of "Bloody" Mary Tudor. On her execution day the oaks around the hall were lopped, and evidence of this can be seen on the old trees.

Bradgate Park is typical of the rest of Charnwood, and go where you will in that compact area, which is wholly contained in a triangle with its points at Leicester, Ashby-de-la-Zouch, and Loughborough, you will find the same areas of fine heathlands and enchanting woods that seem so different from any so far visited in the Midlands. Now, indeed, is the topographical character of the scene changing. The minor undulations of Northamptonshire and Rutland have given place to something a little sterner, something a little more dramatic, yet so gradual has it all been that not until we are reminded of the fact do we realize just what has happened.

At the northwestern edge of the forest is Ashby-de-la-Zouch, (on A50), where the earls of Huntingdon once had their castle. The first Lord Hastings erected the massive keep known as the Hastings Tower. He was executed by Richard III in 1483 and his son Edward fought on Bosworth Field against the king in revenge. The grandson of the first earl was created Earl of Huntingdon by Henry VIII. In 1569 Mary, Queen of Scots, stayed a night in Ashby Castle as his prisoner and in 1586 she was again lodged there.

Anne, wife of James I, visited the Castle in 1603 and the monarch himself came here in 1617, with his entire following. In 1634 Charles I and Henrietta Maria imposed themselves on the earl with their suite. With the outbreak of the Civil War in 1642, Henry Hastings, Earl of Huntingdon, was in charge of the local Royalist forces. Following Edgehill he fortified the castle and provisioned it. Then he commenced to resist the Parliamentarian leader, Lord Grey. The castle became a haven of refuge for Royalists and in May, 1643, the queen again stayed a night at Ashby.

The siege of Ashby Castle began in November, 1644, and continued for more than a year. Finally, the Royalist forces surrendered, Colonel-General Hastings, then Lord Loughborough, having obtained very favourable terms. In 1648 Lord Grey, Hastings' enemy, was appointed Governor of the Castle and the buildings were demolished. After the Restoration, the Hastings family lived at Donington and Ashby Castle was left to decay.

In *Ivanhoe* Sir Walter Scott laid the scene of the famous tournament, in which Ivanhoe and the Black Knight took so prominent a part, at Ashby. Sir Walter's fertile imagination created the Ashby tournament field. The publication of the novel directed attention to the historic remains of the great fortress and the first Marquis of Hastings took measures for their preservation. It is now preserved by the Ministry of Public Building and Works as an ancient monument.

The remains of the castle today comprise the great tower, parts of the walls and towers surrounding the courtyard and various domestic buildings.

East, on A512, is Loughborough, mainly an engineering town and the home of one of the largest bell foundries in England, which has produced bells and carillons that grace the most famous churches and cathedrals in the world.

Derby and Nottingham

A detour to Derby can be made from Loughborough, up the A6. One of the most important industrial cities of the Midlands, and handily situated for Dovedale and the south Derbyshire countryside, Derby has many old buildings which are reminders of its historic past, including All Saints' Church, with its embattled tower dating from the early 16th century. It has important links with the early development of the woollen and silk trades, as well as the manufacture of exquisite Crown Derby china and Rolls Royce engines.

Derby has a professional football side, Derby County, and the Derbyshire County Cricket Club plays many of its home games on a ground close to the city centre. Plays are presented in the *Playhouse,* and concerts at the Art Gallery.

From Loughborough one can go north on A60 to Nottingham, apparently founded by the Danes in the second part of the 9th century. There is much to be seen in the city, which contains a truly magnificent council house, a castle perched on the top of a great crag above the city—built by the Duke of Newcastle in 1679 on the site of an earlier erection and now housing the municipal art collection—and an ancient inn, *Ye Trip to Jerusalem*, which claims to have enjoyed the patronage of the Crusaders towards the close of the 12th century. Since 1963 Nottingham has had an exciting new theatre, which presents its plays in a cylindrical auditorium.

THE MIDLANDS

The *Theatre Royal*, an older house, presents plays, operas and ballets. While here, try to see Wollaton Hall. Formerly the seat of the Willoughby family, it houses a Natural History Museum, and is considered to be one of the finest specimens of Elizabethan architecture.

Some ten miles to the northeast on A612 is Southwell, raised to the seat of a bishopric in 1884 when its truly grand parish church was given the title of a minster, yet in spite of this ecclesiastical distinction Southwell itself has never received rank as a city. Here Charles I stayed at the *Saracen's Head Inn* immediately prior to surrendering himself to the Scottish army.

Newark and Belvoir

Just east of Southwell and on the Great North Road, is Newark-on-Trent, with its grey old castle still standing solidly above an arm of the River Trent and a general look of well-being befitting a town with a treasured historical past and the centre of a thriving agricultural business.

Built by Bishop Alexander of Lincoln in the early part of the 12th century and on the site of an older fortification of sorts, Newark Castle maintained its links with the See of Lincoln until 1547, when it passed to the crown. Prior to that, it had often put up a stout resistance to the monarchs during the troublous times that marked the reigns of kings Stephen and John, albeit the last-mentioned king actually died within its walls in October, 1216. When Royalist and Commonwealth armies fought during the long drawn-out Civil Wars of the first part of the 17th century, however, it stood equally firm in its loyalty to the crown. Three times it had to withstand sieges, and in the end surrender only came at the command of King Charles I himself.

Its church, not only one of the largest, but also one of the most magnificent, in the whole country, is dedicated to St. Mary Magdalene, and although much of its rich interior belongs to the reign of Henry IV, there are parts, such as the Norman crypt and the Early English tower, belonging to an earlier period of history.

With many old inns and a number of other interesting buildings, including the half-timbered Governor's House,

Newark is a fine example of the historic Midlands town that retains so much of its past while still playing an important part in the trade and commerce of today.

Newark is only a few miles from the Lincolnshire border and, indeed, the Great North Road (the A1) crosses the county boundary in a very short time on its way south to Grantham another lovely old town containing much to remind the traveller of its even greater importance in the days of the stage coach.

Like that of so many of these East Midland towns, its church is a gem of ecclesiastical architecture, both outside and within, with the bulk of it in 13th-century work.

One of the greatest glories of Grantham, however, is its wealth of old inns, including the *Angel*, with its lovely 15th-century stone front facing the market place. It was once a hostelry of the Knights Templars and has its links with the English kings—King John holding a court here in 1213 and King Richard III visiting it on the occasion when he signed the death warrant of Buckingham in 1493.

Two of England's finest historic houses lie within easy reach of the town. One, Belton House, the seat of the Earls of Brownlow, virtually joins it on the north and is noted for its fine parklands and Grinlon Gibbons carvings, and seven miles to the west, actually in Leicestershire, is Belvoir Castle, the home of the Duke of Rutland. It has been in the hands of his family, the Manners, since 1525. The castle itself, which is said to be second only to Windsor in magnificence, was founded soon after William of Normandy took over the English throne, but was virtually rebuilt after a fire in 1816.

Grantham makes a good centre for excursions into the country of the fens, formerly a vast region of swamps but now, thanks to a splendidly-kept system of canals and drains which have ensured the reclamation of thousands of acres to land, one of the most important potato-growing districts of England. Here, too, the cultivation of bulbs makes this one of the chief horticultural areas in the country, and no tourist in the vicinity of the East Midlands at the appropriate time of the year should miss the opportunity of paying a visit to the Lincolnshire tulip fields when the colourful flowers present a picture that is unforgettable.

Lincolnshire

Not all, however, is given over to agriculture. The villages contain much of beauty and this is a land of magnificent churches, with the famous "Stump", the 272 foot-high tower of St. Botolph's Church, at Boston, a landmark for miles around.

Boston can be reached from Grantham by way of Sleaford, which is in the centre of the country hunted by another famous pack of hounds, the Blankney. Boston, of course, is of interest to all American visitors who like to recall that it was from this Lincolnshire town that, in 1630, Isaac Johnson and John Winthrop showed their disapproval of the then prevailing conditions by crossing the Atlantic and helping to found the Massachusetts town of the same name. The Puritans had tried to set sail for Holland in 1607, but they were arrested, tried and sentenced; the Guildhall cells in which they and their courageous hopes were imprisoned can still be visited.

The "Stump", which once housed a light that not only guided ships coming to the old port but also served to direct wayfarers crossing the treacherous marshes, has also its links with the Massachusetts town, for in 1931 funds for its restoration were raised on the western side of the Atlantic. The church itself is of interest as one of the largest parish churches in England and containing a good deal of splendid architecture. Climb to the top of the Stump on a clear day and you will see 40 miles of fenland stretching away under the open skies, the towers of Ely Cathedral in the far distance and the ships on the River Witham riding out to sea.

As a port, Boston (originally "Botolph's Town") which had formerly played a big part in the wood trade with the continent, suffered a period of decline between the middle of the 14th and the mid-18th centuries as a result of the silting up of the river, but in 1764, the channel was deepened and since then, the construction of docks and a new river bed has meant that a considerable amount of trade is still handled each year.

Boston's southern neighbour, Spalding, is the capital of "tulipland", and thousands of visitors tour the area in springtime to see its vast acres ablaze with tulips, daffodils and hyacinths. A Tulip Festival with a gay Flower Parade is held in Spalding itself every May. Though not quite such a massive display as in the Dutch Holland across the North Sea,

Lincolnshire's Holland provides, nevertheless, a brilliant show of variegated floral beauty.

While the southern part of Lincolnshire is flat, north of a line taking in the city of Lincoln and the towns of Horncastle and Sleaford, the chalk uplands known as the Wolds stretch north to the Humber, beyond which comes their virtual continuation through Yorkshire, with Flamborough Head as one of the extremities. Compared with the heights of the Pennines and the Lake Country (and even the Cotswold hills of the Midlands), they are insignificant, yet they give a character to the scene which is entirely different from that of the Fen country and, on the western escarpment, provide fascinating long-range views across miles of flat countryside.

A few miles north of Boston on B1192 is the red brick Tattershall Castle, built by Ralph Cromwell, Lord Treasurer to the Crown, in the first part of the 15th century. It was bequeathed to the National Trust, who, of course, permit public access, by Lord Curzon in 1926. Americans should notice the lovely stone carved mantel pieces which so nearly found a home in their own country. Indeed, they were actually sold for export in 1911 and had got as far as Tilbury Docks, when they were reprieved and restored to their rightful setting. Nearby, to the north, are the lovely Spa gardens in Woodhall Spa, a little place famous for its rich springs of iodine and bromine salts, and its superb golf course.

A few more miles or so towards Horncastle is the village of Scrivelsby, the home of the King's Hereditary Champion who, in the days when the British monarchs were crowned in Westminster Hall, had the right of riding into the assembly, clad in a suit of armour, and challenging anyone to mortal combat who dared to dispute the titles of the sovereign. Today, he has the honour of carrying the Standard of England at the coronation ceremony in Westminster Abbey. The office of king's champion was created by the Norman kings and was first held by the Marmions, then passed, by marriage, to the Dymokes. The ancestral tombs of both families are to be seen in the village church.

Horncastle, to the east of Lincoln, is a lovely study of red brick buildings and gabled inns. In the days before tractors became commonplace on the English farms, this land was

THE MIDLANDS

the Mecca of farmfolk from a wide area wanting to buy sound specimens of horseflesh at the annual August fair; even today one is reminded of the scenes described by George Borrow in the pages of his *Romany Rye*.

Lincoln

Journeying westwards, one again sees magnificent stone towers dominating the landscape—those of Lincoln Cathedral, set high on a limestone hill overlooking the town. Like most of the cathedrals in this part of Britain, it was begun in Norman times, suffered fire, natural disaster and pillaging, and has been partly rebuilt, restored and added to at intervals ever since. Inside the cathedral, be sure to look at the intricately-carved font, the rose window at the south end, and its greatest glory—the 13th-century Angel Choir. Lincoln also has its castle, with *two* mounds and a particularly attractive Guildhall, built above the Stonebow Gateway. The insistent notes of the 14th-century Mote Bell on the Guildhall roof still ring out to summon members to council meetings. One of the 19th century's most famous poets, Alfred Lord Tennyson, was born at The Rectory in Somersby, a quiet Lincolnshire village, and you will find an extensive and fascinating collection of the Tennyson family's books and correspondence in the Lincoln City Library.

North-east of Lincoln is the racing centre of Market Rasen, near to which the Tennyson family lived, and between there and the sea is Louth, where perhaps the greatest of them, Alfred, attended the local grammar school. The poet laureate for 42 years died in 1892 and was buried in Westminster Abbey.

The North Lincolnshire coast has great expanses of sandy beach, as well as holiday resorts at Skegness, Mablethorpe, Sutton and Cleethorpes, the last virtually a suburb of the fishing port of Grimsby. Immingham, in the northeast of the county, was the port from which the Pilgrim Fathers made their second, and successful, attempt to reach exile in Holland, whence in 1620 they sailed for the New World.

West from Lincoln, roads go through a succession of interesting villages scattered about the undulating countryside to Newark, and so back to Nottingham.

Sherwood Forest

North of Nottingham is Sherwood Forest, indelibly associated with Robin Hood and his exploits. The road from Nottingham (the A60) passes the grounds of Newstead Abbey (open to the public), which was once a priory of the Black Canons and for many years the home of Lord Byron, who seems to have done everything within his power to ruin the estate he had inherited, cutting down trees, killing the deer, and allowing the hall itself to fall into a terrible state of neglect. Yet Byron's name is still treasured in the vicinity. Nottingham is proud of its association with so great a poet.

Mansfield, the next town, is a strange mixture of old and new. The civic authorities have done much to eradicate some of the less savoury remains of past years, but there are many old buildings still to be seen, as well as some dwellings cut out of the living rock, said to have been used by British refugees at the time of the Roman occupation of the Midlands. It is a convenient centre for exploring the Sherwood Forest, the Dukeries and the Robin Hood country.

Sherwood Forest and the almost legendary Robin Hood are inseparable. Naturally enough, doubts have been expressed as to the existence of such an outlaw, but although history is largely silent, authentic references are not lacking, and it would seem that the stories are based on something rather more substantial than mere legend. Robin Hood, we are told, died in 1247 at the age of 87—you can see his grave at Kirklees, in the Calder Valley, Yorkshire. That was a time when the Normans imposed harsh laws to govern their forests, and many a Saxon defied them and took his share of venison. Naturally, such men assumed the status of local heroes; stories of their exploits were handed down from one generation to another, and it might well be that Robin Hood is but a composite of all who defied the laws of the Norman overlords and endeavoured to preserve the freedom of the forest.

So far as Sherwood Forest is concerned, there is a record of a trial for offences and trespass being held as long ago as 1160 —about the time when Robin Hood seems to have been in action—and it remained a possession of the Crown until the 18th century, when various sections were sold to local landowners. Today, there are still some fine woodland glades and

THE MIDLANDS

outstanding individual trees, of which the Queen, or Major, Oak, near Edwinstowe, is worth a special visit. Although its top was blown off in a terrific storm some 50 or 60 years ago, its trunk still has a girth of over 36 feet.

The northern part of the old forest was long given over to various ducal estates and that produced its name of the Dukeries. Here are the parklands of Rufford, Clumber, Thoresby, and Welbeck, with their grand stretches of woodland, ornamental waters, and spacious areas of turf. Thoresby Hall is still in private ownership, but Rufford Abbey has been taken over by the Ministry of Public Building and Works (who are restoring it) and Welbeck Abbey is now an army training college. The great house of Clumber has been pulled down, but the park, with its magnificent Lime Tree Avenue, is always worth a visit.

South Derbyshire and Staffordshire

We can travel westward on A632 through part of Derbyshire, passing through Chesterfield, with its strange crooked spire, to Matlock, on B6015, where the Derwent River flows through a spectacular gorge, and so by B5036 and 5035 through Wirksworth to Ashbourne. Here the scenery is vastly different from any we have so far encountered. Gone are the rolling pastures and expanses of woodland. Here are moors and crags. We are in the southern Pennine country, a region that falls more appropriately into the North Country section of this book than the Midlands.

South of Ashbourne there are gentler scenes. The Dove can be followed to its junction with the Trent southwest of Derby, if you are good at map-reading. Derby is an industrial town, retaining many old houses and an 18th-century cathedral. From Derby, a westerly route can be taken through the quiet countryside featured by George Eliot in her novels, and so approach Staffordshire.

Staffordshire, it's true, contains much that is unlovely. No one would visit the Potteries for the sake of beauty. The literary pilgrim, however, may care to see something of the "Five Towns", so well described by Arnold Bennett. If fine scenery is your aim, you will find it in Needwood Forest, west of Burton-on-Trent, once a royal hunting ground and still containing many tracts of ancient woodland, and in nearby

Cannock Chase, some 30,000 acres of moorland and bracken-covered slopes near Rugeley.

Lichfield makes a good centre from which to explore these areas, and Lichfield itself contains much of interest. Its cathedral, dedicated to St. Chad, has three lofty spires, known poetically as the "Ladies of the Vale", and in the market place the Johnson Museum is the place where the celebrated Dr. Johnson was born in 1709.

Shropshire and Shrewsbury

South and west of Staffordshire is Shropshire, or Salop, in the old style, one of England's fairest counties. Shrewsbury (or "Shrosebry" as the Salopians call it), stands within a great loop of the Severn River, and few towns in the country can show a greater wealth of magpie-coloured houses. Grope Lane, Fish Street, and Butcher Row, which, appropriately enough, was once occupied by the butchers of Shrewsbury, are packed with treasures in this beautiful form of early domestic architecture. There are also a number of fine old inns, among them the *Lion Hotel,* dating from the 16th century. In the hotel's beautiful Robert Adam ballroom, which has echoed to the magic of Paganini and Jenny Lind, the 'Swedish Nightingale', monthly concerts of classical music are held from September to March and are an outstanding attraction. Tickets for concert and dinner cost around £3 ($7.20). Write to the Manager, Lion Hotel, Shrewsbury, for details.

Shrewsbury, however, has sterner things to show. Near the railway station the red sandstone castle built by Roger de Montgomery and added to by Edward I, stands on a mound dominating the town, and in the Wyle Cop, up which the coaches clattered on their way from London to Holyhead, is the house where Henry Tudor, soon to become Henry VII, stayed in 1485 before the decisive Battle of Bosworth. Shrewsbury also has its associations with Mary Webb, the novelist, for she and her husband came each market day and maintained a stall for the produce grown in their gardens at Pontesbury and Lyth Hill.

The uplands that culminate in the wild ridges of Stiperstones and Long Mynd to the southwest, however, are the most poignant links with Mary Webb. At Pontesbury, southwest of Shrewsbury on A488, we reach the village where she lived for

THE MIDLANDS

many years, and on the opposite side of Pontesbury Hill is Ministerley, a bonny little spot where the church contains relics of the maidens' garlands at one time carried on the coffins of young unmarried girls and, after the funeral, placed over their pews. These consist of thin wooden poles with paper garlands hanging from them. The end of each is carved in the shape of a heart, inscribed with the initials of some girl and the year of her burial.

Ministerley lies near the foot of the narrow ridge of the Stiperstones. From the crest one looks eastward into the heart of England; westward, to the heights that mark the border of England and Wales.

Eastward, too, one often sees a solitary hill rising above the plains. This is the Wrekin, a hill that geologists claim to be the oldest in the land. That may mean little to the average visitor. Far better to record that Housman and others have invested it with some of their poetic charm. Whatever other hill in England is climbed, the Wrekin should not be missed. To stand on its isolated summit and look around is to see what makes up so much of the Midland scene.

Keeping to the west of the county, however, we are within a few leagues of Wales. This was the turbulent Marcher Country, the land where fights and raids and all the turmoil of medieval years made their presence felt and contributed to the local forms of architecture. Down the valley, the road south from Shrewsbury (A49) leads to Craven Arms, a small market town situated in the beautiful countryside of South Shropshire. Almost one mile south of Craven Arms is Stokesay Castle, a unique example of a fortified manor house and the oldest and most complete specimen in the country. Adjacent to the castle is the Church of St. John the Baptist, which was formerly the private chapel belonging to the castle and is now the parish church. West of Craven Arms the road stretches out towards Wales and to that moorish corner of Salop where one may find the four villages of Clunton, Clunbury, Clungunford, and Clun, claimed by the poet as "the quietest places under the sun". But that quietness did not come until after the border uproars had died down. There are castles and fortified houses to show the former state of the land.

See Ludlow, with perhaps a greater display of black-and-white buildings than Shrewsbury itself, and then visit the great castle. There are great hills on either side of Ludlow and its neighbouring dales. To the northwest is the heathery mound of Long Mynd, with the ancient track of the Port Way running along its crest; eastward are the higher Clee Hills and, to the north, the wooded ridge of Wenlock Edge.

Worcestershire and Herefordshire

From Ludlow the Teme Valley can be followed on A456 and A443 through Tenbury and Lindridge, with the great hills rising on either hand, into Worcester, that ever-lovely city with its cathedral that still embraces part of the monastery founded in the 7th century by monks from the Yorkshire Abbey of Whitby. It encompasses, in fact, a whole host of ancient buildings, including the Hospital of St. Wulfstan, known as the Commandery, with its latticed windows and black-and-white walls.

South of the outline of the Malvern Hills, running almost due north and south for a length of nine miles and rising to 1,395 feet at the highest point, is the Worcestershire Beacon. The views from the top are glorious and expansive, and centuries ago early man knew those views, for on the summit of Herefordshire Beacon are remains of one of the best specimens of a fortified British camp in the country. The Malvern towns, noted health resorts, are at the foot.

Herefordshire lies to the west, a beautiful parkland between the Malvern Hills and the uplands of the Welsh Border. Go there to see the loveliest villages in England, matchless gems in black and white, and the rich farmlands with the comfortable-looking native breed of cattle, their white faces looking like masks and contrasting with their brown coats. Go by A4103 from Worcester to Hereford itself, still sleeping beside the River Wye and with its magnificent cathedral containing the *Mappa Mundi*, one of the oldest maps of the world, the work of a monk of the early 14th century, one Richard de Haldingham. Here, too, are black-and-white buildings. Indeed, Hereford, more than any other cathedral city, seems to reflect the unsullied spirit of its surrounding countryside. Hereford is the gateway to the most romantic parts of the Wye Valley, which, if followed, will take the traveller away to Chepstow and the Severn.

THE NORTH

Backbone of England

A glance at a map of northern England shows a long elevated ridge of hills, known as the Pennine Chain, running right down the centre from the Scottish borders to the edge of the Midland shires. School children learn to speak of the Pennine Chain as "the backbone of England", and such a definition is most appropriate.

In the first place, the whole of North Country life owes something to the influence of that range of hills. Its very position means that it acts as the watershed for many rivers, and as these drain to east and west they naturally serve all parts of northern England. On the banks of the rivers are the great towns and cities of Lancashire, Yorkshire, Durham, and Northumberland. Where they enter the sea we find ports and ship-building yards of importance; higher up we have the textile centres, where the waters born among those Pennine hills are possessed with peculiar qualities of their own to enable the wool to be cleansed properly.

On the wilder slopes of the hills sheep farming is carried on, and it is significant that Bradford, the Yorkshire city that lies on the edge of the Pennine chain of hills themselves, is the greatest woollen centre in the world. That elevated barrier has its effect on the climate, arresting the progress of the rain clouds that generally travel from the west across the Atlantic, so giving the central and west sections of the region a heavier annual rainfall than places farther to the east—a factor that the farmer, especially the crop-grower, must take into consideration.

But the term "backbone" has another significance that few North Country people themselves trouble to appreciate. Great chunks of the Pennine hills are, quite literally, composed of bones—yes, backbones—the bones of myriads of fishes and insects that once lived in the shallow seas of which northern England formed the bed. These bones, accumulating on the floor of those seas, built up the limestone that is today a feature of many sections of the Pennines. All that, of course, happened long before recorded history.

Practical Information for the North

HOTELS AND RESTAURANTS

ASHBOURNE (Derbyshire). Good centre for Dovedale. An interesting custom is the "football" match at Shrovetide when the "goals" are at opposite ends of the town and practically every youth in the place takes part in a real rough and tumble affair.

Green Man and Black's Head, 11 rooms, good. Also the *Sunnyside* (Mayfield), 7 rooms.

BAKEWELL (Derbyshire). Handy for the Derbyshire dales and historic houses at Chatsworth and Haddon. Famous for its own brand of tarts, which are, of course, obtainable elsewhere.

Rutland Arms, where Jane Austen wrote much of *Pride and Prejudice*, 30 rooms (3 with bath). First-class reasonable. *Milford House*, 9 rooms. Eat at *Rutland Arms*.

BAMBURGH (Northumberland). Coastal village with spectacular border castle. *Victoria*, 28 rooms, moderate. Good local food at *Lord Crewe Arms*.

BERWICK-ON-TWEED (Northumberland). On coast and close to beautiful Tweed Valley and good coastal scenery. Holy Island a few miles to south. *King's Arms*, first-class hotel with 30 rooms (6 with bath); *Castle*, also first-class, 13 rooms.

BRADFORD (Yorks). First-class superior: *Victoria*, 54 rooms (34 with bath); *Midland*, 81 rooms (23 with bath). Also: *Alexandra*, 45 rooms (2 with bath). Eat at the *Midland*.

BUXTON (Derbyshire). Inland spa town, with orchestral concerts and theatre. Excellent centre for Derbyshire dales and moors. *Palace*, first-class reasonable hotel with 131 rooms (55 with bath); *St. Ann's*, smaller but first-class, 58 rooms (12 with bath); *Lee Wood*, very comfortable with good home-cooked food, 39 rooms (5 with bath); *Old Hall*, 50 rooms (2 with bath).

Also: *Buckingham*, 42 rooms; *Hartington*, 17 rooms; *Portland*, 26 rooms.

CASTLETON (Derbyshire). Centre for Peak District. Interesting caves in immediate vicinity. *Old Nag's Head*. Small hotel with period furniture and a reputation for excellent food. 11 rooms.

CARLISLE (Cumberland). Ancient cathedral city by Hadrian's Wall and Scottish border; near Lake District. *Crown & Mitre*, 80 rooms (25 with bath); *County & Station*, 71 rooms (18 with bath); both first-class reasonable. Also *Central*, 69 rooms (7 with bath).

CATTERICK (Yorks). A good centre, just off the Great North Road at Leeming Bar. Close to race-course, which stages flat racing in summer and steeplechasing in winter.

The *Bridge House* at Catterick Bridge, close to the race-course, is an old coaching inn with 13 rooms (3 with bath). First-class reasonable. Also in the old village is the *Angel*, 9 rooms.

CHESTER (Cheshire). One of the most interesting cities in the north. Good centre for the Cheshire countryside and also for the Welsh borders. The May race meeting on the Roodee attracts the best horses in the country. A convenient country hotel nearby is the *Travel Inn*, at Bruxton. 12 rooms (all with bath).

First-class hotels include the *Blossoms*, 300 years old, 109 rooms (52 with bath); the *Grosvenor*, 103 rooms (all with bath or shower) and the *Queen*, 86 rooms (29 with bath).

Also the *Dene*, 40 rooms (2 with (bath and the *Oaklands*, 20 rooms (3 with bath). Dine at the *Blossoms*.

DARLINGTON (Durham). Biggest hotel is the *King's Head*, 72 rooms (37 with bath). Others include the *Imperial*, 34 rooms (1 with bath), and the *Fleece*, 17 rooms.

Some 6 miles away, at Piercebridge, is the *George*, 7 rooms, a delightful hostelry with first-class food.

DURHAM (Durham). Historic city with castle, cathedral and university. Fascinating views across River Wear. Good place from which to visit the surrounding area.

The *Royal County*, 66 bedrooms (4 with bath) is first-class. Also: *The Three Tuns*, 16 rooms, and the *Waterloo*, 6 rooms.

HARROGATE (Yorks.). Fashionable inland spa with concert hall, theatre (repertory company), and delightfully laid-out gardens. The Yorkshire dales are easy of access, as such cities as Leeds, Bradford and York.

Deluxe hotels are the *Cairn*, 156 rooms (32 with bath); *Majestic* 160 rooms (112 with bath); *Old Swan*, 142 rooms (51 with bath) and *Crown*, 100 rooms (half with bath).

First-class are the *Granby*, 95 rooms (28 with bath) and the *Prospect*, 97 rooms (all with bath).

Also the *Green Park*, 66 rooms (5 with bath); *Russell*, 44 rooms, and *St. George*, 80 rooms (12 with bath).

Best food: *Majestic Hotel*.

HEXHAM (Northumberland). Fascinating market town containing many old buildings, including ancient abbey. Good centre for the Northumberland moors, including the country around the Roman Wall.

Beaumont has been recently reconstructed and is a most comfortable place, with excellent food. 23 rooms (1 with bath). Also: *Royal*, 17 rooms.

At Wall on Tyne (4 miles north of Hexham) is the *Hadrian*, 7 rooms, and at Blanchland (11 miles to the southeast), one of the loveliest villages in the area, is the *Lord Crewe Arms*, 11 rooms (1 with bath), a delightful hostelry almost entirely constructed from the 13th-century Blanchland Abbey. Good food.

HUDDERSFIELD (Yorks.) Best is *George*, 62 rooms (21 with bath). At Farnley Tyas (3 miles southeast) dine at the *Golden Cock*; good Yorkshire food.

HULL (Yorks.). *The Royal Station*, 124 rooms (25 with bath) is a first-class superior hotel, as is the new (1968) *Hull Centre*, 126 rooms (all with bath), and the *White House*, 63 rooms (16 with bath) is a smaller first-class hotel noted for its good food.

KNUTSFORD (Cheshire). Well-placed for visiting Delamere Forest and rural Cheshire. The *Royal George* is an historic inn with excellent food and accommodation. 23 rooms (all with bath).

Best place to eat (one of England's greatest) is *Hat and Feather Buttery*.

LANCASTER (Lancs.). County town containing historic castle and priory church. A convenient place of call on the way north to the Lakes. The *Royal King's Arms* has 60 rooms. Moderate.

LEEDS (Yorks.). Two first-class superior hotels of long standing are the *Queen's*, 200 rooms (all with bath) and the *Metropole*, 120 rooms (61 with bath and 4 with shower). To these must be added the newly-built *Merrion*, incorporated in a new development scheme which includes a cinema and ten-pin bowling alley, and which has 120 rooms (all with bath). Also new (1968), the *Selby Fork Motor Hotel* at nearby South Milford, 72 units (all with bath). *Grove Motel*, 20 rooms (all with bath), is good, at Oulton, 5 miles.

Good hotels include the *Great Northern*, 56 rooms (12 with bath) and the *Griffin*, 112 rooms (9 with bath), and others are the *Golden Lion*, 78 rooms (1 with bath); *Guildford*, 30 rooms, and *Mount*, 127 rooms (18 with bath).

Restaurant: *Jaconelli*.

LIVERPOOL (Lancs.). Two first-class superior hotels are the *Adelphi*, 236 rooms (165 with bath) and the *Exchange*, 110 rooms (8 with bath). Also, due to open in 1970, *St. George's*, 167 rooms (all with bath), an addition to the Trust House hotel group.

Others include *Lord Nelson*, 71 rooms (6 with bath); *Shaftesbury*, 76 rooms (11 with bath) and *Stork*, 84 rooms (17 with bath).

Restaurants: *Golden Phoenix* and *Mariners*.

French Restaurant of the Adelphi is outstanding. Also *La Bussola*, for a good osso buco. For the Liverpool Sound, try *Dino's*, *Triton* or *Beachcomber*.

KIRKBY (Lancs.). Not far from Liverpool is the convenient *Golden Eagle*, 27 rooms (23 with bath), new (1966).

MANCHESTER (Lancs.). The newest luxury hotel is the *Piccadilly*, 260 bedrooms (all with bath), and first-class superior hotels are the *Midland*, 329 rooms (210 with bath); the *Queen's*, 89 rooms (10 with bath), and *Grand*, 153 rooms (138 with bath, balance with shower).

Others include the *Excelsior* at Wythenshaw, 150 rooms (all with bath), the *New Milligate*, 81 rooms. At Ringway is the *Airport*, 150 rooms (all with bath), luxurious.

Restaurants: *Mayflower*; *Manchester Steak House*; *Sam's* and in Hotel Midland, the *French Restaurant*. Nightlife: *Time and Place* or *Drokiweeni*.

MATLOCK (Derbyshire). Set in good scenery in Derwent Valley and handy for the nearby Derbyshire countryside and dales. Interesting caverns close to the town. *New Bath* has 58 rooms (29 with bath). First-class reasonable. Also: *Temple*, 12 rooms. Eat at the *New Bath*.

MIDDLESBROUGH (Yorks.). About half-way between Newcastle and York. Try the new (1966) *Marton Way*, 32 rooms (all with bath).

MONK FRYSTON (Yorks.). *Monk Fryston Hall*, an old house owned by the Duke of Rutland, 17 rooms (5 with bath).

NEWCASTLE UPON TYNE (Northumberland). Newest (1968): *Swallow*, 85 rooms (all with bath); also new, Rank's *Five Bridges*, across the river at Gateshead, 100 rooms (all with bath); *Royal Station*, 140 rooms (38 with bath) is a first-class superior hotel and *Royal Turk's Head*, 110 rooms (49 with bath) and *County*, 86 rooms, are both first-class. Eat at *Royal Turk's Head*.

Others include the *Gosforth Park* (some miles north of the city centre), 102 rooms (all with bath); *Douglas*, 43 rooms (2 with bath) and *Crown*, 78 rooms (3 with bath and 20 with shower).

Restaurants: *Red House*, *Jim's Inn*, *Dante's* (Italian).

OTTERBURN (Northumberland) Near to scene of famous battle. Buy tweeds at local mill. Handy for Cheviot hills and wilder Northumberland dales. The *Percy Arms*, 35 rooms (9 with bath), first-class reasonable. *Otterburn Tower* is smaller, 18 rooms, and of special interest historically.

RICHMOND (Yorks.). Old market town, with ancient castle and church. Excellent centre for Swaledale and other Yorkshire dales. Old theatre. *King's Head*, 20 rooms, moderate.

RIPON (Yorks.). Small but picturesque cathedral city. Good place for Wensleydale and other Yorkshire dales. *Spa*, 47 rooms (9 with bath), first-class reasonable. *Unicorn*, 20 rooms, is smaller, but comfortable. Restaurant: *Old Deanery*.

ROWSLEY (Derbyshire). Pleasant village in Derwent Valley, close to Chatsworth House and Haddon Hall. *The Peacock*, 21 rooms (3 with bath) is first-class reasonable. It was built in 1652 as a dower house at Haddon Hall and was used by the famous Izaak Walton on his fishing expeditions to the district. Excellent trout fishing from the hotel.

SHEFFIELD (Yorks.). *Hallam Tower*, 136 rooms (all with bath) is a luxurious hotel, and first-class superior hotels are *Grosvenor House*, 104 rooms (all with bath); *Grand*, 171 rooms (90 with bath and 3 with shower), and *Royal Victoria*, 65 rooms (19 with bath).

Others include *Kenwood*, 66 rooms (7 with bath) and *Rutland*, 83 rooms (11 with bath). Eat at *Hallam Tower*.

SUNDERLAND (Durham). Shipbuilding and marine engineering centre. Theatre. Football club. Hotels include *Grand*, 53 rooms (5 with bath); *Palatine*, 46 rooms (1 with bath); *Seaburn*, 57 rooms (9 with bath); *Roker*, 50 rooms (16 with bath).

WASHINGTON (Durham). Scheduled to open in 1970: *Post House*.

YORK (Yorks.). Historic medieval walled city in the north. Magnificent Minster, or cathedral, and many ancient churches and historic buildings. Almost completely circled by walls. Unique museums. One of finest racecourses in the land.

Newest (1968) hotel is *Viking*, 112 rooms (all with bath); next is *Royal Station*, 119 rooms (31 with bath). First-class superior. *Chase*, 55 rooms (31 with bath). Close to racecourse. First-class moderate.

York Motel, 14 rooms (all with bath), *Abbey Park*, 40 rooms (9 with bath).

For a magnificent lunch, eat at *Young's Hotel* (said to be birthplace of Guy Fawkes).

SEASIDE RESORTS

Being so easily accessible from the inland centres of population, the northern coastal resorts are usually heavily booked from late May to mid-September, with the "peak" weeks falling in late July and August. It is therefore advisable to book well ahead for accommodation in the summer months. Quite a number of hotels close during the winter. It may be well to write to the publicity manager of the resort favoured, c/o the Town Hall, for a full accommodation list if in doubt.

BLACKPOOL (Lancashire). Unquestionably the gayest and liveliest seaside resort in the north, if not the whole country. Summer brings the stars of variety and vaudeville, while in winter, touring companies often visit the town with plays and musical comedies. Top-class circus during the season. In autumn the famous illuminations are the big attraction.

Imperial, 164 rooms, (106 with bath and 12 with shower) is a first-class superior hotel, and *Cliffs*, 200 rooms (25 with bath) and *Norbreck Hydro*, 400 rooms (many with bath) are first-class.

Others include *Clifton*, 51 rooms (35 with bath); *Redman's Park House*, 100 rooms (3 with bath) and *Savoy*, 150 rooms (30 with bath).

Restaurant: *The Islander*, on Market Street, for Polynesian dishes.

BRIDLINGTON (Yorkshire). Beautifully situated just south of Flamborough Head. Has good entertainment, i.e., plays, orchestra, concerts or revue, in summer months. Good sea fishing. First-class hotels are *Expanse*, 48 rooms (9 with bath) and *Monarch*, 40 rooms (15 with bath).

MORECAMBE (Lancashire). Magnificent situation, with views across Morecambe Bay to the hills of the Lake District. Good entertainment during summer months. Is specially proud of its bathing beauty competitions, held weekly, and its Marineland. Illuminations each autumn.

The *Midland*, 38 rooms (11 with bath) is first-class superior. Other first-class hotels include the *Elms*, 39 rooms (4 with bath); *Grosvenor*, 56 rooms (4 with bath) and *Headway*, 52 rooms.

SCARBOROUGH (Yorkshire). Magnificently situated with superb cliff scenery north and south and two sandy bays. Moorland and dales scenery inland. Old castle. Top-class entertainments, including orchestra and open-air production. Big sporting events include tennis tournament and cricket festival.

First-class hotels, include *Grand* 200 rooms (55 with bath); *Crown* 82 rooms (30 with bath); *Royal*,

141 rooms (46 with bath) and *Pavilion*, 62 rooms (21 with bath).

SOUTHPORT (Lancashire). Good stretches of sand, 6 golf courses, entertainments, and big flower show each August. Ideally placed from Liverpool. First-class hotels include *Prince of Wales*, 100 rooms (36 with bath); *Scarisbrick*, 70 rooms (3 with bath); *Clifton*, 65 rooms, and *Royal*, 58 rooms.

WHITBY (Yorkshire). Historic fishing port with abbey and many links with famous explorer Captain Cook. Entertainments. Wonderful cliff scenery north and south. First-class hotel is *Royal*, 65 rooms (9 with bath).

GETTING AROUND. If you make Manchester your base and wish to drive, *Avis*, one of many rent-a-car agencies, can be found at the airport or 11 Whitworth St. W.

Historic Houses Open to the Public

DERBYSHIRE. *Chatsworth*, near Bakewell. Magnificent home of the first Duke of Devonshire. House open daily except Mons., Tues.; gardens open daily, April to October. *Haddon Hall*, Bakewell. Home of Duke of Rutland and associated with romantic story of Dorothy Vernon. Open weekdays, April through September. *Hardwick Hall*. Splendid Elizabethan house. Open Wed., Thurs., Sat., Sun. Easter through October. Built by "Bess of Hardwick". *Kedleston Hall*, Derby. Perhaps the finest Robert Adam House in England. Open Sunday and Monday afternoons, end of April through September.

LANCASHIRE. *Platt Hall*, Manchester. Georgian mansion, English costume museum. Open daily all year. *Wythenshawe Hall*, Manchester, 15th cent. Open daily all year. *Speke Hall*, Liverpool. Half-timbered Elizabethan house. Open daily all year.

YORKSHIRE. Has over two dozen magnificent historic houses. Among them: *Harewood House*, near Leeds. Home of the Earls of Harewood. Open daily, Easter through September. *Burton Agnes Hall*, near Bridlington. Elizabethan country house. Open daily (except Sat.) May through October. *Castle Howard*, near York. Early 18th-century house by Sir John Vanbrugh for the 3rd Earl of Carlisle. Open daily except Mon. and Fri., Whitsun to October. *Temple Newsam*, Leeds. Tudor-Jacobean house, birthplace of Lord Darnley. Open daily, all year. *Newby Hall*, Ripon. Famous Adam House with tapestries, statuary, gardens. Open Wed., Thur., Sat. and Sun. afternoons, Easter to October.

CO. DURHAM. *Raby Castle*, Staindrop. Home of the Lord Barnard. 14th cent., later alterations. Open Wed. and Sat. afternoons, Easter through Sept. *Washington Old Hall*, near Sunderland. Jacobean manor house, with portions of 12th-cent. house of the Washington family. Open daily, (except Fridays), all year.

NORTHUMBERLAND. *Alnwick Castle*, Alnwick. 12th-century home of the Duke of Northumberland. Medieval fortifications. Open daily, (except Fri. and Sat.) May through September. *Seaton Delaval Hall*, near Newcastle-on-Tyne. Home of Lord Hastings. Open Wed. and Sun. afternoons, May through Sept. Built by Vanbrugh. Now stages nightly medieval banquets at around $6.60 per head. Great fun!

MUSEUMS. Among the many, a few of the best: Accrington: *Haworth Art Gallery* (large collection of Tiffany glass). Aldborough: *The Aldborough Roman Museum* (finds from the Roman town). Bamburgh: *Grace Darling Museum* (relics of the famous lifeboat heroine). Barnard Castle: *The Bowes Museum* (European art). Batley: *Bagshaw Museum* (natural history, Victoriana, etc.). *Oakwell Hall* (Brontë associations, "secret passage"). Berwick-on-Tweed: *Berwick-on-Tweed Museum and Art Gallery* (ceramics and brasswork). Birkenhead: *Williamson Art Gallery and Museum* (water-colours, pottery, Liverpool porcelain). Blackburn: *"Lewis" Textile Museum* (spinning and weaving machines). *Samlesbury Old Hall* (large collection of cabinets). Blackpool: *Grundy Art Gallery* (19th- and 20th-century British artists). Bolton: *Museum and Art Gallery* (Egyptian collection, English water-colours). *Tonge Moor Textile Machinery Museum* (historic textile machines). Bootle: *Bootle Museum and Art Gallery* (Lancaster collection of English figure pottery). Bridlington: *Bayle Gate Museum* (prehistoric relics and farm implements). Burnley: *Towneley Hall Art Gallery and Museum* (Chinese pottery, archeological specimens). *Gawthorpe Hall* (large collection of textiles, costume and accessories). Bury: *Bury Art Gallery and Museum* (Wrigley collection of oil and water-colour paintings).

Carlisle: *Museum and Art Gallery* (Natural history and Roman objects). Castleford: *Castleford Public Library and Museum* (Roman remains). Castle Howard: *Castle Howard Costume Museum* (dresses covering 18th to 20th centuries). Chester: *Grosvenor Museum* (Roman antiquities). *King Charles' Tower* (Chester in the Civil War). *Water Tower* (Chester in the Middle Ages). Chesters: *The Clayton Collection* (Roman inscriptions, tools and ornaments). Chorley: *Astley Hall, Art Gallery and Museum* (Leeds pottery). Coniston: *The Ruskin Museum* (the life and work of John Ruskin).

Darlington: *Darlington Museum* (model engines). Durham: *Gulbenkian Museum of Oriental Art and Archeology* (Egyptian, Mesopotamian antiquities, Chinese pottery and porcelain, Sir Victor Sassoon collection of Chinese ivories, Japanese and Tibetan art). *The Monk's Dormitory, The Cathedral* (Anglo-Saxon crosses, manuscripts, and relics of St. Cuthbert). Grasmere: *Dove Cottage* (home of Wordsworth). *The Wordsworth*

Museum (rural life in Wordsworth's day). Huddersfield: *The Tolston Memorial Museum* (history of the Huddersfield district). Hull: *Ferens Art Gallery* (fine art of the 20th century). *Wilberforce House* (the birthplace of William Wilberforce). *Transport Museum* (coaches and motor-cars). *Maritime Museum* (relics of the whaling days). Ilkley: *Manor House Museum and Art Gallery* (Roman relics). Keswick: *Fitz Park Museum and Art Gallery* (Wordsworth manuscripts).

Lancaster: *Lancaster Museum* (Roman remains). Leeds: *City Art Gallery* (English water-colours, Leeds and Staffordshire pottery). *Temple Newsam* (Tudor/Jacobean house). *Abbey House Museum* (the life of the people of Yorkshire). Lindisfarne: *Lindisfarne Priory* (Anglo-Saxon sculpture). Liverpool: *Walker Art Gallery* (European paintings). *Studley Art Gallery and Museum* (18th- and 19th-century paintings). *Hornby Library* (rare books).

Macclesfield: *West Park Museum and Art Gallery* (Egyptian collection). Manchester: *The City Art Gallery* (pictures of British and foreign schools). *The Athenaeum* (museum of ceramics). *The Gallery of English Costume* (clothing from the 17th century to the present). *Fletcher Moss Museum* (English water-colours). *Queen's Park Art Gallery* (collection of playthings of the past). *Manchester Museum* (geology, botany, zoology). *Whitworth Art Gallery* (English water-colours). Middlesbrough: *Dorman Memorial Museum* (Roman antiquities).

Newcastle-upon-Tyne: *Laing Art Gallery and Museum* (Egyptian and Greek antiquities). *Museum of Science and Engineering* (shipbuilding and other industries). *Higham Place Gallery* (British water-colours). *The Keep Museum* (medieval collections). *The Black Gate* (Museum of local antiquities and bygones). *The Greek Museum* (Greek and Etruscan art). *Museum of Antiquities* (Roman and Anglo-Saxon antiquities). *Museum of the Department of Mining Engineering* (history of mining).

Oldham: *Municipal Art Gallery and Museum* (British paintings of 19th and 20th centuries). Penrith: *Penrith Museum* (local Roman-British objects). Pontefract: *The Castle Museum* (Roman pottery, medieval weapons and armour). Port Sunlight: *The Lady Lever Art Gallery* (Renaissance and British sculpture, Wedgwood ware). Preston: *Harris Museum and Art Gallery* (Victoriana).

Ribchester: *The Ribchester Museum of Roman Antiquities* (includes an excavated area). Richmond: *The Green Howards Museum* (medals, campaign relics). Rochdale: *Art Gallery and Museum* (water colours and oils). *Rochdale Co-Operative Museum* (British and international co-operatives). Rotherham: *Rotherham Museum and Art Gallery* (antiquities from Roman forts).

Salford: *Museum and Art Gallery* (a 19th-century "street"). *Science Museum* (Science in everyday life). Scarborough: *Scarborough Museum of Natural History* (formerly home of the Sitwell family). *Scarborough Museum* (archeological collections). Sheffield: *Sheffield City Museum* (old Sheffield plate). *Graves Art Gallery* (British and European paintings). *Mapping Art Gallery* (the British School of the 18th, 19th and 20th centuries). Southport: *Botanic Gardens Museum* (Victorian room). South Shields: *South Shields Library and Museum* (ship models). *Roman Fort and Museum* (objects found on the site of the Roman Fort). Stalybridge: *The Astley Cheetham Art Gallery* (Greek and Roman antiquities). Stockport: *War Memorial Art Gallery* (Epstein head of Yehudi Menuhin). Stockton-on-Tees: *Preston Hall Museum and Art Gallery* (arms, armour, etc.).

Turton: *The Ashworth Museum* (12th-century Pele tower). Wakefield: *City Museum* (costumes, Victorian rooms). Warrington: *Municipal Museum and Art Gallery* (ceramics and local glass). Whitby: *Whitby Library and Philosophical Society Museum* (Roman relics).

York: *City of York Art Gallery* (collection of paintings). *York Castle Museum* (folk museum of Yorkshire life). *The Railway Museum* (collection of locomotives). *The Yorkshire Museum* (Roman antiquities).

Exploring the North

We can start at Ashbourne, northwest of Derby, not as a place where the Midland scene ends but as one where the northern scene commences. It is a pleasant sort of town, where Dr. Johnson lingered awhile and where the sign of the *Green Man* inn stretches right across one of the streets. Ashbourne, in fact, still wears the unchanging air of the Midlands.

North Derbyshire

Go north on A515 for a mile of two, however, and Dovedale opens ahead, a narrow defile through precipitous sides of white limestone and watered by one of the pleasantest little streams in the whole land. Now you see at once the essential difference between the northern and the Midland scene. In the Midlands we seemed to go from one type to another without ever being conscious of any change. In no place did we encounter anything quite so sweeping and so abrupt as the change that comes within a mile or two of Ashbourne. That sudden impact with the Pennines changes the character of the country, and with it comes a corresponding change in the temper of the people.

Dovedale is one of the outstanding beauty spots of England. Poet and novelist alike have told of its charms. The angler, too, will be interested in the fact that this is one of the most celebrated trout streams in the land. The gentle Izaak Walton, of *Compleat Angler* fame, spent many hours fishing here.

Perhaps one of the advantages of Dovedale is that it must be visited on foot. No road runs its length; only pleasant waterside paths that wind round the feet of limestone buttresses and then cross the green turfed fields that comprise the narrow floor of the dale. That, of course, means that Dovedale remains, for the most part, completely unspoilt. You can enjoy to the full the clear, swiftly-flowing stream and the great limestone pinnacles, carved by Nature to represent a score of odd designs, all along the ten-mile footpath from Ashbourne to Hartington, near the head of the dale.

A few miles to the west and running almost parallel with Dovedale for many miles is the Manifold valley, broader and less dramatic than Dovedale but well worth visiting for the sake of seeing its queer vanishing river.

Some 12 miles to the east is the course of another Derbyshire river, the Derwent; to reach it from Ashbourne, there is a road (B5035) across a windswept plateau through Wirksworth, the capital of the Derbyshire lead mining area, and Cromford (north of Wirksworth on B5036) to Matlock.

Up the Wye to Buxton

It is tempting to suggest that the Derwent be now followed past Chatsworth House to its source in the great moors of the

Peak, but to do this would mean neglecting one of the most interesting sections of the county. At Rowsley (north of Matlock on A6), the Derwent is joined by its tributary, the Wye (not to be confused with the other and better known Wye in the west of England), and we shall do well to turn along its valley, still on A6, and follow this stream, which flows glass-like through the meadows, to reach Haddon Hall, one of England's loveliest mansions. The magnificent baronial mansion is one of the possessions of the Duke of Rutland and well worth a visit. It is associated with the poignant and romantic legend of the elopement of Dorothy Vernon and John Manners.

From here, you may wish to detour to visit Sheffield, a centre of the steel and cutlery industry. Some fine examples of the city craftsmen's work in cutlery are on view in the City Museum. On the edge of the Peak District there is magnificent scenery within a few miles of the city centre. Stop on your way, if you have time to spare, at Hathersage, where Robin Hood's faithful lieutenant, Little John, is buried in the churchyard. His great longbow hung in the church for many years.

As early as 1161 the monks of Kirkstead had four furnaces at nearby Kimberworth, and by 1378 a Sheffield "thwitel" (a knife) was so well known an article of commerce that Chaucer's reference to one in his *Canterbury Tales* was generally understood. With the adaptation of the use of water-power to grinding, Sheffield's cutlery industry developed and by 1614 there were 182 master cutlers. Since the end of the 17th century Sheffield has enjoyed a virtual monopoly of the English cutlery trade. Guided tours of silverware factories are conducted by Chamber of Commerce, Church Street.

Although Sheffield's history is largely that of her major industries it is of interest that in 1530 Cardinal Wolsey, having been arrested near York on a charge of high treason, was entertained for eighteen days in Sheffield by the Earl of Shrewsbury. Nearly forty years later, in 1569, the sixth Earl of Shrewsbury became custodian of the captive Mary, Queen of Scots. For fourteen years she languished in Sheffield Castle or in the Turret House, which may still be seen at the Manor Lodge.

Try to see the ancient Cathedral Church of St. Peter and St. Paul, Church Street, founded early in the 12th century and rebuilt in the 15th.

THE NORTH

Sheffield has two excellent theatres, one, which brings first-class plays and musical comedies to the city, and the other staging repertory.

A mile away from Haddon Hall, having finished with our detour to Sheffield, is Bakewell, with one of the most magnificent churches in the county. Now the Wye begins to feel the presence of the hills, which present well-wooded slopes on either side. At Monsal Dale, the limestone cliffs again begin to take possession of the scene, and henceforward, through Millers Dale and Chee Dale, the river flows through a succession of gorges.

Near the head of the Wye to the west is Buxton, over 1,000 feet up and, like Matlock, renowned for the medicinal qualities of its waters. Indeed, the Romans knew the curative powers of the chalybeate springs and, in all probability, laid the foundations of what has developed into one of the most popular of England's inland spas.

Buxton makes a fine centre from which to explore the surrounding countryside. On one of the hills, Grinlow, is the entrance to Poole's Cavern, which goes underground for nearly 1,000 yards, and further afield there are roads and tracks across the uplands to Axe Edge, a breezy expanse of heather upland commanding some of the widest views in the district. Not far away is the renowned *Cat and Fiddle* inn, just west of Buxton on A537, one of the highest licensed houses in the country.

Back again, eastward, to Rowsley to follow the course of the Derwent. The way north (A623) soon reaches one of the most famous English parks, Chatsworth. Chatsworth House, backed by wooded hills, is one of the finest of England's stately homes and is the seat of the Duke of Devonshire. The interior is packed with wonderful examples of art, furnishings, and rare books. The gardens, designed 100 years ago by the celebrated landscapist Joseph Paxton, are well worth a visit, and are renowned for their fountains and artificial cascades.

Continuing upstream, the valley becomes narrower again and, on the one hand, to the west, we have the limestone uplands, on the other, dark rock, millstone grit of a much later geological age, making rugged edges along the skyline as it thrusts itself through the outer covering of heather and bracken. On these heights is the Langshaw Estate, where the public have access to a great expanse of spreading moor, and here, in early September, take place the annual sheepdog trials that attract visitors from all parts of the north.

Through Grindleford and Bamford (you are now on A622 and A625), there is the same green trench through the hills, and then, above Bamford, the valley has been dammed to form a succession of three artificial lakes which act as reservoirs for several of the north Midland towns and cities.

Moors of the Pennines

It is, however, on the brown uplands beyond these that the infant Derwent itself springs to life. There is neither road nor footpath leading to the actual source among the heathery wastes of Bleaklow Head, one of the two mountain massifs of north Derbyshire, but above the highest reservoir a moorland track leaves the stripling river to make its way over the watershed and out of Derbyshire into Yorkshire, a track leading through some of the wildest scenery in the Pennines.

Castleton, west of Bamford a few miles, is near the northern edge of the Derbyshire limestone area. Here stands Peveril Castle, its grim Norman Keep brooding over a stretch of hilly countryside riddled with caverns, some of them open to the public, and containing "Blue John", a semi-precious rock crystal found nowhere else in the world except around Castleton. Climb the ridge to the north of Castleton and you are on gritstone; not until you have gone north again for another 60 or so miles do you find those gleaming white outcrops of rock in the fields and on the hills that are so familiar a sight on the Derbyshire uplands.

The Peak District

Wildest Derbyshire, however, lies on the other side of that same ridge, the section of Derbyshire known as the Peak, and here it must be pointed out that the Peak is a district and not an individual mountain. Time was when these untamed uplands constituted part of a royal hunting forest, and old Camden, the Elizabethan chronicler, wrote of the area as being "called in the Old English tongue Peac-Land and at this day the Peak".

Having got this matter of a name sorted out, we can turn to Kinder Scout (northwest of Castleton), with its ragged edges of gritstone and its seemingly interminable leagues of heather and peat. All these wild landscapes lie within the boundaries of the Peak District National Park, the first National Park created in Britain.

From Castleton, drive west on A625 and A6 to the gigantic complex of cities around Manchester for a look at modern British industry. On the route is Buxton, situated 1,000 feet above sea level, long known as a health resort. The ill-fated Mary, Queen of Scots, and Lord Leicester, Queen Elizabeth I's favourite, were two of Buxton's many patients. Among its notable buildings is the graceful Crescent, built by the 5th Duke of Devonshire in 1780.

Manchester, long the centre of Britain's cotton industry, is connected to the Mersey by a ship canal and is a thriving port. There is a large modern airport at Ringway, a few miles to the south. The city has a cathedral and many interesting buildings, museums, and art galleries, as well as public parks. An amusement centre and the zoological gardens at Belle Vue are worth visiting, too. Manchester's two large theatres are among the finest in the country and there are two repertory theatres as well as a number of clubs which attract top-class artists. Manchester is the home of the world-famous Hallé Orchestra.

West Riding and the Brontës

North of Manchester and north again of the Calder valley and south of that of the Aire, these same gaunt hills enclose an area that is classical ground, the district immortalized by the writings of the famous Brontë sisters. Haworth, a few miles south of Keighley, is the Mecca of the Brontë enthusiast —a grey west Yorkshire village that certainly might have passed unobserved throughout the years but for the magnetism of the family that lived in the old parsonage, now the museum of the Brontë Society. Every summer thousands of folk toil up the steep main street to visit the hilltop church and the museum, where all too often Brontë enthusiasm stops.

To understand the real spirit of the Brontë books it is necessary to go farther afield. Even to go as far as the Brontë waterfall and beyond that to the ruined farm of High Withens, which everyone calls *Wuthering Heights*, right on the crest of the hills, is to see something of the moors behind, but better still is to cross the watershed to Wycollar, over the Lancashire border, or make that fine walk from Withens to the Hardcastle Crags valley.

East of Keighley are Bradford and Leeds, two of Yorkshire's biggest industrial cities. Bradford, generally regarded as the centre of the world's woollen industry, in recent years has seen a great deal of development in the heart of the city, but its roots still lie in the charter granted by King Henry II early in the 13th century. Its interesting buildings include the cathedral and the Town Hall, with its 200-foot-high tower built after the style of the Palazzo Vecchio at Florence. Its college of technology has lately been given the status of a university. *St. George's Hall* houses some good concerts, and many first-class plays, musical comedies, and variety artists visit the *Alhambra Theatre*.

Leeds is the largest city in Yorkshire and the fourth largest in England outside London. It is an important centre of industry and commerce with a variety of industries and trades. Much of the centre is in the course of development and already a great deal has been achieved. First-class shops, theatres (including the *Leeds City Varieties*, the only music hall in the country, still presenting weekly bills and dating back for some 200 years), and night clubs are abundant. The *Grand Theatre* attracts most of the top English companies each year. Throughout the season there are symphony and other concerts in the Town Hall and the triennial Leeds Festival, established in 1858, is one of the most famous in Europe.

On the west side of the city are the ruins of Kirkstall Abbey, a Cistercian monastery, and an interesting folk museum, and on the other side of Leeds is the mansion-museum of Temple Newsam, where Lord Darnley, ill-fated husband of Mary, Queen of Scots, was born in 1545. Some miles to the north is Harewood House, the former home of the late Princess Royal, aunt of the present Queen.

Leeds possesses some lovely parks, many maintained in almost natural conditions, as at Roundhay, formerly a hunting ground of the Norman barons. The city is well situated for visiting Wharfedale and also the villages of the Plain of York.

North of the gap made by the Aire River (after following it upstream from Keighley on A629, then going west on A65 from Skipton), one enters the Craven country, with its numerous caves and limestone escarpments. Perhaps the most enchanting of Craven villages is Malham, at the head of the Aire, northwest of Skipton, backed by a 300-foot-high limestone cliff at Malham Cove. At hand are secret chasms, such as the great gash in the cliffs at Gordale Scar.

Northwest is Ingleborough Common, most outstanding of all Yorkshire hills, with a host of caves to visit, and, nestling at its foot, Ingleborough Hall, where the great botanist-explorer, the late Reginald Farrer, father of Alpine gardening, laid out a rock garden that is still visited by enthusiasts the world over. Today thousands who have never heard the name of Farrer practise the art he invented.

The Yorkshire Dales National Park

Yorkshire is famous above all for its dales—deep valleys carved by the rivers flowing down from the high moors. Wharfedale, the first of them (approaching from the south), begins to feel the influence of the Pennines at Ilkley, the Roman *Olicana*, northwest of the city of Bradford, and at the northern foot of the spreading brown-to-gold expanse of Rombald's Moor. Six miles up the dale, off A59, is Bolton Priory, where architectural beauty goes hand in hand with loveliness of setting, and from here there are roads (B6160 is best) and riverside paths through the woods to Burnsall, considered by many as the loveliest of Wharfedale villages, standing peaceful and undisturbed beside its spacious green.

Grassington, further north on B6160, a place ancient in both architecture and setting, marks the entry into wilder scenes, and from here the road continues through Kilnsey, clustered under a great bulge of limestone overhanging cottages and dale, Kettlewell and Buckden, beyond which the Wharfe comes dancing through a narrow mountain-girt valley until, with the river now a series of silvery tributaries, only the great fells remain in all their glory.

Nidderdale

The next dale north, Nidderdale, is softer in scene and setting. Harrogate, though outside the confines of the dale proper, makes a capital centre for exploring the nearby countryside. Harrogate, just north of Leeds, has been a health resort for centuries, due to its mineral springs and healthy air. It is also one of England's finest floral towns, with numerous parks and gardens and as a year-round resort, it provides such diverse entertainment as music and drama festivals, French Week and the Great Yorkshire Show (agriculture).

Not far away to the east is the ancient town of Knaresborough, where the Nidd flows through a wide ravine and past the cliff crowned with the ruins of Knaresborough Castle, with its grim traditions emphasized by the equally grim dungeons that remain. Two unusual local sights are Mother Shipton's Wishing Well, and the Dropping Well, whose dripping waters have petrifying properties that will turn to stone any object placed beneath them.

In the North Riding

Wensleydale is even wider and softer in its lower regions. The best approach is from Ripon, north of Harrogate on A61, where the old Cathedral of St. Wilfrid is well worth a visit, and there is a lovely journey upstream through some of the fairest scenery in England. At Middleham (A6108 from Ripon northwest) is the great castle where Warwick the Kingmaker had his home during the stirring years when England was torn between loyalties to the Houses of Lancaster and York contending for a country's throne, and higher up the dale is Bolton Castle (off A684), where Mary, Queen of Scots, was held prisoner for a while. Ahead is Wensleydale at its wildest, a firm contrast with the softer pastures to the east.

Swaledale, at its best from the north clifftop, paralleling the A1, is even wilder, a dale bounded on either side by steep-sided fells and extensive sheep walks. Here, near the head of the dale, originated one of the hardiest of black-faced sheep breeds, the Swaledale itself. The villages take on something of the texture of the fells and fit snugly into little pockets looking as though they, like the Pennines, have been here from eternity.

Richmond and York

Guarding the entrance to Swaledale is one of the finest of all north country towns, Richmond, with its castle standing on the brink of a great cliff. Richmond Castle is one of the noblest specimens of medieval fortification in the land, and its keep is generally regarded as being among the most perfect Norman towers in existence. The Holy Trinity Church is the only one

THE NORTH

in England that has shops built into the walls, a reminder of the town's connections with the dukes of Brittany, who introduced much of what was predominantly continental in atmosphere and architecture.

From Richmond, a short side trip up A6108 and the M1 can be made to Darlington, formerly a market town with links with agriculture, but now chiefly remembered for its early connections with railways and the textile industry. At the main line railway station you can see George Stephenson's famous locomotive, *No. 1*, which hauled the first passenger train in 1825. It is a good center for visiting Teesdale.

Let us leave the shadow of the hills for a while, and journey east across the great plain to York, surely the most entrancing of all English cities. (From Richmond, it is best reached by A1 south and A59 east.) It would take a fat guidebook in itself

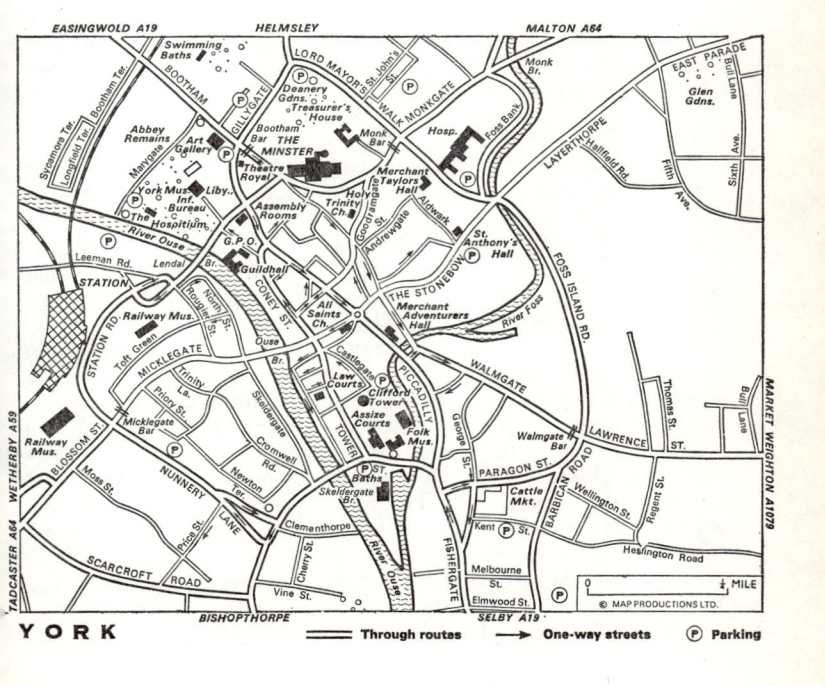

YORK

to do justice to York. Suffice it to say here that no one should leave without walking along the medieval city walls, visiting the historic Minster with its superb collection of stained glass, and wandering along the quaint street known as the Shambles, where the upper storeys of the buildings overhang the narrow cobbled street. The Castle Folk Museum, Railway and Yorkshire (Roman) Museums, and the medieval guildhalls are also places which should not be missed.

From York, it is a short side trip on A1079 east to Hull, a thriving port on the Humber, with the Yorkshire Wolds and southern part of the coast within easy access. The third of the great ports of England, it still has much of historic interest, including Holy Trinity church, the oldest brick building in the country.

Some nine miles north is the noted racing centre of Beverley, the capital of the East Riding of Yorkshire and, of course, much smaller and quieter. The Minster here is one of the finest Gothic churches in the whole of Europe and here is also the beautiful church of St. Mary. Formerly a walled town, Beverley still retains one of its old gateways.

The Yorkshire Coast

From York, the Yorkshire coast calls, and there is a good road (A166) across the chalk escarpments of the windswept wolds to Bridlington, a town combining buildings of historic interest with all the amenities of a modern seaside resort. North is the chalk promontory of Flamborough Head, with two rocky bays where blue-jerseyed fishermen congregate and there are a multitude of caves to explore.

Up the coast is Scarborough, again combining modern amenities with much of historic interest. A ruined castle perches on the summit of a rocky headland, and beside the busy fishing harbour are old houses and inns redolent with the atmosphere of the days when smuggling was rife. Northwards are paths along the edge of the cliffs, passing bays full of the sound of deep-sea music. The roads keep further inland, but whether one goes by road or path, Robin Hood's Bay, a crazy collection of red-roofed cottages crammed together in a little declivity of the cliffs and seemingly about to slip into the North Sea, should not be missed.

Whitby is one of the glories of the Yorkshire coast. The

River Esk comes down a long glen-like ravine cut through the moors and makes a natural harbour of great beauty. Above it, on either side, red-roofed buildings rise tier upon tier, and on top of the cliff are the gaunt ruins of Whitby Abbey, its traceried frame silhouetted against the sky and hurling defiance at the restless North Sea waves. Once a whaling centre, Whitby has a long history of seafaring. The famous explorer, Captain Cook, lived in a house near the harbour, and made his first voyages in Whitby-built sailing ships.

The Northumberland Coast

Perhaps less known, but containing treasures of equal delight, is the Northumberland coast further north from Whitby. Only a few miles east of busy Newcastle upon Tyne is Tynemouth, where castle and priory ruins grace the top of a cliff commanding the entrance to the river.

Newcastle upon Tyne itself is a shipbuilding port at the mouth of the Tyne. A thriving commercial city, but containing much of historical interest, including cathedral and castle keep, it has good theatre and nightclub entertainment. The city is a good place from which to visit the Roman Wall, the Northumberland coast, and the wild hill country of the Northumberland National Park. The city also has a splendid museum filled with fascinating relics and treasures recovered from the Roman Wall country.

Near the mouth of the Coquet, again to the north, is Warkworth Castle, a proud border fortress that belonged to the fighting Percys, lords of Northumberland, and inland is Alnwick Castle, even more spectacular, the centuries-old seat of the Percys and still lived in by the Dukes of Northumberland. North of the Coquet, the Northumberland coast reveals its finest features. Here and there the hard basaltic rock thrusts itself out into the North Sea, making the grand headland crowned with the ruins of Dunstanburgh Castle and the even more striking stronghold of Bamburgh, which legend declares to have been the Joyous Garde of Sir Lancelot du Lac, one of King Arthur's fabulous knights. Off the fishing village of Seahouses, near Bamburgh Castle, however, a seaward extension of this same basaltic rock results in the long line of the Farne Islands, sanctuaries for seals and of some of Britain's rarest sea birds. Go there in June and early July and see the colonies of gulls, terns, puffins, and, most fascinating of all, eider duck.

Continuing north, the long line of Lindisfarne, or Holy Island, cradle of northern England's Christianity and home of St. Cuthbert, shows on the eastward horizon. To reach it, one travels by car along a causeway over three miles of tide-washed sand, a journey possible only at certain times of the day. Go there to see the red ruins of Lindisfarne Priory, built on the site of the first Christian edifice in the north, and the fairylike Lindisfarne Castle, a miniature fortress perched on top of a conical-shaped piece of rock.

Berwick-on-Tweed marks the approach to Scotland, and is the last town of the Northumberland coast. Wandering round its streets, one feels conscious of being in the presence of things that are old. Yet Berwick bore the brunt of the border wars between England and Scotland so fiercely that it is difficult to find any building that is really old still standing intact. Only a few miles from the High Cheviots, in Chillingham Park, roam the unique wild white cattle of Chillingham. Led by a king bull, this herd is descended from the primeval aurochs that lived in Britain thousands of years ago.

The Cheviot Hills and the Roman Wall

Inland, the scene changes to one in which the fells dominate all else. Now the long line of the Pennines merges into the mountain barrier of the Cheviots, the natural boundary between England and Scotland. The political boundary, however, often leaves the summit of the ridge, and in so doing leaves Muckle Cheviot, the highest hill of all, wholly in England.

One can get a fairly good idea of Roman ways by devoting attention to the long line of Hadrian's Wall which runs along the brink of a whinstone elevation just north of the main road between Newcastle to the east and Carlisle, between the North Tyne and the Cumberland border, to the west. (B6318, to the north of A69, is better for viewing, while A69 is faster.) Hadrian's Wall consisted of a long line of camps and fortified sites joined together by a great wall, still five or six feet high in places and wide enough to be walked upon with apparent ease. It is the most impressive of all England's links with the days of the Roman occupation and was built at the order of the Emperor Hadrian himself, about A.D. 120, to serve as a

THE NORTH

kind of fortified boundary between the lands over which the Romans held supreme and unchallenged control, and the area to the north where all attempts at settlement proved transitory when the Picts defied subjection.

The Bastion of Durham

Astride the Wear, the city of Durham, south of Newcastle on the A1, presents a true bastion to invaders from north and south. Its magnificent Norman cathedral and the castle of the Prince Bishops share the summit of a wooded bank rising abruptly from the river, more or less in the centre of the city. Seeing this massive double structure (the finest view is from the railway embankment as the train from the south sweeps round a curve into Durham station), one is reminded of the words of Sir Walter Scott, who wrote of Durham, "Half church of God, half castle 'gainst the Scot." Durham University is one of the leading places of learning in Britain. The city has a quiet gentle air about it, although it is the county town of a mining and shipbuilding region.

Between Durham and Newcastle lies the little village of Washington, a Mecca for American visitors. (Off the A1 at Birtley.) This is the ancestral home of George Washington, and Washington Old Hall, a 17th-century building, contains portions of the original manor house belonging to the first recorded member of the family in 1183. (From here, the branch of the family which produced America's first president moved to Sulgrave Manor, near Banbury.)

West of the Pennines

West of the Pennines are the counties of Cumberland, Westmorland, Lancashire, and Cheshire, each of which contains the general pattern of the north in providing a striking variation of scene and character.

The roads which cross the Pennine barrier are quite interesting. The most northerly (the A69) keeps south of the line of the Roman Wall which although so often originally associated with Northumberland (where, of course, the best preserved sections are to be found), actually bisected the entire country from the mouth of the Tyne, on the east, to the Solway on the west. (The A69's lesser partner, B6318, runs right along the wall from Heddon, near Newcastle, to Greenhead, near Haltwhistle.)

Beyond Haltwhistle, where the South Tyne, which has been its nearby consort for many miles of the way, turns abruptly south to follow a long gap into the hills, the westward road goes over the watershed between east and west, passing the stark pile of Thirlwall Castle (at Greenhead), whereabouts the Picts are said to have breached the Roman defences, and then dropping down into the Irthing Valley and so on Carlisle, capital of the western borderland. Like Berwick-on-Tweed, on the opposite side of the country, Carlisle has a history full of the bitterness and occasional romance of the long continuing strife between two rival nations.

Carlisle

Carlisle is a busy place today, with its industries allowed to flourish unmolested by any thoughts of imminent unrest, yet it has managed to retain much that is reminiscent of the days when kings and military leaders passed through its streets or stayed within its walls as their armies took part in the backwards and forwards surges of warfare. Its history dates from long before Roman times. Slightly to the south of Hadrian's Wall, it became an important Roman settlement (Luguvallium), and the large cavalry camp of Petriana was close by. (The City Museum in Tullie House is particularly strong in Roman remains and information about the wall.)

The castle and city walls were projected by William Rufus (1087–1100) and the city became English in 1092. It was an important border fortress during the wars between England and Scotland, and changed hands several times. During the Civil War, Carlisle surrendered to the Scots after a siege of nearly nine months in 1644–45. Its stormy history continued longer than in any other town in England, and in 1745 the Young Pretender, Bonnie Prince Charlie, entered the town preceded by the famous "hundred pipers", and established his headquarters in English Street. Carlisle remained a walled city for 700 years, having but three entrances: English Gate, Scotch Gate and Irish Gate.

Try to see the cathedral, which is the second smallest in England (started in 1093), the 15th-century Tithebarn, the Market Cross, the Town Hall and the new Civic Centre.

Carlisle's castle, standing on a mound with two rivers washing two sides, has sufficient majesty to summon an impression of its worth as a northerly bastion of England, and its red sandstone cathedral, though diminished from its original size as the result of the Civil Wars between king and parliament in the 17th century, has a dignity in keeping with the seat of a see established as long ago as 1133. Fragments of the walls that once encircled the city are still enough to summon up visions of their former strength.

Carlisle is, of course, the traditional gateway to Scotland on the west, but it is also at the entrance to the Eden Valley, a long, lovely passage from the Cumberland plain back to the Pennine hills, and where the old breed of Dairy Shorthorn cattle still have one of their main strongholds in Britain.

It is on the Eden that Appleby, which that unrivalled chronicler of local life, the late W. T. Palmer, once described as "probably England's quietest and smallest county town", stands, for although Kendal is now the centre of administration for Westmorland, Appleby remains its rightful capital, and there is much that smacks of history, including its castle. Little changed and, perhaps, unfortunately, forgotten by many visitors to the northwest, it is a lovely spot. (Best reached from Carlisle on A6 and A66, south.)

Pennine Fairs

Not far away (on A66 and B6259 south) is Kirkby Stephen, a busy place on market days and even more so on those occasions in autumn when the hardy Swaledale sheep occupy the sales ring and buyers from all parts of the north come to bid for the stout rams reared on the nearby fells. Of almost equal importance are the horse and pony sales of the Cowper Day fair, which falls on September 29 each year (unless, of course, that is a Sunday, in which case the event takes place on either the Saturday or the Monday).

South of Carlisle, the A6 road, the chief communication between England and Scotland, goes on to Penrith, yet another town which bore its share of the troubled times of border strife, retaining its castle as a permanent memorial, and then on to one of the most notorious moorland crossings in the country—the way over the wild and bleak Shap Fell.

Lower levels are reached at Kendal, a major gateway to the

Lake District. From here southwards, the road continues to Levens Bridge, with a fine example of a topiary garden beside the ancient hall, and so out of Westmorland into Lancashire.

Just off the main road (A6) to the west are the villages of Yealand Conyers and Yealand Redmayne, set in a mass of woodlands and as beautiful and unspoilt as their names suggest, and Warton, where the ancestors of George Washington, first president of the United States, once lived. Links survive in the form of a plaque embodying the family coat of arms (said to be the source of the stars and stripes theme), originally incorporated in the masonry of the church tower, but now removed to safer keeping in the building itself.

Beyond Carnforth, the traveller who keeps to the old A6 road rather than take the modern motorway (M6) which bypasses the old city of Lancaster on the way south, has a sight of the broad expanse of Morecambe Bay, bounded by the hills of the Lake District to the north. Low tide reveals a big area of sand, which in former days had to be crossed by travellers on their way to the detached peninsulas of Cartmel and Furness.

The main road continues to Lancaster, but there is a way (A589) along the coast to Morecambe, a popular resort which combines the usual attractions of a seaside holiday town with a situation that makes it a fine centre for exploring the Lake District and neighbouring countryside. A mile or so south is historic Heysham, whose church recently celebrated its 1,000th anniversary of foundation and whose old village street, running down to a cove where St. Patrick is said to have landed, is one of the most picturesque on the northwest coast

Lancaster

Lancaster, unlike York, has allowed much that was historic to disappear, but it does retain its magnificent castle, linked with the dukes of Lancaster (and containing an unrivalled collection of armorial bearings), and its lovely priory church, the two standing almost side by side on a hill overlooking the city and the estuary of the Lune. Open to the public on certain days of the week, this castle is one of the most outstanding examples of medieval fortification in the whole of the British Isles.

Clitheroe, on A59 northeast of Preston, is yet another place with its castle perched on a knoll above the town. It may be regarded as the capital of the Ribble Valley area. A little way to the south are the ruins of Whalley Abbey, once the big religious house of the district and still exhibiting many signs of former wealth and prosperity, but the finest scenery is to the east where, once more, the Pennine hills mould its nature. Like that of the Lune, the Ribble is a vale of comely villages, with Downham (northeast of Clitheroe) one of its gems.

The great hill of Pendle (to the east of Clitheroe) dominates the southern horizon and, although less in area than Bowland, retains the same wildness and feeling of remoteness. It was hereabouts that the famous Lancashire witches practised their debaucheries in the reign of James I, happenings that form the basis of Harrison Ainsworth's story, *The Lancashire Witches*.

The Sea Resorts

West of the Bowland Hills and the road between Lancaster and Preston (A6) are the flatter lands of the Fylde, mainly devoted to farming, but with Blackpool, on the coast, serving as a magnet to those who would enjoy the offerings of what is one of the gayest holiday centres in the whole of Europe.

To visit Lancashire without seeing Blackpool is unthinkable. Each summer, its theatres and homes of entertainment are occupied by the very top personalities of show business, who contrive to play before packed houses from late spring until well into the autumn.

Preston, with a proud history and a general air of well-being, is at the top of the Ribble estuary, and on the sandy coast between the Ribble and the entrance to the Mersey there is Southport, another favourite holiday resort, with an August flower show that claims to be the biggest of its kind in the world, as well as six golf courses within its boundaries.

Liverpool

After Southport, you soon enter Liverpool, the thriving seaport on the River Mersey. The busy airport at Speke is some miles outside the city. One of the most important commercial centres in England, it is a first-class shopping city, and young people will know it as the home-town of the Beatles. Be sure to see the new Roman Catholic Cathedral, the older

(1904) Anglican Cathedral, Speke Hall, the City Museum, and Walker Art Gallery. Two good theatres which have top companies, a repertory theatre, and nightclubs provide plenty of entertainment. Liverpool is the home of the Liverpool Philharmonic Orchestra, which gives regular concerts.

Cheshire

From the hills to the western sea, off the Wirral Peninsula, and to the borders of Wales, Cheshire is mainly a land of well-kept farms, supporting their herds of equally well-kept cattle. Ancient towns, like Sandbach and Tarporley, depend mainly on their links with agriculture. Villages, with Gawsworth in the southeast as one of the gems, contain many fine examples of the black-and-white "magpie" type of architecture more often associated with the Midlands (and every bit as attractive as anything to be found there), and, covering a large chunk of the interior, is Delamere Forest, a region of fine trees and containing some delightful little lakes, or meres.

Chester is its capital, a city steeped in history, with its cathedral, castle, and encircling city walls, as well as a whole host of ancient buildings distributed among its streets, many of them in the bold black-and-white style of Tudor England. The cathedral, originally an abbey dedicated to St. Werburgh, attained its present status in 1536 but still possesses many features, grouped around its cloister, that survive from its monastic past. The castle, built soon after the Norman Conquest and looking out across the River Dee towards Wales, remains a bastion of strength.

Among the unique features of Chester are the famous "Rows", covered-in footways at ground-floor level along many of the main streets, which allow the delights of shopping without fear of any discomfort through wet weather.

Just how these originated does not seem to be clearly known, although some have it they belong to the time when the Saxons rebuilt much of the city on the older Roman foundations, which were not excavated until a somewhat later date. Most are, however, of the opinion that they served a most effective means of defence against the incursions of the Welsh raiders who came to plunder the shops.

THE ENGLISH LAKELAND

A Quietly Beautiful National Park

It is impossible to think of a greater "must" for tourists visiting Great Britain than the inclusion of a visit to the Lake District, which embraces much of the counties of Cumberland and Westmorland and the northern section of Lancashire, in their itineraries.

This part of the northwest, which is now enjoying the protection of National Park status, combines so much that is magnificent in mountain, lake, and dales in a comparatively small space that new and entrancing vistas open out at each corner of the road. Higher mountains there most certainly are in Europe, but none that are finer in outline nor which give a greater impression of majesty; deeper and bluer lakes can be found, but none that fit so readily into the surrounding scene; and while the dales themselves are not so long as many of the glens north of the border, or even those watered by the rivers on the east side of the Pennines, they yield to none so far as beauty is concerned.

Perhaps it is only natural that so lovely an area should have become linked with so many prominent figures in English literature. The poet, William Wordsworth, himself born in the area, lived at Grasmere, and may be regarded as the figurehead of a group which included Samuel Taylor Coleridge and his pathetic son, Hartley, Thomas de Quincey, and Robert Southey, who made their homes in the district in the first part of the last century. Later came Hugh Walpole, and even more recently, the late Graham Sutton and the poet Norman Nicholson have made contributions to Lakeland literature which are every bit as rich and important as those of 150 years ago.

Practical Information for the Lake District

ACCOMMODATIONS. Many old inns are scattered throughout the Lake District, some of them with incredible names. But all are well worth a visit. Although the area has plenty of comfortable hotels, there are few in the modern, luxury category. In food, Cumberland rum butter is a speciality.

AMBLESIDE (Westmorland). At head of Lake Windermere; annual rush-bearing festival, boating, fishing. First-class superior: *Low Wood*, 117 rooms (20 with bath). First-class reasonable: *Salutation*, 31 rooms (1 with bath). *Waterhead*, 28 rooms (5 with bath). Moderate: *White Lion*, 20 rooms.

BUTTERMERE (Cumberland). Good walking and climbing centre, situated between Buttermere Lake and Crummock Water. Moderate: *Bridge*, 25 rooms; *Fish*, 9 rooms.

COCKERMOUTH (Cumberland). An ancient town, birthplace of Wordsworth. Inexpensive: *Globe*, 38 rooms; *Trout*, 18 rooms. Eat at the latter.

CONISTON (Lancashire). At northern end of Coniston Water; sailing, good fell climbing area. Moderate: *Sun*, 13 rooms (2 with bath).

ESKDALE (Cumberland). Beautiful centre for climbing and fishing. The moderate *Bower House* has 12 rooms (5 with bath).

GRASMERE (Westmorland). On the fringe of the lake; burial place of Wordsworth; Grasmere sports held annually in August are an old custom. First-class reasonable: *Prince of Wales*, 42 rooms (2 with bath); *Swan*, 27 rooms (5 with bath). Moderate: *Red Lion*, 26 rooms with bath. Eat at *Swan*.

KENDAL (Westmorland). Ancient town and birthplace of Katherine Parr, wife of Henry VIII, with many historic associations. Moderate: *Heaves*, 17 rooms (all with bath); *Kendal*, 32 rooms; *Woolpack*, 25 rooms.

KESWICK (Cumberland). Famous centre for climbing, set in wide wooded valley. First-class and reasonable: *Armathwaite Hall* (Bassenthwaite Lake), 40 rooms (15 with bath); *Keswick*, 100 rooms (42 with bath); *Queen's*, 37 rooms (10 with bath and 4 with shower); *Royal Oak*, 66 rooms (21 with bath). Eat at *Keswick Hotel*.

NEWBY BRIDGE (Lancashire). Village at foot of Lake Windermere. Good touring centre. Moderate: *Swan*, 30 rooms (20 with bath).

PENRITH (Cumberland). Old market town, castle. First-class reasonable: *George*, 50 rooms (3 with bath).

RYDAL (Westmorland). Charming village beside Rydal Water. Sheep dog trials held each August. Moderate: *Glen Rothay*, 14 rooms.

ST. BEES (Cumberland). Small resort on the coast. Moderate: *Abbots Court*, 25 rooms (4 with bath).

SEASCALE (Cumberland). Small coastal resort. *Scawfell*, 37 rooms (5 with bath).

TORVER (Cumberland). *Church House Inn* has a good dining room.

TROUTBECK (Westmorland). Small, ancient village, east of Lake Windermere. Inexpensive: *Mortal Man*, 12 rooms.

ULLSWATER (Westmorland). Come here to dine at the outstanding *Sharrow Bay Country House*, known through the district for excellent food. You can also stay here—17 rooms (4 with bath).

WHITEHAVEN (Cumberland). Although an industrial town, it is a good centre for the western Lake District. Just south at Eamont Bridge is the *Crown*, which offers free trout fishing for residents, among other amenities. Inexpensive: *Chase*, 14 rooms; *Golden Lion*, 17 rooms.

WINDERMERE (Westmorland). On eastern shore of Lake Windermere and generally known as "Queen of the Lakes". Excellent sailing, walking and other sporting facilities. First-class superior: *Belsfield*, 57 rooms (28 with bath, 2 with shower); *Old England*, 88 rooms (53 with bath). First-class reasonable: *Langdale Chase*, 40 rooms (38 with bath, 2 with shower); *Royal*, 36 rooms; *Windermere Hydro*, 95 rooms (12 with bath). Also *Beech Hill*, 18 rooms (12 with bath), overlooking lake near Bowness.

Historic Houses Open to the Public

In the Lake District there are few great or historic houses that are open to the public, but *Wordsworth House*, Cockermouth, is open on Mondays, Wednesdays and Saturdays, Whitsun through September. Near Kendal, Westmorland, is *Levens Hall*, an Elizabethan house, open daily Tue., Wed., Thur. and Sun. afternoons, May through September. Also *Sizergh Castle*, home of the Strickland family for 700 years (now National Trust), opens Weds., April through September. And in North Lancashire near Grange-over-Sands is *Holker Hall*, 17th-century house with deer park. Open daily (except Fri.), Easter to early Oct.

TRANSPORTATION. The Lake District is served by the London Midland Region of *British Rail*. Penrith is on the main line from London to Scotland; the remainder of the district lies on branches, although through trains are operated to Windermere and Whitehaven from London (Euston). Diesel units are employed in West Cumberland (based on Carlisle). Services of the *Ribble Motor Bus Company* or *Cumberland Motor Services* cover all outlying villages and the towns.

Steamers run on Lake Windermere and motor launches on Derwent Water and Ullswater during the summer months.

MUSEUMS in the Lake District are listed in our chapter on the North. See specifically the towns of Carlisle, Coniston, Keswick, Grasmere and Penrith.

Exploring the Lake District

Approached from the south, the natural gateway to the Lake District is Kendal, briefly mentioned in our chapter on the north of England. A lovely study in grey stone, with reminders of the coaching days in its old inns. Its yards, leading off the main streets, could be closed when news of a visit from the Scottish raiders was imminent. Here you see the remains of its old castle occupying a green knoll above the town.

Some nine undulating miles of roads (A59) separate Kendal from Windermere, showing something of the grandeur that lies ahead from the tops of the rises and of the warmness of the dales as the road drops down to the Kent, near Staveley.

Windermere town, which is also the railway terminus from the south, is a mile or so from the lake, which is reached at Bowness. Windermere, a pleasant open resort, has a 15th-century church with interesting chained books, a "Breeches Bible", and what is probably one of the earliest examples of stained glass windows in the country. In this window is an illustration of the arms of the Washington family, forebears of George Washington, first president of the U.S.A.

Some $10\frac{1}{2}$ miles in length, Windermere Lake may well be regarded as the water passage from the mountain scene to the more tranquil; Bowness comes about midway in the transition. Looking across the water, the general impression is of thickly wooded slopes, rising to no great height, encompassing the waters. The woodlands continue down to the foot of the lake at Newby Bridge and even down the Leven Valley almost to the shores of Morecambe Bay.

The head of the lake at Ambleside, however, is on the threshold of the mountain scene, and although the larger hills themselves are a little too far away from the water to give any sense of overpowering influence, they are still big enough to bring grandeur rather than sylvan beauty to the upper reaches of the lake.

During the summer months there is a regular steamship service from Lakeside, near the southern end, to Ambleside, at the head, with calls at Bowness and other places on the way. At Bowness, too, are the headquarters of the Royal Windermere Yacht Club, one of the foremost inland sailing clubs in Britain, which organizes regular races throughout the season.

From Bowness, the road (A591) keeps sufficiently close to the eastern shore of the lake to allow intriguing glimpses of the water, the woods, and the mountains on the way to Ambleside, where suddenly, one feels to have arrived at the very heart of things. Kendal and Windermere, in turn, gave an impression of something different, but at Ambleside, one feels that the town is itself almost part of the hills and fells. It is not difficult to understand why. Its buildings, mainly of local stone and many built in that local traditional style which forgoes the use of mortar in the outer walls, give the appearance of blending into their setting in a way unequalled elsewhere in the country.

From Ambleside there is a road (A593, then B5343) leading to the top of one of the most interesting valleys, Langdale. It goes by the little lake of Elterwater and along the floor of a wide dale until it comes to a halt near Dungeon Ghyll, with its waterfalls, in the very shadow of the mountains of the Langdale Pikes, perhaps the most exciting in outline of all Lakeland mountains, with higher Bow Fell, on the opposite side of the deep dale. Beyond it, there is a foot pass over the hills to Borrowdale and a climbers' way via Rosset Ghyll to the head of Wasdale, from where the Scafell Pikes can be ascended.

From Ambleside, too, there is a road (B5286, south) over the fells to the idyllic little town of Hawkshead, a fascinating spot of odd nooks and corners where the poet Wordsworth attended the former grammar school. The B5285 road goes over the ridge to Coniston, beside the lake of the same name, where Donald Campbell met his death when breaking the water speed record in the winter of 1966. Near at hand is Brantwood, associated with yet another literary figure, John Ruskin, and towering above the village is Coniston Old Man, which at a height of 2,633 feet, is the highest mountain in Lancashire.

From Ambleside to Keswick

For most, however, the favourite road from Ambleside is

that north to Keswick (A591), perhaps the finest, scenically, of any main highway in the north of England. A short mile from the town and on the right of this road is the place where the famous Vale of Rydal sheepdog trials take place in August.

Rydal Water is the next lake and then comes Grasmere, where the mountains really do exert their influence on the scene, contrasting superbly with the placid lake set in the green hollow.

Grasmere is, of course, packed with Wordsworthian associations. The poet and his family lived at Dove Cottage, on the outskirts of the village, for many years, the house now being a place of pilgrimage for thousands of folk each year. He lies, with the remainder of his family (and with Hartley Coleridge not far away), in the quiet church graveyard, within a stone's throw of the murmuring River Rothay.

Grasmere, too, is the place where possibly the most famous of the traditional Lakeland sports meetings is held in August with the local form of wrestling and races up and down the neighbouring fells as leading attractions.

Beyond Grasmere, the Keswick Road begins the steep climb over Dunmail Raise, at the top of which was fought a battle between the Celtic inhabitants of the area and the Saxons and where, legend has it, a big pile of stones marks the place where the local "king", Dunmail, was slain. Much more certain than the legend, however, is the grandeur of the scene, with the long dale in which Grasmere is situated behind, and the wooded reservoir-lake of Thirlmere ahead.

Thirlmere, which serves as a reservoir for Manchester and other northern centres, covers a once-swampy valley containing a couple of uninteresting shallow pools. Around it, a discerning authority has embarked on a forestry scheme which is a good example of how well-planted trees can be blended into the mountain landscape.

Helvellyn, which at a height of 3,119 feet is the highest mountain in Westmorland, almost overshadows the lake from the east and can be ascended by a well-marked path from Wythburn. There are, however, other longer but more interesting routes to the summit. One leaves Grasmere by Tongue Ghyll and then, by the lonely tarn of Grisedale, there is a mountain track up the slopes of Dollywaggon Pike and on to Helvellyn itself.

The main road keeps to the Helvellyn side of Thirlmere, but there is a quieter and more interesting one (from the point of view of scenery) which branches left after leaving Dunmail and goes along the bottom of the Armboth Fells, commanding more open views of the water and, of course, revealing the full grandeur of Helvellyn itself.

Both roads unite at the north end of Thirlmere before the long drop into Keswick, with commanding views of Skiddaw (3,054 feet) and over Derwent Water to the heights around Borrowdale and Newlands. Older rocks fashion the more urbane slopes of the first, volcanic rocks the more serrated outlines of the second.

Keswick

Keswick, the virtual "capital" of this part of the Lake District, has catering for the tourist as its summer objective, although there are small industries which provide the local folk with work throughout the year. In the past, a good deal of mining was carried out on the nearby hillsides. There are still slate quarries on the heights above Borrowdale, but the scars of those near Keswick have long since been removed and the quarries are not readily noticed from afar.

It was, of course, at Keswick that Coleridge and Southey lived and, at a later date, Hugh Walpole; there are many reminders of all three. In the summer, a festival of plays has become a regular feature.

Only a mile or so from the town is the lake of Derwent Water, often cited as being the loveliest in the area. Certainly, there is much to be said for such a statement, although in a district like this, where each stretch of water has its own individual appeal, it is difficult to make comparisons. Its immediate setting is one of woodland, but beyond, England's grandest mountains make a near circle.

From the head of the lake, Borrowdale runs south, deep into the heart of the hills; it is a magnificent dale with two little hamlets, Seatoller and Seathwaite.

Some four miles or so from the head of Derwent Water, the dale is split by a rocky tongue of land coming down from Glaramara and what may be called the "roof" of the area. On the left, there is a way through Langstroth which leads to the Stake Pass, a track crossing the watershed into Langdale.

The right-hand branch is wilder, going into what Thomas Gray referred to as "that turbulent chaos of mountain behind mountain", a dale deep-set among the grandest peaks. From the head of the watershed, a foot track climbs skywards to the Sty Head Pass, with an even finer aspect as it keeps to a narrow niche on the flanks of Great Gable, to drop into Wasdale on the other side of the watershed.

The crossings of both the Stake and Sty Head passes are walkers' ways, but the motorist can get what might be called the "feel" of these mountain crossings by taking the road (B5289) over Honister Pass from the lower reaches of Borrowdale to the head of the Buttermere Valley. Once this was a popular trip to be made by horse-drawn vehicle, but with the provision of the metalled road the animals found it impossible to get a safe foothold on the smooth surface on some of the worst slopes and today this form of transport is obsolete.

The Buttermere Valley

The Buttermere Valley, which not only contains the lake of the same name, but also Crummock Water and Loweswater, has a quiet grandeur, in keeping with its accessibility. The mountain road over Honister, and another which comes through the Newlands Valley from Keswick and crosses a further pass (B5292), can be used for approaching the head of the dale, but the main roads are from Cockermouth and the western towns, which are somewhat off the beaten track.

Nevertheless, Buttermere is one of the gems of the area, each of its three lakes exhibiting a differing characteristic. Loweswater has a prettiness of its own; at Crummock Water the closeness of the high mountains has a telling effect; and at Buttermere, the great peaks are in command of the setting, exerting their influence in majestic fashion.

Cockermouth, which is reached from Keswick by roads on either side of Basenthwaite Lake (A591 or 594), has a castle and several old buildings, including the house where Wordsworth was born in 1770. Beyond it, the Derwent goes through country which swells into the seaward plain to the coast. But, keeping to the hills again, there is the way south to the Buttermere Valley (B5289 again) and, a little further away, to the even wilder one containing the lake of Ennerdale Water, probably the least-visited of all, and yet one of the most arresting in the country (via A5086).

The western dales are, of course, best approached from the coast, although it is possible to get from one to another by taking climbing, and sometimes tortuous, roads over the lower slopes of the encompassing fells.

Further south along A5086 and A595 is the Wasdale area, with England's deepest lake (Wastwater) filling the upper basin, and its highest mountain (Scafell Pikes) frowning above its head, making an instant appeal to those who wish to see the sheer grandeur of the district. Indeed, there is no other hill in the north quite like Great Gable, which commands the skyline from many parts of the upper dale. Reached by tortuous roads from Gosforth on A595, no wonder that this symmetrical peak was selected by the district's premier climbing club, the Fell and Rock, to be given to the nation as a war memorial to its members.

Wasdale is, indeed, the climbers' dale, with some of the most difficult ascents in the world on the slabs and crags high above the lake. One can watch the experts essaying forth with ropes and other equipment from the farms offering accommodation and from the inn at the top of the dale, but only the skilled can follow them to their fastnesses in the hills.

Running parallel with Wasdale is Eskdale (further south, at Muncaster Castle), which, although containing no lake, is as wild a dale as any in the land, particularly at the head, where the old Roman-way of Hard Knott climbs up the slopes on the way to Ambleside, where the legions had a camp near the top of Windermere Lake. Today, there is a narrow-gauge railway running from Ravenglass, the former Roman port on the coast, up this dale—the trip is one well worth the making.

South is the Duddon Valley, perhaps softer in aspect than the two to the north. From this river, forming the northern boundary of Lancashire, we cross another ridge or two via A593 to get back to Coniston, and so to the vicinity of the southern approaches to Lakeland.

The Eastern Lakes

There still remain the eastern lakes of Ullswater and Haweswater. The first, second in length to Windermere (and also served by steamers in the summer months), is best approached from Penrith, although those coming via Kendal and Windermere have a chance to use one of the most interesting of Lakeland passes, the Kirkstone (on A592), winding over the hills and dropping past the lonely tarn of Brothers Water to Patterdale, at the head of Ullswater.

Ullswater combines sylvan loveliness with mountain setting, and changes its moods as one goes along A592 from Pooley Bridge, at the outlet, southwest to the top of the lake, which, like so many of the others, is deep within a fold of hills.

Hawes Water is another of Manchester's reservoirs, the original lake having been deepened and extended, a change involving the submerging of the entire hamlet of Mardale. Again, the approach is from the east, with Shap or Penrith as the places where the A6 road can be left. Whatever changes have taken place, however, the higher reaches of the valley containing the lake remain the same—a wild declivity among the high fells, over which the Romans had what must have been their most exposed road in the country.

The Coasts

The coasts of North Lancashire and Cumberland, though in places devoted to coal-mining and industry, are not to be ignored. From the A6 at Levens Bridge, south of Kendal, there are roads through the valleys and over the low ridges to Windermere (A5074 and 592) and one which keeps close to the estuary of the Kent to pretty Grange-over-Sands (A590) and then up to the foot of the same lake. While in the vicinity of Grange-over-Sands, be sure to visit nearby Cartmel Priory, dating from 1188, and Holker Hall, set in its own leafy deer park.

Barrow-in-Furness is mainly concerned with ship-building and repairing. A bridge here crosses the narrow channel to Walney Island, which, in spite of a lot of building, has fascinating sands on the opposite shore. Close to Barrow itself is the Cistercian ruin of Furness Abbey, and, near the entrance to the Walney Channel, a fortified island at Piel (not, of course, to be confused with the place of the same pronunciation, spelled Peel, in the Isle of Man).

THE ISLE OF MAN

" Necromancer's Island "

Set almost in the centre of the northern part of the Irish Sea between England and Ireland, and with the coasts of Scotland and Wales also visible from many parts, the Isle of Man combines something of the beauty of all its neighbours in one compact mass of land, covering an area of 227 square miles, with its greatest length only 30 miles and its maximum width little more than ten.

Necromancer's island, some have called it, as a reminder that legend still speaks of its first ruler as one Mannanan-Beg-y-Leir, from whom the name is derived, who was able to cause the mists to descend and so shield it from the eyes of any who coveted its charms.

Today, while linked with Britain in so many ways and, of course, having the Queen as monarch, it has its own Legislative Council, which can be said to correspond to the House of Lords at Westminster, and the House of Keys, which is its equivalent to the House of Commons. They pass the laws of the island, these being proclaimed annually at a fascinating ceremony on Tynwald Hill, in the centre of the island, on old Midsummer Day, which falls on July 5.

Between the fanciful times of King Mannanan and the present, much has happened to mould the story of the Isle of Man, with each successive period making its own contribution to the fabric of one of the most fascinating places within the British Isles.

Interesting and possibly unique as is the history of the island, it is the scenery which most commands attention today; it would be impossible to imagine a greater variation within so small a compass.

Practical Information for the Isle of Man

HOTELS. The Isle of Man is extremely seasonal, and most of the hotels and boarding houses close by the last week of September. The larger hotels in each resort stay open with limited accommodation, frequently catering for conferences, etc. during the winter. Best to book well ahead for the summer season, but the Information Bureau, 13 Victoria Street, Douglas, will help with spur-of-the-moment accommodation.

Castletown. Old town with medieval castle, once the capital; fishing, boating, golf. First-class reasonable: *Golf Links*, 72 rooms (52 with bath and 20 with shower).

Douglas. Largest resort on the island. Plenty of entertainment, and good centre. Principal port. Good hotels include *Castle Mona*, 120 rooms (54 with bath); *Fort Anne*, 57 rooms (20 with bath); *Metropole*, 94 rooms (12 with bath); *Villiers*, 116 rooms (14 with bath) and *Sefton*, 110 rooms (14 with bath). Newest (1966): *Palace*, 100 rooms (all with bath); next to Casino.

Port Erin. Beautiful sandy bay and interesting harbour. Close to magnificent cliff scenery. Hotels include *Cinque's Hydro*, 89 rooms; *Falcon's Nest*, 45 rooms, and *Eagle*, 30 rooms.

Port St. Mary. Fishing port and lovely sands. Good cliff scenery around. The *Balqueen Hydro* has 185 rooms.

Ramsey. Coastal resort and good place from which to visit northern part of island. *Beach Hotel* has 93 rooms and *Grand Island* 65 (22 with bath and 6 with shower).

HOW TO GET TO THE ISLE OF MAN. By steamer from Liverpool to Douglas in 3½ hours, daily in winter, twice daily in summer, by the *Isle of Man Steam Packet Company*. Steamers are also operated seasonally from Belfast, Ardrossan (Scotland), and Dublin to Douglas and Peel.

Cambrian Airways have excellent summer services to Ronaldsway Airport, 8 miles from Douglas, from Liverpool, Manchester, London, and Belfast. Services from London to the island take 75 minutes' flying time. Winters there are daily flights from Liverpool and Manchester; twice weekly from London and Belfast. *Aer Lingus* maintains a seasonal link with Dublin. *British United Airways* fly from Blackpool, Leeds, Birmingham, Edinburgh, Glasgow and other places.

THE ISLE OF MAN

Exploring the Isle of Man

The island's centre is composed of mountain and high moorland, reaching its highest point at the top of Snaefell (2,034 feet), and intersected by thirteen lovely glens, each one of compelling beauty. At the northern extremity of the island, however, a stretch of flat land goes out to the Point of Ayre, which, in clear weather, seems but a stone's throw from the hills of Scotland. To the south there is a similar piece of flatland near Castletown, which houses Ronaldsway, the airport for the island.

Apart from these two sandy sections, however, the coastline is mainly given over to high cliffs, which rise out of the Irish Sea in their majesty and hold within their folds beautiful little bays and coves, some containing villages, others given over entirely to some quiet beach or even the deep sea itself.

Douglas

Douglas, reached by regular sea service from Liverpool, is the largest town on the island and probably the best centre for the visitor. A thriving holiday resort which captures something of the gaiety of Blackpool, its easy access from Lancashire makes it a favourite haunt of people from the mainland towns and cities, many of whom find it hard to tear themselves away from its amusements to explore the mountainous interior of the island.

No one, can deny the grandeur of Douglas Bay, which makes a majestic sweep from Onchan Head to the north to Douglas Head at the south. The promenade follows the same curve, although at the southern end it stops at the harbour, where the River Douglas itself flows between the town and the headland. Here are the larger boarding houses and hotels, one of which, the *Castle Mona*, is interesting on account of its being the residence of the last of the dukes of Atholl to be connected with Man. (It is said that he brought the freestone used in its construction from the island of Arran, off the Scottish coast.) Here, too, are the various places of entertainment, including the lovely *Gaiety Theatre* and the much more modern *Casino*. The horse-drawn tramcars which ply along the promenade are a distinct feature of the town.

Among the most important events of the Isle of Man

calendar are the famous Tourist Trophy races each June, when the finest professional motor-cyclists in the world compete over a 37¾-mile course, incorporating the virtual circuit of Snaefell and calling for the negotiation of some tricky bends and fast stretches of straight road. In September, amateur riders take part in the Manx Grand Prix over the same course.

Outside the actual race weeks, one of the most popular outings is a coach ride over the course, which introduces the visitor to some of the finest scenery of the interior.

On the opposite coast to Douglas is the small cathedral city of Peel, frequently referred to as "Sunset City" because of the magnificent colourings that come to sky and sea when the sun goes down beyond the western horizon, bringing a fairy glow to the warm red sandstone walls of its ancient buildings.

The road from Douglas to Peel passes through a broad valley which separates the northern and southern uplands. On the outskirts of Douglas, this passes the church at Kirk Braddan, the scene of an open-air service each Sunday morning during the summer months, when thousands of people gather on the grassy slopes, and then goes on to St. John's, where the Tynwald ceremony already referred to takes place on July 5 each year.

The Tynwald

Tynwald "hill" itself is an artificial mound, 12 feet high and 240 feet in circumference. There, after a service in the nearby church and a colourful procession, the Lieutenant-Governor, accompanied by the Bishop of Sodor and Man and members of the Legislative Council and House of Keys, gather to hear a recital of the various acts that have received the Queen's signature during the past twelve months and which now become law.

This is claimed as the only outdoor "parliament" in the world and has its origin in the old form of administration carried out by the Scandinavians, who, as we will see later, held sway in the Isle of Man for a lengthy period and who have also left many interesting monuments in the form of carved crosses and the like in different parts of the island.

Peel, a fascinating place of old alleyways, red sandstone buildings, and sandy shore, is the traditional home of the

Manx kipper, and one can see the sheds where the herrings are cured or "kippered".

Most visitors, however, will make for the group of red sandstone buildings on the detached St. Patrick's Isle, which form Peel Castle and Cathedral. The ancient Celts are believed to have had the first church on this spot, where St. Patrick preached in 444 A.D., but this was destroyed in a Viking raid in the eight century. Later, the Norsemen themselves had a fortification of sorts on the little isle, kings Godred and Olaf both dying there.

For several centuries afterwards, the place housed both church and fortress. The cathedral, dedicated to St. German and the cathedral church of the diocese, was rebuilt originally on the site of the older church by one Simon of Iona in 1126, although the diocese itself is said to have been founded by "King" Olaf nearly a century before and, of course, is still maintained. In July each year, Peel remembers its Scandinavian origins with a Viking Festival, during which the townsfolk don Viking warrior garb and re-enact the old Norse invasion.

Later bishops added to the structure, but it was always one of the smaller cathedrals in the British Isles and even in the mid-17th century was in a somewhat dilapidated condition. Although efforts towards restoration have been made, these seem to have been of little avail.

As a fortress, the castellated sections of the buildings have housed prisoners, including the Earl of Warwick, who was confined to one of the towers by Richard II after plotting against the crown in the late 14th century, and one Edward Christian, whom the Earl of Derby had shut away for eight years for supporting the Commonwealth against Charles I.

Ramsey, 16 miles north of Douglas and the chief town of the northern part, is a pleasant coastal resort from where one can visit the Point of Ayre, at the northern extremity of the island, as well as the interesting zoological gardens recently established at The Curraghs, close to the entrance to lovely Sulby Glen, a magic place of woods and waterfalls.

There are two principal routes between Douglas and Ramsey. One climbs across the eastern slopes of Snaefell and commands fine views over the island and across the Irish Sea; the other keeps nearer the coast, going through Laxey and passing the entrances to some delightful little glens leading down to the shore on the way to Maughold, where the cliff scenery is magnificent, before dropping into Ramsey itself.

From Laxey, a valley goes inland towards Snaefell. This was once the centre of a prosperous mining industry, and a feature is the world's biggest pump wheel, 227 feet in circumference and 72 feet in diameter, used for keeping the underground workings, which in places extend to a depth of 2,000 feet, free from water. Although no longer working, it remains as one of the show pieces of the Isle of Man.

Laxey, too, is the terminus of the Snaefell Mountain Railway, which carries visitors to the very summit of the mountain where, on clear days, you can have wonderful views across the sea to the four countries of England, Scotland, Wales and Ireland, not to mention the whole of the island itself, set like a panoramic map below.

In the southern half of the island is Castletown, once the Manx capital, but now simply a pleasant holiday resort whose sheltered harbour is guarded by Castle Rushen, one of the best-preserved medieval fortresses in Britain. The road to Castletown from Douglas passes the grounds of Rushen Abbey, once a Cistercian monastery (founded by King Olaf about 1134) and now laid out in delightful gardens in which an orchestra plays during the summer months.

It is in this southern section of the island that the coastal scenery rises to its full grandeur. Port St. Mary and Port Erin, both picturesque in themselves, are close to the magnificent cliffs, which show their real majesty at Spanish Head, opposite which the isolated rocky isle of the Calf of Man, now a bird sanctuary maintained by the National Trust, rises in abrupt loneliness from the deep sea. And between Port Erin and Peel, Niarbyl Bay is a place for the connoisseur of all that is best in British coastal scenery.

WALES

Land of Poets and Singers

by

JEAN WAKEMAN and JAMES E. THOMAS

(*Jean Wakeman, who was born in the Welsh Marches country, now lives in Oxfordshire. As an author and journalist, she drives 25,000 miles a year seeing countries first-hand. James E. Thomas is a Welshman and cosmopolitan, a lawyer and writer. He has travelled extensively, writing about France, Germany, and, of course, his native Wales.*)

> The land of my Fathers so dear to my soul,
> The land which the poet and minstrel extol.
> Her valiant defenders, her patriots so brave
> For freedom their life blood they gave.

It is indeed rare in this modern world to find a national anthem that stresses so much the artistic, as opposed to the political, aspect of the country. But it is necessary to understand fully this attitude before one can appreciate the subtle change that takes place as we pass the borderline between England and Wales. For no one can cross this frontier into the first little Welsh village without realizing that one is no longer in England. This is due not solely to the question of the language, although Welsh is indeed a sufficient obstacle to most of us who desire to penetrate more deeply into the mysteries of the Welsh character, but rather a profound difference in the way of living, in the attitude towards life of this small, tenacious people.

For the people of Wales represent the remnants of those pugnacious Celtic people who were subjected to centuries of Roman rule, underwent the invasions of the Saxons who drove them to their mountain fastnesses, and endured the phenomenal organizing efficiency of the Norman conquerors without ceding one iota of their cultural independence.

And here, perhaps, is the secret of the essential difference of the Welsh. An old Welsh proverb says, "The Celt always fights and always loses." Militarily and politically this has been true of the Welsh, but, during those centuries of ceaseless strife, the Welshman came to realize that there was something deeper, more important than political or military triumph, something he had always been unconsciously struggling to preserve, an indefinable passion for the music and poetry born of his lonely vigils in mountain and valley when he held solitary converse with the infinite, and, in this last and greatest battle, the Welshman has belied the proverb and emerged victorious.

Thus, very briefly, we have an explanation of the extraordinary tenacity with which this people has clung to its traditions, its customs, its language, and its own way of life, although politically it has been merged long since and has accepted the supremacy of Westminster with much less difficulty than the Irish or the Scots.

This same fierce individualism, running like a flame through national life, explains two striking characteristics of the Welsh people—their non-conformity in religion; and radicalism (or zeal for reform) in the political and social spheres.

At the time of the Civil War, the religious and social upheaval which was tearing England apart spread quickly to Wales. Here the non-conformists, or protesting faction, rapidly gained ground in a country where the people had been neglected for so long. Neither the English nor their language were understood, and here was a new doctrine being preached to them in Welsh. No wonder it spread like wildfire! The oldest non-conformist place of worship in Wales, Maesyronen Congregational Chapel at Glasbury, was built about this time, 1696. Then, not many years later, in 1743, John Wesley and his followers came to preach. Their faith and fervour, and spontaneous hymn-singing were just what the people needed, and soon the Methodist movement became a spearhead for a great religious revival. Little chapels sprang up in every village, but it was a hundred years later, in the middle of last century, that most of those to be seen today were built—at the time of the industrial revolution, when a second religious revival was under way.

This was after the huge South Wales coalfield was discovered; it was to change the face of Wales. Until then, Wales had been almost entirely an agricultural country—bitterly poor, certainly, and often oppressed. A series of catastrophic harvests caused a constant stream of emigrants to the United States, and at the same time a fierce struggle was developing between landlords (who often spoke only English and who frequently lived in England), and the peasants. Side by side with this rural unrest was a greater menace—the discontent caused by the industrial explosion. That had not only laid waste the green valleys, but it made living and working conditions intolerable. People were herded together like animals into houses, which, because of the steepness of the valleys, had to be built in terraces one above the other, till half the population of Wales was concentrated there, and opportunities for oppression were unlimited. There were riots at Merthyr, and a Chartist march on Newport, where the Westbury Hotel was besieged.

The anguish of the valleys was the catalyst that in Wales (England had her own problems) brought about the first corporate moves towards trade, or labour, unions. Ironically, it was Robert Owen, the son of a saddler of Newtown, who first led the way for better conditions for workers; he was the pioneer of factory reform in Scotland. But nothing effective was possible until there was parliamentary reform, and an extension of the franchise. This came in 1867, and a year later, a general election gave the vote to industrial workers. For the first time the valleys had a voice, right inside the British Parliament. It began as Liberal, but they soon returned their own member, which eventually led to a new party, Labour, being born. This naturally became synonymous with the labour unions. A good deal later on, Aneurin Bevan became the voice of the valleys, and he spent his life fighting for what he believed in so passionately.

Many Welshmen have been famous statesmen—one has only to think of Lloyd George as an instance in modern times—but now that non-conformity and radicalism have reached their goals, politics for the Welshman are generally narrowed down to the passionate defence of his language, his customs and his way of living. His true genius flowers most often in the artistic and creative worlds, in music, theatre and poetry. It burns as brightly as ever in the poet Dylan Thomas, a memorable and controversial character; another poet, R. S. Thomas, who is still weaving his magic from an obscure country parish; actor Richard Burton; Emlyn Williams, playwright and actor; Clough Williams Ellis, brilliant architect and landscape artist, who created the dream village of Portmeirion; and Mary Quant, world-famous fashion designer and trend-setter.

Practical Information for Wales

WHERE TO STAY? The places mentioned below are all in or near some of the loveliest parts of Wales. You may find hotels in the small spots simple, but any inconveniences will be compensated for by the scenery. Throughout the summer there are the *Eisteddfodau* (festivals of music and arts), the best places to hear Welsh singing. Wales is a great outdoor country, with ample opportunity for mountaineering, angling, golf and pony trekking. If you plan to visit Wales during either the National Welsh, or International Musical Eisteddfodau, book well ahead.

ABERDOVEY (Merioneth.). Select seaside resort: boating, golf. Good beach. *Trefeddian*, 45 rooms (some with bath), first-class reasonable. *Penhelig Arms*, 7 rooms (2 with bath), moderate.

ABERGAVENNY (Mon.). Busy market town, gateway to Wales and centre for Brecon Beacons, castles. Fishing, boating, golf. *Angel* (Trust House), 32 rooms (4 with bath), first class.

ABERYSTWYTH (Cardiganshire). Popular resort on Cardigan Bay, university, all holiday amenities. *Belle Vue Royal*, 50 rooms (6 with bath), first-class reasonable. *Marine*, 40 rooms; and *Seabank*, 21 rooms, moderate.

BALA (Merionethshire). Market town on Wales's largest natural lake. Mountain scenery; sports centre. Fishing, sailing, golf. *White Lion Royal*, 27 rooms (3 with bath). First-class reasonable.

WALES

BANGOR (Caernarvonshire). University and cathedral city. Penrhyn Castle nearby. Anglesey opposite. *Castle*, 44 rooms (1 with bath), moderate.

BARMOUTH (Merioneth). Has 3 miles of beach, but dangerous tides on Mawddach estuary. *Hendre Mynach Hall*, 10 rooms; *Min-y-Mor*, 59 rooms (4 with bath); *Royal* (Trust House), 17 rooms; all moderate.

BEAUMARIS (Anglesey). Overlooking Menai Straits; popular yachting centre. *Bulkeley Arms*, 40 rooms (6 with bath), first-class reasonable; *Ye Olde Bull's Head*, 15 rooms (4 with bath), moderate.

BETWYS-Y-COED (Caernarvonshire). A lovely village in majestic surroundings; convenient for coast and Snowdonia. *Gwydyr*, 23 rooms; *Royal Oak*, 36 rooms (1 with bath); *Glan Aber*, 22 rooms (3 with bath); all moderate.

BRECON (Breconshire). Centre for Brecon Beacons. Castle ruins, 15th-century church. Good golf, fishing, boating. *Castle*, 23 rooms (4 with bath), first-class reasonable.

BUILTH WELLS (Breconshire). Inland spa; good fishing, ponytrekking centre. *Greyhound*, 14 rooms, moderate; *Lion*, 22 rooms (5 with bath).

CAERNARVON. County town, gateway to Snowdonia. *Royal*, 47 rooms (4 with bath), moderate.

CARDIFF (Glamorgan.). Capital city of Wales; ancient castle, national and folk museums, Llandaff Cathedral. *Angel*, 118 rooms (43 with bath); *Park*, 100 rooms (80 with bath); *Queen's*, 42 rooms (5 with bath); *Royal*, 88 rooms; *Grand*, 33 rooms.

CARDIGAN. County town of Welsh Wales. Near sandy beaches and cliffs. Teifi Valley. Boating, fishing. *Black Lion*, 12 rooms (4 with bath); *Grosvenor*, 21 rooms. *Webley* (Poppit Sands), 10 rooms. All moderate.

CARMARTHEN. County town, focus of Celtic life. *Ivy Bush Royal*, 62 rooms (24 with bath), first-class.

CHEPSTOW (Monmouthshire). Medieval town guarding the Wye valley, with Norman castle, town walls and historic buildings. New Severn Bridge nearby. *Beaufort*, 12 rooms; *Cedars*, 15 rooms (1 with bath); *George*, 18 rooms, all moderate.

CONWAY (Caernarvonshire). Fortified medieval town within city walls, castle and harbour. *Castle* (Trust House), 26 rooms (1 with bath); *Erskine*, 10 rooms. Both moderate.

CRICCIETH (Caernarvonshire). Seaside resort, 13th-cent. castle. *Bron Eifion*, 19 rooms (3 with bath), first class; *Lion*, 31 rooms (3 with bath), moderate.

DEVIL'S BRIDGE (Cardiganshire). Spectacular natural beauty spot near Aberystwyth. *Hafod Arms*, 22 rooms, first class.

DOLGELLAU (Merioneth.). Mountaineering centre at foot of Cader Idris; fishing. *Golden Lion Royal*, 30 rooms (4 with bath), first-class reasonable; *Bontddu Hall Hotel* (Bontddu), 23 rooms (3 with bath), first class.

FISHGUARD (Pembs.). Picturesque town and harbour. Sailing, fishing, port for Ireland. *Abergwaun*, 12 rooms, moderate. *Compton House*, 6 rooms, good food, Welsh specialities.

HARLECH (Merioneth.). Castle. Health resort. Championship golf, good sands. *St. David's*, 70 rooms (7 with bath), first-class reasonable.

HAVERFORDWEST (Pembs.) Small, picturesque town. Good touring centre for county.

Mariners, 25 rooms (2 with bath), moderate. Good food.

LLANBERIS (Caernarvonshire). Mountaineering centre at foot of Snowdon (rack railway to summit) also lakes. *Royal Victoria*, 75 rooms (8 with bath), *Dolbadarn*, 15 rooms.

LLANDRINDOD WELLS (Radnorshire). Leading inland spa; golf, fishing, boating, riding. *Commodore*, 39 rooms (6 with bath); *Glen Usk*, 80 rooms (26 with bath). Both first-class reasonable. *Metropole*, 138 rooms (14 with bath); *Mostyn*, 18 rooms, good food.

LLANDUDNO (Caernarvonshire). Popular coast resort, good beach, rather Coney Island in atmosphere. Pleasure steamers to Liverpool and Isle of Man. Many passable hotels. *Grand*, 140 rooms (40 with bath); *Imperial*, 118 rooms (37 with bath); *Craigside Hydro*, 150 rooms (50 with bath); *St. George's*, 82 rooms (19 with bath). All first-class superior. *Empire*, 33 rooms (4 with bath); *Gogarth Abbey* (where Lewis Carroll wrote *Alice in Wonderland*), 50 rooms (6 with bath); *Marine* (Trust House), 82 rooms (10 with bath). All first-class reasonable.

LLANGOLLEN (Denbighshire). Beautiful old town on R. Dee. Annual venue, International Musical Eisteddfod (2nd week in July). *Royal* (Trust House), 32 rooms (9 with bath); *Hand*, 65 rooms (7 with bath). Both moderate.

MACHYNLLETH (Montgomeryshire). Historic market town near Dovey estuary; centre for mountains, lakes, fishing. *White Lion*, 20 rooms (3 with bath); *Wynnstay* (Trust House), 30 rooms. Both moderate.

MONMOUTH. Ancient county town with unique Norman fortified bridge. Famous Nelson collection. Best centre for Wye Valley, Forest of Dean. *Beaufort Arms* (Trust House), 26 rooms (3 with bath); *Royal George*, 16 rooms. Both moderate.

NEWPORT (Monmouthshire). Ruins of 12th-century castle. Close to Caerleon's Roman ruins. *Queens*, 44 rooms (some with bath).

PEMBROKE. Ancient town, castle, near magnificent cliff scenery. Fishing, boating; nearby car ferry. *Old King's Arms*, 10 rooms (3 with bath), first-class reasonable; *Lion*, 32 rooms (1 with bath) moderate.

PORTHCAWL (Glamorgan). Popular seaside resort, good beaches, (5 lovely bays). Angling, water sports, excellent golf. *Seabank*, 130 rooms (70 with bath), first-class reasonable; *Esplanade*, 88 rooms (25 with bath); *Fairways*, 26 rooms; *Porthcawl*, 31 rooms and *Marine*, 30 rooms, are all moderate.

PORTMADOC (Caernarvonshire). Harbour town in picturesque Snowdonia setting. Fishing, yachting, sands. *Royal Sportsman* (Trust House), 20 rooms, moderate. *Portmeirion Hotel* nearby, luxury centre of famous Italianate village on a small private peninsula.

PWLLHELI (Caernarvonshire). 5 miles of magnificent beach, good touring centre. Near holiday camp, with day tickets for amusements. *Crown*, 18 rooms.

ST. DAVID'S (Pembs.). Cathedral and village. Sandy beaches and rugged coast. Golf, fishing, sailing. Trips to offshore islands, bird sanctuary. *Grove*, 10 rooms (1 with bath); *Warpole Court*, 16 rooms (2 with bath). Both moderate.

SWANSEA (Glamorgan.). University, seaside resort, important port, and second city of Wales. Nearby Gower country. *Dragon,* Trust House. This 8-story hotel has 117 rooms, all with bath; all-day buttery, and restaurant. *Dolphin,* 67 rooms, all with bath. Both first-class superior.

TENBY (Pembs.). Walled town, castle and harbour. Good bathing, boating, trips to Caldey Island, and along coast. *Atlantic,* 49 rooms (16 with bath); *Belgrave,* 50 rooms (20 with bath); both first class. *Royal Gate House,* 66 rooms (6 with bath). Moderate.

TINTERN (Monmouthshire). Charming village in Wye Valley with 12th-century Cistercian abbey. *Beaufort,* 27 rooms (7 with bath); *Royal George,* 7 rooms; both reasonable.

TYN Y MAES (Caernarvonshire). *Snowdonia Park Motel,* 19 rooms with bath. Moderate. New.

WREXHAM (Denbighshire). Industrial town and burial place of Elihu Yale, founder of Yale University. *Wynnstay Arms,* 73 rooms (1 with bath), moderate.

DINING OUT. Drinking laws differ from those in England, and in some counties, by law, no alcoholic beverages may be served on Sundays except to resident guests. All pubs are closed. This applies to all Wales, except Flintshire, Radnorshire, Breconshire, Glamorgan, Monmouth, Montgomery, Pembrokeshire and Denbighshire, and the county boroughs of Cardiff, Newport, Merthyr Tydfil, and Swansea.

Welsh food is simple. Fresh local produce, like poultry, game and fish, is best. Wayside inns and farms provide delicious home cooking. Near the coast, try crabs, shrimps, lobsters, sewin (seatrout) and salmon. Local mutton is a great specialty; so are Welsh curd cakes, Snowdon pudding and home-made wines, when you can get them. There is a growing number of hotels and pubs providing first-class imaginative cooking; but again, book well ahead.

GOOD RESTAURANTS

ABERGAVENNY (near). *Clytha Arms,* on Monmouth Rd. A40. Roadside inn. Fresh local food. Steak bar. Open till 10 p.m. At Llandewi Skirrid, *Walnut Tree Inn.* Excellent.

CARDIFF. Grill Room of *New Continental Restaurant.*

CARMARTHEN. *Ivy Bush Royal.* Grill open till 11 p.m.

FISHGUARD. *Compton House Hotel.* English, French, Spanish dishes. Welsh specialties for lunch. Gay, bistro setting.

HAVERFORDWEST. *Pembroke House Hotel, Chez Gilbert.* Fine original cooking.

LLANARMON DYFFRYN CEIRIOG. *West Arms Hotel.* Fine old Welsh inn. Good roasts. Cheerful atmosphere.

LLANGADOG. *Red Lion.* Outstanding food in French-run restaurant. Small hotel just off A40.

LLANGOLLEN. *Chain Bridge Hotel.* 1½ miles west on A5. Elegant restaurant in old stone inn, built over the Dee.

LLANGURIG. *Black Lion.* Delightful wayside inn, with good, simple food.

LLANHAMLACH. *Old Ford Inn.* Roadside (A40), with interesting, varied food. Good curries. Snacks.

LLANRWST. *Pen-y-Bont Inn.* Outstanding cuisine, dinner by candlelight. No lunches.

NEVERN. *Trewern Arms*, a charming spot.

NEWPORT. *Gaslight Room* of Queen's Hotel is good. Very Victorian.

PANT-MAWR. *Glansevern Arms.* Near Llangurig, on A44. Roadside inn. Simple, excellent local food. Snacks at bar. Plynlimon setting.

PENMAENPOOL. *George III.* Overlooking Mawwdach estuary beside toll bridge. Excellent imaginative cooking. Cellar bar, with home-made buffet food.

PENRHNYDEUDRAETH. *Portmeirion Hotel.* Sophisticated international cuisine, mainly English/German lunch; French at dinner. Superb setting. *Salutation Trattoria* in grounds, good; mainly grills.

RUTHIN. *Ruthin Castle Hotel.* Famous for unique Elizabethan banquet with traditional Welsh dishes, served in luxurious 13th-century castle. Musicians and singers in period costume.

SWANBRIDGE. *Sully House Hotel.* Outstanding French cuisine in modern setting.

Historic Houses Open to the Public

BRECONSHIRE. *Tretower Court*, Crickhowell. Fine medieval house; open weekdays, Sunday afternoons, all year.

CAERNARVONSHIRE. *Caernarvon Castle*, 13th-century and *Conway Castle* are two of Edward I's fortresses for subduing the Welsh. Both are open weekdays, Sunday afternoons, all year. *Penrhyn Castle*, Bangor. Built of Mona marble. Open most weekdays, April to October. At Hafodty, Bettws Garmon, you can see *Nant Mill Falls*, and watch elvers from the Sargasso Sea migrating upstream, June-July; salmon leaping, Sept.-December. Although the gate to Major G. E. Lloyd Jones's property is marked "private", you can go through freely. *Brynawelon Gardens,* the home of the late Lady Megan Lloyd-George, open every Tuesday, May to September.

DENBIGHSHIRE. *Chirk Castle*, near Wrexham. Built 1310 and exterior unaltered, inhabited continuously for 650 years. Open Tues., Thurs., Sat., Sun., May thro' September. *Gwydir Castle*, near Llanrwst. Historic Tudor mansion. Open daily, all year. *Bodnant Gardens*, near Conway. National Trust. Beautiful terraced gardens, open Easter through October, Tues., Weds., Thurs., Sats. *Plas Newydd*, Llangollen. The picturesque, black and white home of the Laides of Llangollen, full of carvings and curios from 18th- and 19th-century celebrities. Superb gardens. Open every day. *Ruthin Castle*, Ruthin. Spectacular 13th-century castle (now hotel that serves medieval Welsh banquets nightly except Sundays), open most of the year.

GLAMORGAN. *Cardiff Castle*, begun in the 11th century. Open daily, May through October. *St. Fagan's Castle*, Cardiff. Welsh Folk Museum, 16th-century house, 13th-century castle. Open weekdays (except Monday) and Sunday afternoons.

MERIONETHSHIRE. *Harlech Castle*, 13th-century, famous in song ("Men of Harlech"). Open weekdays and Sunday afternoons, all year. *Portmeirion*, unique Italian-style village and gardens, open daily, Easter to mid-October.

MONMOUTHSHIRE. *Llanvihangel Court*, Abergavenny. 16th-century manor house. Open afternoons, first and third Sundays, June through August, and Bank Holiday Sundays and Mondays.

MONTGOMERYSHIRE. *Powis Castle*, Welshpool. National Trust. Dates from 13th century and has beautiful gardens. Open most days, June through September (garden from May.)

TRANSPORTATION. *North Wales* is reached by rail from London via Euston Station; *Central and South Wales* from Paddington Station; by air from Manchester and elsewhere to *Glamorgan Airport*, at Rhoose, near Barry (apply to *Cambrian Airways Ltd.*, Wood St., Cardiff). The best *road* approach from London is via the new Severn Road Bridge. The transport system in Wales is well developed; if you are not travelling by car, it is easy to get about by the numerous bus services, day coach tours or by making use of the Holiday Runabout Tickets (apply any *British Rail* station). Day and half-day coach tours are run from all main towns by *Crosville Coach Services, Ltd.* (apply to Crane Wharf, Chester). 8-day coach tours are run from London by *London Coastal Coaches, Ltd.*, Victoria Coach Station, London S.W.1.

Narrow-gauge railway enthusiasts can do five different journeys in Wales. Originally built to carry slate from quarries deep in the mountains to the coast, these Walt Disney-like carriages and engines now take holiday visitors through spectacular scenery. They are: *The Vale of Rheidol* from Aberystwyth to Devil's Bridge through the gorge. *Snowdon Mountain Railway*, from Llanberis to the summit, 3,560 ft. by rack and pinion. *Tallyllyn*, from Towyn to the foot of Cader Idris; *Festiniog Railway*, grandest of all, from Portmadoc to Tan-y-Bwlch; and *Welshpool-Llanfair* from Llanfair up the delectable Banwy Valley

MUSEUMS AND ART GALLERIES. Although every town of importance has some kind of a museum or gallery, we list here only a few of the major collections, in alphabetical order: Aberystwyth: *University College of Wales Museum & Art Gallery* (pottery and wooden items); *The National Library of Wales* (one of 6 copyright libraries in Britain). Bangor: *Museum of Welsh Antiquities* (prehistoric and Roman-British objects); *Penrhyn Castle* (Philippa Judge doll collection and locomotives). Brecon: *Brecknock Museum* (local antiquities and natural history).

Carleon: *The Legionary Museum* (objects from Roman Legion's Isca Fortress). Caernarvon: *Segontium Museum* (on site of Roman fort); *Royal Welch Fusiliers*, headquarters at Caernarvon Castle has a small museum.

Cardiff: *National Museum of Wales* (art, archeology, geology, botany and zoology, excellently displayed). Carmarthen: *County Museum* (Ogham inscribed stones, Roman jewellery, etc.). Conway: *Royal Cambrian Academy of Art* (permanent exhibition of Welsh artists).

Llandrindod Wells: *Radnorshire County Museum* (Roman findings). Llandudno: *Rapallo House Museum & Art Gallery* (fine arts and a Welsh kitchen). Llanelli: *Parc Howard Museum & Art Gallery* (collection of Llanelli pottery). Llangollen: *Plas Newydd Museum* (home of the odd "Ladies of Llangollen"). Llanystumdwy: *Lloyd-George Museum* (relics of the former prime minister).

Merthyr Tydfil: *Art Gallery & Museum* of Cyfarthfa Castle (coins and medals, etc.). Monmouth: *Nelson Museum* (relics of the admiral and Lady Hamilton).

Newport: *Newport Museum & Art Gallery* (Roman relics, Pontypool Japan ware, etc.).

Penarth: *Turner House* (pictures, etc.). Portmadoc: *Festiniog Railway Museum*. Portmeirion: *Architectural Museum* of many buildings from 17th century to present, including barbican gate-house, lighthouse and cloisters.

St. Fagans: *Welsh Folk Museum* (in the castle, re-erected buildings). Swansea: *Glynn Vivian Art Museum* (British paintings, glass, etc.); *Industrial Museum of South Wales*.

Towyn: *Narrow Gauge Railway Museum*.

A Welshman never forgets his national customs, music or dress. At the Royal National Eisteddfod white-robed Druids and blue-robed bards compete in the song and poetry to which the Welsh are so passionately devoted.

The pipers and highland fling dancer of the Scots Guards suggest the vivid martial traditions of the Scots, and this same spirit is reflected in the battlemented cliffs of Castle Rock which dominate Edinburgh's Princes Street.

Exploring Wales

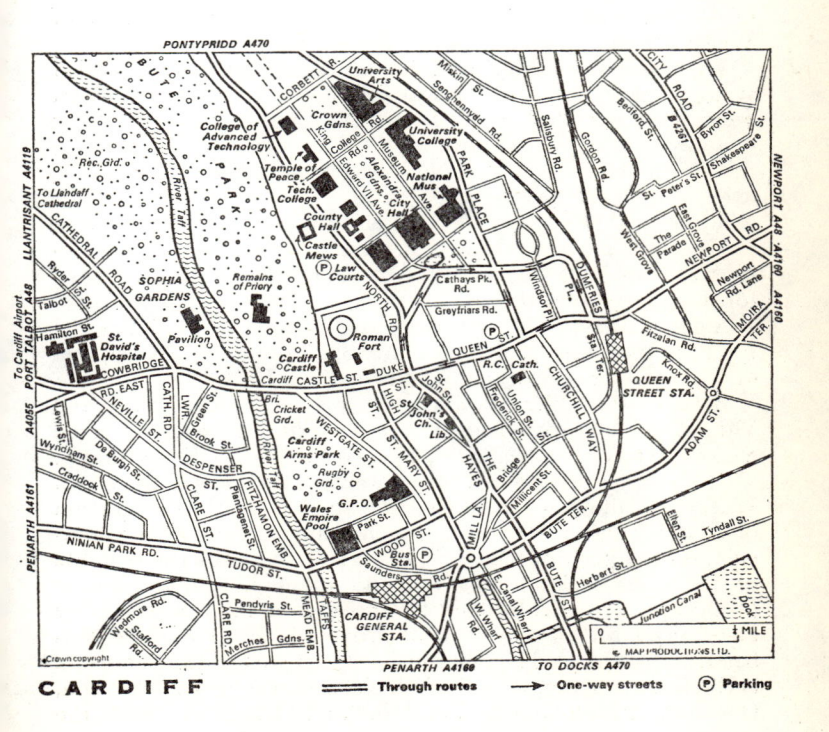

Financially and industrially Cardiff is the most important city in Wales. Hundreds of thousands of the inhabitants of Wales live and work in this town and the adjoining county of Glamorgan, which have drained the valleys and mountains in their ceaseless quest for labour to man the enormous docks through which flows the ceaseless river of coal from the Rhondda Valley on its journey to the ends of the earth. In the roads leading to the docks of Cardiff you will find, much as in Liverpool, Marseilles, or any other great commercial port, the extraordinary mixture of humanity that great ocean-going ships always seem to attract. Chinese, Lascars, and Negroes rub shoulders with Welshmen whose long contact with this cosmopolitan life has deprived them even of that treasured heritage, the Welsh language. Here you will find little that is typically Welsh.

But away from the docks Cardiff is a beautiful city. Among its prized tourist destinations are Llandaff Cathedral with its statue of 'Christ in Majesty' by Epstein, and Cardiff Castle, given to the city by the Marquis of Bute. Partly used as a college of music and drama (connected to the University College of South Wales and Monmouth), it has beautifully-decorated public rooms, which can be seen on a tour. Cathay's Park, the centre of the civic life of the city, with its exceptionally fine group of municipal buildings and its National Museum of Wales, where you will find an enthralling collection of Welsh art and handicraft, is a splendid place.

With the university and its animated groups of Welsh youngsters who swarm around its buildings you touch upon one of the essential enthusiasms of the Welsh people, their passionate love and desire for knowledge. How many small farmers and coal-miners have toiled and deprived themselves even of many of the bare necessities of life in order that their children may have the benefit of an education they themselves have never known? For it is axiomatic in Wales that no talented child shall be deprived of the opportunities necessary for his development.

A few miles to the north of Cardiff lies Caerphilly, noted both for its cheese and for its fine old Edwardian castle, one of whose towers out-leans the one at Pisa, Italy!

Between Cardiff and Swansea runs the delightful, unscarred Vale of Glamorgan; this unexpected world of its own has some charming towns and villages, steeped in antiquarian interests.

Swansea marks the end of the industrial region of the south Wales coastline. And, as if to make amends for the desecration of so much natural beauty, the charming little Gower peninsula, on the neck of which Swansea stands, offers the delights of its wooded landscape and its quiet unspoilt beaches. (Mumbles, a bus ride from Swansea, is a favourite holiday resort and an admirable spot from which to explore this beautiful countryside.) The southwestern part of the peninsula is English-speaking, with English place names such as Cheriton, Overton, Pilton-Green, Fernhill, and Knelston, and the

WALES

inhabitants refer to those living in the eastern districts as those living in the "Welsheries".

Several ruined castles, such as those at Penrice and Oystermouth, prove the importance of Gower in ancient days. At Llanrhidian stands an enormous cromlech known as Arthur's Stone. It is said locally that at night time it comes down to the sea to quench its thirst.

The Carmarthen Valleys

North of Swansea, in the direction of Ammanford, lie the valleys so well described by Richard Llewellyn in *How Green Was My Valley*. But it requires all the vivid imagination of the poet to see these slag-covered hillocks and pit-pocked dales as they were before their virgin beauty was soiled by the advent of the industrial age. Yet, within a few miles, there is an incredible metamorphosis.

As you travel north, the skyline fills with lordly mountains; Carmarthen Van, the triple summits of the Brecon Beacons, and, to the east, the Black Mountains. These wild, windswept uplands stretch from the fertile Vale of Towy to the delectable Usk Valley, and are now protected as the Brecon Beacons National Park. This is the home of the sturdy wild Welsh mountain pony, and also of vast flocks of sheep. Brecon and Abergavenny, the two principal towns in the area, are places where you may well pick up a bargain in the antique shops and local sales—perhaps a hand-carved wooden Welsh love spoon like those in Brecon's little museum. Both towns are also popular centres for pony-trekking, salmon and trout fishing, and climbing in the Beacons. Six miles west of Brecon, hidden away near the remote village of Libanus, is the newly-built Mountain Centre, which has an information bureau, a buffet serving refreshments, and a marvellous panoramic view of the Beacons. Before leaving this scenic corner of Wales, try to fit in a trip to Craig-y-Nos in the Tawe Valley (A40, then A4067 from Brecon). Here you can go on a conducted 45-minute walk *under* a mountain through the spectacular illuminated Dan-yr-Ogof Caves.

Through the town of Carmarthen flows the Towy, famed for its salmon and its coracle-men. There are few of them left today, but if you happen to observe one at work you will see something that has not changed for thousands of years. The coracle is, in fact, a sort of wicker basket over which a leathery skin has been stretched to make it watertight. On the inside, across the middle, is a small wooden plank that serves as a seat, and attached to each end of the seat is a leather thong the coracle-man uses when he carries the coracle on his back. When walking he looks like a giant turtle, and when he poses his frail shell on the water it is fascinating to see the dexterity with which he manoeuvres it.

Carmarthen is a quiet country town with an ancient castle now used as council offices. But on market days the town is full of lively, chattering folk who come in from the surrounding countryside with their wares, and the sing-song lilt of the Carmarthenshire accent fills the narrow streets. (Nearly every county in Wales has a slight difference in accent to distinguish it from the others, but it is difficult for a non-Welshman to appreciate this. Between north and south Wales the difference is very marked.) In the main street of Carmarthen is the stump of an ancient oak tree which is carefully tended, for the legendary magician Merlin prophecied that if the tree sickens and dies, so also will Carmarthen.

Around Carmarthen is a soft, undulating, fertile countryside watered by innumerable little trout streams, and stretching northwards as far as Lampeter and Newcastle Emlyn on the Teifi. This river marks the boundary between Carmarthenshire and Cardiganshire, and as we progress northwards the scenery tends to become less softly undulating, the hills more sharply defined, and the little mountain streams more hurried as they sing their way over pebbly beds. All the roads around Carmarthen are admirable for motoring or cycling, whilst delightful footpaths entice the walker to hidden nooks.

Where the Towy runs into the sea in Carmarthen Bay you may see another sight to remind you sharply that you are in a land where ancient ways of life remain vigorous in spite of the impact of our mechanized civilization. For here the cockle-women set forth at low tide, each on a donkey and with her head enveloped in a shawl fastened in the Arab fashion to protect her against the wind that can at times rage fiercely across the sands. Two, three, or four miles they trot, their donkeys splashing along in the shallow water, and looking exactly like a convoy of Bedouins in a flooded Sahara. The cockles lie hidden just under the surface, and with quick, dexterous fingers the cocklewomen scrape the sand and scoop them into their baskets where they are washed with sea water. With full baskets they trot briskly shorewards to prepare the cockles for the market. In Swansea, or in Carmarthen on market day, you will find them in the streets, where you may enjoy cockles and vinegar for a few pennies a plate.

Laugharne is an ancient township of great charm. It was the home, and is now the burial place, of Dylan Thomas. He lived in the Boathouse, and the neighbourhood is the setting of *Under Milk Wood*. Every three years, there is a local festival.

Pembrokeshire

Down the coast to Tenby and we are in Pembrokeshire, the county that fills the southwestern tip of Wales. Pembrokeshire is in many ways one of the most curious counties in Wales. You may doubt sometimes whether Pembrokeshire is in Wales, for all around are English names like Deeplake, New Hedges, Rudbaxton, and others. Indeed, south of Trefgarn it is difficult to find a Welsh name, whilst off the coast near Milford Haven, the two bird sanctuary islands of Skomer and Skokholm add another (Scandinavian) linguistic complication to the scene. And you may wander over much of south Pembrokeshire without finding anyone who even understands Welsh! South Pembrokeshire, in fact, is known as "Little England beyond Wales".

This curious phenomenon derives its origin from the forcible settling of the English, hard on the heels of the Norman conquerors, and, whether the antipathy was mutual or unilateral, it remains an amazing fact that the two groups of people, living in some places in the same village, have always remained distinct and separate.

The Normans followed up their conquest of Britain by invading and occupying large tracts of Pembrokeshire, so you will not be disappointed if you look for Norman castles there. Tenby, itself, is an antiquarian's delight with its ancient walled town and historical remains, whilst the practical inhabitants have also utilized to the full its unique position on a cliff overlooking Carmarthen Bay and its firm sandy beach to turn it into the most sophisticated seaside resort in South Wales.

Caldy Island, a couple of miles south of Tenby, is tiny but enchanting in the profusion of its bays and coves. The southern part of the island swarms with seabirds whose shrill cries are at times almost deafening. Despite its size Caldy has a recently-built monastery where the monks carry on weaving and metal work, and make their world-famous perfume. It is a pot-pourri of lavender, gorse, ferns and flowers which grow in masses on the island. And, typically Welsh, there is even a printing press.

Manorbier, on the road to Pembroke, is perhaps best known as the birthplace of Geraldus Cambrensis, the 12th-century writer who left us much interesting information about the Wales of his day.

Pembroke is worth a visit if only to see the great moated castle, one of the most impressive in Wales and the birthplace of Henry VIII in 1457. It is easily accessible by road from Tenby, and the drive permits one also to stop a moment at Lamphey, anciently the country seat of the bishops of St. David's. The ruins of the bishop's palace are open for inspection.

The first people to settle Milford Haven here were Quakers who had had to leave Nantucket Island, Massachusetts, in 1793. It is easy to see even now the advantages its magnificent natural harbour with its numerous creeks gave it. Henry II used it in 1172 as the base from which he sailed to conquer Ireland, and until the early 19th century it still retained its importance as a point of departure for more peaceful voyagers to Ireland. It had one of the best fleets of fishing trawlers in Britain, but now it is rapidly becoming a major oil terminus, able to handle tankers of colossal size.

On the banks of the Western Cleddau, which flows into Milford Haven, is Haverfordwest, English in aspect and sentiment. A town such as you might find in one of the English southern counties, with its picturesque steep streets and its purposeful air of a prosperous little market town. The 13th-century Church of St. Mary is probably one of the finest of its kind in Wales.

Fishguard is the terminus of the main South Wales railway line from London, and the port of embarkation for Southern Ireland.

The town itself is perched on a cliff overlooking the harbour, and gives a superb view over the beautiful bay of Fishguard.

On the northern tip of country that juts out over St. Bride's Bay is what has been described as the "holiest ground in Great

Britain", for here, in the midst of a tiny village, is the venerable Cathedral of St. David, and the Shrine of the Saint, where his bones rest in a casket behind the high altar. Unlike any other cathedral it does not seek to dominate the surrounding countryside with its enormous mass, for it is set, quaintly enough, in an enormous hollow, and the visitor must climb down 39 steps (called locally the Thirty-Nine Articles) to enter the cathedral.

The first view of this cathedral is quite extraordinary for, from a distance, only the square tower can be seen, and it is only by approaching the vast hollow that one can see that there is a cathedral built within it.

From the outside, St. David's has a certain simple austerity that harmonizes well with the desolate, windswept countryside where it is built, but the interior is endowed with a richness that more than recompenses for this external severity. In the hush of this ancient building, soaked in centuries of tradition, one can recapture the atmosphere of those days nearly 1,400 years ago when this was almost the solitary outpost of Christianity in the British Isles.

Not far from St. David's are the ruins of the Church of Saint Nonna, the mother of St. David, and tradition has it that St. David himself was born here. As everywhere in this most westerly point of Wales, the coastal scenery is unsurpassed for rugged grandeur, and as such is preserved as the Pembrokeshire Coast National Park.

Cardiganshire

It is Cardiganshire's proud boast that it is the most Welsh of all the counties in Wales, and it is certainly true that nowhere in Cardiganshire will you find anything but Welsh as the predominant language of the people. A county of small farmsteads, fertile valleys watered by the Rheidol, the Aeron, the Ystwyth, the Teifi, and innumerable little mountain streams, it offers a pleasantly undulating landscape which, in the north, with Plynlimon, gives way to rugged and majestic mountain scenery. The coastline, from Aberporth to Borth, teems with delightful sandy beaches, rock-enclosed coves, cliffs, precipitous headlands, and all that is necessary to ensure a perfect seaside holiday. Aberystwyth is probably the best known of the Cardigan seaside resorts. But it is much more than this, for it is the oldest university town in Wales, and it also houses the magnificent National Library of Wales where one can examine the literature of Wales in ancient manuscript and in modern books.

Aberystwyth fully deserves its popularity as a holiday centre. Beautifully situated on the shores of Cardigan Bay, with a fine wide beach curving from the university buildings at the southern end to Constitution Hill at the northern extremity, Aberystwyth stands almost midway between north and south Wales. There are few towns in Wales that can boast such a wide variety of scenery within their immediate neighbourhood. Inland, a magnificent new mountain road goes to the Rheidol power station, and then climbs along the flanks of Plynlimon to the huge Nant y Moch Dam, near the summit, and winds down the other side. But whether you go to Devil's Bridge along the beautiful Rheidol Valley, or up to Plynlimon through the wild but entrancing Llyfnant Valley, or merely stroll over Constitution Hill to the lovely little beach at Clarach, you will see to the north the beginnings of the rugged mountain scenery so typical of north Wales, whilst to the south slope away more gently the hills and valleys of Cardiganshire.

Devil's Bridge is one of the most extraordinary sights in Great Britain, one which you can visit on the Devil's Bridge Railway, the only narrow-gauge line operated by *British Rail*. Clamped between two rocky cliffs through which a torrent of water pours unceasingly into a dark, seemingly bottomless pool far below, this bridge well deserves the name it bears—*Pont y gwr Drwg*, or Bridge of the Evil One, for legend has it that it was the devil himself who built it. There are really three bridges, and the lowest of all is 800 years old.

To the north of Devil's Bridge, Plynlimon raises its hoary head and bids you take heed that you are now on the threshold of north Wales, for its northern slopes stretch down to the River Dovey, which is the natural boundary between north and south Wales. The Severn and the Wye both spring from the flanks of this giant.

To the southeast of Aberystwyth lies the group of Welsh spas, Llandrindod Wells, Llanwrtyd Wells, Builth Wells, and Llangammarch Wells, all on or near the road from Shrewsbury to Swansea. Llandrindod Wells, with its sulphurous, saline, and chalybeate waters, is famed throughout Great Britain, whilst Llangammarch Wells has the distinction of possessing the only springs in Great Britain containing barium chloride, so useful for the treatment of diseases of the heart. Llanwrtyd Wells is popular apart from its reputation as a spa, for there are good golf and fishing.

A few miles to the north of Llandrindod Wells is Rhayader, on the River Wye, well known to all who handle rod and line, and indeed all this superb country, rich in mountain scenery, is a fisherman's paradise, for nearby is the chain of lakes formed by the Elan River, which supplies water to the city of Birmingham over 70 miles away.

Merionethshire

An old song with a plaintive melody, *The Bells of Aberdovey*, has made Aberdovey famous. A legend relates that centuries ago the sea burst the protecting wall and submerged a large part of the town including the church, and it is said that if you listen carefully you will still hear the faint sound of the bells as they sway to and fro with the movement of the water. Debussy's *Cathédrale Engloutie* was probably inspired by this same legend, but lacks the simple charm of the old Welsh melody. Aberdovey is a quiet little town, unpretentious but hospitable, with fine sandy beaches and an equable climate that attract great numbers of visitors.

In 1402 the great Welsh hero, Owen Glendower, was crowned Prince of Wales in Machynlleth (Montgomeryshire) before he began his brilliant but ill-fated campaign to drive out the English. The place in which he is said to have lived, Royal House, may still be seen. Machynlleth today, peaceful and law-abiding, is a favourite spot for anglers.

Barmouth, ideally situated on the northern side of the picturesque estuary of the Mawddach, with its two-mile-long promenade, its wide expanse of golden beaches, its facilities for sea, river, and mountain lake fishing, was even 100 years ago one of the most popular holiday resorts in Great Britain. Tennyson wrote part of his *In Memoriam* whilst staying there, and was inspired to write *Crossing the Bar* by the spectacle of the Mawddach rushing to meet the sea. Darwin worked on *The Origin of Species* and *The Descent of Man* in a house by the shore; Shelley stayed there with his wife in 1812; Ruskin was a constant visitor and was trustee of the St. George's cottages built there by the Guild of St. George in 1871. And indeed, Barmouth, with its superb view of the estuary, the impressive mass of Cader Idris to the south, Harlech Castle to the north, and its efficient transport system which enables the visitor to penetrate easily north, south, or east, is hard to over-rate as a place where the beauties of the Welsh landscape can be seen, as it were, in a concentrated form.

Nearby Dolgellau, the capital town of Snowdonia National Park, is an ancient mountain town where, from the Church of St. Mary, the curfew is still rung every evening as it has been done for centuries. Looming over the town is Mynydd Moel, one of the peaks of the famous Cader Idris. This mountain, whose Welsh name means the Chair of Idris, is connected by ancient legend with Idris, the heroic warrior-bard. It is said that anyone sleeping for a night in that part of the mountain reputed to be the actual chair of the bard, will awaken either a poet or a madman. The Talyllyn narrow-gauge railway runs from Towyn on the coast to within a stone's throw of Cader.

Harlech Castle! What a wealth of legend, poetry, and song is conjured up by the name of this famous castle, towering on its great rock high above the green valleys slumbering far below. The inspiring music of Ceiriog's *Men of Harlech* well typifies the heroic defence of this castle in 1468 by Dafydd ap Eynion, who, summoned to surrender, replied defiantly: "I held a castle in France until every old woman in Wales heard of it, and I will hold a castle in Wales until every old woman in France hears of it!" His proud boast still rings down the centuries in the stirring music of *Men of Harlech*.

From Llanbedr, just below Harlech, begins the long line of mysterious stone steps, called the Roman Steps, which climb inland for about two miles, and whose origins and purpose are still a mystery.

Caernarvonshire

And now to Caernarvonshire, the rugged county of Beddgelert, of Criccieth, Betws-y-Coed, Llanberis Pass, Capel Curig, Nant Gwynant, and of Snowdon. For this is the county where Wales masses all its savage splendour, its fierce beauty, to shatter the complacency of the visitor and instil in his breast some faint echo of the passionate love of their country hymned by the unceasing procession of bards and singers down the long corridors of Welsh history. And yet, standing like a warning finger in this same county stands Caernarvon Castle, "that most magnificent badge of our subjection", wrote Pennant.

The railway, moving northwards up the coast of Merionethshire, swings westwards along Tremadoc Bay and comes to an abrupt halt at Pwllheli. For this is the Lleyn, or The Peninsula, where the inhabitants are reputed to know no English and live in this softly undulating, wooded county cut off from the mainland by the massive rampart of Caernarvon's mountains. Happily, frequent bus services enable the visitor to explore the rest of this delightful countryside. Just off the southwestern tip of Lleyn lies Bardsey Island, the "sacred island", where legend tells that 20,000 saints lie buried in its earth. Known in ancient time as the Gate of Paradise, three pilgrimages to Bardsey Island were counted by the Church as equivalent to one pilgrimage to Rome.

Pwllheli, where the railway ends, is proud of its sands, which it claims to be the finest in Wales. But the view across Tremadoc Bay with its towering background of mountains of Merionethshire would be enough to justify its reputation as one of the leading resorts of the Lleyn. A fascinating tradition surrounds Tremadoc. Long before Columbus sailed on his great journey of discovery, a Welshman named Madog ap Owen Gwynedd set sail for the new world from Ynys Fadog. Though he never returned, many centuries later it was discovered that a remote North American Indian tribe showed inexplicable traces in their language of Welsh phonetics. Whether the two have any connection we shall never know, but it opens up intriguing possibilities.

Criccieth, with its 13th-century castle, has become world famous as the home of Lloyd George. It is a pleasant little place, and again, the panorama of sea and mountain across Tremadoc Bay is breathtaking in its loveliness. Not far away is the village of Llanystumdwy, where Lloyd George went to school, and where he is buried. "Y Gegin", the little theatre, in Criccieth, presents Welsh and English plays, folk dances and singing from time to time.

On the northern shores of the Lleyn is the small summer resort of Nevin, set on a cliff overlooking the delightful little bay of Porth Nevin. And at the very end of the peninsula is the little fishing village from which you can make the trip by boat (weather permitting) to Bardsey Island.

At the opposite end of the Lleyn, where it joins the main body of Wales, a tiny finger of land thrusts into the sandy Traeth Bach estuary. This is the setting for one of the most unusual sights in Wales, the village of Portmeirion, the dream come true of architect Clough Williams Ellis, who has created here a vision of Italy on the threshold of wild Snowdonia, and in doing so has provided one of the most enchanted places imaginable for a restful holiday.

Anglesey

Anglesey, known in early days as Mona, the Mother of Wales, is joined to the mainland by the Menai suspension bridge, one of the most extraordinary engineering feats ever achieved, especially when one considers that it was constructed in 1826. The main railway line from London passes over the Britannia tubular bridge which, although not so graceful as the suspension bridge, is a technical masterpiece, designed by Stephenson and finished in 1850.

Among the many villages on Anglesey is one famous as having the longest name of any place in the world:

LLANFAIRPWLLGWYNGYLLGOGERYCHWYRN-
DROBWLLANTYSILIOGOGOGOCH

The local people are proud of this extraordinary name, and can even repeat it to you from memory, but the ordnance survey authorities firmly refuse to recognize more than the first three syllables, and so it is officially known as Llanfairpwll, much to the relief of visitors and others who may have to expedite correspondence to this locality.

Anglesey still remains the corn-growing country it was in ancient days when its rich cornfields were reputed to be sufficiently extensive to feed all Wales. Hence the name of Mona, the Mother of Wales. Charming, unpretentious seaside resorts are dotted about the northwest tip of Anglesey. From Holyhead a regular steamship service runs daily to Ireland. Holyhead is also a notable holiday resort, and from the granite rock of Mynydd y Twr, called in English, Holyhead Mountain, there is a superb view of Snowdonia, the Isle of Man and, on a clear day, even of Ireland.

Beaumaris is the assize town of Anglesey, and a quiet, dignified, seaside place, with facilities for yachting, bathing, and golf. Its castle was built by Edward I in 1293, to guard Anglesey and Caernarvonshire.

And now back to the mainland to explore Caernarvonshire.

From Anglesey the railway slips over the straits to Bangor, a cathedral and university city which derives its name from *Banchor* or "chief choir", a religious institution founded in the 6th century by St. Deiniol, who also built the original church, destroyed by the Normans and rebuilt by them in the 12th century.

At the southern end of the Menai Straits lies Caernarvon, the grim majestic mass of its castle reflected in the now peaceful waters of the Seiont River. What tragedies and bloody encounters were witnessed by these silent sullen walls, erected by Edward I in the 13th century as a symbol of his determination to reduce the Welsh to complete subjection!

But in 1284, it is said, the crafty monarch thought of an amazing scheme. Knowing that the proud Welsh chieftains would accept no foreign prince, he promised to designate a ruler who could speak no word of English. He sent his Queen, Eleanor of Castile, who was expecting a child, post-haste to Caernarvon that she might be delivered there, and in this cold stone fortress the Queen gave birth to a son. Triumphantly Edward presented the infant to the assembled chieftains as their prince, "who spoke no English, had been born on Welsh soil, and whose first words would be spoken in Welsh". The ruse worked, and on that historic day was created the first Prince of Wales of English lineage. Since then the eldest son of the ruler of England has usually been designated Prince of Wales. In July, 1969, Caernarvon glowed again with pageantry when Queen Elizabeth II presented her eldest son, Prince Charles, to the people of Wales as their prince. This was the first time the ceremony had been held for 58 years, since 1911, in fact, when Prince Edward, now Duke of Windsor, was presented by his father, George V.

Just below the southern slopes of the Snowdon range, and tucked away in a fairyland of sylvan groves and craggy heights where the crystal-clear Colwyn and Glaslyn join together, is the beautiful village of Beddgelert.

Snowdon

Snowdon is the highest mountain in England and Wales (3,560 feet) and can be ascended by foot or by mountain railway from Llanberis. It is the central point of interest in Snowdonia National Park, one of three such parks in Wales. It is impossible to describe the magnificence of the view on a clear day. To the northwest the Straits of Menai, Anglesey, and beyond to the Irish Sea, to the south the mountains of Merioneth, Harlech Castle, and Cader Idris, and all around great towering masses of rock, wild and barren of vegetation. If you take the railway from Llanberis, telephone from the terminus to ascertain whether the peak is free from mist, for you will lose much if you arrive when clouds, as often happens, encircle the monster's brow.

Betws-y-Coed has been so lauded by writers, sketched, painted, photographed, that it is astonishing to find that it is even lovelier than one had been led to believe. It is set in a small green valley, and all around are crags and thickly wooded hills. Owing to its position, it gives an aspect of the Snowdon country that is quite unusual, for although it is within a few miles of the towering peaks, one can see only the hills directly surrounding it. The country around is therefore much less fatiguing to explore, but abounds in spots of enchanting beauty such as the foaming Swallow Falls.

In Orme's Bay, between the rocky precipices of Great Orme's Head and Little Orme's Head, Llandudno pursues its successful career as the most frequented of all Welsh seaside resorts. It is a favourite spot for visitors from the north of England and the midlands, for it provides practically everything that a holiday-maker can desire. A superb sandy beach, a magnificent situation in the shelter of Orme's Bay, safe, first-class bathing facilities, theatres, cinemas, and all the amenities of an up-to-date seaside resort, and yet down the valley of the Conway River, within easy distance by road or rail, lie the mountains and ancient towns, supremely indifferent to the encroachment of modern civilization.

Conway and Llanrwst

Conway, a short distance south, plunges us into medieval times. The massive, tall walls, with their 21 semi-circular towers, still encircle the town as they did when, nearly seven centuries ago, Edward I built them in his crusade to pacify the Welsh, and the castle, with its 15-foot-thick curtain walls, still broods menacingly over the adjacent countryside.

Situated in the estuary of the River Conway, Conway is indeed a beautiful town. From the castle walls you can look down at the yachts lying at anchor in the river, for Conway is a well-known centre for sea and river craft. If you like mussels, don't forget to try them at Conway, where for centuries they have been gathered in the bar of the harbour. They are despatched in sealed bags all over England.

Llangollen

From Bangor to Rhyl the road follows the windings of the coastline between sea and mountain. Rhyl, although popular owing to its accessibility from the English border, lacks the scenic advantages of Llandudno or Colwyn Bay. The surrounding country is quite flat, the mountains visible only in the far distance, but the air is bracing, the sands extensive and for a family holiday, Rhyl has definite advantages in safe bathing and well-organized amenities.

South from Rhyl the road (A525) runs through the pleasant vale of Clwyd, passing Rhuddlan Castle, the pocket-size cathedral of St. Asaph, and Denbigh Castle, to the little town of Ruthin. At Ruthin, in the shadow of the Clwydian hills, the old red sandstone castle has been converted into a comfortable country hotel, renowned throughout Wales for the medieval banquets that take place nightly during most of the year. In Ruthin is also preserved an ancient stone block on which, so legend has it, King Arthur ordered the beheading of Gildas, the historian.

Another 16 miles further south is Llangollen, cradled among tree-covered hills in a hollow beside the River Dee. Spanning the river is a medieval bridge that is one of the traditional Seven Wonders of Wales, but this charming little town is best known for the International Musical Eisteddfod, held here each year in July, with singers and folk dancers from many lands competing with their Welsh hosts. Here, too, is the black-and-white half-timbered home of the eccentric 'Ladies of Llangollen'. Also worth a visit are the noble ruins of Valle Crucis Abbey, founded in 1202 by Prince Madog of Powys, in a hushed valley less than two miles from the town.

The Eisteddfodau

The huge annual Royal National Eisteddfod is certainly the most picturesque and most moving ceremony in Wales. For here the love of song and poetry of the Welsh is organized to provide a spectacle unique in the world. Presided over by white-robed druids with their attendant blue-robed bards, the Eisteddfod summons the people of Wales each year to send forth its singers and poets to participate in this colourful tournament. The culminating event is the choosing of the winning poet, and so intense is the nationwide interest in this ceremony that special newspaper editions are snatched up eagerly by those who are unable to go.

A visit to the Royal National Eisteddfod is unforgettable, for there you will realize the passionate devotion of the Welsh to the things they have guarded so jealously throughout the centuries. And you will hear the Welsh sing! For days they will sing, until you will become as intoxicated as they with the subtle blending of voices and the plaintive beauty of the songs. The National Eisteddfod takes place at varying sites in South Wales (even years) and North Wales (uneven years).

The Founder of Yale University

Not far from the little market town of Corwen is the village of Bryn-Eglwys, and in this village there is a parish church with a chapel bearing a name that has become world famous, for this is the Yale Chapel owned by the family of Elihu Yale, who carried the Welsh passion for education to the New World and founded Yale University. A mile or two away is the Plas-yn-Ial, the former residence of the family.

Elihu Yale is buried in the churchyard at Wrexham, ten miles away.

The progressive shipyards along the Clyde help make Britain a world leader in ship building. Forward-looking in all modern endeavors, the Scots nevertheless devote time and energy to preserving their past in such historical spots as Castle Douglas in Kirkcudbrightshire.

In County Antrim, the Giant's Causeway has inspired a host of ancient legends and tales.

SCOTLAND

Britain's Northern Giant

by

PATRICIA BARCLAY

(The author divides her life between Kitwe, Zambia and Inverness-shire, Scotland. Two hundred of her articles and stories have been published and her first novel, set in Scotland, has just been completed.)

Scotland, most northern country of the British Isles, has only 80 miles of common border with England, which, running from west to east, lies between the Solway Firth and the River Tyne.

Some Scots aver they can tell blindfold the moment they cross the border—either by rail or road—and reach home soil. Though sceptics dismiss this as part of the fertile Celtic imagination, there is an undeniable lift of the heart when contact is first made, or remade, with Scotland's scenery and people. And what if the Celtic imagination is partly responsible? It's also produced much that visitors enjoy in this volatile, wildly beautiful country—hospitality straight from the heart; haunting songs and stories; a pudding called Tipsy

Laird; the massed pipes and drums of the Scottish regiments beating retreat on the floodlit heights of Edinburgh Castle; and the unique blend of greasepaint and grouse moor at Pitlochry Festival Theatre.

Crossing the border by road, rail or air, there's no need to stop or show travel papers as Scotland and England are, despite nationalist sentiment, one nation so far as international affairs are concerned. Besides, there is every reason to speed up the flow across the border. Each year, more people are coming to Scotland in search of the land of their forefathers, or in quest of beauty and the comparatively quiet roads. Each year brings first-timers and many, many others who have been before and just can't keep away.

Scotland is a small country of approximately 30,000 square miles (comparable in size, topography, vegetation and climate to the American state of Maine); this includes 787 islands, 136 of which are inhabited. Within that area, there is tremendous variety of landscape, so that travel is rarely without interest.

Place names are frequently ancient in derivation. *Wick*, Scandinavian for "inlet", appears in Lerwick, while *ness*, meaning "headland", is used in, for example, Stromness. Examples of household words used in Scotland but not in England—acquired during the "Auld Alliance" with France—are *gigot* (chops of mutton) and *ashet*, or serving plate, from the French *assiette*. Gaelic words, too, are used even among the non-Gaelic speaking Scots. There's *ceilidh* (a party with songs) and *bourach*, meaning a bit of a mess.

A Brief Glance at History

Often enough, the people met in pubs, or someone you stop to ask for travelling directions, will expound on the subject of local folklore. The offer of a dram of whisky works wonders in loosening the tongue of even the canniest Scot, who will thereupon hold forth gladly—and entertainingly—about his national heritage. From almost every glen, history exudes—tragic, romantic and violent. And since the story of Scotland is a long one, not unnaturally the countryside is full of things of historical interest.

One of the oldest relics is the Megalithic tomb—a mound over 100 feet in diameter—at Maes Howe, in Orkney. At

SCOTLAND 451

Daviot, six miles south of Inverness, stone circles date back to the Bronze Age, around 1500 B.C. Iron Age *brochs* (large round towers) can be seen in Stirlingshire, Sutherland and Caithness.

An enormous leap in time over wild and pagan years takes us to the reign of King David I (1124–1153). The church flourished then, and monasteries built at the time can be seen, albeit some in ruins, at Melrose and Kelso on the Tweed, Newbattle in Midlothian, Kinloss in Morayshire, Dundrennan on the Solway and, just north of the border, Jedburgh. The Abbey of Holyroodhouse, Edinburgh (Holyroodhouse is the Queen's official residence in Scotland), also dates from King David's time and is open to the public except when the palace is occupied by any member of the royal family or by the lord high commissioner to the General Assembly of the Church of Scotland.

Over the centuries, Scotland was torn asunder by two kinds of strife—intolerance between the churches of Rome and Scotland, and the perpetual menace of England's desire for territorial supremacy.

Scots Wha Hae Wi' Wallace Bled, a rousing song and dramatic pipe-band tune, is generally regarded as the Scottish national anthem. Its subject is William Wallace who, as did Robert the Bruce, waged war against England in the 13th and 14th centuries. At Stirling Bridge and close-by Bannockburn were fought, respectively, the most notable battles of Wallace and Bruce.

Much of Scotland's historical colour was provided by the royal Stuarts, the most memorable figures being Mary, Queen of Scots, and Bonnie Prince Charlie. At the Palace of Holyroodhouse, visitors can see the rooms in which Queen Mary lived, and that in which her secretary, David Rizzio, was murdered. On Loch Leven, Kinross-shire, still stands the castle in which Mary was imprisoned after the Battle of Carberry Hill.

The Highlands set the scene for much of Prince Charles Edward Stuart's tragic and romantic story. At Glenfinnan, there's the monument to mark the 1745 Gathering of the Clans loyal to the prince. And close to Inverness is Culloden battlefield, where, only a year later, they were finally routed by the English army. Eric Linklater's book, *A Prince in the Heather*, gives a memorable account of Prince Charlie's life as a fugitive and is beautifully illustrated.

An Act of Union between Scotland and England finally came about in 1707. Almost inevitably, as the smaller country, some of Scotland's identity went by the board, and to the disgust of most Scots the two countries are often lumped together and referred to as England. It's as well, consequently, for visitors to remember that the expression "You English people . . ." is unpalatable to any rightminded Scot.

How It's Done in Scotland

Although much of Scotland's internal administration is conducted from St. Andrew's House in Edinburgh, the capital, the seat of government is London, where Scotland is strongly represented in both houses of parliament. Quite a number of high offices south of the border are held by Scots. The Queen, of course, is half Scottish (the Queen Mother was, before her marriage, a member of the Strathmore family, whose home is Glamis Castle, in Angus); and since World War II, two prime ministers of Great Britain have been Scots. Although the present parliamentary situation seems to be acceptable to the majority, each year the Scottish National Party (which, since 1934, has advocated home rule) gathers a larger following.

While Scottish currency is the same as English, the Bank of Scotland, the Royal Bank of Scotland, the Clydesdale, National Commercial, and British Linen banks all produce their own rather colourful banknotes.

Scotland has also retained a separate legal system, with her own high courts, law lords, and sheriffs.

Similarly, the Church of Scotland is entirely independent from that of England. It has its own hierarchy and is a considerable strength in the land. The majority of churches are, naturally enough, Scottish Presbyterian, but in all sizeable towns, places of worship of other denominations will be found, and visitors are always welcome. Roman Catholicism, incidentally, is at its strongest in the West Highlands, Glasgow and Dundee.

It is north and northwest of Inverness that the kirk's influence is most strongly felt and there the sabbath day is seriously regarded as a day of rest. To work or take part in pleasurable pastimes is regarded as a sin. Hotels and guest houses do not like guests to arrive or depart on a Sunday, and those landladies described in the Tourist Board list of accommodation as "Sunday Observers" do no work at all on that day of the week. Shops, cafés and petrol (gasoline) stations are closed and very few Sunday newspapers are sold in those areas. Similarly, as some car ferries have no Sunday service, visitors are advised to check beforehand about these. (The Automobile Association or Royal Scottish Automobile Club provides such information.)

But Scotland is a country which likes to be visited. *Ceud mile failte*, the time-honoured Gaelic greeting, is still offered sincerely to Scotland's guests. *Ceud mile failte*—a hundred thousand welcomes!

Particular Facts for Your Trip to Scotland

Most of the practical information in earlier sections of this book, *Facts at Your Fingertips* and *Practical Information for Great Britain*, is applicable to Scotland, of course. There are a few salient points, however, which pertain to this country alone. Those given below, with the data you will find in other sections following, *Practical Information for Scotland, for Edinburgh*, and *for Glasgow* will help you plan the Scottish portion of your trip more accurately, we trust.

WHEN TO GO? The main tourist season in Scotland runs from May to September, and hotels are most fully booked during July and August, when Scottish school children are on holiday. Throughout the summer, there is a wide range of historical, cultural and sporting attractions—festivals, pageants, championship games, working dog trials, shooting and fishing. In winter and spring, there is both rugby and association football (known as rugger and soccer), curling, skiing and mountaineering. The now-important ski season lasts from November to April, although enthusiasts can usually find snow until well on in June. Anyone coming to Scotland during winter would be well advised to check in advance that hotel facilities are available in the district he intends to visit. Many country hotels, even luxury ones such as *Gleneagles* and *Turnberry,* are open only from May until October. If you plan to visit the Highlands and Islands in April and May or in the Fall (after September 21), you can cut the cost of your stay by as much as 20 cents on every dollar you spend. For full details, write to the *Highlands and Islands Development Board*, P.O. Box 7, Inverness. In return they will mail you a 'Highland Holiday Ticket', which is a book of vouchers giving reductions on rail and bus travel, island mini-cruises, car hire, accommodation, meals, golf, salmon and trout fishing, pony-trekking and theatre seats at Pitlochry. Fantastic value, this, especially as many people consider that late spring and fall are the best times to visit the Highlands and Islands.

THE FACE OF BRITAIN

HOW TO GO? The advice given in the section of this volume on England holds good for Scotland. However, you can reach Scotland directly by air (*BOAC*, *KLM*, *Pan Am* and *SAS*) and sea on cargo freighters of following lines: *Blue Star, Fjell-Oranje, Furness Pacific, Manchester, U.S. Lines* from America. There are also daily flights from London to Glasgow (Abbotsinch Airport), Edinburgh (Turnhouse Airport) and Inverness—flying time, 80 minutes to Glasgow and Edinburgh. Direct flights to Scotland from Europe on *BEA*, *BUA*, *Iberia*, *Icelandair*, *Icelandic*, *KLM*, *Pan Am* and *SAS*.

There are services by air to Edinburgh and Glasgow from Belfast and Dublin, and by sea to Glasgow, Ardrossan and Stranraer from Belfast, Larne, Londonderry and Dublin. There are no passport or currency formalities. However, if arriving from Dublin, you should note that Irish banknotes and currency are not generally acceptable in the United Kingdom (though Bank of England notes and coins are acceptable in Eire). Irish notes and currency can be changed at banks in the U.K., but there may be some discount.

By sea, there are regular transatlantic services direct to Gourock and Glasgow, from which smaller vessels sail to the Western Isles. From Rotterdam in Holland, there is a regular 36-hour crossing to Edinburgh on small comfortable cargo and passenger boats of the *Gibson Rankin Line*.

By rail, there are fast services daily from London to Edinburgh and Glasgow—time about 6 hours. Overnight sleepers are comfortable, and hours of wearying driving time can be saved by putting your car and companions aboard the car-sleeper from London and several other English stations. *Scottish Motorail* termini are Aberdeen, Edinburgh, Perth, Stirling and Inverness. Full details can be had from any travel agent or *British Rail* enquiry office, but as bookings for this useful service are heavy, reserve as far ahead as possible.

WHAT TO SEE? By whatever means visitors travel to Scotland—air, sea, rail or road—the great majority will almost certainly arrive either in Edinburgh, the capital, or in Glasgow. Both cities have many attractions in themselves and offer easy access to surrounding districts, with a wonderful range of things to do and see. As they are also within easy reach of each other—45 miles, an hour's trip by rail—the touring regions of either are almost as easily accessible from the other.

Glasgow is the centre from which to visit Ayrshire (Burns country and a golfer's paradise), the Firth of Clyde, Western Isles, Hebrides, Trossacs and Rob Roy country, the central and western Highlands and Galloway.

From Edinburgh, there are many attractive and interesting trips through the Lothians, the Borders and Scott country. North of Edinburgh, across the Firth of Forth, lies the ancient kingdom of Fife, and north again are the glorious lochs and glens of Perthshire, all easily accessible from Perth.

Aberdeen is an excellent centre for Royal Deeside and the Moray coast. Inverness is a popular centre for touring the far north, western Highlands and the Black Isle.

Anyone planning to tour north of Inverness is reminded that it is a region of strict Presbyterianism. Many hotels, restaurants, shops and petrol (gasoline) stations are firmly closed on Sundays.

PAGEANTS. While Scotland may be quiet on the sabbath, it is far from being a land which frowns on fun and games. On its national calendar, there is a long list of pageants and festivals, most of which had their beginnings many centuries ago. The historical pageant at *Arbroath Abbey* during the latter half of August is a colourful event, commemorating the Declaration of Scottish Independence in 1320. This was drawn up by Scottish barons and bishops in the presence of King Robert the Bruce and sent to the pope, asking for his help.

Most spectacular is the *Up-Helly-Aa* procession held in Shetland. A 30-foot replica of a Viking longboat is hauled through the streets, then ceremoniously burned. Flaming torches are carried downhill through the dark streets by people dressed in splendid Viking array and the evening is really gay. Unfortunately, all this takes place at the end of January, a time when few overseas visitors would think of braving the climate, but it's well worth seeing.

Also in January are the *Burns Nicht* suppers, celebrating the national poet. The haggis is first piped into the dining hall, then ceremonially cut while Burns' *Address to a Haggis* is read.

On Candlemas Day the *Callants' Ba'* is played at Jedburgh. Uppies and Doonies, inhabitants of different parts of the town, are the competitors and the ball represents the heads of their slain enemies.

Whuppity Scoorie is a Lanark festival on 1st March, when all the children swing caps and paper balls round their heads, run thrice round the Auld Kirk, then scramble for pennies thrown by the townsfolk.

Many of the border towns—Lauder, Melrose, Hawick, Langholm, etc. have an annual *Riding of the Marches*. The Cornet, Braw Lad or Braw Lass (designations differ from town to town) leads a horseback procession through the streets, climaxing in a tremendous gallop.

Early in the summer term, St. Andrews University has its *Kate Kennedy* procession—an historical pageant enacted by students. The most comely first-year male student (a *bejant*) is selected to represent Kate, who was niece of the university's founder.

Late summer is the season for *Highland Gatherings*. Kilts are everywhere and the air vibrates to the sound of pipes and drums. The athletic events—tossing the caber, putting the weight, and so on—are almost unbelievably arduous. Most famous of these gatherings is at Braemar; it is attended by the Queen and other members of the royal family.

The *Gaelic Mod* is held annually in late summer in one of the Highland towns such as Inverness or Oban. Tartan-bedecked Gaelic speakers arrive from everywhere, singing standards are high and the kilted school choirs from the islands delight both ear and eye. Long into the wee sma' 'oors continue the *ceilidhs,* and all hotels do a roaring trade.

SPORT. The main tourist season comes just too late for visitors to see the climax of the Scottish football season in April. Anyone having the chance to see Glasgow's two renowned soccer teams (*Rangers* and *Celtic*) compete against each other, should not miss it, as the atmosphere alone is worth travelling for. Seven-a-side rugby matches in the border country are also exciting events.

Golf, an all year round sport, has been played in Scotland for more than 600 years. On all its 347 courses, the season really gets under way in spring. Besides the open and amateur championships held in Scotland every second or third year, there is a wide variety of tournaments throughout the summer. Most visitors, however, come to play over one or more of the really great courses—St. Andrews, Carnoustie, Prestwick, Troon and Gleneagles, etc. Many of the lesser-known courses are scenically beautiful and often have fascinating hazards. *Scotland for Golf*, a Tourist Board leaflet, lists all the courses, and most overseas visitors will be agreeably surprised at the low cost of golf in Scotland, often less than $1 a day. A scheme for the hire of clubs is available. Many courses are involved—Gleneagles, Turnberry, Prestwick, North Berwick, Troon and St. Andrews, to mention just a few. For anyone flying from abroad, with only limited luggage allowance, this will be specially helpful, and the Scottish Tourist Board can supply details.

Cricket is gaining an increasing following in central Scotland and some first-class matches between Scotland and English county teams can be watched at Paisley.

Athletics are presented annually at the famous Glasgow Rangers sports ground in early August. It is a comparatively poor year when there are not a dozen or more British, European and American top-rankers competing.

Shinty is an ancient Highland game—a fast, apparently rule-free form of hockey, where all the old ferocity of the Highlander resurfaces. Newtonmore, Kingussie (pronounced *King-yoosie*) and Oban are the best spots to see this game.

Now that Scotland is a major skiing country, hotels which provide ski-hire and instruction have sprung up in the Cairngorm, Glenshee and Glencoe areas. International competitive events are now held on Cairngorm and at all centres; *aprés-ski* entertainment is lively, particularly at Aviemore.

Curling is another native game to Scotland and has been popular for centuries. History, in fact, records that a 16th-century bishop of Orkney was seeverely rebuked for curling on the sabbath day. It can be played at any of the ice rinks or, weather permitting, out of doors, and the most famous Bonspiel of all is held whenever ice is strong enough on Scotland's only lake, the Lake of Mentieth in Perthshire. At Aviemore, there is a splendid curling rink.

Scotland is often, and rightly, described as an angler's dream come true. Although no state licence is needed, almost all fishing belongs to someone (hotelier, landowner, town, etc.), and permission must be obtained—or there are severe penalties. The Scottish Tourist Boards' booklet, *Scotland for Fishing*, gives all necessary information. At Aviemore, there is an angling school, details of which can be had from the Holiday Centre. For sea angling information, contact the Honorary Secretary, *Lockbroom Sea Angling Club*, Ullapool, Ross-shire. (This is where European and Scottish championships are held.)

Deer stalking is rapidly catching on as a sport. As, however, few estate stalkers have time to spend on the preliminary instruction needed by the novice, it is not always easy to arrange. For further information, contact the *Red Deer Commission,* Island Bank Road, Inverness.

Grouse and pheasant shooting are extremely expensive pastimes. As it is also expensive to maintain such moors, visitors are not, naturally, welcome during the nesting season in spring. And from August 12 for about six weeks, it is inadvisable to stroll over grouse moors, lest either a shot or the gamekeeper gets you.

Field trials are run (occasionally in spring, more often in late summer) to test the ability of the gundogs used on sporting moors. There are retriever and spaniel trials, and pointer and setter trials—and the latter especially are fantastically exciting to watch. Anyone who has shot over pointers in the United States will be interested to see the different methods of working these magnificent dogs in Britain. Sheepdog trials also provide much to admire and thrill the spectator, and in summer they are held in many places on the tourist map. For those interested in the show dog, there are about four championships and (in summer) many open shows held in Scotland annually, and at these the topflight breed specimens can be seen.

PREPARING YOURSELF. *Scotland's Magazine,* official month y publication of the Tourist Board, is a good investment, if you want to research your trip. A year's subscription including postage costs 32s ($3.84) (24 Elder Street, Edinburgh) and provides readers with a great deal of background information to just about every part of the country. There are many books on Scotland and many Scottish writers. As a very general guide, however the following authors are superb on their own regions: George Scott-Moncrieff on the Scottish Islands, and Edinburgh; F. R. Banks on the Borders; Jack House on Clydeside. Gavin Maxwell's *House of Elrig* is an excellent mood-setter for anyone who intends to visit the Galloway-Wigtown corner of Scotland. Grace Cambell offers much to interest and fascinate readers in her *Highland Heritage*, but it is Neil M. Gunn whose books take you right into the heart of the Highlands and Highlanders. James Wood gives his readers a good stiff dram of north-eastern flavour, while Compton MacKenzie's *Whiskey Galore* presents a perfect picture of Island life.

Practical Information for Scotland

HOTELS, RESTAURANTS AND AMENITIES. Currently there is considerable activity on the Scottish catering scene. Guests, mercifully, have been released from the attitude which gave rise to such well-known stories as the diner complaining "Waiter, your thumb's in my soup" and being told "That's all right, sir, it's not hot".

Since the inauguration of a Scottish Hotel School, a far more professional approach has been apparent in the services offered. Even so, in some lesser establishments, overseas visitors accustomed to central heating and private bathrooms will notice a difference. There are, unfortunately also a few hotels (and these include one or two of the pricey ones) which apparently lack co-ordination in their correspondence departments. (Generally speaking, incidentally, it is unnecessary to send a cash deposit when booking.)

New hotels are continually being built in Scotland these days, the Tourist Board estimating that around 40 more should be completed by 1970. Licensing hours north of the border are from 11 a.m. to 2:30 p.m. and from 5 p.m. to 10 p.m., although hotel residents can be served alcohol at any time. On Sundays, some pubs *may* serve beer or spirits when meals are ordered, but don't count on it. Of the local brews, McEwan's ale is perhaps the best.

Many Scottish foods are excellent, and well worth trying when they appear upon a menu. Venison, grouse and ptarmigan, for instance, can all be cooked in various exciting ways.

S. Marian McNeill and Elizabeth Craig have written books on Scottish cooking; these can be had from most booksellers. Marian McNeill's *The Scots Kitchen—Its Lore and Recipes* is especially interesting and entertaining, as it describes the old cooking utensils—wooden luggies, plumpchurns, porridge spurtles and so on. Examples of these, incidentally, are to be seen in the splendid *Highland Folk Museum* at Kingussie, Inverness-shire. The book also tells how to make Hebridean Silverweed Bannocks, Hatted Kit (an old Highland pudding), Buttery Rowies (the kind of rolls to be tasted in Aberdeen) and Whim-Wham (a splendid pudding mentioned by Sir Walter Scott in *The Bride of Lammermoor*), besides many others.

National foods more likely to be tasted in hotels nowadays, however, are finnan haddies and Arbroath smokies (fish); porridge, a hot breakfast course made by simmering oatmeal and a little salt in water; haggis, a succulent, spicy mixture (a kind of pudding) of chopped offals (heart, liver, lungs, etc.) and oatmeal held together and cooked in a sheep's stomach.

In some hotels other than the topflight variety, "high tea" is served as the evening meal. This usually consists of a savoury course—often with chips—followed by tea, toast and cakes. Normal time for this meal is about 5:30 or 6 p.m. Tipping, despite the percentage added to bills for staff gratuities, is sometimes expected—and at all times acceptable. Five per cent is abundant if the service charge is added, ten percent is adequate if not on the bill.

Listed below is a selection of holiday towns and villages throughout Scotland's mainland and islands.

ABERDEEN (Aberdeenshire). A convenient motel: *Dee*, 44 rooms (all with bath). *Station*, 60 rooms (13 with bath), reliable in its consistency for excellent food, comfort, warmth and pleasant staff. In town centre, but rooms are quiet. Good bars. Expensive.

Meldrum House is just out of town, the converted ancestral home of the owner. Gracious living at its best, with food of highest quality, splendid furnishings, silver, etc. Costly, but worth it.

Treetops, 27 rooms (4 with bath). Luxury modern hotel two miles from town centre. Excellent decor and food. Plenty of parking and country-club feel about the place.

Moderately expensive are the *Douglas*, 105 rooms, *Gloucester*, 90 rooms, and *Caledonian*, 61 rooms. Less costly are the *George*, 42 rooms, and *Imperial*, 110 rooms.

Royal Athenaeum is perhaps the best restaurant in town.

Aberdeen Steak House provides excellent meals, but is closed Saturday lunchtime and all day Sunday.

ABERFELDY (Perthshire). Try the *Palace*, 19 rooms, of the real old Scottish type. Tartan covers most surfaces and the staff is delightfully welcoming. Accent is on comfort and warmth, and in the dining room, there is some fabulous cooking. Moderately priced.

Other hotels are the *Breadalbane Arms*, 24 rooms, and *Weem*, 19 rooms, both moderately priced. A fraction more expensive is the *Dun Aluinn*, 16 rooms (8 with bath), which provides comfort and very good cooking.

ABERFOYLE (Perthshire). Best is *Covenanters' Inn*, 50 rooms (28 with bath), in class of its own, really geared for tourist enjoyment, without loss of Scottish flavour. Dinner-dancing at weekends, log fires and food to suit both hungry and fastidious. Moderately expensive.

Other good hotels are the *Forest Hills*, 38 rooms, *Rob Roy Highland Motel*, chalets with 64 rooms, and the *Baillie Nicol Jarvie*, 25 rooms. Moderately expensive.

Moderately-priced are *Inverard*, 11 rooms, and *Pavilion*, 10 rooms.

ABOYNE (Aberdeenshire). First is the *Birse Lodge*, 21 rooms (1 with bath), and *Huntly Arms*, 52 rooms (4 with bath), moderately expensive, offer good plain food and solid comfort.

Moderately-priced are *Charlestown*, 7 rooms, and *Balnacoil*, 14 rooms.

ACHARACLE (Argyll). We suggest the *Lochshiel*, 15 rooms. *Old Manse*, 8 rooms and *Acharacle*, 16 rooms, are unpretentious country hotels offering their guests good country fare. Not expensive.

ALFORD (Aberdeenshire). Very good is *Kildrummy Castle*, Mossat (near Alford), 14 rooms. Fairly expensive, but worth it. Tremendous atmosphere in which very old and best modern are successfully blended. Good food.

APPLECROSS (Ross and Cromarty). *Applecross*, 5 rooms, very clean and cozy. Prices moderate and the food homely and plentiful. Because of its inaccessibility, hotel bookings should not be left to chance.

ARBROATH (Angus). Try the *Seaforth*, 19 rooms (5 with bath). Comfortable rooms, pleasant service, and restaurant (open to non-residents) has a menu to be proud of. Moderately costly, but worth it.

Cliffburn, 7 rooms, is comfortable and pleasant. *North Sea*, 14 rooms, *Monksbarns*, 16 rooms, and the *Royal*, 20 rooms, are all of good class, suitable for families with young children.

Auchmithie, in a tiny village a mile or two out of Arbroath. Delightful spot. Six rooms and pleasant food—especially the fish. Exciting for children because of fishing boats. Best to book meals in advance, if non-resident.

Marine Café and *Windmill Restaurant* are consistently reliable for eating out.

ARISAIG (Inverness-shire). We suggest: *Arisaig*, 16 rooms, has bars of character and excellent small restaurant. Comfort, cleanliness and homely food also provided at *Glen House*, 5 rooms.

ARRAN, Isle of (Bute). Look first for *Douglas* and *St. Denys*, Brodick, 46 rooms (some with bath). Modern, comfortable with food of good standard. Moderately expensive only.

Lagg, Kilmory, 18 rooms, has old-fashioned charm. Food very good and the afternoon teas (often served outside among subtropical plants and trees) exceptional. Inexpensive, and good value.

Kildonan, 31 rooms, and *Kinloch*, at Blackwaterfoot, 40 rooms, are moderately priced and offer an honest service.

Teas, coffees, etc., are served in Brodick Castle.

AVIEMORE (Invernessshire). *Strathspey*, 54 double rooms (all with bath), is of the highest possible standard. Luxurious fittings, several excellent bars (to suit different incomes). Food and wines topflight and all bedrooms extremely comfortable. Frankly expensive.

Coylumbridge, 113 double rooms (all with bath). Very attractive place among pine trees and heather, close to Loch Morlich, where yachting takes place just below the ski slopes (simultaneously !). Dancing, food of high quality—and available to non-residents. Very expensive. New (1965).

High Range, chalets of varying size, extreme comfort and attractive decor. Gay evenings to be had in bar, which attracts best of the local characters. Cooking is of high standard. Set in birch wood, close to lovely loch, but only six minutes from station. Restaurant open to non-residents. Expensive, but worth it.

Badenoch, 48 rooms, *Cairngorm*, 27 rooms, and *Lynwilg* (6 miles south of Aviemore) are all good, comfortable hotels. Moderate price.

Winking Owl Roadhouse, 2 rooms, *Dell Private*, 12 rooms and *Alt-na-Craig*, 9 rooms, are convenient for gay life in village.

AYR (Ayrshire). Here try the reliable *Station*, 75 rooms (25 with bath), excellent, with a degree of comfort to delight all travellers. Pleasant decor and wide variation of well-cooked food on menu. Expensive.

Sundrum Castle is six miles out of town and luxurious. Set in splendid grounds and has historic connection. Residents taken only in summer, but excellent restaurant open for dinner all year. Lacks, perhaps, warmth of Scottish welcome, but there is much to compensate. Expensive.

Abbotsford and *Belleisle* are both extremely pleasant, reliable establishments in which to stay or eat out. Close to golf courses and with friendly atmosphere. Moderately expensive.

Rabbie's Bar is a splendid place for eating out. Food of character and atmosphere to match.

BALLATER (Aberdeenshire). The *Invercault Arms*, 25 rooms, is indeed comfortable. Guests made to feel very welcome—and well fed. Fairly expensive.

Loriston, 34 rooms (3 with bath), is comfortable, moderately expensive, and provides plentiful and very good Scottish fare.

Darroch Learg, 19 rooms, is set in lovely grounds. Views all around are magnificent and food is good and plentiful. Inexpensive.

For lunch or tea, try the *Glendee Restaurant*, whose home cooking is good; surroundings pleasant.

BANCHORY (Kincardineshire). The *Raemoir*, 25 rooms, is pleasantly situated but takes a little finding. Food and service consistently of high standard. Not expensive.

Moderately priced hotels are the *Burnett Arms*, 15 rooms, and *Banchory Lodge*, 14 rooms.

BARRA, Isle of (Inverness-shire). *Castle Bay* has 9 rooms, and *Craigard*, 8 rooms, are moderately-priced and quite comfortable. Boarding houses abound.

BETTYHILL (Sutherland). We suggest the *Bettyhill*, 30 rooms (4 with bath), comfortable and provides very good meals. Hospitality is a positive thing here.

BLAIR ATHOLL (Perthshire). *Tilt*, 23 rooms, and *Atholl Arms*, 33 rooms (3 with bath), are similar hotels close to each other. Very comfortable, with consistently plain but good food. Moderately priced.

BOAT OF GARTEN (Inverness-shire). *Craigard*, 22 rooms, is a comfortable family hotel, with nice cocktail bar and proximity to golf courses. Good food. Moderate cost.

Boat, 28 rooms, changed hands recently. Is pleasant and food reputed to be good. Moderate price.

BONAR BRIDGE (Sutherland). Centre of good touring area. Rock-climbing, bird-watching. *Caledonian*, 26 rooms, is a comfortable country hotel in dramatic scenery. Food scheduled to satisfy the appetites of hungry anglers.

Half an hour's motoring from here is *Inveroykel Lodge*, a small hotel where salmon in season is cooked to perfection. Meals should be booked.

BRAEMAR (Aberdeenshire). Try the *Invercauld Arms*, 59 rooms (8 with bath); it has a very high standard in all respects. Impeccable service. Expensive.

Fife Arms, 86 rooms (4 with bath), and *Mar Lodge*, 26 rooms (3 with bath) are also entirely reliable. At the latter, there is usually a young crowd of guests.

BRIDGE OF ALLAN (Stirlingshire). *Allan Water*, 60 rooms (4 with bath), is outstandingly comfortable, in attractive grounds. Quiet surroundings, and very professional atmosphere in the dining room. Expensive.

Queens, 15 rooms, and *Royal*, 34 rooms, both in main street of the town, are moderately priced and of good standard.

Others are *Walmer*, 11 rooms, and *Carmichael's*, 13 rooms.

BRORA (Sutherland). Here, we suggest: *Royal Marine*, 24 rooms (1 with bath), *Links*, 31 rooms. and *Sutherland Arms*, 14 rooms, all excellent for family holidays, Good plain food.

BUTE, Island of. The best hotel is the *Glenburn*, Rothesay, 115 rooms (34 with bath); is palatial and its standards of comfort are equal to best in Britain. Must be booked well ahead (it's advisable even for casual meals) during June-September. Dining room open to non-residents and food sumptuous. Very expensive.

Kyles of Bute Hydro, 80 rooms and *Victoria*, 24 rooms, also good quality. Others too numerous to discriminate.

CALLANDER (Perthshire). *Dreadnought*, 74 rooms, provides some really fine cooking. Scottish foods should be asked for here, and service and comfort generally is of a very high standard. Expensive, but worth it.

Roman Camp, 15 rooms (8 with bath), is another very good place to stay. Lovely surroundings. This was an old hunting lodge and has fabulous gardens bordering river. Costly, but worth it. Food consistently good.

Ancaster Arms, 22 rooms, *Pinewood*, 14 rooms, and *Bridgend House*, 8 rooms, are moderately priced, offering an honest service.

CARNOUSTIE (Angus). Try the *Bruce*, 39 rooms (13 with bath), popular for miles around for the atmosphere of its cocktail bar and excellence of its cooking. Book in advance for dinner if possible. Hotel is comfortable, and on seafront.

Carlogie House, 7 rooms (1 with bath), is moderate in price, clean, but unexciting.

CARRBRIDGE (Inverness-shire). *Carrbridge*, 50 rooms, (12 with bath), is a gay, comfortable hotel with weekend dances and good family food. Reasonably expensive.

Other hotels in village are inexpensive and popular with young skiers. Comfort and food mediocre. *Rowanlea*, 10 rooms, and *Struan House*, 18 rooms.

CASTLE DOUGLAS (Kirkcudbrightshire). *Douglas Arms*, 20 rooms (3 with bath), is a splendid hotel with highly civilized atmosphere. The food, especially shellfish, is really good. Expensive.

King's Arms, 13 rooms, is most reasonably priced. It provides welcome and comfort for its guests, and the cooking is extremely good.

Ernespie House, 16 rooms, and *Balcary Bay*, 13 rooms (the latter at Auchencairn), are delightfully situated, reasonably priced and good.

CRAIL (Fife). We recommend: the *Marine*, 13 rooms, an excellent family hotel on cliff above ancient harbour. Food consistently good. Restful atmosphere. Moderately priced.

Balcomie Links, 12 rooms, *Croma*, 10 rooms, and *Kirkmay House*, 9 rooms, are all good, wholesome establishments, very reasonably priced.

Visit the 14th-century *Smuggler's Inn* at nearby Anstruther—marvellous food served.

COMRIE (Perthshire). It's worth driving from Perth (24 miles), if not further, to this town to dine at the *Royal Hotel*. Superb food. You can also stay here. 12 rooms (3 with bath).

CROMARTY (Ross and Cromarty). *Royal*, 15 rooms, is close to old harbour and has restful atmosphere. Simple but good food and nice afternoon teas. No parking difficulties in this part of the world. Inexpensive.

CULLEN (Banffshire). Here, try: *Three Kings*, 8 rooms; has friendly atmosphere and three delightful bars, always well attended.

Waverley, 14 rooms, *Cullen Bay*, 22 rooms, and *Seafield Arms*, 18 rooms, also good value.

CULROSS (Fife). Best place here is *Dundonald Arms*, 8 rooms, an inexpensive, but pleasant, hotel.

CUMBERNAULD (Dumbartonshire). Scotland's futuristic new town of the 1960's. New (1967) hotel is *Golden Eagle*, 43 rooms (13 with bath, 15 with shower).

DIRLETON (East Lothian). Try the *Open Arms*, 7 rooms (6 with bath, other with shower). A truly excellent hotel—pricey, but worth every penny. Table bookings are

SCOTLAND

advisable as reputation for food is deservedly high.

DORNOCH (Sutherland). Here, try *Dornoch*, 100 rooms (4 with bath), expensive, extremely comfortable, with high standard of cuisine.

Royal Golf, 45 rooms (13 with bath) and *Burghfield House*, 30 rooms (4 with bath), the former residence of Lord Rothermere, with produce from home farm used in high-class cooking, are both highly reliable and only moderately expensive. Families return here year after year.

Others are *Dornoch Castle*, 20 rooms, the old Bishop's Palace, very pleasant. *The Eagle*, 5 rooms, the oldest in town, and *Carlingbank Motel*, 12 rooms.

DUMFRIES (Dumfriesshire). *Cairndale*, 40 rooms (9 with bath), is expensive but excellent. Charming bars, good cuisine and comfortable bedrooms. Burns lived here at one time.

Station, 26 rooms (6 with bath), offers its guests good food, great comfort, as does the *County*, 50 rooms (2 with bath).

The *Mayfair*, 16 rooms, run by an American couple, is also good.

DUNBAR (E. Lothian). Suggest: *Craig-en-Gelt*, 22 rooms, very much a family hotel, conveniently near to all holiday recreations. Moderately priced.

Lothian, 19 rooms, worth searching for. Friendly, efficient, and shows care for guests' comfort and food. Moderately priced.

Other hotels include *Roxburghe*, 40 rooms (4 with bath), *Bellevue*, 47 rooms, and *St. George Old Coach Inn*, 13 rooms, fine food.

DUNDEE (Angus). Best places: *Angus*, 57 rooms (42 with bath), is a new, well-run hotel in centre of city. Food good. Extreme comfort in all rooms—bar, however, best avoided on Saturday nights, as class of clientele plummets. Costly.

Greystanes, Invergowrie, on outskirts of city, has a restaurant with some inspired cooking and excellent service. Except at beginning of week, booking is almost essential because of its justified popularity. Smartly dressed.

Invercarse, 10 rooms (6 with bath), beautifully set above the River Tay, with pleasant garden. Dinner-dancing at weekends and generally good service. Food is very good, indeed. Fairly expensive.

Sandford, Newport. Just across Tay Road Bridge, an excellent place to stay (quietly) or eat either lunch or dinner. Menu consistently good and there is a most pleasant atmosphere. Not unduly expensive. Weekend booking advisable.

Queen's, 48 rooms (1 with bath), is in town centre. Moderately expensive, but food and service are good. Others are *Mathers*, 96 rooms, and *Royal*, 70 rooms.

For lunching out, *Draffens Restaurant* (in shop) is excellent.

DUNFERMLINE (Fife). Here, try: *Pitbauchlie House*, 5 rooms, and situated in pleasant garden. Food good and service excellent. Moderate cost.

In lower-middle price range are *Brucefield*, 9 rooms, and *City*, 27 rooms.

DUNKELD (Perthshire). Suggest: *Dunkeld House*, 22 rooms (6 with bath). All but a few bedrooms extremely comfortable, as are public rooms. Wonderful stretch of river runs through the gardens. Excellent food at all meals and salmon a specialty. Expensive, but worth it.

Cardney House, 14 rooms (6 with bath). This is a private house in splendid grounds, with food grown on estate. Everything is distinguished, and the price is fantastically low. About six miles out of town.

Birnam, 30 rooms (2 with bath), is three miles across the river from Dunkeld. Moderately costly, but is an attractive, spacious hotel with pleasantly old-world atmosphere. Good homely food.

Other hotels are the *Royal*, 32 rooms and *Taybank*, 10 rooms.

DUNNET (Caithness). Here, we suggest: *Northern Sands*, 16 rooms, a typical fishing hotel, not expensive.

DUNOON (Argyll). Best choices: *Argyll*, 22 rooms, *Glenmorag*, 93 rooms, *Selborne*, 87 rooms, and *McColls*, 70 rooms, are moderately expensive and very reliable.

Ardnaheim, 48 rooms, *Dhallaig Lodge*, 18 rooms, and the *Douglas*, 24 rooms, are comparatively inexpensive.

DUNS (Berwickshire). The best: *Barniken House*, 6 rooms, and *White Swan*, 9 rooms, both moderate in all respects.

EAST KILBRIDE (Lanarkshire). New (1968): *The Bruce*, 65 rooms (all with bath).

ELGIN (Morayshire). Our best: *Laichmoray*, 27 rooms, *Gordon Arms*, 26 rooms, and *Royal*, 10 rooms, all moderately priced, reliable, and unexciting. For eating out, it's worth travelling the 12 miles to Forres, where the *Cluny Hills Hotel*, 68 rooms (6 with private bath), is really excellent, fairly expensive, and has a magnificent cuisine.

ELIE (Fife). Our selection: *Marine*, 60 rooms (5 with bath), is first class, with every comfort for all ages. Baby-sitting service, dancing at weekends. Riding, fishing, golf, great comfort and food. Worth every penny, though only moderately expensive.

Golf, 24 rooms, and *Queen's*, 23 rooms (1 with bath), both offer, at moderate cost, good Scottish comfort, food and hospitality.

Other hotels—inexpensive—are the *Victoria*, 22 rooms, and *Earlsknowe*.

FALKIRK (Stirlingshire). Best: *Metropolitan*, 33 rooms (all with bath). Rather an unattractive building, but indoors, much attention has been paid to comfort and convenience of guests. Pleasant decor throughout, and the bars are lush. Dining room service very adequate and food likewise. Although built in busy part of town, there is ample parking space. Expensive.

For eating out, the *Omega Restaurant*, in Newmarket Street, is very good.

FINDHORN (Morayshire). *Culbin Sands*, 16 rooms, and *Crown*, 6 rooms, are small hotels of moderate cost.

FORTINGALL (Perthshire). *Fortingall*, 16 rooms (1 with bath), is moderately expensive and very reliable for comfort and cuisine. Sunday lunches magnificent; during summer season it's as well to book in advance.

FORTROSE (Ross and Cromarty). *Royal Station*, 17 rooms, and *Oakfield*, 10 rooms, are small, homely, moderately-priced hotels.

FORT WILLIAM (Inverness-shire). *Croit-Anna*, 46 rooms (24 with bath), just outside town, is comfortable, spacious, with very good food. Costly, but worth it.

Highland, 51 rooms, *Milton*, 41 rooms (8 with bath), are fairly expensive, but consistently reliable and nicely sited.

Very hospitable, good and less expensive are the *Alexandra*, 34 rooms, and *Commercial*, 8 rooms.

GAIRLOCH (Ross and Cromarty). *Shieldaig Lodge*, 17 rooms (1 with bath), is five miles from Gairloch, but worth the finding. Moderately expensive, it prides itself on simple, homely, excellent cooking. Service is in the hands of a most delightful staff. Grounds are beautiful.

Gairloch, 54 rooms (8 with bath), is also excellent. Near to the beach, it, too, has a happy atmosphere, magnificent setting, good bars and food. Fairly expensive.

GALASHIELS (Selkirkshire). *Douglas*, 25 rooms, *Royal*, 19 rooms, *Kingsknowes*, 15 rooms (2 with bath), and *Kings*, 6 rooms, are all good, moderately-priced hotels.

Less costly are the *Abbotsford Arms*, 8 rooms, and *Waverley*, 4 rooms.

GARVE (Ross and Cromarty). *Strathgarve Lodge*, 22 rooms (3 with bath), is an attractive hotel in an attractive setting. Scottish hospitality at its best. Meals excellent, as are afternoon teas. Cheap at its moderately expensive price.

Garve, 23 rooms, is moderately priced. In great countryside, this hotel has changed hands recently, but reputation in past has been consistently good.

At closeby Contin, the *Craigdarroch*, 12 rooms, produces plentiful, excellent Scottish food. Its bar and dining room are worth travelling miles to enjoy.

GLAMIS (Angus). The *Strathmore Arms* has been converted from village pub into smart restaurant by two of the Queen's relatives, sometimes to be seen lunching or dining there. Food excellent, prices reasonable, and the decor and silver is extremely pleasant.

GLENEAGLES (Perthshire). Try the *Gleneagles*, 212 rooms (160 with bath); has everything—and its reputation is not overdone. Service, food, comfort unsurpassable, with beautiful hills all around. The nearby village of Auchterarder has some fine antique gift and woollen shops. Eat in its *Glen Devon Room* for a fine dining experience.

GLENSHEE (Perthshire). *Dalmunzie*, 23 rooms (5 with bath), is really remote. Has its own golf course and beautiful grounds. Food is of very high standard. Expensive.

Dalrulzion Highland, 11 rooms, and *Spittall*, 19 rooms (5 with bath), are both good, homely and not expensive. The latter usually has a gay, young crowd of guests.

GOUROCK (Renfrewshire). *Bay*, 42 rooms (6 with bath), is a pleasant place to stay. Bars nice and friendly, food good, and there's sometimes dancing. Moderately priced.

Also moderately priced and good value are the *Queen's*, 22 rooms, *Cloch*, 15 rooms, *Fairlight*, 5 rooms, and *Firth*, 14 rooms.

GRANTOWN-ON-SPEY. (Morayshire). *Grant Arms*, 50 rooms (14 with bath), is a first-class hotel with enormous rooms and truly Scottish atmosphere. Comfort of the highest standard, and good food. Fairly expensive.

Craiglynn, 62 rooms (5 with bath), is another popular hotel, with the same families returning year after year. Food consistently good, with own farm produce. Attractive gardens and plenty of parking space. Moderately expensive. White Mountain Ski School headquarters here.

Palace, 44 rooms, and *Ben Mhor*, 28 rooms, moderately

priced, but adequate in service and food. Both have resident ski instructors from the Scottish Norwegian Ski School.

GRETNA GREEN (Dumfriesshire). The convenient *Lovers Leap Motel*, 24 rooms (4 with bath) is a good stopping place.

GULLANE (East Lothian). *Greywalls*, 20 rooms (8 with bath), is expensive but of highest possible standard for comfort, food and service. An attractive building in attractive setting. Only snag is that because of its reputation for excellence, booking is heavy. In the restaurant, all food is good, especially the seafoods.

Other hotels here are all good. *Gables*, 8 rooms, *Queens*, 14 rooms (1 with bath), whose food is reliable, consistent (and occasionally rises to the heights), *Mallard*, 14 rooms, and *Bissett s* 27 rooms. All of these are moderately priced.

HARRIS, Isle of (Inverness-shire). *Harris*, 20 rooms, at Tarbert, is a medium-priced fishing hotel.

HAWICK (Roxburghshire). *Crown*, 36 rooms, *Buccleuch*, 28 rooms, and *Victorian*, 20 rooms—are all moderate in price and quality. Honest, everyday food, which is reliable, but unexciting.

Dine out at the *Wolfelee Hotel*, Bonchester Bridge, nearby—it is a magnificent place with all the right ideas about eating.

HELENSBURGH (Dunbartonshire). *Queen's* 27 rooms (7 with bath), is excellent. Comfortable, nice to look at, and with a clientele which demands and receives the best of service and cooking. Expensive.

Commodore, 30 rooms, *Cairndhu*, 13 rooms, are other good hotels, of moderate price.

INCHNADAMPH (Sutherland). *Inchnadamph*, 30 rooms (2 with bath), is not expensive, but perfect for its type. Mainly for anglers and their families, so that food is good and plentiful. Rooms comfortable and atmosphere friendly; close to hotel, there are pleasant walks.

INVERARY (Argyll). Our choice: *Minard Castle*, 47 rooms (16 with bath), is a new venture, part-owned by a Scot who owns the *Edinburgh Bar*, San Francisco. Tartan and pipers abound and Scottish food is a feature on menus. Castle built 1774, reputed to have genuine ghost. Fairly expensive.

Argyll Arms, 27 rooms (1 with bath), and *George*, 26 rooms (1 with bath), are both extremely good, with consistently high standard of cooking. Moderately expensive.

For a meal out, try *Portsonachan*, a mile or two from Inverary—food is marvellous.

INVERNESS (Inverness-shire). *Station*, 70 rooms, (23 with bath), is expensive, but extremely comfortable. In town centre. Bar and dining room service always of high quality.

Kingsmills, 20 rooms, is moderately expensive and very good indeed. House dates back over two centuries, and the gardens are restful and attractive. Two miles from town centre. Food is very good, if uninspired, and bar traffic entertaining.

Royal, 40 rooms (5 with bath), is in town centre, and expensive. Comfortable public and private rooms and good food.

Caledonian, 120 rooms (all with bath), is planned as being the last word in Highland luxury. Nicely set over River Ness.

Drumossie, 41 rooms (5 with bath), *Cummings*, 30 rooms, and

Columba, 62 rooms, are of moderate price and comfort. (Drumossie is 4 miles from town centre.)

(As the tourist traffic is so enormous in summer, there are too many hotels to mention others.)

For eating out, the *Glenmhor* is good and reasonably priced. For Chinese food, the *New Full Moon* is recommended.

IONA, Island of (Argyll). Try: *St. Columba*, 25 rooms, a fairly expensive hotel, and extremely good in all respects. Views all around are worth the money alone. Advance booking whenever possible.

ISLAY, Isle of (Argyll). Try *Bridgend* at Bowmore, 10 rooms; is fairly expensive but offers its guests great hospitality, good, plentiful, food and splendid scenery.

Seaview at Bowmore, 7 rooms, *Port Askaig Hotel*, 10 rooms, and the *Islay*, 18 rooms, at Port Ellen, are all good value for money. Bars are full of life and dining rooms full of well-fed guests. Book ahead if possible, from June to September.

JEDBURGH (Roxburghshire). The *Spreadeagle*, 13 rooms, *Royal*, 7 rooms, *Jedforest*, 9 rooms, all moderately priced and most comfortable, with plentiful food.

JOHN O'GROATS (Caithness). *John O' Groats House*, 24 rooms, and *Seaview*, 10 rooms, are both moderate in price and amenity.

KELSO ((Roxburghshire). Try: *Ednam House*, 31 rooms (16 with bath), a very fine hotel of 18th-century architecture. It has the right kind of old-fashioned atmosphere and very modern ideas about comfort and quality. Food good and prices only moderately expensive.

Cross Keys, 21 rooms (2 with bath), moderately priced and excellent value in comfort and food.

KILLIN (Perthshire). Suggest: *Killin*, 40 rooms (3 with bath); has a long reputation for high standards of comfort and food. Family hotel with lively bar and its own salmon fishing stretch on Loch Tay. Most welcoming.

All hotels here take pride in pleasing their guests and among them are *Dall Lodge*, 8 rooms, *Bridge of Lochay*, 17 rooms, *Tighnabruich*, 8 rooms and *Morenish Lodge*, 12 rooms. All reasonably priced.

KINROSS (Perthshire). Choice: *Green*, 40 rooms (4 with bath), with food and comfort of high standard. Pleasant outlook over main street and peaceful gardens behind. Bedrooms very comfortable and spacious lounge. Moderately expensive.

Kirklands, 16 rooms and *Bridgend*, 12 rooms, not costly, but more of the commercial type. Excellent breakfasts to be had at the latter.

KIRKCUDBRIGHT (Kircudbrightshire). *Royal*, 22 rooms, pleasant atmosphere typical of town. Food and comfort very adequate and charges moderate.

Mayfield, 30 rooms, is in lovely situation with attractive garden. Comfortable, simple rooms, homely welcome, plentiful food and inexpensive.

Also good is the *Selkirk Arms*, 17 rooms (2 with bath).

KIRKWALL (Orkney). Try these: *Kirkwall*, 46 rooms (2 with bath), is beautifully situated on seafront, and indoors there are no disappointments. Geared to holidaymakers' needs, food and warmth well attended to. Moderately expensive.

Less expensive are the *Queen's*, 5 rooms, and *Royal*, 31 rooms.

KIRRIEMUIR (Angus). Our choice: *Airlei Arms*, 8 rooms, and *Ogilvie Arms*, 8 rooms, are very similar, small Scottish hotels within a stone's throw of each other in town centre. Parking easy enough. Tartan carpets, homely fare and friendly welcomes in bars and other public rooms. Inexpensive.

KYLE OF LOCHALSH (Ross and Cromarty). *Lochalsh*, 36 rooms (5 with bath), luxury class. Expensive, but always good. All rooms, bars, etc., combine Highland comfort and modern efficiency. Situated on seafront rocks, where a day's entertainment can be had watching the boat traffic.

Kyle, 8 rooms, is of moderate price and in very different class from above.

LADYBANK (Fife). A great place: *Fernie Castle* has been converted into a splendid hotel in luxury class. Its history as castle dates from 1353, and many of the rooms can still be discerned in old form (one bathroom, for instance, is cut out of the thickness of a wall). All rooms furnished with taste and the heating is very adequate. Cuisine and service generally of extremely high standard. Expensive, but worth every penny.

LAIRG (Sutherland). Our choices: *Sutherland Arms*, 38 rooms (6 with bath). Fairly expensive, but gives magnificent value in comfort and food, and attracts extremely congenial guests. It has private suites, and with the view over the loch there can be nothing to grumble about here.

Aultnagar, new (1967), 30 rooms, excellent food.

LARGS (Ayrshire). Our best: *Marine and Curlinghall*, 90 rooms (13 with bath), is splendidly situated overlooking the Clyde and is most interesting architecturally. Bookings in advance advisable, if possible, as it is deservedly popular. Expensive, but as everything it offers is of high standard, well worth it.

Mackerston, 55 rooms, is fairly expensive, but reliable. Nice atmosphere, and hotel has attractive gardens.

LERWICK (Shetland). Try the *Queen's*, 22 rooms, *Grand*, 24 rooms, and *Hayfield*, 8 rooms, all good homely hotels, moderately priced.

LINLITHGOW (West Lothian). *St. Michaels*, 6 rooms, *West Port*, 7 rooms, and *Star and Garter*, 9 rooms, are moderately-priced hotels.

LOCHINVER (Sutherland). Try: *Culag*, 45 rooms, is expensive and excellent. Food has caused travellers and writers to wax eloquent and many others to use this wonderful, flower-bedecked hotel as basis for stories. Excellent company in bars and lounges. Food is consistently good.

LOCH LOMOND (Dunbartonshire). Beautiful views of the most famous of Scotland's lakes from the very elegant and well-run *Lomond Castle*, at Balloch, at southern tip of the loch. 12 rooms (3 with bath).

LOCH TORRIDON (Ross and Cromarty). *Loch Torridon*, 25 rooms, not expensive and well worth visiting. Food can be really good, as is comfort. Be sure to book ahead, as it is very much the end of the road and too far to return on an empty stomach. Excellent centre for salmon, sea trout, brown trout sea fishing, deer stalking (Aug.-Feb.), water sports, etc.

LOSSIEMOUTH (Morayshire).

Stonefield, 44 rooms, is a moderately expensive, excellent hotel. Luxurious feel about it, yet eminently suitable for children, too. Bar, lounges and many bedrooms possess splendid views along the Moray Firth.

Laverock Bank, 14 rooms, reasonably priced, beautifully situated on a hill, yet within a minute's walk of the Moray golf course. Good, homely, food.

LUNDIN LINKS (Fife). Try these: *Crusoe*, 10 rooms, faces harbour of infinite charm. Comfortable small hotel which provides excellent food, especially the freshly- and locally-caught fish. Moderate cost.

Lundin Links, 21 rooms (2 with bath), and *Victoria*, 15 rooms, are both really comfortable, with emphasis on hospitable atmosphere and pleasantly served meals.

Others are the *Beach*, 12 rooms, and *Elmwood*, 9 rooms, inexpensive.

MALLAIG (Inverness-shire). Try: *Marine*, 20 rooms, and *West Highland*, 31 rooms, are equally good hotels, very reasonably priced for what they offer. Views abound, as does friendliness. Good, homely fare is plentiful.

Heatherlea Guest House, 12 rooms, and *Parkmohr Guest House*, 11 rooms, are small and inexpensive.

For eating out, the *Jacobite Restaurant* has terrific Scottish food.

MOFFAT (Dumfriesshire). *Annadale*, 25 rooms, is pleasant, not costly and good value. Reasonable in price and amenity are the *Balmoral*, 18 rooms, *Moffat House*, 15 rooms, and *Star*, 12 rooms.

MULL, Island of (Argyll). A new hotel at Salen, the *Glenforsa House*, 14 rooms.

NAIRN (Nairnshire). Best choice: *Newton House*, 30 rooms (10 with bath). Tranquil country house in spacious grounds, where ponies graze and the sea is close. Public rooms are large and comfortable and the bar is superbly run. Dining room service excellent and food consistently of really high standard. Expensive, but first rate.

Golf View, 61 rooms (12 with bath), is also costly, another excellent hotel overlooking the Moray Firth. Cooking generous and excellent.

Alton Burn, 36 rooms, is moderately priced. The service is cheerful. Spacious parking and public rooms, and easy access to beach. Good food.

Royal Marine, 50 rooms, is fairly expensive and gives a reliable service.

Others are *Invernairne*, 16 rooms, *Braeval*, 10 rooms, and *Highland*, 66 rooms.

NETHYBRIDGE (Inverness-shire). *Nethy Bridge*, 74 rooms (15 with bath). This hotel is reasonably priced and offers its guests considerable comfort, good cuisine, and, often, evening entertainment.

NEWTONMORE (Inverness-shire). *Mains*, 42 rooms, is currently changing hands, but has been consistently reliable for years. Service cheerful and the food plain, but excellent. Afternoon teas a specialty. Comfortable rooms and moderate prices.

Balavil Arms, 28 rooms (6 with bath). Pony trekking began here and the hotel is much used by young people with interest in skiing and riding—consequently, gay evenings. Anglers also use it. Plentiful homely fare. Moderate prices.

Badenoch, 14 rooms, *Lodge*, 12 rooms, are inexpensive, homely hotels, where families return year after year.

NORTH BERWICK (East Lothian). *Marine,* 73 rooms (23 with bath), is a luxury hotel, popular over the decades with golfers and families from around Edinburgh. Views of the sea and proximity of golf courses add to its attractions, and there are entertainments galore for young children. Comfort of highest standard and food excellent. Expensive.

Westerdunes, 30 rooms (10 with bath), is a pleasant hotel with high standards of comfort and cuisine which justify its costliness.

Other extremely good hotels, moderately expensive, are the *Royal,* 42 rooms (4 with bath), and *Blenheim House,* 10 rooms (3 with bath).

At *Nether Abbey,* 17 rooms, the cooking is excellent.

There are too many small, inexpensive hotels in this holiday town to discriminate, but generally the standard is high.

OBAN (Argyll). Our choices: *Great Western,* 83 rooms (53 with bath). This is a magnificent place to stay, right on the brilliant blue of the sea. Very gay entertainment laid on and terrific bars. Comfort and food of absolutely top quality, and service to match. Expensive.

Caledonian, 84 rooms (20 with bath). Another excellent establishment, and only moderately expensive. Though large (like several Oban hotels), this has a friendly, homely atmosphere. Food is very good indeed, especially the salmon and shellfish of local extraction.

Loch Melfort Motor Inn, Arduaine, near Oban, 30 rooms (25 with bath and balconies). Country house with distinguished cedar wood annexe situated in large, lovely grounds, with fishing. Views to Jura, Scarba, Luing and Shuna Isles. Excellent cocktail bar, and in grill room, late dinners are served. Expensive.

The choice of hotels here is almost endless, but it is a popular place and should be booked ahead if possible. Expensive, but good, are the *Marine,* 39 rooms (3 with bath) and *Alexandra,* 61 rooms (9 with bath).

Less costly but consistently reliable, are the *Crown,* 20 rooms, *Esplanade,* 26 rooms, and *Regent,* 38 rooms.

For eating out, *McTavish's Kitchen* is a splendid, original place. Scottish dishes a specialty —haggis, kippers, herring in oatmeal, and local prawns. Folk music accompanies them in summer evenings.

PEEBLES (Peeblesshire). We suggest: *Peebles Hydro,* 161 rooms (30 with bath), a big, well-run hotel, with an enviable reputation for good service. Comfort, cuisine, entertainment (and even a physiotherapist) are of high standard. Views of the hills all around are magnificent and the evenings are quite beautiful, full of bird sounds. Expensive.

Tontine, 36 rooms (16 with bath), and the *Parks,* 14 rooms (5 with bath), are expensive, but again, offer their guests all that could be wished for in the way of comfort, surrounding landscape and good cooking.

Moderately priced are the *Cleikum Inn,* 9 rooms, *Green Tree,* 9 rooms, *Lee Lodge,* 11 rooms (1 with bath), and all are reputed to be very reliable.

PERTH (Perthshire). The best: *Station,* 56 rooms (20 with bath). Good food and extremely comfortable rooms. Lively bar.

Royal George, 50 rooms (18 with

SCOTLAND

bath), is sited on River Tay and has a pleasant garden. Darkish, old-fashioned feel about the hotel, our second choice. Bar life entertaining and the food is good. Moderately expensive.

Salutation, 67 rooms (12 with bath), and *Queen's*, 54 rooms (6 with bath), are also good in every way, though unexceptional. Moderately priced.

For eating out, *Huntingtower*, just out of town, is extremely good, either at lunch or dinner time. *Isle of Skye Hotel* is also good.

PITLOCHRY (Perthshire). Try these: *Hydro*, 68 rooms (28 with bath), is probably the best-located for the theatre. Also has a very good restaurant.

Atholl Palace, 114 rooms (16 with bath), is a large, modern hotel with magnificent hilltop setting. Lovely grounds to wander in, and food is usually very good. (Open May-Oct.)

Green Park, 40 rooms (4 with bath), is on Faskally Loch, wonderfully wooded. Views all around are unbelievably beautiful and indoors, too, all is fine. Comfort, cooking, service generally is of first quality.

Moulin, 20 rooms, is a small, moderately-priced hotel approximately 6 miles uphill from Pitlochry, and possesses a magnetic charm. Entirely peaceful. Food homely and excellent.

Fisher's, 70 rooms (12 with bath), and *Pinetrees*, 30 rooms, are moderately priced and very good value. *Fisher's* has a good restaurant.

Others are *Airdaniar*, 11 rooms, *Fasganeoin*, 10 rooms, and *Scotland's*, 54 rooms (21 with bath), the latter being rather expensive for what it offers. Also: *Castlebeigh*, 21 rooms, and *Dundannoch*, 23 rooms.

Eat out at the *Strathgarry Restaurant*. At the Festival Theatre's *Brown Trout Restaurant*, snacks are served during the day, and at night the cold dinner is well worth booking.

PLOCKTON (Ross and Cromarty). *Plockton*, 7 rooms, is very moderately priced. The food is homely and plentiful and the rooms are comfortable.

POOLEWE (Ross and Cromarty). *Pool House*, 21 rooms, is good to look at, well situated, very comfortable and serves really good food. Reasonably priced and excellent value.

Loch Maree, 22 rooms, is about 12 miles from Poolewe and moderately expensive. Beautifully set place with accent on comfort and cuisine. Its reputation is of real worth.

PORTPATRICK (Wigtownshire). *Portpatrick*, 57 rooms (15 with bath), is only moderately expensive and good in all respects. Over the years, the same guests return—which is the best test. The evening entertainment is lively and food good.

Inexpensive other hotels are *Fernhill*, 7 rooms, *Cross Keys*, 12 rooms, and *Melvin Lodge*, 14 rooms.

PRESTWICK (Ayrshire). Try: *Queen's*, 34 rooms (5 with bath), *Links*, 13 rooms, and the *Golden Eagle*, 6 rooms, all moderately expensive and reliable. Scheduled to open by 1970, an *Allied Hotel* of 140 rooms.

ROSEMARKIE (Ross and Cromarty). The best choices: *Marine*, 54 rooms (1 with bath), is an attractive, well-laid out building facing down on to the beach and across the Firth. Moderately expensive, very comfortable and friendly. An excellent place for families. Food is good.

Marita, 13 rooms, is inexpensive and makes every effort to please its guests.

ST. ANDREWS (Fife). The best: *Scores*, 34 rooms (12 with bath), overlooks the sea and the main lounge has long, large windows to make the most of this. Dining room with french windows on to rose garden is attractive and serves extremely good meals. New (1968) hotel, *The Old Course*, 80 rooms (all with bath), definitely in the luxury class. The building is really attractive, overlooking the Royal and Ancient. On top floor is the main restaurant, bar and lounge—all with views across the golf course to the North Sea. Very expensive.

Rusacks, 64 rooms (23 with bath), overlooks the Royal and Ancient golf course, and is comfortable and reliable in all respects. Has its own hairdresser. Expensive.

Cross Keys, 19 rooms (1 with bath), is in centre of town and, although unremarkable to look at, provides excellent meals. Should be booked in advance if possible. Frequented by students and university staff and has undeniable atmosphere. Moderately expensive.

St. Andrew's, 30 rooms (12 with bath), is expensive and pleasantly situated overlooking the sea. Very comfortable.

Rufflets, 20 rooms (7 with bath), and *Golf*, 20 rooms, are moderately-priced hotels which offer a most honest service.

There are too many small hotels in the inexpensive category to discriminate.

For eating out, the *Grange Inn* is excellent. Picturesque setting, candlelight and inspired cooking. Well worth the expense.

SKYE, Isle of (Inverness-shire). *Skeabost House*, 17 rooms (1 with bath). Magnificent country house belonging to the MacLeods, currently run by an American member of the family. Furnishings and furniture throughout of top quality. Bedrooms, dining room and bars all beautifully decorated. Largest log fire imaginable in lounge. Excellent restaurant. Costly, but great value.

Royal, 23 rooms (8 with bath), is at Portree, and has wonderful views over the sea to the hills beyond. All guests are made to feel really welcome in this comfortable place. The food is excellent and pleasantly served. Expensive.

Dunvegan, 18 rooms (2 with bath), is really Highland in atmosphere and appearance. Food is very good and, as often as not, entirely Scottish. Home-made haggis with whisky is served by tartan-clad staff, for instance. Very reasonably priced.

Broadford, at Broadford, 28 rooms, the *Marine*, at Kyleakin, 26 rooms, the *Sligachan*, at Sligachan, 30 rooms (3 with bath), and the *Dunollie*, at Broadford, 21 rooms, are all reasonably priced, and very good indeed.

Excellent restaurant is the *Dolphin*, at Broadford, built out on to the sea. Cooking is very good and meals are served with great civility till late at night.

STEPPS (Lanark). Close to Glasgow is the new (1966) *Garfield*, 17 rooms (all with bath). Very comfortable.

STIRLING (Stirlingshire). *Golden Lion*, 66 rooms (7 with bath), excellent hotel in town centre. Nothing remarkable to look at, but service is always good, bars lively and food of high quality.

King Robert, 20 rooms (all with bath), and the *Portcullis*, 5 rooms, are costly, but very good.

Others are the *Sword*, 5 rooms, and *Station*, 23 rooms.

The *Gateway Restaurant* feeds its guests well and not expensively. Menu range is good, and surroundings pleasant.

STORNOWAY, Isle of Lewis (Ross and Cromarty) Try these: *Caledonian*, 12 rooms, *Newton House*, 14 rooms, *Royal*, 17 rooms, and *County*, 17 rooms; hotels are all reasonable in every respect.

STRANRAER (Wigtownshire). *North West Castle*, 34 rooms (12 with bath). This is a fantastically-built place, something of a cross between a ship and a castle. Other feature is the exceptionally friendly welcome. Only moderately expensive. A thrilling seascape in front. Food is also good.

Lochnaw Castle, 6 rooms, and the *George*, 30 rooms (2 with bath), are reasonably expensive, and very good value indeed is given at both. Food good.

Others are the *Buck's Head*, 18 rooms, and *Ruddicot*, 10 rooms.

STRATHPEFFER (Ross and Cromarty). Among the best: *Ben Wyvis*, 90 rooms, and *Highland*, 100 rooms (12 with bath), are both modern, comfortable hotels with a real Scottish flavour. Food usually very good, indeed. Fairly expensive, but worth it.

Other hotels are *Holly Lodge*, 10 rooms, and *Strathpeffer*, 13 rooms.

TARBERT (Argyll). Best choice: *Stonefield Castle*, 24 rooms (8 with bath and 6 with shower). This is a place which makes its guest feel special. Lovely castle in miraculous surroundings. Dancing, fishing, boating. The comfort and food is worth every penny of its rather expensive prices. Make every effort to get there.

Other hotels — moderately-priced, and rather overshadowed —are the *Tarbert*, 22 rooms (2 with shower), and *Columba*, 14 rooms.

THURSO (Caithness). Try these: *Royal*, 85 rooms (5 with bath), is very good and guests are made to feel comfortable, and well fed. It is moderately expensive.

More moderately-priced are the *Park*, 16 rooms, and *Pentland*, 38 rooms.

For eating out, the *Upper Deck*, excellent Danish food.

TOBERMORY (Argyll). Try the *Western Isles*, 50 rooms (11 with bath), a splendid place with every amenity, own tennis courts, etc. Food is very good, indeed, and service friendly. Walks around the hotel are delightful. Expensive, but well worth it.

Mishnish, 15 rooms, is also good, and moderately priced.

For eating out, try the *Druimard Guest House*, at Dervaig—although booking is necessary. It has fabulous food, often invented recipes of the proprietors, who also run a small theatre in the grounds. An inspired place.

TROON (Ayrshire). We suggest: *Marine*, 90 rooms (4 with bath), is superbly situated for all family entertainments, and for those who want to sit around, the lounges and garden are ideal. All comforts here, and dining room service very good. Expensive and popular. Dinner-dancing at weekends.

Sun Court, 12 rooms (10 with bath), on a much smaller scale, but again extremely comfortable

—rather expensive. Food is good, as is service.

Craiglea, 21 rooms (4 with bath), is right on the seafront, with sun lounges which make even the windy days pleasant for sitting around. Nicely served meals and pleasant attitude to guests. Fairly expensive.

Other hotels are the *Ardneil*, 14 rooms, *Knowe*, 7 rooms, and *Tower*, 6 rooms.

TURNBERRY (Ayrshire). Try the *Turnberry*, 124 rooms (116 with bath and 8 with shower). Luxury hotel of very highest order. Wooded lawns slope down from elegant white building, and there is an indoor swimming pool, dinner-dancing, etc. Food is superlative and the staff is unusually pleasant for such an upper-crust establishment. Very expensive.

ULLAPOOL (Ross and Cromarty). *Royal*, 53 rooms (17 with bath) is a first-class place to stay. Grounds beautiful, public rooms and bars are extremely pleasant to be in. Food excellent and fish is at its freshest here. Costly, but worth every penny.

Caledonian, 32 rooms, moderately expensive hotel and excellent value. Nicely situated on loch side. Food very good, indeed.

Morefield, 21 rooms, moderately priced, reliable hotel. This is an attractive house in lovely grounds. Welcoming staff and consistently good food.

Others are *Riverside House*, 19 rooms and the *Argyll*, 4 rooms.

WICK (Caithness). Our choice: *Station*, 57 rooms (2 with bath), and *MacKay's*, 19 rooms (2 with bath), are reasonably priced hotels which pay attention to their guests' comfort. Food, of the homely variety, is plentiful.

WIGTOWN (Wigtownshire). *Portpatrick Arms*, 57 rooms (15 with bath), is in nearby Portpatrick, and extremely good value for its moderate prices. Food and comfort are both of high standard.

In Wigtown itself, there is the *Galloway*, 11 rooms, which is moderate in all respects.

YARROW (Selkirkshire). Try the *Gordon Arms*, 4 rooms, a small and moderately-priced hotel with desire to please. Homely food is plentiful.

YETHOLM (Roxburghshire). Try: *Plough*, 5 rooms, a small, inexpensive, country-town type of hotel, where food is plain, but cheerfully served.

HOW TO GET ABOUT? *By train:* The north of Scotland is sparsely populated. Rail links are comparatively few, but main lines from Glasgow and Edinburgh run to Inverness and Wick in the north, with a branch to Kyle of Lochalsh, from where a ferry boat leaves for Skye. The line from Edinburgh and Glasgow to Oban is through the most scenic stretches of railroad in the world. Free lineside maps and descriptive booklets are obtainable from the Publicity Officer, *British Rail*, 87 Union Street, Glasgow.

Other fabulous runs are on the observation coaches (the only ones in Britain) between Glasgow and Fort William; Fort William and Mallaig; Inverness and Kyle of Lochalsh. On all these runs the conductor gives a Pleasant, unobtrusive, yet highly instructive commentary. Licensed buffet cars and swivel-type seats all add to the general well-being, comfort and enjoyment of passengers. In popular months these tours tend to become booked.

British Rail also runs Forth Bridge Day Tours which take passengers between Edinburgh and Dunfermline via the Forth Rail Bridge and back by coach over the Forth Road Bridge. These are inexpensive.

Freedom-of-Scotland tickets issued by British Rail are an excellent way of seeing the country and full details can be had from Divisional Manager, British Rail, 23 Waterloo Place, Edinburgh. From this address, it is also possible to obtain details of reduced fares to and from the Scottish ski resorts.

By boat: Most shipping services to the Inner and Outer Hebrides are in the hands of *David MacBrayne's*, an old-established firm with comfortable vessels (some of which carry the royal mail) plying from Oban, Gourock, Mallaig, Tobermory, etc. Services operate frequently, and for certain voyages, sleeping accommodation is provided.

Car ferries operate between many of the islands and cruises of varying lengths are the ideal way of seeing these fabulous islands off Scotland. Full details of all services, car ferries and cruises can be had in an illustrated leaflet from David MacBrayne Ltd., Clyde House, 44 Robertson Street, Glasgow C.2.

Cruises and sailings to Orkney and Shetland. First-class passenger ships sail from Leith (Edinburgh) and Aberdeen from May to September. The cruises vary from 5- or 6-day ones to three-week ones, with longer stays on the islands. Prices are very reasonable. Full details from *North of Scotland, Orkney and Shetland Shipping Co. Ltd.*, Matthew's Quay, Aberdeen. There are regular sailings from Aberdeen to Kirkwall and Lerwick twice weekly, with space on the boats for about 20 cars.

The *Caledonian Steam Packet Company* also runs a comprehensive boat service around the Clyde resorts, calling at some of the most interesting and beautiful of the islands. These tours are linked by train services running to and from Glasgow. Full details to be had from General Manager, Caledonian Steam Packet Co. Ltd., Gourock.

The Caledonian Canal and Loch Ness short cruises run daily except Sunday in the summer season. *M.V. Scot II*, which in winter does service as an ice breaker, is a cheery little boat with accommodation for 65. A bar and light refreshments are laid on and there are morning, afternoon and evening trips up Loch Ness, where everyone hopes to catch sight of the monster. Details from *Caledonian Canal Office*, Clachnaharry, Inverness.

MacFarlane and Son, the Boatyard, Balmaha, Stirlingshire, organize pleasure sailings to glorious Loch Lomond and its islands by mail launch on Mondays and Thursdays.

For visitors from Ireland, two companies offer services by sea. *Burns and Laird Lines*, 56 Robertson Street, Glasgow C.2., have regular services from Belfast, Londonderry and Dublin to Glasgow, while *British Rail* operates drive-on ferries between Larne and Stranraer.

By bus: Bus touring is a popular way of seeing Scotland, and several companies operate tours through fabulous countryside, with stops at some fine hotels. *MacBraynes* run many, some of which are combined with steamer trips. These take in out-of-the-way islands and remote villages. Lengths of trips vary between one day and just over a week. Of the short variety, a popular one is by coach through the Great Glen to Fort William, and thereafter by steamer through Loch Linnhe and the Firth of Lorne. Oban is a stopping-off point, then on to the Isles of Mull, and Erraid, which featured in R. L. Stevenson's *Kidnapped*. At Iona, there is time to visit the cathedral and burial place of the Scottish kings before returning. Details from 44 Robertson Street, Glasgow. *S.M.T.* of Glasgow is another firm with a large selection of coach tours from which to choose, and in just about every sizeable town, local companies arrange tours. In Glasgow, contact *Travel Trips Ltd.*, 22 Renfield Street, or in Dundee, there is *Watson's Tours*, 45 Reform Street, who are renowned for their luxurious vehicles.

By car: If you prefer to rent a drive-yourself car, there are firms who will arrange this in most towns of any importance. Membership of the *Automobile Association* (Fanum House, Leicester Square, London or Fanum House, Glasgow), even for the year, is very inexpensive, and often proves to be money well spent.

Alternatively, there are certain companies who supply cars with drivers. Becoming more and more popular with visitors who want to see as much as possible of Scotland, yet who do not want to be tied to prearranged hotel bookings, is the motorized caravan. These vehicles sleep up to four people comfortably and have built-in cooking and washing facilities. Particularly in the Highlands of Scotland, there is no shortage of secluded overnight stopping places. *Retson Car Rental*, 1143 Argyle Street, Glasgow, can supply vehicles.

By air: Scottish internal air services are flown by *British European Airways*, based at Abbotsinch Airport, Glasgow, and Turnhouse Airport, Edinburgh. All B.E.A. domestic flights to and from Glasgow, let it be stressed, land at Abbotsinch. Glasgow's *other* airport, Prestwick, is used by *B.O.A.C., Pan American, S.A.S.* and *K.L.M.*, so that travellers, direct from the United States may very well arrive at Prestwick whereas those who have changed to B.E.A. plane at London will arrive at Abbotsinch. (Checking in advance re: which airport you use may save much frustration and disappointment.)

From Glasgow there are frequent regular flights to Edinburgh, Aberdeen, Inverness, Campbeltown and Wick on the mainland, and to the islands of Islay, Benbecula, Lewis, Orkney, Shetland and Barra. At most of these airports, the amenities are negligible. There are restaurants at Glasgow and Edinburgh airports, a snack bar at Inverness airport, etc., but at Barra, for instance, there is nothing. Although there are daily flights to and from Barra (except on Sundays), the total community of the island is only 1,400 and the entire airport administration is in the hands of one woman. (Moreover, you land on the beach at low tide!)

SCOTLAND

Historic Houses Open to the Public

Many historic castles and ancestral homes of the Scottish nobility are open to the public at certain times, and the proceeds usually go to charity. The Tourist Board pamphlet, *Scotland's Castles and Historic Centres*, lists many, and a selection of some of the most interesting and beautiful is given below:

(To anyone interested in gardens, there is also a booklet listing those in Scotland open to the public; this can be obtained (price 2s 6d—30¢) from the General Organizer, *Scotland's Gardens Scheme*, 26 Castle Street, Edinburgh.)

Abbotsford House, three miles from Galashiels, was the home of Sir Walter Scott. Open weekdays and Sun. afternoons, end of March through October.

Ardblair, Blairgowrie, Perthshire. 15th-century castle, which is entered only by appointment. Anyone interested in art, architecture or Jacobite relics should phone Blairgowrie 155.

Balmoral Castle, H.M. the Queen's Highland home. Grounds open May to October, except when royal family is in residence.

Balvenie Castle, ancient stronghold of the Comyns, visited by Edward I in 1304 and Queen Mary in 1562. One of the largest, best-preserved castles in Scotland.

Barra Castle, Oldmeldrum, nr. Aberdeen. Close to site of King Robert the Bruce's victory over the Comyns in 1307. Very impressive building with ancient vaulted kitchens. To view, contact Major Irvine, of Barra and Straloch, Oldmeldrum.

The Binns, near Linlithgow, West Lothian. National Trust for Scotland. Historic house with fine 17th-century plaster ceilings. Open daily, mid-June to mid-September.

Blair Castle, Blair Atholl, Perthshire, built in 1269, home of the Duke of Atholl. Jacobite relics, splendid selection of antique toys, firearms, tapestries, etc. Café. Open weekdays and Sunday afternoons, Easter through October.

Brodick Castle, Isle of Arran. Fortress site since Viking times, then seat of dukes of Hamilton. Magnificent gardens. Teas, etc. Open daily (except Sundays) May to September.

Cardoness Castle, Kirkcudbrightshire. 15th-century four-story tower house, ancient home of the McCullochs. Stands on rocky platform above Water of Fleet.

Claypotts Castle, near Dundee, once belonged to John Graham of Claverhouse (Bonnie Dundee). Dates from 1569.

Craigievar Castle, Lumphahan, Aberdeenshire. 17th-century fortified tower, occupied for 350 years. National Trust. Open May to September, Weds., Thurs., and Suns., 2-7.

Crathes Castle, Kincardineshire. 16th-century Jacobean castle with painted ceilings. Gardens date from 1702. Open May to September, daily 2-7, October and April afternoons only.

Cullen House, Banffshire. Contains many art treasures and paintings. Part of house is 700 years old. Open June through September.

Culross Palace, Fife. Built between 1597 and 1611. Fine painted ceilings. Open daily, throughout the year.

Culzean Castle, Maybole, Ayrshire, one of the finest Adam buildings in Scotland, built in late 18th century. Includes flat gifted to General Eisenhower, now a memorial to him. Beautiful gardens laid out in 1783. Open March to October, 10-dusk.

Dalgatie Castle, near Turriff, Aberdeenshire, 13th-century stronghold of the Clan Hay. Rebuilt 14th century, visited by Mary Queen of Scots in 1562. Open July and August, on Wed. and Sun. afternoons.

Dirleton Castle, near North Berwick, East Lothian. Sturdy 13th-century stronghold with lovely gardens. Open daily all year.

Eilean Donan Castle, Ardelve, Ross and Cromarty, built 1220, by Alexander II, to keep out the Danes. Garrisoned by Spanish Jacobite troops in 1719. Open weekdays only, April through October.

Doune Castle, Doune, Perthshire. Old royal castle, one of the best preserved strongholds in Scotland. Open most days, January to November.

Dunrobin Castle, Golspie, Sutherland. Historic seat of the dukes and earls of Sutherland. Open daily (not Sundays), August to mid-September.

Dunvegan Castle, Isle of Skye, dates from 13th century and continuously inhabited by chiefs of Clan Macleod. Open weekdays, April to October.

Falkland Palace, Fife, built in 1542 by James V to replace original castle. Only remaining royal tennis courts in Scotland. Open April to October 10-6.

Glamis Castle, near Kirriemuir, Angus, partly 14th century. Seat of earls of Strathmore and present Queen Mother's childhood home. Open May through September.

Glenapp Castle, near Stranraer, Wigtownshire. Gardens and, occasionally, the castle, open.

Holyrood Abbey and **Palace of Holyroodhouse,** Edinburgh. Only ruins of abbey remain. Palace dates from James IV, is official residence of royal family in Scotland. Relics of Mary Queen of Scots. Open throughout the year, except when the royal family is in residence.

Hopetoun House, South Queensferry, West Lothian. Fine example of 18th-century Adam architecture. Deer parks and grounds laid out on Versailles pattern. Open daily, May through September, (except Thurs. and Fris.).

Kisimul Castle, Isle of Barra. 15th-century seat of the Macneils of Barra. Now largely restored. Tourist Information Office at Castlebay Post Office will supply boat at modest fee (tel. Castlebay 286).

Leith Hall, Kennethmont, Aberdeenshire. National Trust for Scotland. Stately country home with interesting Jacobite relics. Open daily, May to September.

Lennoxlove, Haddington, East Lothian. Historic stately home of the Duke of Hamilton. Admission by appointment (written application only).

Linlithgow Palace, West Lothian, 15th century. Birthplace of Mary Queen of Scots. Open daily throughout the year, 10-7. Suns. 2-7.

SCOTLAND

David Livingtone Memorial, Blantyre, Lanarkshire—tenement of 24 single-room houses built in 1780's. Interesting museum.

Earl Patrick's Palace, Kirkwall, Orkney. Dating from 13th century and, although roofless, is almost intact.

Pluscarden Priory, near Elgin, Morayshire. 13th-century Cistercian monastery, currently being restored by Benedictine Monks.

Scone Palace, near Perth. Home of the Earl of Mansfield. Many treasures to be seen in state rooms. Built in 1803, incorporating parts of old palace originally built on site. Open daily from the end of April through October.

Traquair House, Innerleithen, Peeblesshire. Reputed to be the oldest inhabited house in Scotland, unaltered from 1664. Associated with Mary Queen of Scots and the Jacobite risings. Treasures date from 12th century and include embroideries, glass, manuscripts, silver and pictures. Restaurant. Open July to September.

MUSEUMS. Among the outstanding Scottish museums (outside Edinburgh and Glasgow) are the following: Aberdeen: *Aberdeen Art Gallery & Industrial Museum* (oil paintings, applied arts); *Aberdeen University Anthropological Museum* (remains of the Beaker people); Alloway: *Burns' Cottage and Museum* (where Robert Burns was born); Annan: *Annan Museum* (Thomas Carlyle material); Arbroath: *Arbroath Art Gallery* (local artists); *St. Vigean's Museum* (Celtic Christian artifacts); Ayr: *Ayr Museum & Art Gallery* (local history).

Biggar: *Gladstone Court* (indoor street of old shops); Blair Atholl: *Blair Castle & Atholl Museum* (19th- and 20th-century British artists, arms and Jacobite relics); Blantyre: *Scottish National Memorial to David Livingstone* (birthplace of the great missionary-explorer); Cromarty: *Hugh Miller's Cottage* (birthplace of the renowned geologist); Dumfries: *Dumfries Burgh* (Burns and Barrie manuscripts); Dunblane: *Dunblane Cathedral Museum* (medieval carving); Dundee: *Dundee City Museum & Art Galleries* (British painting, Scottish schools); *Barrack Street Museum* (shipping and industries); *The Spalding Golf Museum* (golf history); *Orchar Art Gallery* (Scottish artists of the 19th century); Dunfermline: *Andrew Carnegie Birthplace Memorial* (memorabilia); *Pittencrieff House Museum* (19th-century costume).

Ecclefechan: *Caryle's birthplace;* Elgin: *Elgin Museum* (Bronze Age Weapons); Glenesk: *Glenesk Folk Museum* (general museum); Fort William: *The West Highland Museum* (Jacobite and Tartan relics) Greenock: *The McLean Museum* (relics of James Watt); *Mary Queen of Scots House* (paintings and engravings); Kingussie: *The Highland Folk Museum* (Highland relics and tartans); Kirkcaldy: *Kirkcaldy Museum & Art Gallery* (arts and crafts); Kircudbright: *The Stewartry Museum,* Broughton House (Burns collection); Kirriemuir: *Barrie's Birthplace* (mementoes and manuscripts).

Newtonmore: *Clan MacPherson House and Museum* (clan relics and memorials); Paisley: *Paisley Museum & Art Galleries* (Scottish painters); Perth: *Perth Art Gallery & Museum* (Scottish School); St. Andrews: *St. Andrews Cathedral Museum* (early Christian monuments); Selkirk: *Selkirk Museum* (local crafts); South Queensferry: *The Hopetoun House*

Museum (Chippendale furniture); Stromness: *Orkney Natural History Museum* (Orkney bygones); Tarbolton: *Bachelors Club* (literary society founded by Robert Burns); Whithorn: *Whithorn Priory Museum* (early Christian monuments).

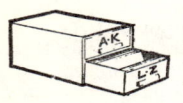

USEFUL ADDRESSES. *Scottish Tourist Board,* 2 Rutland Place, Edinburgh. *Aberdeen Corporation Publicity Department,* 20 Union Street, Aberdeen. *Isle of Arran Tourist Association,* Stroma, Brodick. *Deeside Tourist Association,* 1 Braehead Terrace, Milltimber, Aberdeenshire. *Dunoon Development Association,* Information Centre, Dunoon; *City of Edinburgh Publicity Department* 343 High Street, Edinburgh; *Tourist Bureau,* Fort William; *Information Bureau,* George Square, Glasgow. *Burgh Information Office,* Albany Street, Oban; *Pitochry Tourist Association,* 123 Atholl Road, Pitochry; *Ullapool and Lochbroom Tourist Association,* Quay Street, Ullapool; *Highlands & Islands Develpoment Board,* 6 Castle Wynd, Inverness; *Aviemore Holiday Centre,* Aviemore, Inverness-shire.

EXPLORING SCOTLAND

The Lochs and Highlands

From Carter Bar, on A68 at the summit of the Cheviot Hills, there are extensive views over the Scottish lowlands to the Eildon Hills. And it is from here that the traveller coming north from Newcastle gets his first feel of Scotland.

Bonchester Bridge is the first place to make for, on A6088, passing through the Border National Forest Park. Bonchester has the remains of a hill fort said to have been built in the second century. It also has an excellent hotel for your first meal in Scotland.

Then head northward on A7 through the ancient border towns of Hawick, Selkirk, Galashiels and (on A72) Peebles, where the countryside is lush and green, with its rolling hills deep-cleft by gorges and waterfalls. Border sheep graze in thousands, waiting for their wool, which goes into the making of one of Scotland's important industries—knitted goods, to be shorn. Unfortunately, many of the abbeys hereabouts are in ruin, a reminder of the "rough wooing" by the troops of King Henry VIII of England.

Making steadily for Edinburgh, the capital, the visitor will come upon Howgate, on A6094, an attractive little village possessing an excellent pub.

Four miles southeast of Howgate is Gladstone Reservoir, in winter a favourite roosting place for enormous flocks of greylag and pink-footed geese. On the road into Edinburgh try, too, to see Rosslyn Chapel (off A6094, to the left), which has some really fine carving and sculpture. The chapel was begun in 1446 by the third earl of Orkney, and restored in 1862. Legend has it that the earl's chief mason was sent to Italy to see some pillar which was to be copied at Rosslyn. In his absence, his apprentice, inspired by a dream, built the ornate pillar now known as the 'Prentice Pillar. The mason returned, was beset by jealousy when he saw the magnificent carving, and promptly killed the apprentice.

From Edinburgh, described in a separate chapter later, follow the Queensferry signposts west. This ferry was named after Queen Margaret, who found refuge in Scotland after the Norman conquest and subsequently married the Scottish king, Malcolm Canmore. It was when she travelled between Edinburgh and their other home in Dunfermline, Fife, that the name Queensferry came into being. Fife, lying north of the Forth from Edinburgh, proudly styles itself as a "kingdom", and its long history lends some substance to the boast. From earliest times, its earls were first among Scottish nobility, and crowned her kings. Within its confines many great monasteries were founded, and nearly every village has some remnant of history. Nowadays the Forth can be crossed by car ferry or the new (1964) road bridge. Once over the water into the Kingdom of Fife—a mixture of lovely countryside and awful mining towns—take the road (A92) to Glenrothes.

You can detour for a few minutes to Dunfermline if you wish, with the ruins of the church and abbey built by King David to the memory of his mother, Saint Margaret. It was a place of pilgrimage for centuries. Bruce lay buried there, as did Saint Margaret herself. But the relics of Margaret were hidden for safety during the Reformation, and only a fragment of her tomb remains. The bones of Bruce were found again in 1818 and now lie beneath his memorial statue in the New Abbey Church. Dunfermline's modern prosperity was greatly advanced by the munificence of Andrew Carnegie, who was born here. His birth-place, memorial, and the Carnegie Library are features of the town.

Not far away is Loch Leven, where Mary Queen of Scots was forced to sign the deed of abdication in her island prison in the Loch; she later escaped under romantic circumstances

EXPLORING SCOTLAND

and made her last bid for her throne at the Battle of Langside, near Glasgow, in 1568. The modern fame of Loch Leven stems from the international angling matches that take place there. In one season the catch totalled 50,000 fish.

This town was built in 1949 and was intended to show that a mining town could also be beautiful. Unfortunately, after Britain's top architects and builders had done their work, it transpired that the relevant coal seam was unworkable. A new purpose had to be found for Glenrothes, and soon several light industries (including some with parent companies in the United States) had brought prosperity to the new town. In the Roman Catholic church, open, incidentally, for visitors to look around, there is a really wonderful mural by Alberto Morrocco. Despite the name, Morrocco was born in Aberdeen, now lives and works in Dundee, and is Scotland's foremost portrait painter.

From Glenrothes, it is only a slight diversion to *Fernie Castle Hotel*, with all its delights. Not far away, also, is Largo, where Alexander Selkirk, the original Robinson Crusoe, was born. The house he bought for his father can be seen, and so can Alexander's own statue.

The Golfer's Paradise

St. Andrews, on the east coast, via A92 and 91, is a fine place to spend a few days. Even if you're not a golf addict, there's much to do and see. Here Scots kings were crowned, John Knox preached, and earlier reformers were burned at the stake. Pilgrims came in pre-Reformation times to visit the shrine that traditionally housed relics of St. Andrew the Apostle. Try to see the university and the ruined cathedral and castle. Early in August, there is all the excitement of the Lammas Fair, which dates back to medieval times and was later a Feeing Fair for farm servants. Nowadays, its conglomeration of shooting galleries, dodgem cars and so on completely fills one main street to the exclusion of all traffic. The fishing villages of Crail and Anstruther, roughly 10 miles south of St. Andrews, are well worth visiting.

Head west and north across the Tay Road Bridge (A91, 919 and 92). This fine piece of engineering was opened in the autumn of 1966, just months after its builder, Willie Logan, crashed to death in an aeroplane near his Highland home. This fantastic little man had taken over the debts of a small business not so many years before, and gradually attained the reputation as Scotland's most reliable contractor. A staunch churchman, he refused to allow work on the sabbath—but unlike many firms uncaring of such principles, he always honoured completion dates.

Dundee is a fine shopping place with a long history. Here are the headquarters of D. C. Thomson, the independent publishers of about 40 papers and magazines. Many of Britain's top journalists trained here. Rail travellers approach Dundee by the famous Tay bridge, a spectacle almost as famous as that over the Forth. The first Tay bridge was the scene of the great railway disaster of 1879, when its high girders fell during an exceptional December gale. Queens College at Dundee is part of the University of St. Andrews, and the city possesses a good art school and a teacher's training college. Famed for jute, jam and journalism, Dundee is the fourth city of Scotland, attractive, well situated, industrious. From it you can visit places like Arbroath, whose ruined abbey was the scene of the great Declaration of Independence of 1320; Glamis Castle, with its royal connections; Kirriemuir, where J. M. Barrie was born; and Carnoustie and Montrose for golf.

Next, go along the fast motorway (A85) to Perth, a pleasant market town in rich, gentle farmland. Perth is a pretty, clean, thriving town, whose most famous and vivid literary connection is Scott's *The Fair Maid of Perth*. Other historical memories concern James I (of Scotland) who was murdered here, and John Knox, who preached one of his earliest sermons here. James VI of Scotland (and I of England) is said to have played golf in Perth, and Bonnie Prince Charlie lodged in what is now the *Salutation Hotel*.

A few miles away is Scone, where many of the Scottish kings were crowned on the Stone of Destiny, which was taken to England by Edward I, the "hammer of the Scots", and ever since has performed the same function in Westminster Abbey, London.

Soon after taking the road north of Perth (A9) a sort of excitement touches the traveller to the Highlands. The white-faced, long-legged sheep become fewer, and instead the moors are dotted with the small, grey, black-faced variety, of infinite hardiness. Hills become higher, heather grows right down to the roads, and in the air there is the smell of peat and bog myrtle. Here, too, there is sufficient silence to hear the wild fluting of curlews and the throttly "go-back go-back" of the cock grouse. The approach to Dunkeld—where Scotland's biggest salmon was landed—is truly magnificent, and it's easy to imagine Macbeth and his army on the march.

The whole country to the north holds memories of the Jacobite risings of 1715 and 1745. "Bonnie Dundee" was killed in 1689 at Killiecrankie at the moment of victory. At Dunkeld begins the Great North Road, which was constructed in order to put an end to the inaccessibility of the Highlands as a Jacobite stronghold. Dunkeld also holds the bones of St. Columba, which were removed there from Iona for safety from the Norse pirates in 850.

Pitlochry and its Festival

At the height of the tourist season, cars of just about every nation are to be seen on Pitlochry's main street, and the hotels are busy. (North again on A9.) The Pitlochry Festival Theatre came into being shortly after the war and proudly boasts that visitors can "stay six days and see six plays". On a still summer morning, too, it's fun to drink coffee on the theatre lawn and chat with the actors. In the theatre foyer, original paintings by contemporary Scottish artists can be seen and bought.

After Pitlochry, the countryside really becomes Highland. In the Drumochter Pass on A9, which bears the brunt of Scotland's worst weather, winter snows can drift up to about 18 feet high. The Automobile Association patrolman to be seen on the 21-mile beat between Dalnaspidal and Kingussie—Donald Mackintosh by name—was in 1966 awarded a Special Service medal for all the saving of life for which he has been responsible. Herds of red deer can sometimes be seen on the tops here; the large houses are shooting lodges used mainly during the stalking and grouse-shooting seasons.

Just before Kingussie, instead of taking the main road (A9) through Newtonmore, why not branch off to the right at the A.A. box, where Insh is signposted (onto B970)? Along this pleasantly quiet diversion is Ruthven Barracks, which dates back to the early 18th century, and Jack Drake's nurseries, where all sorts of rare alpine plants and just about every variety of heather can be seen. Bear back on the main road, where the sign points to Aviemore, as the Holiday Centre really shouldn't be missed.

With its comfortable modern hotels, shops, swimming pool, sauna baths, theatre and curling rink, the £2½ million Aviemore Centre has done much to boost tourism in this part of the Highlands. Here you can ski, golf, fish for salmon in the Spey, go pony-trekking, or explore the lochs, mountains and pine forests of the vast Cairngorm National Nature Reserve. At Loch Garten, from a specially-constructed hide, you can watch the only pair of ospreys to breed successfully in Britain, flying around their eyrie in spring and summer. And on the northern slopes of the Cairngorm Mountains, not far from the ski runs, you may see Scotland's only herd of reindeer, owned by an enterprising Swedish Laplander who has settled in Glenmore village.

Via Carrbridge, where you turn east on A938, and Grantown-on-Spey, the road leads straight into a famous whisky area. Distilleries with world-famous names are to be seen every few miles on the long journey to Aberdeen. (Via A95 to Keith and then A96 to Aberdeen.)

Aberdeen to Inverness

Aberdeen itself, holiday centre and busy fishing port, is a fine shopping place, with much of interest historically. It is a brisk city, built largely of granite, which gives it a new look. It stands between the mouths of two rivers, the Don and the Dee, and has a university, which managed to save some of its pre-Reformation treasures, so that its library is well worth a visit by historians. St. Machar's Cathedral (1530) is the only granite cathedral in Britain. The post-Reformation part of the university, the Marischal College, is also magnificent, dominated by the 260-foot-high Mitchell Tower.

Visitors to the city will rejoice in the clean splendour of such monuments as the Wallace and Burns statues. Aberdeen has two miles of perfect sandy beach, stretching from the Don to the Dee. On sunny days in spring and summer it is easy to understand why Aberdeen is called "the silver city with the golden sands".

EXPLORING SCOTLAND

From Aberdeen as a centre you should visit Deeside, westward of the city. Rail and road follow the river for most of its length and the scenery is superb.

Next you come to Balmoral, the Highland residence of the royal family during the shooting season. (The castle is closed to visitors when the Queen is in residence.) Further on is Braemar, scene of the most famous Highland gathering, held in September under royal patronage. Here, too, is the house where Robert Louis Stevenson wrote *Treasure Island*.

Returning to Aberdeen after this excursion down the Dee, head northward to Peterhead (A92 and 952), which is built largely of red local granite and is rather Spartan in appearance. In the 19th century, it was important as a whaling port, but since then has concentrated on herring and white fish. Anyone interested in the lives of the early herring fishermen will enjoy Neil Gunn's novel, *The Silver Darlings*.

Westward along the coast road (A950 and 98) you next go through Macduff, Banff and Cullen to Fochabers. Fochabers, once the stronghold of the powerful Gordon clan, is currently better known as home of the food canners, *W. A. Baxter and Sons*, who (on Tuesdays and Thursdays with prior notice) are glad to show visitors round their factory. Factory, really, is not the word, as the entire place is far more like a large farm kitchen, with its mouth-watering smells of simmering fruit, game and fresh vegetable soups.

The next stop is Elgin, one of the most pleasant towns in all Scotland. Its chief monuments are its ruined cathedral and the restored Greyfriars Abbey Church. The town is a centre of the Jacobite cult, and its historical society collection includes the only surviving copy of the Proclamation offering £30,000 for the betrayal of Prince Charles Edward Stuart, when he was on the run after the Battle of Culloden in 1746. But there were no takers to be found in the Highlands.

Hard by Elgin is Lossiemouth, birthplace of Ramsay MacDonald, one of the Scots prime ministers of Britain, and not far away is Gordonstoun, where Prince Philip, Duke of Edinburgh, and later Prince Charles, went to school.

So we run in through the Macbeth country around Nairn to Inverness. On the way you may wish to stop at the battlefield of Culloden Moor, where in 1746 the Highland army made its last desperate stand for Prince Charlie—and was butchered in defeat. It was the last battle fought on British soil. The burying ground of the clans is a sad and hallowed spot.

The Wild North

From Inverness, described later in the paragraphs on *The Highlands*, a tremendously exciting journey northward starts on the Black Isle at Muiroford on the A9. Between here and Lairg, along A9, then A836, you'll probably use yards of camera film and exhaust your stock of superlatives to describe the views. Highland rivers thunder seawards and, in late summer, the moors shout pink and purple.

From Lairg, you may wish to go east and run along by the coast road to Dornoch, Wick, and Thurso. A detour by road takes you right to John o' Groats and the tip of Scotland. Here you are on the fringe of the land of the midnight sun.

Across the Pentland Firth from John o' Groats lie the Orkney and Shetland groups of islands. Here we are in the ancient sea-kingdom of the Norsemen, for the islands look towards Scandinavia. The ancient Norse festival of Up Helly Aa' is celebrated in Lerwick at the end of January with the pageantry of Norse galleys and Viking warriors.

This ancient kingdom of Zetland, together with Orcadia, was not handed to Scotland until the 15th century, when they formed part of the dowry of a Scandinavian princess about to marry James III, King of Scotland. The islands are virtually bare of trees, due to heavy winter gales, but have a relatively mild climate since the Gulf Stream swirls around them. Seascapes and voes (narrow sea lochs) are unique, and attract visitors from all over Britain. The loch fishing is superb, and free.

Shetland is the *Ultima Thule* of the Romans, the northernmost limits of Britain, where it never really becomes dark during midsummer and the Aurora Borealis flickers in the northern sky. Lerwick, capital of the 100 islands making up the 70-mile long Shetland chain, provides shelter for the trawlers of many nations in its sturdy stone harbour. From Lerwick, buses will take you to Scalloway and its ruined castle, and the excavations of Jarlshof, home of Bronze Age Shetlanders and later, the Vikings. Shetland's coastal scenery is truly awe-inspiring, with seabird-haunted cliffs soaring in places to 1,300 feet.

EXPLORING SCOTLAND

Kirkwall, capital of Orkney, is another fascinating town, with a harbour, narrow paved streets, old stone houses and the splendid cathedral of St. Magnus. Nearby is Scapa Flow, once a great naval base and scene of the scuttling of the German fleet in 1919. If you decide to stay awhile in the Orkneys there are plenty of other interesting places to see, notably the Stone Age village of Skara Brae, Maeshowe burial mound, the prehistoric Standing Stones of Stenness, and the 1,000-ft. cliffs of Hoy. During the last war, when Churchill was in charge of the Admiralty, he ordered Scapa Flow to be shut in from the east by the erection of barriers linking four islands. These Churchill Barriers, built at a cost of two million pounds, are an engineering wonder of the north, and delight Orcadians, who can now drive where formerly they needed to take a series of boat trips.

Back at Lairg, where we interrupted a tour to visit the far north and look at the Orkneys and Shetlands, we find Loch Shin, along the east side of which the A838 road runs. It is Sutherland's largest loch. Maybe the scenery is somewhat stark, but by the time far-away Ullapool is reached (from Laxford Bridge on A838, south on A894 and 835), there can be no complaints. The journey down this miraculous west coast will be sheer beauty, with all sorts of unusual wild flowers colouring the grasses. Gruinard Bay, nearby as the crow flies, but a long auto trip away, is a splendid place for bathing and picnicking, with its pale sands and curving bays.

All down the west coast, and especially between Lochinver and Kyle of Lochalsh, sea lochs thrust salty fingers into the loneliest landscapes in Scotland, carrying the Atlantic's salty tang among the moors and deer forests. Strange, solitary peaks like Canisp and Suilven rear up out of the heather, and you may, if you are lucky, sight a golden eagle soaring overhead in search of the grouse and mountain hares on which this magnificent bird feeds. But you would have to be extremely fortunate indeed to catch even the briefest glimpse of Scotland's most elusive mammal, the wild cat, although several pairs haunt the wild country around Loch Maree. These cats are not merely the domestic variety run wild, but a much larger and more vicious species with flat-topped head and darkly-striped body.

Lochinver, Ullapool, Aultbea and Gairloch are all beautiful little towns, and wonderful stopping places. You can reach the last two from Ullapool on A835 to Braemore Lodge, then onto A832 via Gruinard Bay. A friendly reception is guaranteed by the courteous western Highlanders, but don't expect anything to happen in a hurry. Time means nothing in this part of Scotland—so many other things are of greater importance. After Gairloch, continue south on A832 to Kinlochewe, where you turn onto A896 for Shieldaig, another pretty village.

Over the Sea to Skye

Kyle of Lochalsh, south on A896 again, then onto A890 and 87, has one of the car ferries over to Skye. In the height of summer, there may appear to be endless queues of cars, but they soon disappear. Anyway, it's good entertainment watching the traffic getting on and off. The ferrymen with their knitted, navy-blue caps, skins tanned to the colour of strong tea, and with voices which sound like music, are equally good to see and hear.

Of all the Scottish islands perhaps Skye has most to offer the visitor. It is fey, mysterious and mountainous, an island of sunsets which linger brilliantly till late at night, and beautiful, soft mists. Much-photographed are the really old crofts, still inhabited, with their thick stone walls, earth floors and thatched roofs.

From Kyleakin, the attractive little port with its ruined castle, the road (A850) goes through Broadford and Portree, both pleasant towns. Uig (on A856) is worth a visit while at the north end of the island, as is Dunvegan Castle, home of Dame Flora MacLeod (A863). Down the western side, the road leads through spectacular scenery to Elgol in the south. This tiny village looks across to the Cuillin Hills and to Soay, from which shark fishing was organized by writer Gavin Maxwell shortly after the war. Maxwell wrote his best-seller, *Ring of Bright Water*, from his home near Glenelg, which is just across from the Kyle Rhea crossing. A good idea for the visitor trying to see as much as possible of Scotland, however, would be to plan his itinerary to fit in with boats leaving for the islands of Rum and Eigg—and from there, cross back on to the mainland at Mallaig.

Beyond Skye, in a protective arc, lie the Outer Hebrides—Lewis and Harris, North and South Uist, with the intervening Benbecula, and Barra and Eriskay tagged on at the southern tip. These islands are famous for the quality of their tweed and the sturdy character of their fishermen. They have inspired some of the loveliest songs in the haunting minstrelsy of Scotland, like the *Eriskay Love-Lilt*, *Over the Sea to Skye*, *Will ye no come back again?* and many others. Barra was one of the few corners of Scotland that was never affected by the unsettling currents of the Reformation.

Farther south along the west coast lie other groups of islands that are more accessible from Glasgow—Coll, Tiree, Iona, Staffa, Colonsay, Mull, Jura, Islay, and Arran. The first six may be fairly easily seen by travelling by road or rail from Glasgow to Oban, and thence by boat. (Tiree and Islay can also be reached on BEA flights from Glasgow.) On Mull lies Tobermory Bay, which through the centuries has been the scene of treasure hunts for the Spanish galleon that was wrecked there after the defeat of the Spanish Armada in 1588. Almost every summer a hopeful but none-too-successful search is carried on in the bay under the auspices of the landlord, His Grace the Duke of Argyll. A few precious stones, coins, and pieces of metalwork have been recovered so far.

Iona is famed as the cradle of Christianity in western Scotland. It is the island of St. Columba, though as we noted earlier, his bones were transferred to Dunkeld during the 9th century. Of recent years the Church of Scotland has authorized the establishment of the "Iona Community" scheme here. Fifty-two of the ancient kings of Scotland were buried on Iona, not to mention princes, bishops, and chieftains.

Islay and Arran are best known as holiday resorts, and Arran is particularly well worth visiting. A complete miniature version of Scotland, it has its own mountains, lochs and glens, as well as a castle at Brodick and a delightful bay at Lamlash. The island is best reached by steamer from Ardrossan, on the Firth of Clyde.

On Islay, near the town of Port Charlotte, stands a memorial to a number of American soldiers who lost their lives when the *Tuscania* was torpedoed near the island in 1918. Many of the victims are buried in the local cemetery.

Jura is a wild island with only a scattering of people living on it. Triple peaks, called the "Paps of Jura", attract climbers and hardy walkers who visit the island in summer.

The western isles of Scotland are among the most lovely corners on the earth. Well named the "isles of youth", they reward visitors to their peaty shores with unsurpassed views of charm and loneliness in sunlight and showers.

On the mainland, continuing south via A830, 82, 828 and 85, down the coast road, Oban is the next major stopping place. It is a favourite centre for exploring the Western Highlands and islands. Back here, there will be a marked increase in the number of human beings per square mile—and, indeed, by the time far-distant Dunoon is reached via A816, 83 and 815, there will probably be far too many of them. It's certainly a popular part of the world in summer, with its lure of scenery and yachting and steamer cruises. From here, you can take a car ferry to Gourock, near Glasgow.

South of Glasgow

South of Glasgow, also described in a separate chapter, the road travels initially through endless miles of drab suburb—but the best way to get "away from it all" is through Kilmarnock to Ayr, via A77. At Ayr, in the heart of pastoral Ayrshire, but only five miles from Prestwick Airport, there really is everything for the entertainment of the holidaymaker, as well as much to interest the devotee of Rabbie Burns, the national bard. His cottage is almost a shrine, and the *Tam O' Shanter Inn* is now maintained as a museum. While in that part of the world, do try to see near Maybole the Culzean (pronounced *Cullane*) Castle (in which there is an apartment given to Dwight D. Eisenhower by Scotland), and have at least a meal at *Turnberry Hotel*—a modern pride and joy of the Scots and a great centre for golf.

Lastly, and if possible, lingeringly, go on to the lush green countryside of Galloway and the Solway Firth. (A77 south to 716.) It's a calm corner of Scotland, yet exciting in its reminders of the books of Sir Walter Scott. At Port Logan, the gardens are full of unusual and colourful plants.

Going eastward again (via A716, 715, 75, 755, 711 and 710), and back towards the English border, there are some really fine abbeys to be seen—Dundrennan, New Abbey and Sweetheart Abbey—before reaching Gretna Green. This town (reached from Dumfries on A75) used to be many an eloping couple's first, not farewell, stop in Scotland, and the blacksmith's anvil over which the marriage ceremonies were performed, can still be seen.

The Highlands

An alternative route to Inverness (or a return route from that city, for those who cannot find the time to visit the far north), leads through the heart of the Highlands.

Scottish scenery is at its wildest and most majestic beyond Fort William, north of Glasgow on A82. Ben Nevis, 4,406 feet, the highest mountain in Britain, dominates the vista north of Loch Linnhe; then comes range on range of heathery mountains rolling grandly into remote Sutherland.

You may come by Glasgow to Fort William, and thence by the Great Glen (on B8004 or A82) along the Caledonian Canal that links Loch Lochy and Loch Ness (where you may—or may not—see the Loch Ness "monster"). This is the country of Prince Charlie's wanderings, of bloody Highland feuds, and of the 19th-century "clearances" that depopulated the Highlands and sent much good stock to America and Canada. On the way north from Glasgow to Fort William you can see, south of the latter on A82, the town of Glencoe (Glen of Weeping), the scene of the most tragic massacre in Scottish history.

When King James II fled into exile, some of the Scottish clans, including the MacDonalds of Glencoe, were reluctant to take an oath of allegiance to the new king, William III, which they were ordered to do before the end of 1691. MacIan, chief of the MacDonalds, put off taking the oath until the 31st of December, when he journeyed to Fort William to comply with the edict. Contrary to his expectations, however, there was no magistrate there, and he had to continue to Inverary. Heavy snows delayed him, and it was not until January 6 that he took the oath. Enemies of the MacDonalds reported this to the king, concealing the fact that weather had hindered MacIan from obeying the royal command. A warrant was issued for the extirpation of the clan.

Under the command of Campbell of Glenlyon, a force of 120 men marched to Glencoe, ostensibly to collect taxes. The

MacDonalds entertained them hospitably for twelve days. At 5 a.m. on February 13, 1692, the Campbells set upon the sleeping MacDonalds and massacred them, burning their homes and driving away their livestock. Only a few MacDonalds managed to escape in the darkness, and most of them died of exposure in the hills.

Before leaving Fort William for Inverness, another detour west on A830 will give you a view of Glenfinnan, where Prince Charles Edward raised his standard in 1745.

Along the Great Glen, en route to Loch Ness, visitors will be rewarded by a stop at Fort Augustus Abbey on the southern tip of Loch Ness. Thenceforward the waters of the loch spread in splendour along the road till you join the east coast again at Inverness.

One of the most pleasant features of Inverness is the spectacle of the three suspension bridges. Another is the purity of the English spoken there, equalled only by that of educated Dubliners. In the Town Hall is a portrait of Flora MacDonald, who guided Prince Charlie in his flight to safety and final exile. Her memorial can be seen on the Castle Hill.

This fine city on the banks of the fast flowing River Ness is called "the capital of the Highlands". Interesting buildings include the castle, which now houses the police headquarters and the high court; Abertarff House (17th-century), now a Gaelic Museum; the Town House, containing interesting historical relics, and the Clock Tower, all that remains of Cromwell's Fort. At the foot of the town cross on the Exchange is the Clach-na-Cudainn stone, dating back perhaps 1,000 years. Old washerwomen were supposed to have used it as a resting place on their way down to the river with their tubs. Men from Inverness are still called "Clach-na-Cudainn boys" the world over.

Just outside Inverness is Tomnahurich Cemetery, or "hill of the fairies", which is renowed for its beautiful layout and serene atmosphere. The farming land around Inverness and the Moray Firth is the richest in Scotland. The climate is drier than in most other parts of the country, with invigorating winds and clear skies. This is the unmatched Laich of Moray country.

Six miles from town there is the battlefield of Culloden, the site of the defeat of Prince Charlie in his attempt to regain the throne of his ancestors. Auld Castle Hill marks the legendary site of the castle in which Shakespeare located the murder of King Duncan by Macbeth. On Criag Phadraig Hill, less than two miles from town, is the site of the Pictish King Brude's sixth-century castle and on the summit of the same hill are the remains, dating from about the first century A.D., of an Iron Age vitrified fort.

During July, August and September there are many Highland Gatherings and Games held within easy reach of Inverness, culminating with the Northern Meeting Piping Competitions, held in Inverness in September.

That's it, then—this particular journey round Scotland is over. Many, many visitors on the road south across the border towards Carlisle feel they haven't seen nearly enough of Scotland. And if that's the way you feel, the solution's simple— Haste Ye Back!

EDINBURGH

"Auld Reekie", Scotland's Capital

Edinburgh, Scotland's capital city, is also the most beautiful. It has magnificent skylines, elegant architecture and a very real culture of its own. Its old streets have retained, over the centuries, the atmosphere of romance, tragedy and violence which made up their history.

Saint Margaret, Mary Queen of Scots, Prince Charles Edward Stuart and John Knox all played their roles in Edinburgh, and Robert Louis Stevenson and Sir Walter Scott wrote of it. The castle, towering 270 feet above Princes Street, has garrisoned many famous Scottish regiments. There is a royal palace at Holyrood, and some spectacular buildings, whose doric, ionic and corinthian pillars add dignity to the city. Trees and gardens add colour to the Presbyterian grey backcloth. From the heights, there are sweeping views across farmland to the Firth of Forth and to the Kingdom of Fife. Inland, there are the Pentland Hills. There are theatres, art galleries, good hotels and restaurants, sporting facilities galore, unusual museums, and an annual International Festival of Music and Drama. There is, in fact, something for everyone.

EDINBURGH

For American tourists in particular, there are places associated with familiar names: In South Charlotte Street you'll see the birthplace of Alexander Graham Bell, inventor of the telephone, who later became an American citizen. Edinburgh claims as her sons many other distinguished Americans, among them Andrew Hamilton, who organized the first postal service in the colonies; James Loraine Geddes, the Civil War general who wrote *The Stars and Stripes;* and James Blair, the first president of William and Mary College.

Practical Information for Edinburgh

WHERE TO STAY? There are hundreds of hotels and boarding houses in and around Edinburgh, so that only a small selection can be given here. An Edinburgh Corporation *Register of Accommodation* can be had from travel agents or Edinburgh Corporation Tourist Information Department, 343 High Street (tel. Caledonian 5081). The Tourist Board can only help with festival accommodation. A convenient motel on the outskirts, and new (1966), is the *Derry*, at Dalkeith, on A68. Two new hotels *may* be open by 1970; each 150 rooms, one near stadium, one in centre.

FIRST CLASS

BRAID HILLS, 70 rooms (9 with bath), is even further out of the town. Comfortable, pleasant place to stay. Food always reliable. Fairly expensive.

CALEDONIAN, 173 rooms (110 with bath), and **NORTH BRITISH** 200 rooms (90 with bath or shower), are both old-established hotels. Restaurants are excellent. Expensive.

ESSO MOTOR HOTEL. Brand new (1968) motel in Queensferry Road, 80 rooms (all with bath).

FORTH BRIDGE MOTEL, 60 rooms (all with bath), is new and efficient, with pleasant decor. The setting is undeniably bleak, but convenient for anyone travelling out of Edinburgh northwards. At South Queensferry, west of city. Expensive.

GEORGE, 87 rooms (69 with bath), is a luxurious hotel on historic George Street. All rooms extremely pleasant, food excellent, dinner-dancing. Expensive.

MOUNT ROYAL, right in the heart of things on Princes Street, has 150 rooms (all with bath). Expensive.

PRESTONFIELD HOUSE has only 3 rooms (*none* with private bath). Bathrooms and upstairs corridors really *unmodern*, but in every other respect, it is a luxury hotel. Gracious, peacock-patrolled grounds and the house in its present design dates from 1687. Cuisine of highest possible standard. Expensive.

ROXBURGHE, in Charlotte Square, 73 rooms (60 with bath), Food and service very good indeed. Expensive.

SCOTIA, 50 rooms (15 with bath), is in much quieter surroundings on Great King Street. Converted from several terrace houses. Management goes all out to see that guests are pleased with service, food, comfort — which they invariably are.

HAWES INN at South Queensferry, 7 rooms, has tremendous atmosphere of oldness and serves quite wonderful meals. Bedrooms nothing special, but a good place to stay overnight. Moderately expensive.

CARLTON, 88 rooms (all with bath), is moderately expensive.

MODERATE

FOX COVERT, 46 rooms (30 with bath), is a pleasant easygoing place to stay. Nice food and atmosphere.

MANSION HOUSE HOTEL AND MOTEL, 31 rooms (25 with bath).

RESTAURANTS. Edinburgh is splendidly served by a wide variety of restaurants, including the internationally famous *Pompadour* at the Caledonian Hotel, where during festival time many of the most glittering international stage and concert stars eat. Other hotel restaurants worth a visit are the *North British*, the *Royal British* and the *George*. Rose Street, a narrow lane parallel to Princes Street, contains innumerable pubs, many of which supply lunches. Atmosphere is truly pure Edinburgh. Listed below are some of the good eating places to be found in and around Edinburgh.

ABBOTSFORD, 3 Rose Street. Licensed. Moderate.

ALBYN, 77 Queen Street. Licensed. Can be very good. Downstairs, Swedish foods served. Deservedly popular.

ALLEGRO, 7 Hanover Street. Licensed. Really excellent international cooking. Fairly expensive.

APERITIF, 24 Frederick Street. Licensed. First-class food, especially seafoods, in dim, exciting atmosphere. Fairly expensive.

BEEHIVE INN, Grassmarket. Licensed. Continental cuisine of high standard. Interesting old surroundings. Open late except Saturdays and Sundays. Fairly expensive.

BROWN DERBY, 1 Hanover Street. Unlicensed. Inexpensive.

CAFE ROYAL, 17 West Register Street (behind Royal British Hotel). Historical restaurant with great atmosphere and several dining rooms, bars (the Circle Bar has 30 different whiskies), etc. Marvellous seafood. Expensive. Oyster bar on ground floor is excellent. Upstairs is beautifully decorated (Crown Room is most gorgeous).

CRAMOND INN, just outside Edinburgh. Licensed. Beautifully set village inn close to the sea. Ample parking. Food is of extremely high standard and service friendly. Expensive.

DANIEL BROWN'S, 37 George Street. Licensed. Not expensive.

DORIC TAVERN, 15 Market Street. Licensed. Not expensive. A friendly, informal place for honest food.

EPICURE, 19 Shandwick Place. Licensed. Moderately priced and pleasant.

GEORGE HOTEL, *Des Ambassadors*. Very good food, but rather expensive.

GOLF TAVERN, Bruntsfield Links. Licensed. Splendid place to drink and eat. Moderately expensive.

HANDSEL, 22 Stafford Street. Licensed. Excellent cold food. Moderately expensive.

HAWES INN, South Queensferry. Licensed. Marvellous food here in exciting setting. Expensive.

HENDERSON'S SALAD TABLE, 94 Hanover Street. Licensed. Continental and vegetarian. Pleasant. Not expensive.

LAIGH COFFEE HOUSE, 83 Hanover Street. Unlicensed. This is a fantastic and excellent place to eat. Inexpensive, unusual foods, often truly Scottish. No bookings.

NORTH BRITISH HOTEL, *Grill Room*. Excellent for beef.

POMPADOUR ROOM, *Caledonian Hotel*. Licensed. Luxurious setting and first-class food. Expensive.

PRESTONFIELD HOUSE, on outskirts of Edinburgh. Licensed. Really excellent food. Expensive. Very attractive atmosphere. Peacocks in the grounds. Try the haddock mousse.

OLD HOWGATE INN, Wester Howgate, near Penicuik. Licensed. Delightful restaurant here, with some sumptuous Danish, and other, foods. Moderately priced for value.

QUAICH STEAK HOUSE, Shandwick Place. Licensed. A good, satisfying place to eat. Moderately priced.

TURNHOUSE AIRPORT. Interesting place to eat because you can watch air traffic. Food, too, is good. Moderately expensive.

TRYST, 369 High Street. Unlicensed. Eating place of repute opposite St. Giles Cathedral, frequented by lawyers, etc. Homemade taste to wholesome food. Inexpensive.

RITCHIE'S INTERNATIONAL, 11 Cockburn Street. Licensed. Very old eating house decorated with Italian pictures. All sorts of interesting recipes to be had here. Moderately expensive.

WEE WINDAES, 142 High Street. Licensed. Good wholesome food in interesting atmosphere. Moderately priced.

WHITE COCKADE, Rose Street. Licensed. Modern, with good food. Reasonably priced.

ENTERTAINMENTS. Festival time is, of course, the best for all theatre, music, etc. Programmes for each year can be had from *Edinburgh Festival Society, Ltd.*, 21 Market Street, Edinburgh 1. Details regarding the *Film Festival*, which is concurrent, can be had from the Director, Edinburgh International Film Festival, 3 Randolph Crescent, Edinburgh 3. *Tattoo bookings* and enquiries about the *Highland Games*, which immediately precede the festival, to Edinburgh City Chamberlain's Depar ment, High Street, Edinburgh 1.

Theatres. The *Royal Lyceum*, Grindlay Street is Edinburgh's civic theatre, and has a resident company. Occasionally puts on plays by visiting companies. The *Kings Theatre*, owned by a London company, presents plays and other theatrical productions. In summer, there is mostly revue-style entertainment, with a Scottish flavour. The *Traverse Theatre* is a 60-seater in the Lawnmarket, where experimental plays are put on by a resident, highly professional company. Very interesting set-up, worth visiting. Small theatres putting on occasional amateur and semi-professional productions are the *Gateway* and *Church Hill* theatres.

THE EDINBURGH FESTIVAL

Just after World War II, Edinburgh inaugurated a three-week season that has become world-famous as the Edinburgh International Festival of Music, Drama, and Art. The title gives only a slight idea of the immense range of attractions—exhibitions of painting and handcrafts, ballet, instrumental recitals, a festival of documentary and other films—these are only a few of the items on the varied programme.

Orchestras and opera from America, France, Germany, Italy; dancers from London, Spain, India, America; theatrical companies from France and England; singers, instrumentalists, conductors, writers and film directors from all over the world. Artists of this calibre take part in the festival. New compositions and plays by musicians and playwrights from America, Australia, and Austria have had their premières in halls, graced by the presence of the royal family and cosmopolitan audiences.

Scottish orchestras, choirs, composers, instrumentalists, dramatists and actors participate, too. The quality of their contribution is hotly debated—nowhere more so than among the Scots themselves. Certainly the festival has done more to awaken Scottish and British artistic energies than anything since the great days of Sir Walter Scott and the Edinburgh School. This is an event that no visitor interested in the intellectual life of Europe should miss.

The festival takes place each year during the last two weeks in August and the first week in September. For a detailed programme or other information, write to the Festival Office, 21 Market Street, Edinburgh 1.

NIGHTLIFE. Discotheques include the *Casa Blanca* and one or two others on Rose Street.

Gambling is available at the *Royal Chimes*, 3 Royal Terrace. *Paddy's Bar* and *Scotts*, both on Rose Street, are full of atmosphere. *New Grafton Club*, 16 Home Street, for chemin de fer, brag, black jack, etc.

Manhattan Jazz Club, 8 Carlton Hill, *Pentland Theatre Restaurant* for late night dinner-dancing with cabaret.

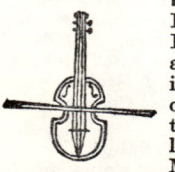

MUSIC. The *Scottish National Orchestra* plays every Friday evening in the Usher Hall, October to March. Principal conductor is Alexander Gibson. Standards are of the highest, and interesting programmes are invariably to be heard. This orchestra gives other concerts besides the main series. From mid-October till end of March there are high-standard weekly lunch-hour *concerts* in the National Gallery, at the Mound. Various *pipe* and *brass bands* play in summer in Princes Street Gardens, where country dancing is also performed.

EDINBURGH

SPORT. There are two first-division football (*soccer*) teams in Edinburgh: Heart of Midlothian, who play at Tynecastle Park, and Hibernian (Hibs), who play at Easter Road Park. At Murrayfield, international *rugby* matches are played. On the several municipal *tennis* courts, play is cheap. *Golf* courses abound in this city, which has been golf-minded since 1457; some privately, some municipally owned. At Portobello, there is a magnificent *swimming pool* with wave-making machine and space for 3,000 swimmers and 6,000 spectators.

For those interested in *horse racing*, there are several meetings at Musselburgh throughout the season. *Greyhound racing* can be seen twice weekly at Powderhall Stadium. *Motor racing* can be seen at Ingliston. *Yachting, riding* and *angling* are all available.

Top sporting event in 1970 is the *Commonwealth Games*, July 16th-25th.

At the *Royal Highland Show*, and others, international show jumpers compete.

Edinburgh this Month is a monthly publication giving a list of events and entertainment in and around the city, and has been found by many visitors to be extremely helpful. It can be had, free of charge, from information bureaux throughout the city.

HOW TO GET ABOUT? *Edinburgh City Transport* have organized coach tours which enable visitors to see the most interesting parts of the city. Details from 14 Queen Street. Many longer tours to the north and west are organized by *Scottish Omnibuses, Ltd.*, Clyde Street.

There are two main-line railway stations, Waverley and Haymarket. Trains run regularly to London, Glasgow, Dundee, Perth, Aberdeen and Inverness, etc.

Leith, the port of Edinburgh, has regular sailings to the continent and Scandinavia.

From Turnhouse Airport (*BEA*), there are air services to Aberdeen, Orkney, Shetland, Glasgow, London and Ireland. From May-Sept., there is a daily direct bus service from Edinburgh to Prestwick Airport, and return.

CAR HIRE. *Alexanders of Edinburgh*, 61 Pitt Street *Avis Rent-a-Car*, 24 East London St. and Turnhouse Airport; *Peter Carnie*; Craighall Garage, Craighall Road; *Godfrey Davis Ltd.*, 195 Dalry Road; *Hertz*, 10 Picardy Place; *Mackay Bros.*, 33 Hanover Street; *Mitchells*, of 32 Torphichen Street; *S.M.T.*, Haymarket Terrace; *Sloans*, Bedford Road and *Wards Car Rentals*, 8 Haddington Place.

EDINBURGH MONUMENTS. *Burns Monument*, Regent Road; *National Monument*, Calton Hill; *Nelson Monument*, Calton Hill; *Scottish-American War Memorial*, West Princes Street Gardens; *Sir Walter Scott Monument*, East Princes Street Gardens; *Wellington Monument*, Princes Street; *Lincoln Monument*,

Calton Old Burying Ground, Waterloo Place; *Mercat Cross*, Parliament Square; *Gladstone Memorial*, Coates Gardens; *Royal Scots Memorial*, West Princes Street Gardens; *Scottish National War Memorial*, the Castle. Most are open from 9.30 a.m. to about 4 or 5 p.m., and closed on Sundays except in summer (when open 11 a.m. to 5 or 6 p.m.)

MUSEUMS, GALLERIES, AND GARDENS. (A highlight or two of each is given.) *Arboretum and Royal Botanic Gardens*, Inverleith Row, open 9 a.m. till sunset, Sunday 11 a.m. to sunset. *Robin Chapel*, Niddrie Mains (Thistle Foundation). Weekdays by appointment. *Scottish National Zoological Park*, Corstorphine. Daily in summer, 9 till 7, in winter 9 till sundown.

Scottish Craft Centre, Acheson House, Canongate. Weekdays 10 to 12:30 and 2 to 5:30. Saturdays, 10 to 12:30. Closed Sundays.

Canongate Tolbooth, Canongate. Highland dress, tartans. Weekdays, 10 to 5.

Huntly House (City Museum), Canongate. Weekdays, 10 to 5 and Wednesday, 6 to 9 p.m. Old-fashioned Scots kitchen.

Museum of Childhood, Hyndford's Close, High Street. Weekdays, 10 to 5. Games, toys and dress.

National Gallery of Scotland, The Mound. Weekdays, 10 to 5, Sundays, 2 to 5. Scottish art to 1900.

National Library of Scotland, George IV Bridge.

National Museum of Antiquities, Queen Street (east end). Weekdays, 10 to 5, Sunday 2 to 5. Relics of Celtic Church, Roman finds.

Royal Scottish Academy, foot of Mound. Annual Exhibition, mid-April to first week August. Festival Exhibition, and others from time to time. Open weekdays, 10 to 9, Sundays 2 to 5.

Royal Scottish Museum, Chambers Street. Monday to Friday, 10 to 6, Saturdays 10 to 5, Sundays, 2 to 5. Largest overall collection in the United Kingdom. Outstanding scale models in Technology Department.

Scottish National Gallery of Modern Art, Inverleith House. 20th-century paintings.

Scottish National Portrait Gallery, Queen Street (east end). Weekdays, 10 to 5, Sundays 2 to 5. Famous Scots.

Lady Stair's House, Lawnmarket. Monday to Friday, 10 to 4, Saturdays, 10 to 1. Relics of Burns, Scott and R. L. Stevenson.

Robert Louis Stevenson Memorial House, Howard Street. Monday to Friday, 10 to 5 (to 4 in winter), Saturdays, 10 to 1. Manuscripts and relics.

John Knox's House, High Street. Daily, 10 to 5. 16th-century religious objects.

USEFUL ADDRESSES. *Scottish Tourist Board*, 2 Rutland Place, (tel. Fountainbridge 1561); *American Consul*, 3 Regent Terrace, Edinburgh 7 (tel. Waverly 2061); *City of Edinburgh Publicity Department*, 343 High Street; *Citizens' Advice Bureau*, 4 Pitt Street; *Automobile Association*, 18 Melville Street; *Royal Automobile Club*, 17 Rutland Square (tel. Fountainbridge 3555); *Tele-*

tourist Information Service for daily events in Edinburgh (May-September), dial ASK 8041.

Exploring Edinburgh

Although there is evidence of habitation in the 10th century, and in the seventh century King Edwin of Northumbria was known to have rebuilt the castle, it was only from the 11th century that reliable records were kept.

King Malcolm III, son of the King Duncan murdered by Macbeth, lived in Edinburgh Castle, and in 1076, Queen Margaret built the chapel within the walls—this can still be visited. As you go in the main gate you can see on either side the statues of the heroes of Scotland's war of independence in the 13th and 14th centuries. Sir William Wallace is on the right, and King Robert Bruce on the left.

From the castle battlements there is a superb view over the city and the Forth River, with the Forth bridges in the distance, reaching across to the "Kingdom" of Fife. On a clear day the vista is one of breathtaking loveliness. On not-so-clear days you will see why Edinburgh is called "Auld Reekie"—though, of course, it is not as smoky as Glasgow. If it is *really* "misty", you can recall that it was in just such a "haar" (or Scotch mist) that Queen Margaret and Mary Queen of Scots first came to their capital.

There, too, are the truly beautiful National War Memorial and the Honours of Scotland. These consist of the sceptre, sword-in-state and crown, remodelled in 1540 by order of King James V, made of Scottish gold, 94 pearls, 10 diamonds and 33 other jewels.

The roadway running between the castle and the Palace of Holyroodhouse is called the Royal Mile. And it is here, in the Old Town, that visitors will find much to interest and entertain them. Before the graciously laid-out New Town was built two centuries ago on the far side of Princes Street, this Royal Mile was the hub of Edinburgh life. Important citizens lived here and all business was done here or hereabouts. Notable street names are the Esplanade, Castle Hill, Lawnmarket, Parliament Square, High Street and the Canongate. On the Esplanade is an iron fountain marking the spot where witches were burned. Ramsay House, now a training college for bankers, was built by the poet Allan Ramsay. The Outlook

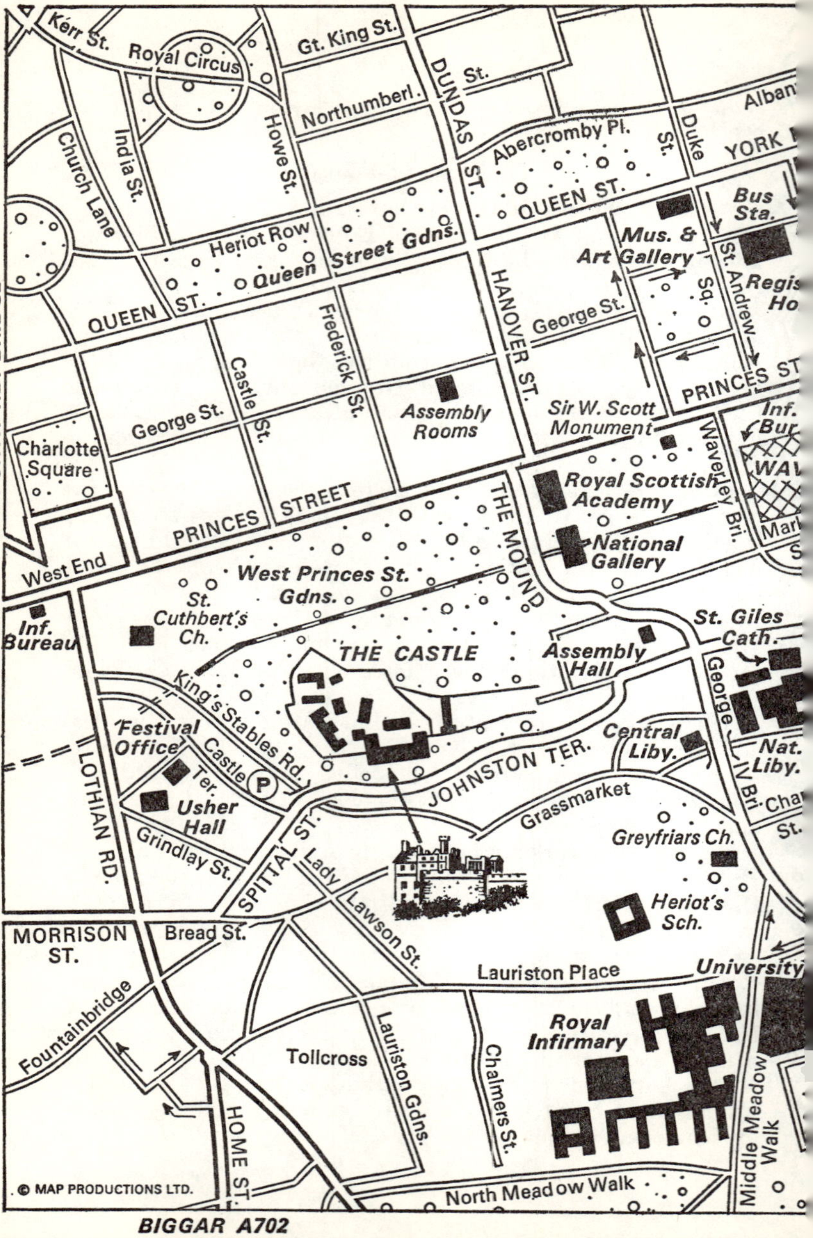
Kerr St.
Royal Circus
Gt. King St.
Northumberl. St.
DUNDAS ST.
Abercromby Pl.
Duke St.
YORK
Church Lane
India St.
Howe St.
QUEEN ST.
Bus Sta.
Heriot Row
Queen Street Gdns.
Mus. & Art Gallery
QUEEN ST.
Frederick St.
HANOVER ST.
George St.
St. Andrew Sq.
A90 FORTH RD. BRIDGE
Castle St.
George St.
Assembly Rooms
Sir W. Scott Monument
PRINCES ST
Charlotte Square
PRINCES STREET
THE MOUND
Royal Scottish Academy
Waverley Bri.
National Gallery
West End
West Princes St. Gdns.
St. Cuthbert's Ch.
Inf. Bureau
THE CASTLE
Assembly Hall
St. Giles Cath.
GLASGOW A8
King's Stables Rd.
Festival Office
Castle Ter.
P
Usher Hall
LOTHIAN RD.
JOHNSTON TER.
Central Liby.
George IV Bri.
Nat. Liby.
Grassmarket
Grindlay St.
SPITTAL ST.
Lady Lawson St.
Greyfriars Ch.
Heriot's Sch.
TO A8
MORRISON ST.
Bread St.
Lauriston Place
University
Fountainbridge
Tollcross
Lauriston Gdns.
Chalmers St.
Royal Infirmary
Middle Meadow Walk
HOME ST.
North Meadow Walk
© MAP PRODUCTIONS LTD.
BIGGAR A702

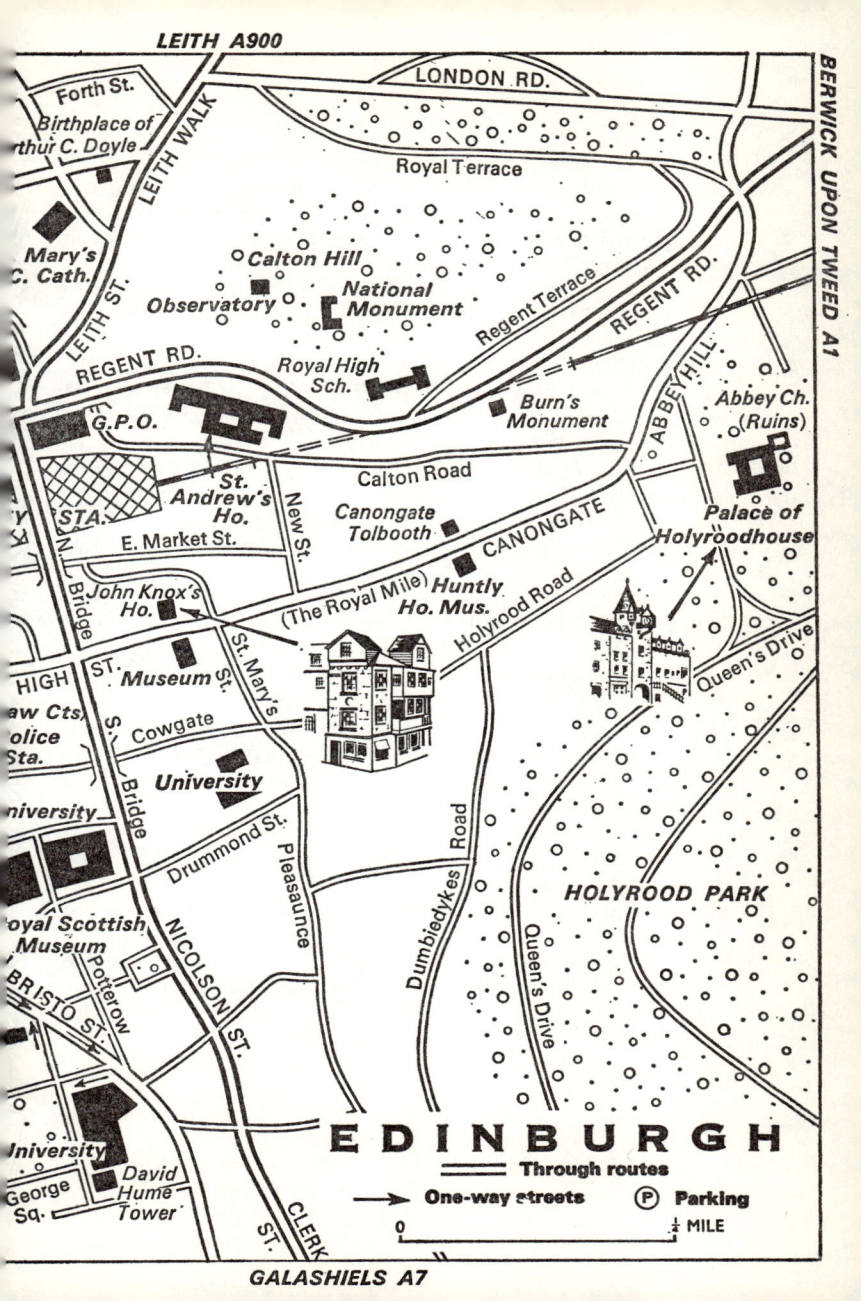

EDINBURGH

— Through routes
→ One-way streets
Ⓟ Parking

0 — ¼ MILE

Tower contains a splendid exhibition of Scottish life through the ages and a *camera obscura*. If your taste runs to the gruesome you can visit the ancient place of execution and the house where the "doomsman" or executioner stayed on these occasions. Here the great Montrose and many another gallant man had a sinister tryst with the hangman. Nearby are the haunts of Burke and Hare and of Deacon Brodie, names familiar to criminologists everywhere.

Gladstone's Land on the Lawnmarket is an exciting 17th-century building, now owned by the National Trust. Special features are an outside stair, interesting gables, painted ceilings and period furniture. At festival time, Scottish music and poetry are heard here.

Lady Stair's House, nearby, is a literary museum concerned with Burns, Scott and Stevenson.

St. Giles Cathedral, the High Kirk of Edinburgh, has had a long, dramatic history of its own. One thing very worthwhile seeing is the Chapel of the Most Ancient and Most Noble Order of the Thistle, the highest order of Scottish chivalry.

Parliament House, behind St. Giles, was the meeting place of the Scots Parliament from 1639 till 1707, and nowadays is the home of Scotland's supreme law courts. In Parliament Hall, there is some fine architecture to be seen, and paintings by Raeburn, Scotland's most renowned portrait painter.

In the High Street, John Knox's house is open to the public, except on Sundays. Built in 1490, it contains interesting timbered galleries and handpainted ceilings.

Directly across the road is the Museum of Childhood. It is a vast collection of historical toys, books, pictures and costumes, most of which are dated between 1850 and 1945, although the oldest toys are about 4,000 years old.

A beautiful cluster of buildings are to be found at White Horse Close, at the bottom of the Canongate. Originally this was a coaching terminus and hostelry, and dates from the 17th century.

The Queen of Scotland's Home

The Palace of Holyroodhouse being the official residence of the Queen in Scotland, is, of course, only open to the public when not occupied by the royal family or by the lord high commissioner. Mainly built in the time of Charles II, some of the work is considerably earlier. Mary Queen of Scots, lived at the palace for six years, and Bonnie Prince Charlie held a ball there in 1745. There are over a hundred royal portraits to be seen and a brass tablet marking the spot where Rizzio's body was left after his murder. State apartments contain magnificent tapestries and furniture, and the Throne Room is utterly beautiful, in green and white Adam style.

South of the Royal Mile is the Grassmarket, a tree-lined square with a long, fabulous history. Bodysnatchers Burke and Hare lived there, and it was a popular execution place; there is a cross marking the spot where many Covenanters died for their beliefs.

Edinburgh University has many buildings in this quarter of the city, the oldest dating from 1582. Its medical school has, over the centuries, produced many famous doctors, including James Young Simpson, the inventor of anaesthetics.

Although in the New Town history hasn't had the same chance to make its mark, there is, nevertheless, plenty to see and do. Robert Adam, most eminent architect of the 18th century, was responsible for the beauty of many squares, Charlotte Square in the west end being one of his noblest. At the other end of Princes Street is St. Andrews Square, which houses the headquarters of many banks, some of which (notably the Royal Bank of Scotland) are impressive.

The Scott Monument in Princes Street is a conspicuous Gothic spire 200 feet high. Anyone with sufficient energy to climb its 287 inside steps will be rewarded with a tremendous all-round view of the city. But as there is an even better one from the castle battlements, where we have been, we shall walk on. The little group of interested spectators there in the gardens is looking at the famous Floral Clock, the pride of the city gardeners.

We have just passed the classical home of the Royal Scottish Academy and the famous Mound. Here on Sunday evenings you can listen to spokesmen for all causes, religious and political, and behind the Academy you will see the National Gallery. Both are well worth a visit from visitors interested in art and history.

In the eastern end of the gardens you can also see the memorial to David Livingstone, the famous Scots missionary whose African meeting with Stanley is part of Scots-American history. At the western end is the American memorial to

Scottish soldiers of World War I. Its beauty and the simplicity of the inscription make it one of the treasures of the capital.

American visitors may wish to walk down over the bridges and climb Calton Hill, with its classical unfinished monument to the dead of the peninsular wars, for in Old Calton Burying Ground is a monument to the combined memories of Abraham Lincoln and the Scottish-American soldiers who fell in the American Civil War.

And each year in late August and early September it is at its gayest. The International Festival has, since 1947, been a "must" in the lives of anyone who loves the arts. Top performers in opera, drama, poetry, choral and orchestral music all come to Edinburgh. Hundreds of soldiers, too, who take part in that most moving spectacle of all—the Military Tattoo—swell the numbers. Unless accommodation has been pre-arranged, therefore, there will be little chance of finding a hotel room. The Tourist Board does well at all times, but at festival time, it does phenomenal work finding last-minute accommodation in private homes. The Festival Club, incidentally, is well worth joining, even as a temporary member. *Note* that as Edinburgh is host city to the Commonwealth Games in July, 1970, this is another time when accommodation will be hard to find.

Excursions from Edinburgh

There are many interesting places to visit within easy and comfortable travelling distance for visitors staying in the city. A start can be made, for instance, at Craigmillar Castle, on the far south of Edinburgh. This is a 15th-century ruined fortress, typical of medieval defence architecture. The Stuart kings stayed here frequently, and after the murder of her secretary and alleged lover, David Rizzio, the tragic Mary Queen of Scots retired here from Holyroodhouse in 1566.

Still driving southward, there's Rosslyn Chapel, another 15th-century building. In this chapel, there is some fantastic sculpture to be seen, in particular the ornate Apprentice Pillar.

Travel onward to Penicuik, a pleasant and prosperous little burgh in the Pentland Hills. Over the centuries it has been famous for paper-making, encouraged by the local lairds, the Clerks of Penicuik. Sir John Clerk, born in 1676, was a patron

EDINBURGH

of the arts and an excellent laird. He built himself a fine Augustan house, but it was burned in 1899—its ruins can still be seen. The present laird and his family live in what were the 18th-century stables.

Go through Lasswade, a village in the north Esk Valley, where the ancient graveyard contains the remains of poet William Drummond, and Henry Dundas, the first Viscount Melville, who virtually ruled Scotland in the early 19th century. Sir Walter Scott spent the first six years of his married life in Lasswade, and was visited there by James Hogg, "The Ettrick Shepherd". De Quincy, the opium-taking writer, also lived here.

Haddington is the next stop. The abbey, in attractive red sandstone, and many fine Adam buildings make this active town very good to look at. Reputed to be the birthplace of John Knox. Going steadily eastward, the next town is East Linton. Here, the River Tyne is crossed by a 16th-century bridge popular with artists. National Trust property is the Phantassie Doocote, an excellent example of the traditional dovecote. Two miles southwest is the beautiful ruin of Hailes Castle, which has a stormy and royal history.

Right on the coast is Dunbar, with its ruined castle and fine harbour. The town house here dates from 1620—and showing how well modern architecture can blend with old are a cluster of fisher houses by Sir Basil Spence.

On the return trip, there is Tantallon Castle, another fine coastal stronghold to be seen. Then the towns of North Berwick (excellent golfing here), Dirleton, and Gullane are all attractive stopping (and eating) places. Cockenzie, next on the itinerary, is an old fishing village, and still has a boat-building yard.

Even in Roman times, Musselburgh was a port of some importance, and on the old bridge, traces have been found of a gate which must have been used for defence. This town has had a long, chequered history since it was granted a royal charter in 1632. The race course dates from 1816, and James IV was reputed to have golfed at Musselburgh in 1504. Each May, the archers of the queen's bodyguard compete for the Musselburgh Silver Arrow—a custom dating back to 1603.

From Musselburgh back into Edinburgh, the journey is through rather unattractive surroundings.

GLASGOW

Scotland's Industrial Heart

Scotland is a warmhearted country, and it is Glasgow's claim that there is no city to equal her in friendliness. Glasgow is indeed a hospitable, uninhibited, bustling place—a friendly, industrial giant astride the Clyde.

Though Glasgow was founded by Saint Mungo before Saint Margaret came to Edinburgh, and though its bishopric had jurisdiction as far south as Carlisle in ancient times and its university was a papal foundation second in age only to Saint Andrews, its importance is almost completely modern and industrial. It is a brash and bustling city, but it has its corners of history. Its cathedral is the finest example of Gothic surviving intact in Scotland. Its university, nobly dominating a noble site at Gilmorehill, celebrated its fifth centenary in 1951. Close by the cathedral is the oldest house in the city, Provand's Lordship, where Mary Stuart may have once stayed.

A 16th-century traveller described Glasgow as "a flourishing cathedral city reminiscent of the beautiful fabrics and florid fields of England". Daniel Defoe in 1727 described it as one of the cleanest, most beautiful and best-built cities in Great Britain. Glasgow, however, with increasing prosperity, soon became less clean and less beautiful. After the Union of the

Crowns, America and the West Indies were allowed to trade with Scotland as well as England, so the Glasgow merchants swiftly seized their opportunity. Cargoes of tobacco from Virginia and sugar from the West Indies were bought, then re-exported to Europe. The "tobacco lords" became wealthy and were able to afford elegant clothes, mansions and even country estates. Soon, too, Glasgow was shipping two million yards of linen a year to America. With the shots fired at Concord in 1775, however, the tobacco lords crashed financially —but Glasgow was securely established as an industrial city. One major activity was the deepening by dredging of the River Clyde, thereby making one of the greatest shipyards and ports the world has ever known.

Practical Information for Glasgow

WHERE TO STAY? There are hundreds of hotels in Glasgow, covering a wide variety of classes. It is possible, therefore, only to give a selection. ***First-class*:** CENTRAL, 245 rooms (115 with bath), is an old-established hotel of great character. Dignified; good service. Food in *Malmaison* restaurant is of highest standard. This is definitely a place to be seen. Expensive. Also due to open late 1970, the *Excelsior Glasgow Airport Hotel* at Glasgow's Abbotsinch airport. It will have 320 rooms (all with bath), air-conditioning, sound-proofing, and covered walkways to airport.

ROYAL STUART, 110 rooms (80 with bath), is really luxurious. Food, comfort and service all of highest order. This is a newish hotel with modern decor. Expensive.

NORTH BRITISH, 82 rooms (20 with bath), and **ST. ENOCH,** 155 rooms (46 with bath), are both eminently respectable, old-established railway hotels, offering their guests a high standard of comfort and cuisine. Only jarring note at the *North British* is occasional appearance of coffee-serving night porter in shirtsleeves and braces. Expensive.

MODERATE

MORE'S, 36 rooms (13 with bath), is an excellent place to stay. Currently somewhat shabby-Victorian in appearance but undergoing modernization. Staff always cheerful and efficient, and food very good indeed. Moderately expensive.

GRESHAM, 7 rooms (1 with bath), is a pleasant, if small, hotel in quiet west-end street. Food and service very good. Moderately expensive.

BATH, 34 rooms, **IVANHOE** 70 rooms (10 with bath), and **KENILWORTH,** 37 rooms (5 with bath), are all good commercial-type hotels. Nothing luxurious about them, and general appearance unexciting, but service good. Reasonably priced.

Others are *Lorne*, 48 rooms (9 with bath) (new), *Delriada*, 13 rooms (new), and *Tinto Fils*, 34 rooms (many with bath) (new),

Cleveden Court, 22 rooms (11 with bath), and *Glassford*, 50 rooms (1 with bath).

Inexpensive are *Hazelcourt*, 8 rooms, *Boswells*, 12 rooms, and *Western*, 15 rooms.

Near Glasgow Airport is the *Airport Hotel*, Renfrew, where truly excellent meals can be had. Smartly dressed clientele, excellent service, utter comfort. Very expensive. 121 rooms (all with bath). Rather unimpressive outside, but don't be put off.

RESTAURANTS. You will find many restaurants in the centre of Glasgow, and the cuisine is of such a standard that any preference is a matter of individual taste in every sense of the word. Apart from hotel restaurants, most are closed on Sundays.

THE BUTTERY, 654 Argyle Street. Licensed. In the *Shandon Bell* pub, this is a friendly eating place. Fine cooking of Scottish and other foods. Inexpensive.

DANNY BROWN'S, St. Vincent Street. Licensed. A virile atmosphere here, and some good plain food. Inexpensive.

CORN EXCHANGE, 88 Gordon Street. Licensed. Snack lunches and Danish sandwiches. Inexpensive.

EPICURE'S, 46 West Nile Street. Licensed. Exciting eastern European dishes here, nice atmosphere. Moderately priced.

FERRARI, 10 Sauchiehall Street. Licensed. Very good food, accent on Italian cooking. Not expensive.

GAY GORDON, 21 Royal Exchange Square. Licensed. Dancing, and very good food indeed. Moderately expensive.

GRANT ARMS GRILL, 186 Argyle Street. Licensed. Good food in interesting surroundings—highly recommended. Moderately expensive.

GROSVENOR, 72 Gordon Street. Licensed. One of Glasgow's most reliable eating places. Fairly expensive.

GUY'S, 196 Hope Street. Licensed. Really super food and lush surroundings. Expensive.

MALMAISON, in the *Central Hotel*. Licensed. Terrific cooking and top-class atmosphere. Expensive.

ONE-O-ONE, 101 Hope Street. Licensed. Lush atmosphere, music, fabulous food. Expensive.

RISTORANTE ITALIANO, 431 Parliamentary Road. Licensed. Italian foods and wines at reasonable prices.

ROGANO'S, 11 Exchange Place. Licensed. Very good food—particularly the fish dishes. Moderately expensive.

ROYAL, 10 West Nile Street. Licensed. Scottish food, pleasantly served in entertaining surroundings. Moderately priced.

ROYAL STUART, Clyde Street. Licensed. Music, surprisingly, accompanies meals. Really excellent cuisine and service. Expensive.

WHITEHALL, 51 West Regent Street. Licensed. Good food, well served. Expensive.

WYLIE AND LOCHHEAD, 45 Buchanan Street. Unlicensed restaurant within exciting shop. Reasonably priced.

ENTERTAINMENTS. Glasgow's entertainments are first-class and splendidly varied till 11 p.m. Thereafter, the city tends to be something of a desert, except for clubs, which are for members and their guests. Best known of these are the *Piccadilly*, 92 Sauchiehall Street; the *R.N.V.R. Club*, H.M.S. Carrick, Customs House Quay. They have late licenses, dancing, resident orchestras and floor shows. (Foreign visitors can sometimes become temporary members at a low fee. Ask your porter to telephone.)

Gambling at the *Chevalier Club* or the *Coronet Club*, 375 Sauchiehall Street.

Theatres. There are three legitimate and two variety theatres in Glasgow. In the first category are the *Alhambra* in Wellington Street, the *Kings* in Bath Street, and the *Citizens'* in Gorbals Street—the latter founded by James Bridie in 1943 as the National Theatre of Scotland. The variety theatres are: *Pavilion*, Renfield St., and *Metropole*, St. George's Rd. Glasgow is home of the *Scottish Opera Company* and is a leading city on the pre-London circuit for new productions. A score of well-appointed *cinemas* dot the city map; their programmes are advertized in the local press.

Music. The *Scottish National Orchestra* gives concerts, usually in June, at the Kelvin Hall. The *BBC Scottish Orchestra* also gives performances, and ticket enquiries should be sent to Broadcasting House, Queen Margaret Drive. International singers and instrumentalists appear regularly.

Dancing. Glasgow is excellently served for dance halls, with outstanding resident bands. The *Plaza*, *Locarno*, *Majestic* and *Albert* are possibly the best known. Discotheques: *Mayfair* and *Joanna's Room*.

SPORTS. There are six first-class football (*soccer*) grounds in Glasgow, including Hampden Park—home of the famous Queen's Park Club and scene of all international matches. Ranking with it are Ibrox Stadium, home of *Glasgow Rangers*, and Celtic Park. There are 11 first-class *rugby* grounds. In and around the city are 9 municipal *golf* courses (4 of them are 18-holers) and about 20 private clubs, four of which offer facilities to visitors without an introduction. (Clydebank; Hayston and Kirkintilloch at Kirkintilloch; and Windyhill at Bearsden.)

There are two *ice rinks*, both of which feature ice hockey matches. Indoor *swimming pools* abound, and many of them are of very high standard. Municipal pools with sunray and Turkish bath facilities are at Govanhill, Whitevale, Ibrox (sunray only), Pollockshaws, Shettleston and Whiteinch.

There are also several international-class *billiard* and *pool* rooms. Possibly the best known are the *Nile*, 222 St. George's Road, and the *Crown*, 8 Sauchiehall Street. *Greyhound* racing can be seen at Carntyne, Shawfield and White City tracks, and on most summer Saturdays, there is *cricket* to be watched. *Horseracing* at Hamilton (11 miles south, May-Sept), and at Ayr (which see).

In summer, there are excellent *sailing* facilities on the Clyde. Usually in late June and early July, there is a gala *sailing week*, when some fine sport can be had.

TRANSPORT. *Bus services* in the city are excellent, as is the *underground* railway, and tours of varying lengths can be taken outside the city. For services to Campbeltown, Fort William and Inverness, contact *David MacBrayne, Ltd.*, 46 Parliamentary Road; to Oban, Aberdeen and further north, contact *W. Alexander and Sons (Midland), Ltd.*, 473 Cathedral Street: for Newcastle, Scarborough, etc., contact *Eastern Omnibuses*, Buchanan Street Bus Station; for London, Birmingham, Manchester, etc., contact *Western S.M.T. Co., Ltd.*, 290 Buchanan Street.

W. Alexander and Sons, Scottish Omnibuses, Ltd., and *David MacBraynes* also operate holiday coach tours of varying lengths. Details can be had from their offices.

There are two main line *railway stations* in Glasgow—Central (for London and south Scotland) and Queen Street (elsewhere). Holiday runabout tickets are available from Glasgow and prove a very inexpensive and interesting way of seeing much of Scotland. *British Rail* booking offices and travel agents can supply details.

Day tours by train and steamer provide an ideal way of seeing the lovely countryside surrounding Glasgow. *British Rail* organize these— for example, to the Trossachs, Loch Katrine and Loch Lomond; Kyles of Bute, Ardrishaig and Oban; to Burns country and Culzean Castle. Or, alternatively, you can go by electric train from Queen Street station to Balloch and there board the *Maid of the Loch* for a cruise of Loch Lomond. The *Caledonian Steam Packet Company* will supply details.

MUSEUMS, GALLERIES, ZOO. Regimental headquarters of the *Royal Highland Fusiliers* has a museum of some military history at 518 Sauchiehall Street. Open Monday to Friday, 9 a.m. to 5 p.m. *Hunterian Museum*, Gilmorehill. Bequeathed to university by Professor William Hunter in early 19th century. Early printing, Roman and archeological exhibits, and very fine collection of coins. Also works by Whistler. Open Monday to Friday, 10 a.m. to 5 p.m., Saturday, 10 a.m. to noon.

Provand's Lordship. Oldest house in Glasgow, built about 1471. King James II and King James IV are supposed to have lived there. Now has fine collection of 17th- and 18th-century furniture and domestic articles. Open daily (except Thursday and Sunday), April to September, 10 a.m. to 12:45 and 2 to 5 p.m. October to March, 11 a.m. to 12:45 and 2 to 5 p.m.

Kelvingrove Park Art Gallery and Museum. Magnificent array of interest and beauty, including part of the Burrell Collection. Armour, ship models, Roman finds, old masters, etc. Set aside plenty of time to see it. Open 10 a.m. to 5 p.m. daily, Sunday, 2 to 5 p.m.

People's Palace, Glasgow Green. This is a museum mainly on the history of Glasgow. Also royal portraits commissioned by the Town Council. Daily, 10 a.m. to 5 p.m., Sunday 2 to 5 p.m.

Tollcross Museum, Tollcross Park, is a children's museum of great interest and charm. Daily, 11 a.m. to 5 p.m., Sunday, 2 to 5 p.m.

Camphill Museum, Queen's Park, has paintings, *objets d'art* and natural history exhibits. Daily, 11 a.m. to 5 p.m., Sunday, 2 to 5 p.m.

Museum of Transport, Albert Drive, Eglinton Toll. A new venture (since 1964) and one of the few transport museums. Includes tramcars, motor cars (many of Scottish manufacture), horse-drawn vehicles, etc. Daily, 10 a.m. to 5 p.m., Sunday, 2 to 5 p.m.

There are 37 public libraries in Glasgow. The *Mitchell Library*, founded in 1874, is largest public reference library in Scotland and one of the most important in Great Britain. Special collections include 3,500 volumes of Robert Burns, Celtic literature, and 20,000 volumes on the history of Glasgow. Daily, 9:30 a.m. to 9 p.m. Sunday, October to March, 2 to 8 p.m.

Zoological Gardens, Calderpark Estate, was opened in 1947. Is on main Glasgow-Uddingston road. Open daily, 9:30 a.m. to dusk.

CAR HIRE. This can be arranged through *Avis,* Clive House, India St., and Prestwick and Abbotsinch airports; *Godfrey Davis,* 3 Broomielaw; *Caledonian Cars,* St. Enoch Square; *S.M.T.,* 39 West Cambell Street, and *Hertz,* 171 Bothwell Street.

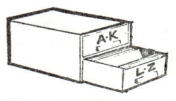

USEFUL ADDRESSES. *American Consul* is in Edinburgh. 3 Regent Terrace, Edinburgh 7 (tel. Waverley 2061). *Automobile Association,* Fanum House, 14 Blythswood Square, C.2 (tel. Central 9191). *Royal Automobile Club,* 242 West George Street, C.2 (tel. City 4444). *Student International Club,* 11 University Gardens, W.2 (tel. Kelvin 1546). *Rotary Club,* 8 Gordon Street, C.1 (tel. City 7826). *Municipal Information Bureau,* George Square, C.2 (tel. Central 9600).

What's on in Glasgow is an extremely useful pamphlet supplying all up-to-date information on exhibitions, theatres, etc., and can be had from travel agents or the *Municipal Information Bureau,* George Square (tel. Central 9600).

Exploring Glasgow

Even today it is possible to walk or drive through Glasgow and trace its stages of growth. First, there was the district containing Provand's Lordship (about five centuries old) and the Tolbooth steeple. These buildings are of grey stone, quarried in the district that was the old centre of Glasgow, the town of the bishop and tobacco lord. Further out, in industrial Glasgow, with its shipyards, foundries, engineering factories and tenements, the buildings are of old red sandstone from north Ayrshire or Arran. Next came the bungalows of the 20th-century private builder, and right up to date are the towns of East Kilbride and Cumbernauld.

The cathedral is the finest surviving example of Gothic architecture in Scotland. The university, nobly dominating a dignified site in Gilmorehill, is over five centuries old. Down the High Street, one-time site of the old university college, there is now a railway goods station, but at the bottom of the street, the old Tolbooth and Mercat Cross (scene of markets and historical proclamations) still stand.

There is also, in the centre of the city, a well-attended art college, in Renfrew Street, designed in a modern adaptation of the Scottish baronial style by Charles Rennie Mackintosh, an architect who has a European and American reputation, though his name is scarcely known in his native city of Glasgow.

Opposite the Art Gallery is the famous Kelvin Hall, largest exhibition hall outside London. Another place to see is the George Square Municipal Chambers, built in Italian Renaissance style and very, very impressive.

The city parks are superb, the city library service is excellent and the Hunterian Museum well worth seeing. There is also plenty of cultural activity in music and drama. Glasgow folk are proud of their Scottish Orchestra, directed by some of the greatest conductors in the world and the principal native contributor to the Edinburgh Festival; their theatres and cinemas, ranging from the largest in Europe to the most cosmopolitan outside London; and their miles of shipbuilding yards, where the *Queen Mary*, the *Queen Elizabeth* and the *Queen Elizabeth II* were built. (Visitors not usually allowed). In claiming these liners, Glasgow is perhaps pirating a glory that rightly belongs to Clydebank, just down the river.

Glasgow's glory is, however, her river—the fabulous River Clyde. And certainly, a most attractive and interesting trip is to sail down the estuary to its meeting place with the Atlantic. Along the north bank, there are glimpses of the Lochs and Trossachs country, all very splendid.

Touring from Glasgow

Leave Glasgow on the main Stirling road and drive through

the suburbs of Bearsden and Milngavie (pronounced *Mulguy*) to Strathblane. Nearby Duntreath Castle dates from the 15th century and its medieval stocks and dungeons are still preserved. Fork right at the Ballat Cross Road and continue into Stirling (26 miles). At Stirling, there is much to see—notably the Field of Bannockburn and the splendid equestrian statue of King Robert the Bruce, the castle, the Wallace Monument, from which there are tremendous views, Old Stirling Bridge, which was the scene of the 1297 battle, and various other old buildings. 29 miles further on is the *Baillie Nicol Jarvie* hotel at Aberfoyle—excellent for lunch.

From Aberfoyle, take the Duke's road (A821) through the Trossachs, a magnificent part of Scotland, where forests, hills and lochs are at their loveliest. One of these, Loch Katrine, provides Glasgow with its beautifully soft water. At A84, turn left for Strathyre—the much sung-about "Bonnie Strathyre." It has an attractive old bridge over the River Balvaig and one or two good examples of 18th-century stone cottages.

On to Lochearnhead, a popular centre for dinghy sailing and water ski-ing. Continuing along the A85, you'll come to Crianlarich, a good stopping place for afternoon tea. Scenery here, where Glen Falloch, Glen Dochart and Strath Fillan all meet, is fairly austere. At the end of the 17th century, two Celtic monasteries were established locally. That at Dull was associated with St. Adamnan, and the other, in Glen Dochart, with St. Fillan. Three miles northwest of Crianlarich, the wall foundations of St. Fillan's Priory still stand, and the saint is alleged to be buried there.

Drive down through Glen Falloch to Loch Lomondside—and this is really thrilling. The loch is 24 miles long, its greatest width is five miles and it contains 30 wooded islands. On Inchmurrin Island, you will see the ruins of an old castle which belonged to the earls of Lennox. Inchcaillach Island has a ruined nunnery and is the burial place of the MacGregors.

From the ancient, go to the modern—and *Loch Lomond Castle Hotel*, at the south end of the loch. This hotel is really luxurious, and is a perfect place to stop either for drinks or dinner before motoring the final 30 miles back into Glasgow.

THE CHANNEL ISLES

England with a French Accent

The Channel Islands of Jersey and Guernsey are the warmest part of Britain, enjoying a mean temperature of a little over 52 degrees. From April to October, day temperatures usually exceed 60 degrees; sharp winter frosts are rare. The archipelago of which Jersey and Guernsey are the chief islands has been called an admirable blend of France and Britain. It lies closer to the French than the British coast. St. Helier, capital of Jersey, is a wonderful centre, full of quaint streets, good hotels and bathing places. You'll be delighted with this touch of France on British soil.

But not only is the climate soothing and the surroundings lush—there's an atmosphere of continental know-how that appeals to all visitors. The food is better cooked and better served than in similarly-priced mainland (England) resorts; the people know a little more about bright living; drinking laws are not so archaic and the atmosphere is flavoured with a touch of the Continent.

Tourism is the biggest industry (70 percent of the economy), and to protect this industry, the States Assembly of Jersey

THE CHANNEL ISLES 519

has been wise enough to introduce a tourism law which requires all hotels and guest houses to register. Tourism officials then grade them according to their standards and inspect them annually to see that the standard is maintained, thus ensuring that the visitor gets a square deal. This, undoubtedly, has been the key stone to Jersey's success in tourism, a point which English hotel keepers, who oppose grading, would be wise to study.

Of course, potatoes, tomatoes, flowers and cattle still play a vital part in the economy, as do the benefits gained from the many wealthy people from Britain who choose to live or retire in Jersey (largely because taxation is much lower than on the mainland—income tax, for example, being only 20 per cent, and there being no capital gains tax or purchase tax).

The States Assembly governs Jersey. It is composed of 12 senators, 12 connetables, and 28 deputies, all elected by the people. Presiding over this is a bailiff, appointed by the Crown, and there's a lieutenant governor as well (representing the Queen), the attorney-general, the solicitor-general, and the dean, who has no vote. The laws and customs present an interesting blend of Norman French and modern British, while the inhabitants are mostly bilingual, speaking a brand of French and a brand of English, both picturesque and distinctive.

Although not many visitors to Britain can be expected to detour to these islands, they have a particular charm which should lure the sophisticated traveller off the beaten path, even if only for a day or two.

Practical Information for the Channel Isles

HOW TO GET THERE? *British Rail* operate a one-class steamer service from Weymouth to Guernsey and Jersey on weekdays, April through August (4 hours to Guernsey, 6½ to Jersey). Additionally, there are some Sunday services, including overnight sailings, during the height of the season. A fast boat train from London (Waterloo) connects with all sailings. Winter services are overnight, with two or three sailings a week. There are also steamer services between the islands. Reduced steamer fares are available for use on Tuesdays, Wednesdays, and Thursdays only, from mid-April to the end of October. *Jersey Lines*, new drive-on, drive-off car ferry, *La Duchesse de Bretagne*, which has a casino and bar on board, operates 5 times weekly from Torquay and Weymouth to Guernsey and Jersey.

Sark can be reached only by boat, from St. Peter Port, on Guernsey, 2 to 4 sailings a day, taking one hour.

British European Airways operate daily services from London and Gatwick airports to both Jersey and Guernsey, with several flights daily during holiday months. Flying time is about 1 hour. *British United Airways* also operate services from Gatwick (1 hour) to Jersey, to Guernsey, and to Alderney. Both airlines have regular flights from main provincial centres. There is also a good inter-island air service, and flights from England on *Cambrian Airways, Channel Airways, Midland, Autair, Westward* and *BKS Air Transport*.

Car Ferries. Cars may be shipped from Weymouth: apply *Continental Car Ferry Centre*, 52 Grosvenor Gdns., London S.W.1; or to the Divisional Shipping Manager, Weymouth Quay, Dorset.

Getting Around. By foot is popular, but by car is better. *Avis* has offices at St. Brelade and St. Saviour (summer only) on Jersey, to mention just one agency.

WHERE TO STAY? Most hotels quote favourable weekly, all-inclusive, rates, but it is essential to book well ahead for the summer season. Hotel accommodation is somewhat limited for the numbers of tourists who go to the Channel Islands.

Newest hotel on Jersey (1969) is the *Mermaid*, 68 rooms (all with bath). It adjoins the airport, and has a swimming pool and ornamental lake in its grounds.

Guernsey's newest (1969) is the *Russell*, 90 rooms (all with bath.)

ST. HELIER (Jersey). Capital of the island, situated on the eastern shores of St. Aubin's Bay; good sporting and entertainment facilities. The new luxury *Hotel de la Plage*, on the beach, has 102 rooms, half with bath and sun balcony; air-conditioned. First-class superior: *Grand*, 138 rooms, 104 with bath; *Pomme d'Or*, 172 rooms, 29 with bath; *Washington*, 40 rooms (10 with bath). First-class reasonable: *Revere*, 40 rooms, 29 with bath; *Royal Yacht*, 43 rooms, 7 with bath; *Hotel de France*, 311 rooms, 63 with bath.

Restaurants: Best is *La Capannina*, in the market place.

ST. BRELADE'S BAY (Jersey). Small resort on southwestern corner of the island; good sands, golf. First-class superior: *L'Horizon*, 90 rooms, 64 with bath. First-class reasonable: *St. Brelade's Bay*, 100 rooms, 50 with bath. Water skiing, ballroom. Also the new *Silver Springs*, 82 rooms (16 with bath).

LA CORBIERE (Jersey). On the extreme southwestern point of the island, with famous lighthouse off-shore. First-class reasonable: *Le Chalet*, 32 rooms, 14 with bath. Continental cuisine.

ST. AUBIN (Jersey). Situated on charming bay with wide, sandy beach, harbour and 16th-century fort. Moderate: *Old Court House*, 10 rooms, and *Somerville*, 44 rooms. Best place to eat is *Old Court House*.

BOULEY BAY (Jersey). *Water's Edge*, 62 rooms, 56 with bath.

PORTELET BAY (Jersey). *Portelet*, 98 rooms, 58 with bath, is first-class superior. Pool and all the usual amenities.

ST. PETER PORT (Guernsey).

Capital of the island, with attractive harbour and Hauteville House, home of Victor Hugo- First-class reasonable: *Old Government House*, 80 rooms, 50 with bath; *Royal*, 76 rooms, 15 with bath; *Fermain*, 24 rooms, and *de Havelet*, 27 rooms. Restaurant: *La Fregate*, expensive, but good. Also good: *Le Nautique*.

ST. MARTINS (Guernsey). Attractive bays; fishing, bathing. First-class reasonable: *Les Douvres*, 38 rooms.

PETIT BOT (Guernsey). Small resort with good sands. Inexpensive: *Manor*, 56 rooms.

ALDERNEY. Third largest of the Channel Islands, with ancient history. First-class reasonable: *Grand*, 28 rooms (7 with bath); *Royal Connaught*, 16 rooms (3 with bath). Open all year: *Bligh's*, 22 rooms, and *Chez Andre*, 20 rooms, both moderate. Eat at *Le Courier* restaurant.

SARK. Privately owned, picturesque island. Great and Little Sark are connected by an unusual natural causeway. First-class reasonable: *Aval du Creux*, 15 rooms (3 with bath), is new (1965); *Petit Champ*, 16 rooms; *Stock's*, 33 rooms; *Dixcart*, 34 rooms, good cuisine. Moderate: *La Sablonnerie*, 20 rooms.

HERM. *White House*, 40 rooms, moderate in price, but excellent.

HIGHLIGHTS OF JERSEY. "*The Battle of Flowers*" on the Thursday before the first Monday in August at St. Helier. *Golf Courses:* one 9-hole and two 18-hole. *Motor* racing and hill-climbs. Ancient *castles and monuments:* Grosnez Castle (St. Ouen); Mont Orgueil Castle (Gorey); St. Aubin's Castle (St. Brelade); Elizabeth Castle (St. Helier); The Hermitage (Elizabeth Castle). *Megalithic Remains:* St. Saviour, Samares, Gorey, Rozel, Trinity, St. Ouen, St. Brelade. Two theatres, three large dance halls, 4 cinemas.

SHOPPING in Jersey is a good idea, as there is no purchase tax here. H.M. Customs allow concessions on perfumes, tobacco and alcohol for personal use only, provided these are declared on arrival in the U.K. Details of these concessions may be obtained from any H.M. Customs and Excise office.

Information. The *States Tourism Committee* is at Weighbridge, St. Helier, Jersey, C.I. Information can be obtained in London from the *Jersey Information Centre*, 118 Grand Buildings, Trafalgar Square, London W.C.2.

Exploring the Channel Isles

Jersey, with an area of 45 square miles, is the largest of the Channel Islands. At one time, two separate railway systems provided transport, but now the ubiquitous bus has completely taken over, together with modern taxis and numerous hire cars and coaches.

St. Helier, a town of 27,000 people, is Jersey's capital. It is a wonderful centre, full of hotels, good bathing beaches, entertainment, and quaint streets. Some of the streets are rather full of traffic, and a one-way system may confuse the visitor for a time. Outside the capital, you'll find secluded coves, beaches for swimming (surfing, too!), rugged rocks, and lovely scenery; in fact, you'll soon appreciate the reason why the French call Jersey "La Reine de la Manche" (Queen of the Channel). Try to see author Gerald Durrell's zoo, at Les Augres Manor, and the Fisherman's Chapel, at Beauport Bay.

The dominant landmark on the west coast is the La Corbière Lighthouse, and on the east coast, it is the Mont Orgueil Castle. The massive walls of the castle reflect the changes that took place between the 13th and 16th centuries to meet defence requirements, but now the castle is a great attraction for tourists; it is floodlit between April and October. Beyond lie the beautiful bays of Anneport and Archirondel, as well as the yachting and fishing areas at St. Catherine's.

Guernsey

Guernsey is some 20 miles north of Jersey, and is rather smaller, possessing only 28 square miles and a total population of some 45,000 persons. It is less sophisticated than Jersey, but its rugged coast, indented with sandy bays and smothered with wild flowers in spring and summer, has great scenic beauty. Although principally concerned with agriculture (the Guernsey cows are world famous) and the export of tomatoes, it is rapidly catching up with Jersey in the tourist trade. Anyone visiting Jersey for a fair period should cross over to Guernsey for a few days; the journey takes only two hours by steamer or 20 minutes by plane.

The chief port and capital is St. Peter Port which, with its terraced narrow passageways and cobblestones, has the appearance of a Mediterranean resort. The granite houses with their mellow red-tiled roofs rise in tiers from the water's edge and make an effective contrast with the grim stronghold of Castle Cornet which dominates the harbour. Among the many places of interest in the old town is the parish church of St. Peter Port, which stands at the foot of the High Street; it is the finest medieval church in the Channel Islands, and has some unusual 13th-century nave arches. An attractive feature of Guernsey's capital is the number of old market halls where local produce, with the emphasis on live lobsters and crabs, is displayed by the friendly stall-holders, many of whom still speak the old Norman *patois*.

Guernsey has its own independent government under the

British Crown, and the opportunity of visiting the Royal Court House while the parliament—or States of Deliberation—is in session should not be missed. Not far from the Court House is Hauteville House, the residence of Victor Hugo when he was exiled from France. The house, which is open to visitors, remains as it was during the lifetime of the great novelist.

St. Peter Port is the largest town on the island, but there are many charming villages and hamlets to which expeditions can easily be made. Torteval Church has a remarkable round tower, and in the grounds of the monastery of Les Vauxbelets is a quaint little chapel, studded with shells and broken china, the work of one of the brothers. Most of the coastal villages are connected by frequent bus services with St. Peter Port.

The Other Islands

Smaller islands in this strange archipelago which is such an admirable blend of France and Britain offer attractive by-ways but little in the way of accommodation. Alderney has an airport and even a capital town (St. Anne) fitted into its tiny area of 1,962 acres on which live about 1,500 people. Most of them are concerned with fishing or agriculture; shellfish are a local industry and are delicious. Should you cross to Alderney, you'll discover quiet solitude, tiny coves, and silver sands, with quite a few comfortable guest or farm houses to cater for you hospitably but not luxuriously. There are a number of old castles and forts on the island. A delightful and unusual feature of Sark is that traffic is banned from the island; instead you can tour in a horse-drawn carriage, a method of transport much more in keeping with Sark's leisurely way of life.

Sark is privately owned, by the Dame of Sark. It can be visited by boat from any of the main islands, most easily from Guernsey. Dame Sibyl Hathaway, who governs the isle, is the widow of Robert Hathaway, an American war hero who joined the British Army in World War I while the U.S. was still neutral.

Herm and Jethou are mere islets, the largest of the many rocks—some barely showing above the sea—that comprise the Channel Islands. Herm has a hotel for visitors and is making a bid for tourist traffic in a small way, touting its unusual beach, composed of powdered shells, with the consistency of sand. Jethou is privately owned, and is only about a half mile wide, but it is open to visitors.

NORTHERN IRELAND

"The Six Counties"

by

MARTIN WALLACE

(*Deputy editor of the* Belfast Telegraph *and a well-known writer and broadcaster, Mr. Wallace is president of the Irish Association for Cultural, Economic and Social Relations.*)

As often as not, Northern Ireland is called Ulster, though it contains only six of the nine counties which made up that ancient Irish province. Unlike other parts of the United Kingdom, it has its own regional parliament and administration, but the major decisions are taken at Westminster, to which it sends 12 elected members of the British parliament. There is no customs barrier between Great Britain and Northern Ireland, and few formalities in crossing the border between the six northern counties and the 26 which form the Republic of Ireland.

As a tourist area, Northern Ireland is underdeveloped. The 240-mile coastline has a number of holiday resorts, but the more remote western counties have largely been neglected, apart from angling. In turn, though, this means unspoiled scenery and a quietness attractive to holidaymakers seeking escape from urban living. The Northern Ireland Tourist Board has worked hard to raise the level of accommodation and amenities—a promising development is improved farmhouse accommodation—and with better communications the west may yet prove the more durable attraction. For the present, however, the best hotels and the more sophisticated entertainments are largely concentrated in the eastern counties of Antrim and Down, and around the capital city of Belfast. But Ulster is a small province, and no part of it is inaccessible. The discerning visitor will probably make the most of Northern Ireland's different attractions.

Ulster's History

To know Ulster today, you must know its past. For centuries, waves of people explored outwards from the European mainland, through or around England and Scotland, ending up in Ireland. It was the end of the known world, until America provided a more distant objective. The first settlers in Ireland crossed the narrow sea from Scotland, spreading along the shore and up the River Bann to Lough Neagh around 6,000 B.C. Later, the Celts (dominating Ireland for the first 800 years of the Christian era), the Vikings, the Normans, the English and the Scots left indelible marks. Of all the Irish provinces, Ulster was the most stubborn and difficult to invade; it was perhaps the most truly Celtic province, and the last to submit to the superiority of English arms. As a result, the native Ulstermen were largely dispossessed of their land, the "plantations" of Englishmen (and particularly, Scots) taking their place in the seventeenth century. The contrast between the Gaelic-speaking Roman Catholic native and the English-speaking Protestant immigrant laid the foundation for the partition of Ireland, which occurred in 1920. The Protestants did not always show as strong a preference for partnership with England and Scotland as they do today, and were often leaders in the historic struggle for home rule for all Ireland, but the religious differences eventually proved a deciding factor.

The principal relics of Ulster's inhabitants are the stone monuments (megaliths) which can be found throughout the province, though it is possible to pick up flint tools in great numbers along parts of the Antrim coast. The first cultivators clung to the lighter soils, principally on the lower slopes of hills, and have left behind burial chambers which were originally covered with "cairns" of small stones; the most striking of the "giants graves" are the dolmens, in which a capstone weighing up to 100 tons is supported by smaller upright boulders. Later inhabitants left behind stone circles, and small round cairns became a familiar sight on hilltops. Single standing stones can also be seen, though some are of little antiquity and were erected as rubbing stones for cattle. There are also artificial mounds and rings of earth, usually known as "forts", though they may simply have been used to enclose cattle. From Celtic times, there are the relics of ancient monastic sites and finely-engraved crosses and pillars. Round towers, sometimes 100 feet high, were probably a defence against the Viking invasions. From the Norman period, there are well-preserved castles at Carrickfergus, Dundrum and Greencastle, and Cistercian abbeys at Inch and Grey Abbey.

In 1607, the so-called Flight of the Earls took Hugh O'Neill and 90 others of the old Ulster aristocracy into voluntary exile. The "plantation" period by the British which followed gave Ulster a number of carefully-planned towns. A few churches and fortified farms or "bawns" survive, though English half-timbering tended to be replaced by native architecture after the burnings of the 1641 rebellion; many of the towns were rebuilt in the eighteenth century.

Ulster Today

Since 1920 when Ireland was divided, Ulster has enjoyed a measure of self-government within the United Kingdom. It has its own parliament—a house of commons with 52 members, a senate of 26—and government to deal with a wide range of domestic affairs like health, education, housing, roads, industry and agriculture. But the major issues of defence, foreign policy and national finance are reserved to the British parliament at Westminster. There is a population of close to 1,500,000, most of it clustered within a 30-mile radius of the capital city, Belfast.

The traditional occupations have been farming, shipbuilding and the linen industry, but all of these employ fewer workers than in the past. In the face of a rising population and a continuing unemployment problem, the Northern Ireland government has made great efforts to bring in new industries, not only from England but from the United States and Europe.

One consequence is that the province has become more cosmopolitan and less parochial than it once was, but it is by no means a sophisticated area. The pleasures it offers a visitor are simple ones. Under Ulster's fourth Prime Minister, Capt. Terence O'Neill, there has been legislation to designate and protect areas of outstanding natural beauty, and to create national parks, the first of which is the Lakeland of County Fermanagh. Steps have been taken to contain the growth of Belfast, so that the green hills surrounding it are not spoiled, and to plan the expansion of other towns in the most modern way.

Ulster and America

For many Americans, visiting Northern Ireland is a return to the home of their forebears. Ulster was the cradle of the Scotch-Irish who made a major contribution to the foundation of the United States. Known in the British Isles as Ulster-Scots, they crossed from the Scottish lowlands into Northern Ireland early in the seventeenth century. Large numbers settled first in counties Antrim and Down; then the western counties were "planted" after the Flight of the Earls. It was a period when plantations were also being undertaken in America; a century later, frustrated by civil and religious disabilities, thousands of Ulster-Scots sailed for the New World in search of liberty and opportunity. Years later, President Theodore Roosevelt was to describe them as "a grim, stern people, strong and simple, powerful for good and evil, swayed by gusts of stormy passion, the love of freedom rooted in their very hearts' core."

While the English settlers in America had divided loyalties during the War of Independence, the Scotch-Irish owed no allegiance to the crown and proved doughty fighters. The Declaration of Independence, composed by Jefferson, was written down by an Ulsterman, Charles Thomson, first secretary of the U.S. Congress; it was printed by another Ulsterman, John Dunlap. Ten presidents have been of Scotch-Irish stock: Andrew Jackson, James Knox Polk, James Buchanan, Andrew Johnson, Ulysses S. Grant, Chester Alan Arthur, Grover Cleveland, Benjamin Harrison, William McKinley and Woodrow Wilson. Jackson, Buchanan and Arthur were the only first-generation Americans to reach this high office; Jackson himself recorded that his parents' ship had barely reached harbor in America when he was born.

Other famous Americans claimed Ulster ancestry—Sam Houston, Davy Crockett, "Stonewall" Jackson, Horace Greeley, Edgar Allan Poe, Stephen Foster, and many of the great businessmen. A century after the Ulster-Scots emigrated, the Irish potato famine encouraged a westward movement of the native Irish Roman Catholics; these Irish-Americans have also made a distinctive contribution to American life.

In recent years, interest in the Scotch-Irish has been revitalised by the work of the Ulster-Scot Historical Society, formed with the help of the Northern Ireland Government to carry out research and to assist people seeking information about their forebears. A leading part has been played by Capt. O'Neill, and a number of historical sites have been identified.

The National Trust has taken over the home of Woodrow Wilson's grandfather, at Dergalt, near Strabane, as well as Gray's printing shop in Strabane, where John Dunlap learned his trade. The ancestral homes of presidents Grant, Arthur and McKinley can still be seen, and not far from Carrickfergus Castle, a plaque marks the site of the home from which Andrew Jackson's parents emigrated in 1765.

The People of Ulster

There are, of course, two peoples. There are the Roman Catholic descendants of the native Irish, whose leaders sailed away in 1607, and who still largely cling to the ideal of a united and independent Ireland, and—twice as numerous—there are the Protestant descendants of the English and Scottish planters. Their religion still means much to both, and they rather look on England as a pagan country. A puritanism still keeps the public houses and cinemas shut on Sundays, though there is less sobriety than is suggested by closed doors and empty streets. Their differences are not merely political and religious; there are also differences of temperament and culture. Yet they share one characteristic common to people of a rural rather than an urban civilization: their interest in people. The Roman Catholic may be more forthcoming, more volatile and extrovert than the Protestant, but both share the desire to be a good neighbor and a good host. They are a sympathetic and generous people, anxious to please. The story is told of a long-legged Englishman who asked a farmer how far it was to walk to the next town. "It's four miles," came the reply, "but with your legs, I think you'll do it in two."

To the conscientious Presbyterians goes much of the credit for building up Ulster industry. But the province has also produced many eminent doctors, scientists and engineers, as well as distinguished soldiers like Alanbrooke, Montgomery, Alexander and Templer in recent time. Few Ulstermen have attained fame as artists or men of letters, but a wealth of folk songs and traditional stories has been handed down from generation to generation. Neighbors still gather for a *ceilidhe* (pronounced "kaylee"), exchanging stories and songs long into the night.

The fireplace is the focal point of the cottage kitchen or living room; the table is placed against wall or window, and there is room around the open hearth to swing the iron crane with its cooking pots—and to sit and talk. (Here is cooked the Irish stew; here the potato bread and soda bread are baked on a griddle.) A peat fire may not have gone out for a hundred years, lest the life go out of the people of the house. Here are passed down the beliefs and superstitions of centuries, the talk of little people and fairy thorns and holy wells, and what happened (or did not happen) long ago becomes as vivid as if it had been yesterday.

Irish is no longer spoken as a first language, of course, but Irish place names are dominant (particularly in the "townland," the smallest division of land, containing perhaps a dozen farms), and Gaelic phraseology is detectable in Ulster speech. Parts of County Antrim could be nearby Scotland, judging from the dialect, and there are other areas where you can hear something very close to Shakespeare's English.

Climate and Scenery

Northern Ireland is small—not much over 5,000 square miles—but within its borders there is a wide variety of scenery. The mild but variable oceanic climate favors an agriculture based on livestock, and small farms cover the countryside. There are few forests, though the government is steadily planting mountain slopes with conifers and the many hedgerow trees give a misleading impression. The large estates or demesnes, many now in public ownership, are often well-wooded; the high walls around them were built as relief measures during the years following the potato famine of the 1840's. The farms are an intricate jigsaw of small fields separated by hawthorn hedge or stone wall; in some areas, it is said, the first harvest was stones. Red brick is gradually replacing the traditional farmhouse built of stone—wood was too inflammable a building material to have much success in Ireland's troubled past—but many traditional whitewashed and even thatched cottages still shelter within a cluster of sycamore trees. The English village never established itself in Ulster; after the break-up of the old Irish pattern of agriculture, with fragmented holdings centred on a group of houses known as a "clachan," each man built on his own land. There are no high mountains—the tallest is under 3,000 feet—but the province's varied geology provides many moorland heights, from which peat or turf is often cut for drying and burning. In spring, the whin or gorse provides a yellow girdle where farmland and mountain meet. In September, the heather is purple, and the hedgerows covered in wild fuschia. There is more coast than inland border, and the indentations are favored equally by yachtsmen and birdlife. Inland, the many small loughs again favor wild life; it has been said that for six months of the year, Lough Erne is in County Fermanagh, and for another six months, Fermanagh is in Lough Erne.

Practical Information for Northern Ireland

WHEN TO GO? Anytime of the year will do, as the climate is neither too severe in winter nor too hot in summer. To help you decide, here is a calendar of events: *Easter:* Circuit of Ireland motor rally. *May:* Lord Mayor's Show in Belfast. Royal Ulster Agricultural Society's annual 4-day show at Balmoral showgrounds, Belfast.

July 12: Annual demonstrations of Protestant Orange Order, commemorating the battle of the Boyne in 1690, with colorful banners and bands. Also in July; the International Rose Trials in Belfast. The largest procession is in Belfast. *August:* Lammas Fair at Ballycastle, best known of Ulster's fairs. *August 15:* Annual demonstration of Ancient Order of Hibernians, a Roman Catholic celebration. *November:* Queen's University arts festival and "Festival '70" in Belfast.

NORTHERN IRELAND 531

HOW TO GET TO NORTHERN IRELAND?
By air: from Birmingham, Blackpool, Bradford, Bristol, Cardiff, Douglas, Dublin, East Midlands, Edinburgh, Exeter, Gatwick, Glasgow, Jersey, Leeds, Liverpool, London, Luton, Manchester, Newcastle-upon-Tyne, Prestwick and Southampton to Aldergrove airport, near Belfast. Also from Prestwick to Londonderry airport.

By sea: Drive-on car ferry services run between Stranraer and Larne (the shortest crossing), Liverpool and Belfast, Ardrossan and Belfast, and from Preston to Larne and Belfast. You can also ship yourself and your car across to Belfast from Heysham, Glasgow, and Douglas, Isle of Man. If you buy a 'Midweek Holiday Return Ticket', you can save 20 percent of the ordinary rail and steamer fare from London during the summer.

By rail and road from the Republic of Ireland.

TRANSPORT INSIDE NORTHERN IRELAND. The *Ulster Transport Authority* has three railway stations in Belfast, linking the capital with other parts of Northern Ireland. Queen's Quay Station—to Bangor. Great Victoria Street Station—the Dublin line, passing through Lurgan and Portadown. York Road Station—to Larne, via Carrickfergus; to Londonderry, via Antrim, Ballymena and Coleraine, with links to Portstewart and Portrush.

In addition, *Ulsterbus* provides a comprehensive road passenger service throughout the province, and issues special holiday tickets giving unlimited travel at a cheap rate. Example: a 7-day "Freedom of Northern Ireland" ticket costs $8.40, gives you a week's unlimited travel by road. During the summer, it operates day, half-day and evening tours from several centres.

Inclusive coach tours are operated by *Ulster Coach Tours*, 2 Glengall Street, Belfast 12; *Devenny's Tours*, Whitehead; *Fawcett's Tours*, Portrush; *Gaston's Tours*, Bangor; *Henry McNeill Ltd.* Larne; *Upton's Reliable Irish Tours, Ltd.*, Ballycastle; and *Grand Metropolitan Hotels Ltd.*, Larne, who can also arrange golfing holidays.

Car hire firms include *Hertz-Rent-A-Car*, 95 Crumlin Road, Belfast 14; *Avis-Rent-A-Car*, 106 Joy Street, Belfast 2; *McCausland*, 77 York Street, Belfast 15; *Ryan's*, 225 York Street, Belfast 15; *Belfast Hire Cars*, 27-31 Grosvenor Road, Belfast 12; *Dick & Co.*, 112 Donegall Street, Belfast 1.

Apart from the immediate vicinity of Belfast, Ulster's well-surfaced and well-signposted roads are free from congestion.

HOTELS AND RESTAURANTS

BELFAST

CONWAY HOUSE (Dunmurry). This Georgian manor, a Trust House 5 miles from city center, has been converted into a deluxe hotel by addition of new wings. Swimming pool, squash, 45 rooms with bath. One of best in Ulster.

CULLODEN (Craigavad). This deluxe hotel is a former bishop's palace in a secluded position overlooking Belfast Lough, 6 miles from city center. 12 rooms with bath. Also one of the best.

MIDLAND, a first-class hotel adjoining the railway to the resorts of Antrim and Londonderry, was acquired by Grand Metropolitan Hotels in 1966 and further modernized. Beef a specialty. 63 rooms with bath.

ROYAL AVENUE, a first-class hotel at city center, comfortably furnished. 131 rooms (49 baths).

Other hotels include *Glenmachan Tower*, in fine grounds overlooking Belfast Lough (11 rooms, 4 baths); *Grand Central*, 170 rooms (76 baths); *Greenan Lodge* (Dunmurry), 11 rooms (3 baths); *Beechlawn* (Dunmurry), 14 rooms (5 baths); *Edenmore* (Newtownabbey), 33 rooms (10 baths); *Glenavna* (Newtownabbey), 13 rooms (5 baths).

Recommended restaurants are *Abercorn*, *Globe*, *Mooney's Grill*, *Thompson's Grill*, *Ulster Tavern*, *Stagecoach Inn* (Derriaghy), *Chimney Corner* (Templepatrick), *Pig'n Chick'n* (Templepatrick).

ELSEWHERE

AGHADOWEY, County Londonderry. *Brown Trout Inn*, 5 rooms (1 bath).

ANTRIM, County Antrim. The county town, 17 miles from Belfast: *Hall's*, 35 rooms (1 with bath). *Skeffington Lodge*, 12 rooms (1 with bath). *Dunadry Inn*, Dunadry, on the Belfast Road, 20 single rooms with showers, 24 double rooms with baths. Recommended roadhouse: *Pig'n Chicken*, at Templepatrick on the Belfast Road.

ARMAGH, County Armagh. *Charlemont Arms*, 22 rooms (11 baths); *Beresford Arms*, 20 rooms (5 baths); *Drumsill House*, 12 rooms (3 baths).

BALLYCASTLE, County Antrim. *Marine Hotel*, 85 rooms (27 baths); *Antrim Arms*, 22 rooms (3 baths).

BALLYGALLY, County Antrim. *Ballygally Castle*, a first-class modern hotel built onto a seventeenth-century castle. At the foot of a winding stone staircase is the *Dungeon Bar*. *Marine Lounge* looks over the sea, and the *Candlelight Inn* offers varied cuisine. 24 rooms (12 baths).

BANGOR, County Down. *Royal*, 34 rooms with bath; *Ballyholme*, 47 rooms (8 baths).

CARRICKFERGUS, County Antrim. *Dobbin's Inn*, 15 rooms (7 baths).

COLERAINE, County Londonderry. *Gorreen House* has good cuisine. Also *Westbrook*. Both moderate.

CRAWFORDSBURN, County Down. *The Old Inn*, a charming seventeenth-century coaching inn with thatched roof, which retains old-world atmosphere in spite of extensive modernization. 25 rooms with bath.

CUSHENDALL, County Antrim. *Cushendall*, 16 rooms (8 baths); *Glens of Antrim*, 14 rooms (2 baths).

CUSHENDUN, County Antrim. *Bay*, 13 rooms (2 baths); *Glendun*, 20 rooms (2 baths).

DONAGHADEE, County Down. *Imperial,* 22 rooms (21 baths or showers).

DUNADRY, County Antrim. *Dunadry Inn.* Deluxe motor hotel created on site of old mill, opened in 1966 and an immediate success; 12 miles from Belfast, 4 miles from Aldergrove airport. 46 rooms with bath.

ENNISKILLEN, County Fermanagh. *Imperial,* 70 rooms (44 baths or showers). *Carrybridge Angling Centre,* 15 rooms.

KILKEEL, County Down. *Kilmorey Arms* 12 rooms (2 baths); *Royal,* 16 rooms (2 baths).

KILLADEAS, County Fermanagh. *Manor House,* 22 rooms (11 baths).

LARNE, County Antrim. *King's Arms,* 56 rooms (7 baths); *Laharna,* 150 rooms (18 baths); *McNeill's,* 62 rooms (14 baths).

LONDONDERRY, County Londonderry. *Broomhill House,* 20 rooms (10 baths); *City,* 73 rooms (28 baths); *Melville,* 62 rooms (19 baths). Also: *Northern Counties,* 35 rooms (14 with bath); *Woodleigh,* 16 rooms; *Ardowen,* 16 rooms (1 with shower); *Quigley's,* 12 rooms.

NEWCASTLE, County Down. *Enniskeen,* 15 rooms (4 baths); *Slieve Donard,* 105 rooms (47 baths), 40 of them renovated in 1968

NEWRY, County Down. *Ardmore,* a well-furnished hotel opened in 1964, with charming grounds featuring a sunken garden 28 rooms with baths.

OMAGH, County Tyrone. *Knock-na-moe Castle,* 28 rooms 8) baths).

PORTADOWN, County Armagh. *Seagoe,* 21 rooms (8 baths).

PORTAFERRY, County Down. *The Scotsman,* recommended restaurant specializing in seafood.

PORTBALLINTRAE, County Antrim. *Bayview,* 23 rooms (3 baths).

PORTRUSH, County Antrim. *Fawcett's Royal Portrush,* 131 rooms (15 baths); *Lismara,* 17 rooms (8 baths); *Northern Counties,* 95 rooms (27 baths); *Skerry-Bhan,* 51 rooms (20 baths).

PORTSTEWART, County Londonderry. *Carrig-na-Cule,* 36 rooms (8 baths); *Strand,* 70 rooms (12 baths); *Montagu Arms,* 30 rooms (8 baths).

ROSTREVOR, County Down. *Great Northern,* 31 rooms (10 baths); *Roxboro,* a center for pony trekking, 20 rooms (3 baths).

STRABANE, County Tyrone. *Abercorn Arms,* 20 rooms.

SPORTS. Many people go to Northern Ireland to *fish.* There are so many rivers and lakes that the angler is never far from good sport, though he must ask permission. Game fish include the salmon, sea trout, brown trout and rainbow trout; the season is from April through September, though some waters are open from March through October. There is no closed season for coarse fish, which include pike, perch, rudd, bream, roach and eels; under-rated by Ulster anglers, these offer excellent sport for the visitor. In addition, there is unlimited sea fishing around the coast. *BEA* offer angling holidays at Enniskillen.

Some of the world's finest ships have been built in Belfast, and the love of the sea is inbred. There are more than 20 *yacht clubs*— one inland on Lough Erne—which make visitors welcome. More recently, *power boats* and *water skiing* have become popular, both at sea and in inland waters like Loughs Neagh, Erne, Aghery and Henney. There is good *canoeing;* a journey through the middle of Ulster begins in the headwaters of the Blackwater River (which separates Counties Tyrone and Armagh), crosses Lough Neagh, and ends at the mouth of the River Bann. In the clear waters along the coast, *sub-aqua swimmers* can touch fish unused to contact with humans.

For the adventurous on land, there is *climbing* in the Mourne Mountains and *pot holing* in the caves of County Fermanagh. There's also *pony-trekking* in the Mournes and at Omagh, where the Carnony Trekking Farm offers daily treks through Gortin Glen Forest Park for $3.60. Ulster is also a land of *golf courses* as varied as the scenery, the climate playing its part in the good grass and true greens. The seaside courses at Portrush and Newcastle are particularly fine, and the Royal Belfast course at Craigavad is beautifully situated overlooking Belfast Lough.

It is also a land of *horses*, which can be hired in most areas. There is *fox-hunting* throughout Northern Ireland during the months of autumn, and the spring brings point-to-point races over the fields. Downpatrick stages the Ulster Grand National, and the Maze, not far from Belfast, has the Ulster Derby. Another highlight of the sporting year is the Ulster Grand Prix *motor-cycling* race at Dundrod, County Antrim.

HISTORIC HOUSES OPEN TO THE PUBLIC. *Ardress House*, near Portadown. Eighteenth-century house. Open April through September, Wednesday, Thursday and Saturday 2-6 p.m.; also Sunday, from July, 2:30-5.30 p.m. *Castlecoole*, near Enniskillen. Eighteenth-century mansion by James Wyatt. Open April through September, 2-6 p.m. daily except Monday and Thursday. Sundays from July only, 2:30-5:30 p.m.

Castleward, near Downpatrick. Open April through September, Wednesday and Saturday, 2-5:30 p.m. Grounds open every day.

Derrymore House, near Newry. Thatched eighteenth-century manor house. Open April through September, Wednesday, Thursday, Saturday, 2-6 p.m.

Florence Court, near Enniskillen. Eighteenth-century house. Hours as for Castlecoole.

Mount Stewart Gardens, near Newtownards. Open April through September, Wednesday, Saturday and Sunday, 2-6 p.m.

Rowallane Gardens, 13 miles southeast of Belfast. Open April to June daily, 10 a.m.-6 p.m. July through September, Wednesday, Saturday and Sunday, 10 a.m.-6 p.m.

Springhill, near Moneymore, County Londonderry. Seventeenth-century manor house; costume museum. Hours as for Castlecoole.

Other places to visit: *Parliament Buildings*, Stormont, Belfast. Monday-Friday, 9:30-4:30; *Belfast City Hall*, Monday-Friday, 8:45-5; *St. Anne's Cathedral*, Donegall Street, Belfast. Monday-Saturday, 9-5. *Queen's University*, Belfast. Monday-Friday, 10-5. Saturday, 10-12 noon.

MUSEUMS. *Ulster Folk Museum.* Craigavad, County Down. Tuesday-Sunday. October through April 2-5 p.m. May through September, 2-9 p.m. *Arts Council Gallery*, Chichester Street, Belfast, Monday-Friday, 10-6. Tuesday, 10-9. *Ulster Museum*, Stranmillis, Belfast. Monday-Saturday, 10-6. Wednesday, 10-9. *Armagh County Museum*, the Mall, Armagh, 10-1 and 2-5. *Regimental Museum*, Royal Irish Fusiliers, The Mall, Armagh,

Monday-Friday, 10-12-30 and 2-4:30. *Natural History Museum,* Tollymore Forest Park, Newcastle. Daily, June through August. Saturday and Sunday, September through May. 12 noon-6 p.m.

Wilson House, Dergalt, Strabane. April through September, Tuesday-Saturday, 2-6 p.m. Sunday, 2:30-6 p.m. *Gray's Printing Shop,* Strabane. April through September. Monday-Saturday, 10-5.

COUNTRY WORKSHOPS in Northern Ireland include the following: County Antrim: tweeds at *Glens of Antrim Tweed Co.*, Cushendall, by Ballymena, and pottery at *Portrush Pottery*, Main Street, Portrush. County Armagh: handmade Carrickmacross lace from *Mrs. Rose Feeney*, Cappy, Crossmaglen. County Down: earthenware at *Donagh Studio Pottery*, New Road, Donaghdee; Aran knitwear at *Inish Saimer*, Innisfayle Avenue, Bangor (by appointment only); stone pendants and brooches, etc. at *Irish Stone Craft*, 12 Beechill Park Avenue, Belfast 8; and jewellery by *Frances Mary McCleery*, Islandbane, Killinchy. County Fermanagh: shillelaghs at *Heather Productions*, Derrygonnelly, Enniskillen (by appointment only), and crocheted lace from *Mrs. Kathleen Owens*, Legatellidy, Coonian, Fivemiletown.

USEFUL ADDRESSES. *Northern Ireland Tourist Board*, 6 Royal Avenue, Belfast 1. *Ulster Transport Authority*, Great Victoria Street, Belfast 2. *Northern Ireland Government Information Service*, Stormont Castle, Belfast 4. *Ulster-Scot Historical Society*, Law Courts, Chichester Street, Belfast 1. *National Trust* (Northern Ireland Committee), 82 Dublin Road, Belfast 2.

Car hire in Belfast: *Hertz Rent-a-Car*, 95 Crumlin Road and at Belfast Airport; *Belfast Hire Cars Ltd.*, 27 Grosvenor Road; *Ryan's (Self-Drive) Ltd.*, 225 York Street. At Enniskillen: *North West Self Drive*, Sligo Road.

Exploring Northern Ireland

Ulster is for the people who want to see Ulster. It is not an area which offers a great deal of indoor entertainment. Neither the live theater nor the music hall is well represented; there are no casinos, and late-night entertainment exists only in good conversation, story and song. As for the climate, the rainfall statistics do not support the picture of perpetual "Irish mist", but there is a grain of truth in the saying "If you can see the hills, it's going to rain; if you can't see them, it's already raining." A slight breeze on a cloudless day is invigorating, but if you want to lie on a beach under the sun, other countries offer more. Without the rain, though, the grass would not be so green.

In short, Ulster itself is the main attraction.

Belfast

For most people, Belfast is their introduction to Northern Ireland. Essentially, it is a creation of the nineteenth-century industrial revolution, and few buildings remain from the eighteenth century; the most notable of the latter is the Charitable Institution, an old people's home. The city hall, crowned by a green dome, was built in 1906; St. Anne's Cathedral is of the same period. Other buildings belong to Northern Ireland's period of self-government, which began in 1921; these include the Royal Courts of Justice, close to the River Lagan, and the parliament building at Stormont on the outskirts of the city. The university quarter contains the expanding Queen's University, established as a college in 1849, the Presbyterian theological college, and the Ulster Museum, where a modern extension is being added to the building left unfinished in 1929. (The university's arts festival each November attracts performers from all over the world.) The Linen Hall Library, facing City Hall, was founded in 1788 and has an admirable collection of Irish works.

It is not a handsome city. The Ulster author who writes autobiographies as Robert Harbinson and travel books as Robin Bryans recalled only one style of architecture from an impoverished childhood in the 1930's—"Victorian Grisly". But it is a friendly place, largely reserving any hostility for its own inhabitants. To be a "good neighbor" is the highest achievement of a rural Ulsterman, and the attitude survives in city streets, where few are far from the soil. "As far as Belfastmen go," said the poet W. R. Rodgers, "every one has hayseeds in the turn up of his pants." The city has its religious tensions, though, and they usually reach a peak around July 12, when the Protestants of the Orange Order march in thousands through the city to the accompaniment of bright banners and flute bands.

Another Ulster poet, Louis MacNeice, wrote: "I was born in Belfast between the mountain and the gantries, To the hooting of lost sirens and the clang of trams." The shipyard is still the city's major employer; rope, tobacco and linen are still prominent, though new industries have carried the burden of the city's post-war expansion.

Belfast's chief virtue is possibly its situation at the head of

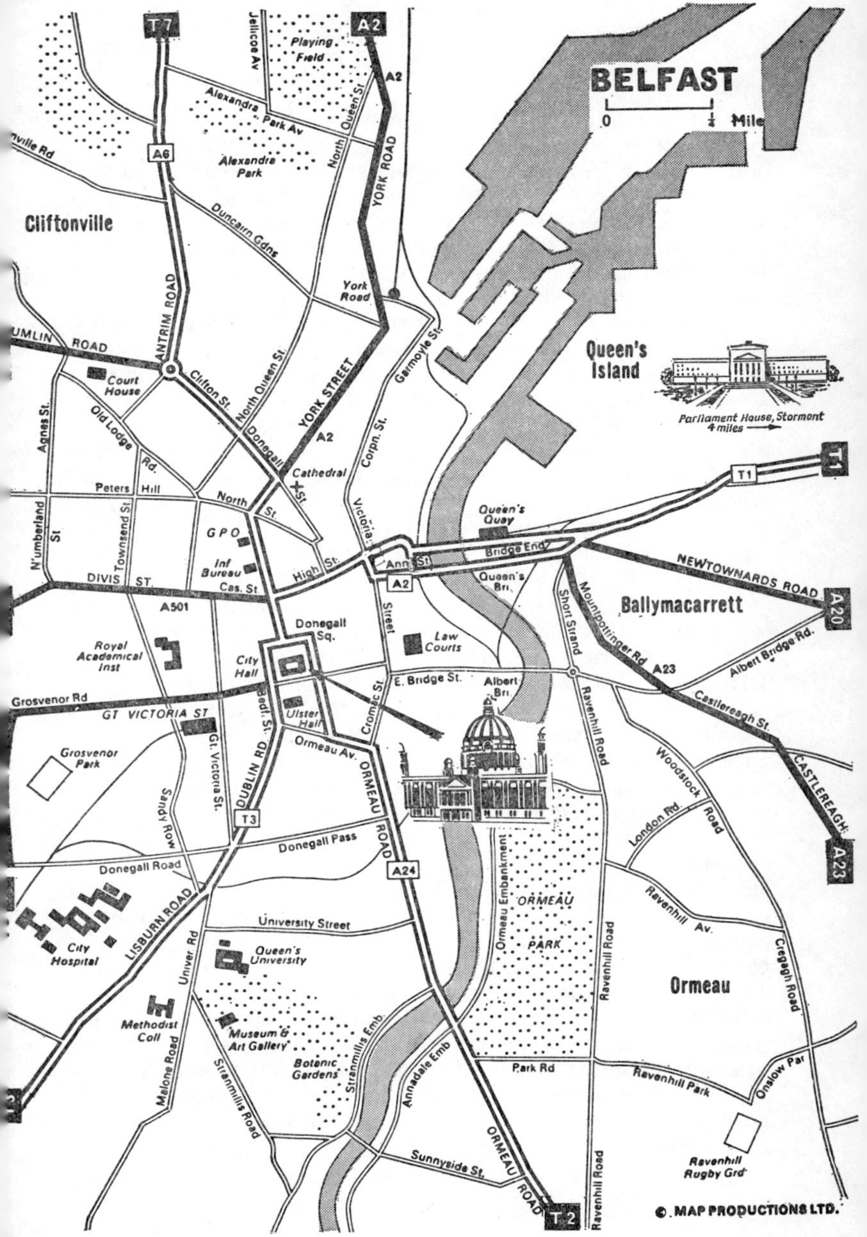
BELFAST
0
¼
Mile
T7
A2
A6
Jellicoe Av
Playing Field
Alexandra Park Av
Alexandra Park
North Queen St.
YORK ROAD
Cliftonville
Duncairn Gdns
York Road
ANTRIM ROAD
Garmoyle St.
Queen's Island
Parliament House, Stormont 4 miles
UMLIN ROAD
Court House
Clifton St.
North Queen St.
YORK STREET
Agnes St.
Old Lodge Rd.
Donegall St.
Corpn. St.
Cathedral
Peters Hill
North St.
Victoria St.
Queen's Quay
T1
N'umberland St
Townsend St.
GPO
Inf Bureau
High St.
Ann St.
Bridge End
Queen's Bri.
NEWTOWNARDS ROAD
DIVIS ST.
Cas. St.
A501
Short Strand
Mountpottinger Rd
Ballymacarrett
A20
Donegall Sq.
Street
Law Courts
Royal Academical Inst
City Hall
E. Bridge St.
Albert Bri.
A23
Albert Bridge Rd.
Castlereagh St.
Grosvenor Rd
GT VICTORIA ST
Bedf. St.
Ulster Hall
Cromac St.
Ravenhill Road
Woodstock Road
CASTLEREAGH
Grosvenor Park
Ormeau Av.
ORMEAU ROAD
Gt. Victoria St.
DUBLIN RD
Sandy Row
T3
London Rd.
Donegall Pass
Donegall Road
A24
Ormeau Embankment
ORMEAU PARK
Ravenhill Av.
LISBURN ROAD
University Street
City Hospital
Univer. Rd
Queen's University
Cregagh Road
Ormeau
Methodist Coll
Museum & Art Gallery
Botanic Gardens
Stranmillis Emb.
Annadale Emb
Malone Road
Stranmillis Road
Park Rd
Ravenhill Park
Onslow Par
Sunnyside St.
Ravenhill Rugby Grd
T2
© MAP PRODUCTIONS LTD.

Belfast Lough (the city's name means "Ford of the Sandbanks" lying in a broad hollow between the Antrim Plateau and the softer Hills of Down. To the north, Cave Hill can be approached through any of three public parks, Belfast Castle, Hazelwood or Bellevue; in 1795, Wolfe Tone, Henry Joy McCracken and other United Irishmen climbed the hill to McArt's Fort to vow an unceasing battle for Irish freedom. The Lagan Valley has been declared an area of outstanding natural beauty, giving protection to its riverside and woodland walks. In Down, the Holywood and Castlereagh hills give fine views across the city and lough. Not far outside Belfast, on the road to Bangor, the Ulster Folk Museum recaptures some of the province's vanishing ways of life; in the grounds of Cultra Manor have been rebuilt, stone by stone, a farmhouse from the Glens of Antrim, an eighteenth-century laborer's house from County Londonderry, a spade mill, and a water mill for turning flax into linen.

County Antrim

North of Belfast, the character of County Antrim is determined by a tilted shelf of basalt. In the west, the basalts sink beneath rich farmland towards the quiet banks of the River Bann, which drains Lough Neagh, the largest fresh water lake in the British Isles. In the east and north, the basalts form rugged cliffs and headlands overshadowing the coast road, and in turn are pierced by deep glens. Almost in the middle of the country rises the steep-sloped mountain of Slemish, where the enslaved Saint Patrick herded pigs; it is now a place of pilgrimage.

Leaving Belfast, there is first of all Cave Hill on the left, shaped (it is said) like Napoleon's nose. Ten miles along the coast road is Carrickfergus, with a well-preserved twelfth-century Norman castle. It changed hands many times in history, and in one siege, the garrison is reputed to have eaten 30 Scottish prisoners before surrendering; on another occasion, a hostage escaped by a rope concealed in a cheese sent by his wife. William of Orange landed at Carrickfergus in 1690, and went on to defeat James II at the River Boyne and conquer Ireland. Near Carrickfergus is Kilroot, where Jonathan Swift, author of *Gulliver's Travels*, preached for a time; his church is now a ruin.

NORTHERN IRELAND

The Antrim coast road proper begins at Larne, a busy port at which in 1914, arms from Germany were landed secretly for the Ulster Volunteer Force's struggle against home rule in Ireland. A nearby raised beach yields primitive flint implements which record the first known inhabitants of Ireland.

Beyond Larne, there are seaside resorts at Ballygally, Glenarm, Carnlough, Waterfoot, Cushendall and Cushendun. The most beautiful of the nine glens of Antrim is Glenariff, behind Waterfoot, in whose upper reaches the river tumbles down a sequence of pretty waterfalls. Thackeray called it "Switzerland in miniature". The main road avoids the rugged coast between Cushendall and Ballycastle, a popular resort which stages the colorful Ould Lammas Fair each August, but the more athletic can explore the cliffs of Torr Head and Fair Head, with the intervening Murlough Bay. Fair Head gives views of Rathlin Island, two and one-half miles away, and of the Scottish coast and islands; the Gray Man's Path leads down to the shore. Rathlin can be reached by boat from Ballycastle; Robert Bruce, the Scottish King, took refuge in one of its caves and saw the persistent spider which persuaded him to "try, try again" for victory. The island teems with puffins, guillemots and razorbills.

Further along the coast is the salmon fishery of Carrick-a-Rede, reached by a nerve-testing rope bridge, the village of Ballintoy, and the sandy crescent of White Park Bay: Carrick-a-Rede was acquired by the National Trust in 1967. The ruined Dunseverick Castle was once the home of a Red Branch knight, Conall Cearnach, who is said to have joined the Roman army and won Christ's robe in a lottery. Another castle is Dunluce, part of which fell hundreds of feet into the sea during preparations for a banquet in 1639; the so-called tinker's window was named after one of the survivors.

Between the two castles is the world-famous Giant's Causeway, a famous geological phenomenon consisting of hundreds of basalt columns, usually six-sided; legend had it that the Irish giant, Finn Mac Coul, built it to reach a Scottish rival, but the cooling of lava is a simpler explanation. A nearby cove, Port-na-Spania, recalls the wreck of the *Gerona*, one of the ships of the Spanish Armada, whose guns were salvaged for Dunluce.

The Antrim section of the coast road ends at Portrush, a

popular resort with an excellent golf course. The limestone caves of the White Rocks are approached by the broad beach east of the town, and boat trips can be made to the Skerries, offshore islands of rock.

Inland, County Antrim has less to offer tourists. Near Dervock is the ancestral home of President McKinley, and the house in which President Arthur's father lived can be seen near Cullybackey. Ballymena is the county town. Nearby, Antrim contains one of the most perfect examples of a round tower; also preserved is the cottage in which lived Alexander Irvine, author of *My Lady of the Chimney Corner*. Lough Neagh is rather inaccessible, and roads that come close to the shore are generally rough and narrow. But it repays exploration with its rather desolate scenery. There is a commercial eel fishery at Toome, bridging the head of the lower Bann, but most of the local fishermen operate from the southern and western shores. Five of Northern Ireland's six counties touch the lough. Like the Giant's Causeway, Lough Neagh is attributed to Finn Mac Coul; a single spade stroke scooped out the lough, according to legend, and the contents were deposited in the Irish Sea to form the Isle of Man.

County Londonderry

The coast of County Londonderry continues the cliffs and beaches of Antrim. Portstewart, like neighboring Portrush, is noted for its bathing and golf. The Bann is crossed at Coleraine, site of Ulster's second university; Castlerock and Downhill are other small resorts on the way to Londonderry, Ulster's second city. At Downhill, the National Trust has taken over Mussenden Temple, a classical folly built in the eighteenth century as a clifftop library by Frederick Hervey, Earl of Bristol and Bishop of Derry. It looks over Magilligan Strand, a six-mile beach which curves to the narrow mouth of Lough Foyle. Farther inland, past the steep slopes of Benevenagh Mountain, is Limavady, where in 1851, Jane Ross wrote down the melody of a wandering fiddler and gave the world *The Londonderry Air*. The Sperrin Mountains are one of the least explored areas of Ulster; narrow, winding roads cross these silent moorlands, and the whitewashed cottages of the foothills belong almost to a past age.

The county was originally Derry (from the Irish for "oakwood"), but the name was extended when it was planted in the seventeenth century under the supervision of the merchant companies of the City of London. The city and seaport of Londonderry originated in a monastery founded by Saint Columba in 546, but it was not until 1600 that English forces gained a permanent grip on the town. The well-preserved city walls, which were completed in 1618, extend about a mile in circumference, and are pierced by old and new gates. Derry is built on a hill, and withstood a famous 105-day siege by James II's army in 1689; eventually an English ship, the *Mountjoy*, broke a boom thrown across the River Foyle below the city and brought relief. Governor Walker's reply to an offer of terms from the besiegers was "No surrender", a phrase since adopted as the city's motto and a Protestant slogan in any crisis. The largest of the cannon used during the siege, *Roaring Meg*, still stands on the walls. Since that time, Derry has been known as the Maiden City; many relics of the siege can be seen in the guildhall and the Protestant cathedral.

County Tyrone

Although Tyrone is the largest of the six counties, much of it is the sparsely populated moorland of the Sperrin Mountains. There are comparatively few tourist amenities, but fishing and shooting both attract visitors, and a forest park at Gortin Glen was opened in 1967. Strabane's links with Woodrow Wilson and James Dunlap have already been mentioned: in another part of the county, at Dergina, close to Ballygawley, is the house once occupied by Hannah Simpson, mother of Ulysses S. Grant. On the shores of Lough Neagh is the Arboe Cross, 18 feet high and the finest example of a high cross in Ulster; its sculpted panels represent scenes from the Bible.

County Down

The largest of County Down's holiday resorts is Bangor, 13 miles from Belfast. A monastery founded in 555 became one of Ireland's finest monastic schools, but the town's reputation today rests on a wide range of tourist amenities. The coast road, less dramatic in Down than in Antrim, passes through quiet resorts like Groomsport, Donaghadee (offshore, there is a bird observatory on one of the Copeland Islands), Millisle, Portavogie, Cloghy and Portaferry—all on the seaward side of the Ards Peninsula, which almost encloses Strangford Lough and its many islands. Greyabbey, on the eastern shore of the lough, contains extensive remains of a twelfth century Cistercian abbey. Nearer Newtownards, an industrial town at the head of the lough, are the gardens of Mountstewart, a National Trust property, in which the mild climate of the peninsula permits eucalyptus groves, bamboos and other subtropical plants.

South of Strangford Lough is the peninsula of Lecale, which has many associations with Saint Patrick. He founded a monastery at Downpatrick; close to the present cathedral, a granite boulder inscribed "Patric" in Celtic characters marks what is believed to be the saint's grave. Close to the town are the ruins of Inch Abbey, another Cistercian foundation. Two miles northeast of Downpatrick is Saul, where Patrick founded Ireland's first Christian church in a barn in 432. A small church of Mourne granite with a traditional round tower as its belfry was built in 1932, and each March 17 (Saint Patrick's Day), pilgrims wend their way from Saul to Downpatrick. A mile away, a Roman Catholic statue of the saint is another place of pilgrimage. Farther east, the village of Strangford occupies a strategic site at the mouth of the lough. Four castles have guarded it in history; one is in the grounds of eighteenth-century Castlewood House, a National Trust property noted for having one front in the Palladian manner and the other in a spidery Gothic style.

South of Strangford are Ardglass—noted for its herrings—the sycamore-lined village of Killough, and the sandy beaches of Tyrella and Dundrum. Then come the Mourne Mountains and the resorts in their shadow—Newcastle (with a fine golf course), Annalong, Kilkeel, Rostrevor and Warrenpoint, strung round the granite heights like a necklace. Although it is possible to drive through the mountains, the greatest rewards go to those who explore the kingdom of Mourne on foot or by pony. Slieve Donard (2,796 ft.), which rises steeply behind Newcastle, is Ulster's highest mountain. Nearby, Tollymore Forest Park covers over 1,000 acres and includes some interesting old trees and unusual plants.

The rest of County Down is largely prosperous farmland, much of it covered with tiny egg-shaped hillocks or "drumlins" left by the retreating ice cap which covered Ulster centuries ago. They give the flat landscape a diversity it would otherwise lack, and create many small lakes. Of the inland villages and towns, Hillsborough most warrants a visit; its Georgian castle is now the official residence of the Governor of Northern Ireland.

County Armagh

The best time to visit Ulster's orchard county is the spring, when the apple trees of the rich lowlands south of Lough Neagh are in blossom. It is a county of neat, well-kept farms, with few stretches of mountain outside the striking volcanic ring of Slieve Gullion in the south.

The city of Armagh is the ecclesiastical capital of Ireland, housing the heads of both the Church of Ireland and Roman Catholicism, one in a sturdy Gothic cathedral and the other beneath soaring spires. Armagh (from the Irish for "Macha's height") was named after a warrior queen who built a great fort west of the hill on which the town later developed. In 1963, a long program of archeological investigation began on the site, which was probably occupied from about 300 B.C. to the fourth century A.D. St. Patrick built his first cathedral in Armagh, probably on the site of the present Anglican cathedral, which is mainly the work of restorations in the eighteenth and nineteenth centuries; the Roman Catholic cathedral was completed in 1873. The town has been destroyed many times in its history, but today enjoys the dignity of some fine Georgian and Regency houses. Armagh Royal School was established in the seventeenth century. Archbishop Robinson founded the public library in 1781 and the observatory 10 years later. In 1967, a planetarium was opened under the direction of Patrick Moore, well-known as a writer and broadcaster.

Portadown, which bridges the upper Bann, is the home of McGredy roses. It is now linked with the neighboring town of Lurgan in a project to create the new city of Craigavon, named after Ulster's first prime minister. A population of 100,000 is expected by the 1980's and a feature of the city will be the development of recreational facilities along the shore of Lough Neagh.

Bessbrook, in southeast Armagh, is interesting as an early example of a model village; it was built in 1846 by the

Richardsons, a Quaker linen family. Nearby is thatched Derrymore House, in which was drafted the 1800 Act of Union, binding Great Britain and Ireland together for over a century.

To the south is Slieve Gullion (1,893 ft.), in the center of a ring of small hills and ridges, and volcanic in origin. The whole region is rich in historical and legendary associations. On Gullion's summit is a bronze age burial place excavated in 1961; to the south is Moyry Pass and remains of a castle.

County Fermanagh

Flowing northwest to the Atlantic, the River Erne divides County Fermanagh in two, widening for much of its length into upper and lower Lough Erne. The county town is Enniskillen, home of two famous Irish regiments, which stands on an island in the river. Of a number of smaller expanses of water, the most notable are Lough Macnean and Lough Melvin in the west. This—despite the size of Lough Neagh—is Ulster's lakeland, a tourist attraction whose potential has only recently been fully recognized. There is now a fast motorway from Belfast and the airport of Enniskillen has reopened.

Little remains of the old castle of Enniskillen, but to the east of the town, a fine example of late Georgian architecture, Castlecoole, has been taken over by the National Trust; it was built by the first Earl of Belmore, who imported Portland stone by sea and bullock cart. The surrounding estate has fine beeches and oaks and a flock of greyleg geese. To the north of Enniskillen, Devenish Island in Lower Lough Erne is a monastic site which retains a perfect round tower; nearby White Island contains the ruins of an early church with seven strange figures carved in one wall. These are but two of the 365 islands scattered across these dreamy waters. For motorists there is a beautiful 40-mile drive around the shores of the loughs, and boats may be hired to explore the lough at Killadeas or at Castle Archdale, where a caravan-cruiser park has been developed. The original Castle Archdale was built and destroyed by fire in the seventeenth century; when its successor in 1776 used "sacred" stones from a ruined abbey, it was prophesied that an heir would never be born in the house. Water sports include swimming, skiing, sailing, cruising and canoeing. Anglers find salmon, pike, perch, bream, rudd, and the Gillaroo and Sonaghan trout of Lough Melvin.

SUPPLEMENTS

AN ENGLISH - AMERICAN VOCABULARY

Explaining the Common Language that Divides Us

by

RANSOM BRADFORD

(*The author, a native of Savannah, Georgia, and resident of London since 1964, has no other qualifications for compiling this glossary than a keen ear, long and sometimes frustrating experiences trying to communicate with the English, and the pedant's compulsion to take notes and compile lists. A graduate of several southern universities, short attender at a number of others, sometime lecturer in English history, he is researching British historiography at the British Museum.*)

Directions, Signs, Travel and Transport

The Briton rarely, if ever, gives directions in terms of "blocks", perhaps because medieval street plans were left largely untouched by the rationalist spirit which governed the grid plans of American cities, and "blocks", as such, do not exist. So be prepared to interpret distances in terms of *linear directions*, i.e., so many hundreds of yards, a half-mile, a mile-or-two; *visual objects*, "as far as the Miller's Arms" (a pub), "down to the bottom" (dead end), "up to the top," (reverse of "down to the bottom," though the points of reference for these seemingly vertical directions are largely imaginary), or "carry straight on until you come to the second set of traffic lights," etc.

British	*American*
coach (railway)	car
carriage (railway)	coach
coach	long distance bus; thus one does not go to the *bus* station, but to the *coach* station
bus	city transport
lorry	heavy transport truck; an "articulated lorry" is a trailer-truck
truck	open railway wagon, or a small open lorry
engine-driver	engineer
goods train	freight train
level crossing	grade crossing
guard (railway)	conductor
booking-hall	ticket office
advance booking	reservations
sleeping-car	pullman (not *sleeper*, see below)
book (verb)	make reservations (in restaurant or for travel)
single-ticket	one-way ticket

AN ENGLISH-AMERICAN VOCABULARY

British	*American*
return ticket	round trip ticket
left luggage	baggage check, baggage room
lost property	"lost-and-found"
enquiry	information
shunt	switch
signal-box	switch-tower
sleeper	cross-tie
terminus	terminal
underground or "tube" (railway)	subway train
zebra crossing (*zeb* rhymes with *deb*)	pedestrian crossing of alternate black and white strips in the roadway anchored at each end by blinking yellow lights: these mark the sacred right of way to pedestrians, but stray out of them and one is fair game to the motorist
footpath, footway, pavement	sidewalk: note Westminster signs, "Please Do Not Permit Your Dog to Foul the Footpath".
straight on	straight ahead
ground floor	first floor
first floor	second floor: "first floor" is never at ground level
lift	elevator
way in	entrance
way out	exit: not hippie language for one's state of being
quay (pron. *kee*)	pier
queue (pron. *cue*)	a concept, one might even say a way of life, peculiar to the British, not really translatable: refers to lines of people standing patiently at bus stops, in front of cinemas, grocers' shops, or perhaps spontaneously at random points; the verb "to queue" means it is mandatory to join one's place and wait patiently, and one may encounter such phenomena in very unlikely places, like shoe shops, etc. *Note;* once the bus arrives, one is perfectly within one's rights to break the queue and race pell-mell for the boarding platform with the rest of the queue.
zed or *z*	"zee", or *z*: the last letter of the alphabet. May cause some trouble, especially when asking for the street guide, *London, A to Z*.
subway	pedestrian crossing under the street
kiosk (telephone) or public telephone	"pay 'phone" (this Americanism is unknown to the British)
gangway (theatre)	aisle
pillar box	letter-box, mail-box
receptionist (hotel)	desk clerk
bonnet (of car)	hood

AN ENGLISH-AMERICAN VOCABULARY

British	American
boot (of car)	trunk
petrol	gasoline
petrol station	filling station (this is gaining in use)
paraffin	kerosene
hooter	horn
windscreen	windshield
fascia (occasional)	dashboard
saloon (car)	sedan
wing (of car)	fender
van	delivery truck
dormobile	small bus, like Volkswagen bus
estate car	station wagon
motorway	express-way
dual carriageway	four-lane highway
roundabout	traffic circle
silencer (of car)	muffler
dipped lights (car)	dimmed lights
side/running lights (car)	parking lights
flyover	overpass
bollard	traffic dividers in middle of streets
"box-junction"	junction of intersections which may not be entered unless the way ahead is clear
reverse (a car)	one reverses a car, but backs a horse
"running-in"	indicates a new car travelling at low speeds
lay-by	places where stopping is permitted on dual carriage-ways and motor-ways
near-side lane	traffic lane nearest to the curb, i.e., the left-hand lane
off/far-side lane	traffic lane nearest the center-line of the road, i.e., the right-hand lane
(arrows in the road)	mean "get in lane" and do not pass: does not mean that road curves in the direction of the arrows
L-driver	Learner-driver, carries white plate with red "L" affixed to front and rear bumper of car
ramp	hump in road
metalled surface	paved road
permanent way	roadbed
cul-de-sac	deadend
loose chippings	loose gravel on the road
call (verb)	to visit in person: it is not normally interchangeable with the verb "to telephone"; if you say "I will call", one will expect you to present yourself bodily; better use the verb "telephone" rather than the Americanism "call"
missile (pron. *miss-isle*)	refers to air propulsion, but pronunciation *miss-el* refers to missal, or prayerbook

AN ENGLISH-AMERICAN VOCABULARY

British	American
cinema	movie theater
hair-dresser (men)	barbershop
loo	toilet, polite term, slightly effete undertones but now in fairly wide use
w.c. (water-closet)	toilet
lavatory	toilet
bathroom	place where one takes a bath, usually separate room from w.c. or lavatory
spend a penny	to use the toilet
kiosk	may refer to a pay telephone, newspaper stand, cigaret stand, etc.
engaged	occupied
vacant	empty

The Mysteries of Money

British	American
penny (1d)	cent
copper (1d)	penny or cent
three-penny bit pron. *thrup'nee bit* (3d)	three-penny piece
tanner (6d)	six-penny piece
bob (1s)	one shilling: note plural, six bob (*not* six bob*s*)
florin (2s)	two-shilling piece
half-crown (2s 6d)	two-shilling & six penny piece
pound note (20s)	a one-pound "bill"
bank note	a bill
quid (20s)	a pound note
guinea (21s, gn.)	twenty-one shillings: a method of computation, no bill or coin corresponding to it
L.s.d.	pounds, shillings, pence, NOT (until recently) drugs
dollar (not used very much)	a crown (5 shillings)

Restaurants

British	American
biscuits	crackers (not sweet)
(sweet) biscuits	cookies
scones	biscuits
cakes	cookies
tarts	often used to describe what Americans would call a pie
buns	rolls
coffee	one should always specify as below:
white coffee	half milk and half coffee; "coffee with cream" almost unknown, so one should say "white coffee with just a little milk," etc.

550 AN ENGLISH-AMERICAN VOCABULARY

British	American
black coffee	one must ask specifically for black coffee for often one gets white coffee if merely "coffee" is asked for
tea	a cup of murky brown liquid with one-third cup of cold milk in the bottom of the cup
lemon tea	plain tea (without milk) served with a slice of lemon (if you are lucky): one always gets ordinary milky tea unless one specifies strenuously that one wants "lemon tea"
jelly	jello
sweet	dessert: an English dessert has aptly been described as "anything with custard poured over it"; names seldom do justice, as "blackberry fool" and "trifle" denote
sweets	candy, chocolates
salad	a salad plate, with sliced meat and salad vegetables; i.e. a chicken salad, more likely than not, will be a piece of cold chicken, sliced tomatoes, and lettuce
elevenses	morning coffee break
afternoon tea	afternoon "coffee break"
tea or high tea	evening meal (occasional)
salad cream	salad dressing
mince	ground meat, when alone, usually refers to ground beef
beetroot	beets
chicory	endives
aubergines	eggplant
lady's fingers	okra (almost unknown)
courgettes	zucchini squash
corn	grain
maize	corn: though corn-on-the-cob is used on menus
treacle	molasses
sultanas	raisins
ice(s)	ice cream
sorbet or water ices	sherbert
prawns	(large) shrimp
scampi	(small) shrimp
cantaloupe (pron. *canta-loo*)	cantaloupe
ogen melon	(similar to) cantaloupe
serviette	table napkin (serviette is a genteel-ism, and you'd be wise to say *table* napkin, but not the word napkin alone)
veg.	vegetable(s)
sippets (croutons)	toasted bread cubes for use in a soup
lollies	frozen ice-cream on a stick
mousse	frozen cream and gelatin dessert
flan	usually fruit in open sponge or pastry case

AN ENGLISH-AMERICAN VOCABULARY

Pubs

British	*American*
pub (public bar)	pub
publican	barkeeper
barman	bartender
barmaid	barmaid

Note: there is a strict caste difference here, and it is only through long acquaintance with English ways that one can ascertain the precise nuances of familiarity used for each one; it is much better to take advantage of one's special status as a tourist and not try to understand them

public bar	working-man's bar, same drinks cheaper here than in other bars
private bar	more formal bar, safe for unaccompanied ladies
saloon bar or lounge bar	both these terms more or less synonymous with private bar; accompanied ladies are often seen in public bars, because this is often where the dart board is found
a bitter	the draught beer usually drunk by Englishmen, though there is a bewildering variety to be had
"best bitter"	slightly more expensive variety of bitter, which varies from pub to pub, depending on the brand
free house	a pub not connected to a brewery chain and thus free to sell many different brands o beer; most pubs are brewery-owned and leased out to individual publicans, thus tying them to selling brands peculiar to a particular brewery company
off-license	"package shop", sells spirits for consumption away from the premises only
licensing hours	hours of opening, strictly adhered to; they vary from area to area, but roughly 11 to 3, 5 to 11, shorter hours on Sundays; and pubs are not closed on election days. See *Practical Information* sections of book.
"time, gentlemen!"	the publican's warning to drink up because it is closing time
half-of-bitter	draught beer is served in half-pint or pint glasses, and one normally asks for "a half" or a "half of bitter", or "a pint". For other varieties (brown ale, light ale, lager, stout) one does not specify the quantity, since they usually come bottled. Here one merely specifies "a brown ale" or a "pale ale".
spirits	"hard" liquor

AN ENGLISH-AMERICAN VOCABULARY

British	American
lager	American-type beer, for the unadventurous (but also Danish or German beer)
martini	sweet vermouth served alone in a glass with a piece of ice and twist of lemon
gin-and-french	a bastard cousin to the American martini, but about 1/3 vermouth to 2/3 gin: not exactly a "dry" martini
martini cocktail	same as "gin-and-french", but often refers to American martini
American martini	American martini: be sure to specify when you say "very dry" that you mean a proportion of about "eight to one," or else you will be very sadly startled
manhattan	similar to the American cocktail, but made usually with Scotch whisky and not bourbon; be sure to specify bourbon, though more often than not, it is not available
whisky	when used alone, it always refers to Scotch whisky
bottle, half-bottle	quantities of whisky or gin: the term "fifth" is unknown, though "pint" would be understood
squash	a very sweet drink made of water and lemon or orange flavouring syrup
shandy	half-beer, half ginger-ale (or lemonade), a demure lady's drink
ice	occasionally kept in a container on the bar, but one must expect to be served spirits without ice unless you specify that you want it
Scotch egg	a hard-boiled egg enclosed in sausage meat, battered and deep fried
sausage roll	sausage wrapped in a pastry covering
"half-round" or "full-round" (sandwiches)	half a sandwich is called a half-round; one asks, for instance for a half-round of cheese, and a round (or full round) of roast beef
crisps	potato chips
chips	french-fried potatoes

Clothing

vest	man's undershirt
waistcoat	man's vest
trousers	man's pants: pants never refer to outer trousers worn by gentlemen
braces	gentleman's suspenders (for trousers)
suspenders	lady's garters
leg suspenders	man's sock garters

AN ENGLISH-AMERICAN VOCABULARY

Miscellaneous

British	American
crackers	firecrackers or fireworks, especially favors used for Christmas decorations; (or) to say someone "is crackers" means they are slightly mad (crazy)
digs	student slang for rented rooms or bed-sitters
vac(s) (pron. *vak*)	student slang for vacations in general
long vacation	summer vacation (student term)
holiday	vacation
yard	any open area connected with a business: i.e. marshalling yard is where goods trains are put together
fortnight	fourteen days (2 weeks)
stone	fourteen pounds: the English do not compute weight by pounds, and often cannot immediately translate "nine stone, six and a half pounds" into pounds avoirdupois
surname	last name
Christian name	first name
verger	those rather unfriendly guardians of cathedral buildings and ancient churches, usually dressed in black gowns who tell you there is no lavatory in that village church
school	high school (never university or college)
university	loose agglomeration of (relatively) independent colleges
college	one's particular college within a university: thus one may be from Cambridge University, but also from Trinity College
Chapel	(usually) refers to a Protestant church, not the Church of England
free church	any sect (other than Roman Catholic or Orthodox) other than the Church of England, i.e. not the established or state church
infant school	primary or "grade" school
junior school	grade school
crêche	kindergarten
public school	private school
secondary modern school	state school on high school level for those who fail to pass qualifying examinations for pre-college study
grammar school	state school on high school level for those who pass qualifying examinations for pre-college study (the difference between "secondary modern" and "grammar" schools corresponds vaguely to the old American division between "commercial" and "classical" courses in high school)
council school	public school

AN ENGLISH-AMERICAN VOCABULARY

British	American
football	soccer (Association football)
rugby	closest analogy to American football
aluminium	aluminum
autumn	fall
bank holiday	legal holiday
caretaker	janitor
ex-service man	veteran
friendly society	fraternal order
pram or perambulator	baby carriage
private soldier	enlisted man
rear (verb)	raise (a family)
bylaw	ordinance
Inland Revenue	Internal Revenue
ticket-of-leave	parole
fag	1. cigarette (adopted Americanism)
	2. new student made to run errands and do chores for older students at boarding schools
chap	"fella"
mate	good friend (male speech)
bloke	"fella"
bloody	exclamation now almost completely acceptable except in the most puritanical surroundings
bleeding	exclamation with stronger overtones which has replaced the now acceptable "bloody"; not used in polite company
brolly	umbrella
loud-hailer	megaphone
cope (verb)	to manage
"not to worry"	mild reassurance
"to get (oneself or something) sorted out"	to reassess one's position, clarify things
(to be) jumped up	to be promoted from menial job to one of higher status: i.e. an interloper
taa (spoken by any waitress)	thanks
t'raa	goodbye
cheers	a toast given when lifting one's glass, or a shortened form of "goodbye"
cheerio	goodbye
to blue (verb)	to blow: i.e. advertisement, "L.E.B. offer you £5 to blue on ice lollies" (trans: "London Electricity Board will give you a £5 discount" for buying a certain appliance)
to give (one) a lift	to give a person a ride
to lift (something)	to steal
Take Courage!	an exhortation to buy a particular brand of beer, not a word of encouragement from Big Brother

INDEX

In the following index, H means *Hotel* listings and R means *Restaurant* listings.

Aberdeen, HR458, 486
Aberdovey, H426, 441
Aberfeldy, HR459
Aberfoyle, HR459
Abergavenny, H426, R429
Aberystwyth, H426, 439-40
Abingdon, HR252, 268
Aboyne, HR459
Acharacle, HR459
Aghadowey, HR532
Alcester, HR348
Aldeburgh, HR332, 341-2
Alderney, HR521, 523
Alford, HR459
Ambleside, HR408, 410-11
Amersham, HR252, 276
Amesbury, HR279
Anglesey, 444-5
Antrim, HR532
Appleby, 403
Applecross, HR459
Arbroath, HR459, 484
Ardblair, 477
Arisaig, HR460
Armagh, HR532, 543
Arran, Isle of, HR460
Ascot, H233
Ascott, 254
Ashbourne, HR380, 388
Ashby-de-la-Zouch, 367-8
Ashford, HR279, 291
Aston Clinton, H252
Avebury, HR279
Aviemore, HR460
Aylesbury, HR252, 275
Ayr, HR460, 492

Bakewell, HR380, 391
Bala, H426
Ballater, HR460
Ballycastle, 530, HR532, 539
Ballygally, HR532
Ballymena, 540
Banbury, HR252
Banchory, HR461
Bangor (Wales), H427, 445
Bangor (N. Ireland), HR532, 541
Barford, HR348
Barkham, 269-70
Barmouth, H427, 441-2
Barrow-in-Furness, 416
Bateman's, 283
Bath, H309, R311, 313-4
Battle, 294
Beaconsfield, 274
Beaulieu, 302
Beaumaris, H427, 445
Belfast, 530, HR532, 536-8, map 537
Berwick-on-Tweed, HR380, 400
Bessbrook, 543-4
Bettyhill, HR461
Betwys-y-Coed, H427, 446
Beverley, 398
Bexhill-on-Sea, HR279, 294-5
Bibury, H252
Biddenden, 292
Birmingham, HR356, 361-2
Blackpool, HR384, 405
Bladon, 261

Blair Atholl, HR461
Blakeney, HR332, 336
Blandford Forum, H309
Bletchingley, H233
Bodmin, 329
Bognor Regis, HR279, 296
Boarstall, 276
Boat of Garten, HR461
Bonar Bridge, HR461
Boston, HR356, 371-2
Bouley Bay, HR520
Bournemouth, HR279, 301
Bourton-on-the Water, HR252, 258
Bowness, 410-11
Box Hill, H233, 249
Bradford, HR380, 394
Braemar, HR461, 490
Braintree, HR332, 339
Brampton, HR356
Brantwood, 411
Bray, 271
Brecon, HR427
Bridge of Allan, HR461
Bridlington, HR384, 398
Brighton, HR279, 295
Bristol, H309, R311, 314-5
Broadstairs, HR279, 293
Broadway, HR252
Brora, HR461
Bryn-Eglwys, 448
Buckingham, 276
Bucklers Hard, 302
Bude, H308
Builth Wells, H427
Burford, HR252, 260

INDEX

Burghfield, HR252
Burnham-on-Crouch, HR332
Bury St. Edmunds, HR332, 340-1
Bute, Isle of, HR461
Buttermere, HR408
Buxton, HR380-1, 391

Caernarvon, H427, 445
Caerphilly, 434
Callander, HR461-2
Cambridge, HR332, 334, 343-5, map 343
Canterbury, HR279-80, 289-90
Cardiff, H427, R429, 432, 433-4, map 433
Cardigan, H427
Carlisle, HR381, 402-3
Carmarthen, H427, R429, 435-6
Carnoustie, HR462
Carrbridge, HR462
Carrickfergus, HR532, 538
Carter Bar, 481
Castle Combe, HR280, 305, 314
Castle Douglas, HR462
Castleton, HR381
Castletown, H418, 422
Castlewood, 534, 542
Catterick, HR381
Chagford, H309-10
Cheddar, H310
Cheltenham, HR252, 257
Chepstow, H427
Chertsey, H233
Chester, HR381, 406
Chichester, HR280, 296
Chiddingfold, 299
Chigwell, R235
Chilham, HR280, 291
Chippenham, 305
Chipping Campden, HR252, 257-8

Chipping Norton, HR252
Christchurch, H280
Church Stretton, HR356
Cirencester, HR252
Cleethorpes, HR359
Cliftonville, HR280
Clitheroe, 404-5
Clovelly, H308, 327
Clun, 377
Clunbury, 377
Clungunford, 377
Clunton, 377
Cockenzie, 509
Cockermouth, HR408, 414-5
Colchester, HR332, 335
Coleraine, HR532, 540
Comrie, HR462
Coniston, HR408, 411
Conway, H427, 446-7
Corby, HR356
Coventry, HR356, 362-3
Craigavon, 543
Crail, HR462
Craven Arms, HR356, 377
Crawley, H233
Crawfordsburn, HR532
Creech Grange, 312
Criccieth, H427, 443
Cricklade, 255
Cromarty, HR462
Cromer, HR332
Croydon, H233
Cullen, HR462
Culloden, 494-5
Cullybackey, 540
Culross, HR462
Culzean, 492
Cumbernauld, H462
Cushendall, HR532
Cushendun, HR532

Darlington, HR381, 397

Dartmouth, H308, R311, 324-5
Deal, HR280, 292
Dedham, HR332
Derby, HR356, 368, 375
Derwent Water, 413
Devil's Bridge, H427, 440
Dirleton, HR462
Dolgellau, HR427, 442
Dorchester, H310, 319
Dorking, H233, R235 249
Dornoch, HR463
Douglas, H418, 419-20
Donaghadee, HR532
Dover, HR280, 292
Drakes Broughton, HR252
Dulwich Village, 246
Dumfries, HR463
Dunadry, HR533
Dunbar, HR463, 509
Dundee, HR463, 484
Dunfermline, HR463, 482
Dungeness, 292
Dunkeld, HR463-4, 485
Dunluce, 539
Dunnet, HR464
Dunoon, HR464
Duns, HR464
Dunster, H310, 316-7
Duntreath, 517
Durham, HR381, 401
Dymchurch, HR280, 292

Eastbourne, HR280, 295
East Kilbride, H464
East Linton, 509
Edinburgh, 496ff, H497, R498, Festival 500, Museums 502, map 504-5
Edington, 306

INDEX

Egham, H233, R235 240
Elgin, HR464, 487
Elie, HR464
Ely, HR332, 345
Enniskillen, HR533, 544
Epping, H233
Epsom, H233, R235, 248
Eskdale, HR408
Eton, 273-4
Exeter, H310, 322-23
Exmoor, 316

Fairford, 258
Falkirk, HR464
Falmouth, H308
Fakenham, HR332
Farnham, 298
Felixstowe, HR332, 341
Findhorn, HR464
Finchingfield, 339
Fishguard, H427, R429, 438
Folkestone, HR280, 292
Fortingall, HR464
Fortrose, HR464
Fort William, HR464, 493-4
Fowey, H308, R311
Framlingham, HR332
Fressingfield, HR332
Frome, H310

Gairloch, HR465
Galashiels, H465
Garve, HR465
Gawsworth, 406
Glamis, HR465
Glasgow, 510ff, H511, R512, Nightlife 513, Museums, 514
Glastonbury, H310, 315-6
Glencoe, 493-4
Gleneagles, HR465
Glenfinnan, 494
Glenrothes, 483

Glenshee, HR465
Gloucester, HR253, 256-7
Godalming, HR280, 298
Godstone, H233
Gordonstoun, 487
Goudhurst, HR280
Gourock, HR465
Grantham, HR356-7, 370
Grantown-on-Spey, HR465-6
Grasmere, HR408, 412
Gravesend, H233, 243
Great Malvern, HR357
Great Yarmouth, HR333
Gretna Green, HR466, 493
Guernsey, HR520-1, 522-3
Guildford, R235, HR281, 297-8
Gullane, HR466

Haddington, 509
Hadley Wood, H233
Hambledon, 273, 300
Hampton Court, H233, 240
Hampton Wick, R235
Harlech, H427
Harlow, HR333
Harris, Isle of, HR466
Harrowgate, HR381, 395-6
Harrow-on-the-Hill, H234, 245-6
Harwich, HR333
Hastings, HR281, 294
Haverfordwest, H427-8, R429, 438
Haverhill, 340
Hawick, HR466
Hawkshead, 411
Haworth, 393
Hayes, H234
Helensburgh, HR466
Hemel Hempstead, H234

Henley-on-Thames, 270-71
Hereford, HR357, **378**
Herm, HR521, 523
Hexham, HR381-82
High Wycombe, 274-5
Hillsborough, 543
Hindhead, HR281
Hingham, 338
Holyhead, 444
Horncastle, HR357, 372-3
Horton-cum-Studley, H253
Howgate, 481
Huddersfield, HR382
Hull, HR382, 398
Hunstanton, HR333
Hythe, HR281

Ilfracombe, H308, 325-6
Ilmington, HR348
Ilminster, H310
Immingham, 373
Inchnadamph, HR466
Inveraray, HR466
Inverness, HR466-7, 495
Iona, Island of, HR467, 491
Ipswich, HR333, **340**
Islay, Isle of, HR467, 491

Jedburgh, HR467
Jersey, Isle of, HR520, 521-2
Jethou, 523
John O'Groats, HR467, 488
Jordans, 274

Kelso, HR467
Kendal, HR408, 410
Kenilworth, HR348, 354
Keswick, HR408, **413**
Kettering, HR357, 364-5
Kilkeel, HR533

INDEX

Killadeas, HR535
Killin, HR467
Kilnsey, 395
Kilroot, 538
Kingsgate, 293
King's Lynn, HR333, 336
Kinross, HR467
Kirkby, HR382
Kirkby Stephen, 403
Kirkcudbright. HR467
Kirkwall, HR467-8, 489
Kirriemuir, HR468, 484
Knaresborough, 396
Knutsford, HR382
Kyle of Lochalsh, HR468, 490

Lacock, HR281, 305
La Corbiere, HR520
Ladybank, H468
Lairg, HR468, 489
Lamphey, 438
Lancaster, HR382, 404
Lauder, 455
Langharne, 437
Langholm, 455
Largo, 483
Largs, HR468
Larne, HR533, 539
Lasswade, 509
Lavenham, HR333, 342
Laxey, 421-2
Leamington Spa, HR348, 354
Leatherhead, H234, 249
Lechlade, R253, 256
Leeds, HR382, 394
Leicester, HR357, 366
Leominster, HR357
Lerwick, HR468, 488
Letchworth, H234
Lewes, 295-6
Lewis, Isle of, HR473
Lichfield, HR357, 376

Limavady, 540
Lincoln, HR357, 373
Linlithgow, HR468
Liphook, HR281
Littlestone, 292
Little Washbourne, HR253
Liverpool, HR382, 405-6
Llanarmon Dyffryn Ceiriog, R429
Llanberis, H428
Llandrindrod Wells, H428, 440-1
Llandudno, H428, 446
Llangadog, R429
Llangammarch Wells, 440
Llangollen, H428, R429, 447-8
Llangurig, R429
Llanhamlach, R430
Llanrhidian, 435
Llanrwst, R430, 446-7
Llanwrtyd Wells, 440
Lochinver, HR468
Loch Lomond, HR468
Loch Torriedon, HR468
London, H136, R166, Museums 153, Nightlife 179, Shopping 184, Other Practical Information 133ff, Exploring 196 ff.
Londonderry, HR533, 541
Long Melford, H333
Looe, H308
Lossiemouth, HR468-9 487
Loughborough, HR357, 368
Louth, 373
Lowestoft, HR333, 341
Ludlow, HR357, 377-8
Lullington, 296
Lundin Links, HR469

Lurgan, 543
Lydford, R311
Lyme Regis, H308
Lyndhurst, HR281, 302
Lynmouth, H308, 326
Lynton, H308, 326

Machynlleth, H428
Maidenhead, HR253, 271
Maidstone, HR281
Mallaig, HR469
Malvern, HR253
Manchester, HR382, 393
Manorbier, 438
Mansfield, HR357, 374
Margate, 293
Market Harborough, HR357, 365-6
Marlow, HR253
Marlow Lock, 273
Matlock, HR383
Max Gate, 319
Melrose, 455
Mere, HR281
Mevagissey, H308
Middleham, 396
Middlesborough, HR383
Midhurst, HR281, 296
Milford Haven, 438
Minehead, 317
Moffat, HR469
Monk Fryston, HR383
Monmouth, H428
Morecambe, HR384, 404
Moreton Hampstead H310
Moreton-in-Marsh, HR253, 258
Mountstewart, 542
Mousehole, 329
Mull, Isle of, H469
Musselburgh, 509

Nairn, HR469
Nether Wallop, 300

INDEX

Nethybridge, HR469
Nevern, R430
Nevin, 443-4
Newark-on-Trent, HR357-8, 369-70
Newbury, HR253, 269
Newby Bridge, HR409
Newcastle (N. Ireland), HR533
Newcastle-upon-Tyne, HR383, 399
Newenden, HR281
Newmarket, HR333, 342
Newport, H428 R430
Newquay, H308-9, 328
Newry, HR533
Newtonmore, HR469
Newtown Linford, 366
Northampton, HR358, 364
North Berwick, HR470
Norwich, HR333, 335, 337-8
Nottingham, HR358, 368-9, 373

Oakham, HR358, 365
Oban, HR470
Old Cleeve, 316
Olney, 272
Omagh, HR533
Otterburn, HR383
Oxford, HR253, 261-7, map 265
Oxted, H234, R235

Paignton, H309
Pant-Mawr, R430
Parkeston, HR333
Paycocke's, 334
Peebles, HR470
Peel, 420-21
Pembroke, H428, 438
Penicuick, 508
Penmaenpool, R430
Penn, 273
Penrhyndeudraeth, R430
Penrith, HR409
Penzance, H309, 329

Perth, HR470, 484
Peterhead, 487
Petit Bot, HR521
Petworth, HR281, 296
Pewsey, 305
Pitlochry, HR471, 485
Plas Newydd, 430
Plockton, HR471
Plymouth, H309, R311, 324
Polesden Lacey, 283
Polperro, H309
Pontesbury, 376-7
Poole, 318
Poolewe, HR471
Porlock, 317
Portadown, HR533, 543
Portaferry, HR533
Portballintrae, HR533
Portelet Bay, HR520
Port Erin, H418, 422
Porthcawl, H428
Porthcurno, 329
Portloe, R311
Port Logan, 492
Portmadoc, H428
Portmeirion, 426
Portobello, 501
Portpatrick, HR471
Portrush, HR533, 539-40
Port St. Mary, H418, 422
Portsmouth, 300
Portstewart, HR533, 540
Preston, 405
Prestwick, HR471
Priddy, R311
Pwllheli, H428, 443

Quinton, HR253 and 348

Ramsey, H418, 421
Ramsgate, 293
Ravenglass, 415
Reigate, H234
Rhayader, 441
Rhyl, 447

Richmond (Surrey), H234, R235, 237
Richmond (Yorks), HR383, 396-7
Ripon, HR383, 396
Rochester, HR281, 293
Roehampton, H234
Romsey, 300
Rosemarkie, HR471-2
Rostrevor, HR533
Rothley, HR358
Rowsley, HR383, 390
Ruthin, R430
Rydal, HR409
Rye, HR281, 294

Saffron Walden, HR333, 339
St. Albans, H234, 245
St. Andrews, HR472, 483
St. Aubin, HR520
St. Bees, HR409
St. Brelade's Bay, HR520
St. David's, H428, 438-9
St. Helier, HR520, 521-2
St. Ives, H309, R311, 328
St. Leonards, HR281
St. Martins, HR521
St. Mawes, H309
St. Peter Port, HR520-1, 522-3
Salcombe, H309, R311, 323-4
Salisbury, HR281, 304
Sanderstead, H234
Sandwich, 292-3
Sark, HR521, 523
Saul, 542
Scarborough, HR384-5 398
Scilly, Isles of, H310, 330
Scone, 484
Scrivelsby, 372

INDEX

Seaford, H281
Seascale, HR409
Sevenoaks, H234, 247
Shaftesbury, H310
Sheffield, HR383, 390-1
Shepperton, H234
Shrewsbury, HR358, 376
Sidmouth, H309, R311
Silbury Hill, 305
Sissinghurst, 291-2
Skegness, HR359
Skye, Isle of, HR472, 490
Sonning, 270
Southampton, HR282, 300
South Mimms, H234
Southport, HR385, 405
Southsea, HR281-2
Southwell, HR358, 369
Spalding, HR358, 371-2
Springhill, 534
Stafford, HR358
Staines, H234
Stanton Drew, 316
Stepps, HR472
Stirling, HR472-3, 516-7
Stockbridge, 300
Stoke Mandeville, 275
Stoke Poges, 272-3
Stokesay, 360
Stonehenge, 304-5
Stornoway, 473
Stourhead, 284
Stowe, 275
Stow-on-the-Wold, HR253, 258
Strabane, HR533
Strangford, 542
Stranraer, HR473
Stratford-upon-Avon, 346-52, HR348, map 351
Strathblane, 517
Strathpeffer, HR473
Strathyre, 517
Studley, HR348

Sulgrave Manor 364
Sunderland, HR383
Sunningdale, H234
Swanage, H309
Swanbridge, R430
Swansea, H428-9, 434

Tarbert, HR473
Taunton, H310, 316
Tavistock, H310, R311
Tenby, H429, 437
Tewkesbury, HR253
Thaxted, HR333, 339
Thetford, H333, 338
Thurso, HR473
Tintern, H429
Tiverton, H310
Tobermory, HR473
Tobermory Bay, 491
Torcross, 324
Torquay, H309, R311
Torver, HR409
Totnes, H310, 324
Towcester, HR358
Tremadoc, 443
Troon, HR473-4
Troutbeck, HR409
Truro, H310, R311
Tunbridge Wells, HR281, 291
Turnberry, HR474
Tynemouth, 399
Tyn y Maes, H429

Uffington, 267
Ullapool, HR474
Ullswater, HR409
Uppingham, 365

Walton-on-Tham H234
Wanborough, 305
Wareham, H309
Warton, 404
Warwick, HR348, 352-3
Washington, 401
Watford, H234, 245
Wells, HR310, 315
Westbury, 305-6
Westerham H234 R235, 248

Westgate, 293
Weston-on-the-Green, HR254
Weston-super-Mare, HR309, 317
West Stoke, HR282
Weybridge, H234
Whitby, HR385, 398-9
Whitehaven, HR409
Whitstable, 293
Wick, HR474
Wight, Isle of, HR288, 302-4
Wigtown, HR474
Wilmcote, 352
Wimbourne Minster, H310, 320
Winchcombe, HR253-4
Winchelsea, 294
Winchester, HR282, 300-301
Windermere, H409, 410
Windsor, H234, R235, 272
Witney, 261
Wolverhampton, HR358
Woodbridge, HR333
Woodhall Spa, HR358, 372
Woodstock, HR254, 261
Wootton, 299
Worcester, HR358, 378
Worksop, HR359
Worthing, HR282
Wrexham, H429, 448
Wye, HR282
Wymondham, 338

Yarrow, HR474
Yealand Conyers, 404
Yealand Redmayne, 404
Yetholm, HR474
York, HR384, 397-8, map 397

(90)

UNITED KINGDOM

(Royaume Uni - Gran Bretaña - Vereinigtes Königreich - Gran Bretagna)

LEGEND – LÉGENDE – LEYENDA – ZEICHENERKLÄRUNG – LEGGENDA

Express highway
Autoroute
Autopista
Autobahn
Autostrada

Main road
Route principale
Carretera principal
Hauptstrasse
Strada principale

Other roads
Autres routes
Otras carreteras
Sonstige Strassen
Altre strade

Distance in miles
Distance en milles
Distancia en millas
Entfernung in Meilen
Distanza in miglia

Railway
Chemin de fer
Ferrocarril
Eisenbahn
Ferrovia

National frontier
Frontière nationale
Frontera de estado
Staatsgrenze
Confine di stato

Regional boundary
Limite régionale
Límite regional
Landesgrenze
Confine di regione

Car-ferry
Bac pour autos
Transbord. p. coches
Autofähre
Chiatta per automobili

Major city
Grande ville
Ciudad grande
Grosstadt
Città grande

Other localities
Autres localités
Otras poblaciones
Andere Orte
Altre località

Airport
Aéroport
Aeropuerto
Flugplatz
Aeroporto

Pass
Col
Puerto
Pass
Passo

Peak
Pic
Pico
Bergspitze
Picco

Castle
Château
Castillo
Schloss
Castello

1 mile = 1.6 km
1 km = 0.625 mile

CONTENTS – SOMMAIRE – ÍNDICE – INHALT – SOMMARIO

② ③ Outline map - Carte de contours
Mapa general - Übersichtskarte
Carta sinottica

④ LONDON

⑤ THAMES VALLEY
London, Oxford, Stratford-on-Avon

⑥ ⑦ SOUTHERN ENGLAND
London, Birmingham, Bristol, Dover

⑧ WALES, DEVON
Manchester, Swansea, Exeter

⑨ CORNWALL, CHANNEL ISLANDS
Torquay, Plymouth, Guernsey

⑩ ⑪ NORTHERN ENGLAND
Newcastle, Liverpool, Manchester, Hull

⑫ ⑬ SCOTLAND, SHETLAND IS.
Edinburgh, Glasgow, Hebrides

⑭ ⑮ NORTHERN IRELAND, IRISH REP.
Belfast, Dublin, Cork

⑯ IRISH SEA
Belfast, Dublin, Liverpool, Isle of Man

Specially prepared for Fodor's Modern Guides by Cartografisch Instituut Bootsma, and printed in the Netherlands by Mouton & Co., The Hague.

Aberdeen

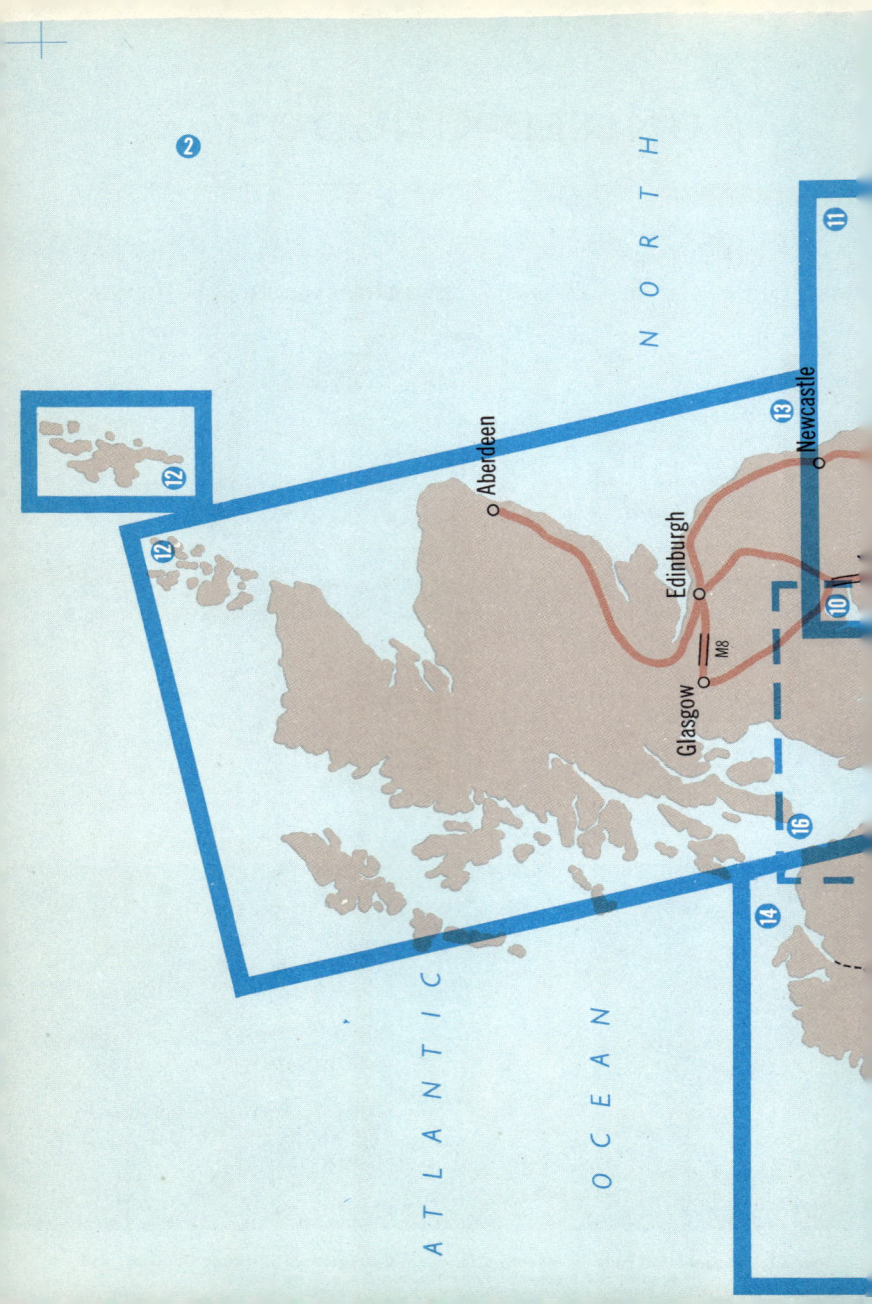

Edinburgh

M8

Glasgow

Newcastle

NORTH

ATLANTIC OCEAN

Motorway

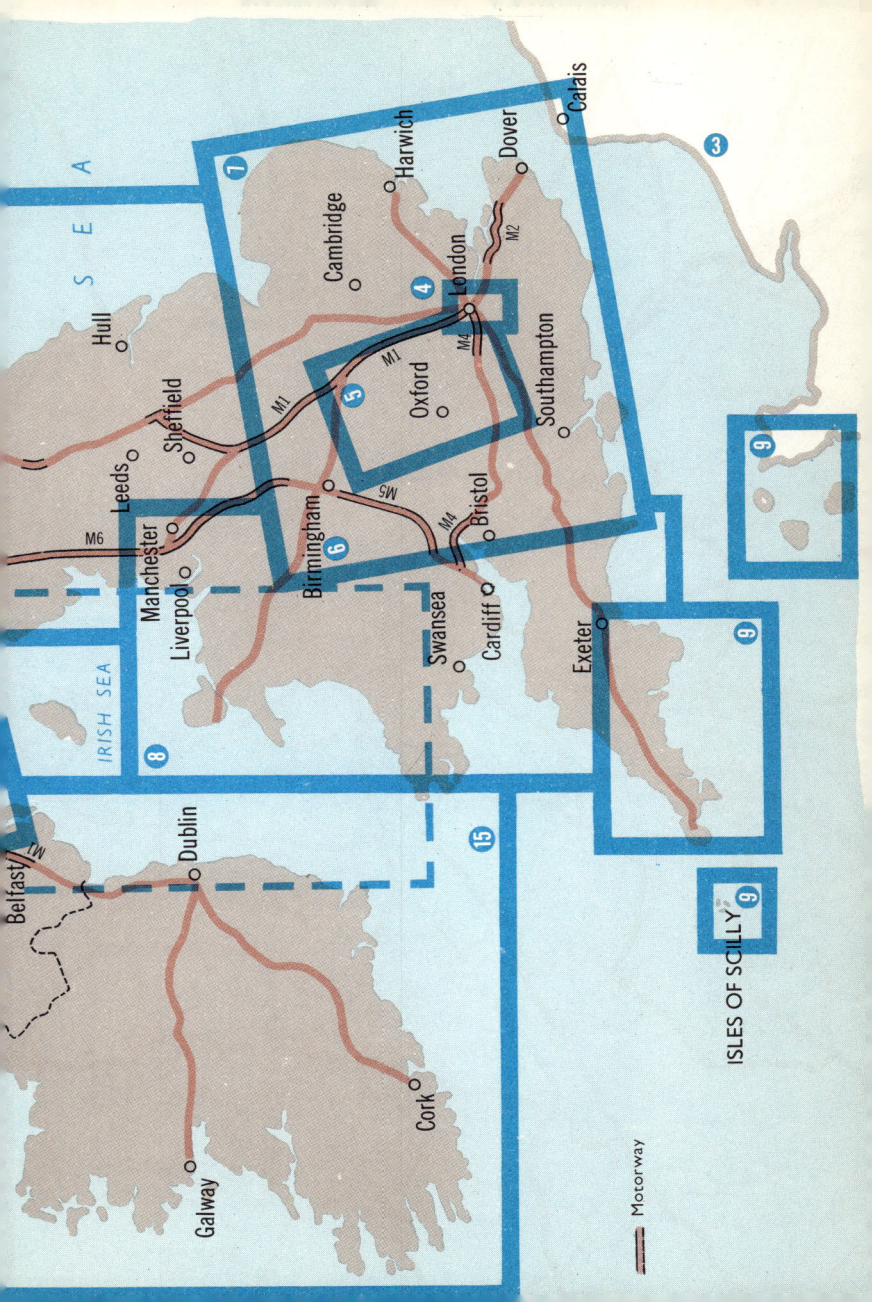

4
Potters Bar
Waltham Cross
A 1
A 5
Barnet
East Barnet
Lough
M1
7
Southgate
CIRCULAR
Edmonton
Chingford
Buckhurst H
ROAD
Edgware
A 1
Wood Green
Tottenham
Woodford
Hendon
Harrow
NORTH
Finchley
Hornsey
Walthamstow
Wanstead
Highgate
Wembley
Leyton
Hampstead
Islington
Stoke Newington
Willesden
A 1
Hackney
WESTERN AVENUE
A 5
St. Pancras
Finsbury
Bethnal Green
East Ham
Marylebone
Ealing
Paddington
St. Paul's
Acton
West Ham
WESTMINSTER ABBEY
Poplar
Kensington
THE TOWER
Thames
M4
Brentford
Hammersmith
BUCKINGHAM PALACE
WEST ROAD
A 4
GREAT
A 30
Chiswick
L O N D O N
Woolwich
Greenwich
A 2
Deptford
Chelsea
Lambeth
Thames
Fulham
Battersea
Barnes
Camberwell
Kew
SOUTH
Putney
Richmond
ROAD
Blackheath
Twickenham
A 3
Wandsworth
CIRCULAR
Lewisham
Dulwich
Wimbledon
A 3
CRYSTAL PALACE
Mitcham
Kingston
Merton
Brom
Hampton Court
A 3
Malden
Beckenham
Beddington
Surbiton
Morden
Carshalton
Croydon
Esher
Wallington
Ewell
Cheam
Chessington
Sutton
Epsom
Purley
Sanderstead
Banstead
Coulsdon
Warlingham
10 km

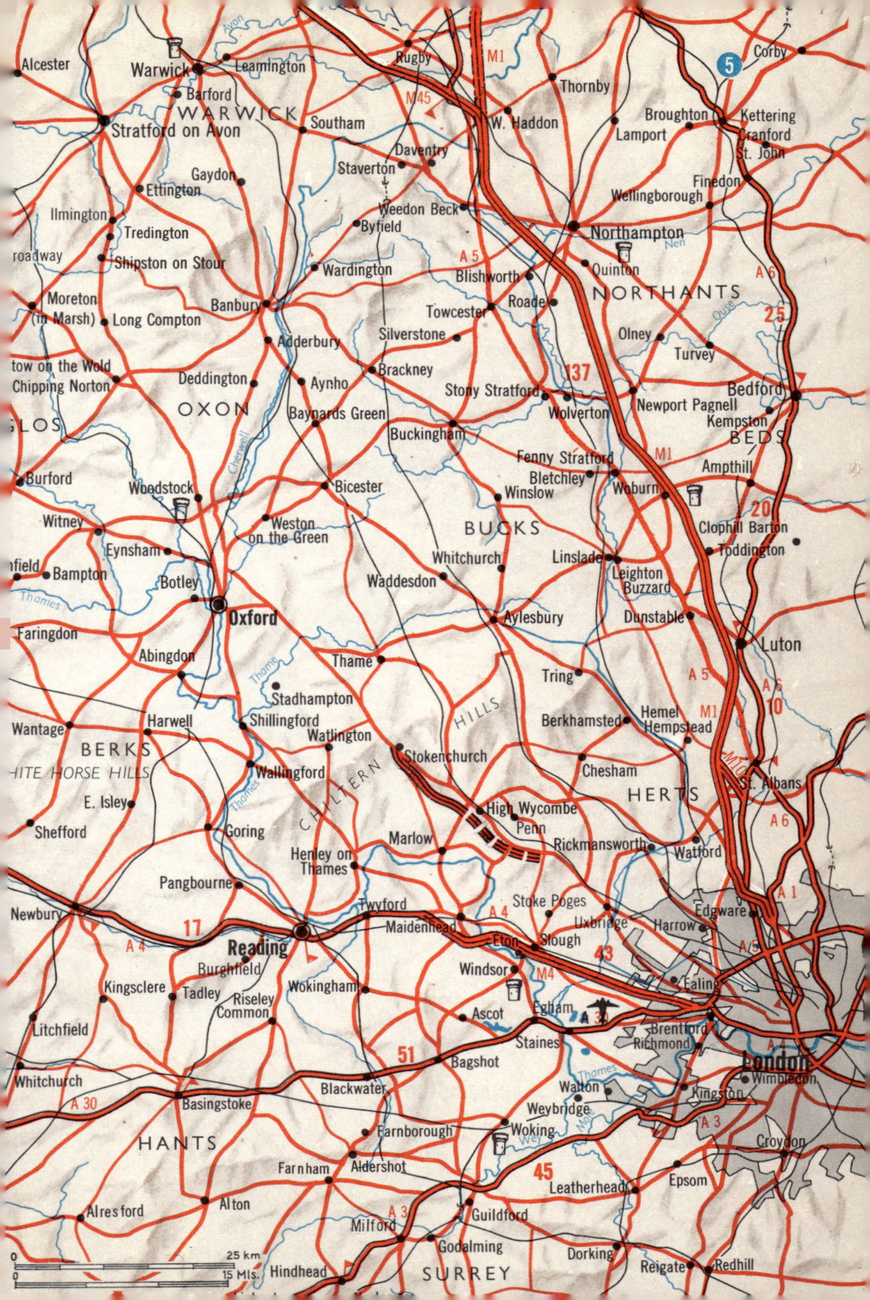

Alcester
Warwick
Avon
Leamington
Rugby
M1
Corby
5
Barford
WARWICK
M45
Thornby
Broughton
Kettering
Stratford on Avon
Southam
W. Haddon
Lamport
Cranford
St. John
Daventry
Staverton
Gaydon
Ettington
Finedon
Wellingborough
Weedon Beck
Byfield
Ilmington
Tredington
Northampton
Nen
Shipston on Stour
A 5
Quinton
Wardington
Blishworth
A 6
NORTHANTS
Moreton (in Marsh)
Banbury
Towcester
Roade
Long Compton
Ouse
25
Adderbury
Silverstone
Olney
Turvey
tow on the Wold
Brackney
Deddington
Aynho
137
Chipping Norton
Stony Stratford
Bedford
Wolverton
Newport Pagnell
OXON
Baynards Green
Kempston
GLOS
Buckingham
BEDS
Cherwell
Fenny Stratford
M1
Ampthill
Burford
Woodstock
Bicester
Bletchley
Woburn
Winslow
Witney
Weston on the Green
20
Clophill Barton
BUCKS
Eynsham
Toddington
nfield
Bampton
Whitchurch
Linslade
Leighton Buzzard
Waddesdon
Botley
Thames
Oxford
Aylesbury
Dunstable
Faringdon
Luton
Abingdon
Thame
Tring
A 5
Thame
A 6
Stadhampton
HILLS
Berkhamsted
Hemel Hempstead
M1
10
Wantage
Harwell
Shillingford
Watlington
Stokenchurch
M10
BERKS
Chesham
St. Albans
HITE HORSE HILLS
Wallingford
CHILTERN
HERTS
E. Isley
Thames
High Wycombe
Penn
A 6
Shefford
Goring
Marlow
Rickmansworth
Watford
Henley on Thames
Pangbourne
Stoke Poges
A 1
Newbury
Twyford
A 4
Edgware
Uxbridge
Harrow
17
Maidenhead
A 4
Reading
Eton
Slough
43
A 5
Burghfield
Windsor
M4
Ealing
Kingsclere
Tadley
Riseley Common
Wokingham
Litchfield
Ascot
Egham
A 30
Brentford
Richmond
Staines
51
Bagshot
London
Whitchurch
Thames
Wimbledon
Blackwater
Walton
A 30
Basingstoke
Kingston
Weybridge
Mole
A 3
Farnborough
Woking
Wey
Croydon
HANTS
Farnham
Aldershot
45
Epsom
Leatherhead
Alton
Alresford
A 3
Guildford
Milford
Godalming
Dorking
25 km
15 Mls.
Hindhead
SURREY
Reigate
Redhill

6
Shrewsbury
20
Stafford
30
Derby
Nottingham
Long Eaton
Newport
Burton upon Trent
Trent
Pontesbury
Wellington
SALOP
A 5
Lichfield
Ashby de la Zouch
Loghbourough
Melton Mowb
Church Stretton
Much Wenlock
Bridgnorth
Walsall
W. Bromwich
Tamworth
A6
LEICS
Wolverhampton
55
M1
Leicester
Oakham
Birmingham
Billesdon
Uppingha
Craven Arms
Dudley
Severn
53
M6
A 5
Market Harborough
Ludlow
Kidderminster
M5
Lutterworth
Coventry
109
Rugby
Co
Ketteri
WORCS
Droitwich
Kenilworth
A6
Leominster
Warwick
Leamington
37
M45
HEREFORD
Worcester
NORTHANT
MALVERN HILLS
Alcester
WARWICK
Stratford on Avon
Daventry
Southam
Wellingborough
Rushden
Hereford
Great Malvern
85
Chipping Campden
Weedon Beck
Northampton
Ledbury
Evesham
Shipston
Olney
Ouse
Towcester
Broadway
M1
M50
Tewkesbury
Long Compton
Newport Pagnell
Ross
Winchcomb
Moreton
Banbury
Wolverton
MONMOUTH
Chipping Norton
Brackley
137
34
Cheltenham
Monmouth
Gloucester
Stow
Buckingham
Bletchley
OXON
GLOS
Woburn
M5
Lydney
Charlbury
Bicester
Leighton Buzzard
Stroud
Burford
Woodstock
Wye
Severn
Chepstow
COTSWOLD HILLS
Witney
Dunstable
Nailsworth
Cirencester
Oxford
Aylesbury
M4
Fairford
Tetbury
Cricklade
Thame
CHILTERN HILLS
Avonmouth
Malmesbury
Amersham
Faringdon
Abingdon
Watford
Castle Combe
Swindon
Wallingford
M4
Wantage
Bristol
Bath
Chippenham
High Wycombe
Thames
Uxbridge
BERKS
Avebury
13
Henley on Thames
Maidenhead
M4
A 4
Hungerford
43
Slough
Marlborough
Avon
Windsor
Devizes
Newbury
Reading
Ascot
Staines
Radstock
Trowbridge
Pewsey
Barkham
Shepton Mallet
SALISBURY PLAIN
Litchfield
Bagshot
Weybridge
Frome
Warminster
A 30
Woking
Whitchurh
Camberley
Deptford
Bruton
Aldershot
Leatherhea
Amesbury
Andover
Basingstoke
Mere
Farnham
115
Wincanton
Dorkir
WILTS
Wilton
Guildford
Salisbury
Alton
HANTS
Godalming
Hindhead
A 30
Shaftesbury
Winchester
SURREY
Sherborne
Liphook
Romsey
Haslemere
Petersfield
Southampton
77
Horsham
Blandford
NEW FOREST
DORSET
Lyndhurst
Midhurst
Petworth
Wimborne M.
Stour
A 3
Fareham
SU
Ringwood
Beaulieu
SOUTH DOWNS
Bere Regis
Poole
Cristchurch
Arun
Dorchester
Frome
Lymington
Gosport
Southsea
Chichester
THE SOLENT
Cowes
Warehan
Bournemouth
Portsmouth
Weymouth
Corfe
Ryde
Bognor Regis
Worthing
Yarmouth
Newport
THE NEEDLES
Portland
Swanage
Sandown
ISLE OF WIGHT
PORTLAND BILL
ST. ALBANS HD.
Shanklin

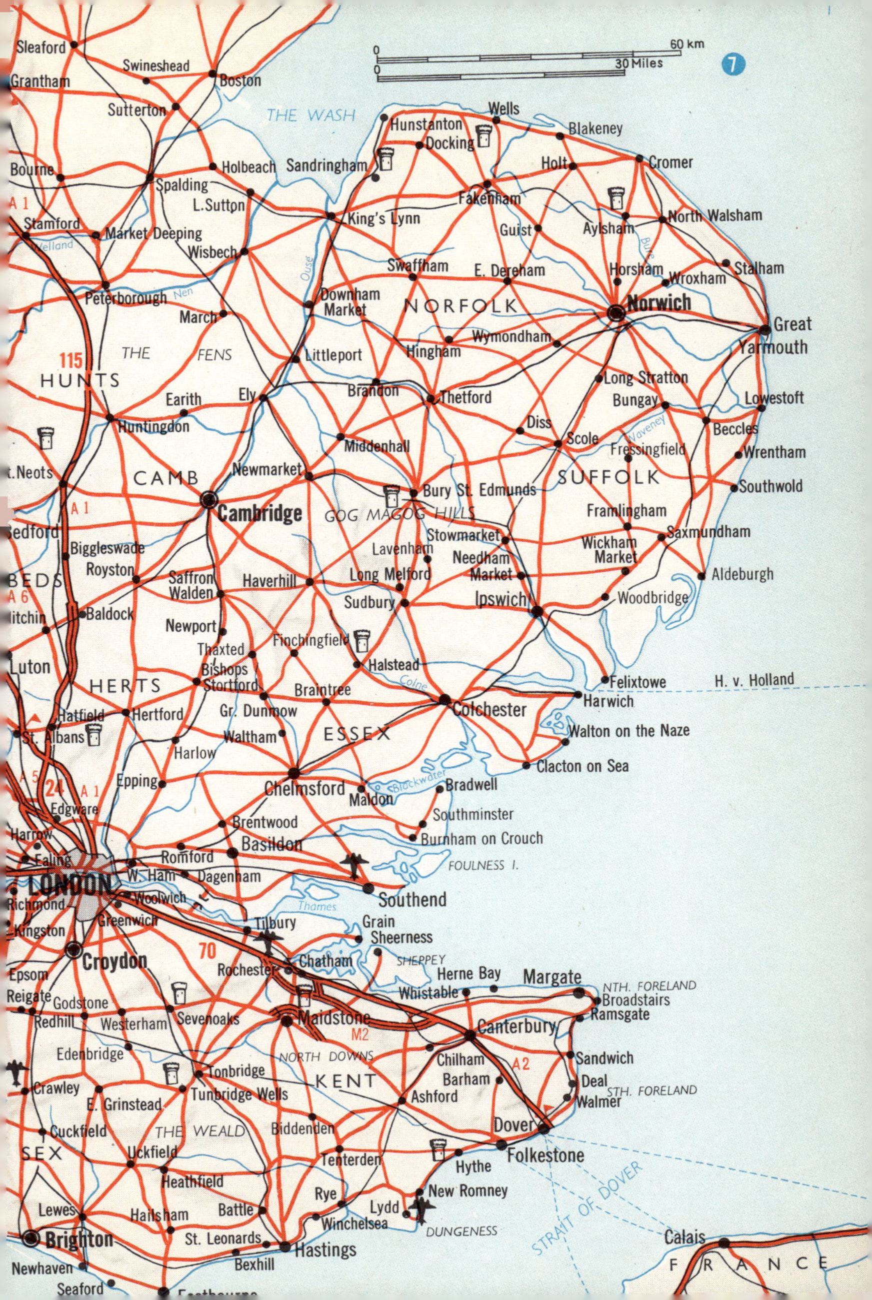

60 km
30 Miles
7
Sleaford
Grantham
Swineshead
Boston
Sutterton
THE WASH
Hunstanton
Wells
Blakeney
Docking
Bourne
Holbeach
Sandringham
Holt
Cromer
Spalding
L.Sutton
Fakenham
A 1
Stamford
King's Lynn
Guist
Aylsham
North Walsham
Market Deeping
Welland
Wisbech
Swaffham
E. Dereham
Horsham
Bure
Stalham
Ouse
Wroxham
Peterborough
Nen
Downham Market
NORFOLK
Norwich
Great Yarmouth
March
Wymondham
115
THE
FENS
Littleport
Hingham
HUNTS
Long Stratton
Brandon
Thetford
Lowestoft
Earith
Ely
Bungay
Huntingdon
Diss
Beccles
Waveney
Scole
Middenhall
Fressingfield
Wrentham
Newmarket
CAMB
SUFFOLK
Southwold
Bury St. Edmunds
A 1
Cambridge
GOG MAGOG HILLS
Framlingham
Stowmarket
Saxmundham
Bedford
Lavenham
Wickham Market
Biggleswade
Royston
Needham Market
Long Melford
Aldeburgh
BEDS
Saffron Walden
Haverhill
Sudbury
A 6
Ipswich
Woodbridge
Hitchin
Baldock
Newport
Finchingfield
Thaxted
Halstead
Luton
Bishops Stortford
Felixtowe
H. v. Holland
HERTS
Braintree
Colne
Harwich
Hatfield
Hertford
Gr. Dunmow
Colchester
St. Albans
Walton on the Naze
Waltham
ESSEX
Harlow
Clacton on Sea
A 5
A 1
24
Epping
Chelmsford
Blackwater
Bradwell
Maldon
Edgware
Southminster
Brentwood
Harrow
Burnham on Crouch
Basildon
Romford
Ealing
FOULNESS I.
W. Ham
Dagenham
LONDON
Richmond
Woolwich
Southend
Thames
Greenwich
Tilbury
Grain
Kingston
Sheerness
70
Croydon
SHEPPEY
Chatham
Rochester
Epsom
Herne Bay
Margate
NTH. FORELAND
Reigate
Godstone
Whistable
Broadstairs
Redhill
Westerham
Sevenoaks
Maidstone
Ramsgate
Canterbury
M2
Edenbridge
NORTH DOWNS
Chilham
Sandwich
A2
Tonbridge
Barham
Crawley
KENT
Deal
Tunbridge Wells
Ashford
STH. FORELAND
E. Grinstead
Walmer
Cuckfield
THE WEALD
Biddenden
Dover
SEX
Tenterden
Folkestone
Uckfield
Hythe
Heathfield
New Romney
Rye
STRAIT OF DOVER
Lewes
Battle
Lydd
Hailsham
Winchelsea
DUNGENESS
Calais
Brighton
St. Leonards
Hastings
Newhaven
Bexhill
FRANCE
Seaford
Eastbourne

LIVERPOOL
BAY
FORMBY PT.
8
HOLYHEAD I.
Amlwch
Ormes Hd.
Llandudno
Rhyl
Liverpool
Wallasey
Birkenhead
Bolton
Wigan
Salford
Manchester
Oldham
Stockport
A 6
Widnes
Mersey
Warrington
Dee
Holyhead
A5
Beaumaris
Conway
Flint
Colwyn Bay
St. Asaph
Denbigh
Ellesmere Port
M6
Northwich
Macclesfield
Middlewich
Llanfairpwll
Bangor
Caernarvon
65
Llanrwst
Mold
Chester
75
Crewe
Ruthin
Nantwich
Llanberis
Betws-y-Coed
Wrexham
Newcastle under Lyme
Stoke on Trent
CAERNARVON B.
SNOWDON
1085
Beddgelert
Ffestiniog
A 5
Whitchurch
Corwen
Llangollen
Criccieth
Bala
Pwllheli
Portmadoc
BERWYN MTS.
Market Drayton
Harlech
CADER IDRIS
892
Oswestry
Stafford
TREMADOC BAY
Llanfyllin
41
BARDSEY I.
Barmouth
Dolgellau
Shrewsbury
Welshpool
Severn
20
A 5
Dinas Mawddwy
Wolverhampton
Towyn
Montgomery
Church Stretton
CARDIGAN
Bridgenorth
Dudley
Aberdovey
Machynlleth
Craven Arms
PLYNLIMMON
752
Newton
Devil's Bridge
Ludlow
BAY
Aberystwyth
Kidderminster
Llangurig
Ystwyth
CAMBRIAN MTS.
Knighton
Droitwich
Rhayader
Llandrindod Wells
Leominster
Aberayron
Teifi
Builth Wells
Worcester
Tregaron
Eardisley
Wye
MALVERN HILLS
Great Malvern
Lampeter
Cardigan
Llanwrtyd Wells
Hereford
Ledbury
Fishguard
Newcastle Emlyn
Talgarth
M50
Tewkesbury
M5
Llandovery
Sennybridge
Cheltenham
St. Davids
BRECON BEACONS
Brecon
BLACK MTS.
Ross
Carmarthen
Llandilo
Gloucester
Strumble Hd.
Towy
Abergavenny
Monmouth
Haverfordwest
Ammanford
Merthyr Tydfil
Brynmawr
Stroud
Lydney
Taff
Pontypool
Usk
38
Tintern
Nailsworth
Milford Haven
Llanelly
Neath
Pembroke
Tenby
Rhondda
Chepstow
Tetbury
CALDY I.
CARMARTHEN B.
Swansea
Newport
COTSWOLD HILLS
St. Govan's Hd.
Port Talbot
Pontypridd
Caerphilly
M4
Malmesbury
Worms Hd.
Porthcawl
Llantrisant
Avonmouth
Chipping Sodbury
Bridgend
Chippenham
Cardiff
Bristol
BRISTOL CHANNEL
Nash Pt.
Barry
26
A 4
Bath
Trowbridge
Weston super Mare
MENDIP HILLS
Axbridge
SOMERSET
Lynton
Porlock
BRIDGEWATER BAY
Cheddar
Frome
Burnham
Wells
Ilfracombe
Minehead
Watchet
Parracombe
Dunster
Braunton
Bridgewater
Glastonbury
Yeo
BIDEFORD B.
Barnstaple
Wiveliscombe
Wincanton
Hartland Pt.
Appledore
Bideford
EXMOOR
Ilchester
Hartland
Bampton
Wellington
Taunton
A 30
BLACKDOWN HILLS
Ilminster
Sherborne
Great Torrington
Yeovil
Merton
Lapford
Tiverton
Stratton
Cullompton
52
Bude
Hatherleigh
Honiton
Axminster
Holsworthy
Taw
A 30
Boscastle
Okehampton
Ottery St. Mary
Lyme Regis
Bridport
Dorchester
Frome
Tintagel Hd.
Lifton
Moreton Hampstead
Exeter
Camelford
Lydford
Teign
Exmouth
LYME BAY
Weymouth
Launceston
Teighmouth
Wadebridge
Portland Bill
Padstow
63
Tavistock
Dart
Newton Abbot
Bodmin
Newquay
Totnes
DARTMOOR
Torquay
Liskeard
Paignton
A 30
Plymouth
Looe
0
75 Km
40 Miles

ALDERNEY
St. Annes
C. de la Hague
Cherbourg
FRANCE
le Pieux
Carteret
GUERNSEY
St. Sampson
St. Peter Port
SARK
CHANNEL ISLANDS
JERSEY
St. Helier
Gorey
St. Aubin
Bradworthy
Merton
Lapford
Bude
Stratton
Holsworthy
Torridge
Hatherleigh
Bow
Crediton
D E V O N
Whitstone
Okehampton
Crackington Haven
Exeter
A 30
41
Boscastle
Sourton
TINTAGEL HD.
Launceston
Lifton
Lydford
Moreton Hampstead
Exminster
Camelford
DARTMOOR
Port Isaac
St. Teath
Bovey Tracey
Dawlish
BODMIN MOORS
22
Princetown
Padstow
Gunnislake
Tavistock
Newton Abbot
Teignmouth
Wadebridge
Callington
Yelverton
Ashburton
Babbacombe
Bodmin
Torquay
CORNWALL
Liskeard
TOR BAY
Saltash
Paignton
Brixham
Newquay
St. Columb
Lostwithiel
Devonport
Ivybridge
Totnes
St. Germans
Plymouth
Dartmouth
Kingswear
St. Blazey
W. Looe
Torpoint
E. Looe
Perranporth
St. Agnes
St. Austell
46
Fowey
Polperro
Modbury
Kingsbridge
A 30
Truro
Grampound
ST. AUSTELL B.
PLYMOUTH SD.
BIGBURY BAY
Tregony
Mevagissey
Salcombe
START PT.
St. Ives
ST. IVES B.
Redruth
DODMAN PT.
Camborne
Hayle
St. Mawes
ENGLISH CHANNEL
CORNWALL
St. Just
Penzance
Marazion
St. Michael's Mount
Falmouth
Helston
FALMOUTH B.
Sennen
MOUNT'S BAY
LAND'S END
Porthcurno
Lizard
LIZARD PT.
40 km
20 Miles
0
TRESCO
ST. MARTINS
ST. MARYS
Hugh Town
ST. AGNES
ISLES OF SCILLY
9

10
Annan
Gretna Green
Longtown
NORTHUMBERLAND
Newcastle
Tynemouth
Sth. Shield
Jarrow
SOLWAY FIRTH
A 7
Haltwhistle
Tyne
Hexham
Corbridge
Gateshead
Sunderla
Brampton
Carlisle
Silloth
Allendale Town
Chester le Street
Wear
Consett
Seaham Harb
Alston
DURHAM
Wigton
Eden
80
893
St. John's Chapel
A 1
Durham
Maryport
Aspatria
CROSS FELL
Crook
Hartlep
CUMBERLAND
A 6
Cockermouth
Penrith
West Hartlepool
Bishop Auckland
Workington
Middleton in Teesdale
Appleby
CUMBRIAN MTS.
Keswick
ULLSWATER
DERWENT W.
Tees
Whitehaven
LAKE DISTRICT
Barnard Castle
Middlesbroug
SCAFELL P. 980
WESTMORLAND
Brough
Bowes
Darlington
Grasmere
Ambleside
A 6
Kirkby Stephen
Stokesley
Tebay
Richmond
Catterick
Coniston
Windermere
Kendal
Sedbergh
Northallerton
Leyburn
112
Swale
Hawes
Middleham
Millom
Newby Br.
Ure
Thirsk
Ulverston
Kirkby Lonsdale
Grange
Ingleton
Ripon
MORECAMBE B.
Barrow
Boroughbri
Grassington
Morecambe
Settle
Ripley
WALNEY I.
Lancaster
Knaresboro
Heysham
Wharfe
Harrogate
Galgate
Skipton
73
Ilkley
Fleetwood
Wetherby
M6
Ribble
Bilsborrow
Clitheroe
Keighley
Tadcaster
Haworth
Aire
Blackpool
Kirkham
Preston
Burnley
Bradford
Leeds
Lytham St. Annes
Accrington
Blackburn
Halifax
Castleford
Tarleton
Pontefract
Dewsbury
Wakefield
Chorley
LANCS
Southport
A 6
A 1
Bury
Rochdale
Huddersfield
Omskirk
Barnsley
Formby
Wigan
Manchester
Oldham
Salford
Ashton
Doncaster
Aintree
Leigh
Liverpool
Eccles
Glossop
Wallasey
Prescot
St. Helens
Stockport
637
LIVERPOOL B.
Rotherha
Birkenhead
THE PEAK
Hoylake
Warrington
Altrincham
PT. OF AIR
Widnes
M6
Sheffield
Rhyl
Prestatyn
Knutsford
79
Mersey
Chapel-en-le-Frith
Worksop
Neston
Hathersage
117
St. Asaph
Ellesmere Port
Buxton
52
Flint
Northwich
M1
Macclesfield
Chesterfield
Denbigh
CHESHIRE
Bakewell
Gt. Rowsley
Clwyd
Mold
Hawarden
Chester
Middlewich
Mansfield
Matlock
Ruthin
Crewe
Leek
Alfreton
Wirksworth
Nantwich
DERBY
Wrexham
Newcastle under Lyme
Ripley
A 5
Llangollen
Stoke on Trent
Ashbourne
Corwen
A 6
41
Whitchurch
Derby
Market Drayton
Uttoxeter
Oswestry
SALOP
M6
STAFFS
Dove
Long Eato
Stafford
Burton upon Trent
M1
BERWYN MTS.
Loughborough
A 5
Shrewsbury
20
Newport
Ashby de la Zouch

Maryport
Cockermouth
Workington
Cockermouth
Kilnhill
Lorton
Keswick
Penrith
Pooley Br.
Distington
Whitehaven
Buttermere
Rosthwaite
Patterdale
CUMBRIAN MTS.
LAKE DISTRICT
Egremont
Gosforth
Seascale
Eskdale Green
Grasmere
Ambleside
Kirkstone Inn
Troutbeck
Windermere
Bowness
Crook
Kendal
Hawkshead
Coniston
Bootle
Broughton
Newby Br.
Levens
Heversham
Lowick Br.
Greenodd
Ulverston
Millom
Grange
Burton
Dalton
Barrow
Carnforth
Morecambe
Heysham
Lancaster
MORECAMBE B.
WALNEY I
HILPSFORD PT.
ST. BEES HD.
SCAFELL P.
980
BASSENTHWAITE LAKE
DERWENT WATER
BUTTERMERE
ENNERDALE WATER
WAST WATER
ULLSWATER
HAWES WATER
CONISTON WATER
WINDERMERE
A 6
A 6
M6
42
11
0
25 km
15 Miles
0
60 km
30 Miles
Redcar
Saltburn
Guisborough
Whitby
Robin Hood's Bay
CLEVELAND HILLS
YORKSHIRE MOORS
Scalby
Scarborough
Helmsley
Pickering
Filey
YORKSHIRE WOLDS
FLAMBOROUGH HD.
Malton
Bridlington
Gt. Driffield
Skipsea
York
Hornsea
Market Weighton
Beverley
Aldbrough
Hull
Hedon
Withernsea
Selby
Howden
Goole
Humber
Barton
Immingham
SPURN HD.
Brigg
Grimsby
Cleethorpes
Hatfield
Scunthorpe
Caistor
Bawtry
Saltfleet
LINCOLN WOLDS
Louth
Gainsborough
Market Rasen
Mablethorpe
Sutton on Sea
East Retford
Alford
Wragby
Horncastle
Ulceby
Lincoln
Ollerton
Woodhall Spa
Spilsby
Tattershall
Skegness
Southwell
Newark
LINCS
NOTTS
Nottingham
Sleaford
Boston
Sutterton
Grantham
Bourne
Hunstanton
Docking
Wells
Blakeney
Holt
Cromer
Fakenham
Aylsham
Sandringham
Holbeach
L. Sutton
Spalding
Gui
Melton Mowbray
Bourne
King's Lynn
NORFOLK
THE WASH
NORTH SEA
A1
A 1
52

ORKNEY
ROUSAY
SANDAY
Stromness
Kirkwall
HOY
St. Margarets Hope
12
0
100 Km
0
60 Miles
BUTT OF LEWIS
C. WRATH
OUTER HEBRIDES
LEWIS
Barvas
Carloway
Stornoway
Tarbert
HARRIS
Leverburgh
SD. OF HARRIS
NORTH UIST
Lochmaddy
SOUTH UIST
NORTH MINCH
LITTLE MINCH
RUDNA HUNISH
SKYE
Uig
Dunvegan
Portree
Sligachan
SD. OF RAASAY
RAASAY
Broadford
Kyleakin
Kyle of Lochalsh
Strome Ferry
Applecross
Armadale
RUM
EIGG
Mallaig
Arisaig
Glenfinnan
ARDNAMURCHAN PT.
COLL
Durness
STRATHY PT.
Melvich
Bettyhill
Tongue
BEN HOPE 927
L. LOYAL
Scourie
EDDRACHILLIS B.
Unapool
Altnaharra
BEN MORE ASSYNT 998
ENARD B.
Lochinver
Inchnadamph
L. SHIN
Ledmore
L. BROOM
Ullapool
Aultbea
Poolewe
Gairloch
L. MAREE
Kinlochewe
Achnasheen
Lairg
Oykell
Carron
Ardgay
BEN WYVIS 1045
Garve
Strathpeffer
Dingwall
Beauly
Farrar
Inverness
L. NESS
Glen Affric
Drumnadrochit
Great Glen
Fort Augustus
L. LOCHY
Laggan Br.
Thurso
Dunnet
PENTLAND FIRTH
DUNCANSBY HD.
John O'Groats
A 9
Halkirk
Watten
Wick
Lybster
Latheron
Kinbrace
Halladale
72
Berriedale
Helmsdale
Brora
Golspie
Dornoch
Tain
81
TARBAT NESS
MORAY FIRTH
Cromarty
Fortrose
Nairn
Forres
Findhorn
Dava
Lossiemouth
Elgin
Fochabers
Rothes
Craigellachie
Buckie
Cullen
Keith
Banff
Macduff
Rosehearty
KINNAIRDS HD.
Fraserburgh
Turriff
Deveron
Huntly
New Deer
Peterhead
Ythan
Grantown on Spey
Spey
Dufftown
Rhynie
47
Carrbridge
Nethybridge
Boat of Garten
Tomintoul
Aviemore
Kingussie
Old Meldrum
Inverurie
Ellon
Alford
UNST
Baltasound
Isbister
YELL
Hillswick
Melby
Voe
Walls
Scalloway
Lerwick
Virkie
SHETLAND ISLANDS

S C O T L A N D
GRAMPIAN MOUNTAINS
Aberdeen
Dyce
Banchory
Stonehaven
Inverbervie
Aboyne
Ballater
Braemar
Balmoral Castle
BEN MACDHUI 1310
BEN DEARG 1081
Dalwhinnie
Fort William
BEN NEVIS 1343
Kinlochleven
L. ERICHT
L. RANNOCH
Glen Garry
Kinloch Rannoch
Blair Atholl
Pitlochry
Laurencekirk
Brechin
Montrose
Kirriemuir
Forfar
Glamis
SIDLAW HILLS
Arbroath
Carnoustie
Broughty Ferry
Dundee
Coupar Angus
Blairgowrie
Dunkeld
Aberfeldy
L. TAY
Tay
Killin
Tyndrum
Dalmally
Crianlarich
Lochearnhead
Glenshee
Perth
Crieff
Gleneagles
OCHIL HILLS
Callander
Aberfoyle
Forth
L. LOMOND
Stirling
Alloa
Kinross
Cowdenbeath
Dunfermline
Newport
Cupar
St. Andrews
FIFE NESS
Crail
Leven
Largo
Methil
Kirkcaldy
FIRTH OF FORTH
North Berwick
Dunbar
Haddington
Leith
Edinburgh
Dalkeith
Linlithgow
Falkirk
Larbert
Glasgow
Motherwell
Wishaw
Hamilton
Lanark
Penicuik
MOORFOOT HILLS
LAMMERMUIR HILLS
Lauder
Eyemouth
ST. ABBS HD.
Duns
Berwick upon Tweed
Coldstream
Kelso
Melrose
Galashiels
Selkirk
Peebles
Tweed
Innerleithen
Biggar
TWEEDSMUIR HILLS
Moffat
Hawick
Jedburgh
Wooler
THE CHEVIOT 816
CHEVIOT HILLS
Belford
HOLY I.
Alnwick
Alnmouth
Rothbury
Otterburn
Morpeth
Ashington
Newbiggin by the Sea
Longtown
Gretna Green
Langholm
Lockerbie
Annan
Ecclefechan
Dumfries
Thornhill
Nith
Dee
Abington
Cumnock
Muirkirk
Strathaven
Kilmarnock
Irvine
Troon
Prestwick
Ayr
Ardrossan
Fairlie
Largs
BUTE
Rothesay
Dunoon
Greenock
Gourock
Helensburgh
Dumbarton
Renfrew
Paisley
Clyde
Arrochar
L. FYNE
Inveraray
ARGYLL
Lochgilphead
Tarbert
Oban
FIRTH OF LORNE
MULL
Salen
Tobermory
MORVEN
Lochaline
Ballachulish
L. LINNHE
IONA
JURA
SD. OF JURA
Craighouse
ISLAY
Port Askaig
Port Ellen
MULL OF OA
KINTYRE
Campbeltown
Machrihanish
MULL OF KINTYRE
ARRAN
Brodick
FIRTH OF CLYDE
Maybole
Turnberry
Girvan
Ballantrae
CORSEWALL PT.
NORTH CHANNEL
Stranraer
Portpatrick
Drummore
LUCE B.
Wigtown
Newton-Stuart
New Galloway
Castle Douglas
Kirkcudbright
Belfast
Larne
Cushendall
Cushendun
Ballycastle
FAIR HD.
A 9
A 8
A 7
A 1
M8
70
45
61
50
48
Crossgates
Culross
Rosyth
Blackness
N. Queensferry
S. Granton
Aberdour
Burntisland
Kinghorn
Kirkcaldy
Leith
Musselburgh
Broxburn
Kirkliston
Mid Calder
Balerno
Loanhead
Newtongrange
Roslin
Rosewell
Penicuik
W. of Leith
13

ATLANTIC
OCEAN
NORTH CHANNEL
IRISH SEA
NORTHERN IRELAND
DONEGAL BAY
Campbeltown
Rathlin I.
Malin Hd.
Tory I.
Inishowen
Giant's Causeway
Portrush
Bushmills
Coleraine
Ballycastle
Fair Hd.
Cushendun
Cushendall
Ballymoney
Antrim Mts.
Clough
Glenarm
Ballygally
Larne
Ballymena
Ballyclare
Carrickfergus
Antrim
Belfast
Glengormley
Bangor
Donaghadee
Newtownards
Lisburn
Strangford L.
Cloghy
Ballynahinch
Portaferry
Downpatrick
Ardglass
Dundrum B.
Newcastle
Sl. Donard 850
Kilkeel
Warrenpoint
Rathfriland
Mourne Mts.
Newry
Newry Canal
Banbridge
Dromore
Lurgan
Portadown
Carlingford
Dundalk (Dun Dealgan)
Dundalk Bay
Dunany Hd.
Drogheda (Droichead Atha)
Balbriggan
Skerries
Ashbourne
Malahide
Londonderry
Limavady
Dungiven
Maghera
Bann
Main
L. Foyle
L. Swilly
Buncrana
Johnstown
Strabane
Sperrin Mts.
Newtown Stewart
Tobermore
Cookstown
Dungannon
L. Neagh
Pomeroy
Omagh
Fintona
Irvinestown
Clogher
Ballygawley
Aughnacloy
Armagh
Monaghan
Newtown Hamilton
Ballybay
Castleblayney
Carrickmacross
Kingcourt
Ardee
Slane
Rosapenna
Errigal 752
Donegal Mts.
Aran Is.
Dungloe
Letterkenny
Glenties
Ballybofey
676 Blue Stack
Rosses Pt.
Killybegs
Carrick
Donegal
L. Derg
Ballyshannon
Bundoran
Belleek
L. Erne
Enniskillen
Manorhamilton
Sligo
Sligo B.
Dromahair
Upper L. Erne
Ballinamore
Cavan
Cootehill
L. Oughter
Bailieborough
Virginia
Kells (Ceannannas)
L. Sheelin
An Uaimh (Navan)
Castlepollard
Boyne
Mullinggar
Kinnegad
Kilbeggan
Moate
L. Ennell
Athlone
Ballymahon
Royal Canal
Edgeworthtown
Longford
Drumod
Carrick on Shannon
L. Allen
L. Arrow
L. Key
Boyle
L. Gara
Ballaghaderreen
Tulsk
Castlerea
Ballymoe
Roscommon
L. Ree
Mount Bellew
Ballinasloe
Suck
Ballymote
Ballysadare
Enniscrone
Ox Mts.
Tubbercurry
Swinford
Ballina
Killala B.
Erris Hd.
Benwee Hd.
Balmullet
Bangor
Mts. Mayo
L. Conn
Nephin 807
Keel
Achill I.
Mallaranny
Clew B.
Clare I.
Westport
Castlebar
Claremorris
Ballyhaunis
Dunmore
Tuam
Ballinrobe
L. Mask
Cong
L. Corrib
Headford
Oughterard
Leenane
819 Mweelrea
Mts. of Connemara
Clifden
Maam Cross
Slyne Hd.
Inishturk
Inishbofin

EIRE
Dún Laoghaire (Kingstown)
Bray
Greystones
Wicklow
WICKLOW HD.
WICKLOW MTS.
930
Avoca
Aughrim
Arklow
Baltinglass
Tullow
Gorey
Naas
Newbridge
Kildare
Tullamore
Portarlington
Port Laoighise (Maryborough)
SL. BLOOM
Athy
Carlow
Barrow
Slaney
Bagenalstown (Muine Bheag)
Newtownbarry (Bunclody)
CAHORE PT.
Enniscorthy
Wexford
Rosslare
CARNSORE PT.
Duncormick
New Ross
Thomastown
Kilkenny
Castlecomer
Durrow
Roscrea
Birr
Portumna
DERG
Shannon
Loughrea
Galway (Gaillimh)
Costelloe
KILKIERAN
GALWAY B.
ARAN I.
Gort
SLIEVE AUCHTY
Lisdoonvarna
Ennistymon
Lahinch
Milltown Malbay
Ennis
Killaloe
Nenagh
Templemore
Borrisoleigh
Thurles
Limerick (Luimneach)
695
SILVERMINE MTS.
Kilkee
Carrigaholt
Kilrush
Foynes
LOOP HD.
MOUTH OF THE SHANNON
Tarbert
Rathkeale
Adare
Oola
Cashel
Callan
Fethard
Carrick-on-Suir
Nore
Suir
Listowel
Newcastle West
Abbeyfeale
Kilmallock
Tipperary
920
GALTEE MTS.
Cahir
Clonmel
TRALEE B.
Tralee (Tráighlí)
Charleville (Ráth Luirc)
Buttevant
Castleisland
Dingle
Ventry
DINGLE B.
Castlemaine
Killorglin
Newmarket
Kanturk
Mitchelstown
KNOCKMEALDOWN MTS.
Cloghean
Fermoy
Cappoquin
The Sweep
Waterford (Port Láirge)
Tramore
WATERFORD HARB.
HOOK HD.
L. LEANE
Farranfore
Blackwater
Mallow
Lismore
Dungarvan
Glenbeigh
Killarney
Glencar
Millstreet
Banteer
BOGGERAGH MTS.
Cahirciveen
MACGILLYCUDDYS REEKS
Waterville
Parknasilla
Kenmare
Cork (Corcaigh)
Midleton
Youghal
MINE HD. OF KINSALE
YOUGHAL HARB.
Macroom
Cloyne
Cobh (Queenstown)
CORK HARB.
Glengariff
CAHA MTS.
Dunmanway
Ballinhassig
Crosshaven
Bandon
Kinsale
BANTRY B.
Bantry
OLD HEAD
Clonakilty
Skibbereen
MIZEN HD.
ROARINGWATER B.
C. CLEAR
ST. GEORGES CHANNEL
St. Davids
0
100 km
0
60 Miles

15

FAIR HD.
Ballycastle
Cushendun
16
Cushendall
ANTRIM
Clough
MTS.
Glenarm
Larne
Ballymena
Ballyclare
21
Carrickfergus
Antrim
Glengormly
Belfast
BELFAST L.
Bangor
Donaghadee
Newtownards
Lurgan
Lisburn
51
STRANGFORD L.
Ballynahinch
Dromore
Portaferry
Banbridge
Downpatrick
Clough
MOURNE MTS.
DUNDRUM B.
Newry
Newcastle
Rathfriland
SL. DONARD 850
Warrenpoint
Kilkeel
Carlingford
Newry Canal
Main
NORTH CHANNEL
Girvan
Ballantrae
CORSEWALL PT.
Stranraer
Portpatrick
LUCE B.
Drummore
MULL OF GALLOWAY
New Galloway
Newton-Stuart
Wigtown
Kirkcudbright
WIGTOWN B.
BURROW HD.
Thornhill
Dumfries
Castle Douglas
Dee
Ecclefechan
Lockerbie
Langho
Longtown
Annan
SOLWAY F.
Silloth
Carlisle
Wigton
Maryport
Cockermouth
Workington
Whitehaven
ST BEES HD.
Egremont
CUMBRIAN MTS.
SCAFELL 979
Keswi
Grasm
Ambleside
Windermer
Coniston
Newby Br
Millom
Ulverston
Barrow
Morecam
MORECAMBE B.
Heysha
Fleetwood
Blackpool
Southport
FORMBY PT.
Liverpool
Wallasey
Birkenhead
0 75 km
0 40 Miles
PT OF AYRE
ISLE OF MAN
Ramsey
620 SNAEFELL
Peel
St. John's
Laxey
Douglas
Port Erin
Port St. Mary
Castletown
CALF OF MAN
DUNDALK BAY
DUNANY HD.
IRISH SEA
Drogheda
(Droichead Atha)
Balbriggan
53
Skerries
Ashbourne
Malahide
Howth
Dublin (Baile Atha Cliath)
Dùn Laoghaire (Kingstown)
Bray
Greystones
Wicklow
WICKLOW HD.
Avoca
Arklow
Gorey
CAHORE PT.
LIVERPOOL BAY
HOLYHEAD I.
Amlwch
Ormes Hd.
Llandudno
Conway
Rhyl
Colwyn Bay
Flint
St. Asaph
Denbigh
Mold
Ches
Holyhead
A 5
Bangor
65
Cearnarvon
Llanrwst
Llanberis
Betws-y-Coed
Ruthin
Wrexham
CAERNARVON B.
SNOWDON 1085
Ffestiniog
Corwen
Llangollen
A 5
Criccieth
Portmadoc
Bala
BERWYN MTS.
Pwllheli
Harlech
CADER IDRIS 892
Oswestry
TREMADOC BAY
Llanfyllin
BARDSEY I.
Barmouth
Dolgelley
Welshpool
Dinas Mawddwy
Towyn
Montgomery
Aberdovey
Machynlleth
CARDIGAN BAY
PLYNLIMMON 752
Newton
Aberystwyth
Ystwyth
CAMBRIAN MTS.
Llangurig
Knighton
Rhayader
Llandrindod Wells
Aberayron
Teifi
Builth Wells
Tregaron
Wye
Lampeter
Cardigan
Llanwrtyd Wells